THOROUGHBRED
HANDICAPPING

THOROUGHBRED
HANDICAPPING

STATE
OF THE ART

William L. Quirin, Ph.D

QUILL / WILLIAM MORROW AND COMPANY, INC.
NEW YORK

Library of Congress Catalog Card Number: 84-60211
ISBN: 0-688-11215-3

Printed in the United States of America

3 4 5 6 7 8 9 10

BOOK DESIGN BY BERNARD SCHLEIFER

For my father

FOREWORD

Once my first book, *Winning at the Races*, gained critical acclaim, several doors opened for me. One led to the marketing offices at Belmont Park, where I was asked to conduct seminars on handicapping in conjunction with the Breakfast at Belmont and Saratoga programs. The seminars were to help launch the NYRA's program for newcomers. My task was to outline for novices the meaning and use of the various symbols found in the *Daily Racing Form*, while at the same time adding enough insight to keep seasoned players interested. Those seminars became the seeds for this book. I would like to thank Ted Demmon and Howard Giordano of NYRA for providing the opportunity.

Winning at the Races was unique in its field, presenting the results of computer studies into the relevance of the various aspects of past performances. In some sense, it brought to a climax the "Tom Ainslie Era" of handicapping analysis, verifying to a great extent the teachings of the sport's most prolific and revered writer. The book also ushered in handicapping's scientific era, giving impetus to the use of the computer as a handicapping aid.

However, despite the reputation *Winning at the Races* may have won for me, both as a speed handicapper and a proponent of the scientific approach, I have always placed the major emphasis in my own handicapping on the interpretive side of the game. There, indeed, is an art to Thoroughbred handicapping. Understanding how to fit together the various pieces of the handicapping puzzle, including those provided by speed figures or scientific analysis, and determine the logical play in a race, is the key to successful handicapping. That will be the focus of this book.

FOREWORD

The handicapping process must always be at least slightly incomplete. We all would like to be able to ask the trainer how his horse is doing, and what he thinks of its chances, and to ask the horse how it feels that day. Unfortunately, most of us can do no such thing. To help bridge that gap, and to provide the reader with some insight into the sport as seen from the trainer's point of view, I prepared and distributed a questionnaire to New York trainers, and their input has been incorporated into the text. To those eleven trainers who replied to the questionnaire, my sincerest thanks for finding time in an already packed schedule to acknowledge the importance of you, the informed bettor, to their industry.

I would also like to thank, first and foremost, my good friend Anton Hemm, for not only freely sharing ideas and theories on handicapping over the years, but also for his untiring efforts in digging up examples and past performance clippings for this book.

And thanks to the following:

My friends Glenn Magnell and Phil Zipse, who have contributed significantly to my growth as a handicapper. My colleagues Jim Quinn and Scott McMannis for reading the manuscript and offering suggestions that have improved the final work. And colleagues John Pricci and Paul Mellos for critiquing the chapter on trip handicapping, and otherwise sharing their thoughts on handicapping. Tom Ainslie, for helping me to get started as an author, guiding my earlier works, and creating a marketplace for books on this subject. Tom Pappas, George Stohood, Steve Shoemaker, and Ed Lakso for sharing their thoughts on handicapping. Rex Franciotti, Gary Tobey, John Southard, and Lou DeGregorio of the Adelphi Computer Center for their assistance with my programs and tapes. And last, but certainly not least, my wife Diane for sharing my interest in handicapping and pointing out several of the examples used in this book, and my daughter Kristin, for her love of Belmont Park, and her three-hour naps.

CONTENTS

CONTENTS

CONTENTS

THOROUGHBRED
HANDICAPPING

Chapter 1

INTRODUCTION

We start with an obvious premise: that a winning afternoon or evening at the races is far more pleasant than a losing one. And furthermore, that one's pleasure is enhanced many times over when the winners result from an in-depth personal analysis of the day's races, rather than simply from playing favorites, or hunches, or colors, or jockeys, or following the selections of a tip sheet purchased when entering the track. Winning is fun, but "being right" is far more satisfying, especially to the ego.

Those who analyze the contestants in each race are engaging in what is commonly termed "handicapping." They are likely to be "right" far more often than those who rely strictly on guesswork or hearsay when making their selections.

☐ THE PAST PERFORMANCES ☐

Where does a prospective handicapper begin? The answer is simple. The initial step must be a familiarization with the format of the past performances of Thoroughbreds as they appear in the *Daily Racing Form* or one of its reasonable facsimiles, such as *The Racing Digest* in California, or *Sports Eye*, which is now a national publication.

One's first encounter with the *Racing Form* is somewhat akin to trying to decipher the hieroglyphics on the Rosetta stone, or read the *Iliad* in the original Greek. So many symbols can be found in the past performances of just one horse that the handicapper must be fluid in the language of past performances or he will never have the time to probe to the heart of matters.

Yet, even after the meanings of the various symbols have been mastered, the novice handicapper is still likely to be overwhelmed. Because there is so much information to be extracted from the past performances, where does one begin? I distinctly remember my first attempts at handicapping. My eyes would jump from one horse to the next, and from one handicapping consideration to another, usually in a rather haphazard manner. In a short period of time, I would scan many useful pieces of information with little understanding of their significance. What I lacked was a cohesive, orderly way of looking at the past performances of a race, or of an individual horse in a race. With experience my focus became sharper, and after fifteen years, a basic plan of attack has emerged. That approach will be summarized in Chapter 15. Its components will be discussed throughout the book.

□ GOALS □

Our goal is to introduce the newcomer to the fascinating pastime (hobby, obsession, profession) of Thoroughbred handicapping, and help the seasoned player become more proficient at it. Consequently, the book is written on two levels, aimed at two separate audiences. The novice handicapper will find an explanation of each symbol that might appear in the *Daily Racing Form* past-performance lines, together with a discussion of its relevance in the total handicapping picture. The more experienced player will be offered many suggestions on how to read between the past-performance lines, and how to interpret the information found therein.

The novice handicapper will probably find it useful to read the book twice, concentrating on the basics of what's what in the past performances the first time through. Several items are mentioned (in examples) before they are formally introduced and discussed in detail in a later chapter.

We ask that the seasoned practitioner bear with us while we discuss the elementary points, and that he not skip the early chapters—there are many interesting points to be found, both in the text itself, and in the examples. The beginning handicapper should be made aware that no one piece of information found in the *Form* has overriding significance standing alone. Everything found in the *Form* is interrelated. Each item becomes more relevant when viewed side-by-side with several others.

Because of the differences in format between the Eastern and Western editions of the *Daily Racing Form*, it would in many cases be necessary to demonstrate the positioning of information with examples from each. For the most part, however, we have chosen to use the Eastern format when presenting examples of *Form* symbols or handicapping points. A brief appendix will note the key differences between Eastern and Western editions.

□ THE KEY QUESTIONS OF HANDICAPPING □

The handicapping process usually comes down to answering (or attempting to answer) four basic questions about each race, its individual contestants in particular, and their relationships and expected interactions with each other. The reader should keep these questions in the forefront of his thoughts as he proceeds through the book.

Ability

The first question deals with the ability of the individual horse. Is the animal capable of winning the race? Does he belong on the same racetrack as his opponents? Are the distance, surface, track conditions, and race classification within his proven capabilities? Is there evidence in the horse's historical record supporting these conclusions?

The answers to these questions will usually be provided either by "class handicapping" or "speed handicapping," or a combination of the two. The reader will find that Chapters 2, 6, 8, 9, and 10 specifically contain significant amounts of information about these topics.

Class handicappers who attend the races on a daily (or regular) basis find that awareness of the local "pecking order" among horses is their most reliable barometer. Based on personal observations, they simply know, or think they know, that one horse is better than another.

Speed handicappers, in particular, prefer to rate horses numerically. Their numbers are commonly called "speed figures," the terminology we shall use throughout the book.

Class and speed are closely related. The "class" horse is usually the one able to run the distance fastest when pitted against the strongest opposition and/or faced with the strongest pace.

Fitness

The second question looks at the flip side of the coin. Will the horse run to its capabilities today? Is the horse at its peak physically? Is it well-meant by its connections? Or do they look upon the race as just another part of the horse's conditioning program?

The answers to these questions lie in the bailiwick of "form," an elusive concept that encompasses such important matters as consistency, recency, a detailed analysis of the horse's most recent races, and an awareness of the *modus operandi* of the horse's conditioner. The reader will find Chapters 3, 4, 6, 7, 11, and 13 especially relevant to understanding form.

Class and form cannot be separated. A horse's "class" is measured by its performances when fit and capable of doing its best. When off form, it may easily be fair game for a fit horse of lesser stature.

The handicapper is usually on uncertain ground when dealing with form. Form often proves to be a guessing game. The clues are complex and often multifaceted. They are frequently self-contradictory, leaving open two completely opposing interpretations. They can often be used to explain why a horse should win, or why the same horse is a likely loser. Should a handicapper's analysis of a race leave too many questions about form unanswered, he is best advised to proceed cautiously, possibly even to pass the race.

A horse that ran a superior race in its last start, possibly overcoming severe traffic problems, perhaps earning the best speed figure of its life, is obviously at the peak of its form. Or is it? Perhaps the effort expended in running so well tapped the horse's energy reserves, leaving the animal with little fuel in its tank for a repeat performance. Should the horse be given extra credit for the big effort last out? Or should it be penalized for possibly having overexerted itself? Is the horse still at, or approaching, the peak of its form cycle? Or did the last race represent that peak? Only the horse's handlers know "for sure." And even they are quite often fooled.

The preceding discussion highlights two important aspects of the form riddle.

Is the evidence to be taken at face value? Or is there room for anticipation? Are we to look for obvious form? Or should hints of hidden form be sought out?

If the evidence may, or may not, be reliable, or can be interpreted in both a positive and negative sense, is there not the need to find corroborating evidence, a series of clues all leading to the same conclusion?

The answer to both questions is a resounding "YES." It is in this manner that we must deal with form.

Extenuating Circumstances

The third question looks at each horse in context, rather than as an individual. Are there extenuating circumstances that might conspire for or against a particular horse or horses? How will the race be run in terms of pace? What is the condition of the racing surface?

If a horse likes to contest the early lead, will it have any serious rivals at that stage? If so, will the pace be too fast for all concerned? Will any of the early contenders be able to overcome the pace and still hold something in reserve for the stretch run? Will a lone pacesetter be able to set such slow fractions that no rival will be able to get close enough to mount a serious challenge in the stretch?

Will the horses that race from behind find the pace so fast that their late charge will have maximum effect? Or so slow that their late run will prove totally ineffective?

Will a horse's post position place it at a disadvantage in the run to the first turn? Will the horse have to take that turn three or four wide? It is an established fact that each path away from the rail costs a horse one length around a turn.

Will a horse's post position force it to run over the best, or the worst, part of the racing surface? At many tracks, Belmont and Saratoga being two examples, the rail becomes the worst place to race when the surface is wet. But ordinarily, the rail provides the shortest path home.

Will a horse's running style work to its advantage on a hard track favoring front-runners? Or over a drying-out surface favoring closers?

In general, will a horse's post position and/or running style force it to race with, or against, a possible track bias?

Is the horse overmatched? Overall, or just for the early lead? Often, a supposedly outclassed horse wins because it was anything but overmatched for the early lead.

A colleague in the teaching profession once asked me if Thoroughbreds "ran true to form." I had to reply that his was a difficult question to answer. Some horses, and some trainers, were very reliable. Others were not. Confusing the issue was the fact that many that appeared on paper to be inconsistent were in actuality victims of circumstances. The makeup of a field of horses and the condition of the racing surface often decisively influence the outcome of a race.

Preconceived notions about a race can be dangerous. One should never make a "firm commitment" to a horse until after learning the scratches and estimating the effect of track conditions on the outcome of the race.

Chapters 3, 10, and 11 will shed more light on the types of questions just raised.

Value

The fourth, and final, question, puts the other three in proper perspective. What price is the horse worth? At what odds would the horse be considered a good (or fair) bet?

Some handicapping clues might say "Yes" to a horse's chances of winning, others, "No." The player must weigh the pros and cons, decide if the horse is worth a bet, and if so, at what odds.

All handicappers have had this experience time and again. After investing a fair amount of time analyzing a race, we find a few interesting "angles" in one horse's record, and decide to play that horse. Or, we notice something in a horse's performance one day, and eagerly await its return. Then, it seems that everybody had noticed the same angles, or was waiting for the same horse. The odds are disappointingly low. We hate to bet against the horse, yet find it difficult to accept the miserly odds.

To be successful, a handicapper must come to realize that there is a significant difference between a good selection and a good bet. A handicapper must shop for value on the tote board. He must seek out what are termed "overlays," horses whose odds are higher than their probable chances of winning. To do this, the handicapper must be able to estimate the relative chances of each contestant, or at least those of the more likely contenders.

One should never decide who or how to bet until seeing the odds. From a long-range perspective, the best horse to bet may not be one's original selection. Or even the winner!

The wise player plies his trade at the racetrack itself, and not offtrack at an OTB parlor or through his neighborhood bookie. One of his major weapons is the ability to adjust his thinking, to adapt his selections to changing circumstances, such as late scratches or track conditions.

One must play the races with the attitude that it is possible to beat the races, over the long haul. Many times, however, it is necessary to "sacrifice" an individual race, playing a horse other than the one judged most likely to win, simply because it is this horse that represents value.

Part of one's betting strategy revolves around the race favorite. Before the betting begins, one should ask "Which horse will the crowd make its favorite? How solid are its credentials? Does the horse have sufficient negative points that betting against it would appear an attractive proposition?"

Should the crowd instead make another horse its favorite, a closer look at that animal's record is called for. Is it a legitimate favorite on paper? Or is the horse receiving a surprising amount of play, likely a sign of stable confidence?

On the other hand, if a horse is being offered at high odds, look for a couple of positive signs in its record that might make it an exciting longshot possibility. In many cases, however, this will not be possible. Not every longshot is an overlay with reasonable expectations of winning. For that matter, many favorites are legitimate overlays, despite their relatively short odds.

The handicapper must overcome the temptation to say, "I'm going to bet such-and-such horse in the fifth race today." Rather, he must learn to reason "This horse appears worth 2–1 in today's fifth race, if I can get it. If not, a second horse appears worth 5–1 as an alternative, or some other at 20–1 as a possible longshot play." And then, bet the preferred horse if the odds are decent. If not, the player has three options:

(1) pass the race altogether,
(2) play his second or third choice, if their odds are enticing,
(3) use his preferred horse as the key in an exotic wager, combining that horse with the other reasonable contenders.

Chapter 14 will shed more light on the matter of betting strategies.

Let us mention once again the value of anticipation. Handicappers who wait for the evidence to appear in black and white usually find that they forfeit price as a result. If the evidence is there for all to read, it will usually be reflected in the betting pools. The handicapper can stay one jump ahead of the crowd if he makes it a practice to bet horses first time on the grass, or first try at a distance, if the pedigree is right. Or first race off a layoff, if the workouts signal readiness and a top rider is aboard. Until evidence of ability or fitness appears in the Form, many in the audience will look elsewhere.

□ SUPPLEMENTING THE FORM □

Several of the crucial pieces of the handicapping puzzle do not appear in the lines of the Racing Form. The serious handicapper, one who attends the races on a daily basis, will probably supplement the information he can extract from the *Form* in as many as four ways:

(1) Accurate speed figures of his own making, taking into account daily variances in the speed of the racing surface (see Chapters 9–10).
(2) Accurate trip notes, including track bias information, resulting from his personal viewing and reviewing (on the track's reruns, or on cable television) of the day's races (see Chapter 11).
(3) An in-depth knowledge of the strengths, weaknesses, and methodology of the trainers on his circuit (see Chapter 4).
(4) A basic familiarity with the physical appearance, idiosyncrasies, and problems of the horses that compete on his circuit. The book *The Body Language of Horses,* coauthored by Bonnie Ledbetter and Tom Ainslie, is an excellent reference on this subject.

Each of the above is an important facet of handicapping. All the more so, in fact, because what they reveal cannot be found in the *Form*, and therefore is less likely to be reflected on the odds board.

The ideal handicapping "syndicate" would consist of four people, working as a team, each expert in one of the four areas just outlined. Perhaps a fifth could be added, responsible for observing trends on the odds board. It would be his task to spot imbalances (signifying betting action) between the win, place, and show pools, and the exotic betting pools. More about this in Chapter 14.

☐ STATISTICAL TERMINOLOGY ☐

Although this book will not be nearly as statistically oriented as *Winning at the Races*, there will be occasions when results of statistical surveys will be presented. Our findings will be listed in as many as six categories, under the following headings:

NH   The number of horses (cases) studied.
NW   The number of horses studied that won their race.
WPCT   The percentage of horses studied that returned winners.
MPCT   The percentage of horses studied that finished in the money (i.e., first, second, or third).
I.V.   The "Impact Value," an improvement over the straight win percentage, this number takes field size into consideration. It compares the percentage of winners sharing the characteristic being studied to the percentage of starters

having that same characteristic, by dividing the latter into the former. For example, if 50 percent of the starters in sampled races carried 117 pounds or more, while 75 percent of the winners did, the impact value for "117 pounds or higher" would be $^{75}/_{50}$, or 1.50. An impact value of 1.00 is average. One above 1.00 signifies a factor producing more winners than it should.

$NET   The "Dollar Net," or "Average Payoff," is a statistic calculated by totaling the win payoffs produced by the winners in the study, then dividing by the total number of horses studied. From a betting point of view, the break-even point is $2.00. It is a well-documented fact that public favorites produce a $NET of approximately $1.80 over the long run, representing a loss of 20 cents per $2 bet, or 10 percent on investment.

When perusing the statistics we present, you should look for a high impact value (well above 1.00), complemented by an average payoff above $2.00. This will point out a type of horse, or handicapping characteristic, likely to win consistently more often than expected at good enough odds to produce a long-term profit for investors.

Chapter 2

THE RACE CONDITIONS

The launching pad for the handicapping process must be a reading of the race conditions. These are the short paragraphs that appear above the past performances for each race, to the right of the oversized race number, track name, and diagram of the course for the race. They describe the conditions under which the race is to be run.

It is the job of a track's racing secretary to write the conditions for the day's races. This is done several days ahead of time, and reflects the secretary's assessment of the available horse population on the grounds. The race conditions are published in a booklet called the *Condition Book* for distribution to the horsemen—the trainers and jockey agents in particular. The typical condition book covers two weeks' racing, and usually appears a few days before the first day of that period. For a nine-race card, the book probably will include conditions for at least eleven races. It is hoped the first nine listed will constitute the day's racing program. But should one of these races fail to attract sufficient entries ("fail to fill," in the jargon of the backstretch), one of the extra races will be used in its stead. Any relationship between the numbering of the races in the condition book and their eventual placement on the program is purely coincidental. As a rule, the races that attract the larger fields are reserved for the daily double or triple races. Large fields often produce huge exotic payoffs. This, in turn, entices the gambling instincts of the smaller bettor, offering him the chance for a big "score," and this, of course, is good for business.

The reader will find on the following page a sample day's conditions from a recent Belmont condition book (reproduced with the permission of the New York Racing Association).

☐ MAIL-ORDER TOUTS ☐

Did you ever receive a letter offering inside information about a horse set to win easily three Saturdays hence, guaranteed to pay in double figures? Some actually will go so far as to tell you the exact race on the program in which the horse will compete. Don't fall for this ploy. Not even the racing secretary knows the kinds of races that will be scheduled for that day until well after such letters have reached their prospective marks.

Several years ago, after I had been playing the horses for a couple of years, I saw an ad in the paper for a booklet offering fifteen keys to successful handicapping. Since the price tag was just $3, I sent for it. The booklet told me not to bet horses that had bled in their most recent start, along with fourteen other equally revolutionary rules. Most significantly, by purchasing this product, my name had been placed on the seller's mailing list.

A short time later, I received a letter like the one previously described, giving a telephone number to call the day of the race, and asking that I place a $10 wager on the horse for them (to be mailed in before their next release). Rather than respond, I asked a friend to purchase the booklet and get his name on the mailing list too. The next time they had a "sure thing" going, we would be prepared to test their veracity! When we called the morning of the race, we were not surprised to find that we had been given different horses. One was the prerace favorite, the other among the more obvious contenders.

Apparently, it was their standard operating procedure to release different horses to different customers. Possibly they distributed the entire field to their customers, guaranteeing that some would be satisfied at day's end, likely to respond to their next solicitation, and send them the proceeds of the winning bet to insure that future winners would keep coming.

Beware of the mail-order touts. Enough said. End of digression.

FORTY-FIRST DAY — SUNDAY, JULY 3
(Entries close Friday, July 1)

1st Race—Black Pool   Five Furlongs
Purse $20,000. For Two-Year-Olds which have never won a race other than Maiden or Claiming
Non-winners of a race other than claiming since June 15 allowed ..... 3 lbs.
Of such a race since June 1 ..... 5 lbs.

2nd Race—Claiming   One Mile
Purse $15,500. For Fillies and Mares Four Years Old and Upward
Non-winners of two races at a mile or over since June 1 allowed ..... 3 lbs.
Of such a race since then ..... 5 lbs.
..... 2 lbs.
Claiming price $25,000; for each $2,500 to $20,000.
(Races when entered to be claimed for $18,000 or less not considered.)

3rd Race—Maiden   One Mile and a Sixteenth (Turf)
Purse $24,500. For Maiden Fillies and Mares Three Years Old and Upward Foaled in New York State and Approved by the New York State-Bred Registry.
Three-Year-Olds ..... 116 lbs.   Older ..... 122 lbs.
(Purse reflects $5,500 from New York Breeding Fund enrichment.)

4th Race—Lord Avie Handicap   Seven Furlongs
(Closing Thursday, June 30)
Purse $35,000. A Handicap for Fillies and Mares Three Years Old and Upward.
Weights Thursday, June 30.   Declarations by 10:00 A.M., Friday, July 1.

5th Race—Claiming   Six and a Half Furlongs
Purse $16,500. For Four-Year-Olds and Upward ..... 122 lbs.
Non-winners of two races since June 1 allowed ..... 3 lbs.
Of a race since then ..... 5 lbs.
Claiming price $35,000; for each $2,500 to $30,000 ..... 2 lbs.
(Races when entered to be claimed for $25,000 or less not considered.)

24

6th Race—Maiden   One Mile
Purse $19,000. For Maidens Three Years Old and Upward.
Three-Year-Olds ..... 116 lbs.   Older ..... 122 lbs.

7th Race—Navajo   One Mile and a Sixteenth (Turf)
Purse $21,000. For Three-Year-Olds and Upward which have never won a race other than Maiden, Claiming or Starter.
Three-Year-Olds ..... 116 lbs.   Older ..... 122 lbs.
Non-winners of a race other than claiming at a mile or over since June 15 allowed ..... 3 lbs.
Of such a race since June 1 ..... 5 lbs.

8th Race—Ribero   One Mile (Turf)
Purse $32,000. For Three-Year-Olds and Upward which have never won four races other than Maiden, Claiming or Starter.
Three-Year-Olds ..... 116 lbs.   Older ..... 122 lbs.
Non-winners of two races other than maiden or claiming at a mile or over since June 1 allowed ..... 3 lbs.
Of such a race since then ..... 5 lbs.

NINTH RACE—THE TIDAL HANDICAP
$75,000 Added
(Grade II)

For Three-Year-Olds and Upward. By subscription of $150 each, which should accompany the nomination; $600 to pass the entry box; with $75,000 added. The added money and all fees to be divided 60% to the winner, 22% to second, 12% to third and 6% to fourth. Weights Tuesday, June 28. Starters to be named at the closing time of entries. Trophies will be presented to the winning owner, trainer and jockey. The New York Racing Association reserves the right to transfer this race to the main course.
Nominations close Wednesday, June 15, 1983.

ONE MILE AND THREE FURLONGS (Turf Course)

Substitute Race No. 1—Claiming   One Mile and a Sixteenth (Turf)
Purse $20,500. For Four-Year-Olds and Upward ..... 122 lbs.
Non-winners of two races at a mile or over since June 1 allowed ..... 3 lbs.
Of such a race since then ..... 5 lbs.
Claiming price $50,000; for each $2,500 to $45,000 ..... 2 lbs.
(Races when entered to be claimed for $40,000 or less not considered.)

Substitute Race No. 2—Claiming   One Mile and a Sixteenth
Purse $11,000. For Four-Year-Olds and Upward ..... 122 lbs.
Non-winners of two races at a mile or over since June 1 allowed ..... 3 lbs.
Of such a race since then ..... 5 lbs.
Claiming price $14,000; for each $1,000 to $12,000 ..... 2 lbs.
(Races when entered to be claimed for $10,000 or less not considered.)

CLOSING FRIDAY, JULY 1
THE INDEPENDENCE HANDICAP — Purse $37,000
Three-Year-Olds and Upward   Two Miles (Turf)
To be run Monday, July 4

25

☐ **PROPER PLACEMENT** ☐

A horse can have basically two kinds of excuses for a poor performance. One is bad racing luck, over which the trainer has no control, and the bettor no forewarning. The other is poor race selection. Trainers and owners pick the spots for their horses, often not wisely. But astute handicappers can take advantage, eliminating poorly managed horses from consideration as possible contenders.

No horse, no matter how sharp it is, can be considered a good bet unless properly placed in a race that befits its ability and experience. A reading of the race conditions helps the handicapper separate the true contenders from pretenders that may be unsuited by the distance or surface, or that may be entered against far superior opponents.

As we discuss each component of the race conditions, I will point out where that piece of information will reappear in the running lines of the past performances, once the race in question becomes part of the historical record. I emphasize that many of the items discussed here are given specific, individual attention in this chapter alone.

☐ **THE RACE NUMBER** ☐

9 **AQUEDUCT** **1 MILE** AQUEDUCT

1 MILE. (1.33⅓) CLAIMING. Purse $17,000. 3-year-olds and up. Weights: 3-year-olds, 120 lbs.; older, 122 lbs.; non-winners of 2 races at a mile or over since Oct. 15 allowed 3 lbs.; of such a race since then, 5 lbs. Claiming Price $35,000; for each $2,500 to $30,000 allowed 2 lbs. (Races where entered to be claimed for $25,000 or less not considered)

The first piece of information encountered in the race conditions is the race number, appearing encircled and in large type, followed by the name of the track. This information is carried over directly into the running lines, preceded by the date, which does not appear in the conditions, but is a vital piece of information that will be discussed in detail in Chapter 7. The date appears in day-month-year format.

The race number is of little, if any, use to handicappers. Some feel that the incidence of chicanery is higher in races featuring exotic betting such as exactas and triples; consequently they are suspicious of the results of such races. Nowadays, however, it seems that almost every race offers some form of exotic wagering, yet one cannot function effectively at the track while in a state of paranoia. If there are dishonest things happening, they can just as easily work in favor of an unwitting handicapper as against him, at least often enough to alleviate the concern. At least one instance occurs where the race number might prove helpful, however. It follows a day of changing weather and/or track conditions. For example, a strong wind might kick up late in the afternoon, blowing briskly into the faces of the horses as they run down the backstretch. Such conditions make things extremely difficult for the front-running types, who take the brunt of the wind. It is worth recalling the conditions under which these animals ran when they make their next start, and the race number might prove the key to jogging the handicapper's memory.

☐ THE TRACK ☐

The identity of the track at which a horse ran its most recent races can prove quite significant. It will be one of the main points of discussion in Chapter 7. A complete list of abbreviations for North American tracks is published regularly in the Form and is reproduced on page 25. In the past performances, the symbol ♦ preceding the race number denotes a foreign track. (See the past performances of Mary Mitsu on page 43.)

Knowing the track at which the day's races will be run can be quite helpful. By this, we are not referring to the inconvenience of driving to Aqueduct when the day's races are being held at Belmont, but rather to understanding the track and its personality. Each race track, and each racing surface, has its own individual characteristics. Some are more hospitable to early speed. Others become quite cuppy after prolonged use, and tend to favor stretch runners when in that condition. Some dry out faster after a period of rain, returning quickly to normal. At others, the rail becomes quite deep and sticky during the drying-out phase, severely penalizing horses attempting to take the shortest route home. The handicapper aware of the existence of any such "track bias" holds a distinct advantage over his competitors, the lesser-informed players in the audience. More about this in Chapter 11.

Abbreviations and Purse Value Index For North American Tracks

The following table may be used as an adjunct to Daily Racing Form's past performance feature of showing the value of allowance race purses. The number in bold face type following the name of each track (except hunt meets) represents the average net purse value per race (including stakes and overnight races), rounded to the nearest thousand, during the track's 1982 season. A comparison thus can be made of the value of an allowance purse in a horse's current past performances with the average value of all races at that track the preceding season. The purse value index in the track abbreviation table will be changed each year to reflect the values of the previous season. If no purse value index is shown in the following table. the track did not operate a race meeting last year.

AC — (Agua) Caliente, Mexico—3
Aks — Ak-Sar-Ben, Neb.—10
Alb — *Albuquerque, N. Mex.—7
AP — Arlington Park, Ill.—11
Aqu — Aqueduct, N.Y.—20
AsD — *Assiniboia Downs, Canada—4
Atl — Atlantic City, N.J.—7
Ato — *Atokad Park, Neb—1
BD — *Berkshire Downs, Mass.
Bel — Belmont Park, N.Y.—25
Beu — Beulah Race Track, Ohio—4
Bil — *Billings, Mont.—1
BM — Bay Meadows, Cal.—11
Bmf — Bay Meadows Fair, Cal.—10
Bml — Balmoral Park, Ill.—3
Boi — *Boise, Idaho—1
Bow — Bowie, Md.—9
CD — Churchill Downs, Ky.—12
Cda — *Coeur d'Alene, Idaho—1
Cen — Centennial Race Track, Colo.—2
Cka — *Cahokia Downs, Ill.
Cls — *Columbus, Neb.—2
Com — *Commodore Downs, Pa.—2
Crc — Calder Race Course, Fla.—9
CT — *Charles Town, W. Va.—3
DeD — *Delta Downs, La.—3
Del — Delaware Park, Del.—8
Det — Detroit Race Course, Mich.—5
Dmr — Del Mar, Cal.—19
Dmf — Del Mar Fair, Cal.—9
Elm — *Elma, Wash.
EIP — Ellis Park, Ky.—5
EnP — †Enoch Park, Canada
EP — *Exhibition Park, Canada—6
EvD — *Evangeline Downs, La.—4
FD — Florida Downs, Fla.
FE — Fort Erie, Canada—7
Fer — *Ferndale, Cal.—1
FG — Fair Grounds, La.—10.
FL — Finger Lakes, N. Y.—5
Fno — Fresno, Cal.—4
Fon — *Fonner Park, Neb.—3
FP — Fairmount Park, Ill.—4
GBF — *Great Barrington, Mass.—2
GD — †Galway Downs, Cal.
GF — *Great Falls, Mont.—1
GG — Golden Gate Fields, Cal.—11
GP — Gulfstream Park, Fla.—12
Grd — *Greenwood, Canada—10
GrP — *Grants Pass, Ore.—1

GS — †Garden State Park, N. J.
Haw — Hawthorne, Ill.—10
Hia — Hialeah Park, Fla.—13
Hol — Hollywood Park, Cal.—25
HP — *Hazel Park, Mich.—6
Imp — *Imperial, Cal.
JnD — *Jefferson Downs, La—5
Jua — Juarez, Mexico
Kee — Keeneland, Ky.—17
Key — Keystone Race Track, Pa.—8
LA — *Los Alamitos, Cal.—10
LaD — Louisiana Downs, La.—13
LaM — *La Mesa Park, N. Mex.—2
Lar — Nuevo Laredo, Mexico
Lat — *Latonia, Ky.—4
Lbg — Lethbridge, Canada
Lga — Longacres, Wash.—6
LnN — *Lincoln State Fair, Neb.—4
Lrl — Laurel Race Course, Md.—9
MD — *Marquis Downs, Canada—2
Med — Meadowlands, N.J.—13
Mex — *Mexico City, Mexico
MF — *Marshfield Fair, Mass.—2
Mth — Monmouth Park, N. J.—10
Nmp — *Northampton, Mass.—2
NP — *Northlands Park, Canada—5
OP — Oaklawn Park, Ark.—14
OTC — †Ocala Training Center, Fla.
Pay — †Payson Park, Fla.
Pen — Penn National, Pa.—4
Pim — Pimlico, Md.—11
PJ — *Park Jefferson, S. D.—1
Pla — *Playfair, Wash.—2
Pln — Pleasanton, Cal.—8
PM — Portland Meadows, Ore.—3
Pmf — Portl'nd M'd'ws Fair, Ore.
Poc — *Pocono Downs, Pa.
Pom — *Pomona, Cal.—12
PR — Puerto Rico (El Com'te)
Pre — *Prescott Downs, Ariz.—1
RD — River Downs, Ohio—4
Reg — *Regina, Canada—2
Ril — *Rillito, Ariz.—1
Rkm — Rockingham Park, N. H.
Rui — *Ruidoso, N. Mex—4
SA — Santa Anita Park, Cal.—26
Sac — Sacramento, Cal.—5
Sal — *Salem, Ore. (Lone Oak)—1
San — *Sandown Park, Canada—2
Sar — Saratoga, N.Y.—26

SFe — *Santa Fe, N. Mex.—3
ShD — *Shenand'h Downs, W. Va.
SLR — †San Luis Rey Downs, Cal.
Sol — *Solano, Cal.—6
Spt — *Sportsman's Park, Ill.—11
SR — *Santa Rosa, Cal. —6
Stk — Stockton, Cal.—5
StP — *Stampede Park, Canada—5
Suf — Suffolk Downs, Mass.—6
SuD — *Sun Downs, Wash.—1
Sun — Sunland Park, N. Mex.—3
Tam — Tampa Bay Downs, Fla.—3
        (Formerly Florida Downs)
Tdn — Thistledown, Ohio—4
Tim — *Timonium, Md.—5
TuP — Turf Paradise, Ariz.—3
Vic — *Victorville, Cal.
Was — Washington Park, Ill.
Wat — Waterford Park, W. Va.—2
WO — Woodbine, Canada—13
YM — Yakima Meadows, Wash.—1

HUNT MEETINGS

Aik — Aiken, S. Carolina
AtH — Atlanta, Ga.
Cam — Camden, S. Carolina
Clm — Clemmons, N. Carolina
Fai — Fair Hill, Md.
Fax — Fairfax, Va.
FH — Far Hills, N. J.
Fx — Foxfield, Va.
Gln — Glyndon, Md.
GN — *Grand National, Md.
Lex — Lexington, Ky.
Lig — Ligonier, Pa.
Mal — Malvern, Pa.
Mid — Middleburg, Va.
Mon — Monkton, Md.
Mor — Morven Park, Va.
Mtp — Montpelier, Va.
Oxm — Oxmoor, Ky.
Pro — Prospect, Ky.
PW — Percy Warner, Tenn.
RB — Red Bank, N. J.
SH — Strawberry Hill, Va.
SoP — Southern Pines, N. C.
Try — Tryon, N.C.
Uni — Unionville, Pa
War — Warrenton, Va
Wel — Wellsville, Pa.

Tracks marked with (*) are less than one mile in circumference. †Training facility only.

Another important aspect of a track's "personality" are the people involved—specifically the trainers and jockeys. Knowing which are competent, and which are not, is crucial to playing the races successfully at that track.

☐ THE DISTANCE ☐

The next piece of information found in the conditions is the distance of the race. It is usually preceded by a diagram depicting the course for the race, and possibly followed by a parenthetical note (TURF) indicating that the race is to be run on the grass course.

This information is carried over into the past performances, as indicated, preceded by a description of the condition of the racing surface. The symbol "f," for furlong, is used to designate sprint distances, such as "6f" for a six-furlong race. No special symbols are used for route races. The symbol "1" represents a one-mile race, while "1⅛" means a race of a mile and one eighth, to give two examples.

An encircled Ⓣ is used to indicate races run over a grass course. At tracks such as Belmont and Saratoga which use two separate grass courses, the inner (nearer the infield) course is designated by the symbol ⊤. At Aqueduct, which has the dubious distinction of having two dirt courses, the symbol ▣ is used for the inner (winterized) dirt course. An asterisk before the distance means the race was run at "about" (approximately) that distance. This is common in grass racing, where the inner rail is moved a few feet out to allow the grass along the (former) rail to grow back in. The course becomes slightly longer when this is done.

America's Thoroughbred races are run over a wide variety of distances, on either dirt or grass courses. The standard yardstick for measuring distance is the "furlong," the commonly used terminology for an eighth of a mile (220 yards). Races run at distances up to (but not including) one mile are termed "sprints." Those run at distances of one mile or longer are called "routes." Sprints can be as short as the three-furlong "nursery" distance used for newly turned two-year-olds early in the year. However, the most popular sprint distance is six furlongs. Older horses quite frequently run at six and one half and seven furlongs, while two-year-olds run mostly at five and five and one half furlongs during the summer months.

The standard route races are at the "middle distances," from one mile to a mile and three-sixteenths. However, many important stakes races (as well as lesser events) are run at the "classic distances" between a mile and a quarter and a mile and a half. Races at times are scheduled for marathon distances up to two and a quarter miles, the distance of Aqueduct's Display Handicap, North America's longest stakes event. Most grass races are run over a distance of ground, although some tracks card grass sprints at distances ranging from five to seven furlongs.

Some Thoroughbreds are specialists. Some prefer the sprint distances, quite a few of these the shorter sprint distances up to six furlongs. Others are best suited to the route distances. A few require the marathon distances before turning into high gear. Some can handle only the dirt course, while others are more at home on the grass.

On the other hand, many Thoroughbreds are versatile, able to handle both grass and dirt, sprints and middle distance routes. It is the task of the handicapper to judge whether a horse is suited to the particular distance and surface it is being asked to handle. Reading the race conditions and scanning the distance column in the running lines often provides a quick answer to that question. It is also important for the handicapper to make note of the prevailing track conditions, then refer to the historical record to determine if a horse can handle those conditions. Track condition designations for the main dirt track include:

FAST	denoted	Fst
GOOD	"	Gd
SLOW	"	Sl
SLOPPY	"	Sly
MUDDY	"	My
HEAVY	"	Hy
FROZEN	"	Fr

A *sloppy* (or wet) track will often pass through *good* before reverting back to *fast*. After a considerable amount of rainfall, a track will usually become *muddy* or *slow*, or possibly even *heavy*, during the drying-out phase. It is important to note that a sloppy track usually favors front-runners, as does a frozen track, an occasional occurrence during the frigid winter months. Frozen tracks often produce exceptionally fast running times as well. On the other hand, the traditional belief has been that the typical track will favor stretch-runners while drying out. My statistical studies, documented in *Winning at the Races*, found the latter to be untrue, however. All types of racing surfaces, as a general rule, favor front-runners. Some horses seem to revel in the wet going. Others can't handle it at all. We shall discuss how breeding and/or conformation might play a role in this phenomenon in Chapter 5.

The *Daily Racing Form* has in the past assigned a mud-mark (an asterisk following the horse's name) to denote fair mud-runners. Good mud-runners receive an X rather than the *, while superior mud-runners are assigned the symbol ⊗. However, in recent years the *Form* has become rather lax in its assignment of mud-marks. Therefore, the handicapper is best advised to make his own evaluation of a horse's mud-running ability by looking to the record for evidence of races run over wet tracks. Keep in mind that the *Form's* symbols represent the subjective opinion of one of their employees, and are seldom altered even when subsequent information suggests the original rating may have been incorrect.

On the grass, the possible track conditions are:

HARD	denoted	Hd
FIRM	"	Fm
GOOD	"	Gd
SOFT	"	Sf
YIELDING	"	Yl

The usual status of the grass course is *firm*. A *hard* course is likely to develop after a prolonged period of hot and dry weather, and usually favors front-runners quite noticeably. *Soft* and *yielding* courses result from recent rains, and are the most conducive conditions for stretch-runners. Soft conditions are the worst, and often favor horses that raced well abroad under other than firm conditions. A course termed "good" by European standards is equivalent to conditions American tracks usually term "soft." *Good* is used for the in-between status, somewhere between completely dry and noticeably damp. Also note that long grass tends to be tiring, and so hurts the chances of speed horses.

Some grass runners prefer a firm course, while others favor a more resilient surface. Likewise, there are runners that perform well over a sloppy track, but nowhere near as well as on a muddy track, which can be a quite different type of surface. It is always wise to look for a variance in form between dry and wet conditions, or between the various types of wet conditions. Many horses exhibit some kind of preference.

CASE STUDY: NASKRA'S BREEZE AND ZOOPHILE

Americans handicap dirt races with an eye toward track conditions. But when it comes to turf racing, they seem to reason that "grass is grass," and the relative firmness of the course doesn't matter. Read any report from a European correspondent to *The Blood-Horse* or *The Thoroughbred Record* magazines, and you will soon think otherwise. European horsemen and handicappers alike are well aware of the preferences of individual horses for firm or soft conditions underfoot.

Naskra's Breeze — **B. g. 5, by Naskra—Tropical Heat, by Tropical Breeze**
Own.—Broadmoor Stable — **Br.—Davis C C (NY)** — **Tr.—Johnson Philip G** — **119**

Lifetime								
25 9 6 3		1982	2	0	0	0	$3,288
$281,927		1981	10	3	2	2	$139,207
		Turf	5	3	0	1	$118,135

19May82- 7Bel	fst	1	:45⅘	1:09⅘	1:34⅕	3↑Alw 35000	2	5	55½	68	614	616	Samyn J L	121	2.60	79-14 ConquistdorCielo11311SwingingLight119¾BchlorBoo1243¼	Outrun	7
5May82- 8Aqu	fst	6f	:23⅕	:46⅖	1:10⅘	3↑[S]Pelham H	6	2	31	42¼	52¼	4½	Samyn J L	118	8.20	86-22 Kim's Chance 119no Dedicated Rullah 116nk Prosper112nk	Rallied	8
12Dec81- 8Lrl	fst	1⅛	:48⅗	1:13	1:50	3↑W Haight H	3	3	33	23	22½	21½	Samyn J L	117	*1.30	94-21 SunnyWinters1111½Naskra'sBreeze11710PoorDd1131	Second best	6
25Nov81- 8Aqu	fst	1	:48⅖	1:14	1:38⅖	3↑[S]Handicap	6	3	22	12½	15	14¾	Samyn J L	117	*.80	74-32 Nskr'sBreeze1174¾NorthCountryBlue112½RomnChef1081¼	Handily	6
3Nov81- 6Aqu	gd	1⅜	(T):49⅖	1:39⅘	2:18⅖	3↑Kn'ckerb'r H	5	3	33	11	2hd	31½	Samyn J L	115	2.90	77-26 Euphrosyne110¾OurCaptinWillie115¾Nskr'sBreeze115¾	Weakened	8
3Nov81-Run in two divisions sixth & eighth races.																		
17Oct81- 6Med	fm	1 1/16	(T):47⅖	1:10⅘	1:41	3↑Jersey Blu H	2	9	96¼	87¼	59	56½	Samyn J L	117	*2.50	90-10 Acaroid 1162¾ War of Words 114no Data Swap 1173	No threat	10
9Sep81- 8Bel	sf	1 1/16	(T):47⅘	1:13⅕	1:45⅗	3↑Britn Bch H	9	7	64½	1hd	16	111	Samyn J L	112	8.70	69-31 Naskra's Breeze 11211 Manguin 107¾ Restless Thief 107½	Easily	9
21Aug81- 8Sar	fm	1 1/16	(T):46⅖	1:10	1:41	3↑[S]W. Point H	12	9	95	76	53	1nk	Samyn J L	117	12.20	92-15 Naskra's Breeze 117nk Ta Ho Tom 1122¼ Adlibber 122½	Driving	12
10Aug81- 9Sar	fm	1	[T]:47⅗	1:12⅕	1:37	3↑[S]Handicap	3	6	67½	53	2½	1½	Samyn J L	116	3.00	91-11 Naskra's Breeze 116½ SirAck1213¾NorthCountryBlue1061½	Driving	10
10Aug81-Disqualified from purse money.																		
20Jly81- 8Bel	sly	1	:45⅖	1:09⅗	1:35	3↑[S]EvanShipman	1	5	45½	44¼	45	33¼	Samyn J L	117	18.70	90-15 Fio Rito 1172½ Sir Ack 121¾ Naskra's Breeze 117nk	Mild Rally	7

LATEST WORKOUTS **May 1 Bel tr.t 6f fst 1:15⅕ b** **Apr 26 Bel tr.t 6f fst 1:19 b** **Apr 22 Bel tr.t 5f fst 1:00⅖ h** **Apr 17 Bel tr.t 4f fst :50⅗ b**

Naskra's Breeze provides a good example of a horse that moves up several lengths when the footing is soft. After struggling to win twice in state-bred company over a firm course at Saratoga, the gelding exploded in open company over a very damp course at Belmont on September 9.

His next race was dismal, over a firm course at the Meadowlands, but notice that he ran much better next out over a good Aqueduct course.

As a five-year-old, Naskra's Breeze's best performance came in the Grade I United Nations Handicap at Atlantic City, over a course softened by recent rains. Those who remembered his preference for soft footing were rewarded with a $13.00 mutuel.

Zoophile is a prime example of a soft-course specialist. Prior to May of 1983, her only two races over yielding turf were sharp, while most of her efforts on firm grass were dismal. And judging by the slow times on November 8, the course that day was probably closer to soft than firm. When entered on a yielding course May 22, 1983, Zoophile "woke up." She returned a nice $21.60 to those who paid attention to track conditions. But when raced next on June 12, Zoophile caught a firm course. True to form, she did little running.

Other horses have quite the opposite preference—they prefer a firm course, and the harder it is, the better they like it.

Hard-turf conditions during the summer months are fertile grounds for upsets, as front-runners that tired over softer courses during April and May suddenly "improve" when the conditions become more favorable to their running style. European imports are likely to run below their best form under such conditions, which seldom are seen on the other side of the Atlantic. The foreign horses can be expected to show marked improvement during the fall months, when conditions soften up more to their liking.

□ ONE-TURN ROUTES □

The handicapper is also advised to glance at the diagram of the race course/distance, especially when dealing with route races. How close is the start to the first (clubhouse) turn? If very close, horses in outside post positions are severely handicapped. At certain tracks (Aqueduct, Belmont, and Arlington), races at one mile (and longer at Belmont) are run around just one turn. The diagram will point this out. Such races feature a long straightaway run to their only turn, a run that frequently works against front-running types. It is a statistically proven fact that front-runners do better in two-turn routes than in the one-turn variety, even though the latter may be the shorter races. At one turn, the front-runners are forced to run a considerable distance on the same lead foot while battling for the lead. At two turns, they get an additional change of leads on the clubhouse turn, aiding them to fight off fatigue.

AQUEDUCT　(**1 MILE**)　1 MILE. (1.33⅓) CLAIMING. Purse $17,000. 3-year-olds and up. Weights: 3-year-olds, 120 lbs.; older, 122 lbs.; non-winners of 2 races at a mile or over since Oct. 15 allowed 3 lbs.; of such a race since then, 5 lbs. Claiming Price $35,000; for each $2,500 to $30,000 allowed 2 lbs. (Races where entered to be claimed for $25,000 or less not considered)

The race distance is followed by a number indicating the track record for that distance. Although speed ratings (see Chapter 9) are based on the track records, the record itself is of no use to the handicapper at this stage.

AQUEDUCT　(**1 MILE**)　1 MILE. (1.33⅓) CLAIMING. Purse $17,000. 3-year-olds and up. Weights: 3-year-olds, 120 lbs.; older, 122 lbs.; non-winners of 2 races at a mile or over since Oct. 15 allowed 3 lbs.; of such a race since then, 5 lbs. Claiming Price $35,000; for each $2,500 to $30,000 allowed 2 lbs. (Races where entered to be claimed for $25,000 or less not considered)

☐ THE ELIGIBILITY CONDITIONS ☐

Next encountered is the word or two that describes the classification of the race. Broadly speaking, Thoroughbred races are divided into two categories: claiming races and those that are not claiming races. We will take a look at the claiming race first.

Claiming Races

Every horse running in a claiming race is for sale. Any owner who has started a horse at the current meeting is eligible to claim a (one)

AQUEDUCT   **1 MILE**
AQUEDUCT

1 MILE. (1.33¼) **CLAIMING**. Purse $17,000. 3-year-olds and up. Weights: 3-year-olds, 120 lbs.; older, 122 lbs.; non-winners of 2 races at a mile or over since Oct. 15 allowed 3 lbs.; of such a race since then, 5 lbs. **Claiming Price $35,000, for each $2,500 to $30,000** allowed 2 lbs. (Races where entered to be claimed for $25,000 or less not considered).

horse from a claiming race. He assumes ownership of the horse, dead or alive, after the race has been run, without sharing in any possible earnings from the race. It has happened on several occasions that more than one owner entered a claim for the same horse, only to watch the animal suffer a fatal injury during the running of the race. The owners were then forced to draw lots for the right to purchase the horse, then pay for its burial expenses.

Claiming races are designed to provide competitive contests. The conditions force the entrants to race for nearly equal claiming prices. In the example, the range is from $35,000 down to $30,000. Horses entered at a price below the top price listed receive a break in the weights, in our case two pounds for each $2,500 below $35,000. A horse entered for $30,000 will carry four pounds less than had it been entered for $35,000 instead. As a general rule, a $10,000 claimer will be a $10,000 horse wherever it competes. At times, however, an abundance of talent at a given claiming level will overflow into neighboring classes. If one track has an overload of $10,000 animals, its $8,500 ranks also will be unusually strong and very likely competitive against $10,000 claimers at nearby tracks. At the minor tracks, however, there is some question regarding the true value of those horses competing at the higher claiming levels. Are they really cheaper horses moving up into a vacuum to help fill races at an unrealistically high level for that track? Can they compete successfully against horses of similar value at nearby major tracks? The answer, no doubt, differs from one minor track to another. Serious handicappers at these tracks are best advised to do the research that will uncover the answer in their locale.

Now, imagine that you are the owner of a $50,000 claiming horse. Would you race it in a $25,000 claiming race? Perhaps so, if you are desperate to win a purse, or if the animal is developing severe physical problems. Otherwise, you would do so fully aware that a sound-looking $50,000 animal entered at half its market value would almost certainly be claimed. The loss on the value of the horse would hardly be compensated for by the purse it would almost certainly win. A claiming horse dropping slightly in price may be doing so to find its proper level, or to win a purse, but the horse dropping drastically must be looked upon suspiciously. The horse probably has physical problems, and a good paddock and/or post parade inspection could confirm the suspicion.

The claiming price for which a horse is entered appears somewhat to the right of the horse's name, immediately above the column revealing claiming prices from previous starts. Note that the claiming price is listed after the symbol Clm, which denotes Claiming race. Should the horse have been claimed from one of its previous starts, the symbol c- will precede the claiming price, as on the third line of Creme de La Fete's past performances.

Note in passing that a horse claimed must move up at least 25 percent in claiming price for thirty days after being claimed. That, or race in allowance or starter company, or remain on the sidelines for that amount of time. During those thirty days, a recent claim is said to be "in jail."

When a top outfit claims a horse, they give it a thorough physical checkup. Small things, like improperly fitted shoes, can retard a horse's performance. An abscessed tooth can lead to a loss of appetite, and a consequent loss of form. Attention to details separates the leading trainers from those seldom seen in the winners' circle.

CASE STUDY EXQUISITE GAL

When a top trainer claims an apparent "dog," take notice. You might not be able to determine what he saw in the horse. But perhaps just a slight change in treatment or equipment will brighten the animal's outlook on life, and help turn it around as a racehorse.

What Oscar Barrera saw in Exquisite Gal is certainly not obvious to the naked eye. The six-year-old mare had lost eleven consecutive races during the early part of 1983, without being close at any stage in most of those races. She had shown little speed, and no apparent interest in racing. Yet, just three days after being claimed, she was able to move up into $16,000 company and win rather easily, after stalking the pace in the early stages of the race. The usually sharp New York crowd, well aware of Barrera's magic with his claims, let this one escape at $29.80.

Exquisite Gal — Ch. m. 6, by Canonero II—Summer Time Gal, by Summer Tan
$14,000 Br.—Dimauro S A (NY)
Own.—Barrera Oscar S — Tr.—Barrera Oscar S
1067 — Lifetime 44 3 4 8 $84,656 — 1983 11 0 1 1 $9,390 — 1982 16 2 2 2 $36,300 — Turf 2 0 0 0

27Apr83- 1Aqu	fst	1⅛	:47⅘	1:13	1:53	ⒻClm c-9000	4	7	715	714	612	612	Messina R5	108	6.00	58-17	DoubleDcqure1121¼HrritonJmie1125¼ProvoctiveGlnce114¾	Outrun	7
25Mar83- 9Aqu	fst	6f	:23⅗	:48⅘	1:13⅘	ⒻⓈAlw 27000	1	7	89	78½	56½	48	Thibeau R J7	110	17.00	65-36	Klara Balint 1142¾ Final Bow 1174 Lady Accipiter1171¼	No factor	12
19Mar83- 9Aqu	my	1	:47	1:12⅘	1:39⅕	ⒻClm 16000	9	3	42½	52½	911	108¼	Barnett W A7	112	10.60	62-21	La Foresita 117¾ Canino Vera 112hd Nicely Naskra 1171½	Tired	10
13Mar83- 9Aqu	fst	1 1/16	⊡:47⅖	1:12⅖	1:44	ⒻClm 20000	8	7	89½	716	611	511	Murphy D J7	106	5.80	82-08	Huffy's Turn 1127½ Talented Jet 117nk Shofoose 1081½	No factor	11
4Mar83- 7Aqu	fst	170	⊡:48	1:13⅘	1:45	ⒻⓈAlw 28500	3	9	1013	911	55½	22	Thibeau R J5	112	26.30	75-19	Reserve Decision 1172 ExquisiteGal112nkKlaraBalint1171¾	Rallied	10
24Feb83- 1Aqu	fst	1⅛	⊡:48⅕	1:13⅘	1:55⅘	ⒻClm 14000	5	5	517	516	516	310	Alvarado R Jr5	108	6.30	58-24	Baby Bonnie 1139BrightSky1081½ExquisiteGal1082¼	Checked turn	7
14Feb83- 3Aqu	fst	1 1/16	⊡:47⅖	1:13⅕	1:45⅖	ⒻClm 14000	5	9	918	89¾	77½	69¾	Powers T M5	109	10.30	76-13	Klara Balint 1125 Committ 1171¾ Baby Bonnie 115¾	No factor	11
6Feb83- 3Aqu	fst	1 1/16	⊡:48⅖	1:14⅕	1:48	ⒻⓈAlw 28500	2	6	610	65½	66¾	66¼	Barnett W A7	110	17.50	67-22	Onyx Beauty 1122½ HailtoFrance1171¾SwoonLake1121¼	No factor	10
27Jan83- 9Aqu	fst	6f	⊡:23⅖	:47⅕	1:13⅕	ⒻClm 14000	10	12	1116	1115	1012	73½	Barnett W A5	108	47.70	74-19	Mary Of Winloc 110nk Onyx Fox 117nk Miscast 110nk	Outrun	12
14Jan83- 6Key	fst	170	:47⅘	1:12⅖	1:44	ⒻClm 11000	12	8	912	1117	922	1014	Vega A5	b 111	8.10	66-22	Whitewalls 115½ Holly's Silver 1193½ Sugar Pockets 1101	Outrun	12

LATEST WORKOUTS Apr 28 Bel tr.t 4f fst :49⅘ b Apr 22 Aqu 4f fst :52 b

CASE STUDY: ROCK LIVES

When a trainer reclaims one of his former charges, he is telling the public in no uncertain terms that he believes the animal is relatively free of physical problems. He knows the animal better than most, and feels it worth repurchasing, usually at a price higher than he received for the animal. He is willing to give the other owner an immediate profit. Obviously, he must feel that he can make money with the horse.

Rock Lives provides a good example. Claimed from Roy Sedlacek at the end of the Meadowlands meeting, the three-year-old was immediately reclaimed by his former outfit from his first start at Aqueduct. The transaction cost the Tresvant Stable $15,000, but they regained possession of a horse that was soon to become a stakes winner. Nothing in the past performances points out the fact that the horse was a reclaim. Only those handicappers who make note of such things will be in a position to profit from such transactions.

Rock Lives — Dk. b. or br. c. 3, by Rock Talk—In Camelot, by Joust
Br.—Torre J E (NJ)
Own.—Tresvant Stable — Tr.—Sedlacek Roy
120 — Lifetime 15 5 2 2 $84,755 — 1983 5 2 1 1 $53,280 — 1982 10 3 1 1 $31,475 — Turf 1 0 0 0

27Feb83- 8Aqu	fst	1⅛	⊡:48	1:12⅗	1:52⅗	Lucky Draw	3	1	11½	11	13	13	Davis R G	117	11.20	83-20	Rock Lives 1173CommonSense117hdInstantAlamode117nk	Driving	7
17Feb83- 6Aqu	fst	6f	⊡:23⅕	:46⅘	1:11⅗	Alw 20000	4	1	11	1hd	13	14½	Davis R G5	112	*1.30	86-17	Rock Lives 1124½ PersonalityCrisis1173Significantly1174½	Driving	7
31Jan83- 7Aqu	fst	1 1/16	⊡:48⅕	1:12⅗	1:44	Alw 21000	2	2	31½	42½	35	36½	Alvarado R Jr5	112	*1.40	87-15	A NativeYank1176½Flip'sLittleBoy117noRockLives1123	Weakened	8
21Jan83- 8Aqu	fst	1⅛	⊡:46	1:10⅗	1:50⅘	Alw 21000	5	3	43½	23	1½	21	Alvarado R Jr5	112	*2.20	91-15	EspritDeRomeo1191RockLives1125¾TallTleTeller117no	Weakened	8
7Jan83- 7Aqu	gd	1 1/16	⊡:47⅕	1:12	1:45⅘	Clm c-55000	3	1	1hd	2hd	22	44¾	Miceli M	113	3.00	79-16	Rushing Water 1154½ Ghent 113hd Whipped Cream 112½	Tired	7
20Dec82- 9Med	fst	1	:47⅕	1:12	1:37⅖	Clm c-40000	3	1	12	11½	15	18	Delgado A5	112	*1.10	95-18	Rock Lives 1128 Kegley 1201½ Dispensation 1136	Ridden out	7
7Dec82- 7Med	fst	6f	:22⅘	:46	1:11⅕	ⓈAlw 15000	2	4	1hd	1hd	2½	22	Delgado A5	109	4.60	85-22	Billdear 1142 Rock Lives 1093½ Always Up 1179	Best of others	7
27Nov82- 6Med	fst	6f	:22⅘	:46⅖	1:11⅘	ⓈN J Fut'y	9	1	42½	42¾	45½	47	Delgado A	122	22.70	77-21	Diamond Patrol122¾AmericanDiabolo122¾Billdear1225½	Weakened	10
9Nov82- 5Med	fst	6f	:22⅖	:46⅖	1:12⅖	Clm 40000	1	4	1hd	3nk	42	43½	Davis R G5	112	*1.60	78-18	TriRum'nCoke1131½Acclimtd1121½Chtnoogchuchu115¾	Weakened	7
30Oct82- 1Med	fst	1	:47⅕	1:12	1:38⅖	Clm 28000	6	2	12½	14	15	17	Delgado M Jr5	108	6.70	90-13	Rock Lives 1087 Par Avion 1172½ Friendly Sign 113no	Ridden out	8

LATEST WORKOUTS ●Mar 21 Aqu 5f fst 1:00⅕ h

CASE STUDY: FRIENDLY SIGN

When a horse's record shows several recent claims, one usually can assume that the animal looks sound; otherwise, it would not have attracted so much interest. If, during the same time span, the horse has been able to move up several notches in claiming value, all, no doubt, is well with the horse. However, if the claims are followed immediately by drops in price, something is likely amiss. Friendly Sign, claimed from each of four consecutive starts, is a prime example. After being claimed by Joseph Ferraioli for $25,000 on January 12, out of a race in which he closed strongly, Friendly Sign was suspiciously absent for six weeks before returning at a reduced price. Apparently, Ferraioli had to battle some kind of physical (or mental) problem with the horse, and was content to lose him for $19,000.

The second claimant, Dominick Galluscio, attempted to take advantage of the horse's apparent good form and strong finishing kick, bringing Friendly Sign back six days later in a $25,000 route. Although the horse faltered in the stretch, Galluscio realized a quick $6,000 profit when the horse was once again claimed.

Sue Sedlacek, the third claimant, apparently struggled with the same problems Joseph Ferraioli faced. She rested the horse for seven weeks, then brought him back at a reduced level on April 23, only to have him claimed by Oscar Barrera.

When a trainer is forced to rest a recent claim, then drop it in value upon returning it to the races, one might suspect either that the horse has problems, or that the trainer was not especially competent. When the pattern repeats with a second trainer, it is the horse that must be suspect. Although Friendly Sign managed to win (as favorite) when dropped in class on April 23, his recent performance profile did not bode well for his future. Entered for $20,000 on May 5, the horse rallied smartly into contention around the turn, only to bear out badly under pressure in the final furlong. Even the Barrerra magic failed to help. Another layoff followed, and another drop in class, but the horse showed even less.

Friendly Sign — Dk. b. or br. c. 3, by Steve's Friend—Sign Play, by Pet Bully
$14,000 Br.—Keyes F (Fla) Tr.—Barrera Oscar S — **112**5
Own.—Barrera O S
Lifetime 18 2 3 2 $22,965 — 1983 7 1 1 0 $10,990 — 1982 11 1 2 2 $11,975

12Jun83-	9Bel	fst	7f	:22⅘	:46⅕	1:25⅘	Clm 15000	10	8	97¾	108¾	84¼	54¼	Thibeau R J	b	110	2.30	69-13	Rock N' War 1141½ Pipe Creek 1172 Kerino 117¾	Bumped 12
5May83-	3Aqu	fst	6f	:22⅕	:45⅗	1:11⅘	Clm 20000	7	5	46	45¼	45½	52½	Cordero A Jr	b	117	2.40	79-21	Gourmet 106no TrueCoverup1141¾ValidDecision117¾	Wide into str. 7
28Apr83-	7Aqu	fst	1	:44⅘	1:09⅖	1:35	Alw 21000	8	8	84¾	95¾	67	611	Davis R G5	b	112	13.30	80-16	Intention 1171¾ Wild Chorus 117hd Cold Remark 1177	No factor 11
23Apr83-	4Aqu	fst	6½f	:23	:46⅗	1:18⅘	Clm c-16000	3	6	21½	2½	1½	1hd	Davis R G5	b	112	*1.80e	81-24	Friendly Sign 112hd Valid Decision 1172 Swift Aid 119¾	Driving 9
4Mar83-	5Aqu	fst	1¹⁄₁₆	⊡:47⅕	1:13⅗	1:47	Clm c-25000	5	4	612	53¼	55	612	Migliore R	b	117	*1.20	66-19	FleetPirte1177½NewMember1171Fendy'sPrince113hd	No response 8
26Feb83-	2Aqu	fst	6f	⊡:23⅖	:48	1:13⅘	Clm c-19000	8	10	118¾	85¾	34	22	Zuniga M	b	115	2.70	73-25	Gourmet 1172 Friendly Sign 1152 Irish Act 1083¼	Rallied 14
12Jan83-	3Aqu	fst	6f	⊡:23⅕	:47⅕	1:12⅘	Clm c-25000	4	8	85½	96½	65	4¾	Asmussen S M7		110	3.90	79-19	Feisty Lad 113nk Iron Sovereign 117no GallantGeorge110½	Rallied 12
28Dec82-	7Med	fst	6f	:22⅖	:45⅘	1:11⅘	Clm 20000	6	3	79	46	23	2¾	Delgado A5		112	3.10	83-18	My Son Jason 115¾ Friendly Sign1123GallantGeorge1172½	Rallied 8
18Dec82-	1Med	fr	6f	:22⅖	:45⅕	1:10⅗	Clm 25000	4	7	77¾	69½	57½	46½	Barnett W A5		112	6.50	83-07	Fungun 1172 Elite Class 1131¼ Mi Te Syd 1173¼	No menace 8
9Dec82-	9Med	fst	170	:47⅖	1:13⅕	1:44⅘	Alw 13000	4	5	67½	69	511	57½	Delgado A5		109	4.60	69-23	CaseBack114nkHedoftheHouse1203½Kevin'sTurn1093½	No menace 6

LATEST WORKOUTS Jun 10 Bel tr.t 4f fst :48⅘ b — Jun 5 Bel tr.t 4f fst :49⅕ b — Apr 27 Bel tr.t 3f fst :36 h

CASE STUDY: URBANIZED

The claiming box is not the only vehicle by which horses change hands. A horse may be sold at public auction in a "horses of racing age" sale, or a horse may be purchased privately. Urbanized provides a good example of what may happen after a horse is purchased privately. Braulio Baeza purchased this well-bred three-year-old from his breeders, Tartan Farms, in late October, just prior to his pair of victories. We are not trying to imply that Baeza is a better trainer than Jan Nerud. The son of Hall-of-Famer John Nerud has consistently been among the leaders on the tough New York circuit. The significant point is that Urbanized went from being a "small fish in a big pond" to the opposite, "a big fish in a small pond." With numerous stakes runners in his barn, Nerud doubtlessly had little time to devote to this reluctant dragon. Baeza wanted the horse, and had far more time to give him. Add to this the fact that it was Braulio Baeza who rode Tartan's Dr. Fager to his greatest triumphs, and one can surmise there was nothing seriously wrong with the animal. Tartan would not have sold an ailing horse to their old friend Baeza. Consequently, improvement in form would come as no surprise. This situation is oft repeated each year, as the larger "class" stables cull their lesser runners. Sharp handicappers quick to spot such changes in ownership will often find nice mutuels as their reward. These changes are not mentioned in the past performances.

Horses are often entered at a price below the top value for the race. Some trainers do this to receive a break in the weights. Perhaps others do so to add a touch of confusion to their horse's past performances. A $25,000 claiming race usually allows a range of prices down to $20,000. The next classification down from $25,000 happens to be $20,000, with possible prices ranging down to $18,000 or $16,000. When the symbol Clm 20000 appears in the past performances, one cannot be certain that the horse ran last in a $20,000 claiming race. It could have been running at a reduced price against $25,000 claimers. When entered today against

$20,000 competition, it might actually be taking a hidden drop in class. This clever maneuver with the claiming prices might have been engineered by a manipulating trainer seeking to insure decent odds for the day's race, when the horse is set to give its best effort. Peregrine Power (see Case Study in Chapter 14) had this feature in his past performance profile.

Maiden Races

Before moving on to the allowance race, which is the most common form of nonclaiming race, we shall discuss the maiden race. A maiden is a horse that has never won a race. A maiden race is a contest restricted to maidens—none of the entrants has ever won. Some may not have raced before, others may have tried and failed many times over. When a horse wins for the first time, it is said to have "graduated" from the maiden ranks, or "broken its maiden." Slightly less than half of all horses never accomplish even one victory.

Some maiden races are, in fact, claiming events. These are the so-called maiden claiming races, of which the following is typical.

4 **AQUEDUCT**

6 FURLONGS. (1.08⅕) MAIDEN CLAIMING. Purse $10,000. Fillies and mares, 3-year-olds and upward. Weight, 3-year-olds, 112 lbs. Older, 124 lbs. Claiming price $35,000; for each $2,500 to $30,000, 2 lbs.

As a rule, these races are filled with beasts whose connections harbor little (if any) illusions of greatness, but every so often, a graduate of the maiden claiming ranks goes on to great accomplishments. A recent case in point was the ill-fated Timely Writer, who broke his maiden for a mere $30,000 at Monmouth Park.

Notice that the maiden claiming conditions appear in the classification column of the past performances as Md 30000.

Timely Writer — B. c. 3, by Staff Writer—Timely Roman, by Sette Bello
Own.—Nitram Stable — Br.—Davis Dorothy C (Fla) — Tr.—Imprescia Dominic F — **122**

	St.	1st	2nd	3rd	Amt.
1982	1	0	0	0	$250
1981	7	4	1	2	$218,061

24Feb82- 9Hia	fst	7f	:23⅖	:46	1:22⅕	Allowance	6	7	9^{5}	$9^{5\frac{3}{4}}$	$9^{7\frac{1}{2}}$	$6^{8\frac{1}{2}}$	Fell J	b 119	3.00	83-19	Distinctive Pro $119^{4\frac{1}{2}}$ D'Accord $119^{2\frac{1}{4}}$ Cecis LilBandit$115^{\frac{3}{4}}$	Outrun	9
10Oct81- 7Bel	fst	1	:46⅘	1:11⅕	1:36⅖	Champagne	6	11	7^{4}	3^{nk}	1^{1}	$1^{4\frac{3}{4}}$	Fell J	b 122	8.20	86-14	TimelyWriter$122^{4\frac{3}{4}}$BeforeDwn119^{3}NewDiscovery122^{nk}	Ridden out	13
26Sep81- 8Bel	fst	7f	:22⅖	:45⅖	1:23⅘	Cowdin	1	7	5^{3}	7^{3}	3^{3}	$2^{4\frac{1}{2}}$	Cordero A Jr	b 122	3.20	78-17	Native Raja $115^{4\frac{1}{2}}$ TimelyWriter$122^{1\frac{1}{2}}$NewDiscovery115^{no}	In close	9
12Sep81- 8Bel	fst	7f	:23⅗	:47	1:24⅖	Futurity	7	4	3^{1}	$3^{1\frac{1}{2}}$	$3^{2\frac{1}{2}}$	$3^{2\frac{1}{2}}$	Danjean R	b 122	*.80	77-26	Irish Martini 122^{no}Herschelwalker$122^{2\frac{1}{2}}$TimelyWriter$122^{3\frac{1}{2}}$	Evenly	8
22Aug81- 8Sar	fst	6½f	:22⅕	:44⅘	1:16⅕	Hopeful	3	4	$6^{7\frac{1}{2}}$	$5^{7\frac{1}{2}}$	3^{2}	$1^{4\frac{1}{4}}$	Danjean R	b 122	6.50	91-11	Timely Writer $122^{4\frac{1}{4}}$ Out Of Hock 122^{2} Lejoli $122^{1\frac{1}{4}}$	Driving	8
3Aug81- 8Sar	fst	6f	:22⅕	:45⅗	1:10⅗	Sar Spec'l	7	4	$4^{1\frac{1}{2}}$	$6^{5\frac{1}{4}}$	$7^{4\frac{3}{4}}$	$3^{1\frac{3}{4}}$	Danjean R	122	5.30	85-18	ConquistdorCielo$117^{\frac{1}{2}}$Herschelwlker$117^{1\frac{1}{4}}$TimelyWriter$122^{1\frac{1}{4}}$	Wide	10
4Jly81-10Suf	fst	5½f	:22	:46⅕	1:04⅘	Mayflower	12	1	$4^{2\frac{1}{2}}$	$4^{2\frac{1}{2}}$	1^{hd}	1^{1}	Danjean R	114	9.70	99-19	Timely Writer 114^{1} Ring Proud $114^{\frac{3}{4}}$ BrightTalisman114^{no}	Driving	13
9Jun81- 3Mth	fst	5f	:23⅕	:47⅕	:59⅗	Md 30000	1	3	1^{hd}	$1^{\frac{1}{2}}$	1^{4}	1^{8}	Thornburg B	118	4.90	88-21	TimelyWriter118^{8}MnInTrouble$116^{1\frac{1}{4}}$WrOnTheRis114^{nk}	Drew clear	9

LATEST WORKOUTS Mar 1 Hia 7f fst 1:26⅘ h Feb 18 Hia 5f fst 1:00⅕ h Feb 13 Hia 1 fst 1:41 h ●Feb 8 Hia 4f fst :45⅗ h

The average maiden claiming winner is considerably overvalued by open claiming standards. As a general rule, figure at least a 25 percent reduction in price before the animal reaches its proper level, unless, of course, racing experience brings improvement.

CASE STUDY: PRETTY PRETENSE

Pretty Pretense provides a good example of a betting coup gone wrong, as well as underlining the recognized relationship between the open and maiden claiming ranks.

John Campo claimed the three-year-old filly from her racing debut. Entered against $16,000 winners that day, she raced midpack, within six lengths of the lead, for the first half mile in a promising effort. With normal improvement, she figured to be competitive against $20,000 or $25,000 maiden fillies. Lack of opportunities at that level forced Campo to choose a $50,000 maiden race against males five weeks later for her next start. Pretty Pretense had worked well at four and five furlongs in the interim, and although severely outclassed, she raced well, advancing to fourth in midstretch before tiring. Campo had the filly primed to win in the proper spot, but again had trouble finding her a race. He entered her twice for maiden $20,000, but on both occasions failed to draw in from the also eligible list. Pretty Pretense finally got to race again on July 24, against $25,000 maiden fillies. Her odds were only 7–1, contrasted with 29–1 in both previous starts, suggesting stable confidence. After racing up close over a speed-favoring wet track, she took command entering the stretch, looking every bit the winner, but she hung inside the final sixteenth, allowing two opponents to pass her.

Pretty Pretense Ch. f. 3, by Big Bluffer—Pretty Fussy, by Dark Armor
$25,000 Br.—Luro Mr-Mrs H A (Fla)
Own.—Saj Stable Tr.—Campo John P
116
Lifetime 2 0 0 0 1983 2 M 0 0 1982 0 M 0 0
8Jly83- 2Bel fst 6f :22⅘ :45⅘ 1:11⅘ 3♦Md 45000 5 4 5^5 5^{9½} 4^{11} 6^{15} Santos M H^7 b 105 29.70 68-18 Importunity 116^3 Mock Court 116^{6¾} Piston Lift 116^{¾} No factor 10
5Jun83- 3Bel fst 7f :22⅘ :46⅕ 1:25⅗ ⒻClm c-16000 9 10 6^{6¼} 5^6 8^{9¼} 7^{11} Bailey J D 116 29.50 63-17 Marvelous Montauk 107^{hd}LilMissScarlet113^{1¾}MissB.P.116^{2¾} Tired 11
LATEST WORKOUTS Jly 6 Bel 5f fst 1:00⅖ hg Jun 30 Bel 5f fst 1:00⅘ hg Jun 26 Bel 4f fst :48 hg Jun 22 Bel 5f fst 1:00⅗ hg

Nonclaiming maiden races are called "Maiden Special Weights" in the East, and simply "Maiden" in the West.

3 AQUEDUCT 6 FURLONGS INNER DIRT TRACK AQUEDUCT (START / FINISH)

6 FURLONGS. (INNER-DIRT). (1.08⅘) MAIDEN SPECIAL WEIGHT. Purse $19,000. Fillies and Mares. 3-year-olds and upward. Weights, 3-year-olds, 120 lbs. Older, 122 lbs.

In the running lines of the past performances, the symbol MdSpWt (Mdn in the West) designates a maiden special event. We shall use the abbreviation MSW to refer to such races.

Copelan B. c. 2, by Tri Jet—Susan's Girl, by Quadrangle Lifetime 1982 1 1 0 0 $10,200
Br.—Hooper F W (Fla) 119 1 1 0 0
Own.—Hooper F W Tr.—Griffin Mitchell $10,200
13Jly82- 6Bel fst 5½f :22⅘ :46⅘ 1:05⅘ Md Sp Wt 1 1 12½ 13 12 1½ Migliore R 118 3.00 86-22 Copelan 118½ Rising Raja 1185¾ Torpedo Los 1181 Driving 10
LATEST WORKOUTS Jly 27 Sar 5f fst 1:02⅖ b ●Jly 21 Sar tr.t 4f fst :49⅗ b Jly 7 Sar tr.t 5f fst 1:04⅕ b Jly 2 Sar tr.t 6f fst 1:15⅘ b

Future champions begin their careers in MSW events, often with losing efforts. These races are also cluttered with steeds that will never break their maidens, and others that will eventually be forced into the claiming ranks before winning. Most owners with the slightest delusion of "stakes potential" will not risk their prized possessions in claiming races until the harsh evidence of numerous failures forces the reality upon them.

Maiden races are probably the easiest to handicap. The horse with numerous starts, and no luck yet, is seldom worth backing. First-time starters are worthy of consideration, as a rule, only when they show some life on the tote board. Exactly what defines "life" depends on the outfit involved. For a small stable, odds as low as 10–1 might represent a significant amount of action. For some large barns, odds as high as 4–1 might be a bad sign. On the other hand, too much "life" often makes for an unattractive betting proposition. Inexperienced horses can find too many ways to lose a race to warrant a bet at low odds.

The most positive sign in maiden races is the obvious one—a strong in-the-money finish (second or third) last out. The horse becomes all the more interesting should its speed figure from that race be high. All published statistical studies of maiden races have found this a strong predictor of impending success, yet not enough, over the long haul, to guarantee wagering profits.

Allowance Races

Horses running in allowance races are not for sale. The term "allowance" comes from the fact that weights are assigned according to the horse's recent record. The less a horse has accomplished lately, the greater the weight allowance (break) it receives. More on this later, when we discuss weight in more detail.

The term "allowance race" covers a wide variety of conditions. The weakest restrict eligibility to horses that have won no more than a maiden race. The strongest may allow entry even to major stakes winners. In between is a hierarchy with which all serious handicappers must be familiar. We shall now study this hierarchy from bottom to top, offering suggestions on the types of horses best suited to each kind of race.

Restricted Allowance Races

We start our discussion with the restricted allowance races, allowance races for "limited winners." We begin with the NW1 race, restricted to horses that have never won even one allowance race. Maiden winners usually make their next start in such races. The conditions may take the form

3 BELMONT (6 FURLONGS, BELMONT PARK)

6 FURLONGS. (1.08¾) ALLOWANCE. Purse $19,000. Fillies, 2-year-olds which have never won a race other than maiden or claiming. Weight, 121 lbs. Non-winners of a race other than claiming since September 1 allowed 3 lbs. Of such a race since August 15, 5 lbs.

Copyright © 1984, by DAILY RACING FORM, INC. Reprinted with permission of copyright owner.

or

5 BELMONT (1 1-16 MILES, BELMONT PARK)

1 1/16 MILES. (TURF). (1.39½) ALLOWANCE. Purse $20,000. Fillies and Mares. 3-year-olds and upward which have never won two races. Weights, 3-year-olds, 113 lbs. Older, 124 lbs. Non-winners of a race other than claiming at a mile or over since May 1, allowed 3 lbs. Of such a race since April 15, 5 lbs.

Copyright © 1984, by DAILY RACING FORM, INC. Reprinted with permission of copyright owner.

which excludes winners of nonmaiden claiming races, or the West Coast version

4th Santa Anita

(6 FURLONGS, SANTA ANITA)

6 FURLONGS. (1.07⅗) ALLOWANCE. Purse $21,000. Fillies. 3-year-olds which are non-winners of $2,000 other than maiden or claiming. Weight, 120 lbs. Non-winners other than claiming since December 25 allowed 3 lbs.; of such a race since November 1, 6 lbs. (Winners preferred.)

Copyright © 1984, by DAILY RACING FORM, INC. Reprinted with permission of copyright owner.

which allows entry of more seasoned winners from smaller tracks such as Caliente.

The ideal contender in an NW1 race is the lightly raced three-year-old that required no more than three starts to break its maiden, then followed up with a strong effort against nonwinners-of-one company. Or the lightly raced animal that broke its maiden in especially fast time, and is now trying allowance competition for the first time.

Least deserving of support are recent maiden claiming winners,

MSW winners that required several starts before finally winning, slow MSW winners, and horses that have been unsuccessful several times in NW1 company, regardless of whether or not they were competitive. Note that the conditions of an NW1 race often penalize recent maiden winners, forcing them to carry the maximum weight prescribed by the eligibility conditions. This, among other reasons, makes the recent maiden graduate a high risk the first time out against other winners. The step up from maiden company is possibly the steepest that the average horse will be asked to take in its racing career. When you encounter a horse that just beat maidens by several lengths, look at the records of its opponents. You'll be surprised how many of them broke their maiden in similar style, and have since been unable to reproduce that form against winners.

Many of the higher-priced older claimers on the grounds have, in their younger days, worked their way through the restricted allowance races. Those among them who have not, but who compete successfully at the higher claiming levels, often hold a class and experience edge over all but the most promising of the younger allowance runners. This is especially true in the NW1 races, particularly late in the year when the more promising three-year-olds are no longer eligible. At any age, claiming horses pose less of a threat under the "nonwinners of two races" conditions than under the more typical "nonwinners of a race other than maiden or claiming" conditions. Those eligible have yet to win an open claiming race, much less an allowance. On the other hand, the same thing definitely *cannot* be said for the high-priced three-year-old claimer, which is probably overpriced and more likely than not has never been close to savoring victory in allowance company. Unless, of course, the animal has very recently run a strong race against older claimers.

The NW1 event for two-year-olds presents a somewhat different picture. The maiden-claiming winner can no longer be ruled out, if its times are competitive. Class among two-year-olds, especially at the shorter sprint distances, very often is strictly a matter of time—the fastest horse is the "class" of its field.

CASE STUDY: OFFICER'S BALL AND BOTTLE TOP

Juvenile allowance (and stakes) races often ask the player to choose between a hotshot recent maiden winner and a horse that has been racing competitively, if not successfully, in stakes competition. During the summer months, two-year-old winners often are forced into stakes competition for lack of allowance opportunities. The experience they gain helps them immeasurably, yet they often are looked upon as early season "flashes-in-the-pan," unlikely to continue racing successfully when the better prospects get to the races. And that impressive maiden winner, especially a debut-winner, is usually considered among the "better prospects."

That the bettors at Saratoga on July 27, 1983 chose Officer's Ball as their even-money favorite in the Schuylerville Stakes was to be expected. Bottle Top, her main rival and eventual conqueror, appeared to be going backwards. Her figures from her two stakes appearances were five lengths behind Officer's Ball's debut figure. Yet the experience Bottle Top gained from stakes competition proved decisive when she hooked Officer's Ball in the stretch.

The basic concept of the NW1 race extends upwards to the NW2, NW3, and occasional NW4 events:

⑤ BELMONT — WIDENER TURF COURSE — 1 MILE, BELMONT PARK

1 MILE. (TURF). (1.33) **ALLOWANCE.** Purse $21,000. Fillies and Mares, 3-year-old and upward **which have never won two races other than maiden, claiming or starter.** Weight, 3-year-olds, 119 lbs. Older, 122 lbs. Non-winners of a race other than maiden or claiming at a mile or over since September 1 allowed 3 lbs. Of such a race since August 15, 5 lbs.

⑦ AQUEDUCT — 6 FURLONGS, INNER DIRT TRACK, AQUEDUCT

6 FURLONGS. (INNER-DIRT). (1.08⅘) **ALLOWANCE.** Purse $27,000. 4-year-olds and upward. Fillies and mares **which have never won three races other than Maiden, Claiming or Starter.** Weights, 122 lbs. Non-winners of two races other than Maiden or Claiming since November 15 allowed 3 lbs. Of such a race since then 5 lbs.

Each allows alternate forms, such as "nonwinners of three races," and "nonwinners of $2500 twice," both of which are basically NW2 races. These races provide step-by-step advancement opportunities for young developing horses. They also often provide havens for untalented but well-bred fillies, who otherwise would have no place to race. The ideal contender in any of these races is the horse that has made no more than three attempts since advancing from the preceding classification, preferably one showing a good effort since its win in the lower class, or exceptionally high speed figures on that occasion. Or, the horse that has proven competitive in higher allowance or stakes company. Advanced "nonwinners" conditions (NW3 and higher) often demand a touch of stakes quality.

CASE STUDY: MARY MITSU, KAZANKINA, AND TARGHESE

Restricted allowance races often prove to be soft touches for lightly raced European horses that may have won a maiden race and one (possibly graded) stakes race, while competing steadily in top-class company. As a rule, the better European horses race less often than their American counterparts, and win less often as a result. This leaves them eligible for lesser allowance events when they come to this country, and they often hold a decided class advantage, provided the race is on grass. Mary Mitsu provided a good example when entered in a mile allowance event for "nonwinners of two" at Belmont, October 9, 1982. Her one victory since breaking her maiden came in a Group 3 stakes at The Curragh in Ireland. And she had run fifth, beaten just four lengths, in the classic 1000 Guineas prior to that. Normally, Mary Mitsu would have been an outstanding bet in such a field of limited winners. However, her workout line warned otherwise. It was not typical Leroy Jolley. There was no string of exceptionally fast handy works, and the odds board confirmed these suspicions—Mary Mitsu was "ice" at over 4–1. A Jolley horse ready to roll would have been bet rather heavily.

Indeed, Mary Mitsu was not ready for her best effort. She finished off the board on October 9.

***Mary Mitsu** — **Dk. b. or br. f. 3, by Tarboosh—Misty Hill, by Hill Clown**
Own.—Brant P M — **Br.—Asigh Farm Ltd (Ire)** — **Tr.—Jolley Leroy** — **114**

	Lifetime				
	6 2 3 0				
	$38,254				
1982	4	1	2	0	$30,695
1981	2	1	1	0	$7,559
Turf	6	2	3	0	$38,254

11Sep82♦6Curragh(Ire) gd 1	1:41$\frac{3}{5}$	(T) (F)GilltownStudStakes(Gr3)	1^3	Roche C	121	8.00	— —	Mary Mitsu 121^3 Kazankina $125^{1\frac{1}{2}}$ Aloe 121no	Bid, drew clear	12
4Aug82♦5Brighton(Eng) fm 1	1:35	(T) Lanes Stakes	2^2	Carson W	118	*.15	— —	Mubhedj 121^2 Mary Mitsu 118^3 Ballyseedyhero 117^{10}	Bid,led	6
22May82♦4Curragh(Ire) gd 1	1:40$\frac{2}{5}$	(T) (F)Irish 1000 Guineas(Gr1)	5^4	Carson W	126	8.00	— —	Princ'sPolly126^1 Woodstrm126^{no} OnThHous$126^{\frac{1}{2}}$	Bid then evenly	24
22Apr82♦3Epsom(Eng) fm $1\frac{1}{16}$	1:42$\frac{3}{5}$	(T) (F)PrincessElizabethStkGr3	$1^{\frac{3}{4}}$	Carson W	121	10.00[D]	— —	[D]MaryMitsu$121^{\frac{3}{4}}$ ClareIsland121^1 RoseofMonteaux$124^{1\frac{1}{2}}$	Bore in	9
22Apr82-Disqualified and placed second.										
19Jun81♦1Ascot(Eng) fm 5f	1:02$\frac{2}{5}$	(T) Windsor Castle Stakes	2^3	Kinane M J	127	*2.25	— —	Tender King 130^3 Mary Mitsu $127^{2\frac{1}{2}}$ Captain Henry 123^1	Led 4f	6
2May81♦1PhoenixPk(Ire) gd 5f	:59$\frac{4}{5}$	(T) (F)Enfield Plate(Mdn)	1^2	Kinane M J	126	*2.50	— —	Mary Mitsu 126^2 Miss Lilian 126no Wolary 126^2	Well up,dr.clear	17

LATEST WORKOUTS **Oct 6 Bel 5f fst 1:02 h** **Sep 30 Bel [T] 5f fm 1:06 b (d)**

Kazankina's European form resembled that of Mary Mitsu quite closely. They faced each other twice in Ireland, with each filly getting the nod once. But when brought to this country, Kazankina was tested immediately in stakes competition, before trying her luck in a "nonwinners of two" allowance at Aqueduct on May 14, 1983. This time, the workout line told quite a different story. Her sharp :58.2 workout on

May 11 suggested quite strongly that Kazankina was acclimated and ready to run back to her best European form. And indeed she was, overcoming the sharp turns and speed bias of the Aqueduct course to win a three-horse photo as the 2–1 favorite of the sharp New York audience.

Those same "experts" were not heard from, however, when Targhese made her American debut on June 3, 1983. As a two-year-old, the granddaughter of Round Table had twice placed in Group 3 events in France. Her :47h workout on May 19 signaled readiness, and the "nonwinners of one" field she faced was ordinary, with the second choice (and eventual runnerup) also coming off a layoff. Yet the European "class" filly paid a stunning $33.60 after winning off by almost seven lengths.

CASE STUDY: STEADY NASKRA

Be especially watchful for a horse entered under restricted conditions dropping from a higher classification allowance race in which it was reasonably competitive. Steady Naskra provided such an example on October 28, 1982. He moved directly from an impressive MSW win at the Meadowlands to classified allowance company at Aqueduct where he narrowly missed running in the money, despite traffic problems through much of the race. Then he was placed back where he belonged, in NW1 company, on October 28. In this case, trainer P. G. Johnson's "best laid plans" didn't work out as designed. Steady Naskra found either the mile-and-a-half distance or the extremely soft grass conditions to his disliking, and finished a disappointing third at odds of 9–10. Obviously, Johnson's class maneuver did not go unnoticed! Those giving Steady Naskra an "excuse" (for the marathon distance, or the wet course) on October 28 were further disappointed on November 12, when the horse ran out of the money (as favorite again) over a firm course at a mile and an eighth. His taxing effort on October 28 apparently had dulled his sharp edge.

Steady Naskra — **B. c. 3, by Naskra—Steady Wind, by Sea-Bird** — Lifetime 7 1 0 1 $10,500 — 1982 5 1 0 1 $10,500
Br.—Meadowhill (Ky) — **110**5 — 1981 2 M 0 0
Own.—Meadowhill — **Tr.—Johnson Philip G** — Turf 3 1 0 1 $10,500
28Oct82- 3Aqu sf 1½ Ⓣ:52⅖ 2:14⅖ 2:41⅖ 3↑Alw 20000 4 3 36½ 43 1hd 31½ Samyn J L 114 *.90 32-66 Courage In Gold114nk Kanduit1091½SteadyNaskra114nk Weakened 6
13Oct82- 3Aqu fm 1⅛ Ⓣ:48 1:12 1:50 3↑Alw 35000 3 4 78½ 711 68½ 45¼ Davis R G7 105 2.30e 89-13 No Neck 1152¼ Winds of Winter 1152¾ Ghazwan119nk No menace 9
2Oct82- 5Med fm 1 Ⓣ:46⅘ 1:11⅘ 1:37⅕ 3↑Md Sp Wt 3 9 912 68¾ 22½ 17 Davis R G7 109 5.80 88-15 Steady Naskra 1097 Arctic Blast 1164 Nobleline 116½ Drew clear 10
2Oct82-Evening Program
13Sep82- 6Bel fst 7f :23⅕ :46⅗ 1:25⅖ 3↑Md Sp Wt 1 4 109¼1111 910 910 Samyn J L 118 14.70e 65-19 Waitlist 1182¾ To The Penny 118½ Penny Bank 118nk Far back 11
4Sep82- 4Bel fst 6f :23 :46⅕ 1:11⅕ 3↑Md Sp Wt 1 2 915 914 812 511 Samyn J L 118 27.20 75-13 My Liphard 1181 CricketDrummer1185½NorthernSpell108¾ Outrun 9
29Nov81- 6Aqu fst 7f :23⅗ :48⅖ 1:28⅖ Md Sp Wt 9 1 45 66½ 911 813 Samyn J L 118 8.90 46-33 Katana 1185¾ Straight Main 118nk Fort Monroe 1131 Tired 9
22Nov81- 4Aqu fst 6f :23 :47⅗ 1:11⅘ Md Sp Wt 6 7 77¼ 65 64½ 58¾ Samyn J L 118 14.10 73-18 GntlSun118nkHntrHwk118nkHollywoodHndrson1184 Lacked room 7
LATEST WORKOUTS Nov 8 Bel tr.t 6f fst 1:17 b Nov 3 Bel tr.t 3f fst :36⅘ b Oct 23 Bel tr.t 3f fst :38⅗ b Oct 9 Bel tr.t 4f fst :51 b

Before proceeding, we point out that rock-bottom claiming races at the smaller tracks are structured in much the same manner as allowance events at the larger tracks. If $2,500 is the bottom classification, there will be $2,500 claiming races restricted to horses yet to win two, three, or four times in their lives. There will also be $2,500 claiming races of a less restrictive nature, similar to the classified allowances about to be discussed. Consequently, the symbol Clm 2500 can refer to a broad spectrum of possible eligibility conditions. Sharp handicappers at the minor-league tracks collect result charts (see Chapter 12), or record the exact conditions under which all races were run for future reference. Not a bad example for their brethren at the major tracks to follow.

The numbers of previous races have their most significant application at the minor tracks. Most tracks card their better races toward the end of the program. Consequently, if the majority of a track's races are for rock-bottom claimers, one can presume that the seventh race will attract a better field than the second. Yet the Form will report Clm 2500 for both. A horse that ran in the seventh race last week and is now entered in the second is probably dropping significantly in class, a maneuver many in the crowd will miss.

Classified Allowance Races

Once a horse becomes ineligible to compete in the restricted allowance races ("runs out of conditions," to use the racetrack vernacular), it will most likely race in what are termed "classified" allowance events. That, test its mettle in stakes competition, or drop down into the claiming ranks. The term "classified allowance" covers a broad spectrum of possible eligibility conditions. With these races, more than any other, the handicapper must read the conditions carefully. They usually point very clearly to the logical contenders, often spotlighting the eventual winner.

The following is an example of typical classified conditions that are likely to attract a strong field, possibly including stakes runners preparing for future engagements. The race was run on June 5, 1982 at Belmont.

7 FURLONGS. (1.20¾) **ALLOWANCE.** Purse $35,000. 3–year–olds and upward which have not won two races of $12,500 since April 1. Weight 3–year–olds, 114 lbs. Older, 122 lbs. Non–winners of three races of $15,000 since December 1 allowed 3 lbs. Of two such races since January 1, 5 lbs. Of such a race since then, 7 lbs. (Maiden, claiming, starter and state–bred races not considered.)

Very few horses on the grounds had won two (or more) races with a winner's share as high as $12,500 within the relatively short time span specified. Very few horses, therefore, would be ineligible to compete in this race, should it fit into their schedule.

At the opposite extreme is the following race, run November 27, 1982 at Aqueduct:

7 FURLONGS. (1.20½) **ALLOWANCE.** Purse $32,000. 3–year–olds and upward which have not won a race of $15,000 in 1981–82. Weight, 3–year–olds 120 lbs.; older, 122 lbs. Non–winners of two races of $12,500 since May 1 allowed 3 lbs.; of such a race since then 5 lbs.; of such a race in 1982 7 lbs. (Maiden, claiming, starter and state–bred races not considered.)

No established allowance runner on the grounds will be eligible under these conditions, unless it has been away from the races for an extended period of time. This race will likely attract (if it fills) a weak field of infrequent winners, and could very well be won by a claiming animal.

In between these two, we have the typical "first race of the year" conditions, a race likely to attract (among others) stakes runners making their first start since returning from a winter's respite.

6 FURLONGS. (1.08½) **ALLOWANCE.** Purse $35,000. 3–year–olds and upward which have not won a race of $15,000 since December 1. Weight, 3–year–olds, 112 lbs. Older 124 lbs. Non–winners of two races of $12,500 since January 1 allowed 3 lbs. Of a race of $15,000 since August 1 5 lbs. (Maiden, Claiming, Starter and State–bred races not considered.)

This race, run April 22, 1983 at Aqueduct, attracted an especially strong field of stakes runners, and figured to be won by one of them. Horses that had raced all winter in New York, and were still eligible to such a race, figured to be severely outclassed.

Handicappers must be careful, however, that a stakes horse is not just using an allowance race for conditioning purposes. Possibly, the distance is too short. Often, a look at the workout line, or knowledge of the trainer's usual tactics, including his selection of rider, will provide the clue. On the other hand, a big allowance win often preps a horse both physically and psychologically for an upcoming stakes engagement.

Route conditions often exempt winning efforts at sprint distances, requiring only that the horse has not won a certain number of races of a specified value within a designated time frame at a mile or over.

The following conditions likely would attract a weak field. The race was run April 3, 1982 at Aqueduct:

1 MILE. (1.33½) ALLOWANCE. Purse $35,000. 4-year-olds and upward which have not won a race of $12,500 at a mile or over in 1981–82. Weight, 122 lbs. Non-winners of two races of $15,000 at any distance since January 1 allowed 3 lbs. Of two such races since June 1, 5 lbs. Of a race of $10,800 at a mile or over since February 1, 7 lbs. (Maiden, claiming and starter races not considered.)

Copyright © 1984, by DAILY RACING FORM, INC. Reprinted with permission of copyright owner.

And the following conditions for May 1, 1983 at the same track were likely to attract a stronger group of horses:

1 1/16 MILES. (TURF). (1.41) ALLOWANCE. Purse $37,000. 3-year-olds and upward which have not won two races of $15,000 at a mile or over since January 1. Weights, 3-year-olds, 113 lbs. Older, 124 lbs. Non-winners of two races of $15,000 at any distance since January 1 allowed, 3 lbs. Of three races of $15,000 at a mile or over in 1982–83, 5 lbs. (Maiden, Claiming, Starter and State-Bred races not considered.)

Copyright © 1984, by DAILY RACING FORM, INC. Reprinted with permission of copyright owner.

Certain "classified" conditions tend to attract fields that would otherwise be contesting restricted allowance races. New York, where the winner of a classified allowance race earns approximately $20,000, once carded classified races for "nonwinners of a race for $15,000." No horse that had won a classified allowance in New York would be eligible for such a race! These races often were easy targets for shippers from the classified ranks at nearby tracks, where purse schedules were considerably lower than New York's. In their absence, sharp animals still eligible under NW3 or NW4 conditions usually proved the class of the field. Similarly, conditions like "nonwinners of two races of $12,000" ruled out all classified winners—in fact, they ruled out any horse that might have won both an NW2 and NW3 race in New York. Handicappers on other circuits may find similar conditions written, and should handle them in like fashion. How do the restrictions relate to the winners' share under various allowance conditions? That is the key question.

Some route conditions rule out horses that have previously won once or twice at a mile or longer. Others, those that have won a race or two of a specified value at a mile or over during a designated period of time. In some races of these types, the handicapper will be left guessing which sprinter is best suited to stay a distance of ground. If he is lucky, just a few of the contenders will have demonstrated the ability to race well at route distances, and they will contest the issue.

CASE STUDY: I'M FOR FUN

A superficial analysis of eligibility conditions may have quickly eliminated I'm For Fun as a serious contender when she was entered in the following classified allowance race at Belmont on July 4, 1983:

WIDENER TURF COURSE

9 **BELMONT** (1 MILE / BELMONT PARK) 1 MILE. (TURF). (1.33) ALLOWANCE. Purse $37,000. Fillies & Mares. 3-years-old and upward which have not won a race of $12,500 at a mile or over in 1982-83. Weights, 3-year-olds, 116 lbs. Older, 122 lbs. Non-winners of two races of $15,000 at any distance since April 1 allowed 3 lbs. Of two such races since January 1, 5 lbs. (Maiden, claiming, starter and State-bred races not considered.)

The four-year-old filly was still eligible under NW2 conditions, and had never competed for a purse larger than $22,000. How could she be expected to race well in a $37,000 race? In actuality, no filly that had captured an NW2 route in New York would have been eligible for this race! In midsummer, I'm For Fun might have found stiffer competition in NW2 company, racing against developing young fillies possibly on their way to stakes competition later in the season. In this particular race, I'm For Fun's opponents included fillies that had advanced into higher allowance company at sprint distances or at tracks with purse schedules lower than those found in New York, and refugees from the claiming ranks hoping to find a soft spot in allowance competition. The 6–5 favorite Top Of The Barrel was legitimate—she was a sharp classified filly, but had been winless for eleven months. I'm For Fun was certainly not outclassed in this field. When she was solidly supported at the betting windows, there was little doubt that she was ready to go a mile. Eddie Kelly's horses are always ready, and placed where they can win. I'm For Fun won easily, and returned $8.80 to those who understood the conditions of the race.

I'm For Fun — Ch. f. 4, by What Luck—I'm All Ready, by Amerigo
Own.—Brookfield Farms — Br.—Isaacs H Z (Ky) — Tr.—Kelly Edward I — 117

Lifetime				Year					
				1983	1	0	1	0	$4,840
10	2	2	3	1982	9	2	1	3	$35,780
$40,620				Turf	6	1	0	3	$18,780

26Jun83- 5Bel	fst	6f		:23⅖	:46⅘	1:12⅕	3↑ⒻAlw 22000	2	1	32	1hd	2½	22¾	Cordero A Jr	b 117	5.50	78-24	MedievlMoon1142¾I'mForFun1171¼Prid'sCrossing1143	Ducked in	8
22Nov82- 7Aqu	fst	6f		:23⅖	:47⅖	1:12	3↑ⒻAlw 20000	8	3	1hd	1hd	22½	21¼	MacBeth D	b 120	*1.60	80-23	Maggie Gold 1171¼ I'm For Fun1201¾LeapoftheHeart115½	Gamely	9
12Nov82- 6Aqu	fst	7f		:23⅕	:45⅘	1:24⅕	3↑ⒻAlw 20000	1	4	4¾	52½	52¼	45½	MacBeth D	b 120	*1.60	74-21	Flag Waver 1173¼Metbychance117¾LadyHatchet1101½	Lacked bid	8
28Oct82- 5Aqu	fst	6f		:22⅘	:46	1:09⅘	3↑ⒻAlw 19000	2	2	21½	1½	12	13¼	MacBeth D	b 114	5.00	92-14	I'm For Fun 1143¼ Versailles 1081½ Lady Noble 114½	Ridden out	8
9Oct82- 5Bel	fm	1	Ⓣ	:45	1:09⅘	1:36⅘	3↑ⒻAlw 21000	8	3	31	2½	41	43¾	MacBeth D	b 114	3.40	77-17	Fair Rosalind 1221¾ Superheat 114no Baby Duck 1142	WEakened	10
25Sep82- 9Bel	fm	1 1/16	Ⓣ	:45⅕	1:09	1:40⅘	3↑ⒻAlw 20000	12	1	11	1½	31½	37½	Fell J	b 118	10.80	84-12	Street Dance 1134½ Lady Mandarin1133I'mForFun1181	Weakened	12
12Sep82- 9Bel	fm	1 1/16	Ⓣ	:45⅖	1:10⅕	1:43⅘	3↑ⒻMd Sp Wt	3	1	1½	1½	13	1¾	MacBeth D	b 118	*1.70	77-23	I'm For Fun 118¾ Lovely Duckling 1221 For All Time1183	Driving	10
30Aug82- 9Sar	fm	1	[T]	:46⅖	1:10⅘	1:35⅘	3↑ⒻAlw 20000	6	5	48½	46½	56	65¾	MacBeth D	b 112	9.10	91-09	Compatability1141¾LdyMndrin1121¼Bishop'sFling112½	Weakened	10
8Aug82- 2Sar	fm	1 3/16	Ⓣ	:47⅗	1:12⅖	1:57⅖	3↑ⒻMd Sp Wt	9	4	22	1hd	1hd	3nk	MacBeth D	b 117	4.70	79-08	All AboutEve117hdLovelyDuckling122nkI'mForFun1176	Weakened	11
29Jly82- 9Bel	yl	1 1/16	Ⓣ	:47⅖	1:13	1:46⅖	3↑ⒻMd Sp Wt	6	4	41½	41½	44	34	MacBeth D	b 116	3.50	60-38	Nettlesome 1162 Dedelightful 1162 I'm For Fun 1162¼	Came out	10

LATEST WORKOUTS Jun 23 Bel 5f fst :59⅘ h Jun 14 Bel 6f fst 1:16⅗ b Jun 9 Bel tr.t 6f fst 1:14⅘ b Jun 4 Bel tr.t 3f sly :38⅖ b (d)

Finally, allowance conditions at times may exclude the entry of (recent) stakes winners:

6 BELMONT

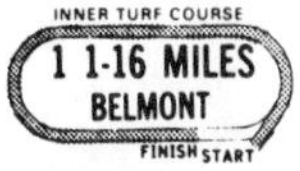

1 1/16 MILES. (INNER-TURF). (1.40⅕) ALLOWANCE. Purse $40,000. Fillies and Mares, 3-year-olds and upward which have not won a sweepstakes in 1981-82. Weight, 3-year-olds, 119 lbs. Older, 122 lbs. Non-winners of two races of $15,000 at a mile or over since August 1 allowed 3 lbs. Of two such races since June 1, 5 lbs. Of two such races since January 1, 7 lbs. (Maiden, claiming, starter and State-bred races not considered.)

Horses that have raced well in stakes competition without winning, or against stakes runners in allowance contests, are the best bets in such races. The ideal contender in any type classified allowance race is the horse that fits the conditions most snugly, almost as if the race were written with that particular horse in mind. Look for the horse that comes closest to not qualifying under the conditions of the race. If that horse has a minimal number of recent failures under similar conditions, or possibly several recent wins under slightly weaker conditions, it may be a very strong play. For example, should the conditions restrict eligibility to horses that have "not won two races of $15,000 since November 1," a horse that won such a race in late October, then another early in November fits the conditions very snugly. Should the second win have been followed by a winter freshening, and then a decent effort in a recent prep race, the horse will likely be a powerful contender.

CASE STUDY: TOUGH CRITIC VS. MORTGAGE MAN

The clever handicapper is acutely aware that a good performance under weak classified conditions is not as good as a fair performance under strong conditions. For this purpose, handicappers keep detailed notes on the race conditions under which classified allowances are run. This is "class handicapping" at its finest. These considerations helped separate the 2–1 co-favorites for the fifth race at Aqueduct on April 23, 1983. Mortgage Man had just won on a clear lead in a race for "nonwinners of a race of $12,500 at a mile or over in 1982–83." Tough Critic, on the other hand, raced an even third in a stronger race which was restricted to "nonwinners of three races of $15,000 since May 1." The past performances, however, reported simply Alw 37,000 for both races.

Clearly, Mortgage Man had found a soft spot for his first try of the year at more than six furlongs. Tough Critic had raced well against a pair of sharp sprinters. The fact that trainer Warren Pascuma thought the horse was good enough to compete in the Westchester Handicap after just one six-furlong prep race, combined with his victory over the top sprinter Maudlin at seven furlongs the previous summer, hinted that Tough Critic was a slightly better horse than Mortgage Man. Indeed he was, wearing his rival down through the stretch, and eventually beating him a length.

[Daily Racing Form past-performance chart for Mortgage Man and Tough Critic]

Regardless of type, classified or restricted, allowance races are denoted in the past performance lines by the symbol Alw (Aw in the West) followed by the purse for the race. Form readers are not told the exact allowance conditions. They must use their knowledge of the track's purse structure, or recognition of the horses competing in the race, to determine what those conditions were.

[Daily Racing Form past-performance chart for Illuminate]

The purse for a particular type of allowance race may well vary from circuit to circuit. This should not be taken to imply that the better runners in any given classification at one track would not be competitive in the same classification at a track with a higher purse structure. This may or may not be true. Other factors, such as accurate speed figures, help determine. Remember, most horses race where their owners find it convenient to attend the races, and this has no bearing on their inherent class.

The fact that the allowance purse value now appears in the past performances reveals what in the past may have been a hidden drop in class. It is convenient to be spoon-fed such information, but far better to have uncovered it oneself. At least the pari-mutuel payoff wasn't hurt that way. Handicappers at the minor tracks still have the same opportunity, however. The different classifications hidden under the claiming price remain hidden.

Stakes Races

At the top of the race classification ladder are the stakes races, from the Grade I Belmont Stakes, run at equal weights:

1 ½ MILES. (2.24) 114th Running THE BELMONT STAKES (Grade I). Purse $200,000 added. 3-year-olds. By subscription of $100 each to accompany the nomination; $1,000 to pass the entry box; $2,000 to start. A supplementary nomination of $5,000 may be made on Wednesday, June 2 with an additional $15,000 to start, with $200,000 added of which 60% to the winner, 22% to second, 12% to third and 6% to fourth. Colts and Geldings, 126 lbs. Fillies, 121 lbs. Starters to be named at the closing time of entries. The winning owner will be presented with the August Belmont Memorial Cup to be retained for one year, as well as a trophy for permanent possession and trophies will be presented to the winning trainer and jockey and mementoes to the grooms of the first four finishers. Closed Tuesday, February 16, 1982 with 332 nominations.

and the country's premier sprint stakes, the Grade I Vosburgh, which now is run under weight-for-age conditions:

7 FURLONGS. (1.20½) 43rd Running THE VOSBURGH (Grade I). $100,000 Added. 3-year-olds and upward at Weight for Age. By subscription of $200 each, which should accompany the nomination; $800 to pass the entry box, with $100,000 added. The added money and all fees to be divided 60% to the winner, 22% to second, 12% to third and 6% to fourth. Weight for Age. 3-year-olds, 123 lbs. Older, 126 lbs. Starters to be named at the closing time of entries. Trophies will be presented to the winning owner, trainer and jockey and mementoes to the grooms of the first four finishers. Closed Wednesday, September 29, 1982 with 20 nominations.

to the Grade II Lawrence Realization (America's equivalent of Europe's St. Leger Stakes), which is weighted under allowance conditions:

8 BELMONT

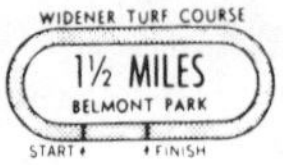

1 ½ MILES. (TURF). (2.24⅘). 90th Running THE LAWRENCE REALIZATION (Grade II). $75,000 Added. 3-year-olds. Weight, 126 lbs. By subscription of $150 each, which should accompany the nomination; $600 to pass the entry box, with $75,000 added. The added money and all fees to be divided 60% to the winner, 22% to second, 12% to third and 6% to fourth. Non-winners of two races of $70,000 at a mile and a furlong or over in 1982 allowed, 3 lbs. Of such a race of $50,000 in 1982, 5 lbs. Of such a race of $35,000 in 1982, 9 lbs. Of such a race of $25,000 in 1982, 12 lbs. Starters to be named at the closing time of entries. Trophies will be presented to the winning owner, trainer and jockey and mementoes to the grooms of the first four finishers. The New York Racing Association reserves the right to transfer this race to the Main Course. Closed Wednesday, September 8, 1982 with 31 nominations.

and the Grade III Roamer Handicap:

8 AQUEDUCT

1 $\frac{3}{16}$ MILES. (INNER-DIRT). (1.55⅗) 34th Running THE ROAMER HANDICAP. $50,000 Added. (Grade III). 3-year-olds. By subscription of $100 each, which should accompany the nomination; $400 to pass the entry box, with $50,000 added. The added money and all fees to be divided 60% to the winner, 22% to second, 12% to third and 6% to fourth. Weights, Monday, December 13. Starters to be named at the closing time of entries. A trophy will be presented to the winning owner. (Nominations close Wednesday, December 1). Closed with 27 nominations.

with weights assigned by the track handicapper on December 13, all the way down to the conditioned stakes. Some, like the Bolsa Chica Stakes at Santa Anita,

8th Santa Anita

6 FURLONGS. (1.07⅗) 3rd Running of THE BOLSA CHICA STAKES, $60,000 added. 3-year-olds. Non-winners of a sweepstakes since December 25. (Foals of 1980) (Allowance). By subscription of $50 each to accompany the nomination, $100 to pass the entry box and $600 additional to start, with $60,000 added, of which $12,000 to second, $9,000 to third, $4,500 to fourth and $1,500 to fifth. Weight, 122 lbs. Non-winners of a race at of $50,000 or two of $25,000 allowed 2 lbs.; of a race of $25,000 or two of $15,000, 5 lbs.; of a race of $13,000, 8 lbs. (Claiming races not considered.) Starters to be named through the entry box by the closing time of entries. A trophy will be presented to the owner of the winner. Closed Wednesday, February 16, 1983 with 16 nominations.

bar recent (previous) stakes winners. Others, like the same track's Bradbury Stakes,

8th Santa Anita

1 ⅛ MILES. (1.45⅘) 10th Running of THE BRADBURY STAKES. $60,000 added. 3-year-olds which have never won *$13,000. (Special Weight). By subscription of $50 each to accompany the nomination, $600 additional to start, with $60,000 added, of which $12,000 to second, $9,000 to third, $4,500 to fourth and $1,500 to fifth. Weight, 118 lbs. Starters to be named through the entry box by the closing time of entries. A trophy will be presented to the owner of the winner. *A race worth $13,000 to the winner. Closed Wednesday, March 23, 1983 with 22 nominations.

bar the winners of a specified amount of first money during a designated period of time—in this case, $13,000 lifetime. The Bradbury is a prep for the Santa Anita Derby, and is designed to attract developing horses that have won no more than an NW1 allowance contest.

The stakes name, or an abbreviation thereof, is shown in the classification column of the past performances. The letter H after the name means that the race was a handicap stakes.

Copyright © 1984, by DAILY RACING FORM, INC. Reprinted with permission of copyright owner.

The best advice regarding graded stakes races is to regard as contenders (with few exceptions) horses with proven ability at the same stakes level (grading) or higher. Restricted stakes leave the handicapper more freedom, from horses competitive in graded stakes to lightly raced developing horses with top speed figures that might be contesting a stakes event for the first time in their career. Stakes contestants are weighted either under allowance conditions, based on previous successes, or by the racing secretary, under handicap conditions. Occasionally, racing secretaries card overnight handicaps, such as this one, scheduled for July 3, 1982 at Belmont:

7 BELMONT

W. DESER TURF COURSE

1 1-16 MILES
BELMONT PARK

1 ¹⁄₁₆ MILES. (TURF). (1.39½) HANDICAP. Purse $35,000. 3-year-olds and upward. Weights Wednesday, June 30. Declarations by 10:00 a.m., Thursday, July 1.

Copyright © 1984, by DAILY RACING FORM, INC. Reprinted with permission of copyright owner.

An overnight handicap is designated Handicap in the past performances. Note the appearance of the July 3 race in the past performances of Illuminate. These are basically allowance races, but the weights are assigned by the secretary. Weights, as determined under allowance conditions, will be discussed later in this chapter.

Starter Races

We conclude our discussion of race classifications with the starter race, a nonclaiming event for claiming horses, often under handicap conditions. In the East, "Starter Handicap" is the common terminology. Western tracks also card "Starter Allowances."

① AQUEDUCT — 1½ MILES INNER DIRT TRACK AQUEDUCT

1 ½ MILES. (INNER-DIRT). (2.30½) STARTER HANDICAP. Purse $17,000. 4-year-olds and upward which have started for a claiming price of $16,000 or less since January 1, 1982. Weights Wednesday, January 12. Declarations by 10:00 a.m., Thursday, January 13. (Closing Wednesday, January 12)

To become eligible for one of these events, a horse must have started at a specified claiming price (or lower) during a designated time interval. In our example, for $16,000 (or less) since January 1, 1982.

At many tracks, the conditions also limit what the horse might have accomplished after becoming eligible:

9th Golden Gate

1⅛ MILES GOLDEN GATE — START ▲ ▲FINISH

1 ⅛ MILES. (1.46⅜) STARTER ALLOWANCE. Purse $8,500. 4-year-olds and upward, which have started for a claiming price of $8,500 or less in 1982–83 and since that start have not won a race other than maiden, starter or claiming, or a claiming or starter race exceeding $8,500. Weight, 120 lbs. Non-winners of two starter races since February 1 allowed 3 lbs.; two such races since January 1, 5 lbs.; one such race since February 1, 7 lbs. (Maiden, starter and claiming races for $7,500 or less not considered.)

In this case, the conditions stipulate that the horse must not have won an allowance race, nor a claiming nor starter race with a purse exceeding $8,500 since becoming eligible. Two symbols are used in the past performances for starter races. For example, the symbol Hcp 10000s is used for a starter handicap, and Alw 10000s for a starter allowance, each requiring that a horse have raced for a claiming tag of $10,000 or lower sometime within the past year. We note in passing that such a starter race will always carry a higher purse value than a straight $10,000 claiming race.

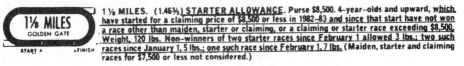

At most tracks, an owner must have started a horse in a prior race at the meeting to be eligible to make a claim. Such rules exclude all owners from claiming from the first race run at the meet. This gives a maneuvering trainer a free shot at dropping a horse in value, winning a purse, and making the animal eligible for starter races, without the fear of losing the horse through the claiming box, provided, of course, that the meet's first race is a cheap claiming event.

Trainers often go to extremes to make a horse eligible for their track's starter series, disguising the horse's form over a series of races before dropping it to the appropriate claiming level. That drop in price will often be accompanied by large bandages on all four legs, warning all concerned that the animal has serious physical problems. It's amazing how these problems heal almost overnight, after the horse has escaped being claimed, and become eligible for the starter series!

Starter races present problems for class handicappers. How does one establish the class level of such a race? A good rule of thumb advises that the value should be established at 50 percent more than the claiming value for eligibility. This would make a SCAP 10000 equivalent to a CLM 15000. However, it is better practice to classify such races based on the established class of the horses that prove to be contenders. Class, however, is often the key to successfully handicapping starter races. Which horse is worth more on the open claiming market? The answer may be all the handicapper needs to know. If fit, that animal likely will win several races in the series. Many knowledgeable handicappers believe, and rightfully so, that the best bet in a starter race is a "class" horse that has already won such a race.

□ PURSE □

The next item encountered in the race conditions is the purse for the race. As for providing insight into the nature of the race and its likely contenders, the purse is practically useless. However, some handicappers calculate a numerical rating estimating a horse's class (or earnings ability), and they may factor the purse value into their equation. More on this in Chapter 6.

The purse is divided in some ratio among the first four finishers (five or more at some tracks). The most commonly used formula is 60–22–12–6, meaning 60 percent of the purse to the winner, 22 percent to the place horse, 12 percent to the third finisher, and the last 6 percent to the animal that finished fourth. This formula is used at many of the country's major tracks, but not in Southern California, where the purses are highest. That circuit (Santa Anita, Hollywood, and Del Mar) uses instead the formula 55–20–15–7.5–2.5, with the purse being divided among the first five finishers. As noted above, the purse for allowance races becomes part of the past performance lines. This is not true, however, for claiming races, where the claiming price appears instead.

It is important that the serious handicapper know what price claiming horse fits with the various types of allowance conditions written on his home circuit. Observation—knowing who has been successful where of late—helps. Awareness of the relationship between claiming purses and those for allowance races also sheds considerable light on the problem.

□ AGE □

Next are the age and sex restrictions for the race. We shall tackle age first.

7 AQUEDUCT TURF COURSE $1\frac{1}{16}$ MILES AQUEDUCT

$1\frac{1}{16}$ MILES. (TURF). (1.41) ALLOWANCE. Purse $35,000. Fillies and Mares. 3-year-olds and upward, which have not woin two races of $15,000 at a mile or over since April 15. Weights, 3-year-olds, 119 lbs. Older, 122 lbs. Non-winners of two races of $12,500 at a mile or over since August 15, allowed 3 lbs. Of such a race of $15,000 since August 1, 5 lbs. Of such a race since June 1, 7 lbs. (Maiden, claiming, starter and State-Bred races not considered.)

Thoroughbreds begin racing at age two. Injury withstanding, they can hold top form through age six. A very small percentage are still going strong at age ten or older.

Port Conway Lane * Gr. g. 14, by Bold Commander—Grey Taffety, by Grey Sovereign
Br.—Creek Hill Farm (Ky)
Own.—Sheppard J M Tr.—Kuhn Marvin H
115 Lifetime 228 50 37 34 $421,691 | 1982 22 4 5 2 $18,685 | 1981 12 3 1 1 $12,502 | Turf 5 0 0 0 $1,050

3Dec82-	2Lrl	sly	1	:47	1:13	1:39⅗	3 ♦ Clm c-5000	3	5	5^{8}	2^{8}	2^{6}	2^{8}	Passmore W J	b	119	*1.30	66-23	RiseChrger115^{8}PortConwyLne119$^{3\frac{1}{2}}$Profools110$^{4\frac{1}{4}}$	Best of others	7
24Nov82-	2Lrl	fst	1	:47⅖	1:13⅗	1:39⅘	3 ♦ Clm 5000	5	4	3^{3}	$3^{1\frac{1}{2}}$	$2^{1\frac{1}{2}}$	$1^{\frac{1}{2}}$	Passmore W J	b	115	*.80	73-28	Port ConwayLane115$^{\frac{1}{2}}$ClassyMac115^{2}AppearInCourt115$^{3\frac{1}{4}}$	Driving	9
18Nov82-	2Lrl	fst	6f	:23	:47⅘	1:13⅕	3 ♦ Clm 4000	5	7	$6^{5\frac{1}{4}}$	4^{3}	$4^{2\frac{3}{4}}$	1^{1}	Passmore W J	b	115	*1.40	77-25	PortConwyLn115^{1}MioHost110$^{1\frac{1}{4}}$King'sDominion119$^{\frac{1}{2}}$	Bumped, dr	10
10Nov82-	2Lrl	fst	6f	:23	:47⅘	1:14	3 ♦ Clm 4000	5	5	10^{9}	6^{6}	$4^{3\frac{1}{4}}$	2^{hd}	Passmore W J	b	115	*1.70	73-25	King's Dominion 117^{hd} Port ConwayLane115^{nk}MioHost110^{1}	Wide	12
20Oct82-	1Lrl	fst	6f	:23⅗	:47⅘	1:13⅗	3 ♦ Clm 4000	4	6	$5^{4\frac{1}{2}}$	$4^{4\frac{1}{2}}$	3^{3}	2no	Passmore W J	b	115	3.60	75-30	LookngForwrd110^{no}PortConwyLn115$^{2\frac{1}{4}}$EpcQust120$^{1\frac{1}{4}}$	Just missed	12
1Oct82-	9Bow	fst	6f	:23	:46⅕	1:12⅕	3 ♦ Clm 4000	7	8	$7^{7\frac{1}{2}}$	$7^{9\frac{1}{4}}$	7^{12}	$7^{8\frac{3}{4}}$	Passmore W J	b	117	*1.30	70-21	Fight at Night 117^{1} King's Dominion 112$^{\frac{1}{2}}$ BelBaie117^{2}	No factor	11
10Sep82-	3Bow	fst	6f	:23⅕	:46⅗	1:11⅕	3 ♦ Clm 6250	1	6	6^{6}	$6^{9\frac{1}{2}}$	6^{12}	6^{16}	Passmore W J	b	116	3.20e	68-25	Surge 114^{7} Best Arbitrator 117^{3} Curious Butler 114no	Outrun	8
23Aug82-	1Mth	fst	$1\frac{1}{16}$	:48⅖	1:12⅘	1:46	3 ♦ Clm c-5000	5	3	$3^{4\frac{1}{2}}$	2^{4}	3^{4}	$4^{3\frac{1}{2}}$	Tejeira J	b	115	*2.20	71-19	Parofools 112^{nk} Ball OfFire115^{2}MyFriendWilliam108$^{1\frac{1}{4}}$	Weakened	8
4Aug82-	3Mth	fst	1⅛	:49⅗	1:14	1:52⅘	3 ♦ Clm 6250	2	4	$2^{1\frac{1}{2}}$	$2^{1\frac{1}{2}}$	2^{4}	$3^{1\frac{1}{2}}$	Tejeira J	b	115	6.20	69-19	AboveTheTitle116$^{\frac{3}{4}}$CaptainPhil112$^{\frac{3}{4}}$PortConwyLne115^{6}	Weakened	7
26Jly82-	2Mth	fst	1^{70}	:47⅖	1:12⅖	1:43⅖	3 ♦ Clm 6500	5	4	5^{2}	$5^{6\frac{3}{4}}$	4^{7}	$3^{9\frac{1}{2}}$	Tejeira J	b	115	5.60	69-22	ChicgoNtive115^{7}Fgr'sPrinc115$^{2\frac{1}{2}}$PortConwyLn115^{1}	Steadied early	6

The racing world is very fortunate, indeed, when its great stars like Seattle Slew, Spectacular Bid, Affirmed, and Alydar are permitted to race at age four, rather than being shipped off to the breeding shed, where they have enormous value. The two-year-old Thoroughbred ("juvenile," as it is called) races in closed competition, exclusively against other juveniles. But the three-year-old, still immature and not yet fully developed physically, is often asked to compete against its elders. Does he (or she) stand a chance? The answer is yes and no. When dealing with maiden and restricted allowance races, the answer is basically yes. But when speaking about claiming races, the answer becomes no. And the logic behind these divergent answers is quite sound.

Eligibility conditions for maiden and restricted allowance races are predicated on what the horse has failed to accomplish thus far in its career. Against which horse is it a more serious knock not to have won a race other than maiden or claiming, a young three-year-old or an older horse? Obviously, the older horse. It has at least one more full year of failure under its belt. Consequently, unless one is dealing with a lightly raced four-year-old from a top barn that economically is able to bring its prospects along with extreme caution, one must assume that a four-year-old (or older horse) competing in maiden or restricted allowance races is somewhat lacking in talent and/or soundness. All things being equal, the three-year-old should be preferred in these races. On the other hand, imagine that you own a three-year-old. Aware that horses don't reach physical maturity until late in their third year, at the earliest, wouldn't you be willing to string along with your horse for a while, hoping that with maturity, it would be able to realize its "assumed" potential? Of course you would! Most owners would react that way.

All young horses have "potential," at least in the eyes of their owners. Consequently, the eventual claiming horse often is not recognized as such at three. Or if entered in claiming events, does not sink to its true level very quickly. The three-year-old claiming animal is usually overpriced, often by a large amount. A three-year-old entered with a $35,000 claiming tag might actually be worth just $20,000. When entered against older $35,000 horses that likely are worth that amount, it is probably severely outclassed.

The young claiming horse is probably the most difficult to analyze. The animal is immature, both physically and mentally, and of moderate and still-developing ability. Its past performances are confounded by awful performances as its trainer(s) attempts to identify its true preferences regarding distance, surface, and classification.

The fact that a race was open to both three-year-olds and older horses is indicated in the past performances by the symbol 3↑ preceding the race classification. Otherwise, for races restricted to three-year-olds, or to horses aged four and up, no symbol appears in this place.

□ SEX □

During the 1970s and into the 1980s, female Thoroughbreds have been winning their share of the world's major races. Witness France's Prix de L'Arc de Triomphe, one of the most significant races in the world. Fillies have won seven of the last thirteen editions of this classic. How does one explain this? The excellent book *The Body Language of Horses*, by Bonnie Ledbetter and Tom Ainslie, presents a viable explanation. To quote:

> Female horses seldom race with the reckless impetuosity of males. The blinding burst of speed is a specialty of colts and geldings. Fillies and mares seem to be governed by a more keenly developed sense of self-preservation.
>
> Why, then, have Dahlia, Allez France, Waya and so many other great fillies and mares defeated the best males of their generations in races at classic distances on grass? The answer is simply that such races favor the running styles and temperaments of females. Some of them can run all day, galloping along at a characteristically even pace and retaining ample energy for the crucial final stages. Not many males are so patient.
>
> The kind of race in which females are at the most disadvantage is sprint and middle-distance competition on dirt tracks—the racing that predominates in North America. This is only partly because the burst of speed is a powerful asset in racing of that kind.

Bonnie goes on to explain that the female Thoroughbred must race at a level reflecting her value as a racehorse plus her residual value as a broodmare. The typical male Thoroughbred's value is established solely on the basis of his racing ability. Consequently, the average filly is overpriced relative to the average colt, if considering racing ability alone, and therefore usually is not a good bet when facing the boys.

North American racing affords fillies far more opportunities to race within their own league, against other fillies, than does European racing. Consequently, very few average-class fillies challenge males in this country. They don't have to, they can win the same purses competing against other fillies. Those that take on the males do so for the major stakes awards, and fare very well, as do their European counterparts.

Races restricted to fillies and mares are identified by the symbol Ⓕ appearing before the race classification in the past performances.

☐ STATE-BREDS ☐

Some races are restricted to horses bred and/or foaled in the state in which the race is to be run.

⑨ **AQUEDUCT** (**6 FURLONGS** INNER DIRT TRACK AQUEDUCT)

6 FURLONGS. (INNER-DIRT). (1.08⅗) ALLOWANCE. Purse $26,500. 4-year-olds and upward, fillies and mares foaled in New York State and approved by N.Y. State-Bred Registry which have never won a race other than Maiden, Claiming or Starter. Weights, 122 lbs. Non-winners of a race other than Claiming since December 1 allowed 3 lbs. Of such a race since November 15, 5 lbs. (Purse reflects $5,500 from N.Y. Breeding Fund enrichment)

The fact that a race was restricted to state-breds is indicated by the symbol Ⓢ appearing before the race classification in the past performances. This symbol, actually, is now used to represent all races of a restricted nature. A race may be restricted to the get of certain stallions, or to horses owned by residents of a certain state, to cite two more examples.

State-bred programs exist in many racing states, including New York, New Jersey, Maryland, Pennsylvania, Florida, Louisiana, Illinois, and California. In many states, the state-breds are a few notches below open competition in any given classification, yet the purses usually are higher, including a supplement from the state breeders fund.

Cupecoy's Joy ✕ — **B. f. 3, by Northerly—Lady Abla, by Alsina**
Own.—Ri-Ma-Ro Stables — **Br.—Perez R (NY)** — **Tr.—Callejas Alfredo**

111

Lifetime									
19	6	7	4	1982	11	4	5	1	$286,146
$377,960				1981	8	2	2	3	$91,814

26Jun82- 8Bel	fst	1½	:47⅕	2:02⅕	2:28⅘	ⒻC C A Oaks	4	1	13½	2hd	22	26	Velasquez J	121	*2.30	71-20	ChristmasPast1216Cupecoy'sJoy121noFlyingPartner1213	Held 2nd	10
4Jun82- 8Bel	fst	1⅛	:45⅘	1:09⅘	1:48⅖	ⒻMotherGoose	2	1	11½	1½	11½	1¾	Santiago A	121	*1.20	85-18	Cupecoy'sJoy121¾ChristmsPst1213½BlushWithPride1214¾	Driving	12
22May82- 8Bel	fst	1	:46	1:09⅗	1:34⅕	ⒻAcorn	5	2	1½	11½	12	12¾	Santiago A	121	7.60	95-11	Cupecoy's Joy 1212¾ Nancy Huang 1213½ Vestris 1212¼	Driving	9
17May82- 8Aqu	fst	7f	:22	:44⅗	1:23⅕	ⓈAlbany H	3	8	43½	31½	1hd	2½	Santiago A	121	*1.80	84-22	MjesticKt112½Cupecoy'sJoy121½FdedPostr1182¾	Bumped, drifted	9
1May82- 8CD	fst	1¼	:46⅕	1:37⅕	2:02⅖	Ky Derby	1	1	13½	1½	83	1011	Santiago A	121	8.90f	74-13	Gato Del Sol 1262½ Laser Light 126nk Reinvested 1262½	Gave way	19
27Mar82- 9Lat	fst	1 1/16	:46⅗	1:11⅗	1:44⅗	Spiral	10	4	2hd	23	25	35	Santiago A	115	9.30	82-29	Good N' Dusty 1205 Fast Gold 120noCupecoy'sJoy1154	Weakened	12
17Mar82- 8Aqu	gd	6f	:22⅘	:46	1:11	ⓈCatskill	5	2	31	31½	32	2nk	Santiago A	115	1.60	86-26	Pay or Play 112nk Cupecoy's Joy 115¾ Faded Poster1172¼	Gamely	7
20Feb82- 8Aqu	fst	6f	⊡:22⅗	:45⅘	1:11	ⒻCicada	4	3	2hd	1hd	14	2hd	Santiago A	121	*2.10	89-17	Bold Ribbons 116hd Cupecoy's Joy 1215½ Adept 114¾	Sharp	11
3Feb82- 8Aqu	sly	6f	⊡:22⅕	:46⅘	1:14⅘	ⒻⓈSag Harbor	2	—	—	—	13	1nk	Santiago A	121	*.70	70-37	Cupecoy'sJoy121nkHastyDmscene1123½LdyHoot113½	Fog, driving	7
6Jan82- 8Aqu	fst	6f	⊡:22⅕	:45⅕	1:10⅕	ⓈMontauk	8	1	1hd	1½	2hd	1no	Santiago A	114	3.40	93-16	Cupecoy's Joy114noAskMuhammad1224Jan'sKinsman1141	Driving	8

LATEST WORKOUTS Jly 23 Bel Ⓣ 3f fm :34 b Jly 18 Bel 1 fst 1:38⅘ h Jly 10 Bel 5f fst :59⅖ h Jly 9 Bel 3f fst :38 b

Just five years ago, the breeders programs in New York and New Jersey were laughable. They are definitely improving. In 1982 alone, New York-bred Naskra's Breeze won the Man O'War and United Nations, both grade I events, New York-bred Cupecoy's Joy won the first two jewels of New York's triple crown series for three-year-old fillies, New York-bred Slewpy won the Grade I Young America at the Meadowlands, New York-bred Thunder Puddles won the Grade II Rutgers at the Meadowlands, and New Jersey-bred Castle Royale took home the Grade II Sheepshead Bay Handicap at Belmont.

CASE STUDY: NEW YORK COMPANY

Although state-bred programs are improving, there often can be a dramatic difference between a state-bred race and an open race of the same (or even weaker) classification. New York Company provides a good example of this, and a trainer angle as well. Allowed to debut in open company, New York Company was a complete unknown as far as New York-bred competition was concerned when brought back against fellow state-breds. That Nick Zito started this horse in open company suggested two interesting possibilities. Perhaps Zito was trying to make the horse appear cheap on paper by starting it against claimers, but open maiden $35,000 claimers tend to run faster than state-bred MSWs in New York. So perhaps Zito was intentionally trying to darken the horse's form, hoping to cash a bet when he placed the animal against more suitable opponents. Also speaking well for this darkhorse's chances was the fact that Zito, like his mentor Johnny Campo, does his best work with young horses. Our analysis of New York trainers (see Chapter 4) revealed that six of Zito's thirty-seven winners during 1979 were two-year-olds making the second start of their career. That New York Company showed improvement in his second start was no surprise. The $47.40 payoff was surprisingly high, though.

New York Company Dk. b. or br. c. 3, by Circle Home—Moon Over Hawaii, by Cool Moon
Own.—Jablow Andrea Br.—Binn O M (NY)
Tr.—Zito Nicholas P **117**
Lifetime 2 1 0 0 $14,400
1983 1 1 0 0 $14,400
1982 1 M 0 0

3Jan83- 7Aqu fst 6f ⊡:23⅘ :48⅖ 1:14⅖ Ⓢ Md Sp Wt 4 4 2hd 1hd 1hd 12¼ Martens G 122 22.70 72-25 NwYorkCompny1222¼Buck'sSprt1226ClrlyOtFront115¾ Drew clear 9
26Dec82- 6Aqu fst 6f ⊡:23⅘ :48 1:13⅖ Md 35000 4 9 87½ 812 516 516 Martens G 118 8.50 61-24 HeySilor1187NothingIsForever1184½UpprCountry1134¾ No factor 9
LATEST WORKOUTS Jan 19 Bel tr.t 4f fst :48⅘ h Jan 12 Bel tr.t 4f fst :49⅗ b Dec 20 Bel tr.t 4f fst :49 b Dec 11 Bel tr.t 4f fst :50 b

□ WEIGHT □

The last topic we shall discuss is weight, one which occupies a good portion of the race conditions. With the exception of maiden and handicap races, weight is assigned under allowance conditions. Whether the race be claiming or allowance, the basic principle is the same:

9 AQUEDUCT

1 MILE. (1.33⅕) CLAIMING. Purse $17,000. 3-year-olds and up. Weights: 3-year-olds, 120 lbs.; older, 122 lbs.; non-winners of 2 races at a mile or over since Oct. 15 allowed 3 lbs.; of such a race since then, 5 lbs. Claiming Price $35,000; for each $2,500 to $30,000 allowed 2 lbs. (Races where entered to be claimed for $25,000 or less not considered).

Working from a specified top weight (122 pounds in our example), horses are given weight allowances based on age (120 pounds for three-year-olds, in our example), sex (not shown, but a standard five-pound break early in the year, three pounds after September 1), and recent lack of success. Horses that have won two (or more) races at a mile or longer since October 15 will be forced to carry the top weight. Those that had won just one such race are given a three-pound break. And those that had not won such a race since then are given the maximum break, five pounds. Note the parenthetical remark "races where entered to be claimed for $25,000 or less not considered." A horse's weight assignment (and, in some cases, eligibility) is determined solely on the basis of its races at a comparable (to $35,000) level, or higher.

What this all means is quite simple. The horses carrying the higher weights are the ones that have won recently, and appear, at least on paper, to be in form. Horses carrying lower weights have done little lately to earn a higher weight assignment, or warrant our support at the betting windows. In other words, the higher weights tend to be assigned to those horses that look best on paper off recent form.

Weight is a dependent variable, a function of form. Statistical studies documented in *Winning at the Races* prove that weight is an insignificant factor in evaluating Thoroughbred performance. Horses seemed to run (slightly) faster under higher weights. This is especially noticeable at sprint distances. Yet the high weight cannot improve the horse's chances, nor increase its speed. The trainers responding to our questionnaire indicated without exception that they read the weight allowances in the race conditions very closely, and were influenced in their selection of races by the weight their horse would be assigned. Clearly, then, trainers place considerable emphasis on the weight their horses will be asked to carry. Whether they are right or wrong is not the point. It is what the trainer is thinking that is important. When a trainer makes a move designed to put less weight on his horse, one can usually conclude that he thinks his horse will run well, and is trying to improve its chances.

Most horses can carry the top weights assigned in allowance and claiming races. Apparent failures result not from the weight, but rather from the deterioration in form resulting from the efforts put forth earning the high-weight assignment. Horses lose under 115 pounds, and nobody blames the weight. Rather, they point the finger at the form cycle, the competition, or the trip.

Handicaps are no different. The better horses carry the higher weights. Yet we are told that each horse has its breaking point. But unless the record suggests what that weight might be, the handicapper is best advised to ignore small weight increases and evaluate the topweights on the basis of other handicapping factors alone.

To summarize, then, weight is of little significance unless excessive and being toted over a distance of ground. In such cases, the reader is best advised to check if the horse has ever successfully carried as much weight (or more) at a similar (or longer) distance under handicap or allowance conditions. Bounding Basque, for example, may have appeared capable of handling his 126-pound assignment in the Dwyer at Belmont on July 2, 1983. After all, he had carried the same package while winning the Wood Memorial at the same distance. However, the Wood had been at equal weights, and the Dwyer was an allowance stakes, and Bounding Basque was being asked to concede weight to his

Bounding Basque — Ch. c. 3, by Grey Dawn II—La Basque, by Jean-Pierre — 126 — Lifetime 11 5 2 0 $223,522 — 1983 6 3 1 0 $175,022 — 1982 5 2 1 0 $48,500
Own.—Wimpfheimer J D — Br.—Wimpfheimer J D (Ky) — Tr.—Sedlacek Woodrow

23Jun83- 8Bel fst 1 1/16 :47⅗ 1:11⅘ 1:43⅗ 3↑Alw 37000 2 1 2½ 1hd 1½ 11¾ McCarron G b 111 5.60 84-22 BoundingBsque1111¾NicePirte117¾ExclusiveOne117hd Ridden out 6
30May83- 8Bel my 1 :44⅖ 1:08⅕ 1:33⅘ 3↑Metroplt'n H 10 10 11¹³ 13²² 13¹⁹ 13¹⁷ McCarron G b 112 16.10 79-11 Star Choice 1131½ Tough Critic 1103¾ John's Gold 1112 Wide 13
23Apr83- 7Aqu fst 1⅛ :48⅕ 1:12⅖ 1:51⅖ Wood Mem 4 3 2½ 1hd 1hd 1no McCarron G b 126 2.30 78-24 BoundingBsqu126noCountryPin1264AztcRd1262 Lost whip,driving 8
23Apr83-Run in two divisions 7th & 8th races
2Apr83- 7Aqu fst 1 :44⅕ 1:09⅗ 1:35⅘ Gotham 6 2 2⁴ 2hd 1½ 22¾ McCarron G b 123 3.90 84-23 AssultLnding1142¾BoundingBsque1231½Jcque'sTip123hd Bore out 9
2Apr83-Run in Two Divisions: 7th & 8th Races
20Mar83- 8Aqu fst 7f :22⅕ :44⅗ 1:22⅗ Bay Shore 1 9 9¹³ 8¹⁵ 7¹⁴ 59¾ McCarron G 121 4.90 78-27 StrikGold1144¼AssultLndng114nkChsConrly1143 Slow St.,Bore In 9
15Jan83- 8Aqu sly 6f ⊡:22⅘ :46⅗ 1:13 Rockaway 4 8 7⁸ 4⁶ 3² 11¼ McCarron G 121 *2.10 79-22 BoundingBasque1211¼Stashed1172¾AtomSmsher1172 Going away 8
22Dec82- 8Aqu fst 6f ⊡:23⅕ :47⅕ 1:12 Alsab 2 6 5³ 3¹ 2½ 13¼ McCarron G 113 2.50 84-22 BoundingBsqu1133¼ChsConrly1134Jff'sCompnon113no Drew clear 6
27Nov82- 8Aqu fst 1 :46⅕ 1:12 1:37⅗ Nashua 6 8 79¼ 89¾ 7¹⁰ 59¼ McCarron G 114 13.80 69-29 I Enclose 1142½ LooseCannon1142½MomentofJoy114¾ No menace 11
14Nov82- 7Aqu fst 7f :22⅘ :45⅗ 1:23⅕ Alw 19000 2 7 52¼ 66¾ 6⁴ 43½ McCarron G 122 9.20 81-23 RisingRj1222¾ChsConrly117hdVnishngPrnc117¾ Passed tired ones 10
30Oct82- 4Aqu fst 6f :22⅘ :46⅕ 1:11⅕ Md Sp Wt 7 6 2hd 2hd 1¹ 12½ McCarron G 118 3.30 85-16 BoundingBsqu1182½AvidDncr118½Jff'sCompnion1182¼ Drew clear 12
LATEST WORKOUTS Jun 18 Aqu ⊡ 5f fst 1:02 b — Jun 13 Aqu ⊡ 4f fst :49 b — Jun 6 Aqu Ⓣ 3f gd :39 b (d) — May 29 Aqu ⊡ 3f fst :38 b

rivals. He was unsuccessful, as might have been expected, finishing fifth. New Yorkers weren't fooled, sending the horse off at odds of almost 11–1.

Another point to be on the lookout for is the three-year-old spotting actual weight to older horses. It may be carrying only 118 pounds against its older rivals' 116, but it is being asked to concede a lot of weight, theoretically. Three-year-olds should be getting weight from older horses, not giving it.

The weight a horse has been assigned for its upcoming race is shown in large numerals slightly to the right of center at the top of the past performances. If followed by a superscript in smaller print, the animal is being ridden by an apprentice rider with the weight allowance indicated. The weight carried in previous races is listed as indicated:

Psychosis Gr. h. 8, by Highbinder—Gray Pixie, by Gray Phantom
$20,000 Br.—Stavola M J (Fla) 108⁵ Lifetime 123 15 21 16 $271,495 | 1982 28 2 6 7 $49,190 | 1981 18 2 1 1 $28,520 | Turf 3 0 0 0
Own.—Barrera O S Tr.—Barrera Oscar S

27Dec82- 2Aqu	fst	6f	⊡:23⅖	:47⅕	1:12⅖	3+Clm 18000	7	3	76½	77	56	34½	Cordero A Jr		113	*2.40	77-22	Abelardo 117nk Moon Glider 1174½ Psychosis 113no	Rallied 9
23Dec82- 1Aqu	fst	6f	⊡:23⅖	:47⅖	1:12⅗	3+Clm 20000	2	2	52½	21½	1hd	2½	Davis R G5		108	8.00	80-27	Happy Cannibal 117½ Psychosis 108¾SpaceMountain1122¾	Gamely 6
17Dec82- 6Aqu	gd	1⅛	⊡:48⅕	1:14⅕	1:54⅕	3+Clm 18000	11	10	107¼	53	41½	31	Alvarado R Jr		108	5.30	74-25	Ultra Suede 117½ Two Too Many 117½ Psychosis 108no	Rallied 12
9Dec82- 9Aqu	fst	1¼	⊡:49⅘	1:42⅕	2:09⅗	3+Clm c-10000	4	3	34	24	24	27¾	Venezia M		117	*1.50	62-30	Soudan 1107¾ Psychosis 1179 Howzat 1085¼	Gamely 10
5Dec82- 2Aqu	gd	1 1/16	⊡:48⅕	1:13⅘	1:46⅖	3+Clm 12500	2	7	65½	47	48	37	Venezia M		117	4.50	74-16	Lite Ahoy 1172¾ ReadMeTheNames1194¼Psychosis117no	Steadied 12
26Nov82- 2Aqu	fst	1⅛	:51	1:16	1:55⅕	3+Clm 12500	8	6	76¼	63¾	41¾	4½	Santiago A		117	7.40	58-26	Cincelari 117nk T. Formation 117hd Flying Straight 119hd	Rallied 8
17Nov82- 9Aqu	fst	1	:47⅕	1:12⅗	1:38⅕	3+Clm 12500	7	6	55½	55½	54	53½	Alvarado R Jr5		112	*2.20	71-18	Read Me The Names 1171 Two Tangos113hdLouhoum1152	Evenly 11
8Nov82- 3Aqu	fst	1⅛	:50⅖	1:15	1:53⅕	3+Clm 12500	1	3	31½	3½	1hd	23¾	Alvarado R Jr5		112	5.30	65-26	Return For Glory1173¾Psychosis112hdTwoTangos112no	Led, wknd 7
23Oct82- 2Aqu	fst	1	:47⅘	1:12⅗	1:37⅘	3+Clm 2[illegible]000	2	6	57	411	512	511	Alvarado R Jr5		112	7.60	66-21	SpartanMonk1135FortunteWether1084½Tullie'sSlugger112nk	Tired 7
11Oct82- 2Bel	fst	1½	:49⅖	2:06⅗	2:33⅘	3+Clm 2[illegible]000	11	4	44	812	718	828	Davis R G7	b	112	10.70	– –	Brave The Reef 1171¼ Desperado 1141 Care Taker 1141¼	Tired 12

LATEST WORKOUTS Dec 22 Bel tr.t 3f fst :38 b Dec 15 Bel tr.t 4f fst :50⅕ b

☐ CONCLUSION ☐

We have been able only to touch the surface of this important matter. For more details, the reader is referred to James Quinn's *The Handicapper's Condition Book*, an excellent text written specifically to shed light on race conditions.

Chapter Three

THE RUNNING LINES

The running lines occupy the middle portion of the past performance lines, and play a central role in the handicapping process. Up to ten lines appear for each horse, describing the animal's performance in each of its most recent races. These races appear in chronological order, with the top line representing the most recent. Using them, we can make judgments about a horse's present state of fitness. Is the animal in shape? Could its fitness possibly be hidden by lackluster races at inappropriate distances or over unfriendly footing? Is the horse simply and obviously out of shape, and in need of a rest? Is the horse approaching its best form? Or has it possibly passed that peak? The running lines, and what we can read from between them, shed light on these questions.

A quick glance at the running lines helps the handicapper visualize the race beforehand. How will it be run? Which horses will contest the early lead? Which will stalk the pace, then attempt to take control around the turn? Which will lay far behind in the early stages, then try to make one run through the stretch? Which horses will race along the rail? And which on the far outside? The experienced handicapper can "get the picture" rather quickly, simply by glancing through the running lines.

The running lines consist of a series of six numbers denoting a horse's position at six successive points of call during the running of the race. The last four positions are supplemented with indications of how far (in terms of lengths) the horse was from the lead, or in the lead, should that have been the case.

Far Out East — B. c. 3, by Raja Baba—Bambar, by Ambehaving — Br.—Schiff J M (Ky) — Tr.—Kelly Thomas J — Own.—Schiff J M — **114**

	St.	1st	2nd	3rd	Amt.
1980	7	3	3	1	$43,060
1979	0	M	0	0	

16Aug80-	2Sar	fst	7f	:22⅘	:45	1:22⅘	3↑Allowance	2	5	44	42	11½	11¾	Cordero A Jr	b 114	*2.00	88-13	FrOutEst1141¾PecefulCountry1176½MilHighClub1143¾	Ridden out	7
28Jly80-	7Bel	fst	7f	:23⅗	:46⅗	1:24⅗	3↑Allowance	1	4	42	32	11½	14½	Lovato F Jr5	b 106	*.80	79-22	Far Out East 1064½ Crosscut 117hd Operable 113no	Ridden out	7
19Jly80-	6Bel	fst	6f	:22⅗	:45⅘	1:11	3↑Allowance	6	6	810	77½	61¾	2no	Lovato F Jr5	b 106	3.70	87-20	Fly North 111no Far Out East 106nk Dr.Johnson1133	Sharp effort	10
4May80-	9Aqu	fst	6f	:23	:46⅗	1:11	Allowance	10	1	97½	86	54½	31¼	Velasquez J	b 122	5.60	87-25	I'ma Hellraiser 122¾ Kick 117½ Far Out East 1225	Rallied	10
19Apr80-	3Aqu	fst	6f	:22⅘	:46⅕	1:11⅕	Md Sp Wt	6	3	75½	44½	32	12	Velasquez J	b 122	*1.80	87-17	Far Out East 1222 Preferred List 1221¾CreativePlan122nk	Driving	7
23Feb80-	8Hia	fst	6f	:22⅗	:46⅖	1:11⅗	Md Sp Wt	6	5	66½	31	22	21½	Fell J	120	1.90	83-19	Kick 1201½ Far Out East 1206½ Another Dragon 1202	Gamely	10
9Feb80-	1Hia	fst	6f	:22⅘	:46⅘	1:13	Md Sp Wt	4	7	53	45	32	21	Solomone M	120	4.10	77-28	Bombay Flight 1201 Far Out East1201½ValiantOrder1203½	Held on	12

LATEST WORKOUTS Aug 28 Bel (T) 3f fm :38 b Aug 23 Sar 3f fst :35⅘ h Aug 14 Sar 3f fst :36 h Aug 6 Sar 5f fst 1:01 h

□ FIELD SIZE □

The information found in the running lines must be analyzed in light of the number of horses competing in the race. That number appears at the far right of the past performance line, and will be the starting point of our discussion. On August 16 at Saratoga, Far Out East ran in a seven-horse field.

Far Out East — B. c. 3, by Raja Baba—Bambar, by Ambehaving — Br.—Schiff J M (Ky) — Tr.—Kelly Thomas J — Own.—Schiff J M — **114**

	St.	1st	2nd	3rd	Amt.
1980	7	3	3	1	$43,060
1979	0	M	0	0	

16Aug80-	2Sar	fst	7f	:22⅘	:45	1:22⅘	3↑Allowance	2	5	44	42	11½	11¾	Cordero A Jr	b 114	*2.00	88-13	FrOutEst1141¾PecefulCountry1176½MilHighClub1143¾	Ridden out	7
28Jly80-	7Bel	fst	7f	:23⅗	:46⅗	1:24⅗	3↑Allowance	1	4	42	32	11½	14½	Lovato F Jr5	b 106	*.80	79-22	Far Out East 1064½ Crosscut 117hd Operable 113no	Ridden out	7
19Jly80-	6Bel	fst	6f	:22⅗	:45⅘	1:11	3↑Allowance	6	6	810	77½	61¾	2no	Lovato F Jr5	b 106	3.70	87-20	Fly North 111no Far Out East 106nk Dr.Johnson1133	Sharp effort	10
4May80-	9Aqu	fst	6f	:23	:46⅗	1:11	Allowance	10	1	97½	86	54½	31¼	Velasquez J	b 122	5.60	87-25	I'ma Hellraiser 122¾ Kick 117½ Far Out East 1225	Rallied	10
19Apr80-	3Aqu	fst	6f	:22⅘	:46⅕	1:11⅕	Md Sp Wt	6	3	75½	44½	32	12	Velasquez J	b 122	*1.80	87-17	Far Out East 1222 Preferred List 1221¾CreativePlan122nk	Driving	7
23Feb80-	8Hia	fst	6f	:22⅗	:46⅖	1:11⅗	Md Sp Wt	6	5	66½	31	22	21½	Fell J	120	1.90	83-19	Kick 1201½ Far Out East 1206½ Another Dragon 1202	Gamely	10
9Feb80-	1Hia	fst	6f	:22⅘	:46⅘	1:13	Md Sp Wt	4	7	53	45	32	21	Solomone M	120	4.10	77-28	Bombay Flight 1201 Far Out East1201½ValiantOrder1203½	Held on	12

LATEST WORKOUTS Aug 28 Bel (T) 3f fm :38 b Aug 23 Sar 3f fst :35⅘ h Aug 14 Sar 3f fst :36 h Aug 6 Sar 5f fst 1:01 h

Relative position is important. A horse that finishes third in a five-horse field will earn more than a horse finishing fourth in a fourteen-horse field of comparable class. But there is a strong possibility the latter accomplished more. After all, it finished ahead of ten horses, while the other beat just two!

When handicapping a race with a small field (five, six, or maybe seven runners), one must remember the racing secretary, and those two extra races in the condition book each day. The secretary would like each of his first nine races to fill, and often will go to some lengths to ensure they do. He might approach a particular trainer, reminding him (or her) of how he worked overtime recently, filling a race featuring that trainer's star runner. He will then also point out that another of the trainer's charges looks in need of some exercise, which it very well might obtain in a race scheduled for two days hence, a race that at the moment is rather light in entries. How can the trainer refuse? The point is that races with small fields very frequently may contain one or two entrants recruited in this manner, horses that would not have been entered otherwise. Racing secretaries with whom I have talked agree that the typical six-horse field includes one such horse. Obviously, they are not very likely winners. Or are they? Trainers questioned rated their chances anywhere from practically none to 25 percent. Racing secretaries, on the other hand, thought "fillers" had an excellent chance of winning. They recruited horses that fit the race, and often were able to point this out to trainers who otherwise might have thought the race would come up too tough for their horse.

An experienced handicapper often will be able to spot "fillers" in short fields—they stand out as not belonging in that particular race. Other times, he will unsuspectingly bet one of them because it did, in fact, fit the race. He does not even bother to look for "fillers" in large fields, however, simply because their presence was not required to help fill the race.

☐ POST POSITION ☐

The first of the six position numbers in the running lines tells the horse's post position for that race. On August 16, Far Out East broke from post 2.

Post positions for the race at hand are not to be found in the past performances. However, the *Form* does list entrants in post position order, so a horse's scheduled post can be determined rather easily, after scratches. There are basically four situations in which post position takes on critical importance. Otherwise, it can be ignored almost completely.

(1) When a race starts near a turn, the horses in the outer part of the gate (as a rule, posts 9 through 12) are placed at a severe disadvantage. They will likely be forced to take that turn two or three wide, and often will be outside the entire trip. They will be penalized approximately one length for each horse they race outside around a complete turn.

(2) The chances of a front-runner often depend to a great extent on the

number of speed horses breaking inside it, horses that must be out-run in order to gain control of the race before reaching the first turn. This is especially critical when a race starts near a turn.

(3) Horses breaking from post one are often intimidated by horses out-side of them scrambling for position, or confused by the absence of a rail to their left, where a chute joins the main oval. The latter is most noticeable in mile-and-a-sixteenth races on Belmont's inner grass course.

(4) When a track is wet or drying out, the rail often becomes the most difficult part of the track to navigate. Horses with inside post positions that appear unlikely to escape the rail are more than slightly inconvenienced.

Regardless, post one has been proven statistically to be the most advantageous place to start. Horses breaking from post one are often asked for quick speed away from the gate. They must establish position, or risk being pinched back. Apparently, this works to their advantage.

Post position considerations must be applied when analyzing the upcoming race, and also must be used to help interpret performances in previous races found in a horse's record. One can easily excuse a lack-luster performance from post position 11 at a mile and a sixteenth at Pimlico, or a floundering performance from post one over a muddy track at Saratoga. A speed type that romps from post one at a flat mile at Monmouth will find things less to its liking when breaking from post eight next time. For each horse inconvenienced by the draw for posts, there is another for whom the same draw proves favorable. For each horse breaking wide into a turn, there is another enjoying the advantage of an inner post. And for each horse trapped along a sticky rail, there is another racing over the more favorable outer portion of the racing strip. If the horse you fancy figures to be among the disadvantaged, you can always switch to another contender without the extra burdens to over-come. And then come back to your original selection next time it races, when its form might appear partially clouded, and its odds higher as a result.

All of this comes under the banner of trip handicapping. This newest trend in handicapping will be the topic of discussion in Chapter 11.

☐ THE START ☐

The second number among the six running positions relates the horse's position shortly (a few yards) after the start of the race. (Actually, this is true for sprints only. For routes, this number has a different meaning, described below.) Far Out East broke fifth in his field on August 16.

Far Out East — B. c. 3, by Raja Baba—Bambar, by Ambehaving — Br.—Schiff J M (Ky) — Tr.—Kelly Thomas J — **114**

Own.—Schiff J M

	St.	1st	2nd	3rd	Amt.
1980	7	3	3	1	$43,060
1979	0	M	0	0	

16Aug80- 2Sar	fst	7f	:22⅖	:45	1:22⅘	3↑Allowance	2	(5)	4^{4}	4^{2}	$1^{1\frac{1}{2}}$	$1^{1\frac{3}{4}}$	Cordero A Jr	b	114	*2.00	88-13	FrOutEst114$^{1\frac{3}{4}}$PecefulCountry117$^{6\frac{1}{2}}$MilHighClub114$^{3\frac{3}{4}}$	Ridden out	7
28Jly80- 7Bel	fst	7f	:23⅖	:46⅗	1:24⅗	3↑Allowance	1	4	4^{2}	3^{2}	$1^{1\frac{1}{2}}$	$1^{4\frac{1}{4}}$	Lovato F Jr^{5}	b	106	*.80	79-22	Far Out East 106$^{4\frac{1}{4}}$ Crosscut 117^{hd} Operable 113no	Ridden out	7
19Jly80- 6Bel	fst	6f	:22⅗	:45⅘	1:11	3↑Allowance	6	6	8^{10}	$7^{7\frac{1}{2}}$	$6^{1\frac{3}{4}}$	2no	Lovato F Jr^{5}	b	106	3.70	87-20	Fly North 111no Far Out East 106^{nk} Dr.Johnson113^{3}	Sharp effort	10
4May80- 9Aqu	fst	6f	:23	:46⅗	1:11	Allowance	10	1	$9^{7\frac{1}{4}}$	8^{6}	$5^{4\frac{1}{2}}$	$3^{1\frac{1}{4}}$	Velasquez J	b	122	5.60	87-25	I'ma Hellraiser 122$^{\frac{3}{4}}$ Kick 117$^{\frac{1}{2}}$ Far Out East 122^{5}	Rallied	10
19Apr80- 3Aqu	fst	6f	:22⅘	:46⅕	1:11⅕	Md Sp Wt	6	3	$7^{5\frac{1}{4}}$	$4^{4\frac{1}{2}}$	3^{2}	1^{2}	Velasquez J	b	122	*1.80	87-17	Far Out East 122^{2} Preferred List 122$^{1\frac{3}{4}}$CreativePlan122^{nk}	Driving	7
23Feb80- 8Hia	fst	6f	:22⅗	:46⅖	1:11⅗	Md Sp Wt	6	5	$6^{6\frac{1}{2}}$	3^{1}	2^{2}	$2^{1\frac{1}{2}}$	Fell J		120	1.90	83-19	Kick 120$^{1\frac{1}{2}}$ Far Out East 120$^{6\frac{1}{2}}$ Another Dragon 120^{2}	Gamely	10
9Feb80- 1Hia	fst	6f	:22⅘	:46⅘	1:13	Md Sp Wt	4	7	5^{3}	4^{5}	3^{2}	2^{1}	Solomone M		120	4.10	77-28	Bombay Flight 120^{1} Far Out East120$^{1\frac{1}{2}}$ValiantOrder120$^{3\frac{1}{2}}$	Held on	12

LATEST WORKOUTS Aug 28 Bel [T] 3f fm :38 b Aug 23 Sar 3f fst :35⅗ h Aug 14 Sar 3f fst :36 h Aug 6 Sar 5f fst 1:01 h

Some horses break quickly from the gate, time after time. Others break tardily, as a rule. This is reflected in the overall consistent pattern of their running lines. The former will be on the pace in most of its races, while the latter usually will trail in the early stages. What the handicapper must look for, however, are the exceptions. The usually alert starter that broke poorly last time out, then wasted its energy rushing up to challenge for the lead nevertheless. Or the slow starter that broke sharply in its last race, after a series of dull performances. If that good start heralded an improved effort overall, it could very well spotlight an animal approaching its best form, both physically and mentally. Some horses have ongoing problems with the starting gate, getting away poorly more often than not, compromising their chances severely when they do so. Such horses should be recognized for what they are, poor risks. Racing is competitive enough, without giving the opposition a head start.

□ THE RACE CALLS □

We come finally to the four race "calls," which tell us the position of the horse at four critical junctures during the running of the race. The first two can cause confusion because what they represent differs with the distance of the race. The latter two are always taken in midstretch, an eighth of a mile from the finish, then at the finish itself. Two numbers are given for each call. The larger figure indicates the horse's running position (1 = first, 2 = second, and so on), and the smaller one its total margin behind the leader. In his August 16 race at Saratoga, Far Out East was running fourth at the first call, trailing the early leader by four lengths. He was still fourth at the second call, although just two lengths behind. Far Out East had taken the lead by the stretch call, a length and a half clear of his closest pursuer, and increased his advantage to a length and three-quarters at the wire.

Far Out East B. c. 3, by Raja Baba—Bambar, by Ambehaving
Br.—Schiff J M (Ky)
Own.—Schiff J M Tr.—Kelly Thomas J

114

	St.	1st	2nd	3rd	Amt.
1980	7	3	3	1	$43,060
1979	0	M	0	0	

16Aug80- 2Sar	fst	7f	:22⅖	:45	1:22⅘	3↑Allowance	2	5	4^{4}	4^{2}	$1^{1\frac{1}{2}}$	$1^{1\frac{3}{4}}$	Cordero A Jr	b 114	*2.00	88-13	FrOutEst$114^{1\frac{3}{4}}$PecefulCountry$117^{6\frac{1}{4}}$MilHighClub$114^{3\frac{3}{4}}$	Ridden out 7
28Jly80- 7Bel	fst	7f	:23⅖	:46⅗	1:24⅗	3↑Allowance	1	4	4^{2}	3^{2}	$1^{1\frac{1}{2}}$	$1^{4\frac{1}{4}}$	Lovato F Jr^{5}	b 106	*.80	79-22	Far Out East $106^{4\frac{1}{4}}$ Crosscut 117^{hd} Operable 113no	Ridden out 7
19Jly80- 6Bel	fst	6f	:22⅗	:45⅘	1:11	3↑Allowance	6	6	8^{10}	$7^{7\frac{1}{2}}$	$6^{1\frac{3}{4}}$	2no	Lovato F Jr^{5}	b 106	3.70	87-20	Fly North 111no Far Out East 106^{nk} Dr.Johnson113^{3}	Sharp effort 10
4May80- 9Aqu	fst	6f	:23	:46⅗	1:11	Allowance	10	1	$9^{7\frac{1}{4}}$	8^{6}	$5^{4\frac{1}{2}}$	$3^{1\frac{1}{4}}$	Velasquez J	b 122	5.60	87-25	I'ma Hellraiser $122^{\frac{3}{4}}$ Kick $117^{\frac{1}{2}}$ Far Out East 122^{5}	Rallied 10
19Apr80- 3Aqu	fst	6f	:22⅘	:46⅕	1:11⅕	Md Sp Wt	6	3	$7^{5\frac{1}{4}}$	$4^{4\frac{1}{2}}$	3^{2}	1^{2}	Velasquez J	b 122	*1.80	87-17	Far Out East 122^{2} Preferred List $122^{1\frac{3}{4}}$CreativePlan122^{nk}	Driving 7
23Feb80- 8Hia	fst	6f	:22⅗	:46⅖	1:11⅗	Md Sp Wt	6	5	$6^{6\frac{1}{2}}$	3^{1}	2^{2}	$2^{1\frac{1}{2}}$	Fell J	120	1.90	83-19	Kick $120^{1\frac{1}{2}}$ Far Out East $120^{6\frac{1}{2}}$ Another Dragon 120^{2}	Gamely 10
9Feb80- 1Hia	fst	6f	:22⅘	:46⅘	1:13	Md Sp Wt	4	7	5^{3}	4^{5}	3^{2}	2^{1}	Solomone M	120	4.10	77-28	Bombay Flight 120^{1} Far Out East$120^{1\frac{1}{2}}$ValiantOrder$120^{3\frac{1}{2}}$	Held on 12

LATEST WORKOUTS Aug 28 Bel T 3f fm :38 b Aug 23 Sar 3f fst :35⅗ h Aug 14 Sar 3f fst :36 h Aug 6 Sar 5f fst 1:01 h

Special symbols might be used in place of the smaller number. Margins are estimated to the nearest quarter length, unless two horses are extremely close to each other. In that case, you might see:

no	denoting	a nose
hd	"	a head
nk	"	a neck

Two noses are equivalent to a head, two heads to a neck, and two necks to a quarter of a length. The call 1no means the horse won (or led) by a nose, while 3^{hd} means the horse was running (finished) third, just a head behind the lead horse.

As we have already mentioned, the first two calls are taken after certain distances have been run, and these distances vary with the overall distance of the race. For the standard six-to-seven-furlong sprint, a call is taken after a quarter mile, another after a half mile. For middle distance routes (one mile up to a mile and three-sixteenths), the first call occurs after the first half mile, and the second after six furlongs have been run. The call at the "start" really comes after a quarter of a mile has been run; however, only the running position is printed. Lengths behind (or ahead) at this stage are omitted. In most cases, the first call is taken at some point along the backstretch, and the second anywhere from midway around the turn to the head of the stretch. For more detailed information, the reader is referred to the table on the following page, which lists, by distance, the exact position in the race at which each call is made.

We mention that there are times when a running line may be missing or incomplete. Weather conditions, such as snow or fog, may prevent the race caller from seeing the horses on the backstretch, or at the top of the stretch. A horse may lose its rider or suffer an injury, and be unable to finish the race. In all such instances, dashes are used to replace the missing calls, as in the case of Dr. Farr on February 11 and February 23.

POINTS OF CALL AND FRACTIONAL TIMES IN PAST PERFORMANCES

The points of call and the fractional times in the past performances vary according to the distance of the race. The points for which the fractional times are given correspond to the points of call of the running positions (except in some races at odd distances). In all races, the stretch call is made 1/8 mile from the finish. The points of call and fractional times for the most frequently raced distances are:

Distance of Race	1st Call	2nd Call	3rd Call	4th Call	5th Call	Fractional Times Given At These Points of Call
2 Furlongs	Start	—	—	Stretch	Finish	— — Finish
2 1/2 Furlongs	Start	—	—	Stretch	Finish	— — Finish
3 Furlongs	Start	—	—	Stretch	Finish	1/4 — Finish
3 1/2 Furlongs	Start	1/4	—	Stretch	Finish	1/4 3/8 Finish
4 Furlongs	Start	1/4	—	Stretch	Finish	1/4 1/2 Finish
4 1/2 Furlongs	Start	1/4	3/8	Stretch	Finish	1/4 1/2 Finish
5 Furlongs	Start	3/16	3/8	Stretch	Finish	1/4 1/2 Finish
5 1/2 Furlongs	Start	1/4	1/2	Stretch	Finish	1/4 1/2 Finish
6 Furlongs	Start	1/4	1/2	Stretch	Finish	1/4 1/2 Finish
6 1/2 Furlongs	Start	1/4	1/2	Stretch	Finish	1/4 1/2 Finish
7 Furlongs	Start	1/4	3/4	Stretch	Finish	1/4 3/4 Finish
1 Mile	1/4	1/2	3/4	Stretch	Finish	1/2 3/4 Finish
1 Mile 70 Yards	1/4	1/2	3/4	Stretch	Finish	1/2 3/4 Finish
1 1/16 Miles	1/4	1/2	3/4	Stretch	Finish	1/2 3/4 Finish
1 1/8 Miles	1/4	1/2	3/4	Stretch	Finish	1/2 3/4 Finish
1 3/16 Miles	1/4	1/2	3/4	Stretch	Finish	1/2 3/4 Finish
1 1/4 Miles	1/4	1/2	1 mile	Stretch	Finish	1/2 1 mile Finish
1 5/16 Miles	1/4	1/2	1 mile	Stretch	Finish	1/2 1 mile Finish
1 3/8 Miles	1/4	1/2	1 mile	Stretch	Finish	1/2 1 1/4 Finish
1 1/2 Miles	1/2	1 mile	1 1/4	Stretch	Finish	1/2 1 1/4 Finish
1 5/8 Miles	1/2	1 mile	1 3/8	Stretch	Finish	1/2 1 1/2 Finish
1 3/4 Miles	1/2	1 mile	1 1/2	Stretch	Finish	1/2 1 1/2 Finish
1 7/8 Miles	1/2	1 mile	1 5/8	Stretch	Finish	1/2 1 3/4 Finish
2 Miles	1/2	1 mile	1 3/4	Stretch	Finish	1/2 1 3/4 Finish
2 1/16 Miles	1/2	1 mile	1 3/4	Stretch	Finish	1/2 1 3/4 Finish
2 1/8 Miles	1/2	1 mile	1 3/4	Stretch	Finish	1/2 1 3/4 Finish
2 1/4 Miles & Longer	1/2	1 mile	2 miles	Stretch	Finish	1/2 2 miles Finish

NOTE: When the 1/4 mile or 1/2 mile call is substituted for the start call, only the horse's position at that point is indicated. The margin separating the horse from the leader is not given.

Dr. Farr — Dk. b. or br. g. 4, by Key To The Kingdom—Chagrin Falls, by Polic

Own.—Margulies D W — $12,000 — Br.—Classen T F (Ohio) — Tr.—Toscano John T Jr — 113

Lifetime		1983	5	1	0	0	$5,700
9 1 0 0		1982	4	M	0	0	$570
$6,270							

2May83- 2Aqu	fst	6f		:22⅖	:45⅗	1:12⅕	Clm 9000	3	7	65½	77½	67	52	Rogers K L	b 113	34.20	78-24	Florid'sJoy117nk KingofClssics114no PrincofSport115no	Stride late	9
28Apr83- 1Aqu	fst	6½f		:22⅕	:45⅕	1:17⅖	Clm 12500	2	10	1010	1013	1011	1012	AntongorgiWA7	b 110	39.20	76-16	AnotherRodger115¾ BrightCurrent1082½ KingofClssics112½	Trailed	10
23Feb83- 1Aqu	fst	6f	⊡	:22⅘	:46⅘	1:12⅖	Clm 16000	10	12	1217	1224	—	—	McKnight J	b 119	19.30f	— —	KingBelgian1171 HerefordMn117hd AnotherRodger117hd	Distanced	12
11Feb83- 4Aqu	fst	6f	⊡	:23⅗	:47⅘	1:13⅖	Md 18000	8	—	—	—	34½	1nk	Beitia E	b 118	38.50	77-24	Dr. Farr 118nk CricketDrummer115¾ HughCapet1171½	Snow, jst up	14
13Jan83- 2Aqu	fst	6f	⊡	:23⅘	:47⅗	1:13⅖	Md 13000	9	2	2½	33½	38	511	Beitia E	118	37.50	66-26	Ierax 1185¼ Roi Rajas 1181½ Hold Your Prince 111¾	Tired	13
29Dec82- 9Aqu	fst	6f	⊡	:23	:46⅗	1:13⅗	3↑Md 15000	4	3	45	813	715	812	Beitia E	120	17.50	64-24	Sixth Cavalry 1152 Rexexplode 120nk Merry Go Round109no	Tired	11
19Dec82- 4Aqu	fst	6f	⊡	:23⅕	:47⅘	1:14⅕	3↑Md 20000	1	9	78	711	713	89	Beitia E	120	18.90	64-23	Kinderhook 1091½ I'm The Heir1202¼ SixthCavalry1111½	No factor	13
24Nov82- 2Aqu	fst	6f		:23⅖	:49	1:14⅖	3↑Md 20000	10	1	1½	2hd	35½	49¾	Graell A	120	57.60	59-36	NoDrilling1163¼ SignalNine1065¾ CapitalColonel113¾	Lug'd in tired	13
19Nov82- 3Med	fst	6f		:22⅗	:46⅕	1:12⅖	3↑Md Sp Wt	5	7	713	720	726	729	Foresta R10	109	12.80	52-19	Starve Easy 1191½ Pro 1191½ Spit The Pit 112¾	Drifted in	7

LATEST WORKOUTS May 11 Bel 5f fst 1:00 h — Apr 21 Bel tr.t 4f gd :51⅗ b — Apr 13 Bel tr.t 4f fst :50 bg — Apr 5 Bel tr.t 5f fst 1:02⅕ h

Some horses are front-runners, going immediately for the lead on most occasions. Others are closers, lagging early and saving their energy for the stretch run. But many are versatile, able to run either way, depending on how the race sets up. A quick glance at the running lines reveals the horse's tendencies.

☐ EARLY SPEED ☐

The computer discoveries presented in *Winning at the Races* proved conclusively that the recent first call is a more reliable predictor of success in the upcoming race than is the previous finish position. Horses that led at the first call in their most recent race fared better than those that had won their latest start.

Early speed is very closely tied to winning. Five of the nine races on a typical card are won by horses that flashed early speed—were among the first three at the first call. And significantly, among these could be found the vast majority of longshot winners. Apparently, long-shot systems must have early speed (or pace) as an integral component, or be doomed to failure. Possibly the most powerful angle in all handicapping is the fit horse that appears to be the only front-runner in its field. Often, accurate pace figures uncover horses in this position that otherwise would go unnoticed.

In *Winning at the Races,* we presented a concept called "early speed points." Our intent was to allow handicappers to rate numerically the early speed potential of each horse. The speed points have proven a very useful tool for myself and many others since, but they lack one thing. They fail to spotlight the erratic horse that shows high early speed every so often, and when it does, runs its best races, often carrying that speed wire-to-wire. It is these horses that produce the tremendous profits found on the front end.

The speed points, or a simple glance at the first-call tendencies of all entrants, give the handicapper a quick, though rather qualitative, picture of the probable early pace in the race. We shall defer a more quantitative approach until Chapters 9–10, where we will discuss pace figures and pace handicapping.

Getting Into Position

A question that relates to early speed is the following: "Is the horse always out of position to win?" In sprint races, horses that have never been on the lead (in the lead, or in a photo for the lead) at the stretch call of any of the sprint races in their past performances win less than 65 percent of their fair share of races. In routes, those never in the lead, or within one length of the lead, at the stretch call of any of the route races in their past performances win just 75 percent of their share of races. Both cost their supporters at least 25 percent of dollars invested.

	NH	NW	WPCT	MPCT	I.V.	$NET
Sprints	2404	170	7.1%	25.3%	0.64	$1.33
Routes	891	79	8.9%	31.2%	0.75	$1.50

When dealing with closers, therefore, it is wise to ignore those incapable of making an early move on occasion, and sustaining it to the wire. Horses that don't come into view until midstretch should be avoided, unless the track is biased in their favor.

☐ PATTERNS ☐

As documented in *Winning at the Races*, certain types of performance in a horse's latest start bode especially well for its next engagement. We shall discuss these here, including several not previously published.

Ainslie's Big Win

Horses coming off wins do as well as any others, and better than most. Our statistics revealed that they repeat approximately 17 percent of the time, but cost their backers in excess of 10 percent of their wagered dollar. Are certain styles of winning performance more potent than others? Tom Ainslie coined the term "Big Win" for the following kind of victory:

(1) The horse must have won its last race by at least two lengths, at basically the same distance (sprint or route).
(2) The horse must have been in the first three, and within two lengths of the lead (if not leading), at the second call in that race.
(3) If leading at the stretch call in that race, the horse must have gained at least one length on the field in the run to the wire.

Far Out East's victory on July 28 provides us with an example of a big win. His victories on April 19 and August 16 do not.

Far Out East — B. c. 3, by Raja Baba—Bambar, by Ambehaving — Br.—Schiff J M (Ky) — Tr.—Kelly Thomas J — **114**

Own.—Schiff J M

	St.	1st	2nd	3rd	Amt.
1980	7	3	3	1	$43,060
1979	0	M	0	0	

16Aug80- 2Sar	fst	7f	:22⅘	:45	1:22⅘	3↑Allowance	2	5	4^{4}	4^{2}	$1^{1\frac{1}{2}}$	$1^{1\frac{3}{4}}$	Cordero A Jr	b	114	*2.00	88-13	FrOutEst$114^{1\frac{3}{4}}$PecefulCountry$117^{6\frac{1}{2}}$MilHighClub$114^{3\frac{3}{4}}$	Ridden out 7
28Jly80- 7Bel	fst	7f	:23⅖	:46⅗	1:24⅗	3↑Allowance	1	4	4^{2}	3^{2}	$1^{1\frac{1}{2}}$	$1^{4\frac{1}{2}}$	Lovato F Jr^{5}	b	106	*.80	79-22	Far Out East $106^{4\frac{1}{2}}$ Crosscut 117^{hd} Operable 113no	Ridden out 7
19Jly80- 6Bel	fst	6f	:22⅗	:45⅘	1:11	3↑Allowance	6	6	8^{10}	$7^{7\frac{1}{2}}$	$6^{1\frac{3}{4}}$	2no	Lovato F Jr^{5}	b	106	3.70	87-20	Fly North 111no Far Out East 106^{nk} Dr.Johnson113^{3}	Sharp effort 10
4May80- 9Aqu	fst	6f	:23	:46⅗	1:11	Allowance	10	1	$9^{7\frac{1}{2}}$	8^{6}	$5^{4\frac{1}{2}}$	$3^{1\frac{1}{4}}$	Velasquez J	b	122	5.60	87-25	I'ma Hellraiser $122^{\frac{3}{4}}$ Kick $117^{\frac{1}{2}}$ Far Out East 122^{5}	Rallied 10
19Apr80- 3Aqu	fst	6f	:22⅘	:46⅕	1:11⅕	Md Sp Wt	6	3	$7^{5\frac{1}{4}}$	$4^{4\frac{1}{2}}$	3^{2}	1^{2}	Velasquez J	b	122	*1.80	87-17	Far Out East 122^{2} Preferred List $122^{1\frac{3}{4}}$CreativePlan122^{nk}	Driving 7
23Feb80- 8Hia	fst	6f	:22⅗	:46⅖	1:11⅗	Md Sp Wt	6	5	$6^{6\frac{1}{2}}$	3^{1}	2^{2}	$2^{1\frac{1}{2}}$	Fell J		120	1.90	83-19	Kick $120^{1\frac{1}{2}}$ Far Out East $120^{6\frac{1}{2}}$ Another Dragon 120^{2}	Gamely 10
9Feb80- 1Hia	fst	6f	:22⅘	:46⅘	1:13	Md Sp Wt	4	7	5^{3}	4^{5}	3^{2}	2^{1}	Solomone M		120	4.10	77-28	Bombay Flight 120^{1} Far Out East$120^{1\frac{1}{2}}$ValiantOrder$120^{3\frac{1}{2}}$	Held on 12

LATEST WORKOUTS Aug 28 Bel (T) 3f fm :38 b Aug 23 Sar 3f fst :35⅗ h Aug 14 Sar 3f fst :36 h Aug 6 Sar 5f fst 1:01 h

We found positive results for this "angle" in sprint races only, where a sample of 190 horses produced 20 percent winners, although still costing their fans in excess of 10 percent of the amount wagered. Of these, however, 118 were returning within 14 days of their big win, and did exceptionally well:

	NH	*WPCT*	*I.V.*	*$NET*
Big win, then right back	118	24.6%	2.21	$2.17

These proved one of the best types of repeat winners found in our studies. We note that a "Big Win" accomplished with the aid of a biased racetrack probably is less powerful than it appears on paper. A speed horse may look impressive drawing away through the stretch over a sloppy surface, but no doubt was greatly aided by the conditions.

The Taxing Stretch Drive

The "taxing stretch drive," during which a horse is engaged in close combat with at least one rival for no less than the last eighth of a mile of its most recent race, has always been considered a negative sign, a warning signal of a fatigued horse. Our research, surprisingly, proved that quite the opposite was true.

A "taxing stretch drive" is defined to mean that the horse was never more than a length ahead or behind during the duration of that drive.

Jennifer's Julep engaged in a taxing stretch drive on September 22, then again on November 26. She followed the latter with a much stronger performance, as so often happens.

Jennifer's Julep B. f. 4, by Speak John—Peter's Pet, by Bald Eagle
Own.—Daly J R Br.—Daly J R (Ky) Tr.—Healy Paul A
117 Lifetime 10 2 2 0 $35,020 1982 7 2 2 0 $35,020 1981 3 M 0 0

8Dec82- 9Aqu	fst	1 1/16 ⊡	:48⅗	1:14⅕	1:47⅖	3+ Ⓕ Alw 22000	2	1	1hd	1 1½	14	12¾	Hernandez R	115	*.80	76-21	Jennifer'sJulep1152¾DncdAllNight117¾NtivNwYorkr1151½	Driving	11
26Nov82- 1Aqu	fst	1	:46⅔	1:12	1:38⅕	3+ Ⓕ Alw 20000	7	1	11	1hd	2hd	2nk	Hernandez R	115	*1.50	75-26	Golden Summer 115nk Jennifer'sJulep1152LadyNoble1152¾	gamely	7
22Sep82- 5Bel	gd	1⅛	:46⅕	1:10⅗	1:48⅘	3+ Ⓕ Alw 20000	4	1	15	12	2hd	2nk	MacBeth D	113	2.10	83-16	SavedGround114nk Jennifer'sJulep1133¾DeepRapture1131	Brushed	8
15Sep82- 3Bel	fst	1⅛	:46	1:10⅖	1:48⅖	3+ Alw 20000	2	1	1hd	3½	47½	411	Vasquez J	115	5.40	74-14	Trenchant 1134¾ Chapter One 1173¼ Condition Red 1053¼	Tired	7
27Jun82- 5Bel	fst	1	:45⅖	1:10⅕	1:36⅗	3+ Ⓕ Alw 20000	1	8	813	813	815	713	Migliore R	114	5.90	70-21	Gerldine'sStore1092½Alzbell112hdNicoleMonAmour109hd	Dwelt st.	9
11Jun82- 3Bel	fst	1 1/16	:46	1:10⅖	1:42⅘	3+ Ⓕ Md Sp Wt	4	4	11½	14	18	113	Vasquez J	114	4.70	88-15	Jennifer's Julep 11413 Gabfest 1143¼ Legis 1143¾	Ridden out	7
3May82- 4Aqu	fst	6f	:22⅗	:46	1:11⅖	Ⓕ Md Sp Wt	5	10	77½	69½	512	49½	Vasquez J	121	33.00	74-24	WimbledonStr1217½Gerldine'sStore121¾MjsticMm1211¼	No factor	10
23Sep81- 3Bel	fst	6f	:22⅘	:46⅖	1:12	Ⓕ Md Sp Wt	8	12	1212	1215	1118	916	Skinner K	b 117	18.90	66-18	Pert 112nk Broom Dance 1172¼ Christmas Past 117¾	Broke slow	13
14Sep81- 7Bel	fst	7f	:23⅗	:47⅖	1:25⅖	Ⓕ Md Sp Wt	10	13	42	65	1218	1224	Migliore R5	112	13.50	51-26	SheWon'tTell1178SavedGround117nkFoolishLuck1171½	Slow Start	13
5Sep81- 4Bel	fst	6f	:22⅗	:45⅘	1:11⅖	Ⓕ Md Sp Wt	10	10	79	78½	610	613	Velasquez J	117	4.60	72-14	Vain Gold 1173¾ Nafees 117nk Pert 1126	Broke slowly	10

LATEST WORKOUTS Apr 10 Bel tr.t 5f sly 1:02 b Apr 5 Bel tr.t 6f fst 1:15⅗ h ●Mar 31 Bel tr.t 6f fst 1:15⅕ b Mar 26 Bel tr.t 5f fst 1:01⅗ h

Statistics proved that the longer a horse engaged its rivals, the better. Horses able to withstand such pressure from the second call to the wire came back stronger than those able to do so from midstretch to the finish line. And, for sprint races only, horses coming off consecutive efforts of this type fared even better.

	NH	*WPCT*	*I.V.*	*$NET*
From stretch call	617	18.3%	1.59	$1.85
From second call	388	20.1%	1.75	$2.11
From stretch call twice	248	21.0%	1.89	$1.98
From second call twice	141	22.7%	2.04	$2.42

The traditional belief has been that one such effort knocked a horse out. Perhaps this is true of the horse that turns in a good effort only once in a while. But overall, the statistics are telling us that a horse able to withstand such pressure is both game and durable, and worthy of our support. Whether it won or lost the recent stretch battle did not seem to matter.

The Rallier

The horse that rallies in the stretch, passing horses and gaining ground, is generally a bad risk, unless the track is exhibiting a strong bias against front-runners. Horses that attempt a rally from the rear half of their field at the first call win only half their fair share of races. One exception highlighted in our studies was the sprinter able to rally to win, or at worst lose in a photo. Such horses proved profitable in their next start, producing a 14.5% profit, though winning only 13.9 percent of the time. Had such a horse finished its last quarter in 24 seconds or less, or its last eighth in twelve seconds or better, its performance can be considered all the more powerful and impressive. A rallier's performance is most impressive when it catches a legitimate front-runner early in the stretch, and then draws away through the lane.

CASE STUDY: TRUE KNIGHT AND LITTLE CURRENT

Among Lou Rondinello's early pupils as trainer for the Darby Dan Stable was the top handicap horse True Knight, who numbered Forego among his victims. True Knight had no speed—he showed so little promise at two that he was allowed to break his maiden under a claiming tag. True Knight "came from the clouds" in all his races. His style of racing seemed to have a telling effect on his trainer's philosophy of training.

True Knight ✻ — **Dk. b. or br. h. 5, by Chateaugay—Stealaway, by Olympia**
Own.—Darby Dan Farm — **Br.—Galbreath J W (Ky)** — **Tr.—Rondinello T L** — **126**

	St.	1st	2nd	3rd	Amt.
Turf Record	1	0	0	0	
1974	11	4	3	0	$352,518
1973	12	3	2	4	$200,858

14Sep74- 8Bel	sly	1⅛	:46	1:10⅖	1:46⅗	3↑Marlboro H	4	8	10^{14}	$10^{5\frac34}$	5^{7}	$5^{6\frac12}$	Cordero A Jr	124	11.20	87-12	Big Spruce $120^{2\frac34}$ Arbees Boy $119^{1\frac14}$ Forego $126^{\frac12}$	No threat 10
2Sep74- 8Bel	fst	1⅛	:45⅖	1:09⅖	1:46⅕	3↑Governor	8	10	10^{26}	10^{19}	10^{17}	8^{14}	Cordero A Jr	128	5.50	82-09	Big Spruce $118^{2\frac12}$ Arbees Boy $121^{1\frac12}$ Plunk $121^{1\frac14}$	Outrun 10
20Jly74- 8Aqu	fst	1¼	:47⅖	1:11⅕	2:01⅖	3↑Suburban H	1	10	10^{23}	7^{11}	$5^{4\frac12}$	$1^{1\frac12}$	Cordero A Jr	127	4.10	89-12	•True Knight $127^{1\frac12}$ Plunk 114^{hd} Forego $131^{2\frac12}$	Drew off 10
13Jly74- 8Mth	fst	1¼	:46⅖	1:10⅘	2:02	3↑Haskell H	5	9	9^{22}	4^{3}	$1^{1\frac12}$	$1^{3\frac34}$	Rivera M A	124	*1.60	92-14	True Knight $124^{3\frac34}$ Ecole Etage $112^{\frac34}$ Hey Rube $111^{\frac34}$	Handily 9
16Jun74- 9Suf	fst	1⅛	:47⅗	1:11⅕	1:48⅗	3↑Mass. H	6	7	7^{18}	7^{19}	$5^{8\frac12}$	4^{3}	Cordero A Jr	121	*.60	95-19	Billy Come Lately 109^{nk} Forage $114^{\frac12}$ North Sea $111^{2\frac14}$	Rallied 7
27May74- 8Bel	fst	1	:44⅗	1:09	1:34⅖	3↑Metropol'n H	5	8	8^{20}	8^{13}	$7^{9\frac34}$	$6^{8\frac14}$	Rivera M A	125	7.00	88-11	Arbees Boy 112^{2} Forego $134^{\frac12}$ Timeless Moment 109^{hd}	Outrun 8
6Apr74- 8GS	sl	1¼	:47⅗	1:12⅖	2:06	3↑Trenton H	4	6	6^{10}	4^{3}	$2^{1\frac12}$	$1^{\frac34}$	Cordero A Jr	125	1.30	70-34	True Knight $125^{\frac34}$ Prove Out $123^{6\frac12}$ Play the Field 116^{nk}	Driving 6
23Mar74- 9Hia	fst	1¼	:47⅕	1:11	2:01⅕	3↑Widener H	3	7	7^{27}	$7^{7\frac12}$	$3^{2\frac12}$	2^{1}	Cordero A Jr	124	1.80	91-12	Forego 129^{1} True Knight 124^{2} Play the Field 114no	In close 7
9Mar74- 8Bow	fst	1¼	:48⅕	1:13⅗	2:05⅖	3↑J B Campbell	4	14	14^{17}	10^{10}	$5^{4\frac34}$	$1^{\frac12}$	Cordero A Jr	123	*.60	96-25	True Knight $123^{\frac12}$ Delay $113^{1\frac12}$ Ecole Etage 110no	Steadied, driving 14
23Feb74- 9GP	fst	1¼	:46⅘	1:10⅘	1:59⅘	3↑Gulf Park H	4	6	6^{20}	$4^{5\frac12}$	2^{hd}	$2^{\frac12}$	Cordero A Jr	123	*1.10	97-14	Forego $127^{\frac12}$ True Knight 123^{6} Golden Don 118^{3}	Held on 6

LATEST WORKOUTS **Sep 27 Bel 3f gd :39⅖ b** **Sep 23 Bel 1 fst 1:38⅘ h** **Sep 20 Bel 4f fst :49 b** **Sep 12 Bel 4f fst :50 b**

When Little Current first came to the races as a two-year-old, he was blessed with natural speed. He set the pace in his debut, at five-and-a-half furlongs, despite breaking slowly. But Rondinello had the classics in mind for this colt, and taught Little Current to relax, to come from behind. The rest is history. Little Current won the Preakness and the Belmont, but lost on several other occasions, including the Kentucky Derby, when his stretch run came too late, or was slowed by traffic problems.

Little Current — **Ch. c. 3, by Sea-Bird—Luiana, by My Babu**
Own.—Darby Dan Farm — **Br.—Galbreath J W (Ky)** — **Tr.—Rondinello T L** — **126**

	St.	1st	2nd	3rd	Amt.
1974	8	2	0	0	$198,022
1973	4	1	1	1	$9,170

18May74- 8Pim	gd	$1\frac{3}{16}$	:47	1:10⅗	1:54⅗	Preakness	2	12	12^{11}	10^{5}	3^{1}	1^{7}	Rivera M A	126	13.10	97-09	Little Current126^{7} NeapolitanWay126^{1} Cannonade$126^{\frac34}$	Steady drive 13
4May74- 8CD	fst	1¼	:46⅗	1:11⅘	2:04	Ky. Derby	10	23	21^{22}	17^{18}	7^{13}	$5^{6\frac12}$	Ussery R	126	22.60	70-15	Cannonade $126^{2\frac14}$ Hudson County $126^{3\frac14}$ Agitate $126^{\frac34}$	Closed gap 23
25Apr74- 6Kee	fst	1⅛	:46⅗	1:10⅗	1:49⅕	Blue Grass	7	13	12^{13}	4^{3}	$4^{2\frac14}$	$4^{4\frac14}$	Rivera M A	114	5.40	87-15	Judger 123^{4} Big Latch 117^{hd} Gold and Myrrh 114^{hd}	Rallied 14
30Mar74- 9Hia	fst	1⅛	:47⅖	1:11	1:49	Flamingo	2	9	9^{10}	$6^{9\frac12}$	$7^{7\frac34}$	$4^{4\frac12}$	Cordero A Jr	122	6.30e	82-16	Bushongo $122^{2\frac14}$ Hasty Flyer 122^{1} Judger $122^{1\frac14}$	Lacked room 10
20Mar74- 9Hia	fst	1⅛	:46	1:10⅕	1:49⅕	Everglades	9	9	9^{12}	6^{9}	3^{1}	$1^{\frac12}$	Cordero A Jr	113	3.50	86-17	Little Current $113^{\frac12}$ Bushongo 112^{hd} Hasty Flyer 117^{2}	Driving 11
4Mar74- 9GP	fst	1⅛	:46⅖	1:11⅕	1:49	Florida Dby	12	14	15^{23}	13^{11}	7^{11}	$5^{6\frac34}$	Cordero A Jr	118	11.80	82-11	Judger $118^{\frac34}$ Cannonade 122^{5} Buck's Bid 118^{nk}	Bumped 16
20Feb74- 9GP	fst	$1\frac{1}{16}$	:45⅗	1:09⅘	1:42⅖	Ftn Youth	1	14	14^{25}	11^{17}	11^{11}	$6^{4\frac14}$	Cordero A Jr	113	8.70	85-18	Green Gambados $112^{\frac34}$ Judger $115^{\frac34}$ Eric's Champ $112^{\frac12}$	Stride late 15
6Feb74- 9GP	fst	7f	:22⅕	:44⅗	1:22⅖	Hutcheson	6	13	13^{17}	12^{16}	$7^{5\frac14}$	$4^{2\frac34}$	Cordero A Jr	112	21.10	89-16	FrnkieAdms$114^{2\frac34}$ [DH]Judger110^{hd} [DH]TriningTble113^{hd}	Belated rally 13
5Dec73- 3Aqu	fst	7f	:22⅘	:45⅗	1:22⅗	Md Sp Wt	11	2	$10^{7\frac14}$	$6^{4\frac34}$	$3^{\frac12}$	$1^{1\frac34}$	Cordero A Jr	122	*1.70	88-11	LittleCurrent$122^{1\frac34}$ RubeTheGret122^{2} SplittingHedch122^{hd}	Drew out 12
24Nov73- 2Aqu	fst	6f	:22⅖	:45⅗	1:11	Md Sp Wt	10	11	$8^{7\frac14}$	6^{7}	4^{5}	$2^{2\frac34}$	Cordero A Jr	122	5.40	85-13	Nile Delta $122^{2\frac34}$ Little Current 122^{4} Whoa Boy 122^{1}	Bore in 14
8Aug73- 2Sar	fst	5½f	:22⅗	:46⅖	1:06⅕	Md Sp Wt	1	5	$2^{1\frac12}$	2^{2}	$4^{4\frac12}$	$5^{4\frac34}$	Cordero A Jr	b 119	*2.20	81-13	Ding Dong Bell 119^{nk} Lea's Pass 119^{nk} Buck Hill $119^{1\frac14}$	Tired 9
21Jly73- 2Aqu	fst	6f	:23	:46⅕	1:11⅖	Md Sp Wt	4	9	$1^{\frac12}$	$1^{1\frac12}$	1^{1}	$3^{\frac12}$	Cordero A Jr	b 118	3.00	85-14	MonsieurLafitte$118^{\frac12}$ ThirdCvlry118^{no} LittleCurrent118^{nk}	Weakened 10

LATEST WORKOUTS **Jun 7 Bel 4f fst :49⅕ b** **Jun 3 Bel 1 sly 1:44⅕ b** **●May 30 Bel 7f fst 1:28 b** **May 26 Bel 5f fst 1:01⅘ b**

Lou Rondinello handles most of his horses as if they were budding Little Currents or True Knights. Standard Rondinello workouts are slow, slower, and in reverse. Should any of his runners have natural speed, it will likely be trained out of them. Most of his charges ultimately race from far behind, and find themselves at a severe disadvantage in the sprint and middle-distance route racing so predominant in this country. During 1979, not one of Rondinello's winners was able to repeat, a reflection not on the trainer's ability, but rather on the tactical disadvantage his horses, and all that race from far behind, must overcome.

Bid, But Hung

Surprisingly, the horse that made its move sooner, but failed to carry through, proves to be a more interesting betting proposition. If a horse passed rivals and gained ground between the first and second calls, or between the second and stretch calls, into the front half of its field and within five lengths of the lead, only to lose position from that point to the wire, it is said to have "bid and hung." This "angle," by itself, proved profitable over a sample of almost five hundred cases. The profit was 5 percent, combined with a solid 19 percent winning percentage.

The "bid and hung" performance can be a good omen, or a bad sign. Was the horse's previous effort good or bad? Did the "bid" tip off the fact the horse is approaching its best form? Or was the "hung" a sign that the "bid" was the animal's "last hurrah," a sign that the horse had run out of gas, and tapped its energy supply, leaving nothing left in the tank for its next battle? The most recent race of Gnome's Gold would have been a nice example of the former, coming in his first start after a considerable layoff. However, its significance was diminished by the fact that Gnome's Gold did not race again until March 5.

CASE STUDY: FOUR BASES

After a ten-week absence, Four Bases returned to the races on April 6, only to bid, then hang. A repeat performance on April 22 set the colt up for his winning performances on May 8 and May 15. Not coincidentally, these wins came over Four Bases' favorite surface, the grass course. A glance at his earnings box (see Chapter 6) reveals that the four-year-old now had six victories to his credit, five of which came on the turf. We must presume that his one victory at age two came on the dirt, and that Four Bases had since become a grass specialist. Therefore, on May 8, we had a classic example of a horse approaching peak condition while at the same time returning to its proper milieu. Those who noted the connection were rewarded to the tune of $12.40.

Copyright © 1984, by DAILY RACING FORM, INC. Reprinted with permission of copyright owner.

CASE STUDY: CENERENTOLA

After sharp performances on January 26 and February 18, Cenerentola bid and hung on March 3. It was a bad sign, forecasting an even worse performance on March 25. One might suggest that the filly's "deterioration" in form was only apparent, better explained by the fact that she was moving up in class, first into a higher claiming bracket, and then into allowance company. But among the three-year-olds that spend

Copyright © 1984, by DAILY RACING FORM, INC. Reprinted with permission of copyright owner.

the winter in New York, the difference between $40,000 and $55,000 claiming and NW1 allowance races is practically negligible, especially at the route distances. The better explanation is that Cinderella (Cenerentola, in Italian) turned into a pumpkin in midstretch on March 3.

Closer to the Lead

The horse "closer to the lead" in its latest start, compared to its previous start, has traditionally been thought to be in the "improving" category. Our statistical studies found very positive results for sprint races, but nothing of the kind for routes. Wide variances in route pace likely account for the latter.

Focusing on horses entered in a sprint today that had sprinted in both of their latest two starts, we demand that the animal had been "closer to the lead" at both the second and third call. By this we mean in the front half of its field and within five lengths of the lead in its most recent start, after having been in the rear half and more than five lengths from the lead in its previous start. Crockford Lad satisfied these requirements, prior to winning a six-furlong sprint at Aqueduct on March 5, 1983, returning $5.40.

***Crockford Lad** B. h. 6, by Klairon—War Lass, by Whistler Lifetime 1983 4 0 1 2 $11,920
$70,000 Br.—McEnery W J (Ire) 113 43 6 10 6 1982 22 4 6 3 $68,740
Own.—Spiegel R Tr.—Schaeffer Stephen $102,498 Turf 15 2 2 1 $16,888
20Feb83- 3Aqu fst 6f ⊡:23 :46 1:11 Clm 70000 3 4 31½ 32½ 22 21 Cordero A Jr b 113 4.80 88-20 Mighty Nasty 1171 Crockford Lad 1134¼ King'sWish1171¼ Rallied 7
31Jan83- 5Aqu fst 6f ⊡:22⅕ :45⅖ 1:10⅕ Clm 70000 5 1 55 65½ 48 34¼ Cordero A Jr b 113 3.90 89-15 KentuckyEdd1082¾HappyHooligan1131½CrockfordLd1131¼ Rallied 6
16Jan83- 2Aqu sly 170 ⊡:47 1:12⅘ 1:43⅗ Clm 85000 6 6 510 58 48 614 Cordero A Jr b 116 7.40 70-20 LarkOscilltion116½AccountReceivble1124TenBore1096½ No threat 10
9Jan83- 1Aqu fst 6f ⊡:23⅗ :47 1:10⅗ Alw 37000 2 6 53½ 64½ 34½ 35 Cordero A Jr b 115 5.20 86-17 Let Burn 1154 Main Stem 1101 Crockford Lad 1152 Evenly late 6
22Dec82- 4Aqu fst 6f ⊡:23⅖ :47⅕ 1:12⅕ 3+Clm 50000 8 11 74¼ 31½ 1½ 12 Cordero A Jr b 119 4.60 83-22 Crockford Lad 1192 Palimony 112hd Cut High 1192 Drew clear 12
11Dec82- 1Aqu fst 6f ⊡:23 :46⅘ 1:12⅕ 3+Clm 45000 7 2 32½ 32 1hd 11¾ Cordero A Jr b 114 3.10 83-20 CrockfordLad1141¾NorthernRegent1131½HerefordMn108½ Driving 7
27Nov82- 8Med fst 1 1/16 :47 1:12 1:45⅖ 3+Alw 25000 1 2 21 2hd 65 66½ Migliore R b 115 20.10 75-21 Boogie Woogy 117hd Deedee's Deal 1152 Aye's Turn 1152¼ Tired 8
12Nov82- 5Aqu fst 7f :22⅘ :45⅕ 1:23⅖ 3+Clm 50000 3 4 2½ 2hd 2hd 2no Bailey J D b 117 6.30 84-21 Surf Club 113no Crockford Lad117¾NorthernRegent113nk Gamely 8
25Oct82- 6Aqu sly 7f :23⅖ :47 1:25⅖ 3+Clm 70000 4 4 31½ 34 48½ 34¾ Bailey J D b 113 9.50 69-33 SpeedyReality1081¾GauguinNtive1123CrockfordLd1132 No excuse 6
6Oct82- 5Bel fst 6f :22⅗ :46⅖ 1:11⅘ 3+Clm 70000 3 3 45 32½ 53 53½ Bailey J D b 113 2.70 79-28 GoodbyeStarter117noFanny'sFox115½BrasherDoubloon113no Tired 8
LATEST WORKOUTS Mar 3 Bel tr.t 3f fst :35⅕ h Feb 17 Bel tr.t 5f my 1:02⅗ h Jan 28 Bel tr.t 3f fst :37 h Jan 7 Bel tr.t 4f my :48⅖ h

The statistics are quite impressive for this angle, all the more so (see second line) if we demand the horse be returning within ten days of its improved effort, and have won at least once in its latest ten tries:

	NH	*NW*	*WPCT*	*MPCT*	*I.V.*	*$NET*
Closer to lead	250	43	17.2%	37.2%	1.59	$2.40
Returned in 10 days	66	14	21.2%	40.9%	1.90	$3.18

As mentioned above, all investigations of this sort into route racing proved fruitless.

Surprise Early Speed

Handicappers have also believed that horses showing unexpected early foot in their most recent start are set to win next time. Studies substantiated this for sprints only, and also pointed out that many bettors are well-attuned to this signal.

"Surprise early speed" is defined by demanding first that a horse's three most recent races were at basically the same distance as today's race—all sprints, or all routes. Further, that the horse was either first, second, or third at the first call, and within two lengths of the lead, in its latest race, after achieving no such position early in either of its prior two starts. Dr. Farr satisfied our requirements on February 11. Indeed, he did so in spades, flashing surprise speed in a race with an exceptionally quick pace for its class (see Chapter 10). Although moving up slightly in class, usually an insignificant matter when dealing with cheap maidens, he was able to win, and returned a delicious $79.00.

Copyright © 1984, by DAILY RACING FORM, INC. Reprinted with permission of copyright owner.

The statistics for these horses were hardly outstanding, especially for routes:

	NH	NW	WPCT	MPCT	I.V.	$NET
Sprints	253	42	16.6%	38.7%	1.53	$1.88
Routes	187	21	11.2%	31.6%	0.92	$1.66

Carried Speed Farther

Another early speed angle that failed to stand up to our statistical testing asserts that a horse able to carry its early speed farther last time will go even farther today. To define this concept, we demanded that a horse's two most recent efforts were at basically the same distance (sprint or route) at which it is entered today, that it had raced within two lengths of the early lead on both occasions, and that it had remained within two lengths of the lead last time for at least one call longer than on the previous occasion.

Stage Gossip demonstrates this pattern, leading up to her $10.20 win on February 28.

While hardly discouraging, the statistics uncovered were far from profitable:

	NH	NW	WPCT	MPCT	I.V.	$NET
Sprints	374	68	18.2%	44.7%	1.64	$1.72
Routes	73	14	19.2%	49.3%	1.66	$1.79

Best results were obtained from those horses able to carry their speed at least through midstretch last time in an improved effort.

Two Moves

The last angle has been around for years, and has held up exceptionally well over a small sample of nearly one hundred sprints (31 percent profit from 23 percent winners). We refer to the horse that started quickly in its latest race, then dropped back some during the middle stages of that race, only to come on again at the finish. The qualifying race also must have been a sprint.

Fortuis was coming off just such an effort when entered May 20 in a seven-furlong maiden race at Belmont. Second early, he fell back to fourth before coming on again through the stretch. Fortuis' much-improved effort on May 10 was tipped by his sharp half-mile workout May 6, long a hallmark of a ready Nerud horse. Fortuis won May 20, returning a fair $5.80.

A Warning

When using these angles, it is wise to make sure they are legitimate. Accurate speed and pace figures help immensely in this regard. Make sure the stretch rally was with some authority, and not only apparent because the pace was so strong everything was slowing down to a walk in the stretch. A move at any stage of the race is all the more powerful against opponents that are doing some running of their own. A horse can be deceptively closer to the lead if the pace of the race is noticeably slower than expected. Speed and pace figures help identify such situations.

Chapter Four

THE HORSE'S CONNECTIONS

Four names appear in the past performances of each horse: its breeder, owner, jockey, and most importantly, its trainer. The identity of its breeder remains constant throughout a horse's lifetime. On the other hand, a horse may have several different owners and trainers during its racing career. And even if it has had just one of each, it nonetheless may have been ridden on different occasions by any number of different jockeys.

□ THE BREEDER AND THE OWNER □

First discussed is the breeder and owner of the horse, neither of whom are of much importance to handicappers. The breeder is the person (farm, stable) that had owned the dam (mother) when the horse was foaled (born). Appearing in parentheses next to the breeder's name is an abbreviation of the state in which the horse was bred. Silver Buck, for example, was bred in Kentucky by C. V. Whitney, who still owned the four-year-old colt.

Silver Buck — Gr. c. 4, by Buckpasser—Silver True, by Hail to Reason — Br.—Whitney C V (Ky) — Tr.—Burch Elliott — Own.—Whitney C V — 126

Lifetime 14 7 1 2 $347,856 — 1982 4 3 1 0 $249,480 — 1981 10 4 0 2 $98,376

7Aug82- 8Sar	fst	1⅛	:47⅖	1:11	1:47⅘	3+Whitney H	6	6	6^{11}	$5^{5½}$	3^{nk}	$1^{1½}$	MacBeth D	115	*.80	96-14	Silver Buck $115^{1½}$ Winter's Tale 119^{nk} Tap Shoes 113^{4}	Driving	6
4Jly82- 8Bel	fst	1¼	:47⅖	1:35⅗	1:59⅗	3+Suburban H	4	4	$4^{6½}$	$3^{1½}$	$1^{½}$	1^{3}	MacBeth D	111	2.80	102-14	SilverBuck111^{3}It'sTheOne$124^{3¾}$Alom'sRuler$112^{½}$	Lugged In, Clear	8
31May82- 8Bel	fst	1	:45	1:09	1:33	3+Metropolt'n H	3	10	$8^{5¼}$	5^{6}	$4^{6½}$	$2^{7¼}$	Hernandez R	111	4.10	94-12	ConquistadorCielo$111^{7¼}$SilverBuck$111^{2½}$StarGlint$111^{1¼}$	Slow start	14
7May82- 8Aqu	fst	1⅛	:50⅕	1:14	1:50⅗	3+Alw 27000	5	3	$3^{1½}$	$1^{½}$	$1^{1½}$	1^{1}	Maple E	119	*.80	82-21	Silver Buck 119^{1} Rahway II $119^{6½}$ Nice Pirate $119^{½}$	Driving	6
12Nov81- 6Med	fst	1¼	:47⅕	1:36⅗	2:02⅖	3+Med Cup H	7	5	$9^{7½}$	7^{10}	$6^{7¼}$	$6^{5½}$	Hernandez R	114	3.50	84-14	Princelet $110^{¾}$ Niteange $114^{¾}$ Peat Moss 121^{2}	No threat	14
31Oct81- 8Aqu	fst	1⅛	:47⅗	1:11⅗	1:48⅘	3+Stuyvesant H	9	7	$10^{5¾}$	7^{6}	$4^{4½}$	$3^{1¾}$	Hernandez R	112	*1.80	89-15	Idyll 114^{1} Spoils Of War $113^{¾}$ Silver Buck $112^{¾}$	Rallied	12
22Oct81- 7Aqu	fst	1⅛	:48⅗	1:12⅘	1:50⅗	3+Alw 22000	4	4	$4^{7½}$	$3^{4½}$	1^{hd}	1^{nk}	Hernandez R	114	*.30	83-21	Silver Buck 114^{nk}SpoilsOfWar$117^{½}$NephewScott$112^{7¼}$	Ridden out	6
10Oct81- 8Bel	fst	1½	:48	2:02⅕	2:28⅖	3+J C Gold Cup	9	6	$7^{6¼}$	$3^{2½}$	$3^{1½}$	4^{1}	Velasquez J	121	8.40	77-14	John Henry 126^{hd} Peat Moss $126^{¾}$ Relaxing 123^{hd}	Rallied	11
23Sep81- 7Bel	fst	1	:47⅗	1:12	1:36⅕	3+Alw 21000	5	5	5^{2}	$4^{2½}$	$1^{½}$	$1^{2¾}$	Hernandez R	118	*.70	87-18	Silver Buck $118^{2¾}$ Spoils OfWar$117^{1¼}$TroonRoad$113^{2¼}$	Ridden out	7
6Sep81- 6Bel	fst	1⅛	:47⅗	1:11⅘	1:48⅕	3+Alw 20000	6	2	$3^{1½}$	2^{hd}	1^{5}	1^{13}	Hernandez R	114	*.60	86-15	Silver Buck 114^{13} Piling 108^{nk} My Friend Willie 113^{5}	Ridden out	7

LATEST WORKOUTS ●Sep 1 Bel 5f fst :58⅕ h ●Aug 28 Bel 6f fst 1:12 h Aug 22 Sar 4f fst :52⅖ b Aug 16 Sar 3f fst :36 b

Should a horse have been foreign-bred, the country of its birth is given instead. The fact that a horse is foreign-bred is also noted by an asterisk preceding its name. Lark Oscillation, for example, was born in France.

***Lark Oscillation** B. h. 8, by Mara Lark—Oscillation, by Honest Boy
Own.—Princeway Farms Br.—Alperson & Doumen Mrs C F (Fra)
Tr.—O'Connell Richard **109**

Lifetime 64 10 10 11 $250,618 | 1983 2 1 1 0 $26,200 | 1982 11 0 1 2 $18,260 | Turf 2 0 0 0

16Jan83- 2Aqu	sly	1 70	⊡	:47	1:12⅘	1:43⅗		Clm 85000	1	2	25	21½	11½	1½	Hernandez R	116	3.70	84-20	Lark Oscillation116½AccountReceivable1124TenBore1096½ Driving	10
8Jan83- 7Aqu	fst	1 70	⊡	:47	1:12	1:42		Alw 40000	5	8	67	55½	26	22	Hernandez R	115	8.90	90-16	Way, Jr. 1102 Lark Oscillation 1156 Rain Prince110¾ Fin. Strongly	9
5Dec82- 3Aqu	gd	1 70	⊡	:46⅖	1:11	1:41⅖	3↑	Clm 75000	5	8	814	711	58½	58¾	Maple E	117	2.70	86-16	ⒹWay Jr. 1083¾ Ten Bore 1132 Gauguin Native 1081½ No menace	9
12Nov82- 8Aqu	fst	1		:45⅗	1:09⅗	1:35⅕	3↑	Alw 35000	4	7	65½	64¼	35½	35¾	Maple E	115	14.00	84-21	Sing Sing 1102¼ Stiff Sentence 1223½ LarkOscillation1151 Rallied	8
23Oct82- 6Aqu	fst	1		:46⅗	1:12	1:36⅘	3↑	Alw 40000	3	6	62¾	4nk	34	45¼	Bailey J D	115	3.50	77-21	WestOnBrod117¾StiffSentenc1172½SwingingLight1152 Weakened	8
14Oct82- 8Aqu	fst	7f		:23⅘	:46⅘	1:22⅘	3↑	Alw 32000	6	1	52	31½	31½	21¾	Maple E	115	5.80	85-20	StiffSentence1151¾LrkOscilltion115noInFromDixie1154¾ Game try	6
3Oct82- 7Bel	fst	1		:45⅖	1:10⅗	1:36⅕	3↑	Alw 35000	5	8	77½	64	42¾	43¾	McCarron G	115	12.90	80-20	Otter Slide 114hdRiseJim117nkJohnCasey1153½ Lacked a response	8
29Aug82- 5Sar	fst	7f		:22⅘	:45⅕	1:22⅕	3↑	Clm 75000	1	5	79¼	77	74½	31¼	McCarron G	117	10.80	90-15	JiggsAlarm117noGrandFelice1171¼LarkOscilltion117no Raced wide	7
16Aug82- 2Sar	fm	1 1/16	Ⓣ	:46	1:10	1:41⅘	3↑	Clm 75000	8	9	912	812	77½	711	McCarron G	117	15.20	77-13	Deedee's Deal 115no King Neptune 119¾ DiscoCount1131½ Outrun	9
7Aug82- 7Sar	fst	7f		:22⅖	:45	1:21⅖	3↑	Alw 32000	1	7	75¼	86	63	54	McCarron G	117	27.60	91-14	Rivalero 1172 Ring of Light 117no Cut High 1171¾ No threat	8

LATEST WORKOUTS Jan 2 Bel tr.t 3f fst :36⅗ h Dec 24 Bel tr.t 4f fst :50 b Dec 19 Bel tr.t 4f fst :51⅖ b Nov 28 Bel 6f fst 1:18⅖ b

Some horses are home-breds, meaning they were bred by their owner from one of his mares. Those great arch rivals of the late 1970s, Alydar and Affirmed, were home-breds, as was the legendary Secretariat. Others were purchased at public auction, for prices ranging as high as a few million dollars. Some handicappers take note when an expensive purchase makes its racing debut, expecting the horse to immediately display the ability that such a high price presumes. They have no guarantees, no more so than do the owners of such animals. Many of the highest priced yearlings on record have proven dismal failures as racehorses for one reason or another. Some of our greatest stars, though, sold for "a mere bag of shells," Seattle Slew for only $17,500 and Spectacular Bid for just $37,000 to mention just two.

The identity of the owner is of little use to the handicapper, unless he happens to be a personal friend. There are exceptions, however. The horses of C. V. Whitney, long a prominent owner on the New York circuit, always seem to find their best form at Saratoga, where Mr. Whitney is able to attend the races. But cases like his are few and far between.

□ THE JOCKEY □

The identity of the jockey selected to ride a particular horse is an important piece of the handicapping puzzle. The particular talents of an individual jockey may match up better with one horse than another. Some ride especially well on the front end. Others are better able to get a horse to relax, and rate early. Some excel over a distance of ground, others on sharply turning grass courses. Some have a special touch with fillies. Others help two-year-olds learn their lessons more quickly.

Successful riders are well aware that they must ride a horse according to its style, rather than their own. A horse must be asked to produce its run when it is ready. If asked too soon, the horse may expend its energy, and flatten out in the stretch. If too late, the animal may already have become frustrated, and refuse to extend itself at all. The leading riders do not move a horse up, or make it run faster than it is capable. Rather, they give the horse a better chance to run its race, by staying out of trouble, getting good position, and correctly judging the pace. They excel particularly in route races, especially those on grass, where their superior strength and/or experience comes into play more frequently. And they win more than their share of the close finishes.

One can usually count on jockeys adjusting to happenings in previous races. If two horses engaged in a speed duel last time, tiring each other out, don't bet on another killing speed duel this time. At least one of the riders will attempt to rate his mount today.

The identity of the jockey is best used as a window to the trainer's intentions. Is the horse well-meant today? Or is it just being sent out for some exercise? The trainer may "tip his hand" by the jockey he chooses. A glance at the identities of the riders from his horses' good performances might provide some insight as to how and when the trainer chooses his riders.

The better horses tend to attract the better riders. For this reason, the jockey factor can be looked upon as a "dependent variable," to use the popular statistical terminology. The identity of the rider can be used to confirm or refute other clues to the horse's fitness found in the past performances.

The names of the jockeys from each of a horse's previous starts appear in the past performances, where indicated:

A number appearing after the jockey's name means the rider was an apprentice taking the weight allowance listed. The name R. Alvarado, Jr., appears seven times in Mouse Corps' past performances. The first two times, he was still a relatively inexperienced rider, receiving an allowance of seven pounds. The next three times, the allowance was only five pounds, because Alvarado had by then won thirty-five races, the cutoff point between a five- and seven-pound apprentice. On the two most recent occasions, Mouse Corps was contesting a stakes race, and so his rider received no break in the weights.

The name of the jockey scheduled to ride a horse appears nowhere in its past performances, for good reason. Although supposedly against the rules, one rider may be scheduled (listed) on two or three different horses in a given race. This is especially true of the leading riders, particularly the hot apprentice rider. Which horse he eventually chooses may very well provide the player with some "inside information."

The jockey is just one half of a team. The other half is his agent, who must be part salesman and part handicapper. A good handicapper, as a rule, privy to the secrets of the backside, where he plies his trade. It is he who schedules his jockey's mounts, based on feedback from his rider, his own handicapping acumen, and what he hears along the backstretch grapevine.

When a leading rider suddenly turns up on a longshot, the astute handicapper should ask himself two questions. First, why did the trainer bother to seek out a leading rider? And second, why did the agent agree to the ride? Especially when he could have possibly ridden one of the more fancied entrants? The answer could be simply that the jockey has a commitment to the stable (trainer) to ride all (or most all) its horses, or that the agent booked his rider on a "dog" to insure a future mount on its stakes-winning stablemate, or that there is more to the horse than meets the eye.

Chic Belle was a case in point when entered May 22, 1983, after a five-week layoff. The filly's two placings came in January against much weaker competition than she would face at Belmont. Her performances in early spring at Aqueduct were poor. Her workouts—two at three furlongs during the week preceding her race, following an absence of three weeks—hardly suggested readiness. Yet New York's hot apprentice, Declan Murphy, chose to ride her, and she won off by three lengths at 21–1. Obviously, somebody—trainer Sally Bailie and jockey agent Lenny Goodman, included—knew something. This was just the first of three consecutive victories for Chic Belle at that meet.

Chic Belle — **Dk. b. or br. f. 3, by Mr Prospector—Sleek Belle, by Vaguely Noble** — **113**
Own.—Aisco Stables — **Br.—Aisco Stable (Fla)** — **Tr.—Bailie Sally A**
Lifetime 6 1 1 1 $17,140 — 1983 5 1 1 1 $17,140 — 1982 1 M 0 0

22May83- 6Bel	my	6f	:22⅗	:46	1:11	3↑ⒻMd Sp Wt	2	4	43¼	31½	12	12¾	Murphy D J7	106	21.40	87-14	Chic Belle 1062¾ Beneficence 1132¾ Sauce Of Life 1082¾	Driving	10
16Apr83- 4Aqu	sly	1	:46⅖	1:12⅖	1:39	ⒻMd Sp Wt	5	2	2½	22	69¼	716	Graell A	121	5.50	55-26	Lyndamar 121½ Granchira 1143½ Gnome Junction 114¾	Bore out	9
31Mar83- 6Aqu	fst	6f	:22⅕	:45⅘	1:11⅖	ⒻMd Sp Wt	4	4	67½	78	69½	610	Graell A	121	8.50	74-21	Far Flying 1213¾ Teriyaki Stake 1211 Angelic Imp 1211½	Outrun	9
23Jan83- 6Aqu	sly	6f	⊡:23⅕	:47⅕	1:14⅕	ⒻMd Sp Wt	11	4	2hd	2hd	2½	33¼	Graell A	121	2.50	70-26	Growing On Trees121nkShawneeCreek1213ChicBelle1212	No rally	11
6Jan83- 4Aqu	sly	6f	⊡:23	:47	1:12⅖	ⒻMd Sp Wt	7	2	2½	21½	31½	25¾	Graell A	121	2.20	76-17	Tornada 1165¾ Chic Belle 121¾ Squaw Island 111¾	Best of others	12
28Dec82- 6Aqu	fst	6f	⊡:23⅕	:47	1:13	ⒻMd Sp Wt	5	8	86¼	76½	910	66¾	Alvarado R Jr5	112	*2.30	72-22	Kal'sCornishGirl117¾TyroleanMiss117½WhtmiWood1172¾	Checked	14

LATEST WORKOUTS May 29 Bel 3f fst :35⅗ h — May 21 Bel 3f fst :39 b — May 16 Bel 3f fst :38⅖ b — Apr 23 Bel 4f fst :51 b

The top ten riders at a meet (over a season, on any given circuit) dominate that meet's (season's) statistics, winning approximately two thirds of the races. Unfortunately, this fact is relatively useless to the handicapper. Several of these riders compete in each race. But where the very best riders at a meeting are well-known to all, and have their followings at the betting windows, there may be several others, just slightly below them in talent and ability, who are well worth following. One doesn't give up a whole lot in terms of ability when betting these riders. Yet they usually are worth a few points on the odds board, as the majority of the crowd tags along with their better-known peers. When given a live mount, they can usually be counted upon to give a competent ride.

The most popular apprentice jockey riding at a meet usually has his choice of live mounts. As a rule, he rides well-meant horses, and his presence in the saddle must be regarded as a positive sign from that standpoint. Apprentices are young, however, and they do make numerous mistakes. For that reason, the serious player should think twice before supporting a horse ridden by an apprentice in a grass contest, where the sharp turns give rise to a higher incidence of traffic problems.

The important thing to remember about apprentices is that they are inexperienced. Most of them are several notches below the established journeymen riders at their track, in terms of ability, a fact easily proven by the immediate lack of success most apprentices experience upon losing their "bug." But when an apprentice suddenly becomes "fashionable," weight-conscious trainers surround the rider's agent, demanding the young jockey's services.

☐ THE TRAINER ☐

Whereas the ten leading jockeys dominate their peers at any given track, no such thing is true among the trainers. A study of a full twelve-month season in New York (1979) revealed that only twelve trainers won as many as forty races that year. A total of ninety-one won ten or more. Frank "Pancho" Martin, the perennial leader on the New York circuit, topped the list with 105 victories, the only one to break the century mark. At the opposite extreme was the Greentree Stable, long a potent force on the New York (and national) scene. They won an Eclipse Award with Bowl Game that year (he won twice in New York), and only one other race, that one in a dead heat, no less.

The leading trainers are well-known to the racing public. Their names and current records appear daily in the track program, and consequently they have some impact on the odds. Statistics on the vast majority of trainers, however, are not readily available to the public. It is incumbent upon the individual handicapper to become familiar with these people, their strengths and weaknesses. The sharp handicapper is aware of the identities of the current "hot" trainers on his circuit, and tends to play along with them during their "roll." The stable's success may be due to a new assistant trainer, medication, drug, or feed, but this is of no concern to the handicapper. The winners all may be logical, or come totally unexpected. The smart player tags along.

An in-depth statistical analysis of trainers would be invaluable, but is a massive undertaking, even for one circuit. My study of 108 New York trainers encompassed well over two hundred hours of research time. Just a few specific details of that study are presented in this book, some in this chapter, others in the form of examples where appropriate in other chapters. The facts uncovered would be practically useless to readers other than those who frequent the New York tracks, or encounter the New York trainers during their winter sojourns to sunnier climates. It is our methodology, however, that is important. How does one go about organizing a trainer study?

Statistically speaking, the number of starters, winners, and in-the-money finishes was calculated for each trainer, then each's win and money percentage for the season. We also totaled the payoffs on all winners, permitting calculation of each trainer's $NET for the year. It pays to compare a trainer's win percentage with his in-the-money percentage. If a large percentage of a trainer's in-the-money finishes are, in fact, winning efforts, that trainer must be considered very efficient, from a betting standpoint. When he sends out a sharp horse, it will, more likely than not, get the job done. In general, a 15–20 percent win percentage (and 40–50 percent in-the-money percentage) must be considered good. Anything higher is well above average, and achieved by the rare few.

Among the top twelve trainers in New York during 1979, only Allen Jerkins had a win percentage above 20 percent (he scored with 24 percent of his 196 starters), and only Jan Nerud, producing a $NET above the break-even point (a 25 percent profit from 243 runners). None of the eleven others came near $2.00 for their average return on investment.

New Yorkers, therefore, were forced to look elsewhere, to trainers not listed among the leaders in the track program, to find some betting advantage. This was particularly true with grass racing. Eight of the top ten trainers together combined for a mere eleven wins on the grass that season. Their "bread and butter" was the claiming horse, which has limited opportunities on the grass in New York.

Not surprisingly, several of the lower volume trainers proved profitable betting propositions that year. Unless this was due to one extremely high payoff skewing the statistics, or was based on a rather small sample, it can be concluded that it is possible to get a reasonable price on that trainer's horses when they are set to win. The question then becomes one of identifying the signs of a forthcoming victory, of discovering the trainer's *modus operandi*, and of learning his strengths and weaknesses before the public catches on.

Serious handicappers attempt to learn as much as possible about the trainers on their circuit. They scrutinize the form of race winners, often after the fact. They take a close look at surprise losers as well. It takes only a minute or two after each race to justify why a particular horse won, or another lost, and to store that information in one's memory for future reference. On the other hand, knowledgeable handicappers are aware that some trainers will remain a mystery, no matter how much they dig. Some trainers themselves don't know when their horses are going to win. Others often find it necessary to darken their horses' form. They rely on cashing bets at decent odds to supplement the moderate income produced by their racing stable. And they must disguise their better runners' fitness from fellow trainers who might be inclined to step in and claim away their meal ticket.

For year, authors of handicapping books, articles, and systems have warned their readers to avoid horses returning from a layoff of more than thirty days, switching from a leading rider, dropping back from a route to a sprint, among numerous other negative signs. In *Winning at the Races*, I demonstrated that most of these axioms were valid by presenting statistics based on numerous cases. However, while these generalities have their value, they can be misleading. They are best used as broad guidelines, with the understanding that there are numerous exceptions relating to specific horsemen and their individual talent and style of training.

Here then are some of the points that were looked at:

THE ODDS: The payoffs were noted on the trainer's winners, and the odds on the losers as well, to determine that trainer's reliability when running a favorite, especially one at odds-on, and the threat he poses when starting a longshot. If a high percentage of a trainer's winners fall into the longshot category, take note, and try to discover if they have anything in common.

THE JOCKEY: We noted the rider on each winner, attempting to identify jockey preferences. Some trainers, like Laz Barrera, use name riders ex-

clusively. Others, of whom Allen Jerkins is a notable example, give winning mounts to almost anyone capable of climbing in the saddle. Some
barns use a stable jockey who gets almost all of its "live" mounts. Many
weight-conscious conditioners like the seeming advantage they get by
riding an apprentice. Some trainers tip their hand by switching to one of
the meet's leading riders when they feel their horse has reached its peak.
Therefore, jockey changes on winners were duly noted.

REPEATERS: The number of horses able to repeat a victory was noted,
especially from the maiden ranks. Some trainers take a lot out of a horse
preparing for, and achieving, a win. Others waste winning form by
foolishly placing their horses in subsequent starts. It is important to
know which trainers are able to keep a horse at a peak level of performance for more than just a race or two.

GRASS: Special note was made of grass winners, especially those doing
so in their first start on that surface. It is helpful to know which trainers
are serious about grass racing, and which are aware of the potential inherent in grass bloodlines (see Chapter 5). New Yorkers Mack Miller and
Phil Johnson seem to try everything in their barn on the grass, and are
quite successful. They have their counterparts on every circuit featuring
grass racing.

AGE/SEX: The age and sex of each winner was recorded. Some trainers
have their greatest success with horses of a particular age or sex. Johnny
Campo has long had a reputation as a trainer of juveniles. Five of his
young charges won their debuts in 1979, and all were heavily bet. Jim
Maloney, on the other hand, is widely recognized for his prowess with
fillies and mares.

LAYOFFS: Victories immediately following a layoff were noted, especially those coming in a horse's racing debut. Some trainers, like Elliot
Burch in New York and Charles Whittingham in Los Angeles, use the
first few starts of a horse's career for educational purposes. Others like
to wind their horses up for a serious try first time out. For some of these,
the tip-off lies in the workouts. For others, readiness will be signaled on
the odds board.

RECENCY: The number of days since each winner's previous start was
recorded. Some trainers like to race their stock frequently, and will
bring an especially sharp horse back within the week, while others prefer to give the horse a few weeks to recuperate, yet have the skill to keep

the animal at its peak while doing so. New Yorker David Whiteley, who won with 39.3 percent of his starters in 1979, almost never brings a horse back within ten days. Eddie Kelly, Sr., can race a horse once a month, and have it always at its peak. But for Oscar Barrera, New York's "action" trainer, the term "right back" means the next day!

FORM: Special note was made of each winner's performance in the races leading up to its victory. It helps to know whose horses are formful, and whose often win as surprises. Some trainers use prep races to fine-tune their charges for peak efforts. Many need just one race to bring a freshened horse back to a peak of fitness. For some, there are telltale signs in the first race back, such as sharp early speed or a middle move. For others, the improvement might come unexpectedly. Some trainers are able to keep a horse going in top form for several races. Others can't, usually getting the best from a horse when it is relatively fresh. Still others race their horses two or three times before cracking down. Some trainers tend to waste races at inappropriate distances. Others persistently race their horses over their heads. Some do so out of stupidity, others for conditioning purposes. Some don't know when to stop with a horse. They fail to respond to signs of wear and tear, and instead "squeeze the lemon dry," making it all the more difficult to bring the horse back to its previous peak.

CLASS CHANGES: Each winner's race classification was noted in comparison with the classification from its previous two starts. It is important to identify trainers able to improve their charges, and win on the "raise" in price. As a general rule, the failure to move a recent winner up in class is a tip-off that the conditioner feels the horse is no longer at its best. When a recent claiming winner is not moved up, it must be considered prime claim bait. In that respect, the trainer is telling one and all that he considers the animal most useful to him in someone else's barn, with the check for the claim deposited in his account. It is also critical to understand what a drop in class means for any given trainer, especially a sharp drop. For many, a drop in class signals an all-out effort to win a purse. For others, dropdowns represent "damaged merchandise" to rival trainers. The player must learn whose dropdowns can be bet and whose should be avoided among the trainers on his local circuit.

CLAIMS: Some trainers have excellent reputations at the claiming box, and are able to move a recent claim up in class quickly. Others are often forced to drop their claims back to (or below) their purchase price before winning. Special note was made of recent claims that won, and the name of the trainer from whom the claim had been made was recorded. This will help the researcher identify the truly talented claiming trainers on his circuit.

DISTANCE: Some trainers are successful when stretching young horses out to a route distance for the first time. Allen Jerkins is noted for this. Others do their best work with sprinters. A few are capable of winning regularly when dropping a horse back in distance, which is no mean feat. Some use sprints to sharpen a horse for a route engagement. Others employ routes to build a sprinter's stamina. It was found helpful to use shorthand notation such as SSR to note the distances of a horse's two races preceding its victory. So for example, SSR means that the horse prepped twice in sprints before winning the present race at a route distance.

SHIPPERS: Some trainers are very successful with shippers. When they arrive on a circuit, their horses run well immediately. New Yorkers Phil Johnson and Jim Maloney traditionally arrive from winter quarters in the spring with barns full of horses ready to roll. Laz Barrera usually arrives at Saratoga with California horses ready to whip their New York-based rivals. Others give their horses a race or two of seasoning before cracking down. Some ship to a neighboring track to pick up an easy win. Others do the same to take advantage of different drug rules.

WORKOUTS: Each winner's workout pattern from the day of its most recent race was noted. Some trainers work their horses regularly, every five days. Others, rather infrequently. Some train with fast works, while others employ more leisurely breezes. Some prefer short works, while others like long works at six furlongs or a mile. Some regularly work their horses between engagements, others do not. Many cap off their workout schedule with a sharp "blowout" of three or four furlongs a morning or two before the race.

THE TIME OF THE YEAR: Some trainers aim to have their stable at its peak for a certain meeting. They may lay low at the end of the preceding meeting, resting some horses and culling others, while at the same time claiming fresh horses they feel will help them at the upcoming meet. Therefore, the date and track of each winner were noted.

STABLE BETTING: Some trainers bet, others don't. Some do so successfully, supplementing their income. Others lose, like the majority of players. Some stables' betting activity can be spotted in the pari-mutuel pools. Some bet early, others late. Some hide their activity in the exotic pools. Certain trainers are overbet by the public. With others, it is often possible to get an overlay price on a sharp horse, while for some, a surprisingly good price might mean "ice," the surprising absence of betting action signaling a dull effort forthcoming. It helps to chart the odds on a trainer's horses. Next to the morning-line odds in the track program, record the opening flash, then the odds ten minutes before post time, then again with five and two minutes to go, and finally the closing odds. With a large enough sample, stable betting patterns should become clear, and those that tend to bet at the right time will soon be identified.

We emphasize that one can be easily misled if looking solely at a trainer's winners. It may be insignificant that 65 percent of a conditioner's winners were ridden by a certain jockey—the same rider may have been on 75 percent of the outfit's starters. On the other hand, if 95 percent of a trainer's winners were coming back within ten days, the researcher has uncovered a strong elimination factor for that trainer—don't bet any of his starters away from the races more than ten days.

Most of the topics just mentioned will receive more attention in later chapters.

CASE STUDY: CHARGING THROUGH

Trainers often repeat a winning pattern, and the handicapper is well-advised to look at the sequence of events leading to a horse's previous wins. Although possibly stretching the point, notice that Charging Through laid off the pace on March 30, then moved too soon, only to hang slightly in the stretch. That race came after a five-week layoff, and was followed by a front-running score on April 13.

Trainer John Veitch repeated the exact pattern on May 29 and June 11. After a six-week layoff, the horse bid and hung, then came back two weeks later to score wire-to-wire. On the latter occasion, he returned $20.60 to those who noticed the similarities.

The past performances list only the present trainer of each horse. A horse may have had a few other conditioners during the time span covered by the races appearing in its printed record. Unless the handicapper has kept notes, or has a sharp memory, he will never know.

When a horse is claimed, we have no information about from whom it was claimed. If claimed by Joe Backstretch from the leading trainer at the meeting, one would hardly anticipate improved form. Should the situation be reversed, however, improvement can be expected, unless the former trainer has left the horse in such poor condition that no one could straighten it out.

CASE STUDY: RUSTIC LOVE

Here is a good rule to follow with the typical recent claim. Give the horse one race in its new barn without your support at the pari-mutuel windows. If it shows improvement, especially in a higher classification, then string along in subsequent starts, until the animal appears to have reached its potential and leveled off. Perhaps the new trainer has found the animal's hole card, and the horse will continue to improve over a series of races.

Note the improvement exhibited by Rustic Love after she was claimed by Sue Sedlacek on February 9. After a promising first effort for her new barn on March 5, Rustic Love won at $17.20 on March 21 with the help of a slight drop in class. Moved up one notch on April 11, she again raced promisingly, and then came back to win in that same class, this time at $16.20. Ten days later, she narrowly missed when raised three classes. The improvement cycle should have continued at the $30,000 level, but instead her trainer chose to drop her to the $25,000 level. The sharp player might have backed off at this point, and would have guessed correctly. The filly raced poorly, and her cycle of improved form ended.

□ CONCLUSION □

Training is not an easy profession. The hours are long, and the patients don't speak. Good help is hard to find. I have been an avid golfer for many years, but as each year passes, it becomes more noticeable that the sharp feeling and smooth swing one day may become labored and shaky the next. So it must be with the physical condition of horses from race to race. Indeed, from day to day. Many little things can go wrong. Not every horse racing is at its physical best. The effective trainer, however, must detect ailments as they develop, before they become critical.

Recall the career of Secretariat. His loss in the Wood Memorial was due to an abscess in his mouth. Trainer Lucien Laurin was unaware of its presence until the week before the Derby. Secretariat lost the Whitney because he was in the early stages of an illness that became apparent to his conditioner a couple of days later. He lost the Woodward because he wasn't properly prepared for the race, being a last-minute substitute for stablemate Riva Ridge, who was forced to scratch because of wet track conditions. This is Secretariat we are talking about, the most publicized horse of the last half-century, whose every cough made headlines. Not even his trainer knew (immediately) why he had lost two of those races. Not to mention the general public!

How could one have anticipated the victory of Deputed Testamony in the 1983 Preakness? After all, the colt had shown nothing in the Bluegrass Stakes, when pitted against the same caliber of horses, over similar sloppy conditions. What the majority of people didn't know, however, was that the colt was running a 103° fever the day after the Bluegrass, so he obviously wasn't at his best for that race. How many other horses race poorly because of a fever or cough, and then produce a remarkable reversal of form once recovered?

What about the average, everyday horse? The racing public has no way of knowing their personal histories. We can only hope to make valid inferences concerning their present fitness by becoming familiar with their trainer, his level of competence, and his *modus operandi*.

CASE STUDY: TIME TO EXPLODE

The past performances of Time To Explode failed to hint at the numerous problems that plagued this fleet son of Explodent during the formative stage of his racing career.

Time To Explode — **Ch. c. 4, by Explodent—Timely Queen, by Olden Times**

Own.—Rutherford M G — **121** — **Br.—Lin-Drake Farm (Fla)** — **Tr.—Jones Gary**

1983	**2**	**1**	**1**	**0**	**\$72,550**
1982	**9**	**5**	**1**	**0**	**\$133,300**
Lifetime	**11**	**6**	**2**	**0**	**\$205,850**

5Feb83-8SA	$1\frac{1}{16}$	$:46^1$	$1:10^4$	$1:43^1$sy	*$2\frac{1}{4}$	121	2^{hd}	2^{hd}	2^{hd}	$2\frac{1}{2}$	PincayLJr^6	Sn Psql H	84	RglFlcon,TimToExplod,WstOnBrod	7
2Jan83-8SA	7f	$:22^1$	$:44^3$	1:21 ft	*8-5	117	$2^{1\frac{1}{2}}$	$2\frac{1}{2}$	$1^{2\frac{1}{2}}$	1^{nk}	Pincay L Jr^6	Malibu	95	TmTEpld,PrncSpllbnd,WvrngMnrch	8
18Dec82-8Hol	7f	$:21^4$	$:44^2$	$1:20^3$ft	*8-5	118	1^{hd}	2^{hd}	1^{hd}	1^2	PincayLJr^4	Yuletide H	94	TmToExplod,Dv'sFrnd,TrvllngVctor	8
14Nov82-8Hol	6f	$:21^2$	$:43^3$	$1:08^1$ft	*2	118	6^3	4^3	3^2	$4^{1\frac{1}{4}}$	PncLJr^9	Ntl Sprt Chp	95	Mad Key, Shanekite, Dave's Friend	9
14Nov82—Run in two divisions, 8th & 9th races															
3Jly82-8Hol	6f	$:21^2$	$:43^3$	$1:08^4$ft	*2-3	117	$8^{6\frac{3}{4}}$	7^9	$8^{8\frac{1}{2}}$	6^5	PincayLJr^8	Hol Exp H	88	RmmbrJohn,PompCort,LghngBoy	10
26Jun82-4Hol	7f	$:21^4$	$:43^3$	$1:19^2$ft	*4-5	117	2^{hd}	1^{hd}	$1^{2\frac{1}{2}}$	1^6	Pincay L Jr^2	Aw24000	100	Time To Explode, Okubo, Shashy	6
31Mar82-8SA	$6\frac{1}{2}$f	$:21^3$	$:44^1$	$1:15^1$ft	*2-5	120	3^2	3^{nk}	$2\frac{1}{2}$	$2\frac{3}{4}$	Pincay L Jr^6	Baldwin	93	RmmbrJohn,TmToExplod,CrystlStr	7
6Mar82-8SA	1	$:44^3$	$1:09^1$	$1:34^2$ft	4	119	$1\frac{1}{2}$	1^{hd}	1^{hd}	4^1	Hawley S^1	Sn Rafael	96	PrincSpllbound,Muttring,Unprdctbl	9
17Feb82-8SA	6f	$:21^2$	$:43^4$	$1:08^3$ft	$3\frac{3}{4}$	117	2^{hd}	1^1	$1^{2\frac{1}{2}}$	1^3	Pincay LJr^7	Blsa Chca	95	TmToExplod,RmmbrJohn,JornytS	10
30Jan82-7SA	6f	$:21^2$	:44	$1:09^1$ft	$2\frac{1}{2}$	120	$3^{3\frac{1}{2}}$	$3^{1\frac{1}{2}}$	$1\frac{1}{2}$	1^{nk}	Pincay L Jr^7	Aw19000	92	TimeToExplode,JourneytSe,SrdSpy	8

Feb 12 SA 3f ft :37 b — Jan 30 SA 6f gd 1:14 h — Jan 26 SA 6f sl $1:13^3$ b — Jan 14 SA 5f ft $:59^3$ h

We include here quotes taken from articles appearing in *The Thoroughbred Record*. They are worth reading, if only to make the point that what appears in the *Racing Form* past performances is not necessarily the whole story.

The January 30 allowance race

> "He was short for that race, though," claimed his trainer Gary Jones before the Bolsa Chica. "But he has no excuse today. I was able to get as much work into him as he needed."

Apparently, the January 30 race was better than it appeared to be on paper.

The Bolsa Chica

> "The little fellow tries so hard," said Jones. "He tried so hard in his race that he left some grain in his tub for the first time."

In this case, a superior performance may be tainted, and *Form* readers would be caught unaware.

The San Rafael

> As with many one-mile races on one-mile racetracks, the tactics of the San Rafael were dictated by the post position draw. Trainer Gary Jones was chagrined to find his Bolsa Chica Stakes

winner, Time To Explode, had received the No. 1 post, just inside of the San Vicente winner Unpredictable, an incendiary son of Tri Jet who knows only one way to run. "Delahoussaye will be clocking my colt all the way around," said Jones of Unpredictable's rider, Eddie Delahoussaye.

Time To Explode was forced into a suicidal speed duel in the San Rafael, costing him the race, but making his game performance all the more impressive.

The Baldwin

Time To Explode, under Pincay, may have been a bit shy of his best for the Baldwin. Gary Jones had to lose some training time with the energetic son of Explodent due to minor nags like a burned heel and a cough.

Prior to his world-record-equaling performance on June 26

Then the hinges began to come off. Jones had the spotted chestnut primed for the San Felipe Handicap in March, but Time To Explode threw a shoe, then came down with a throat ailment. When he came back to the races in late April he was beaten by Remember John in the Baldwin Stakes, and came out of the race hurting again. "He pulled a muscle in back of his right forearm," said Jones, "and then he caught that thing that was making the rounds here. In the meantime we pulled off his shoes one day and found an old abscess, probably from when he threw that shoe at Santa Anita."

The Hollywood Express

Whetted by that 1:19.2 seven furlongs, trainer Gary Jones decided to spin his Explodent colt right back in the Express one week later. He felt confident, with only the lingering doubt that nags most trainers after such a stunning performance: How much did it take out of the horse that I cannot see?

About a dozen jumps out of the gate the question was rendered moot. Remember John, breaking like a shot under McCarron, swerved into Time To Explode just enough to throw him off stride. After that he had very little to do with the Express.

"My colt came back with leg cuts, one ankle filled, and real body sore," Jones added. "I'm just thankful we got him back in one piece."

The National Sprint Championship

The chestnut son of Explodent with the surrealistic white markings had not raced since his roughhouse trip in the Hollywood Express last July. In June, he equaled the world record for seven furlongs. "He got sick a couple times," said trainer Gary Jones, "otherwise he would have been back sooner. I think I've got him fit enough, but I'm not sure he won't get a little tired running over the Hollywood surface after all his training has been at Santa Anita."

The Yuletide Handicap

"I really had to hone him to get him ready for that one," Jones said of Time To Explode. "It was asking a lot of him to run him in a tough race like that after such a long layoff. And I had trained him at Santa Anita, vanning him to Hollywood for the race. I guess maybe I learned a lesson because this time I brought him to Hollywood from Santa Anita for his last work before the race. I think it helped him to do that."

Two weeks after the Malibu

Pincay would not have been aboard Water Bank had Time To Explode stayed healthy. But the chestnut fireball came down with a temperature just four days before the San Fernando, and now will have to miss the Strub as well.

The San Pasqual (from Gordon Jones' column in the LA Herald-Examiner)

But the runnerup was giving Regal Falcon six pounds and maybe a race in terms of current condition. Trainer Gary Jones had legitimate excuses in defeat. "I figured Regal Falcon was the horse to beat, and I think my horse ran a super race," he said. "What beat him was the weight and the fact he lost a shoe."

The San Antonio (to which the past performances above refer)

While Bates Motel got all the best of the luck, Time To Explode got the worst. Loading last, he was unsettled in the gate when the stall door opened. He broke on his left lead, and promptly grabbed a quarter. The cut on the bulb of Time To Explode's heel puts him out of the Santa Anita Handicap.

Chapter 5

BLOODLINES

Thoroughbred racing is, above all else, a fascinating sport. Part of that fascination lies in the continuity of its bloodlines. Although many of racing's stars are on stage for only a year or two, fans usually can look forward to watching their offspring race. A horse's bloodlines are listed front and center in the past performances, preceded by the animal's color, sex, and age:

Slew O' Gold — **B. c. 3, by Seattle Slew—Alluvial, by Buckpasser**
Br.—Claiborne Farm (Ky)
Tr.—Watters Sidney Jr
Own.—Equusequity Stable
124

Lifetime	1983 7 3 2 1		$264,990
10 5 2 1	1982 3 2 0 0		$22,200
$287,190			

11Jun83- 8Bel	fst	1½	:47⅖	1:59⅘	2:27⅘	Belmont	1	3	21½	1½	21	23½	Cordero A Jr	126	*2.50	77 14	Caveat 1263½ Slew O' Gold 1261¾ Barberstown 126no	Led, wknd	15
29May83- 8Bel	fst	1⅛	:45⅗	1:09⅕	1:46⅘	Peter Pan	5	4	2½	12½	18	112	Cordero A Jr	126	*.80	93 11	Slew O' Gold 12612 I Enclose 1233¾ Foyt 1176	Ridden out	5
7May83- 8CD	fst	1¼	:47⅕	1:36⅘	2:02⅕	Ky Derby	1	7	78	75½	33	43¼	Cordero A Jr	126	10.10	83 10	Sunny's Halo 1262 Desert Wine 126nk Caveat 1261	Bothered start	20
23Apr83- 8Aqu	fst	1⅛	:48⅕	1:12⅕	1:51	Wood Mem	1	6	52	41¾	1hd	1nk	Maple E	126	*1.30	80 24	Slew O' Gold 126nk Parfaitement 126½ High Honors 1269¾	Driving	7
23Apr83-Run in two divisions 7th & 8th races																			
13Apr83- 1Aqu	fst	1⅛	:48⅗	1:12⅗	1:50⅘	Alw 23000	4	2	1hd	11	16	17¾	Cordero A Jr	117	*1.00	81 19	Slew O' Gold 1177¾ Law Talk 1171¼ El Cubano 117¾	Ridden out	6
19Mar83-10Tam	fst	1$\frac{1}{16}$	:48	1:13	1:47⅕	Tampa Dby	2	5	42½	43½	23	2¾	Rivera H Jr	118	2.30	82 21	Morgnmrgnmrgn118¾SlwO'Gld118¾QckDp1186	Steadied, checked	14
5Mar83-10Tam	fst	1$\frac{1}{16}$	:47⅘	1:13⅖	1:47⅖	Sam F Davis	4	7	86¾	43	32½	33¾	Molina V H	118	*.40	76 23	Silverton 1181¼ Two Turns Home 1202 Slew O Gold1181¼	Mild bid	8
13Nov82- 8Aqu	gd	1⅛	:48⅖	1:12⅘	1:50⅕	Remsen	11	4	52½	53	610	612	Lovato F Jr	115	*1.80e	72 20	Pax In Bello 1131¾ Chumming 1158 PrimitivePleasure113hd	Tired	11
23Oct82- 9Aqu	fst	1	:47	1:12⅕	1:37⅖	Alw 20000	8	2	2½	1hd	11½	11¾	Lovato F Jr	117	3.70	79 21	Slew O' Gold 1171¾ Last Turn 1172¾ Chumming 1222¾	Ridden out	9
15Oct82- 3Aqu	fst	6½f	:23⅖	:47	1:18⅘	Md Sp Wt	8	1	2½	2½	1½	1nk	Cordero A Jr	118	*.60	81 26	SlewO'Gold118nkCountrtrd1186MstyCov1182½	Lugged in, driving	8

LATEST WORKOUTS **Jly 28 Mth 4f fst :47⅘ b** **●Jly 23 Bel 5f fst :59⅖ h** **●Jly 18 Bel 1 fst 1:38⅖ h** **●Jly 14 Bel 6f fst 1:12⅖ h**

Possible color designations are:

Blk	denoting	black
B	"	bay
Br	"	brown
Dr. b. or br.	"	dark bay or brown
Ch	"	chestnut
Gr	"	gray
Ro	"	roan
Wh	"	white

Color is of no significance to the serious player. I do have one friend, however, who refuses to bet the gray offspring of Hoist The Flag on the grass, reasoning that the stallion's failure to transmit his own bay coloring is correlated somehow with a failure to transmit grass-racing ability. Possibly he's right!

Male horses are termed:

c	denoting	colt
h	"	horse
g	"	gelding
rig	"	ridgling

and female horses:

f	denoting	filly
m	"	mare

A male Thoroughbred is designated a colt until becoming a horse at age five. Likewise, a filly becomes a mare when she turns five.

Gelding is the term reserved for the altered (castrated) male. A ridgling is a male with a testicle that has failed to drop into the sac. A gelding has no future as a stallion. A ridgling may, should the testicle eventually fall into place. Why are horses gelded? For some, it is necessary to slow their growth. For others, to calm them down, and make them amenable to training. The gelding supposedly has its mind on business, rather than the filly three stalls down the shed row. For this reason, some handicappers prefer geldings to unaltered males among cheaper stock, especially when competing in the presence of a member of the opposite sex. And some like to take their chances with recently gelded horses, expecting a dramatic turnaround in form following the operation. It takes a sharp memory or extensive bookkeeping, however, to keep on top of such situations.

Listed in the past performances are the sire (father), dam (mother), and broodmare sire (mother's father) of the horse, in that order. Are bloodlines of any use? Possibly, but only before the horse establishes its preferences for distance and surface conditions. Once an animal has been around for a while, few handicappers pay much attention to its lineage.

Slew O'Gold, for example, was a three-year-old bay colt by the stallion Seattle Slew from the broodmare Alluvial, herself a daughter of

Buckpasser. As such, he was the son of a Triple Crown winner and a mare that had already produced a Belmont winner in Coastal. Slew O'Gold nearly gave his dam a unique place in racing history.

A Thoroughbred's name may consist of as many as eighteen characters, and may not duplicate the name of a horse currently active in racing or breeding. Owners of Thoroughbreds often must submit several names to the Jockey Club before having one accepted. Slew O'Gold was named by my good friends Bob and Mary Colgan. The name was the last on the list they submitted.

As we discuss breeding in this chapter, the emphasis will be placed rather heavily on the sire. Keep in mind, however, that each horse has two parents, and that its inherited aptitudes may have been passed along from either. We also emphasize that bloodlines should be used as an incentive to take a shot with a horse at a decent price. Don't bet a favorite that is untested on the grass or unproven at the distance, simply because of its sire. The horse may take after its dam instead! Or it may not be ready for a top effort. Breeding means nothing if the animal is not in shape.

☐ SPRINTERS ☐

Some horses are bred to be sprinters, expected to run out of oxygen after traveling more than six or seven furlongs. Physically, such horses are blocky and quite muscular looking. The stallions listed below are known to be sires primarily of sprinters, horses with an abundance of speed and very little stamina:

Blade	Loom
Christopher R	Our Michael
Cutlass	Princely Native
Distinctive	Rollicking
Duck Dance	Shecky Greene
Full Pocket	Time Tested
Hard Work	Tumiga
Insubordination	What Luck
Kaskaskia	

Sprint types often are precocious, and usually do well as two-year-olds, before the distances begin stretching out. They are likely candidates to win their racing debuts.

□ **ROUTERS** □

Other horses can't get going until they have traveled half a mile or six furlongs. They prefer races over a distance of ground. For some, the longer the better. Physically, they tend to be longer and slimmer than the typical sprinter.

The following stallions tend to produce progeny with little speed and an abundance of stamina:

Big Spruce	London Company
Cougar II	One For All
Good Counsel	Proud Clarion
Grey Dawn	Run The Gantlet
High Echelon	Tom Rolfe
Le Fabuleux	

Routers tend to develop more slowly than sprinters. Some come around toward the end of their juvenile season, others not until becoming three-year-olds. Smart handicappers give extra credence to such horses when they stretch out for the first time, especially if they had shown any signs of ability at shorter distances. Astute handicappers are also aware that certain precocious types are able to stay farther as two-year-olds than at any other time in their careers, simply because many of the true routers have yet to come to hand.

CASE STUDY: LEAP OF THE HEART

Bloodlines often point the handicapper toward a horse likely to improve when entered at a distance or over a surface that usually favors the get of its sire (or dam, or both). Breeding can also warn the handicapper to be suspicious of a horse in apparent good form. Such was the case with Leap Of The Heart, who was entered in a six-furlong allowance sprint at Belmont on September 4, 1982.

Fashionably bred by the great Nijinsky from the stakes-winning mare Ivory Wand, and trained by the astute Mack Miller, she had every right to be "any kind." Speed figures earned in her previous two starts placed her well above her competition, suggesting she might possibly be of stakes caliber. But after winning at six furlongs, and then racing strongly at seven furlongs, why was she being dropped back to six furlongs again? Mack Miller did not earn his reputation training sprinters. If Leap Of The Heart were a top prospect, Miller's logical next move would have been a middle-distance route, probably on the grass. That he chose a shorter sprint instead was a warning that all was not as rosy as appeared on paper.

Any astute handicapper would have passed her, especially at odds-on. Leap Of The Heart ran well, rallying to finish a close third. But as a three-year-old, she won just one allowance race, and did not compete in any stakes races.

□ SLOP BREEDING □

Certain horses seem to race especially well over wet surfaces. At least, they seem to endure such conditions better than most. Later in this chapter, we shall mention the possible role conformation might play in this phenomenon.

It seems valid to conclude that the offspring of certain stallions inherit an aptitude for racing under adverse conditions. Particularly noteworthy in this respect are the following:

Bagdad	Key To The Mint
Bosun	King's Bishop
Cinteelo	Native Charger
Damascus	Proudest Roman
Graustark	Ridan
Grey Dawn	Spanish Riddle
Herbager	The Pruner
In Reality	Truxton King

The top handicap mare Love Sign was born with water wings. By the outstanding offtrack runner Spanish Riddle and from a Graustark mare, she paid over $70 winning her career debut on a sloppy track, then went on to capture such major prizes as the Ruffian Stakes at Belmont in the slop.

Love Sign X — Dk. b. or br. m. 5, by Spanish Riddle—Native Nurse, by Graustark
Own.—Clark S C Jr — Br.—Clark Mrs S C Jr (Va) — Tr.—Watters Sidney Jr — 124

Lifetime						
35 16 6 4	1982	6	3	1	1	$144,493
$875,897	1981	13	3	4	1	$343,750
	Turf	4	2	1	0	$133,122

11Aug82- 8Sar	fst	7f	:22⅕	:44⅗	1:22⅘	3↑ⒻBallerina	8	1	5¾	31	63½	43¼	Hernandez R	126	*.90	85-16	ExpressiveDnce1221¼TellASecret113½SproutdRy1131½	Raced wide	8
1Aug82-10Del	fst	1¼	:47⅗	1:37	2:02⅗	3↑ⒻDelaware H	2	1	11½	2½	21½	35¼	Hernandez R	125	*.80	82-22	Jameela 1212 Zvetlana 1113¼ Love Sign 1253	Weakened	9
14Jly82- 8Bel	fst	1 1/16	:45⅗	1:10⅕	1:43	3↑ⒻImp	5	1	11	12	13½	12	Hernandez R	125	*.50	87-20	Love Sign 1252 HittingIrish1162¾DebonairDancer1161	Ridden out	5
21Jun82- 8Bel	fst	1	:46⅘	1:11	1:35⅗	3↑ⒻTwlight Tear	3	2	3nk	1hd	2½	21	Hernandez R	125	*.50	87-14	Andover Way 1251 Love Sign 1257 Prismatical 1201½	Bobbled st.	4
6Jun82- 8Bel	sly	1⅛	:46	1:09⅗	1:48	3↑ⒻHempstead H	3	1	1hd	1hd	15	17¾	Hernandez R	123	*.50	87-20	Love Sign 1237¾ Anti Lib 1162 Jameela 1223¾	Handily	4
24May82- 8Bel	sly	7f	:22⅘	:45⅗	1:21⅘	3↑ⒻAlw 32000	4	1	12	12	15	19½	Hernandez R	121	*.40	93-18	Love Sign 1219½ Prime Prospect 11911Scherzo'sLast1195	Handily	4
1Nov81- 8Aqu	fst	1¼	:48⅕	1:37	2:01⅘	3↑ⒻLadies H	3	1	1½	44	49½	416	Hernandez R	123	*.60	71-16	Jameela 1206 Discorama 1151 Tina Tina Too 1128½	Tired	8
11Oct81- 8Bel	fst	1¼	:48⅖	1:37	2:01⅘	3↑ⒻBeldame	6	1	11½	1½	12½	17	Shoemaker W	123	2.30	91-16	Love Sign 1237 [DH]Jameela 123 [DH]GloriousSong1235½	Ridden out	7
27Sep81- 8Bel	fst	1⅛	:46⅖	1:10⅖	1:47⅗	3↑ⒻRuffian H	4	1	11	1½	2hd	2¾	McCarron C J	120	7.00	88-19	Relaxing 123¾ Love Sign 1205¾ Jameela 1222	Gamely	4
6Sep81- 8Bel	fst	1	:46⅖	1:10⅕	1:35	3↑ⒻMaskette	5	1	11	2hd	2½	22	Hernandez R	123	1.40	91-15	Jameela 1232 Love Sign 1236½ Island Charm 1164	Gamely	5

LATEST WORKOUTS Aug 17 Sar 3f fst :36 b — Aug 8 Sar 4f fst :48 b — Jly 27 Bel 5f fst 1:00⅖ b — Jly 21 Bel 5f gd 1:01⅕ b

As a rule, large horses do not like the slop, Forego being a very notable example. Because of the length of their strides, they tend to slide, and cannot get a good grip on the slippery surface. Horses with short, quick strides do better when the track becomes wet.

Also, the handicapper must be aware that there are different kinds of wet tracks. A sloppy track is vastly different from one termed muddy. And sloppy conditions at Aqueduct differ significantly from conditions termed sloppy at either Belmont or Saratoga. Some horses have their preferences. Some wet tracks favor horses that like that particular kind of wet track. The sharp handicapper proceeds with caution when analyzing wet-track form.

□ GRASS BREEDING □

CASE STUDY: FIRST SEA LORD

As I drove to Aqueduct April 25, 1981, a major bet was the last thing on my mind. Heavy overnight rains had washed out the day's grass races, I'd presumed. I had some business to attend to, would watch a few races, then return home. But as I walked through the parking lot, I noticed the starting gate out on the grass course. It was nearing post time for the fourth race, which had been scheduled for the turf. My interest, however, leaped ahead to the sixth race, also scheduled for the grass. Among the entrants was First Sea Lord, a son of Little Current, set to make his grass debut. Little Current had been literally phenomenal as a sire of grass-runners. First Sea Lord's form on the dirt was reasonably good. If he moved up at all on the grass, he could be a stakes-class runner, competing here against a mediocre field of allowance runners. Based on his dirt form alone, First Sea Lord should have been among the favorites. However, the usually alert New York crowd let him get away at 12–1, presumably because of his lack of form (experience) on the turf. Little Current had not yet gained notoriety as a sire of grass runners.

It would be nice to report that First Sea Lord blew that field away. He didn't. But given a perfect ground-saving trip by young Richard Migliore, he came out at the head of the stretch and got up right at the wire. As I left Aqueduct that day, I knew that grass-breeding handicapping was still alive and kicking.

Since my publication *Turf Racing in North America* first appeared in 1975, the face of grass-race handicapping has changed. Some grass sires highlighted in that booklet have died, others have been retired from stud, and still others have aged to the point where they are represented by only tiny crops of offspring. More significantly, bettors across the country are now aware of certain stallions whose progeny show marked and immediate improvement when introduced to grass racing. The get of these stallions are bet more heavily now than in 1975. This simple approach of picking grass winners off their pedigree remains viable today. New grass sires have emerged to replace the old standbys. The key to success is early recognition of those new sires, and the courage to back their offspring when they go greensward the first few times, no matter how bad their dirt form. While there are some maiden and allowance races cluttered with first-time grass starters whose bloodlines suggest grass potential, awareness of the truly effective grass sires and a quick glance at the prevailing odds often point out a horse or two worth playing, often at hefty odds. Additionally, exotic wagering offers the opportunity to box two, three, or even four horses with grass bloodlines.

The study presented in this chapter focuses on progeny of anticipated or reputed grass sires in their first two attempts at grass racing. We allow two starts, rather than one, to give a second chance to a horse that may have had an excuse (poor racing luck, or too ambitiously placed) in its grass debut. We restrict ourselves to the first two starts, because it is there that true grass aptitude can be identified. The statistics presented here reflect racing through August 22, 1983. In addition, with the availability of more complete *Daily Racing Form* statistics, we have been able to look backward through the years to identify horses missed in earlier studies. Consequently, the sample sizes are larger than before, and the results more thorough and reliable.

When you look at the figures for the stallions, remember to check the WPCT and MPCT statistics as well as the $NET statistic. The former pair tell of the stallion's consistency as a grass sire, while the $NET reflects the surprise element, the magnitude of improvement demonstrated by the stallion's debuting grass runners. A high $NET alone, however, may simply be the result of one high-priced winner, and may thus give a misleading clue to a sire's true effectiveness. Some might complain that a large number of bad horses that can't run on any surface might ruin a stallion's statistics. But these same people will be the first to point out the bad horses that jump up to win at a big price first time out on the grass. Both contribute to our statistics. Note that grass sprints, especially those at five or five and a half furlongs, can often produce misleading results concerning grass breeding. Such races seldom feature horses with true grass bloodlines, and often go to the fastest horse able to handle the grass. Do not be influenced by the breeding of the winners of such races.

From a betting point of view, there are two kinds of grass sires: those the public is aware of, and those whose exploits have gone unheralded (so far). Hoist The Flag, Nijinsky, Northern Dancer, Le Fabuleux, and Tom Rolfe all are outstanding grass sires. But it seems that too many people know it. Betting on their first-time grass starters, as a rule, will not result in long-term profits. The win odds, on the average, are too low. Progeny of these sires must be respected first out on the grass, but the wise player looks for runners by less fashionable, though no less formidable grass sires.

Here is our current list (as of August 22, 1983) of the top ten grass sires. Our criterion is a combination of wagering profitability and consistency from at least fifty starters.

(1) Little Current
(2) Stage Door Johnny
(3) Exclusive Native
(4) One For All
(5) Tell
(6) Advocator
(7) Star Envoy
(8) Roberto
(9) Big Spruce
(10) Ambernash

Little Current is presently the "hot" young grass sire. All of his runners should be bet first time on the grass, regardless of previous form. Perhaps Little Current will someday catch on with the betting public, as did Hoist The Flag, and Nijinsky, and Le Fabuleux, after a few crops branded them as grass sires. Stage Door Johnny never did "catch on," despite his enormous reputation. Betting profits can still be had with this fine stallion.

Grass-breeding specialists are constantly on the lookout for the emerging grass stallions. They rely on early recognition. Once everyone else catches on, betting profits usually disappear. But in the first few years of a stallion's career, the profits can be plentiful. At this moment, the emerging grass sires might be Blood Royal, Caro, Champagne Charlie, Empery, Majestic Light, Mississippian, Tom Tulle, and Tom Command. Next year at this time, the list may well be quite different.

□ THE PRINCEQUILLO LINE □

Turf Racing in North America, and later *Winning at the Races* (which updated the earlier work) both focused attention on the Princequillo-line stallions, specifically Round Table, Prince John, and the latter's son Stage Door Johnny. The first two mentioned were for many years the basic staple for grass-breeding players, and rightfully so. Even at an advanced age, Round Table's record for 1981–82 read five winners from nine starters among his small crops of three-year-olds. However, Round Table is now retired from stud duties and Prince John is deceased. Unfortunately, Round Table, Prince John, and Stage Door Johnny have not been prolific sires of important sires. The Princequillo influence at major tracks can be found only in a very limited number of stallions.

Round Table

Round Table thus far has sired only two sons that have been successful as sires of grass runners in the United States: Advocator and Tell. King Pellinore, a major stakes winner on both sides of the Atlantic, had little success with his first two crops, but it is far too early to dismiss him as a grass sire. The beautifully bred European-raced Apalachee, with just five crops to race, has yet to demonstrate ability as a grass sire. Another son, King's Bishop, appears more a mud sire than a grass sire. Among the young sons and grandsons of Round Table to recently enter stud, six in particular should be watched as potential grass sires: Star Spangled, Banquet Table, Take Your Place, Told, Clev Er Tell, and Agitate. Likewise, Upper Case, who has recently returned to this country from stud duties in Europe.

Stallion	NH	NW	WPCT	MPCT	$NET
Round Table	142	35	24.6%	54.9%	$3.60
Advocator	169	25	14.8%	39.6%	$4.09
Tell	73	13	17.8%	42.5%	$2.94
King Pellinore	24	2	8.3%	20.8%	$1.42
Apalachee	43	3	7.0%	37.2%	$1.19
King's Bishop	84	8	9.5%	33.3%	$1.32

Prince John

Prince John also has had just two sons noted for passing on grass-racing ability: the incredible Stage Door Johnny, still a potent force, and the steady, less-publicized Speak John. The latter has sired Verbatim, sire of 1981 Belmont winner Summing, and just as effective a grass sire as his father. Summing's next-to-final prep for his Belmont Stakes was a victory in the Hill Prince Handicap at Belmont in his grass debut. He paid a generous $22.20! Stage Door Johnny, however, simply has not been a sire of sires. His best grass runners to date have been fillies or geldings, with the notable exception of the brilliant Shredder, a non-stakes winner now at stud in New York, where his offspring will have the opportunity to display their innate ability on the grass. Text and Improviser, both sons of Speak John, and Prince Valiant and Jack Sprat, sons of Stage Door Johnny, all have recently entered stud and bear watching as potential grass sires.

Stallion	NH	NW	WPCT	MPCT	$NET
Prince John	149	23	15.4%	33.6%	$3.12
Stage Door Johnny	189	52	27.5%	48.1%	$3.24
Speak John	157	23	14.6%	33.1%	$2.50
Verbatim	126	19	15.1%	46.0%	$2.90

We point out in passing that the offspring of Stage Door Johnny are particularly effective when grass conditions are damp.

Although weak in numbers, the Princequillo line is noted for its consistency. Most Princequillo-line stallions produce offspring with a fondness for the grass. Worth mentioning are Ramsinga, a grandson of Princequillo; Ole Bob Bowers, another grandson, and sire of Horse of the Year and all-time leading money winner John Henry, a grass champion; Diplomat Way, a son of Nashua from a Princequillo mare; and High Echelon, a son of Native Charger from a Princequillo mare. Worth watching is Jockey Club Gold Cup winner On The Sly, who is inbred to Prince Rose, sire of Princequillo.

Stallion	NH	NW	WPCT	MPCT	$NET
Ramsinga	49	7	14.3%	42.9%	$2.30
Ole Bob Bowers	24	6	25.0%	62.5%	$2.76
Diplomat Way	191	33	17.3%	39.3%	$3.07
High Echelon	63	10	15.9%	34.9%	$2.66

A genealogical chart of the Princequillo line appears on page 110.

With the Princequillo line thinning out, it becomes necessary to look elsewhere for potential grass sires. Specifically, we shall study three other primary sources: Hyperion, Native Dancer, and most significantly, Nearco.

☐ **HYPERION** ☐

The Hyperion influence in American grass racing can be found in four stallions, each of whom traces back to Hyperion through a different son of that great European champion. They are Forli (sire of Forego), Nodouble, Rock Talk, and Star Envoy. All are potent sires in the United States, with Forli being quite influential in Europe as well. His son Thatch was a leading sire in Europe, and another son, Forceten, appears a potential grass sire in this country. Curiously, Noholme II, sire of Nodouble, has been an abject failure as a grass sire in this country.

Stallion	NH	NW	WPCT	MPCT	$NET
Forli	113	15	13.3%	36.3%	$2.26
Forceten	13	2	15.4%	46.2%	$4.58
Intrepid Hero	17	2	11.8%	29.4%	$3.27
Noholme II	199	17	8.5%	30.2%	$1.03
Nodouble	138	25	18.1%	37.7%	$2.69
Rock Talk	107	17	15.9%	37.4%	$2.59
Star Envoy	58	8	13.8%	50.0%	$2.81

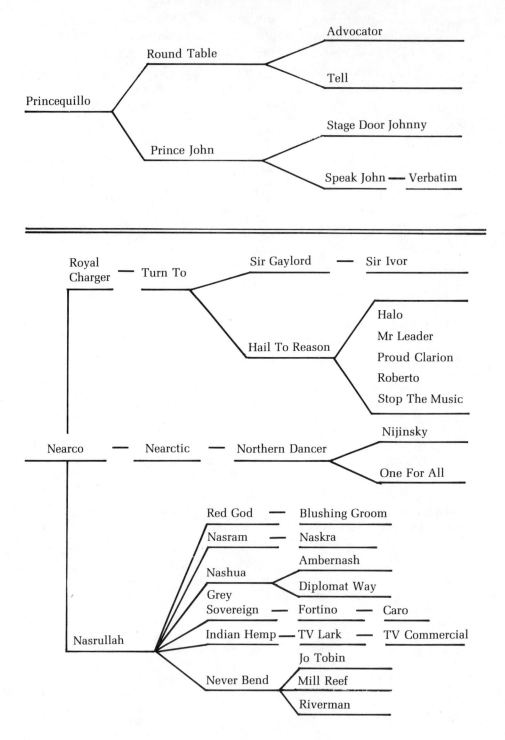

CASE STUDY: NODOUBLE

Probably the one stallion most slighted by earlier grass studies, as presented in *Winning at the Races*, was Nodouble. The "Arkansas Traveler" was a durable stakes campaigner across the country, yet never even placed in a grass stakes. He was not included in previous studies.

Undoubtedly the greatest feat in grass breeding annals belongs to Nodouble. It occurred in the Esquire, a minor $25,000 stakes for two-year-olds at Louisiana Downs. The date was October 4, 1980. Only two of the twelve starters in the Esquire were maidens, and both were sons of Nodouble. Nine of the other ten were multiple winners, and the tenth was a son of Quack, a "potential" grass sire at that time. The other nine had absolutely no grass breeding at all.

Nobubble — **Ch. c. 2, by Nodouble—Breezle Berry, by Craigwood**
Br.—Smreker J & Young C (Fla) **1980 3 M 0 1 $550**
Own.—Dixie Stable **114** **Tr.—Frazier Roy C**

20Sep80-9LaD 6½f $:22^4$ $:46^3$ $1:18^3$ft 23 113 $7^{3\frac{1}{4}}$ 11^{11} 11^{14} 10^{22} SnyderL[1] Hits Parade 67 CircleofStl,BoysNitOut,MggiB.Min 11
5Sep80-8LaD 6½f :23 $:46^2$ $1:18^3$ft 12 113 $8^{5\frac{1}{4}}$ $8^{8\frac{3}{4}}$ $7^{9\frac{1}{2}}$ $6^{9\frac{3}{4}}$ Snyder L[8] Alw 79 MggieB.Mine,SpkthVrb,CirclofStl 10
4Jly80-4LaD 5½f $:22^4$ $:46^4$ $1:06^3$ft 2¼ 120 $8^{6\frac{1}{4}}$ 6^7 4^7 3^{12} Romero R P[3] Mdn — Adesperado,Masterworth,Nobubble 9
Sep 19 LaD 3f sl :37 b **Sep 14 LaD 5f ft $1:02^3$ h** **Aug 30 LaD 3f sl $:37^3$ bg** **Aug 24 LaD 6f ft 1:15 h**

Spanish Double — **Ch. c. 2, by Nodouble—Spanish Relic, by Flying Relic**
Br.—Early Bird Stud (Fla) **1980 4 M 0 0**
Own.—Fast Track Stable **114** **Tr.—Spencer Ray**

20Sep80-9LaD 6½f $:22^4$ $:46^3$ $1:18^3$ft 38 113 $5^{2\frac{1}{4}}$ $5^{4\frac{1}{2}}$ 5^6 6^{12} RmrRP[11] Hits Parade 77 CircleofStl,BoysNitOut,MggiB.Min 11
5Sep80-4LaD 6½f $:22^4$ $:46^1$ 1:18 ft 96 114 $5^{1\frac{1}{4}}$ 3^4 $6^{7\frac{3}{4}}$ 6^{13} Whited D E[9] Alw 79 BoysNiteOut,Dr.Spanky,JudgeIrby 11
29Aug80-7LaD 6f $:22^4$:47 1:13 ft 57 120 $9^{5\frac{1}{2}}$ $8^{4\frac{3}{4}}$ 7^5 6^{12} Bourque K[2] Mdn 72 SpektheVerb,DoubleQuck,Cptense 11
23Aug80-1LaD 6f :23 $:46^4$ $1:13^3$ft 15 120 $5^{2\frac{1}{4}}$ $7^{4\frac{3}{4}}$ $8^{8\frac{1}{2}}$ 8^{10} Romero R P[5] Mdn 71 BoysNitOut,DoublHssl,MronCounty 9
Sep 27 LaD 4f ft $:49^2$ h **Sep 19 LaD 3f sl :37 b** **Sep 13 LaD 5f ft 1:03 b** **Aug 17 LaD 6f ft $1:18^2$ b**

Nodouble's sons were dismissed as the longest prices on the board. Yet they finished first and second, with the $5.00 exacta returning a sensational $3019.00.

TENTH RACE
La. Downs
OCTOBER 4, 1980

7 ½ FURLONGS.(turf). (1.30⅗) 2nd Running ESQUIRE. ALLOWANCES. $25,000 Added. 2-year-olds. Weight, 122 lbs. Winners of $9,000 twice other than maiden or claiming an additional 2 lbs. Non-winners of $9,000 other than maiden or claiming allowed 3 lbs.; $6,000, 5 lbs.; $4,500, 8 lbs. (Nominations close Saturday, Sept. 24, at $50.00 each; with $100.00 to pass the entry box on Thursday, Oct. 2, and $100.00 additional to start on Saturday, Oct. 4.) Closed with 15 nominations.
Value of race $28,150, value to winner $16,890, second $5,630, third $2,815, fourth $1,689, fifth $1,126. Mutuel pool $98,244. Exacta Pool, $113,220.

Last Raced	Horse	Eqt.	A.	Wt	PP	St	¼	½	Str	Fin	Jockey	Odds $1
20Sep80 ^{9}LaD^{10}	Nobubble	b	2	114	7	10	$8^{1\frac{1}{2}}$	$9^{1\frac{1}{2}}$	$6^{\frac{1}{2}}$	$1^{3\frac{1}{2}}$	Frazier R	59.70
20Sep80 ^{9}LaD^6	Spanish Double	b	2	114	4	2	6^1	$8^{1\frac{1}{2}}$	$3^{\frac{1}{2}}$	$2^{\frac{1}{2}}$	Rini A	49.10
12Sep80 ^{7}LaD^1	Double Quack		2	114	9	7	$9^{1\frac{1}{2}}$	7^{hd}	5^{hd}	$3^{\frac{1}{2}}$	Romero R P	3.40
20Sep80 ^{9}LaD^3	Maggie B. Mine	b	2	114	11	8	$7^{\frac{1}{2}}$	$4^{\frac{1}{2}}$	1^{hd}	4^1	Agnello A	9.80
23Aug80 ^{9}LaD^3	Lark's Mist	b	2	122	5	6	5^{hd}	5^{hd}	$4^{1\frac{1}{2}}$	$5^{\frac{1}{2}}$	Whited D E	14.70
20Sep80 ^{9}LaD^2	Boys Nite Out		2	117	3	3	2^{hd}	3^{hd}	$2^{\frac{1}{2}}$	6^3	Ardoin R	2.90
20Sep80 ^{6}Alb^1	Bin A Battle		2	114	2	5	$3^{\frac{1}{2}}$	$6^{\frac{1}{2}}$	7^2	$7^{4\frac{1}{2}}$	Poyadou B E	9.40
19Sep80 ^{4}LaD^1	Captive Rey		2	116	6	12	10^{hd}	11^2	$10^{1\frac{1}{2}}$	$8^{\frac{1}{2}}$	Maple S	19.40
25Sep80 ^{8}LaD^1	Sky Moon		2	116	1	1	1^{hd}	2^{hd}	$9^{1\frac{1}{2}}$	$9^{1\frac{1}{2}}$	Walker B J	2.60
24Sep80 ^{4}LaD^1	Close Out	b	2	114	10	4	$4^{\frac{1}{2}}$	1^{hd}	$8^{\frac{1}{2}}$	10^1	O'Shaughnessy M	46.50
23Aug80 ^{9}LaD^8	Bay Blaze	b	2	114	8	11	12	12	11^{10}	11	Holland M A	47.80
6Sep80 ^{8}AP^{15}	Contorsionist	b	2	122	12	9	$11^{1\frac{1}{2}}$	10^{hd}	12	—	Trosclair A J	12.90

Contorsionist, Distanced.

OFF AT 5:53 CDT Start good. Won driving. Time, :24, :47⅗, 1:13⅕, 1:31⅗ Course firm.

$2 Mutuel Prices:	7–NOBUBBLE	121.40	58.40	16.20
	4–SPANISH DOUBLE		37.40	16.40
	9–DOUBLE QUACK			4.20

$5 EXACTA (7–4) PAID $3,019.00.

Ch. c, by Nodouble—Breezie Berry, by Craigwood. Trainer Frazier Roy C. Bred by Smreker J & Young C (Fla).

NOBUBBLE came between horses in upper stretch for room and reached the front in deep stretch to win going off. SPANISH DOUBLE rallied to the lead in deep stretch but was no match for the winner. DOUBLE QUACK finished willingly outside. MAGGIE B. MINE rallied to the lead in upper stretch but flattened out in the final furlong. LARKS MIST lacked a stretch bid. BOYS NITE OUT set or forced the pace and weakened. BINA BATTLE saved ground vying for the early lead and tired. SKY MOON was used vying for the early lead. CLOSE OUT set or forced the pace and faltered in the drive. CONTORSIONIST dropped far back through the stretch.

Owners— 1, Dixie Stable; 2, Fast Track Stable; 3, Strapro Stable; 4, Franks J; 5, Evans G Jr; 6, Lafleur C & Soileau J Y; 7, Jones R C; 8, Powers Robin; 9, Trotter W E II; 10, Camelot Farm; 11, Moore B & Winburn A; 12, Corley E R.

Overweight: Captive Rey 2 pounds.

* I would like to thank George Connor of Dallas for providing the past performances and result chart from this race.

Hyperion is a major influence in world-class racing today because of the exploits at stud of his great-grandson Vaguely Noble. Strangely, the American-based offspring of Vaguely Noble have shown absolutely no preference for grass racing. Consequently, it is difficult to predict what the future might hold for Exceller, nearly the American champion grass and handicap horse of 1978, who is now at stud in this country. Two other sons of Vaguely Noble, Empery and Mississippian, are off to good starts as grass sires.

Stallion	NH	NW	WPCT	MPCT	$NET
Vaguely Noble	43	4	9.3%	34.9%	$1.06
Mississippian	27	4	14.8%	25.9%	$2.97
Empery	20	4	20.0%	35.0%	$2.78

□ NATIVE DANCER □

Native Dancer is the grandsire of European champion Sea-Bird, a noted grass sire in his own right. Sea-Bird's best American son was Preakness-Belmont winner Little Current, presently the most effective grass sire in this country. Ironically, Little Current suffered a career-ending injury in his only attempt at grass racing.

Stallion	NH	NW	WPCT	MPCT	$NET
Little Current	73	13	17.8%	54.8%	$4.27

Native Dancer also is sire of the brilliant Raise A Native, whose career was ended by injury in the middle of his juvenile season. While Raise A

Native's reputation is as a sire of sprinters, and few of his offspring have excelled at grass racing, several of his sons have proven to be effective grass sires. Most notable among these has been Exclusive Native, sire of Triple Crown winner Affirmed and numerous top-class grass performers, such as Native Courier, Sisterhood, Erwin Boy, and Qui Native. Exclusive Native's son, Our Native, has started at stud as if he intends to become a potent influence as a grass sire.

Stallion	NH	NW	WPCT	MPCT	$NET
Exclusive Native	110	22	20.0%	48.2%	$2.31
Our Native	38	7	18.4%	31.6%	$3.22
Teddy's Courage	12	1	8.3%	50.0%	$0.80

During his first few years at stud, Exclusive Native was not a good grass sire. But once he made his mark at stud, and began getting better mares, his statistics as a grass sire improved significantly. This is not an uncommon phenomenon. As this is being written, the same thing appears to be happening with both Explodent and His Majesty (see below).

Two other sons of Raise A Native have proven to be effective grass sires: Marshua's Dancer and Native Royalty. Raise A Bid and Son Ange have not, while at present Raise A Cup can be termed a possibility. Although not a consistent sire of grass runners, Majestic Prince has sired a grass champion in the hot young stallion Majestic Light, who looks to be the emerging grass sire.

Stallion	NH	NW	WPCT	MPCT	$NET
Marshua's Dancer	57	8	14.0%	40.4%	$2.19
Native Royalty	58	9	15.5%	31.0%	$3.22
Raise A Bid	48	5	10.4%	25.0%	$1.39
Raise A Cup	29	5	17.2%	31.0%	$1.46
Son Ange	44	4	9.1%	27.3%	$0.47
Majestic Prince	90	15	16.7%	44.4%	$1.64
Majestic Light	19	5	26.3%	47.4%	$4.93

Six young stallions from the Raise A Native line bear watching when their progeny begin their grass-racing careers: Alydar and To The Quick, both sons of Raise A Native, the latter from a Princequillo mare; Affirmed and Valdez, sons of Exclusive Native; and Coastal and Sensitive Prince, both sons of Majestic Prince.

I vividly recall my first impression of Affirmed, as Alydar ran past him in the stretch of the Great American Stakes early in their juvenile year—"a nice-looking animal that could develop into a major contender on the grass as a three-year-old." How ironic that the rest of his career would be wasted chasing such illusive goals as the Triple Crown, Horse Of The Year, and Alydar!

☐ THE NEARCO LINE ☐

Nearco, like Ribot after him, was an undefeated champion of Europe, perhaps the greatest of his era. From Nearco descend such champions and noted sires as Bold Ruler, Northern Dancer, Hail To Reason, and T. V. Lark. His is the predominant sire line in modern world-class racing. For years, the Bold Ruler branch of the Nearco line was the dominant force on the American scene. The progeny of Bold Ruler were noted for their speed and precocity, but few of them excelled on the grass. As a result, the turf-racing ability found in other branches of the Nearco line may have been overshadowed to an extent by the lack of same in the more publicized Bold Ruler branch. Unjustly so, to say the least. There are enough grass sires tracing to Nearco to warrant close scrutiny of the entire Nearco line. A genealogical chart of the Nearco line, featuring his most prominent sons, can also be found on page 110.

The Nearco line flourished through the efforts of three of his sons: Royal Charger, Nasrullah, and Nearctic. A fourth line traces to American grass champion Hawaii, sire of such splendid European runners as Epsom Derby winner Henbit, Hawaiian Sound, and Hunza Dancer. Hawaii's overall record as a grass sire, however, has been sporadic.

Stallion	NH	NW	WPCT	MPCT	$NET
Hawaii	131	15	11.5%	29.0%	$1.79

Royal Charger

Given a look at the names appearing in the Royal Charger branch of the Nearco line, the casual race fan would probably guess the primary grass influences to be Sir Ivor and Mongo. The facts, however, prove quite the opposite to be true. The grass sire's descendant from Royal Charger can be found among the sons of Hail To Reason, most notably Epsom Derby winner Roberto. Note that our figures for Hail To Reason are far from complete. Yet the win and in-the-money percentages suggest that Hail To Reason may well have been a grass sire the equal of

Northern Dancer or T. V. Lark. Young Hail To Reason-line stallions to watch include Darby Creek Road, a son of Roberto, and Cure The Blues and Temperence Hill, both sons of Stop The Music. Why Sir Ivor has failed to become a significant influence on the grass in this country is difficult to explain. Like Vaguely Noble, Sir Ivor's European runners have far overshadowed his American-based progeny. Strangely, Sir Ivor's sire, Sir Gaylord, is still going strong as an American grass sire, especially since his return from stud duty in Europe.

Stallion	NH	NW	WPCT	MPCT	$NET
Mongo	148	17	11.5%	38.5%	$1.49
Sir Gaylord	77	15	19.5%	40.3%	$3.82
Sir Ivor	125	18	14.4%	38.4%	$1.10
Cyane	147	20	13.6%	38.8%	$1.41
Drone	39	6	15.4%	23.1%	$1.42
Hail To Reason	53	10	18.9%	52.8%	$1.83
Roberto	110	19	17.3%	49.1%	$2.60
Halo	60	7	11.7%	33.3%	$1.44
Hail The Pirates	32	3	9.4%	40.6%	$2.13
Stop The Music	49	6	12.2%	38.8%	$1.66
Good Counsel	53	4	7.5%	39.6%	$1.00
Mr. Leader	176	22	12.5%	35.2%	$2.06
Personality	68	2	2.9%	26.5%	$0.44
Proud Clarion	145	21	14.5%	31.0%	$2.00

Nasrullah

The Nasrullah line is generally not known for its production of grass sires. Yet Nasrullah's great son Bold Ruler is the sire of a grass champion in the incomparable Secretariat (from a Princequillo-line mare), and a budding young grass sire in Top Command. Nasrullah's son Indian Hemp is the sire of T. V. Lark, a grass champion and prominent sire of grass sires. Another son of Nasrullah, Never Bend, has sired European champions in Mill Reef, Riverman, and J. O. Tobin. With just a few crops at the races, Mill Reef and Riverman have already established themselves as major sires in Europe, Mill Reef having sired an Epsom Derby winner and Riverman consecutive winners of the Arc de Triomphe. Naskra, a grandson of Nasrullah, has been a surprising success at stud, and an effective sire of grass runners in particular. The recently deceased Nashua, a son of Nasrullah, was sire of the consistent Ambernash and Diplomat Way, the latter already mentioned as a maternal grandson of Princequillo. Finally, the exciting young European imports Blushing Groom and Caro both descend from Nasrullah.

Stallion	NH	NW	WPCT	MPCT	$NET
Secretariat	96	13	13.5%	40.6%	$1.51
Top Command	9	3	33.3%	44.4%	$3.89
Chieftain	71	7	9.9%	43.7%	$1.80
Singh	46	4	8.7%	37.0%	$0.98
Blushing Groom	14	1	7.1%	35.7%	$1.30
Caro	20	4	20.0%	40.0%	$2.22
T. V. Lark	120	22	18.3%	42.5%	$1.64
T. V. Commercial	150	20	13.3%	39.3%	$2.30
Buffalo Lark	32	3	9.4%	18.8%	$4.69
Mickey McGuire	47	6	12.8%	38.3%	$2.36
Quack	61	7	11.5%	34.4%	$2.09
Ambernash	96	18	18.8%	39.6%	$2.56
Naskra	122	15	12.3%	28.7%	$1.87

Nearctic

Without question, Nearco's greatest legacy as a grass sire, and as an international sire, comes through his Canadian-raced son Nearctic, sire of Northern Dancer, the most influential sire in the world today. Northern Dancer is himself sire of two of the world's leading stallions, Nijinsky and Lyphard. From a betting standpoint, however, it is apparent that the prowess of Northern Dancer and Nijinsky as grass sires has not escaped notice among the American betting public. While their offspring show a remarkable win percentage in their initial grass outings, they do so (usually) at relatively low odds. At this point in time, Lyphard has sired only a handful of American-based grass runners, so whether he will fall into the same category remains an open question.

We note in passing that One For All, a son of Northern Dancer with Princequillo blood on his dam's side, remains one of our most effective grass sires. Northern Dancer's European-raced sons The Minstrel, Nureyev, and Storm Bird all bear watching as potential grass sires, as do Czaravich, Caucasus, and Upper Nile, all sons of Nijinsky.

We also point out that Explodent and Icecapade, both sons of Nearctic, are doing fairly well as sires of grass runners.

Stallion	NH	NW	WPCT	MPCT	$NET
Northern Dancer	277	57	20.6%	49.5%	$1.78
Nijinsky	152	37	24.3%	53.3%	$1.74
Lyphard	28	5	17.9%	42.9%	$1.98
Explodent	84	12	14.3%	40.5%	$1.93
Icecapade	72	10	13.9%	36.1%	$1.88
Champagne Charlie	18	3	16.7%	66.7%	$5.20
North Sea	46	2	4.3%	17.4%	$0.91
Northern Fling	42	3	7.1%	31.0%	$1.02
Northern Jove	52	4	7.7%	36.5%	$0.62
One For All	137	24	17.5%	40.9%	$3.65
Caucasus	16	2	12.5%	31.3%	$1.09
Upper Nile	10	0	0.0%	30.0%	$0.00
Dance Spell	34	3	8.8%	38.2%	$2.17
Dancing Champ	27	3	11.1%	40.7%	$1.50
Far North	17	2	11.8%	23.5%	$0.47

☐ RIBOT ☐

Unlike Nearco, European champion Ribot has not been an effective grass influence, at least not on this side of the Atlantic. Two of his greatest sons, Graustark and Arts & Letters, both top-class sires, have been dismal failures as grass sires. Graustark's best son to date, Key To The Mint, a half-brother to grass champion Fort Marcy, has had mixed reviews thus far as a grass sire—a high percentage of winners, but a low dollar return. Shady Character, a son of Graustark, who won stakes on grass, has done next to nothing thus far as a sire of grass runners. Curiously, Graustark's full brother His Majesty, who was unlucky never to have displayed his full talents on the racetrack, did not catch on immediately at stud, nor did his runners seem to take to the grass. But in the early 1980s, His Majesty has become a major stallion, and his recent crops have shown a fondness for the grass. Our statistics cover only these recent developments.

Stallion	NH	NW	WPCT	MPCT	$NET
Graustark	117	13	11.1%	36.8%	$0.84
His Majesty	23	6	26.1%	30.4%	$2.50
Key To The Mint	54	10	18.5%	40.7%	$1.20
Shady Character	27	2	7.4%	11.1%	$1.70
Arts & Letters	60	3	5.0%	23.3%	$0.51

There are, however, at least three grass influences in the Ribot family tree. His California-based grandson Unconscious, based on a relatively small sample, can be termed a grass sire. Blood Royal, a young European-raced son of Ribot, is off to an impressive start as a sire of grass runners. But the most significant grass influence in the Ribot family is Tom Rolfe, sire of numerous stakes winners over the turf, including champions Run The Gantlet and Bowl Game. Tom Rolfe's second dam was a daughter of Princequillo, probably explaining his progenies' affinity for the grass more so than the Ribot sire line. Tom Rolfe's major grass-stakes-winning sons Droll Role and London Company have failed to be influential sires, although the latter is now doing well as a grass sire. Until 1981, Run The Gantlet had fallen into the same category, but the exploits of his European runners have elevated him to the status of an important stallion on the world scene.

Tom Rolfe's greatest legacy, both as a sire and as a sire of grass sires, has been his brilliant son Hoist The Flag, whose international reputation as a grass sire rivals that of Round Table, Stage Door Johnny, and Nijinsky. Another young son of Tom Rolfe off to an excellent start as a grass sire is Tom Tulle. Hoist The Flag's sons Alleged and Fifth Marine would appear excellent prospects to inherit their late father's position as a leading grass sire. And, as this chapter was being revised for the final time, Tom Rolfe's son Tom Swift, from the immortal mare Shuvee, sent out a $138.00 winner from his second crop. Tom Swift also had a longshot winner from his first crop, and certainly deserves serious attention as a potential grass sire.

As mentioned in *Winning at the Races,* Ribot mares have been more reliable producers of grass runners than have Ribot or his sons. Cannonade, a maternal grandson of Ribot, is off to a good start as a grass sire.

Stallion	NH	NW	WPCT	MPCT	$NET
Unconscious	32	5	15.6%	37.5%	$2.97
Cannonade	20	3	15.0%	50.0%	$5.15
Blood Royal	18	3	16.7%	38.9%	$3.58
Tom Rolfe	246	31	12.6%	36.2%	$1.45
Droll Role	54	5	9.3%	35.2%	$0.76
London Company	44	8	18.2%	36.4%	$4.04
Hoist The Flag	145	31	21.4%	45.5%	$1.79
Fifth Marine	9	2	22.2%	33.3%	$4.78
Tom Tulle	29	6	20.7%	48.3%	$4.03

☐ HERBAGER ☐

Herbager and his sons, especially Grey Dawn, have reputations as grass sires, and justifiably so. Yet if a similar study were made of wet-track racing and breeding, Herbager could easily play the leading role as the "Princequillo of mud racing." Witness Big Spruce and Tiller, sons of Herbager, and Vigors, a son of Grey Dawn. Each first came to prominence as a grass runner, yet were to win major graded stakes later when switched back to damp main tracks. Dike, a classics contender from the great crop of 1969, and Gleaming, a major stakes winner on the grass (both sons of Herbager), have experienced difficulty at stud. Neither has proven a noted grass or mud sire.

CASE STUDY: HERBAGER, GREY DAWN, AND SANTA ANITA

When the storms of winter blow in off the Pacific and collide with the winter meeting at Santa Anita, the tribe of Herbager and his son Grey Dawn celebrate. During the past five years, the likes of Tiller (a son of Herbager), Vigors, and Mr. Redoy (both sons of Grey Dawn) all have won stakes races at this meeting over tracks listed other than "fast." Both Tiller and Vigors previously had been known as turf specialists. Yet when some of the most destructive storms of recent years put a damper on the 1983 Strub series, Californians failed to recall the lessons of previous winters. Swing Till Dawn, a son of Grey Dawn, improved dramatically in the mud, narrowly missing at 50–1 in the San Fernando Stakes, his final tune-up for the Strub.

In the Strub itself, the Santa Anita audience focused their attention on the first three finishers in the San Fernando. Swing Till Dawn went to the post at 38–1, and the grey colt stunned the crowd with a front-running victory in the slop. Players searching for value on the odds board should have seized this tremendous overlay. Those with an awareness of bloodlines would have made the colt their bet of the meeting.

We note that Vent Du Nord remains a quietly successful grass sire. His European sire lines are quite similar to those of Herbager.

Stallion	NH	NW	WPCT	MPCT	$NET
Herbager	145	21	14.5%	38.6%	$1.82
Grey Dawn II	255	34	13.3%	30.2%	$2.37
Big Spruce	79	14	17.7%	32.9%	$3.19
Dike	35	2	5.7%	20.0%	$0.49
Gleaming	43	3	7.0%	34.9%	$1.87
Vigors	11	2	18.2%	36.4%	$1.76
Vent Du Nord	89	11	12.4%	33.7%	$2.32

☐ OTHERS ☐

Other sires and bloodlines were studied, with few producing positive results. French champion Le Fabuleux has always been an extremely effective grass sire, and now has the reputation to prove it. His runners are usually well supported when switching to the grass. His sons Ben Fab, Effervescing, and Fabled Monarch, all stakes winners on the grass, should be scrutinized closely when their first crops reach racing age.

The Rough 'n Tumble influence through Dr. Fager and Minnesota Mac is especially worth noting, and figures to be carried on by the latter's son Mac Diarmida, a grass champion. In Reality, a son of deceased grass sire Intentionally from a champion Rough 'n Tumble mare, suffered from a severe case of "seconditis" (on grass) during his early years at stud. However, runners from his five most recent crops have turned that around, winning almost 24 percent of their initial grass outings while producing a profit margin in excess of 48 percent. Tentam, also a son of Intentionally and a superior grass runner in his own right, has yet to show any penchant for siring grass runners. With Tentam now deceased, In Reality remains the only major stallion at stud carrying on the male line of Man O'War. Likewise, with Dr. Fager gone, Minnesota Mac, Mac Diarmida, and Ack Ack alone carry on the Domino line. And Ack Ack has shown little inclination toward earning a reputation as a grass sire, despite having Princequillo and Nearco blood on his dam's side. Four stallions from these lines worth following are Youth (by Ack Ack), Known Fact (by Tentam), and Believe It and Relaunch (both by In Reality).

Pretense, whose dam was by Hyperion, shows no proclivity toward siring grass runners, nor does his top-class son Sham. With Executioner showing signs of a potential grass sire, we studied his sire, The Axe, and Al Hattab, another son of The Axe. The results were generally negative. The statistics for L'Enjoleur, a son of Buckpasser from the great Northern Dancer mare Fanfreluche, can no longer be ignored. L'Enjoleur definitely merits recognition as a sire of grass runners. Finally, West Coast star Cougar, sire of 1982 Kentucky Derby winner Gato Del Sol, has shown little consistency siring grass runners. We base this on a small sample of mostly Eastern runners, which consequently may not represent his true ability. More evidence is clearly needed, specifically from racing on the Southern California circuit.

Stallion	NH	NW	WPCT	MPCT	$NET
Le Fabuleux	117	23	19.7%	44.4%	$1.77
Dr. Fager	162	25	15.4%	31.5%	$2.05
Minnesota Mac	166	25	15.1%	31.9%	$3.05
In Reality	100	14	14.0%	39.0%	$1.62
Tentam	93	11	11.8%	40.9%	$1.20
Ack Ack	93	10	10.8%	38.7%	$0.94
Youth	12	1	8.3%	25.0%	$0.32
Pretense	97	10	10.3%	35.1%	$1.14
Sham	20	0	0.0%	5.0%	$0.00
The Axe II	192	18	9.4%	31.8%	$1.33
Executioner	65	8	12.3%	35.4%	$1.67
Al Hattab	142	19	13.4%	32.4%	$1.60
L'Enjoleur	40	9	22.5%	42.5%	$3.12
Cougar II	50	5	10.0%	28.0%	$0.70

CASE STUDY: ANCIENT BARRISTER

Bob DeBonis trains a large public stable on the New York circuit, and has been among its leaders in a number of wins during the past five seasons. Unlike the other leading "claiming" stables in New York, however, the DeBonis barn excels in grass racing, with sixteen wins over that surface during 1979 alone. In contrast, Frank Martin, who sent out 105 winners during 1979, had only two grass winners that year. DeBonis' success on the grass came mostly with horses of nondescript breeding. But the case of Ancient Barrister, a son of leading grass sire Advocator, was astounding. Entered in an NW1 allowance on the grass, November 12, 1982, Ancient Barrister was facing seven rivals, none of whom had ever competed in claiming events. Ancient Barrister had just broken his maiden for $25,000. In his favor was the fact that five of his seven opponents were also coming out of maiden races. All but one of them had raced well on the grass, although none of these had earned an exceptional speed figure on that surface. On dirt, Ancient Barrister came within five points of their grass figures.

Ancient Barrister's major rival, based primarily on class and figures, appeared to be Pitchpipe, a son of Key To The Mint from a Northern Dancer mare. He had broken his maiden in exceptionally fast time, then run a credible second to Bet Big, the Meadowland's top juvenile that fall, in the Montclair Stakes. Like Ancient Barrister, Pitchpipe was making his grass debut, yet figured to be the betting favorite. On paper, the others appeared hard to separate. If Ancient Barrister improved on the grass, as many of the Advocator's do, he likely would be competitive with most of this field. Whether he could beat Pitchpipe was another question. The race offered quiniela wagering, making the logical bet a win-quiniela combination. Pitchpipe failed to reproduce his dirt form on grass, ruining the quiniela bet. But Ancient Barrister came from behind and won a three-horse photo for the win. He paid an amazing $130.40! At 64–1, the thought that Ancient Barrister might take to the grass should have been quite enticing. And as 2–1 favorite, the possibility that Pitchpipe might not like the grass should have discouraged a serious bet.

CASE STUDY: MIDDLE STAGE

When Middle Stage appeared in the entries for the Athenia Handicap at Aqueduct, October 13, 1982, there had to be some question of her ability to handle grass. Although a daughter of Stage Door Johnny, the three-year-old filly had just one prior start on the grass. She finished off the board on that occasion, which doesn't show in her past performances. Did she handle the grass so poorly that trainer Campo chose to keep her out of subsequent grass opportunities? Or did poor form on that occasion prevent her from showing to good advantage on footing she might very easily favor?

Save your old *Racing Forms!* You never know when one might come in handy. Those able to look back at the rest of Middle Stage's career would have known that her first grass try came in the second start of her career. In neither of those first two races did she run a step, trailing throughout in both. She simply may not have been ready for the races at that time. One might easily consider her to have been making her grass debut in the Athenia, at a distance favorable to progeny of Stage Door Johnny. Given her background in graded stakes, her victory in the Athenia should have come as no surprise. Apparently it did surprise many New Yorkers. She paid a more than generous $22.20

Middle Stage — Dk. b. or br. f. 3, by Stage Door Johnny—Patelin, by Cornish Prince
Own.—Buckland Farm | Br.—Evans T M (Va) | Tr.—Campo John P | **112**
Lifetime 16 1 3 2 $69,609 | 1982 9 0 2 1 $47,579 | 1981 7 1 1 1 $22,030 | Turf 1 0 0 0

15Sep82- 8Bel	fst	1⅛	:46⅗ 1:10⅕ 1:47⅗	(F)Gazelle H	5	4	52¼	77	612	59¼	Miranda J	b	111	29.30	80-14	Broom Dance 121nk Number 1132¾ Mademoiselle Forli1141¼	Tired	7
21Aug82- 3Sar	fst	1⅛	:48⅕ 1:12⅕ 1:50	3↑(F)Alw 20000	1	3	1hd	2hd	2½	2nk	Miranda J	b	115	*.70	85-14	NicoleMonAmour112nkMiddleStage1152SvedGround1145½	Gamely	6
24Jly82- 9Mth	fst	1⅛	:47⅘ 1:11⅖ 1:49⅖	(F)Mth Oaks	4	8	812	89¼	611	55	Lovato F Jr	b	112	23.80	83-14	ChristmasPst1211½Milingo1191½MdemoiselleForli1121½	No factor	9
26Jun82- 8Bel	fst	1½	:47⅕ 2:02⅕ 2:28⅗	(F)C C A Oaks	6	9	920	711	610	49	Lovato F Jr		121	17.20e	68-20	ChristmasPst1216Cupecoy'sJoy121noFlyingPrtner1213	No Factor	10
14May82- 8Pim	fst	1 1/16	:47⅕ 1:11⅘ 1:44⅗	(F)Blk Eyed Su.	1	6	68	711	511	48¼	Miranda J		111	9.10	74-21	Delicate Ice 1141¾ Trove 1211½ Milingo 1215	No factor	10
14Apr82- 8Aqu	fst	1	:47⅕ 1:13 1:38⅖	(F)Rare Perfume	6	5	57	42½	42	21½	Miranda J		112	21.00	72-26	Nafees 1121½ Middle Stage 1121¾ Beau Cougar 1121¾	Rallied	7
14Feb82- 8Aqu	fst	1⅛	[•]:48⅕ 1:13 1:51	(F)Ruthless	2	4	49	48	48	411	Skinner K		114	6.30	80-18	Polite Rebuff 1184 Girlie 1183¾ Thoughtless Doll 1143	Poor start	4
30Jan82- 8Aqu	fst	1 1/16	[•]:48⅘ 1:13⅗ 1:46⅗	(F)Searching	8	8	89¼	87½	35	35	Hernandez R		113	9.70	75-21	Girlie 116½ Adept 1124½ Middle Stage 1137½	Rallied	8
16Jan82- 8Aqu	fst	1 1/16	[•]:46⅗ 1:11⅗ 1:44⅕	(F)Busanda	4	4	68½	68	56½	48½	Hernandez R		113	3.90	83-10	Polite Rebuff 1143¾ Girlie 1163¾ Thoughtless Doll 1131	Evenly	7
12Dec81- 8Key	fst	1 1/16	:47 1:12⅗ 1:46	(F)Villager	6	7	77½	55¾	67	57½	Nemeti W		112	3.10	66-22	Chasuble 112¾ Fairy Tooth 1121½ Martie's Double1121¾	No factor	12

LATEST WORKOUTS Oct 7 Bel (T) 5f fm 1:02 h (d) Oct 2 Bel tr.t 5f fst 1:02⅖ b Sep 29 Bel tr.t 4f fst :49⅗ b Sep 12 Bel tr.t 4f fst :48⅖ h

CASE STUDY: DOODLE

Doodle presented a different problem for handicappers when entered in the other division of the Athenia that day. A proven grass runner at the middle distances, would she be able to handle the longer mile-and-three-eighths route? Considering her sire is Dewan, it wasn't likely—his offspring seem to favor the longer sprints and middle distance routes. On the other hand, Doodle's broodmare sire is Round Table—his get could run all day. Who would have the greater influence?

Doodle — B. f. 3, by Dewan—Actual, by Round Table
Own.—Perry W H | Br.—Claiborne Farm (Ky) | Tr.—Kelly Edward I Jr | **119**
Lifetime 11 4 3 2 $75,295 | 1982 9 4 3 2 $73,435 | 1981 2 M 0 0 $1,860 | Turf 5 3 2 0 $57,295

1Oct82- 8Bel	fm	1 1/16	(T):47 1:11 1:42⅖	(F)Lamb Chop H	2	5	51¾	84¼	42	2hd	MacBeth D	b	115	11.80	84-16	Vocal 110hd Doodle 115no Dance Number 114nk	Rallied	10
11Sep82- 8Med	fm	1 1/16	(T):47 1:10⅘ 1:41⅖	(F)Boil Sprg H	6	4	2½	2hd	2½	24	Pincay L Jr	b	115	2.50	91-09	Larida 1194 Doodle 115½ Distinctive Moon 114¾	Good try	11
11Sep82-Evening Program																		
11Sep82-Run in two Divisions 6 & 8 Races.																		
4Aug82- 9Sar	fm	1 1/16	(T):48⅖ 1:12⅘ 1:42⅘	3↑(F)Alw 25000	6	8	67	52½	1½	1no	Cordero A Jr	b	114	2.20	83-12	Doodle 114no Hush Dear 1172½ Immense 1142	Driving	11
4Jly82- 6Bel	fm	1	(T):46⅘ 1:11 1:36⅖	3↑(F)Alw 21000	9	3	32	21	2½	1nk	Cordero A Jr	b	113	*2.50	83-17	Doodle 113nk Little Bullet 1121 Doblique 1111½	Bobbled, driving	10
13Jun82- 6Bel	sly	1 1/16	:47⅗ 1:12⅕ 1:44	3↑(F)Alw 21000	5	6	53½	32½	35¼	37¾	Samyn J L	b	109	*1.20	74-15	La Ninouchka 1144 Doblique 1133¾ Doodle 1092	Wide	6
2Jun82- 7Bel	fst	1 1/16	:46⅖ 1:11⅖ 1:43	3↑(F)Alw 21000	5	4	42	31½	1hd	2½	Samyn J L	b	109	4.60	86-11	Broom Dance 111½ Doodle 1092 Zany 1126¼	Gamely	6
13May82- 6Aqu	gd	6f	:22⅖ :45⅗ 1:11⅕	(F)Alw 20000	7	5	22	1hd	2½	31¾	Maple E	b	118	2.10	83-17	Rosa D'Argent 116hd Lady Lothario 1161¾Doodle1182¾	Weakened	8
5Apr82- 8GP	fm	*1	(T) 1:37⅘	(F)Alw 13000	2	4	42	11½	2hd	1½	Fires E	b	116	*2.40	92-13	Doodle 116½ Miss Frampton 1163½ Your Live 1166	Driving	10
27Mar82- 4GP	fst	6f	:22⅕ :45⅘ 1:11⅗	(F)Md Sp Wt	6	6	42	21	1hd	11¼	Fires E	b	121	2.70	81-19	Doodle 1211¼ Sterling Blue 121¾ Sans Pareil 1213½	Drew clear	12
18Oct81- 6Aqu	fst	6f	:22⅘ :46⅕ 1:11⅘	(F)Md Sp Wt	8	8	58½	510	49	47	Maple E		117	3.00	75-22	Favored Times 1174 Sassy 'nBright117noDearlyToo1123	No factor	10

LATEST WORKOUTS Sep 6 Bel 6f fst 1:14 h Aug 30 Sar (T) 6f fm 1:17⅗ b Aug 19 Sar 5f fst 1:02⅖ h Aug 13 Sar 3f fst :39 b

Doodle was more like a Round Table than a Dewan. She was a grass specialist, like so many of the Round Tables, and so few of the Dewans.

So, like Round Table, she probably would also like the marathon distance.

Doodle rallied strongly in the Athenia, as favorite, only to be passed in the final yards by Mintage, a filly with considerable experience at the extended distance.

CASE STUDY: HERO'S HONOR

When Hero's Honor first reached the races in April of his three-year-old season, I immediately marked him down as a grass prospect. Being a son of Northern Dancer alone would have been sufficient reason. Hero's Honor was particularly interesting, however, because his dam was Glowing Tribute, a brilliant racemare whose forte was grass racing.

When Hero's Honor showed steady improvement in his early races, leading up to his predictable maiden win on May 21, I feared that he would be a short-priced favorite when Mack Miller finally sent him greensward. Instead, the colt disappeared for three months. When he finally reappeared at Saratoga, he turned in an uncharacteristically dull performance, then followed with a carbon copy ten days later at Belmont.

How was the grass-breeding advocate to react to Hero's Honor on September 3, when he was entered for the first time in a grass contest? Did the horse have a physical problem? Was he now a lesser animal than he had been in the spring, unlikely to race well over any surface? Knowing Miller's reputation, one might easily have concluded that there was nothing physically wrong with the horse. If there was, Miller would not race him. On the other hand, many horses have (or develop) psychological problems that truly test their trainer's mettle. Some sour on racing and need a change of scenery to rekindle their interest. Grass racing often proves to be the right tonic. In fact, such was the case with Hero's Honor. His victory (at $23.20) on September 3 was the first on three straight on the grass for the well-bred colt.

Hero's Honor B. c. 3, by Northern Dancer—Glowing Tribute, by Graustark
Br.—Mellon P (Va)
Own.—Rokeby Stable Tr.—Miller Mack
113
Lifetime 5 1 1 0 $14,760
1983 5 1 1 0 $14,760
1982 0 M 0 0

27Aug83- 9Bel	fst	7f	:22 2/5	:45 2/5	1:23 3/5	3↑ Alw 24000	2	9	6^4	$8^{9\frac{1}{4}}$	10^{18}	10^{23}	Bailey J D	b	113	6.40	61-12	American Standard 112^7 Brave Squire 117^1 Nivernay 113^{nk}	Outrun 11
17Aug83- 9Sar	fst	6f	:22 1/5	:45	1:09 3/5	3↑ Alw 20000	7	6	7^7	8^{11}	10^{15}	10^{19}	Bailey J D	b	113	5.30	73-11	Cozzene $112^{2\frac{1}{4}}$ Stop Card $114^{5\frac{3}{4}}$ Cagle Springs 112^{hd}	Bumped 12
21May83- 4Bel	gd	7f	:22 4/5	:45 1/5	1:22 4/5	Md Sp Wt	2	2	3^2	$4^{1\frac{1}{2}}$	1^3	1^3	Bailey J D	b	122	3.40	88-07	Hro'sHonor 122^3 JohnnyofWnloc 122no DrngGroom $115^{2\frac{3}{4}}$	Drew clear 8
12May83- 6Aqu	fst	7f	:23 1/5	:47 1/5	1:25 1/5	Md Sp Wt	9	3	$7^{4\frac{3}{4}}$	5^3	$3^{\frac{1}{2}}$	$2^{2\frac{1}{4}}$	MacBeth D		122	5.40	73-20	Naskra's Gold $122^{2\frac{1}{4}}$ Hero's Honor $122^{\frac{3}{4}}$ Humbug I 122^4	Wide str. 10
30Apr83- 6Aqu	fst	6f	:22 2/5	:45 4/5	1:12 3/5	Md Sp Wt	7	4	$2^{2\frac{1}{2}}$	3^3	$1^{\frac{1}{2}}$	$5^{1\frac{3}{4}}$	MacBeth D		122	2.90	76-22	Entropy 122no Real Stubborn 122^1 [D] ConchaYToro 122^{hd}	Lugged in 8

LATEST WORKOUTS Sep 2 Bel 3f fst :35 1/5 h ●Aug 24 Bel 3f fst :35 h Aug 14 Sar 6f fst 1:14 2/5 h Aug 8 Sar 4f fst :47 4/5 hg

Handicappers at the country's smaller tracks will find the information in this chapter only marginally useful. The offspring of our major stallions seldom perform at their tracks. However, the children of sons of these stallions do. Therefore, it is most helpful to become familiar with the pedigrees of those stallions that crop up frequently in the past performances of horses racing on one's local circuit. And also to make note of those stallions whose offspring do especially well on the grass, or in the slop.

□ CONFORMATION □

There are some who believe that grass-racing and mud-racing ability do not mix. A horse able to do well in one milieu will not handle the other. There are many counterexamples, however, the offspring of Herbager mentioned above, for example. Both Tiller and Vigors captured Grade I stakes on the grass and in the mud during their racing careers. Yet there is some logic behind this conjecture, much of it having to do with conformation. It is the animal's feet that provide the clue. The grass foot is thought to be large, wide, and dishlike, with little or no heel, and set at a rather flat angle with the ground. The mud foot, on the other hand, is reputedly small, cuplike, with a high vertical heel, set at a sharp angle with the ground.

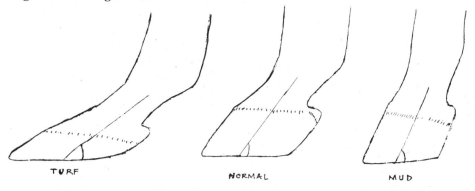

TURF   NORMAL   MUD

On a wet track, the small foot penetrates quickly to the base, providing the horse with a firm grip. The larger foot tends to slide. In addition, the large foot creates more suction, making the horse work harder than one with a small foot. On grass, especially soft grass, the small foot again penetrates deeper, slowing the horse's progress, while the large foot does not, allowing the horse to skip along on top of the ground. At a seminar I gave recently in San Francisco, Bob Miller drew an analogy that made sense. Imagine jabbing a finger into the grass and contrast that with hitting the palm of your hand on the grass and you will understand the difference.

CASE STUDY: LOOSE CANNON

I have always felt that a horse with grass bloodlines and a proven record of futility in the slop is all the more likely to take to the grass. As a son of Nijinsky and a stakes-winning Graustark mare, Loose Cannon had the bloodlines to become a stakes winner on the grass or a monster in the mud. After a fairly promising debut, the colt raced miserably in the slop, discounting the latter possibility, and in my mind lending further credence to the possibility of the former. The proof came immediately, in the colt's next start. Loose Cannon ran a much improved race first try on the turf, returning $17.60 to the bloodlines experts in the crowd.

Loose Cannon — Ch. c. 2, by Nijinsky II—Java Moon, by Graustark
Own.—Galbreath D M — Br.—Galbreath J W (Ky) — Tr.—Rondinello Thomas L — **119**
Lifetime 3 1 0 0 $10,800 — 1982 3 1 0 0 $10,800 — Turf 1 1 0 0 $10,800

10Oct82- 3Bel	fm	1$\frac{1}{16}$	[T]:48⅗ 1:12⅘ 1:44	Md Sp Wt	2	6	4$2\frac{1}{2}$	3$3\frac{1}{2}$	2^{hd}	1^{hd}	Velasquez J	b	118	7.80	81-17	Loose Cannon 118^{hd} Eskimo $118^{1\frac{1}{4}}$ So Intent 118^{4}	Driving	8
27Sep82- 4Bel	sly	7f	:22⅖ :45⅘ 1:25⅖	Md Sp Wt	7	9	9^{14}	7^{17}	7^{14}	7^{14}	Velasquez J	b	118	11.60	61-25	Hypertee 118no Fibak 118no The Whole Ticket 118^{nk}	No factor	9
25Jly82- 4Bel	fst	6f	:22⅘ :46⅘ 1:11⅗	Md Sp Wt	1	10	$6^{9\frac{1}{2}}$	3^{6}	4^{11}	5^{15}	Brumfield D	b	118	8.40	69-21	NumberOneSpecil118^{7}RoylHostg$118^{3\frac{3}{4}}$MoonSpirit118^{2}	Off slowly	10

LATEST WORKOUTS Nov 6 Bel 6f fst 1:16⅗ b — Nov 1 Bel 5f fst 1:04 b — Oct 27 Bel 4f gd :51 b — Oct 22 Bel 3f fst :36⅘ h

Copyright © 1984, by DAILY RACING FORM, INC. Reprinted with permission of copyright owner.

The trainers we surveyed agreed that bloodlines and conformation were the predominant reasons for trying a horse on the grass. They also mentioned "desperation" as another reason. If a horse has failed at everything else, they give it a chance on the grass before dropping it down through the claiming ranks. A trainer looks very foolish if he drops a horse first, has it claimed, and then watches as the new trainer "transforms" the horse into a first-rate runner on the grass. Another reason mentioned why a horse might prefer the grass is the simple fact that some horses don't like having dirt kicked in their faces, a discomfort they don't face on the grass.

□ CONCLUSION □

An age-old axiom of handicapping warns against betting a horse to do something it has not done previously. Not true! Anticipation often leads to nice mutuels. And the bloodlines often are a powerful source of information upon which to base the anticipation. Grass racing is a completely different ball game from dirt racing. Strange form reversals do occur, and often can be predicted solely on the basis of a horse's breeding.

Chapter 6

THE EARNINGS BOX

Class in the Thoroughbred relates to its ability to race competitively at a given level of competition. Whatever that level is, wherever the horse fits most comfortably, is said to define the class of the animal. A horse's class rating may change several times during its racing career, due to injuries, maturity, a different trainer, or simply the wear and tear that comes with racing. Where the horse fits today is the crucial question. The answer may prove to be far different from where it fit two months ago, or where it will fit in four weeks.

Defining class in broad generalities is relatively easy. Putting the definition into practice can be quite another matter. How does one go about evaluating a horse's class? One approach uses the claiming tags, or the allowance purses, of recent races in which the horse performed well. The class estimation is based on an average, or a projection of a trend evident in these races. Now that the *Daily Racing Form* gives the purse for allowance races, rather than grouping all types under the one word "Allowance," this approach has become more workable. At least if a horse has raced strictly in claiming races, or exclusively in allowance company. But what of the horse that races in both claiming and allowance competition? Unless able to equate allowance races with their claiming equivalents, through common purse value or par times, the handicapper is at a loss.

Another possible way to define class can be found in the "earnings box," located in the upper right-hand corner of the past performances.

The earnings box has been expanded twice in recent years, and now includes four lines. One summarizes the horse's lifetime record, another

Tantalizing — B. c. 4, by Tom Rolfe—Lady Love, by Dr Fager
Br.—Phipps O M (Ky)
Own.—Phipps O M — Tr.—Penna Angel — 115

Lifetime	1983	5	4	1	0	$150,920
5 4 1 0	1982	0	M	0	0	
$150,920	Turf	3	2	1	0	$132,320

19Jun83- 8Bel fm 1⅜ (T):48⅗ 1:37⅖ 2:14⅘ 3+Bwlg Green H 7 4 46 32 43½ 1¾ Vasquez J 113 *1.80 83-25 Tantalizing 113¾ Sprink 1131 Majesty'sPrince122¾ Brushed drvng 7

11Jun83- 5Bel fm 1½ (T):47⅖ 2:00⅘ 2:25⅖ 3+Handicap 7 6 67 1hd 11½ 2no Bailey J D 113 *1.50 97-06 Field Cat 116no Tantalizing 113nk Highland Blade 1264 Just failed 12

25May83- 7Bel gd 1¼ (T):49 1:39 2:04⅖ 3+Alw 27000 8 4 312 1½ 14 17¾ Bailey J D 121 3.80 72-33 Tantalizing 1217¾ Silver Ring 1193¾ Groomed 119½ Ridden out 8

12May83- 5Aqu fst 1 :46⅖ 1:12⅗ 1:38⅖ 3+Alw 21000 3 5 49 44½ 2½ 1nk Bailey J D 121 *.90 74-20 Tantalizing 121nk Nepal 1102½ Starhitch 1162¾ [illegible] 7

29Mar83- 4Hia fst 7f :23⅕ :46⅗ 1:24⅕ Md Sp Wt 7 10 85¾ 33 12 17 Bailey J D 122 *.80 82-19 Tantalizing 1227 Rexson's Rock 1221¼ Hazard Man 1225 Handily 11

LATEST WORKOUTS Jly 18 Bel 6f fst 1:14⅗ h Jly 12 Bel 5f fst 1:00⅘ h Jly 1 Bel 4f fst :47⅘ h Jun 18 Bel 3f fst :36⅖ b

gives its record for the present year (to date), still another for the preceding season, and the final one covers just its races on grass. The first and last mentioned are the new ones, having appeared after the data-base used for *Winning at the Races* was completed, preventing computer analysis of their relative worth.

Each line in the earnings box lists the appropriate number of starts, wins, seconds, thirds, and earnings. The symbol M in the wins column indicates the horse was a maiden at the end of that year, or is presently still a maiden. The four-year-old colt Tantalizing, for example, was a maiden at three (unraced, in fact), and was a winner of four out of five starts at four (matching his lifetime totals), including two of three races on the grass.

Some handicappers like to manipulate these figures arithmetically, with the net result being a "class rating" for the horse. We shall now discuss various techniques that are popular, plus a new one of our own making.

Before proceeding, though, some words of warning: All earnings figures fail to account for recent form and are the weaker for it. They do not ask when the horse earned its money, only how much it earned. Nor do these ratings take into consideration the distance or surface preferences of horses, or their consistency when placed against suitable opposition. Earnings figures are also confounded by differences in purse distribution at comparable tracks (such as New York and Florida), and by changes in purse levels at a given meeting (if business is good, purses go up). Additionally, in many states, races for state-breds have higher purses than open races of the same classification, even though the state-breds may be (far) inferior runners. This, of course, further confuses the issue.

New Yorkers calculating class ratings based on earnings will regularly underestimate the chances of shippers from nearby tracks, such as Monmouth, where purses fall far short of those offered in New York. They will overrate horses that spend the winter months in New York at the direct expense of those that winter in Florida, where the purses are smaller but the competition stronger. Handicappers in New Jersey and

Florida, on the other hand, will overstate the cases of New York shippers, if earnings are their primary consideration.

The *Racing Form* now provides handicappers with a guide to the relative class of different tracks, as seen through their purse structure. Included in the table of track abbreviations (see page 25) is a number indicating, in thousands of dollars, the average purse value per race run at each track during 1982. At Belmont Park, for example, the average race run during 1982 (including stakes) offered a purse of $25,000.

Handicappers choosing to calculate earnings figures must decide at the outset how much information they will use. Should ratings be based on the current year's figures whenever possible? Or is it better to combine the totals from the present and previous year? Our computer studies found this a difficult photo finish to call. One approach works as well as the other, on paper. Each has its own obvious advantages and disadvantages, but the final totals were quite similar. The statistics presented below are based on earnings over two seasons. They relate to horses rated first in the four categories mentioned. Our sample included 946 races. A small number of ties in rank explain the slightly higher number of horses in each category.

	NH	WPCT	MPCT	I.V.	$NET
Gross Earnings	958	18.0%	47.3%	1.56	$1.41
Average Earnings	950	20.6%	48.1%	1.75	$1.67
Average Purse (60–22–12–6)	948	15.4%	40.4%	1.32	$1.54
Average Purse (20–45–80–30)	947	17.4%	39.1%	1.50	$2.16

☐ GROSS EARNINGS ☐

Advocates of the "gross earnings" approach consider only the horse's gross (total) earnings from the past year or two. This approach favors durability at the expense of ability. Talented, lightly raced allowance runners, especially, could easily come out second best in the ratings to veterans of the claiming wars, rivals they might handle easily.

☐ AVERAGE EARNINGS ☐

On the other hand, the "average earnings" technique (divide total earnings by number of starts) favors consistency at the expense of quality. A horse that runs consistently in the money against $20,000 rivals, and is now moving up into $25,000 company for the first time, may rate higher than a $35,000 animal dropping down, if that classier animal had its record sullied by frequent unsuccessful excursions into higher claiming or allowance competition. Also, this approach often overrates lightly raced MSW winners moving into allowance company.

One useful statistic to remember is that the horse whose average earnings figure falls below 10 percent of the purse for which it is now competing is probably outclassed:

NH	WPCT	MPCT	I.V.	$NET
3437	7.9%	27.0%	0.69	$1.44

□ AVERAGE PURSE □

The "average purse" approach to earnings figures attempts to rate horses according to the average purse for which the horse has, in the past, raced "successfully." It is the basis for several devices on the market, including one popular line of products. The approach has serious flaws.

First, it is closely tied to the purse distribution formula used at the local track. Since this formula can vary from one track to another, monies earned elsewhere can be distorted. To describe this procedure, we will use the popular 60–22–12–6 formula used at many North American tracks. The "average purse" technique tells the handicapper to:

multiply wins by	0.60
multiply seconds by	0.22
multiply thirds by	0.12
multiply fourths by	0.06

add the points so obtained, then divide them into the earnings.

For example, should a horse's earnings line read:

13–5–3–0–1–$80,877

(note that fourth-place finishes do not actually appear in the earnings box), we would calculate:

$$5 \times 0.60 = 3.00$$
$$3 \times 0.22 = 0.66$$
$$0 \times 0.12 = 0.00$$
$$1 \times 0.06 = \underline{0.06}$$
$$3.72$$

and then divide:

$$\$80,877 \,/\, 3.72 = \$21,741$$

to obtain the horse's rating. This horse's "successful" efforts were given in races whose average purse value was $21,741.

To better understand how this works, take a look at how a $25,000 purse is divided, based on the 60–22–12–6 distribution formula:

Finish	Percent of Purse	$25,000 Purse
1	60%	$15,000
2	22%	$5,500
3	12%	$3,000
4	6%	$1,500

Note the arithmetic that follows. It is the key to understanding the logic of this technique, and also its fatal flaw.

$$\$15,000 \,/\, 0.60 = \$25,000$$
$$\$5,500 \,/\, 0.22 = \$25,000$$
$$\$3,000 \,/\, 0.12 = \$25,000$$
$$\$1,500 \,/\, 0.06 = \$25,000$$

If a horse earned $15,000, based on one win in a race for a $25,000 purse, its point total would be 0.60, which when divided into $15,000, gives us back the $25,000 value of the purse. Likewise, a horse earning just $1,500 based on one fourth place finish in a $25,000 race (point total 0.06) would also be rated at $25,000.

Most horses have a mixture of wins, places, shows, and fourths in their records, these coming for a variety of purses. The net result, however, is an average which closely (but not exactly) approximates the purse value for which the horse has, in the past, competed "successfully."

What is wrong? Quite simply, the method fails to distinguish between the various shades of "successful." A win for $25,000 is rated equal to a fourth-place finish for the same purse.

To give an extreme example, suppose that four horses competed against each other in a series of ten races, each with a purse of $25,000. Further, assume that the order of finish was the same in each of the ten races. Their earnings records would read:

Horse A: 10–10–0–0–0–$150,000
Horse B: 10–0–10–0–0–$55,000
Horse C: 10–0–0–10–0–$30,000
Horse D: 10–0–0–0–10–$15,000

Using the average purse technique, each would be rated at $25,000, because each has been running "successfully" in $25,000 races. No matter that they have established a very definite "pecking order." The formula treats them as equals.

To make matters worse, a horse that has run ten times, winning once for a $25,000 purse,

Horse E: 10–1–0–0–0–$15,000

rates the equal of Horse A, who won ten times in as many starts for that purse. And a horse with just one fourth-place finish, that in a $25,000 race,

Horse F: 10–0–0–0–1–$1,500

rates the equal of the other five. Apparently, consistency is worth nothing with this formula.

No race in recent memory better highlights the fallacy of this technique than the 1979 Jockey Club Gold Cup which featured Affirmed, Spectacular Bid, and Coastal. The fourth-place finisher in this great race was an allowance runner called Gallant Best. The "average earnings" technique rated him the equal of the three superb horses he trailed home by some thirty-one lengths.

To make this kind of approach reasonable, weights other than 60, 22, 12, and 6 would have to be used, so that one might be able to distinguish between first-, second-, third-, and fourth-place finishes. We used the statistical technique known as "multiple regression" in an attempt to determine the best possible set of weights, and came up with 20, 45, 80, and 30. These produce the desired effect of making a win worth more than a second, a second worth more than a third, but produced the (possibly) undesirable effect that a fourth-place finish is worth slightly more than a third-place finish. On the other hand, fourth-place finishes not among the ten races appearing in the past performances are not counted, possibly justifying the high weight assigned to those that do appear.

For example, with a $25,000 purse, we get:

$$\$15,000 \ / \ 0.20 = \$75,000$$
$$\$5,500 \ / \ 0.45 = \$12,222$$
$$\$3,000 \ / \ 0.80 = \ \ \$3,750$$
$$\$1,500 \ / \ 0.30 = \ \ \$5,000$$

Our mythical horse whose earnings line looked like:

$$13-5-3-0-1-\$80,877$$

would now be rated:

$$5 \ \times \ 0.20 = 1.00$$
$$3 \ \times \ 0.45 = 1.35$$
$$0 \ \times \ 0.80 = 0.00$$
$$1 \ \times \ 0.30 = \underline{0.30}$$
$$2.65$$

with $80,877/2.65 = $30,520 being the horse's rating. Note that this rating is higher than before. The horse has been "rewarded" for its impressive number of wins, even though they may have come against cheaper stock.

The ratings produced by this formula can no longer be interpreted in the "average purse" sense. They probably don't "mean" anything, and should be viewed simply as ratings. Nor do they resolve the problem with consistency mentioned above. A horse that wins ten consecutive $25,000 races will still be rated the equal of a horse winning just one such race, and earning nothing in its remaining starts. Both will be rated at $75,000. Each method attempts to tell how good a horse is when it runs well, without making any pretensions of telling whether or not the horse will run well today. What is important here is that this new technique outperforms the other earnings methods, specifically in the dollar net category. Players using the 20–45–80–30 formula will be betting "against the grain," in many cases against those using the popular 60–22–12–6 formula. Whenever a handicapper is able to incorporate something sensible into his handicapping that is not known or appreciated by the masses, he will be rewarded often enough with decent payoffs to make his efforts worthwhile.

In head-to-head competition, the 20–45–80–30 formula clearly out-performed the 60–22–12–6 formula. In the 702 races where the two formulae rated different horses on top, the new formula picked the winner 111 times, the old formula just 92 times.

Since our three approaches to earnings (gross, average, and average purse) measure three different aspects of a horse's earning power, and in fact complement each other quite well, it would be interesting to see how well they worked together. In our sample of 946 races, we found 149 horses that were ranked first by all three methods (using the new formula for average purse). Here are their statistics:

NW	NH	WPCT	MPCT	I.V.	$NET
149	43	28.9%	61.1%	2.60	$1.91

Quite interesting, especially in light of the fact that no other handicapping factors were considered.

☐ CONSISTENCY ☐

After determining that a horse is fit, suited by the distance, surface, and track conditions, and entered against suitable opponents, the handicapper still must be concerned with the horse's reliability. How often does the horse win, or at least run well? Does it like to win? Or is it content simply to run close? Are the animal's wins (good efforts) predictable? Or do they seem to occur at random? Does the horse ever run consecutive good (winning) races? Or does one all-out effort set the horse back for weeks?

Some Thoroughbreds are winners, fiercely competitive animals seemingly aware of what is expected of them. Others are professional losers, some of these the perennial bridesmaids that are always knocking on the door, but seldom (if ever) entering the winner's circle. Most horses fall somewhere between these extremes. They win their share, but not a great deal more. They cannot be discarded as potential winners, based on consistency alone. They must be respected as possible contenders when fit and properly placed.

A horse's reliability, or consistency, can be measured (rather superficially) by consulting the results of the ten races showing in its past performances, or by looking at its earnings box. The serious handicapper will dig a little deeper, however. He will look for races of comparable class, distance, and surface as the upcoming race, disregarding races that shed little light on how the horse might perform under today's conditions. For example, if a horse shows only two wins in its latest fifteen starts, with both coming over sloppy tracks, that horse may be considered incapable of winning over today's fast surface. But should heavy rains dampen the racing surface, the horse might become a powerful factor. The grass line in the earnings box might reveal a horse to be a grass specialist, an animal not worth considering when entered to race on the main track.

When dealing with consistency, one should look for the extremes. Our computer studies documented in *Winning at the Races* revealed the worst profile belongs to the horse winless in its last ten starts, while best were those whose winning percentage over the past two years was at the 40 percent level, or higher.

	NH	WPCT	MPCT	I.V.	$NET
No wins last ten starts	5011	8.0%	28.2%	0.70	$1.30
Win percentage 40% up	162	24.1%	45.7%	2.09	$2.43

We would like to mention one angle play here. It deals with horses that had won at least three of their latest ten starts, but whose most recent performance could not be termed "good," as we shall define the term in the next chapter. If such horses are given at least ten days rest before starting again, they often return to winning ways at decent mutuels, as the following statistics prove:

NH	NW	WPCT	MPCT	I.V.	$NET
235	31	13.2%	29.4%	1.19	$2.21

The Bridesmaid

New York fans probably will never forget Jacques Who, a gray stud who turned almost pure white during his later years on the racetrack. Jacques Who became a stakes winner in the final start of his racing career, on a New Year's Eve at Keystone. Prior to that, however, he had sent many New Yorkers to the track bars (rather than the cashier's windows), muttering to themselves about his penchant for finishing second. Jacques Who was the prototype of the bridesmaid, the "sucker bet" that looks so good on paper, but always manages to get beaten. Jacques Who was far from unique. Each track has its own version, indeed several of them each year. New York will certainly have its share. Jacques Who stands at stud in that state, and runners from his first crop are just getting to the races as this is being written. Surprisingly, they are doing well. One of them, Jacques' Tip, is already a multiple stakes winner in state-bred competition, and has placed in open stakes such as the Gotham Mile.

Most bridesmaid types have the tendency to lose ground during the stretch run, perhaps "allowing" one horse to edge ahead of them. Pour L'Oiseau is an excellent example of what is called the "professional maiden." At this point in her career, the filly had accumulated eight seconds in twelve lifetime starts.

Pour L'Oiseau — B. f. 3, by Groton—Partridge, by Mito — $55,000 — Br.—Levinson & Thomas (Ky) — Tr.—Kelly Michael J — **117**

Own.—Levinson S

Lifetime 12 0 8 1 $20,260 — 1983 6 M 4 0 $11,970 — 1982 6 M 4 1 $8,290

25Mar83- 4Aqu	fst	1		:48⅘	1:15⅘	1:43	ⒻMd 45000	1	1	13	16	11	2hd	Davis R G5	b	112	5.50	51-36	Crown's Heart 121hdPourL'Oiseau1124¾Pentecost1195	Just failed	8
16Mar83- 4Aqu	fst	1⅛		:48⅘	1:14⅗	1:55	ⒻMd Sp Wt	6	3	52	32	614	616	Samyn J L	b	121	7.50	44-27	Cains Dusty 116½ Pentecost 1211¼ Granchira 1142¼	Tired	8
3Mar83- 2Aqu	fst	1 1/16	⊡	:48	1:14⅕	1:48	ⒻMd 35000	5	1	13	11½	2hd	2¾	Davis R G5	b	116	*1.20	72-21	CosmicSeaQueen119¾PourL'Oiseu116¾Pentecost1217¾	Just failed	12
27Feb83- 6Aqu	fst	6f	⊡	:23⅖	:47⅘	1:13⅕	ⒻMd 50000	9	2	73¼	75	45	47¾	Davis R G5	b	116	*1.20	70-20	GrndeYBonit119¾KinglyMiss1173¾CommndrNThif1143¼	No Threat	12
6Feb83- 4Aqu	fst	1 1/16	⊡	:49⅕	1:15	1:49	ⒻMd 45000	1	1	12	12	11	2nk	Davis R G5	b	112	*1.70	68-22	BonEglogue121nkPourL'Oiseau1123¼MybeMorgen1121	Just failed	8
29Jan83- 9Aqu	fst	6f	⊡	:22⅘	:47	1:13⅕	ⒻMd 45000	3	6	54	41¼	31	21	Davis R G5	b	112	2.70	77-20	Real Jenny 1171 PourL'Oiseau1121¼MinuteByMinute1172½	Rallied	12
28Dec82- 2Crc	fst	6f		:23	:46⅖	1:13	ⒻMd 40000	3	4	2½	21½	24	33¾	Smith A Jr		115	*1.70	83-13	Crimson'sFirst1092¼RoylMillinry1191½PourL'Oisu1151½	Weakened	9
10Dec82- 3Crc	fst	6f		:22⅕	:46⅗	1:14	ⒻMd 40000	1	1	21	33	21½	23½	Solis A5		110	*1.50	78-19	LegalWard1153½PourL'Oiseau1102¾PompnoGirl117hd	Nudged out	7
15Nov82- 1CD	fst	6½f		:23⅗	:47⅗	1:20⅕	ⒻMd 30000	1	6	21	2½	1hd	21¼	Day P		120	*1.60	78-22	Naughty Madam 1201¼ Pour L'Oiseau 1208 Julie Poolie 1202¾		12
10Nov82- 3CD	fst	6½f		:23	:46⅕	1:20⅕	ⒻMd Sp Wt	11	1	74¾	98¾	87¼	810	McKnight J		120	2.70	69-22	Hotsy Totsy 120½ Big Dreams 1202½ Tilloo Bound 120nk		12

LATEST WORKOUTS Mar 15 Bel tr.t 3f fst :37 b Feb 23 Bel tr.t 5f fst 1:03 b Feb 20 Bel tr.t 4f fst :51 b

Copyright © 1984, by DAILY RACING FORM, INC. Reprinted with permission of copyright owner.

Another typical bridesmaid profile belongs to the horse that time after time rallies strongly through the stretch, passing all but the winner. However, the typical bridesmaid is usually competitive, often found leading at some point in the stretch, though not at the finish.

CASE STUDY: FORTUIS

Fortuis had the standard bridesmaid profile when entered in a seven-furlong sprint at Belmont September 18, 1982. During the 1982 season, he had finished second five times in eight starts, while winning just once. Extremely versatile, Fortuis had run close seconds at both six and seven furlongs, as well as at a mile and a sixteenth, on both dirt and grass. He appeared capable of losing a photofinish under any conditions. But there is a fine point to be made here. Unlike most with his earnings box profile, Fortuis was a fighter. In only one of his last seven races had he lost ground from the stretch call to the wire. Two of his losses were by just a nose, another pair by merely a head. The horse probably didn't know he had lost any of those races. He ran well enough to be considered a winner, and should be considered as such by intelligent handicappers. Fortuis lay over his field on September 18. His major rivals were a recent maiden graduate making its first try in allowance company, and a horse that had been away from the races since late March. Even still, was he worth a wager at 1–2 odds? Did the low odds take into consideration the possibility the horse might have a mental block against winning?

We point out once again that Fortuis was atypical of the horse having a tendency to finish second. Most of them show signs of faintheartedness in the stretch. This could hardly have been said of Fortuis. While we do not encourage betting such a horse, we would have found it difficult betting against this one.

Fortuis — Gr. c. 3, by Native Charger—Zenith Star, by Vertex
Own.—Nerud J A — Br.—Nerud J A (Fla) — Tr.—Nerud Jan H — **113**
Lifetime 10 1 5 1 $33,380 — 1982 8 1 5 1 $33,380 — 1981 2 M 0 0 — Turf 1 0 1 0 $4,400

9Sep82- 8Bel	fst	6½f		:22⅖	:46	1:17	3↑Alw 19000	6	7	46	34½	31½	2no	Venezia M	b 113	*2.20	91-21 King Naskra 106no Fortuis 113no Tarantara 1134	Raced Wide	9
22Aug82- 7Sar	fm	1 1/16	T	:47⅗	1:11⅖	1:42⅖	3↑Alw 20000	4	4	31½	31½	32	2no	Cordero A Jr	112	3.70	98-11 Forkali 117no Fortuis 112nk Bandwagon 1172	Just missed	10
29Jly82- 7Bel	fst	1 1/16		:47⅘	1:12⅕	1:42⅗	3↑Alw 20000	2	3	51¾	1hd	1½	2nk	Cordero A Jr	113	*1.30	89-17 Words By The Wise 112nk Fortuis 1134 I'm So Merry1128	Gamely	7
8Jly82- 7Bel	fst	7f		:23⅕	:46⅕	1:24	3↑Alw 19000	2	4	1hd	32	3nk	2hd	Cordero A Jr	113	*.90	92-23 Le Washingtonian 116hd Fortuis 1132½ King Naskra 1112¾	Sharp	13
20Jun82- 9Bel	fst	7f		:23⅕	:46⅕	1:22⅗	3↑Alw 19000	5	3	64¼	74¼	43	33	Cordero A Jr	112	6.00	86-10 Exclusive One 1141½NathanDetroit1131½Fortuis112no	Wide, rallied	11
20May82- 6Bel	fst	6f		:22⅖	:46⅕	1:11	Md Sp Wt	5	4	35½	32	2hd	1½	Cordero A Jr	122	*1.90	87-18 Fortuis 122½ Uniontown 1224 Bambolino 1221¼	Driving	8
10May82- 7Aqu	fst	6f		:23	:47	1:12⅖	Md Sp Wt	4	3	24	47½	36	2hd	Cordero A Jr	122	21.00	79-29 Groomed 122hd Fortuis 1222½ Arctic Avenger 1223¾	Sharp	10
23Apr82- 6Aqu	fst	6f		:22⅗	:46⅕	1:11⅖	Md Sp Wt	11	7	97¾	99½	815	715	Velasquez J	122	65.60	69-25 Pams McAllister1221¾ToryWillow1225¼Woodberry1221½	No factor	14
19Dec81- 6Aqu	fst	6f	⊡	:23⅕	:47⅗	1:12⅖	Md Sp Wt	1	6	42½	43	45½	58¼	Cordero A Jr	118	19.50	74-17 Shananie 1183¾ Found The Money 1182½ Shore Leave1132	Evenly	12
9Sep81- 4Bel	fst	6f		:22⅖	:45⅘	1:11⅗	Md Sp Wt	14	14	87½	89	108½	117¾	Foley D3	114	64.60	76-17 Boomie's Luck 112¾ Bambolino 1172½ Arctic Avenger1171	Outrun	14

LATEST WORKOUTS Sep 7 Bel 4f fst :48⅕ h — Sep 2 Bel 4f sly :48⅘ h — Aug 20 Sar 4f fst :48⅘ h — Aug 15 Sar 4f fst :49⅖ b

What can a handicapper do with a horse like Fortuis? Should there be little apparent opposition, the odds will be unacceptably low. Certainly not worth the risk the animal will once again run a close second. What had its previous conquerors looked like beforehand? Had their form been sharp? Or did they inexplicably upset the dope? Could it happen again? Who might the darkhorse be this time? On the other hand, should there be other legitimate contenders, the bridesmaid type still may be favored. More than likely, one of its rivals should be preferred. Bridesmaids often present prime betting opportunities—playing against them—should one of their rivals make good handicapping sense.

Numerically, a horse's bridesmaid tendencies can be measured by the formula:

$$2 \times wins - (seconds + thirds)$$

For example, our 13–5–3–0 horse would be rated +7. Horses rated +3 or higher place the bettor at the breakeven point:

	WPCT	*I.V.*	*$NET*
+3 or higher rating	16.7%	1.50	$1.99

Horses rated −3 or lower show the distressing signs of being bridesmaids.

The Betting Tool

At the opposite extreme is the "betting tool," the relatively infrequent winner whose record features few seconds and thirds. Such a record implies that the trainer is usually successful when he goes for the win (at least with this horse). Second- and third-place finishes carry with them the stigma of a horse that was meant to win, but failed. The typical betting tool is trained by a relatively unknown conditioner, one who is able to give plenty of attention to each of the few horses he handles. Bright Sky is a prime example—a winner of three of fifteen starts, with one third-place finish the only semblence of failure marring an otherwise "perfect" record. Notice that the mare's two most recent wins both came in $15,000 company, when stretching out from six furlongs to a route, suggesting that trainer Sidney Cole knew how to prepare his horse for a winning effort, and place it properly when it was ready.

Bright Sky — B. m. 5, by Mr Right—Light the Sky, by Jacinto
Own.—Mil-Bert Stable — $20,000 — Br.—Decap Stable (NY) — Tr.—Cole Sidney Jr — 117
Lifetime 41 4 0 9 $61,254 — 1983 1 1 0 0 $7,800 — 1982 14 2 0 1 $14,094 — Turf 4 0 0 1 $5,100

7Jan83- 5Aqu	gd	1⅛	[•]:48⅗	1:13⅘	1:54⅗	ⒻClm 16000	1	8	9^{11}	$9^{5\frac{3}{4}}$	2^{3}	1^{nk}	Attanasio R	117	8.80	73-16	Bright Sky 117[nk] Baby Bonnie 113[2] Beaverboard 112[hd]	Driving	10
19Dec82- 3Aqu	fst	6f	[•]:24	:48⅘	1:14	3↑ⒻClm 16000	4	9	$8^{5\frac{1}{2}}$	$7^{5\frac{1}{4}}$	$5^{3\frac{1}{2}}$	$4^{3\frac{1}{2}}$	Attanasio R	117	27.30	70-23	Gold Zeda 117[1½] Limited Lady 115[2] Rouge Galop 115[no]	Rallied	9
15Aug82- 9FL	fst	1[70]	:48⅕	1:13⅕	1:44⅗	3↑ⒻS B Anthny H	2	7	$7^{4\frac{3}{4}}$	$7^{7\frac{1}{4}}$	7^{11}	7^{16}	Annonio A	113	18.10	62-22	CrackerBonBon115[2½]TalentedJet112[no]Fneuil'sJewel117[no]	Outrun	7
8Aug82- 9FL	fst	1[70]	:47⅘	1:13	1:44⅘	3↑ⒻⓈClm 15000	6	8	8^{10}	7^{9}	$7^{7\frac{1}{2}}$	$6^{7\frac{1}{2}}$	Annonio A	119	7.60	69-13	WiggleWaggle110[2½]WitSpeedToSpare116[½]Vin'sClover112[2]	Outrun	9
17Jly82- 6FL	fst	1[70]	:48⅗	1:14⅖	1:47⅕	3↑ⒻⓈClm 15000	2	6	$5^{4\frac{1}{4}}$	$5^{3\frac{3}{4}}$	$4^{\frac{3}{4}}$	1no	Annonio A	115	12.80	65-22	Bright Sky 115[no] Beaverboard 113[1] Zepha 113[nk]	Driving	8
10Jly82- 8FL	fst	6f	:22⅕	:45⅘	1:12⅖	3↑ⒻⓈAlw 11100	5	9	9^{15}	9^{17}	9^{14}	8^{16}	Annonio A	119	22.40	71-23	Amazing Maj 113[6½] Rootabebin 113[1½] Wittles Lane 113[2]	Outrun	9
2Jly82- 7FL	fst	5½f	:22	:46	1:06⅖	3↑ⒻⓈAlw 9800	3	9	9^{12}	9^{14}	9^{12}	$9^{7\frac{3}{4}}$	Annonio A	119	11.50	82-25	Misty Empress 119[3] Jet Lag Jane 108[nk] Sherry's Girl 113[nk]	Tired	9
13Jun82- 9FL	fst	6f	:23⅕	:47	1:12⅘	3↑Alw 5000	1	10	$11^{9\frac{1}{4}}$	11^{14}	11^{11}	9^{9}	Annonio A	b 114	39.30	76-16	Jodhpur 115[2] Mister Kite 114[no] Grandange 113[½]	Outrun	11
21May82- 8FL	fst	6f	:23⅖	:47⅗	1:14⅕	3↑ⒻⓈAlw 9800	5	7	7^{12}	6^{14}	5^{12}	3^{8}	Dosher K	b 119	3.40	70-22	Wit Speed To Spare119[2]Sherry'sGirl113[6]BrightSky119[2]	Mild rally	7
14May82- 7FL	fst	6f	:22⅘	:47⅕	1:14⅕	3↑ⒻⓈAlw 9000	10	10	$10^{9\frac{3}{4}}$	8^{7}	4^{1}	$1^{1\frac{1}{2}}$	Annonio A	b 116	16.70	78-25	Bright Sky 116[1½] O. Kauai 107[3] Lady Pam 122[1]	Driving	12

LATEST WORKOUTS Jan 2 Bel tr.t 4f fst :50⅖ b — Dec 28 Bel tr.t 4f fst :53⅕ b — Dec 9 Bel tr.t 4f fst :49 h — Dec 4 Bel tr.t 5f gd 1:02⅘ bg

Many betting tools share this characteristic—a very definite trainer pattern leading up to their wins.

Chapter 7

RECENCY

A horse's odds today usually reflect form exhibited in its most recent starts, rather than the animal's present state of fitness. The odds board tends to run one race behind reality. Handicappers tend to take a horse at face value, presuming it will perform today exactly as it did in its last start. They often jump on the bandwagon one race too late. Some horses are in and out, running well one time and not so well the next. Others just appear that way, due to trips or poorly selected races. Some horses, however, are clearly improving toward winning form.

In many cases, a horse's most recent race provides a strong clue to its future success. A good race last out is (statistically) significant. However, it is far too obvious, and this is reflected on the odds board. Horses coming off good races win far more than their fair share of races. But betting profits are our primary concern, not percentages. One would do just as well financially if betting at random rather than betting simply because a horse's most recent effort was good. In *Winning at the Races*, we took a positive approach to the recent good performance. We sought to strengthen it, supplement it with other positive signs from the past performances. We looked for something that would insure, at least often enough, that good form on paper would likely be reproduced today.

Defining a good performance to be a finish either first, second, or third, or within two lengths of the winner (three lengths if a route), we found the following statistics as a starting point:

	WPCT	I.V.	$NET
Good Race Last Start	15.5%	1.41	$1.65
Won Last Start	17.0%	1.52	$1.77
Won Last Two Starts	20.2%	1.76	$1.53

139

Among positive supplements to a recent good race were:

	WPCT	I.V.	$NET
*Raced within last ten days	18.9%	1.74	$1.96
3 + wins last ten starts	20.9%	1.90	$1.87
*Carries 120 pounds or more	26.3%	2.34	$2.18
Ranked first in Average Earnings	24.9%	2.26	$1.90
Ranked first in Speed Figures (average last 2 good races)	28.9%	2.40	$1.90

*indicates sprint races only

We now suggest an alternate approach. We recommend that the handicapper play the role of devil's advocate with a horse's form. If the horse ran well last time, try to knock its performance. Could it possibly have overexerted itself? Did it enjoy a perfect trip? Was the pace compatible with its running style, weakening its front-running rivals? Or possibly so slow it was able to coast on an easy lead? If moving up, has it proven incapable of the rise on previous occasions?

Whatever the reason, should a recent performance prove not as strong as appears on paper, the horse likely will be an underlay nevertheless, placing at least one of its rivals in an overlay situation where it has a solid chance to upset the dope. Should a horse's last effort been less than good, might it have had an excuse, and possibly still retain winning form? In other words, could its winning form be hidden? Did the horse suffer from a poor trip, perhaps starting from a disadvantageous post, running into interference, or racing against a track bias? Was it competing at other than its favorite distance, or over an unfamiliar surface? Had it been entered over its head, against rivals it had little chance to beat? Did the poor race occur immediately before a layoff, signaling to the trainer a need for some rest and relaxation? Or right after a layoff, before the animal had reached a reasonable state of fitness? Any of the above could have been true, masking the animal's present fitness. Should the horse have been competitive at some call, despite the obstacles placed in its path, we have a strong sign of fitness, and possibly an excellent betting opportunity at good odds. All the more so, should the animal be a proven, consistent winner in its classification. In any case, the horse's performance rating should be upgraded.

CASE STUDY: JE'DA QUA

The best time to bet a consistent horse is when it is coming off a pair of excusably poor performances. The price is usually right, and the horse likely will rebound if properly placed. Je'Da Qua's two most recent performances probably were the worst of her career. Usually right there, she had won an NW1 route at Gulfstream and then a seven-furlong NW2 sprint at Hialeah. In between, she had finished sixth in her first try on the grass, although experiencing traffic problems in that race. On April 1, however, she finished a dismal eighth in the Coral Gables, then rested six weeks before finishing a distant fifth on the grass behind the brilliantly fast Sabin (although only four lengths behind the second-place filly). Outclassed on one occasion, and racing over a possibly unsuitable surface on the other, good form could have easily been hidden. Entered in an allowance race at seven furlongs on May 28 at Belmont, Je'Da Qua returned to form, winning easily at 5–1 odds.

Je'Da Qua — Dk. b. or br. f. 4, by Fleet Nasrullah—Font, by Double Jay
Br.—Quammen L D (Ky)
Own.—Quammen L D — Tr.—Skiffington Thomas
119 — Lifetime 18 3 6 4 $60,410 — 1983 6 2 0 0 $16,330 — 1982 12 1 6 4 $44,080 — Turf 2 0 0 0 $170

13May83- 5Aqu	fm	1 ①	:47	1:12⅖	1:35⅕	3↑ⒻAlw 27000	9	7	77½	79	712	515	Velasquez J	b 121	26.40	87 —	Sabin 112¹¹ Bedazzle 1211½ Cryptic 1142¼		Off slowly	10
1Apr83- 9Hia	fst	1⅛	:46⅘	1:11⅗	1:50	3↑ⒻCoral Gables	7	5	55	65	716	822	Vasquez J	b 116	7.90	60-17	Vany 1187½ Van Lingen 1164 Congress Flier 1161		Tired	10
23Mar83- 8Hia	fst	7f	:23	:46	1:24⅗	ⒻAlw 11000	2	7	62¾	43	31	1½	Vasquez J	b 119	*1.80	80-16	Je'Da Qua 119½ Petet Gold 119½ Heavy Spender 1162		Driving	11
24Feb83- 7GP	yl	*1 1/16 ①			1:49⅕	ⒻAlw 17000	7	8	74¼	42½	63¾	64	Velasquez J	b 122	4.10	56-33	Baklawa 1222½ La Vamp 122no Native New Yorker 122nk		Checked	10
24Feb83-Placed fifth through disqualification																				
7Feb83- 8GP	gd	1 1/16	:47⅘	1:13	1:44⅘	ⒻAlw 15000	2	5	41½	1hd	14	19	Velasquez J	b 117	*1.70	77-21	Je'Da Qua 1179 Nasty Lark 1171½ Mavoureen 1172		Ridden out	9
14Jan83- 6GP	fst	6f	:22⅗	:46⅕	1:12	ⒻAlw 14000	6	11	109¾	66½	63½	41½	Samyn J L	b 119	*1.10	77-20	Iceland Spar 1121Jove'sDaughter117hdJusticeAtDawn117½		Rallied	12
16Dec82- 7Aqu	sly	6f ⊡	:23	:47	1:12⅘	3↑ⒻAlw 21000	6	2	41¾	2hd	1hd	2½	Samyn J L	b 115	*1.00	79-23	Jennine'sSuite115½Je'DQu1152IncredibleMomnt1103		Couldn't last	6
6Dec82- 8Aqu	my	6f ⊡	:22	:45⅕	1:10	3↑ⒻAlw 21000	1	4	45½	25	26	26¾	Samyn J L	b 115	2.90	87-15	VisulEmotion1156¾Je'DQu1154IncredibleMomnt110no		Best others	7
27Nov82- 6Aqu	fst	6f	:23⅘	:47⅘	1:12⅖	3↑ⒻAlw 19000	5	1	51¾	31½	22½	22¾	Samyn J L	b 120	4.90	76-29	Chime 1152¾ Je'Da Qua 1208 Backstage Whisper 108nk		No match	6
31Oct82- 7Aqu	fst	6f	:22⅖	:46⅕	1:11	3↑ⒻMd Sp Wt	1	4	36	32½	2hd	13¼	Samyn J L	b 119	*1.10	86-18	Je'Da Qua 1193¼ What An Act1194LoyalDiplomat119¾		Ridden Out	8

LATEST WORKOUTS May 26 Bel 4f fst :47 h — May 10 Bel 5f fst 1:00⅘ h — May 5 Bel 4f fst :49 b — Apr 28 Bel tr.t 6f fst 1:14⅖ h

Copyright © 1984, by DAILY RACING FORM, INC. Reprinted with permission of copyright owner.

□ RECENT ACTION □

The races in the past performances of the typical horse are, as a rule, unevenly spaced. One race may be followed by another eight days later, that by another in twenty-two days, then still another twelve days later. While an occasional trainer may prefer to space his charges' races a few weeks apart, a three-week gap between races usually can be taken to mean one of two things. Either the horse's physical condition prevented it from returning sooner, or the event for which it was pointing failed to fill, leaving the animal with nowhere to race.

When contemplating how (and why) a trainer has spaced a horse's recent races, keep the condition book in mind, because the trainer has! That suspicious-looking twenty-four day gap might well be the result of a specific race not filling. Or possibly the type of event the trainer really wanted for his horse might not have appeared in that condition book. The distance or classification of another race might have been his only choice. Still another race "chosen" for the horse might have been at the request of the racing secretary, to help fill a race. On the other hand, with the proliferation of racing dates, especially in the Northeast, many trainers are forced to race (rather than train) their stock into top shape, and often do so at the request of the racing secretary.

Some trainers have their own theories on the spacing of races, and adhere to them rather rigidly. For most, however, the best approach is to let the individual horse dictate the moves. Some thrive on work, and do best when raced every week. Others like time between races, and many need it. The astute handicapper will glance through the past performances attempting to discover if an individual horse has any such preferences. Most don't, but some do have preferences, and awareness of them often provides a valuable clue that a horse will perform to the best of its ability in the upcoming contest.

□ LAYOFFS □

Horses racing for the first time after a layoff of a month or longer are usually at a disadvantage. All statistical studies of racing have verified this fact. Layoff horses win only 70 percent of their share of races. A recent sharp race, suggesting fitness, is especially important over a tiring surface, such as Calder, or almost any track drying out after recent rains. What has just been alluded to holds true more so for sprints than routes. To win, a horse must be physically fit and mentally sharp, as well as suited to the conditions of the race. Racing sharpness is honed in recent competition, and appears especially important at the sprint distances. For routes, fitness and ability at the distance remain the primary concerns. Lack of recent activity becomes less alarming the farther a horse must race. The older a horse, the longer it will take to come to hand, as a general rule. In addition, an older horse is less likely than its younger rivals to bounce back from a poor effort.

Horses returning from layoffs should not be automatic throwouts, however. Some trainers have reputations for winning with freshened horses, and it pays to learn who they are. Some horses race well when fresh. A few do their best immediately after a layoff. The evidence might be right there in the past performances for all to see, or it may be filed away in the handicapper's memory, waiting to be used when the occasion arises. Romaldo, for example, shows three wins and two seconds in his record. All were achieved in first or second starts after layoffs. The January 4, 1982 win came after an eight-month layoff, and the February 28, 1983 win after nearly seven months on the sidelines.

One note of warning here. A horse able to win its racing debut is not necessarily a layoff type. Maiden races are filled with first-time starters and horses returning from layoffs. They often are won by a horse yet to

Romaldo — Ch. h. 5, by Gallant Romeo—Aldonza, by Bold Bidder
Br.—Wimpfheimer J D (Ky)
Own.—Wimpfheim J D — Tr.—Sedlacek Woodrow — **112**

Lifetime	1983	1	1	0	0	$21,000
20 5 2 5	1982	9	2	2	0	$45,552
$99,912	Turf	1	0	0	0	

28Feb83-	8Aqu	fst	6f	⊡:22 4/5	:46	1:11	Alw 35000	8	4	1 1½	12½	13	13	McCarron G	b 115	1.80e	89-25	Romaldo 115 3 Jan's Kinsman 115¾ Cannon Royal 110no	Driving	8
15Aug82-	1Sar	fst	6f	:22 3/5	:44 4/5	1:09 3/5	3♦Alw 32000	5	4	33	47	57	43¾	McCarron G	b 115	3.60	88-11	Victor's Gent114½DashO'Pleasure1151¾Starbinia1151½	No menace	6
25Jun82-	8Bel	fm	1	Ⓣ:46	1:09 4/5	1:34	3♦Alw 27000	7	2	2hd	21	58½	58¾	McCarron G	b 117	24.50	86-11	Hrmonizer1171¾HollywoodHendrson1141¾Erin'sTigr1193½	Used up	11
30May82-	5Bel	fst	7f	:23	:45 3/5	1:22 2/5	3♦Alw 32000	3	3	11	11½	12	2nk	McCarron G	b 121	10.70	90-13	Wild Moment 119nk Romaldo 1214½ Sten 1191¼	Just failed	8
10May82-	8Aqu	fst	6f	:23	:46 4/5	1:11 4/5	3♦Alw 25000	4	1	1hd	12	1hd	21½	McCarron G	b 119	18.40	80-29	Baby Kobe 1131½ Romaldo 119nk Maudlin 1192	Gamely	6
5Mar82-	8Aqu	gd	6f	⊡:22 1/5	:45 1/5	1:09 3/5	Alw 29000	1	4	11½	21	65½	76¾	McCarron G	b 117	7.50	89-12	Gallant Dance 1171¼MightyNasty117½Fanny'sFox1151¼	Done early	7
15Feb82-	8Aqu	fst	6f	⊡:22 3/5	:45 1/5	1:10 2/5	3♦Sprtng Plt H	3	3	32	32½	76¼	96¾	McCarron G	b 118	3.40	85-16	Contare 114hd Feathers Lad 112¾ In From Dixie 116½	Stopped	9
31Jan82-	8Aqu	my	6f	⊡:23	:47 2/5	1:13 3/5	Coaltown	5	7	53½	54½	56½	47¼	McCarron G	b 114	*2.60e	69-46	Royal Rollick 1144¼ Main Stem 1171½ Samba Boy 1141½	Evenly	10
16Jan82-	7Aqu	fst	6f	⊡:22 1/5	:45	1:09 4/5	Alw 29000	5	1	1hd	2hd	1hd	11¾	McCarron G	b 115	*1.50	95-10	Romaldo1151¾TravellingMusic110hdBrazendBold119nk	Drew clear	6
4Jan82-	8Aqu	sly	6f	⊡:22	:45 1/5	1:11 1/5	Alw 17000	1	2	—	—	13	14	McCarron G	b 117	2.10	88-25	Romaldo 1174 Feel Good 1171½ Creme DeLaFete1121½	Fog. easily	6

LATEST WORKOUTS Feb 23 Aqu ⊡ 5f fst 1:03 2/5 b — Feb 15 Aqu ⊡ 5f fst 1:02 h — Feb 2 Aqu ⊡ 4f fst :48 2/5 h — ●Jan 26 Aqu ⊡ 3f fst :37 2/5 b

reach its peak of fitness or sharpness. Debut winners may later prove incapable of winning when they are fresh and pitted against seasoned rivals. Most handicappers know little about the majority of trainers, and their abilities or intentions with fresh horses. Even so, they can often read the signs when a first race back is not to be taken seriously. The stable's second- or third-string jockey may be scheduled to ride. A router may be entered at a sprint distance. A horse that does its best at six furlongs may be entered instead at seven. A claiming horse may be returned in a higher bracket, possibly even in allowance company, where it can gain conditioning without the threat of being claimed.

One note about two-year-olds: The juvenile away from the races two or three months may have been on the sidelines due to "bucked shins," a malady almost all young horses must face. Some buck before getting to the races, delaying the start of their career as a result; others do so in a workout, or during the running of a race. When assessing the chances of a juvenile that stopped abruptly in its latest start and since has been among the missing, be mindful of the probable cause. It is by no means serious.

The timing of a horse's return to competition can be quite revealing. If started within the first week or two of a meeting, things are likely going well for the horse, with everything proceeding right on schedule for its comeback. A New York horse absent from mid-June until the first week at Saratoga probably was resting, and not ailing. But if most of the other runners in a barn return to the races in April or early May, the one coming out in July no doubt had serious problems that delayed the start of its campaign.

□ THE RECENCY CYCLE □

It pays to notice where a horse is in its recency cycle. Once a horse gets back into the swing of things, and its form becomes established, the handicapper is often left guessing whether the status quo will remain unchanged. With the relatively fresh horse, however, dramatic improvement is possible, and often predictable. They provide the handicapper with one of the prime situations where anticipation may prove extremely effective. Sprinters making their second, third, or fourth starts after a layoff have a statistical advantage, and from this point of view they are unique. Their advantage becomes especially noteworthy if they ran well in their most recent start—a good race, or at least a finish in the first half of their field. Here are the figures for those that beat at least half their opponents last time out:

	WPCT	I.V.	$NET
Second race back	15.3%	1.43	$1.85
Third or fourth race back	16.1%	1.50	$1.83

Signs of improvement, either within that last race (bid and hung, surprise speed, etc.) or since (sharp workouts, a positive rider change, etc.) are all the more encouraging. Should that last race qualify as a "good race," all the statistics seem to improve. Sharp horses making their third or fourth start after a layoff, and returning within ten days of their previous race, are especially powerful. The following table reveals how the "improvement" angles discussed in Chapter 3 come to life (for the most part) when restricted to freshened horses making their second, third, or fourth start after a layoff. The statistics that follow are for sprint races only:

Angle	NH	NW	WPCT	MPCT	I.V.	$NET
Ainslie's Big Win	64	16	25.0%	51.6%	2.26	$2.51
Taxing Stretch Drive	124	25	20.2%	50.8%	1.90	$2.67
Bid, Hung	111	27	24.3%	46.0%	2.29	$2.94
Stretch Rally	98	18	18.4%	50.0%	1.71	$3.08
Closer To Lead	105	19	18.1%	40.0%	1.75	$3.24
Surprise Speed	91	13	14.3%	36.3%	1.35	$1.48
Carried Speed Farther	124	21	16.9%	47.6%	1.62	$1.92
Two Moves	23	3	13.0%	34.8%	1.27	$1.24

Horses that return to the races with a fair effort are eligible to improve in their second start, and often do. Those that return with a strong race may suffer through a period of disappointment before running back to that race.

CASE STUDY: MUSKOKA WYCK AND KATERINA THE GREAT

Beware the horse that was severely tested through the stretch run on its return to the races. Overexertion at this point in a horse's campaign usually does no good. Many of these horses will run lethargically as favorites in their next starts. They come back from their first start "muscle sore," and often need time and/or racing to work out the soreness. Muskoka Wyck is a case in point. As a three-year-old, the son of Tentam ran his best races at six furlongs. For his 1983 debut, however, the colt was overtaxed. He was forced to fight tooth and nail with Pinstripe through the length of the stretch in a seven-furlong race, only to lose by the bob of a head at the wire. Seasoned handicappers would have marked him down as a horse to avoid in his next start. That he went backward on that occasion should have come as no surprise.

Muskoka Wyck — B. c. 4, by Tentam—Lachesis, by Iron Ruler
Own.—Rokeby Stables
Br.—Marydel Farm (Md)
Tr.—Miller Mack
117
Lifetime 14 3 5 1 $61,110
1983 2 0 1 0 $5,500
1982 10 3 3 1 $51,870
Turf 1 0 0 0

25May83- 9Bel	fst	7f	:22⅘	:45⅘	1:23⅘	3↑Alw 25000	10	7	21½	3½	33½	54¼	Fell J	b 119	2.60	79-16	Mr. Badger 119hd Fortuis 1193 Chapter One 1191	Wide	11
4May83- 8Aqu	fst	7f	:22⅖	:44⅘	1:22⅕	3↑Alw 25000	3	2	12	1½	1½	2no	Fell J	b 121	2.10	90-20	Pinstripe 121no Muskoka Wyck 1212 Groomed 121½	Just Failed	7
17Nov82- 6Aqu	fst	6f	:22⅘	:45⅗	1:10	3↑Alw 32000	5	5	42	42	32	2½	Fell J	b 117	*1.30	90-18	Fleet Saber 113½ Muskoka Wyck 1171 This Is Smith1104¼	Rallied	6
31Oct82- 1Aqu	fst	6f	:23	:46⅖	1:10⅗	3↑Alw 20000	4	4	32	1hd	1hd	12¼	Fell J	b 114	*1.00	88-18	Muskoka Wyck 1142¼ El Bombay 117½HenryWilliams122¾	Driving	5
7Oct82- 1Bel	fst	1⅛	:46⅕	1:10⅘	1:50	3↑Alw 21000	3	1	1hd	2hd	52½	55½	Fell J	b 114	*2.00e	71-20	Skin Dancer 1141 Rigid 117no Tides Of Chance 114hd	Tired	7
25Sep82- 5Bel	fst	1 1/16	:48⅕	1:12⅖	1:42⅖	3↑Alw 21000	4	4	63¼	63¼	57	58¾	Fell J	b 113	5.40	81-15	Trenchant 118¾ Faces Up 1135 Skin Dancer 1131	Tired	7
18Sep82- 9Bel	fm	1 1/16 Ⓣ	:45⅖	1:09⅘	1:40⅖	3↑Alw 21000	8	6	75½	89½	820	820	Fell J	b 113	6.80	74-08	Lamerok 1134 Lord Lister 1133 Broadly 115½	No factor	9
2Sep82- 7Bel	sly	7f	:22⅖	:45	1:22⅕	3↑Alw 20000	1	3	11½	14	22	24¼	Fell J	b 113	*1.50	87-19	PuritanChief1194¼MuskokWyck113hdShiftySheik1134½	Weakened	7
22Aug82- 6Sar	fst	6f	:22⅗	:45⅕	1:09⅗	3↑Alw 20000	7	6	41½	31	33	33	Fell J	b 112	*.80	89-12	TheTimeIsNow1173JetStm113hdMuskokWyck1122	Lacked a rally	7
3Jly82- 8Del	fst	6f	:22	:45⅖	1:10⅘	Icecapade	7	3	41¾	3½	32½	21¾	Molina V H	b 119	3.00	85-21	Tiny Rollick 1121¾ Muskoka Wyck 1191½Wyetown112nk	Game try	8

LATEST WORKOUTS ●May 31 Bel 4f sly :48⅕ h May 22 Bel 4f sly :49⅗ b May 16 Bel 5f fst :59⅗ h ●May 10 Bel 4f fst :46⅖ h

At first glance, Katerina The Great might appear an inconsistent filly, with a fifth-place finish sandwiched between two wins. In fact, her June 13 race probably came too close on the heels of an exceptional effort in her seasonal debut ten days earlier, and she had yet to get over the muscle soreness that resulted. On June 3, Katerina The Great pressed a fast pace, then took over upon entering the stretch and held sway under "strong handling." She was the only speed type to win over the Belmont grass during the first four days of June. Indeed, earlier on the June 3 card, the fillies that contested the early pace under similar allowance conditions all faded far out of the picture. And Katerina The Great ran against a much faster pace in her division. Although her June 3 race does not appear (on paper) as taxing as Muskoka Wyck's upon his return to the races, in fact it was. The mare likely developed sore muscles as a result, seriously affecting her performance ten days later. Given seventeen days to recuperate before her next start on June 30, Katerina The Great recovered, and returned to winning ways.

***Katerina The Great** — B. m. 5, by Great Nephew—View Mistress, by Kings Troop
Own.—Hancock R E
Br.—Molins D W (Eng)
Tr.—Turner William H Jr
117
Lifetime 23 3 5 2 $67,842
1983 3 2 0 0 $26,400
1982 7 0 3 0 $12,359
Turf 23 3 5 2 $67,842

30Jun83- 8Bel	fm	1 Ⓣ	:45⅘	1:11	1:36	3↑Ⓕ Alw 23000	12	4	34	31½	1½	15	Maple E	122	7.60	85-27	KaterinTheGret1225GoldenSummer1121½HonedEdge119no	Driving	12
13Jun83- 5Bel	hd	1 1/16 [T]	:47	1:10⅗	1:42⅖	3↑Ⓕ Alw 23000	3	1	11	1hd	2½	51½	Maple E	122	2.20	87-08	Idle Gossip 113½ NeverKnock117noGoldenSummer112	Weakened	8
3Jun83- 7Bel	gd	1 1/16 Ⓣ	:46⅕	1:11⅘	1:45⅖	3↑Ⓕ Alw 21000	8	2	21	2½	11½	11	Maple E	117	*2.70	69-31	KterinThGrt1171Topin1133WhiskyAndEggs1101¼	Strong handling	12
15Aug82 ♦3Deauville(Fra)	gd	*1			1:37⅘	Ⓣ Grand Hcp deDeauville						105¾	Lefevre J P	117	21.00	— —	King James 127¾ Silver Ring 117nk Kebir 115nk	Well pl,wknd	21
13Jly82 ♦5Evry(Fra)	gd	*6½f			1:16⅖	Ⓣ Prix Hampton						56½	Lefevre J P	127	*1.75	— —	Try To Smile 123½ MorseCode119½ Pampabird1261½	Well pl,wknd	7
30Jun82 ♦5Evry(Fra)	gd	*7f			1:26⅖	Ⓣ Prix le Sancy						2nk	Lefevre J P	122	12.00	— —	Pampabird119nk KaterinaTheGret122no Alkmr1201½	Strong finish	11
6Jun82 ♦5BadenBaden(Ger)	gd	*1			1:38⅕	Ⓣ Badener Meile(Gr.3)						6	Lefevre J P	117	9.00	— —	[D]Elektrant 1212¼ Torgos 1211½ Justus 119¾	No threat	10
21May82 ♦4MLaffitte(Fra)	sf	*6f			1:14⅘	Ⓣ Prix Cor de Chasse						2½	Lefevre J P	124	12.00	— —	Kind Music 118½ KaterinaTheGreat1243 SkyLawyer1301½	Fin.well	9
8Apr82 ♦4Evry(Fra)	gd	*1			1:39⅖	Ⓣ Prix de Ris Orangis(Gr3)						88	Lefevre J P	120	19.00	— —	Big John 1231½ Tonar 1232 Vablinis 123nk	No threat	9
27Mar82 ♦6StCloud(Fra)	gd	*1			1:50⅖	Ⓣ Prix le Capucin						2½	Lefevre J P	118	19.00	— —	WaterMelon121½ KaterinaTheGret118no Vblinis1262	Game finish	9

LATEST WORKOUTS Jly 21 Bel [T] 4f yl :51⅘ b (d) Jly 14 Bel Ⓣ 5f fm 1:03 b (d) Jly 7 Bel [T] 5f fm 1:01⅘ h (d) Jun 23 Bel [T] 5f fm 1:03 b (d)

Whether or not a horse develops muscle soreness depends to a great extent on the foundation the trainer has built under the horse prior to its return to the races. Indeed, the horse severely tested in its second or third start off a layoff, when it is better prepared for the strain, is more likely than not to profit from the experience. The exertion at this stage of its campaign often advances the horse's conditioning to a winning peak.

CASE STUDY: CHRISTMAS PAST

Christmas Past's easy victory in the Ruffian Handicap was predictable. Ignore the (significant) fact that she was the only filly in the field with Eclipse Award aspirations. Our interest lies in the fact that she was repeating a pattern, one concerned with her recency cycle. Look back to her performance in the Acorn Stakes on May 22. Entered in a route stakes for her first start in two months, and given considerable support in a strong field, she raced wide and evenly to Cupecoy's Joy, on a track favoring the latter's early speed. Trainer Angel Penna, Jr., was looking ahead, however, using the Acorn as a prep race for longer events to follow. Benefiting from the conditioning she gained in the Acorn, Christmas Past finished a much-improved second to the same Cupecoy's Joy in the Mother Goose, then thwarted that filly's bid for New York's "Triple Crown for Fillies" with a smashing triumph in the mile and a half Coaching Club American Oaks.

Given a brief respite after winning the Monmouth Oaks, Christmas Past failed as odds-on favorite when returned to the races in the mile and an eighth Gazelle, repeating her Acorn pattern. In actuality, her effort in the Gazelle was somewhat better than her performance in the Acorn—she made a big (though premature) move, then hung through the lane. Her much-improved effort in the Ruffian should have come as no surprise, repeating the improvement pattern first seen in the Mother Goose. Her good third to the older male Lemhi Gold in the mile and a half Jockey Club Gold Cup on October 9 completed repetition of the full form cycle, and stamped Christmas Past as this country's best distance filly in 1982.

Christmas Past — Gr. f. 4, by Grey Dawn II—Yule Log, by Bold Ruler
Br.—Phipps Cynthia (Ky)
Own.—Phipps Cynthia — Tr.—Penna Angel Jr
122 — Lifetime 13 6 2 3 $437,040 — 1982 11 6 2 1 $432,960 — 1981 2 M 0 2 $4,080

9Oct82- 8Bel	fst	1½	:47⅘	2:04	2:31⅕	3↑J C Gold Cup	7	6	6^{19}	$3^{4½}$	2^{5}	$3^{6½}$	Vasquez J	118	7.00	57-25	LmhiGold126^{4½}SilvrSuprm126^{2}ChristmsPst118^{17}	Wide, weakened	10
26Sep82- 8Bel	fst	1⅛	:46⅕	1:10⅕	1:48⅘	3↑(F)Ruffian H	8	7	$7^{4¼}$	1^{hd}	$1^{1½}$	1^{5}	Vasquez J	117	2.50	84-19	ChristmsPst117^{5}MdemoiselleForli112^{2¼}LoveSign123¾	Ridden out	8
15Sep82- 8Bel	fst	1⅛	:46⅗	1:10⅕	1:47⅗	(F)Gazelle H	2	6	$6^{2¾}$	2^{1}	$4^{4½}$	$4^{4¼}$	Vasquez J	123	*.70	85-14	BroomDnce121^{nk}Number113^{2¾}MdmoisllForli114^{1¼}	Bid, weakened	7
24Jly82- 9Mth	fst	1⅛	:47⅘	1:11⅖	1:49⅖	(F)Mth Oaks	9	6	$6^{2¼}$	3½	1½	$1^{1¼}$	Vasquez J	121	*.40	88-14	Christmas Past121^{1¼}Milingo119^{1¼}MademoiselleForli112^{1½}	Driving	9
26Jun82- 8Bel	fst	1½	:47⅕	2:02⅕	2:28⅗	(F)C C A Oaks	1	4	4^{12}	1^{hd}	1^{2}	1^{6}	Vasquez J	121	2.50	77-20	Christmas Past 121^{6}Cupecoy'sJoy121^{no}FlyingPartner121^{3}	Driving	10
4Jun82- 8Bel	fst	1⅛	:45⅘	1:09⅘	1:48⅖	(F)Mthr Goose	6	5	5^{9}	4^{7}	$2^{1½}$	2¾	Vasquez J	121	7.10	84-18	Cupecoy'sJoy121¾ChristmasPst121^{3½}BlushWithPride121^{4¾}	Rallied	12
22May82- 8Bel	fst	1	:46	1:09⅗	1:34⅕	(F)Acorn	9	5	5^{3}	$4^{4½}$	$5^{6½}$	$5^{9½}$	Vasquez J	121	4.30	85-11	Cupecoy's Joy 121^{2¾} Nancy Huang 121^{3½} Vestris 121^{2¼}	Wide	9
24Mar82- 9GP	fst	1$\frac{1}{16}$	:47⅘	1:11⅘	1:44⅕	(F)Bonnie Miss	2	6	$4^{1¾}$	3^{1}	$1^{1½}$	1^{3}	Vasquez J	121	*.40	80-22	Christmas Past 121^{3} Norsan 113^{1} Our Darling 112^{1½}	Ridden out	6
4Mar82- 9Hia	fst	1⅛	:48⅕	1:12⅕	1:49⅖	(F)Poinsettia	6	5	$3^{1½}$	$2^{1½}$	$1^{1½}$	1^{6}	Vasquez J	113	7.20	85-23	Christmas Past 113^{6} Larida 114^{7} Smart Heiress 112½	Handily	8

LATEST WORKOUTS Feb 8 Hia 4f fst :48⅕ b ●Feb 2 Hia 5f fst :59 b Jan 27 Hia 4f fst :47⅕ b ●Jan 18 Hia 5f fst :58⅖ h

☐ RACE OVER THE TRACK ☐

Thoroughbreds are always on the move. Only a small minority make one track their year-round home. Horses that race the summer and fall in New Jersey may spend their winter in Miami, then stop off in Kentucky during the spring before returning to the Garden State. Horses that race at Keeneland in April arrive from Florida, Arkansas, and Louisiana, as well as the smaller tracks on the Kentucky and Ohio circuits. Those that don't remain in Kentucky to race at Churchill Downs ship out to destinations such as New York, New Jersey, and Chicago. Even in New York, where racing is a year-round proposition, there is a significant turnover in the horse population. In early December, many of the major stables ship out to warmer climates, and New Yorkers are treated to an influx of cheaper stock from neighboring circuits, all in quest of the higher New York purses. At winter's end, the classier stables return, forcing their winter stand-ins to return home. Later in the season, when Saratoga opens, New Yorkers welcome back Laz Barrera and others returning from Southern California for the fall championship races.

How does the handicapper deal with all this moving about? Does a horse, as a rule, need a race over the local racing surface? Unfortunately, there is no simple answer to this question. For one thing, there are two kinds of shippers. One is the "ad hoc" shipper, sent from a nearby track for a specific race, to be returned home immediately thereafter (unless claimed). The other type is from a stable that has just arrived on the local scene, where it will remain for the duration of the meeting or season. The handicapper can distinguish one from the other simply by noting where the horse lives. This usually can be done by looking at the site of its most recent workout.

There is a sense of immediacy with the "ad hoc" shipper. At least with most of them. The trainer is answering one of our key handicapping questions for us. Yes, the horse is fit and well-meant. Why else would the owner pay for the shipping expenses? The stable is going all-out to win the race in question. If the horse were in need of exercise, that could have easily been obtained in a race at its home track. There are exceptions, of course. Allowance horses shipping from Belmont or Aqueduct to nearby Northeastern tracks may actually be dropping in class, although racing in the same classification. Some of these may be sharp horses, looking for an easy win. Others may be fit, but only marginally talented by New York standards. They ship hoping to find the competition elsewhere more to their liking. Their trainers are just hoping for the best. They are willing to settle for a smaller purse, rather than nothing at all, and they are telling one and all that their horse is probably not good enough to win the same kind of race in New York.

After finishing a respectable third in the Nassau County Handicap, Otter Slide appeared capable of winning a classified allowance in New York, and picking up the winner's share of a $35,000 purse. Instead, trainer P. G. Johnson sent the horse to Monmouth, where he easily captured the same kind of race, and the major share of a $20,000 purse. When returned to Belmont, Otter Slide ran off the board as 7–5 favorite in another classified allowance route. Apparently, Johnson had his reasons for shipping to Monmouth.

Otter Slide — B. c. 4, by Far North—Ms. Bloomers, by Carlemont
Br.—Rosenthal M (Ky)
Own.—Rosenthal Mrs M — Tr.—Johnson Philip G — **119**

Lifetime						
19 7 1 5	1983	6	1	0	3	$27,504
$139.911	1982	13	6	1	2	$112,407
	Turf	5	1	1	2	$39,927

25Jun83- 8Mth	fst	1 1/16	:47⅕	1:10⅘	1:42	3↑Alw 20000	2	1	1^{1}	1^{1}	1^{4}	$1^{5\frac{1}{2}}$	Perret C	115	*.80	95-15	Otter Slide $115^{5\frac{1}{2}}$ CastleGuard$115^{3\frac{1}{2}}$DoubleLeader$117^{\frac{1}{2}}$	Ridden out	6
10Jun83- 8Bel	fst	1⅛	:46⅖	1:09⅘	1:47	3↑Nassau Cty H	6	5	$4^{1\frac{1}{2}}$	$3^{2\frac{1}{2}}$	3^{8}	3^{6}	Samyn J L	113	8.90	86-11	Winter's Tale 117^{3} Fabulous Find114^{3}OtterSlide113^{13}	Evenly late	8
30May83- 8Bel	my	1	:44⅖	1:08⅕	1:33⅘	3↑Metroplt'n H	7	6	7^{9}	8^{12}	9^{11}	$9^{9\frac{1}{2}}$	Samyn J L	110	32.60	86-11	Star Choice $113^{1\frac{1}{2}}$ Tough Critic $110^{3\frac{3}{4}}$ John's Gold 111^{2}	Wide	13
15May83- 1Aqu	fst	1	:46	1:09⅘	1:35	3↑Handicap	6	4	5^{4}	$4^{5\frac{1}{2}}$	4^{6}	$3^{4\frac{1}{4}}$	Maple E	113	1.80e	87-18	West On Broad $109^{2\frac{1}{2}}$ Star Choice $115^{1\frac{3}{4}}$ OtterSlide113^{nk}	Mild bid	6
1May83- 7Aqu	fst	7f	:23	:46	1:23	3↑Alw 35000	1	7	$5^{2\frac{1}{2}}$	$5^{3\frac{1}{2}}$	$4^{4\frac{1}{2}}$	$3^{2\frac{1}{2}}$	Samyn J L	124	*.60e	83-21	Satan's Charger $101^{\frac{3}{4}}$ Acaroid $109^{1\frac{3}{4}}$ Otter Slide $124^{\frac{3}{4}}$	Mild rally	7
22Apr83- 8Aqu	fst	6f	:22⅖	:45⅗	1:09⅖	3↑Alw 35000	6	8	$8^{5\frac{1}{2}}$	$9^{6\frac{1}{2}}$	$7^{5\frac{1}{2}}$	$6^{6\frac{1}{2}}$	Samyn J L	121	3.80e	87-16	Fit to Fight $121^{1\frac{1}{2}}$ Star Gallant $121^{3\frac{1}{4}}$ Sepulveda 119^{nk}	No threat	11
12Oct82- 6Med	fst	1 1/16	:48⅕	1:11⅘	1:44	Handicap	5	3	$3^{\frac{1}{2}}$	$1^{2\frac{1}{2}}$	1^{4}	$1^{5\frac{1}{2}}$	Samyn J L	122	*.50	89-19	Otter Slide $122^{5\frac{1}{2}}$ Nemrac $114^{2\frac{1}{4}}$ Real Twister $115^{\frac{1}{2}}$	Easlily	6
3Oct82- 7Bel	fst	1	:45⅖	1:10⅗	1:36⅕	3↑Alw 35000	2	5	$4^{2\frac{1}{2}}$	$4^{2\frac{1}{2}}$	3^{nk}	1^{hd}	Samyn J L	114	19.00	84-20	Otter Slide 114^{hd} Rise Jim 117^{nk} John Casey $115^{3\frac{1}{2}}$	Driving	8
23Sep82- 8Bel	gd	1	Ⓣ:47⅖	1:11⅘	1:35⅕	3↑Alw 27000	6	5	$2^{1\frac{1}{2}}$	$2^{1\frac{1}{2}}$	$3^{2\frac{1}{2}}$	$3^{4\frac{1}{2}}$	Samyn J L	113	4.50	84-17	Disco Count $119^{2\frac{3}{4}}$ Santo's Joe $112^{1\frac{3}{4}}$ Otter Slide 113^{1}	Weakened	8
18Aug82- 7Sar	fm	1	[T]:48	1:11⅗	1:35⅖	3↑Alw 27000	7	6	$6^{4\frac{1}{2}}$	5^{5}	$5^{6\frac{1}{2}}$	$5^{7\frac{1}{4}}$	Samyn J L	112	4.70	92-15	Reinvested $112^{4\frac{3}{4}}$Bucksplasher117^{no}DoubleLeader117^{nc}	No factor	8

LATEST WORKOUTS Jly 2 Bel tr.t 3f fst :36⅕ b ●Jun 22 Bel tr.t 4f fst :47⅕ h ●Jun 17 Bel tr.t 5f fst :59⅕ h ●Jun 6 Bel tr.t 4f fst :47 h

Many horses travel to nearby states where the rules permit racing on drugs such as phenylbutazone (bute) or furosemide (Lasix). Bute is a pain-killer which allows ouchy horses to race when they otherwise would probably be confined to their stalls. Bute relieves the pain, but does not cure the problem, giving the horse a false sense of security. Lasix helps bleeders, those horses that bleed internally through the nostrils from the strain of racing. When a horse bleeds during competition, it will stop suddenly, and often lose its coordination to some extent.

The 1983 Preakness spotlighted the drug problem in this country. It was not until the day of the race that the participation of Derby runner-up Desert Wine and Derby favorite Marfa was assured. The controversy centered around the different rules for using Lasix in California, Maryland, and Kentucky.

Different racing jurisdictions have different sets of rules. Some, such as Kentucky and Pennsylvania, allow horses to race on both bute and Lasix. Others, like Maryland and New Jersey, allow just Lasix. And still others, such as New York, permit neither. In some states, a horse must bleed during a race or workout before being allowed to race on Lasix. In others, a simple note from a veterinarian is sufficient. Some states, such as Florida, indicate in the track program those horses that are racing on Lasix. Others, such as California, reveal no such information. In most states where drugs are allowed, pertinent information can be found in the *Daily Racing Form* concerning which horses are scheduled to race on drugs that day.

It would be useless at this point to present the reader with a listing of tracks that permit racing on bute and/or Lasix. Several, no doubt, will change before this book reaches its audience. In fact, as this is being written, Florida is attempting to ban the use of both drugs, and the trainers are boycotting the entry box in protest. What this country needs is a uniform set of rules applying in all states, and full disclosure in the *Racing Form* past performances of each horse's prior and current use of drugs.

When a trainer ships a horse to a nearby drug state, he is telling everybody that his horse has physical problems, and needs the drugs to race effectively. Many of these trainers are hoping the drugs will provide the remedy. They often do—"first time on Lasix" is a powerful angle. However, even if such a horse wins on the drugs, don't expect the "improved" form to continue when the animal returns home. The Otter Slide story is typical of what likely will happen. Don't be influenced by a winning effort on drugs if the animal is later racing without them. Be careful with shippers from tracks where drugs are permissible. They may be well-meant, but unable to produce their best effort without that "little help from their friends."

CASE STUDY: OSCAR BARRERA

Seldom has a trainer enjoyed a season to compare with Oscar Barrera's during 1983. With a small stable of runners, he led the New York circuit in races won, totaling almost 100 victories for the year. His bread and butter was the claiming animal. Time after time, Barrera would reach in for a claim, then bring the horse back within a few days and have it ready. Notable examples of the Barrera magic were:

DANCER'S MELODY, a winner of two out of nineteen starts prior to being claimed for $8500, won first out for Oscar four days later for $14,000, then easily stretched out to a mile and five-sixteenths—no easy feat. The colt won an allowance contest at Aqueduct on April 9.

Dancer's Melody — **Dk. b. or br. c. 4, by Dance Spell—Dulia, by Dunce**
Own.—Barrera O S — **Br.—Gentry T (Ky)** — **Tr.—Barrera Oscar S** — **117**^{5}

Lifetime								
23 4 2 3	1983	10	3	2	1	$29,000
$40,610	1982	13	1	0	2	$11,610
	Turf	2	0	0	0	$330

31Mar83- 5Aqu	fst 1		:45⅘ 1:10⅕ 1:36⅖	Alw 21000	6	3	2^{1}	$2^{\frac{1}{2}}$	1^{hd}	$2^{1\frac{1}{4}}$	Samyn J L	b	122	*.70	83-21	BlazingComet117$^{1\frac{1}{4}}$Dancer'sMelody122$^{2\frac{1}{4}}$HughCapet119$^{2\frac{3}{4}}$	Gamely	9
23Mar83- 7Aqu	fst 7f		:22⅗ :45⅘ 1:24	Alw 20000	2	8	4^{6}	4^{3}	$2^{1\frac{1}{2}}$	$2^{\frac{1}{2}}$	Samyn J L	b	122	*2.30	80-28	Bambolino117$^{\frac{1}{2}}$Dancer'sMelody122^{5}CauseForAppluse117^{2}	Gamely	9
17Mar83- 3Aqu	fst 1 5/16		:47⅘ 1:38⅘ 2:11	Hcp 7500s	7	3	$2^{1\frac{1}{2}}$	1^{3}	1^{7}	1^{10}	Samyn J L	b	109	*1.50e	84-27	Dancer'sMelody109^{10}Hopehrd114$^{2\frac{3}{4}}$ElevtorShoes114$^{1\frac{3}{4}}$	Ridden out	9
14Mar83- 5Aqu	fst 6f	⊡	:22⅗ :45⅖ 1:09⅗	Clm 14000	4	6	$4^{3\frac{1}{2}}$	$3^{1\frac{1}{2}}$	1^{hd}	1^{4}	Samyn J L	b	113	7.80	96-10	Dancer'sMelody113^{4}RulerComeBack117$^{1\frac{3}{4}}$Recidin112$^{\frac{3}{4}}$	Drew clear	7
10Mar83- 1Aqu	sly 6f	⊡	:22⅘ :46⅘ 1:11⅗	Clm c-8500	7	11	7^{7}	$9^{7\frac{3}{4}}$	$6^{6\frac{1}{4}}$	$3^{7\frac{1}{2}}$	Graell A	b	117	4.20	78-17	Daddy Frank 110^{4} Golly Golly 108$^{3\frac{1}{2}}$ Dancer'sMelody117^{nk}	Rallied	14
27Feb83- 2Aqu	fst 6f	⊡	:23⅕ :47 1:12⅖	Clm 7500	8	8	$5^{2\frac{3}{4}}$	$5^{2\frac{1}{4}}$	$1^{\frac{1}{2}}$	$1^{3\frac{3}{4}}$	Graell A	b	117	6.20	82-20	Dancer's Melody 117$^{3\frac{3}{4}}$ Implosion 112^{1} Ierax 117^{2}	Driving	14
17Feb83- 1Aqu	fst 6f	⊡	:23⅕ :47 1:12⅗	Clm 10000	9	14	13^{9}	12^{12}	10^{15}	8^{11}	Graell A	b	117	10.90f	70-17	Foxmoor Flight 115$^{\frac{1}{2}}$ Omas Josh110^{1}OnTheCharles110^{2}	No factor	14
7Feb83- 9Aqu	my 6f	⊡	:23⅗ :47⅕ 1:12	Clm 10000	6	11	$8^{3\frac{3}{4}}$	$7^{5\frac{1}{2}}$	$4^{5\frac{1}{2}}$	5^{8}	Graell A	b	117	14.00	76-17	Phi Beta Key 112$^{3\frac{3}{4}}$ Come UpPence117$^{1\frac{1}{4}}$Joan'sPoker117^{2}	Rallied	12
31Jan83- 9Aqu	fst 6f	⊡	:22⅘ :46⅖ 1:12	Clm 12500	9	11	$11^{5\frac{1}{4}}$	9^{14}	9^{11}	6^{7}	Miranda J	b	117	18.40	77-15	Alturas 119$^{\frac{1}{2}}$ Extradite 113$^{1\frac{1}{2}}$ Christopher Star 108$^{1\frac{3}{4}}$	Far back	12
3Jan83- 3Aqu	fst 6f	⊡	:23⅗ :47⅖ 1:13⅖	Clm 16000	8	2	6^{7}	5^{7}	7^{11}	9^{10}	Venezia M		117	12.50	67-25	Busy Hilarious 112^{hd} RoguishManner107$^{4\frac{1}{2}}$Dark'NBold117^{nk}	Tired	9

LATEST WORKOUTS **Apr 6 Bel tr.t 4f fst :50⅗ b** **Mar 27 Bel tr.t 4f fst :49⅖ b** **Mar 7 Aqu ⊡ 4f sly :51⅕ b (d)** **●Feb 24 Aqu ⊡ 3f fst :35⅖ h**

ARDENT BID was two for twenty-three in 1982–83 prior to being claimed. This gelding won five of his first seven starts for Barrera, moving from $8500 claiming into allowance company. His first win for Oscar came four days after being claimed, two classes higher.

Ardent Bid — Gr. g. 4, by Buck's Bid—Ardent Amelia, by First Landing
Br.—Bright View Farm Inc (NJ)
Tr.—Barrera Oscar S
Own.—Barrera O S
114 — Lifetime 36 8 2 7 $90,465

	Starts	1st	2nd	3rd	Earnings
1983	16	7	0	3	$72,960
1982	16	0	2	3	$11,270
Turf	2	0	0	1	$1,920

6Jun83- 2Bel	gd	1⅜	[T]:48⅖ 1:39⅕ 2:18	3↑Hcp 16000s	5	7	7^{14}	$5^{6½}$	4^{5}	$3^{2¼}$	Smith A Jr	b 120	3.10e	65-31	Campus Capers 122^{1} Could It Be $114^{1¼}$ Ardent Bid 120^{3}	Fin. well	11
26May83- 7Bel	gd	1¼	[T]:49 1:39 2:04⅖	3↑Alw 27000	1	8	8^{21}	8^{19}	7^{19}	6^{18}	Davis R G^{5}	b 116	9.60	54-33	Tantalizing $121^{7¾}$ Silver Ring $119^{3¾}$ Groomed 119½	Outrun	8
21May83- 3Bel	gd	1 1/16	:44⅘ 1:08⅘ 1:41	3↑Alw 23000	4	10	10^{12}	$9^{9¾}$	$3^{7½}$	1¾	Davis R G^{5}	b 116	*3.20	97-07	ArdentBid116¾JmesBoswell119^{2}RockyMrrig$113^{4¾}$	Came out,drvng	12
15May83- 7Aqu	fst	1⅛	:47⅖ 1:12 1:51⅗	3↑Alw 23000	4	7	7^{9}	7^{11}	$6^{8½}$	$4^{7¾}$	Murphy D J^{7}	b 117▲	3.30e	69-18	Count Normandy $121^{1¼}$ Blazing Comet $121^{1½}$ Bishen108^{5}	Mild bid	7
15May83-Dead heat																	
13May83- 3Aqu	fst	1⅛	:47⅘ 1:13⅕ 1:52⅕	Clm 32500	3	7	7^{13}	$7^{8¼}$	5^{3}	1^{2}	Davis R G^{5}	b 112	*1.10	74-28	Ardent Bid 112^{2} Brae Axe 112½ Rollix 115^{2}	Drew clear	8
1May83- 2Aqu	fst	1⅛	:47⅗ 1:12⅕ 1:51⅕	Clm 35000	1	7	$6^{9½}$	$6^{7½}$	$3^{6½}$	$3^{4½}$	Murphy D J^{5}	b 114	*1.90	74-21	Startop's Ace 112^{4}LetterFromLucy116½ArdentBid114^{5}	Wide Str.	7
25Apr83- 6Aqu	my	1⅛	:48⅕ 1:13⅕ 1:50⅕	Alw 23000	9	3	$3^{2½}$	3½	$1^{2½}$	$1^{2½}$	Smith A Jr	b 117	*1.90e	84-20	Ardent Bid $117^{2½}$ Blazing Comet 119½ I'm So Merry 112^{5}	Driving	10
20Apr83- 9Aqu	gd	1	:46⅖ 1:11⅖ 1:36	Clm 16000	10	7	$5^{1¼}$	1½	1^{3}	$1^{6½}$	Davis R G^{5}	b 112	3.30	86-19	Ardent Bid $112^{6½}$ Inner Circuit 112^{5} Atractivo 113no	Driving	11
15Apr83- 1Aqu	fst	1⅛	:49⅗ 1:15 1:54⅘	Clm 12500	10	10	$9^{7¼}$	$6^{4½}$	$5^{2¾}$	1¾	Davis R G	b 114	4.20	61-29	ArdentBid114¾Milliard110¾AmericanRoyalty117¾	Blocked, driving	12
11Apr83- 9Aqu	my	1⅛	:48⅗ 1:13⅘ 1:52⅘	Clm c-8500	3	9	$9^{7¾}$	$8^{6¾}$	$7^{4¼}$	1½	Thibeau R J^{7}	b 112	*1.60	71-23	Ardent Bid 112½ Signoreante 117¾ Return For Glory 113^{3}	Driving	9

LATEST WORKOUTS Jun 10 Bel tr.t 3f fst :38 b Jun 5 Bel tr.t 3f fst :37 b May 11 Bel tr.t 4f fst :50 b Apr 30 Bel tr.t 3f fst :37⅗ b

Copyright © 1984, by DAILY RACING FORM, INC. Reprinted with permission of copyright owner.

COUNT ADVOCATE, also claimed for $8500, won three of his first seven starts for Oscar, with three seconds and a third, while competing in state-bred allowance and starter handicap company as well as in the high-priced claiming ranks.

Count Advocate — B. c. 4, by Turn and Count—Lucky Sari, by Advocator
Br.—Bricken Mrs J & Tantivy Inc (NY)
Tr.—Barrera Oscar S
Own.—Barrera O S
114^{5} — Lifetime 20 7 4 2 $83,900

	Starts	1st	2nd	3rd	Earnings
1983	11	5	4	1	$65,210
1982	6	1	0	0	$5,610

7May83- 3Aqu	fst	1⅛	:49⅘ 1:14⅕ 1:51⅖	Clm 45000	10	2	3^{3}	4^{3}	2^{6}	2^{9}	Smith A Jr	b 115	5.50	69-19	BrshrDoubloon119^{9}ContAdvoct$115^{2¼}$NphwScott117½	Best others	10
28Apr83- 8Aqu	fst	1⅛	:47⅖ 1:12 1:50⅘	3↑[S]Alw 41000	1	1	2^{hd}	2^{hd}	3^{3}	2^{3}	Davis R G^{5}	b 114	1.70	78-16	Shy Groom 124^{3}CountAdvocate114^{nk}Rajab'sSon$119^{2¼}$	Gained 2nd	8
18Apr83- 1Aqu	fst	1 5/16	:48⅖ 1:38⅗ 2:11⅗	3↑Hcp 10000s	1	3	3^{5}	3^{2}	1½	1¾	Smith A Jr	b 122	*.70e	81-25	Count Advocate 122¾ Atop ItAll108^{hd}FriendlyLetters112½	Driving	7
5Apr83- 5Aqu	fst	1 5/16	:47⅕ 1:38 2:11	3↑Hcp 12500s	6	6	3^{5}	2^{1}	2^{hd}	2no	Smith A Jr	b 117	*1.30	84-22	Soudan 115no Count Advocate 117^{5} Imaromeo $122^{3¼}$	Brushed	7
29Mar83- 6Aqu	gd	7f	:23⅖ :47⅘ 1:25⅗	[S]Alw 27000	4	7	4^{3}	2^{hd}	1^{1}	$1^{1¾}$	Davis R G^{5}	117	8.00	73-28	Count Advocate$117^{1¾}$OceanScandal117^{hd}Celia'sFirst$122^{1½}$	Driving	11
19Mar83- 1Aqu	my	1¼	:47⅕ 1:38⅖ 2:04⅗	Hcp 10000s	3	4	$3^{4½}$	1^{3}	1^{5}	1^{6}	Smith A Jr	b 113	5.30	73-21	Count Advocate 113^{6} Imaromeo 124¾ Ardent Bid 111^{5}	Driving	9
10Mar83- 7Aqu	sly	1 1/16	[•]:48 1:12⅘ 1:44⅖	[S]Alw 28500	4	3	2^{1}	$3^{2½}$	3^{5}	$3^{4¼}$	Alvarado R Jr^{5}	b 112	8.60	87-17	[D]ProvMWrong117^{no}DoblAtom$112^{4¼}$ContAdvoct$112^{7¼}$	Weakened	8
5Mar83- 2Aqu	fst	1¼	[•]:48⅗ 1:40⅖ 2:07	Clm c-8000	6	1	1^{6}	1^{8}	1^{5}	1^{3}	Hernandez R	b 114	*1.10	83-16	Count Advocate 114^{3} Ohno 108^{3} Cincelari 113^{6}	Driving	8
24Feb83- 9Aqu	fst	170	[•]:48 1:13⅘ 1:45⅗	Clm 8000	5	1	1^{5}	$1^{1½}$	1½	$1^{1½}$	Hernandez R	b 113	5.40	74-24	Count Advocate $113^{1½}$ Click Off$113^{1½}$KingofClassics$112^{3½}$	Driving	10
10Feb83- 9Aqu	fst	6f	[•]:23 :47⅕ 1:12⅗	Clm 8500	5	2	2½	$3^{1½}$	$4^{2¼}$	$5^{2¾}$	Cordero A Jr	b 117	*2.30	78-18	RomnSpry117^{nk}MickeyRooney$110^{2¼}$SouthrnPrinc108^{nk}	Weakened	12

LATEST WORKOUTS Apr 27 Bel tr.t 3f fst :37 b Apr 15 Bel tr.t 3f fst :39⅘ b Mar 27 Bel tr.t 4f fst :49⅕ h

Copyright © 1984, by DAILY RACING FORM, INC. Reprinted with permission of copyright owner.

HOT WORDS, three for twenty-three in 1982–83 prior to being claimed, won two of his first four starts for Barrera, including a powerful win four days after being claimed, and an allowance race two weeks later.

Hot Words — B. h. 8, by Verbatim—Napalm, by Nilo
$45,000 Br.—Nuckols Bros (Ky)
Tr.—Barrera Oscar S
Own.—Barrera O S
108^{5} — Lifetime 71 15 10 13 $241,698

	Starts	1st	2nd	3rd	Earnings
1983	11	4	1	3	$60,430
1982	16	1	2	2	$17,295
Turf	3	0	0	0	$75

13Jun83- 9Bel	fst	1	:45⅖ 1.09 1:34⅘	3↑Alw 37000	1	1	2^{hd}	1½	1^{2}	$2^{1¼}$	Samyn J L	b 117	4.30	90-12	Shy Groom $117^{1¼}$ Hot Words 117^{2} Silver Express 117^{hd}	Gamely	9
5Jun83- 7Bel	fst	7f	:22⅖ :45 1:22⅗	3↑Alw 35000	1	3	2^{3}	$2^{2½}$	$1^{1½}$	$1^{3¾}$	Thibeau R J^{5}	b 112	3.90	89-17	Hot Words $112^{3¾}$ Warcry 119¾ To Erin $117^{1¼}$	Drew clear	6
2Jun83- 2Bel	fst	1 1/16	:46⅖ 1:10⅘ 1:42⅕	Clm 72500	1	2	2^{hd}	3^{1}	3^{1}	$3^{2¾}$	Thibeau R J^{5}	b 110	*1.70	88-20	Act It Out 117^{hd} BrasherDoubloon$113^{2¾}$HotWords110^{4}	Weakened	6
23May83- 9Bel	my	1 1/16	:45⅖ 1:09⅘ 1:40⅘	Clm 35000	4	1	1^{hd}	1^{3}	1^{6}	1^{7}	Thibeau R J^{5}	b 112	4.00	98-16	Hot Words 112^{7} Letter From Lucy 115^{10} Mingo 112½	Ridden out	9
18May83- 3Bel	fst	6½f	:23 :46⅖ 1:17	Clm c-25000	9	13	$13^{7½}$	$13^{9¼}$	$9^{8¾}$	8^{5}	Davis R G^{5}	112	*3.00e	86-15	Cold Trailin' 117^{1} DealingDiplomat115^{nk}HerefordMan117½	Outrun	14
7May83- 9Aqu	fst	7f	:22⅗ :45⅗ 1:23⅕	Clm 25000	6	4	$4^{2½}$	9^{7}	$7^{5¼}$	3^{2}	Thibeau R J^{5}	112	7.30	83-19	Quick Rotation 117^{1} Mingo 110^{1} Hot Words 112no	Rallied	12
28Apr83- 3Aqu	fst	1⅛	:48⅘ 1:13 1:51⅖	Clm c-20000	1	1	1^{hd}	2^{hd}	1^{hd}	3^{2}	Cordero A Jr	117	*1.00	76-16	Cartucho 117½ Friendly Letters $117^{1½}$ Hot Words 117^{1}	Weakened	8
1Apr83- 7Hia	fst	7f	:22⅖ :44⅘ 1:22⅕	Clm 25000	7	4	$5^{2¾}$	$8^{7¼}$	$8^{7¼}$	$4^{4¼}$	Velez J A Jr	122	2.80	88-17	NocturnalPhantom120^{3}GustofReson116¾RoughDuck120½	Late bid	11
5Mar83-12GP	fst	1 1/16	:48⅘ 1:13⅖ 1:45⅖	Clm 20000	10	1	1½	1^{2}	1^{3}	$1^{7½}$	MacBeth D	119	*1.80	74-19	Hot Words$119^{7½}$Two'sNotEnough117^{nk}GovernorBob$117^{2½}$	Driving	12
16Feb83-10GP	sly	7f	:22⅖ :45⅗ 1:23⅘	Clm 25000	9	1	$3^{3½}$	$4^{3½}$	$4^{3½}$	5^{3}	MacBeth D	122	*2.20	82-23	GreatFanfre$113^{2½}$BishopsPride112^{nk}Tumig'sFlme122^{hd}	Weakened	10

LATEST WORKOUTS Jun 30 Bel tr.t 3f fst :38 b ●Jun 12 Bel tr.t 3f fst :35⅘ h Jun 1 Bel tr.t 3f gd :37 b

Copyright © 1984, by DAILY RACING FORM, INC. Reprinted with permission of copyright owner.

KENNY J., two for thirty-two over two years prior to being claimed for $7500, won five of six starts for Oscar before being lost for $10,000 after winning for as much as $20,000.

Kenny J. Dk. b. or br. g. 5, by Droll Role—Jennie Murphy, by Royal Serenade
Own.—Amendola R J $14,000 Br.—Carter Donald W (Ky) Tr.—Siravo Robert D 122
Lifetime 69 11 12 6 $122,663 | 1983 9 5 1 0 $39,070 | 1982 28 2 4 4 $20,103 | Turf 2 0 0 0

16May83-9Aqu	sly 7f	:23 :47 1:26⅖	Clm c-10000	7 1 1hd 1½ 12½ 1¾	Davis R G5	b 117	*1.50	69-28 Kenny J. 117¾ Whambang 107¾ Page Six 108¾	Driving 8
12May83-9Aqu	fst 6½f	:23⅕ :47 1:18⅖	Clm 15000	1 9 11½ 11½ 13 1½	Davis R G5	b 112	*1.50	83-20 Kenny J. 112½ Southern Shade 1172 Rasselas 1171½	Driving 12
5May83-9Aqu	fst 7f	:22⅕ :44⅘ 1:22⅖	Clm 30000	1 7 24 24 77½ 814	Thibeau R J5	b 108	3.70	75-21 Fanny'sFox1175AlecGeorge117½RaiseABuck1061¼	Stumbled break 10
17Apr83-2Aqu	gd 6f	:22⅖ :46⅖ 1:11⅖	Clm 19000	1 4 42½ 22½ 11½ 12	Davis R G5	b 112	*1.80	84-23 Kenny J. 1122 No Heir 1172 Spartan Monk 1171½	Steadied, clear 9
8Apr83-2Aqu	my 7f	:22⅗ :45⅖ 1:22⅗	Clm 20000	10 1 21 1½ 12½ 1nk	Davis R G5	b 108	4.60	88-17 Kenny J. 108nk Need A Penny 1121 DealingDiplomat115hd	Driving 13
5Apr83-2Aqu	fst 1	:46⅗ 1:11⅗ 1:37⅕	Clm 11500	9 2 1hd 16 16 13	Davis R G5	b 110	*2.60	80-22 Kenny J. 1103 Atop It All 1196½ Two Too Many 1152	Ridden out 10
29Mar83-3Aqu	gd 1	:47⅕ 1:12⅖ 1:38⅖	Clm c-7500	10 1 1½ 1½ 22 21½	Miranda J	b 117	5.70	72-28 Delta Leader 1121½ Kenny J. 1179 Irish Poplar 1121¼	Bumped 12
19Mar83-1Aqu	my 1¼	:47⅕ 1:38⅖ 2:04⅗	Hcp 10000s	2 1 2½ 714 829 835	Graell A	b 109	16.50	38-21 Count Advocate 1136 Imaromeo 124¾ Ardent Bid 1115	Used early 9
26Feb83-9Aqu	fst 6f	⊡:23⅕ :47⅘ 1:13⅕	Clm c-10000	2 5 21½ 32 56½ 68	Rogers K L	b 117	4.50	70-25 Foxmoor Flight 117½ Rapido's Repeat 1122¾AManShort1124	Tired 12
28Dec82-9Haw	sly 6½f	:22⅗ :45⅖ 1:18⅗	3↑Clm 15000	8 3 41½ 42 42¼ 811	Strauss R	b 115	4.70	69-26 Mr. Cleve T. 117½ Marty's First 1143 Thebian Ruler 1171¼	Tired 9

LATEST WORKOUTS Apr 15 Bel tr.t 4f fst :49⅗ b

THE MANGLER, purchased for $4,800 at a "horses of racing age" sale at Belmont Park on June 14, won four of his first six starts for Barrera. Prior to that, the five-year-old gelding had achieved only a maiden win in twenty-six career starts.

The Mangler Ch. g. 5, by Quadrangle—Manda Merelia, by Hasty Road
Own.—Barrera O S $16,500 Br.—Hosta Mr-Mrs V L (Va) Tr.—Barrera Oscar S 115
Lifetime 32 5 8 1 $67,210 | 1983 16 5 2 0 $40,565 | 1982 9 M 5 1 $20,170 | Turf 5 0 1 0 $5,055

20Jly83-2Bel	gd 1⅛	:47⅖ 1:12⅕ 1:52⅖	Clm 12000	6 3 1½ 3½ 32 1¾	Samyn J L	118	*2.30	65-25 The Mangler 118¾ Port On 1101¾ Spirited Song 1151	Driving 12
1Jly83-2Bel	hd 1⅜	[T]:46⅗ 1:36 2:13⅘	3↑Hcp 16000s	6 3 46 38 616 818	Velasquez J	112	*.90e	70-15 Could It Be 1174 American Royalty 1091¼ Exuberance 1114	Tired 11
11Jly83-2Bel	fst 1½	:49⅕ 2:05 2:31⅕	Clm 12000	5 3 34½ 1½ 11½ 14	Samyn J L	115	*1.40e	64-21 The Mangler 1154 Friendly Letters 108nk Milliard1126	Ridden out 10
3Jly83-4Bel	fst 1 1/16	:47⅕ 1:12 1:44⅘	Clm 17000	10 3 3½ 11 11½ 13¾	Samyn J L	115	3.60	78-20 The Mangler 1153¾ Milliard 1171½ Firstee 1171	Drew clear 13
25Jun83-4Bel	fst 1¼	:48⅗ 1:39⅖ 2:05⅘	Clm 19000	4 1 11 1½ 32 77¾	Samyn J L	115	*1.50e	61-22 Cartucho 117nk Joycapade 112no Port On 1081¾	Tired 8
22Jun83-3Bel	fst 1⅛	:47⅕ 1:11⅖ 1:50	Clm 12000	5 1 12 12½ 12 11¼	Samyn J L	113	*1.60e	77-22 The Mangler 1131¼ Friendly Letters1132¾Signoreante1154	Driving 10
10Jun83-3Bel	fst 6f	:23 :46⅕ 1:10⅖	Clm 12000	4 1 62½ 84¼ 77½ 77¾	Rogers K L	113	21.30f	82-11 RulerComBck1101¼ThisIsSmith117nkAnothrRodgr1081	Early foot 14
14May83-2Aqu	fst 1⅛	:49⅖ 1:14⅕ 1:54	Clm 10500	6 6 107 1113 1119 1121	Rogers K L	113	23.00	44-20 Letter Perfect 1122¾ Hopehard 1125 Signoreante 117½	Far back 12
30Apr83-3Aqu	fst 1⅛	:48 1:12⅖ 1:53⅘	Clm 15000	2 2 24 26 911 97¾	Santagata N	115	12.90	58-22 Oscar My Love 1171¾ Care Taker 117hd PerfectBidder1122½	Tired 10
20Apr83-9Aqu	gd 1	:46⅖ 1:11⅖ 1:36	Clm 16000	3 5 62¾ 63¾ 59½ 512	Migliore R	117	5.90	74-19 Ardent Bid 1126½ Inner Circuit 1125 Atractivo 113no	Evenly 11

LATEST WORKOUTS Jly 9 Bel tr.t 4f fst :49⅕ b   Jun 16 Bel tr.t 4f fst :49 b   Jun 5 Bel tr.t 4f fst :48⅘ h

JOYCAPADE AND WALKIN' ON AIR, the highly publicized daily double of June 1. Both horses won powerfully within a few days of being claimed while being moved up two classifications. Both were bet heavily at the track, with the double paying just $18.40.

Joycapade Ro. g. 5, by Icecapade—Our World, by Our Michael
Own.—Barrera O S $22,500 Br.—Winchell V H Jr (Ky) Tr.—Barrera Oscar S 110^5
Lifetime 54 4 5 10 $54,602 | 1983 8 0 1 4 $8,330 | 1982 14 3 1 4 $25,923 | Turf 9 0 1 3 $5,865

29May83-2Bel	fst 1⅛	:46⅗ 1:10⅘ 1:49⅘	Clm c-15000	8 4 43 31½ 21 21¼	Hernandez R	b 115	3.80	77-11 Inner Circuit 1171¼ Joycapade 1153¾AtopItAll107½	Best of others 8
19May83-2Bel	fst 1 3/16	:49⅖ 1:13⅖ 1:57⅗	Clm 15000	2 6 53½ 45½ 46 33	Davis R G5	b 110	7.40	89-12 Perfect Bidder 112hd Letter Perfect 1123 Joycapade 1105	Rallied 9
17Apr83-9Aqu	fst 7f	:23⅗ :47 1:25⅖	Clm 12500	9 8 87¼ 87 44 33¼	Santagata N	b 117	6.60	71-23 Hopehard 1122 Delta Leader 1101¼ Joycapade 1172¾	Rallied 9
5Apr83-3Aqu	fst 1	:48⅖ 1:14 1:39⅕	Clm 12500	7 4 42 2½ 32 32¼	Santagata N	b 117	6.30	68-22 Christy's Ridge 1191¼ SoAwesome1171Joycapade1171¼	Weakened 8
10Mar83-3Aqu	sly 1 1/16	⊡:47⅕ 1:12⅗ 1:46⅖	Clm 16000	5 12 1214 99 56 42¾	Santagata N	b 117	8.10[D]	78-17 On The Charles 1061½ BenMarino117½Rout113¾	Dw st.; came over 12
10Mar83-Disqualified and placed twelfth									
28Feb83-9Aqu	fst 1⅛	⊡:48⅕ 1:13 1:53⅘	Clm 14000	8 9 712 56 45 32	Santagata N	b 113	7.80	75-25 Mr. October 1121¼ Perfect Bidder 117¾ Joycapade 1131½	Rallied 11
31Jan83-1Aqu	fst 1½	⊡:49 2:06⅘ 2:33⅗	Hcp 10000s	1 6 65½ 55 56½ 66¾	Santagata N	117	7.50	76-15 Could It Be 1131¾ Soudan 118hdFairangle1052¾	Hesitated at start 8
14Jan83-9Aqu	fst 1¼	⊡:48⅗ 1:40⅕ 2:07	Hcp 10000s	2 — — — — —	Santagata N	b 122	5.70	— — Soudan 1144¾ [D]Tantivy 1091¾ Hail to Hardin 113no	Dwelt 10
19Dec82-1Aqu	fst 1 1/16	⊡:49 1:13⅘ 1:45⅘	3↑Clm 50000	3 6 67½ 67½ 613 613	Santagata N	b 117	6.80	71-23 Subordinate 1083½ GrandFelice1172¾NorthernRegent1133¾	Outrun 6
5Nov82-8Grd	my 1	:49⅘ 1:14⅘ 1:43⅖	3↑Clm 47500	4 9 914 79¾ 69½ 33¾	Beckon D	b 116	10.55	59-40 Snow Swoop 1161¼ Another Rodger 1112½ Joycapade 116½	Rallied 9

LATEST WORKOUTS May 31 Bel tr.t 4f my :50⅘ b   May 14 Bel tr.t 4f fst :53⅗ b   Apr 29 Bel tr.t 4f fst :51 b   Apr 2 Bel tr.t 4f fst :52 b

Walkin' On Air B. c. 3, by Step Nicely—Vent d' Amour, by Vent du Nord
Own.—Barrera O S $22,500 Br.—Mittman E (Fla) Tr.—Barrera Oscar S 110^5
Lifetime 12 1 1 2 $10,660 | 1983 9 1 1 2 $10,660 | 1982 3 M 0 0

27May83-3Bel	sly 7f	:23 :46 1:24⅕	Clm c-16000	13 1 1111 88½ 78¼ 45¼	Samyn J L	b 117	7.20	75-15 Talking Stranger 1082½ Ghent 1172½ Elite Class 117½	Mild bid 13
18May83-9Bel	fst 6f	:23 :46⅘ 1:12	Clm 16000	5 7 86¾ 65 65¼ 34¾	Samyn J L	117	7.20	77-15 Prohibited 1173¾ Leroy Beasley 1101 Walkin' On Air117hd	Rallied 10
5May83-3Aqu	fst 6f	:22⅕ :45⅗ 1:11⅘	Clm 20000	1 6 613 612 67 64¼	Samyn J L	119	29.60	78-21 Gourmet 106no True Coverup 1141¾ Valid Decision 117¾	Outrun 7
14Apr83-2Aqu	fst 6f	:23 :46⅘ 1:12⅘	Md 18000	7 4 42½ 22 21½ 1nk	Samyn J L	118	14.40	77-25 Walkin' On Air 118nk Upper Country 1182¼ Londono1181¾	Driving 10
1Apr83-4Aqu	fst 6f	:23⅗ :48⅖ 1:14⅗	Md 20000	7 7 97 97¾ 813 87	Asmussen S M5	113	11.20	61-30 Brightest Hope 115hd Mutiful 1222½ First Speaker 1221¾	Outrun 14
21Mar83-2Aqu	sly 7f	:22⅖ :45⅘ 1:25⅗	Md 18000	6 5 76½ 811 711 613	Asmussen S M5	113	3.90	60-26 J. Daniel B. 1221¾ Another Dunham1181¼SteelPier1202¼	No factor 14
18Feb83-4Aqu	fst 6f	⊡:23⅗ :49 1:15	Md 15000	6 7 65¼ 66½ 42½ 32½	Asmussen S M5	117	*3.10	66-27 Bishen 122¾ Brightest Hope 1221¾ Walkin' On Air 1171¾	Rallied 14
21Jan83-4Aqu	fst 6f	⊡:24 :48⅕ 1:13⅖	Md 15000	10 13 126¾ 72¼ 32 2¾	Asmussen S M5	117	7.60	76-15 Mugsy'sBoss118¾Wlkin'OnAir1171¾ResonbleWish118¾	Fin. strong 14
5Jan83-4Aqu	fst 1⅛	⊡:49⅕ 1:15⅕ 1:55⅗	Md 18000	10 5 47 34 412 617	Asmussen S M7	111	4.00	51-24 KingoftheSlopes1229¾SpiritOfAlm1171¼VeryRewrding1153¾	Tired 12
23Dec82-9Aqu	fst 1 1/16	⊡:48⅕ 1:14⅗ 1:49⅖	Md 20000	1 1 1hd 2½ 21½ 511	Miranda J	118	8.40	55-27 Monmrtre1163SpendYourCpitl1141¼VeryRewrding1115	Weakened 12

LATEST WORKOUTS May 31 Bel tr.t 3f my :38⅕ b   May 1 Aqu 4f fst :49 b

GOURMET, usually gasping for air after going five furlongs, won at a flat mile first time out for Oscar, then ran his "career race," blazing seven furlongs in 1:22.3 on the heels of a blistering :44.4 half. That effort set the three-year-old up for a sharp effort in a good allowance field on May 23.

Gourmet — Ch. c. 3, by Sauce Boat—Deep Dish Pie, by George Lewis
Br.—Farish W S III & Jones W L Jr (Ky)
Own.—Barrera O S — Tr.—Barrera Oscar S
1045 — Lifetime 22 7 6 1 $76,550 — 1983 10 5 3 0 $55,480 — 1982 12 2 3 1 $21,070

23May83-	7Bel	my	6f	:22⅕	:45⅖	1:10	3↑Alw 22000	7	3	2hd	1hd	1½	21¾	Davis R G5		108	2.60	90-16	Ski Jump 1161¾ Gourmet 1083 Structure 112nk	Gamely 10
15May83-	9Aqu	fst	7f	:22	:44⅘	1:22⅗	Clm 25000	10	1	12½	13	13	13¾	Davis R G5		114	*1.50	88-18	Gourmet 1143¾ Forty More 1105 Valid Decision 1106	Driving 10
11May83-	3Aqu	fst	1	:47⅘	1:13	1:38⅖	Clm 25000	10	1	11½	1½	12¼	12¼	Davis R G5		112	3.80	74-30	Gourmet 1122¼ Speier's Luck 1126½ Valid Decision 117½	Driving 11
5May83-	3Aqu	fst	6f	:22⅕	:45⅗	1:11⅘	Clm c-18000	2	3	1hd	1hd	11½	1no	Murphy D J7	b	106	*2.00	82-21	Gourmet 106no True Coverup 1141¾ Valid Decision 117¾	Lasted 7
8Apr83-	5Aqu	my	6f	:22⅕	:45⅗	1:11⅕	Clm 25000	6	4	53½	54½	57½	79	Cordero A Jr	b	113	*.90	76-17	Sir Prize Birthday 1153IronSovereign115¾OliverList112½	Checked 12
18Mar83-	7Aqu	sly	6f	:23⅕	:46⅘	1:11⅘	Clm 30000	1	4	11	13	14	2½	Smith A Jr	b	115	*2.00	81-27	Brooder's Tip 112½ Gourmet 115no Forty More 1065¾	Just failed 9
9Mar83-	9Aqu	gd	6f	⊡:23	:46⅘	1:11⅖	Clm 27500	5	2	11½	11	11½	11	Smith A Jr	b	115	*2.40	87-09	Gourmet 1151 Our Man Valentine 112¾GallantGeorge110¾	Driving 10
26Feb83-	2Aqu	fst	6f	⊡:23⅖	:48	1:13⅘	Clm 20000	11	3	11½	11½	14	12	Smith A Jr	b	117	*2.30	75-25	Gourmet 1172 Friendly Sign 1152 Irish Act 1083¼	Driving 14
19Feb83-	2Aqu	fst	6f	⊡:23⅕	:47⅕	1:13	Clm 30000	13	4	11	12½	1½	56½	Cordero A Jr	b	113	*3.00	72-20	J. Strap 1152¾ Feisty Lad 117nk Medieval's Son 110¾	Gave way 14
9Feb83-	1Aqu	fst	6f	⊡:22⅖	:45⅘	1:11⅕	Clm c-12500	5	3	44½	41½	2½	22¾	Alvarado R Jr5	b	112	3.20	85-20	Pleasure Jig 1172¾ Gourmet 1127GallopingDomino1172¼	Game try 6

LATEST WORKOUTS May 10 Bel tr.t 3f fst :38⅘ b — May 7 Bel tr.t 4f fst :48 h — Apr 18 Bel tr.t 3f fst :39⅕ b

THUNDER BRIDGE, perhaps the most astonishing of them all, had failed to win in his first twelve starts of the year before being claimed by Barrera, while competing at the $25,000 claiming level or lower. But in his first two starts for Oscar, Thunder Bridge blew out allowance fields by eleven and then eight lengths, beating stakes horses on the latter occasion.

Thunder Bridge — Ro. g. 5, by High Echelon—Successfully Yours, by Successor
Br.—Lake Donald (Ky)
Own.—Barrera O S — Tr.—Barrera Oscar S
1175 — Lifetime 50 7 5 7 $110,245 — 1983 14 2 2 2 $47,130 — 1982 23 3 3 3 $50,040 — Turf 1 0 0 0

10Jly83-	6Bel	fst	1 1/16	:46⅕	1:10⅗	1:42	3↑Alw 37000	5	7	42½	3½	15	18	Thibeau R J5	b	112	*1.40e	92-15	Thunder Bridge 1128Starbinia1173MortgageMan1141¼	Ridden out 8
6Jly83-	5Bel	fst	1⅛	:45⅘	1:09⅘	1:47⅖	3↑Alw 23000	3	4	3nk	15	18	111	Thibeau R J5	b	112	3.30	90-10	ThunderBridge11211InstntAlmode112noElPerico1131¼	Ridden out 7
2Jly83-	9Bel	fst	1⅛	:47⅕	1:11⅗	1:50⅕	Clm c-25000	3	9	73¾	74¼	41¾	2¾	Alvarado R Jr5		112	3.60	75-16	Imaromeo 117¾ Thunder Bridge 1123¾ Starhitch 117½	Steadied 11
20Jun83-	3Bel	gd	1 1/16	:46⅗	1:11	1:43	Clm 25000	8	4	35½	33½	43	51½	Alvarado R Jr5		112	3.70	85-14	LetterFromLucy117nkInnerCircuit1101Joycpde115hd	Wide stretch 8
8Jun83-	3Bel	fst	7f	:23⅕	:45⅘	1:23⅗	Clm 25000	12	11	116	911	87	31¾	Alvarado R Jr5		112	25.70	82-22	King Belgian 1121¾ Hereford Man110noThunderBridge112nk	Wide 13
21May83-	2Bel	gd	1 1/16	:46⅘	1:10	1:41⅕	Clm c-19000	3	5	43	25	35	45¼	Thibeau R J5		110	2.60	91-07	King Belgian 1084¾ HailtoHardin117noRaiseABuck117½	Weakened 7
11May83-	9Aqu	fst	1⅛	:49⅕	1:14⅕	1:52	Clm 18000	2	6	66	84¼	64½	33	Thibeau R J5		108	4.30	72-30	Friendly Letters 1122½ColdTrailin'117½ThunderBridge108¾	Rallied 10
28Apr83-	3Aqu	fst	1⅛	:48⅘	1:13	1:51⅖	Clm 20000	5	5	3½	41¾	33	53½	Maple E		117	12.10	74-16	Cartucho 117½ Friendly Letters 1171½HotWords1171	Wide stretch 8
8Apr83-	2Aqu	my	7f	:22⅗	:45⅖	1:22⅗	Clm 22500	12	2	1210	1113	815	79¼	Graell A		115	7.80e	79-17	Kenny J 108nk Need A Penny 1121 Dealing Diplomat 115hd	Wide 13
21Mar83-	5Aqu	sly	7f	:22⅕	:44⅘	1:23⅗	Clm 25000	4	10	1011	1216	713	511	Maple E		117	5.20	72-26	The Bloody Best1104¾HerefordMan1125¼ColdTrailin'117nk	Rallied 12

LATEST WORKOUTS Jly 18 Bel tr.t 4f fst :48 h — ●Jly 9 Bel tr.t 3f fst :35⅕ h — Jly 4 Bel tr.t 4f fst :48⅕ h — Jly 2 WO tr.t 4f fst :50 bg

Serious handicappers make it a point to keep abreast of recent developments in the claiming wars. They are well aware of who currently has the hot hand at the claiming box.

Some horsemen are particularly adept at spotting horses with physical ailments affecting their performance, and then correcting those problems, perhaps with just a simple change of equipment. Others have the knack for claiming durable types with a touch of "back class" capable of performing frequently and in higher claiming brackets. Both—the equipment change and the back class—were often parts of Barrera's pattern.

Of course, when a claiming trainer suddenly develops a hot hand the question of drugs arises. It is entirely conceivable that an illegal drug will fall into the hands of a dishonest trainer, with an inexplicable hot streak the usual result. The trainer will ride the crest of the wave until the streak is broken, when the racetrack's chemists devise a test to identify the drug.

Although patently unfair to rival horsemen, situations of this sort actually favor the alert handicapper.

Whether the trainer involved is using tender loving care or black magic should be of no concern to handicappers. Their primary worry should be how to get their money safely from the vault to the racetrack so they can invest it on that trainer's recent claims.

When a horse ships in from a lesser track, and its form there appears dull, beware! Look at its record carefully. If one of your circuit's leading riders has accepted the mount, look again. Find out what the horse is capable of doing when at its best, because it probably is set for a peak effort. Has the trainer "raided" your circuit successfully in the past? Watch the odds board. The horse should be a longshot. If it isn't, you can be sure the stable is betting rather heavily.

CASE STUDY: SNOWGUN

Why would Fred Federico ship Snowgun to New York? The animal finished "absolutely" in its latest start at Suffolk Downs, beaten twenty-two lengths while losing fourteen lengths in the last eighth mile. And why would the New York crowd bet the horse down to 6–1, lower than its odds at Suffolk? It wasn't the drop in class—where this horse fit in New York was anybody's guess, based on its Suffolk form. And if New York money lowered the odds, it was only following New England money to the windows. Credit trainer Federico for knowing that his horse was fit, and especially for placing it properly in New York, and mark his name down for future reference, so that when he ships another horse, you'll know he is a man to be respected.

CASE STUDY: J. R. COLLINS

When J. R. Collins shipped over to Aqueduct on May 14, 1983, New Yorkers looked at his three most recent efforts and laughed. They should have looked more carefully. The clues were plentiful. The horse was entered in a "nonwinners of one" grass marathon at a mile and three-eighths, exactly what a son of Majestic Light from a Santa Claus mare would prefer. If the horse were not ready for such a challenge, trainer Chase could have easily arranged for some exercise at Monmouth, but the gelding's bullet workout on April 22 hinted of improving form, and jockey Fell's willingness to accept the mount confirmed this.

J. R. Collins had raced once previously on the grass, as a two-year-old at the Meadowlands. Note three things about that race. The obvious one is that he raced well on that occasion. More significantly, he improved noticeably when introduced to the grass, suggesting a true aptitude for grass racing. And, most interestingly, the horse's odds dropped sharply on that occasion. Apparently, someone knew beforehand that the horse would take to the grass, and now he was being given his second chance. New Yorkers who recognized Majestic Light as a "potential" grass sire, and took the time to dig into this horse's history, were rewarded to the tune of $48.60. The colt led all the way, drawing off nicely through the lane.

One might bring up two points against believing J. R. Collins. First, the grass marathon may have been a desperate move on the part of the trainer, all else having failed. But there was considerable evidence that this was not the case. Second, the horse had raced poorly in April when shipped to New York. On that occasion, however, the race was obviously meant for exercise, the stable having shipped into Monmouth well before that track opened for racing. When J. R. Collins returned (to Belmont) two weeks later for another grass marathon, New Yorkers were

J. R. Collins — **B. g. 3, by Majestic Light—Biwa, by Santa Claus**
Own.—Turvan Stable — **Br.—Stonereaty Farm & Westerly Stud Fm (Ky)**
Tr.—Chase Baden P — **110**

	Lifetime				
15 2 2 4	**1983**	4 1 0 0	**$12,750**
$29,250	**1982**	11 1 2 4	**$16,500**
	Turf	2 1 0 1	**$13,810**

14May83- 1Aqu	fm 1⅜ Ⓣ	:49 1:40⅗ 2:18⅖	3↑Alw 21000	9	1	$1^{1\frac{1}{2}}$	1^{1}	1^{4}	$1^{3\frac{1}{4}}$	Maple E		113	23.30	79-14	J. R. Collins $113^{3\frac{1}{4}}$ So Intent 110^{hd} Jeffers West $121^{2\frac{1}{2}}$	Driving 12
29Apr83- 5Mth	fst 170	:46⅕ 1:10⅖ 1:41⅖	3↑Alw 10500	2	4	$6^{8\frac{1}{4}}$	6^{12}	6^{14}	6^{13}	Rocco J	b	109	15.20	76-14	Courteous Majesty $111^{1\frac{1}{2}}$ Dashing Duke $109^{3\frac{1}{2}}$ Kvell 114^{2}	Tired 9
6Apr83- 7Aqu	fst 6f	:22⅕ :45⅖ 1:10⅘	Alw 20000	2	9	11^{16}	11^{20}	11^{22}	11^{22}	Melendez J D5	b	112	71.10	65-22	Now's The Time$117^{\frac{3}{4}}$AgileShoebill$112^{1\frac{3}{4}}$ARomanKaper$117^{\frac{1}{2}}$	Outrun 11
7Feb83- 6GP	gd 1 1/16	:47⅖ 1:12 1:44⅖	Alw 15000	2	4	4^{5}	7^{12}	9^{17}	9^{23}	McCauley W H	b	122	14.90	56-21	Asked To Run 122^{2} Moon Spirit $117^{2\frac{1}{2}}$ Catch And Run $117^{\frac{1}{2}}$	Tired 10
29Dec82- 5Med	fst 170	:47⅖ 1:12⅖ 1:43⅖	Md Sp Wt	1	2	$3^{1\frac{1}{2}}$	4^{3}	$2^{\frac{1}{2}}$	2^{hd}	McCauley W H	b	118	2.00	84-18	[D]Manspray 118^{hd} J. R. Collins 118^{2} Tina's Double 118^{5}	Bumped 8
29Dec82-Placed first through disqualification																
11Dec82- 4Med	fst 170	:47⅗ 1:14 1:45⅖	Md Sp Wt	10	2	2^{1}	1^{4}	1^{1}	$2^{2\frac{1}{2}}$	McCauley W H	b	118	7.20	71-21	Bannow Rambler $118^{2\frac{1}{2}}$ J. R. Collins118^{1}DiscoDom$113^{\frac{1}{2}}$	Weakened 10
1Dec82- 7Med	sly 1 1/16	:47⅖ 1:12⅖ 1:47⅕	Md Sp Wt	1	4	4^{5}	3^{4}	2^{5}	$3^{5\frac{1}{2}}$	Cordero A Jr	b	118	2.60	67-20	HedofthHous$118^{\frac{1}{2}}$ApchCompny118^{5}J.R.Collins$118^{\frac{3}{4}}$	Bid, weakened 8
2Nov82- 4Med	gd 1 Ⓣ	:47⅕ 1:11⅘ 1:38⅖	Md Sp Wt	3	4	$4^{2\frac{1}{2}}$	$2^{1\frac{1}{2}}$	$2^{\frac{1}{2}}$	$3^{\frac{3}{4}}$	McCauley W H	b	118	*2.70	81-18	Mucho Frio 118^{nk} Bannow Rambler $118^{\frac{1}{2}}$ J.R.Collins$118^{2\frac{1}{2}}$	Gamely 10
7Oct82- 1Med	fst 1	:46⅘ 1:12⅖ 1:40⅗	Md Sp Wt	4	5	6^{9}	$6^{9\frac{1}{2}}$	4^{8}	$5^{9\frac{1}{2}}$	Verge M E	b	118	5.20	69-19	Tarpaulin $118^{2\frac{1}{2}}$ Sir Wajima 118^{3} Fight Inflation 118^{3}	Drifted Out 8
23Sep82- 3Med	fst 6f	:22⅗ :46⅗ 1:13	Md Sp Wt	4	4	4^{7}	3^{10}	6^{12}	5^{15}	Verge M E	b	118	3.50	63-24	Bet Big $118^{4\frac{1}{2}}$ Arctic Lark 118^{6} Sixisenough 118^{3}	No factor 7

LATEST WORKOUTS May 13 Mth 3f fst :36 b ●Apr 22 Mth 7f fst 1:27 h Apr 2 GP 3f fst :37 b Mar 28 GP 6f fst 1:18 b

faced with a standard dilemma. If favored, he won May 14 because of a track bias favoring early speed. If a decent price, he was an impressive winner on that occasion, a horse with stakes potential, and likely to repeat. Handicappers are faced with interpretations of this sort every day, and the odds often decide the issue. In the case of J. R. Collins, the odds were 3–1 on May 28. The colt ran a game race on the front end, but faltered late to finish fourth to older horses.

With shippers other than the "ad hoc" type, the question comes down to the ability or preference of the individual trainer or horse. Layoffs may also be involved. Some trainers like to (try to) win first out after a layoff, or at a new track. Others give their horses a race or two before cracking down. Some horses run well when fresh. Many are able to carry their form from one track to another with little difficulty. It is helpful to be aware of how a barn is doing since arriving on the local circuit. Sometimes, it seems the entire string goes well first time out. Other times, the entire barn needs a race or two of preparation. This simply reflects what the trainer was able to accomplish with his horses before shipping in.

Does a horse need a race over the track? Can a horse learn from the experience of one race how to handle a (possibly different) surface? Not at all! A horse is not going to make adjustments in its stride to handle a deeper, or harder, surface. The trainers answering our questionnaire were unanimous in their response to this question. Either a horse likes a surface, or it doesn't. Variances in its form cycle might suggest the opposite, as might differences in the surface from one day to the next. Some horses simply prefer the sandy New York courses, while others like to hear their feet rattle over the hard California surfaces. And still others appreciate the deep cushions found at places like the Fair Grounds and Churchill Downs.

CASE STUDY: POLITE REBUFF

Polite Rebuff provided an excellent example of "horses for courses" when entered in the second division of the Affectionately Handicap at Aqueduct on January 22, 1983. The two victories that appear in her past performances were over Aqueduct's Inner Course, the surface on which the Affectionately would be contested. In addition, Polite Rebuff was a fresh horse, having raced just twice since returned to the races for a winter campaign. Her rallying effort at six furlongs was promising. Her tiring performance over a route distance January 3 was deceptive—she raced three-wide around both turns on that occasion, her first distance race in months. Improvement should have been expected from Polite Rebuff in the Affectionately. And when 3–5 favorite Cheap Seats, carrying 121 pounds, found herself embroiled in a suicidal speed duel, Polite Rebuff's chances of staging an upset were enhanced considerably. Returning to her form of the previous winter, Polite Rebuff came on in the stretch to win, and paid a generous $31.80.

Polite Rebuff — B. f. 4, by Wajima—Merely, by Dr Fager
Br.—Spendthrift Farm (Ky)
Own.—El Rancho Murietta — Tr.—Kay Michael
110 — Lifetime 19 4 3 2 $115,820 — 1983 1 0 0 0 — 1982 9 2 0 1 $73,626 — Turf 1 0 0 0

3Jan83- 8Aqu	fst	1^{70} ⊡	:50⅕ 1:15⅘ 1:45⅘	ⒻAlw 35000	5	4	$3^{1/2}$	4^{1}	$5^{4 1/2}$	$6^{4 1/2}$	Lovato F	b	117	*1.00	69-25	Halo Again 117^{1} Debonair Dancer 117^{hd} HarlemQueen$112^{1 1/2}$	Wide	7
22Dec82- 7Aqu	fst	6f ⊡	:23 :46⅘ 1:12⅘	3↑ ⒻAlw 37000	4	7	$4^{5 1/2}$	$4^{4 1/2}$	4^{4}	$3^{2 3/4}$	Cordero A Jr	b	113	3.20	78-22	ChristmsBonus$115^{1 3/4}$ExplosivKingdom110^{1}PoltRbuff113^{nk}	Rallied	8
14Aug82- 8Sar	fst	1¼	:48⅖ 1:36⅘ 2:02⅕	ⒻAlabama	4	6	6^{4}	$6^{6 1/2}$	$6^{6 1/2}$	$6^{8 1/2}$	Vasquez J	b	121	18.40	80-11	Broom Dance 121^{hd} Too Chic $121^{2 1/4}$ MademoiselleForli$121^{1/2}$	Tired	7
24Jly82- 9Mth	fst	1⅛	:47⅘ 1:11⅖ 1:49⅖	ⒻMth Oaks	6	4	$4^{3/4}$	$4^{3/4}$	$5^{7 1/2}$	6^{10}	Brumfield D	b	121	28.30	78-14	Christmas Past $121^{1 1/4}$ Milingo $119^{1 1/4}$MademoiselleForli$112^{1 1/2}$	Tired	9
4Jun82- 8Bel	fst	1⅛	:45⅘ 1:09⅘ 1:48⅖	ⒻMthr Goose	1	4	$3^{7 1/2}$	$3^{6 1/2}$	6^{11}	8^{15}	Fell J	b	121	57.00	70-18	Cupecoy'sJoy$121^{3/4}$ChristmasPast$121^{3 1/4}$BlushWithPride$121^{4 3/4}$	Tired	12
22May82- 8Bel	fst	1	:46 1:09⅗ 1:34⅕	ⒻAcorn	2	8	$7^{4 1/2}$	7^{6}	$6^{7 1/2}$	6^{10}	Fell J	b	121	25.60	85-11	Cupecoy's Joy $121^{2 3/4}$ Nancy Huang $121^{3 1/2}$ Vestris $121^{2 1/4}$	No factor	9
14Apr82- 8Aqu	fst	1	:47⅕ 1:13 1:38⅖	ⒻRare Perfume	1	7	$7^{8 1/2}$	6^{11}	6^{16}	6^{21}	Samyn J L	b	121	1.90	53-26	Nafees $112^{1 1/2}$ Middle Stage $112^{1 3/4}$ Beau Cougar $112^{1 3/4}$	Poor start	7
14Feb82- 8Aqu	fst	1⅛ ⊡	:48⅕ 1:13 1:51	ⒻRuthless	3	2	2^{4}	2^{2}	1^{2}	1^{4}	Cordero A Jr	b	118	*1.20	91-18	Polite Rebuff 118^{4} Girlie $118^{3 3/4}$ Thoughtless Doll 114^{3}	Driving	4
30Jan82- 8Aqu	fst	1 1/16 ⊡	:48⅘ 1:13⅗ 1:46⅗	ⒻSearching	5	4	$5^{1 3/4}$	$5^{3 1/4}$	4^{7}	4^{13}	Cordero A Jr	b	118	*.40	67-21	Girlie $116^{1/2}$ Adept $112^{4 1/2}$ Middle Stage $113^{7 1/2}$	Wide	8
16Jan82- 8Aqu	fst	1 1/16 ⊡	:46⅗ 1:11⅗ 1:44⅕	ⒻBusanda	6	5	3^{7}	$3^{1 1/2}$	1^{2}	$1^{3 3/4}$	Cordero A Jr	b	114	*1.70	92-10	Polite Rebuff $114^{3 3/4}$ Girlie $116^{3 3/4}$ Thoughtless Doll113^{1}	Ridden out	7

LATEST WORKOUTS Jan 20 Bel tr.t 4f fst :49⅘ h Jan 13 Bel tr.t 4f fst :49⅕ h Jan 2 Bel tr.t 3f fst :38 b Dec 21 Bel tr.t 3f fst :36⅖ b

Possibly the most significant factor confounding this issue is the matter of acclimatization. Horses often need time to become accustomed to new surroundings. This is especially true of nervous types. The different noises and smells associated with a new stall can put a horse off its feed for days. For that matter, different feed and water found in another locale can have the same effect. If raced while still unhappy or uneasy about its living quarters, a horse will probably race poorly, its mind not on the business at hand. After all, how would you feel if taken from your stall at warm, beautiful Hialeah, placed on a van heading north to Belmont Park, then dropped off in a stall overlooking noisy Hempstead Turnpike?

Foreign imports pose a special problem. Many are accustomed to a more relaxed style of training, and riders who exert little pressure in the early stages of a race. Because of this, many imports race well right off the plane, then go downhill thereafter, until fully acclimated.

□ DISTANCE CHANGES □

The typical past performance profile will include races at both sprint and route distances. A distance change may be an experiment on the part of the trainer, attempting to discover the animal's true distance preferences. Or it may be for the sake of conditioning. A sprinter may be entered in a route to build up its stamina, or a router entered in a sprint to sharpen its speed. Do distance changes really advance a horse's conditioning? Are there certain signs in the horse's performance at the opposite distance worth looking for?

Horses switching distances generally are at a disadvantage. For those stretching out from a sprint to a route, the disadvantage is relatively small. Early speed sharpened in sprint competition usually places such horses on or near the early lead in a subsequent route—a favorable position. When a proven router rallies smartly in a sprint race just prior to stretching out, it is telling one and all that it is fit and ready for a top effort at its preferred distance.

Astute handicappers are familiar, however, with the "rallying sprinter" type. The horse will rally smartly at sprint distances, as if it would appreciate a longer race. But when given the opportunity to go farther, its rally fizzles, or it tires after setting the pace to the stretch. The horse can travel just so far, and no farther. When dealing with a horse stretching out for the first time, the handicapper must be aware that a strong finish at a shorter distance is no guarantee that the horse will appreciate the longer trip.

CASE STUDY: FACES UP

An occasional horse becomes a specialist at seven furlongs. Possibly limited by its breeding to the sprint distances, the horse for some reason is not quick enough to contend at six furlongs. Unable to win over shorter distances as a two-year-old, Faces Up won four races at three, each at seven furlongs. He was too slow to catch up at six furlongs, and hung the only time he reached contention at a distance.

As a son of What A Pleasure, one might have anticipated that Faces Up would be a sprinter, but not one totally devoid of early speed. His dam, Magic, interestingly, was an unraced daughter of Horse of the Year Buckpasser and a half-sister to another champion, the incredibly fast Dr. Fager.

Faces Up — **B. c. 3, by What a Pleasure—Magic, by Buckpasser**
Br.—Tartan Farms (Fla)
Own.—Tartan Stable — **Tr.—Nerud Jan H**
111

Lifetime								
16 4 1 4	1982	10	4	1	2	$58,200
$63,480	1981	6	M	0	2	$5,280
	Turf	1	0	0	0	

19Nov82- 7Aqu	fst	7f	:23⅕	:46⅕	1:23⅕	3↑ Alw 23000	8	8	$8^{5\frac{1}{2}}$	4^{4}	$1^{2\frac{1}{2}}$	$1^{4\frac{3}{4}}$	Cordero A Jr	b	117	*1.00	85-23	Faces Up $117^{4\frac{3}{4}}$ King Naskra 110no HailEmperor$117^{1\frac{3}{4}}$	Ridden out	8
10Nov82- 7Aqu	fst	7f	:23⅖	:46⅗	1:23⅗	3↑ Alw 20000	3	7	6^{5}	$5^{2\frac{1}{4}}$	$1^{\frac{1}{2}}$	$1^{3\frac{1}{4}}$	Cordero A Jr	b	115	2.00	83-24	FcesUp$115^{3\frac{1}{4}}$DeterminedBidder$120^{1\frac{3}{4}}$HnryWillims119^{no}	Drew clear	7
27Oct82- 6Aqu	fst	1	:46⅕	1:10⅗	1:35⅕	3↑ Alw 21000	5	9	$8^{6\frac{3}{4}}$	$5^{5\frac{1}{2}}$	$5^{5\frac{1}{2}}$	$4^{4\frac{1}{4}}$	Cordero A Jr		114	4.20e	86-17	Exclusive Era $114^{1\frac{1}{2}}$CountNormandy110^{1}ConditionRed$106^{1\frac{3}{4}}$	Wide	9
25Sep82- 5Bel	fst	$1\frac{1}{16}$	:48⅕	1:12⅖	1:42⅖	3↑ Alw 21000	2	7	$3^{1\frac{1}{2}}$	2^{1}	2^{hd}	$2^{\frac{3}{4}}$	Cordero A Jr		113	7.40	89-15	Trenchant $118^{\frac{3}{4}}$ Faces Up 113^{5} Skin Dancer 113^{1}	Off slowly	7
11Sep82- 5Bel	fst	6f	:22⅘	:45⅗	1:10⅖	3↑ Alw 20000	2	7	$6^{6\frac{1}{2}}$	$6^{7\frac{3}{4}}$	$3^{6\frac{1}{2}}$	3^{3}	Skinner K		113	*1.50e	87-12	Roughcast $122^{1\frac{1}{4}}$ Citius $118^{1\frac{3}{4}}$ Faces Up $113^{2\frac{1}{2}}$	Wide	7
20Aug82- 7Sar	fm	1½ Ⓣ	:50	2:04⅖	2:28⅗	3↑ Alw 21000	4	5	$6^{7\frac{1}{2}}$	$7^{7\frac{1}{2}}$	7^{10}	7^{17}	Cordero A Jr		112	13.30	82-11	Half Iced $112^{7\frac{3}{4}}$ Natomas Breeze 117^{nk} Lamerok 114^{hd}	Outrun	8
29Jun82- 7Bel	sly	$1\frac{1}{16}$	:46	1:10⅕	1:41⅕	3↑ Alw 21000	1	4	$4^{6\frac{1}{2}}$	3^{7}	$3^{7\frac{1}{2}}$	3^{15}	Cordero A Jr		113	8.10	81-13	Exclusive One $112^{1\frac{1}{4}}$ Singh Tu 112^{14} Faces Up $113^{2\frac{3}{4}}$	Evenly	6
5Jun82- 2Bel	gd	7f	:22⅘	:45⅖	1:23	3↑ Alw 19000	10	5	$4^{2\frac{1}{4}}$	4^{2}	$3^{\frac{1}{2}}$	$1^{\frac{1}{2}}$	Cordero A Jr		113	3.90	87-11	Faces Up $113^{\frac{1}{2}}$ Straight Main 110^{hd} Hardy Hawk 110no	Driving	10
10May82- 6Aqu	fst	1⅛	:50⅗	1:16	1:53⅕	Alw 20000	3	7	$8^{4\frac{1}{4}}$	$7^{6\frac{3}{4}}$	$6^{4\frac{3}{4}}$	6^{4}	Cordero A Jr		117	*1.80	65-29	Otter Slide 122^{nk} Dom And Jerry $122^{\frac{1}{2}}$ Half Iced 117^{2}	Dull	8
21Apr82- 6Aqu	fst	7f	:23	:46⅕	1:24⅕	3↑ Md Sp Wt	1	6	$7^{5\frac{3}{4}}$	5^{8}	3^{5}	1^{1}	Cordero A Jr		114	2.30e	80-24	Faces Up 114^{1} Roulette Wheel 112^{hd} Fulton $114^{5\frac{1}{2}}$	Driving	7

LATEST WORKOUTS **Dec 2 Bel tr.t 4f sly :52⅖ b** **Nov 27 Bel 4f fst :48 b** **Nov 4 Bel tr.t 4f fst :50 b** **Oct 25 Bel 3f fst :38⅗ b**

Many tracks are unable to card races at seven furlongs. Seven-furlong specialists, then, must either ship out to find a race at their favorite distance, rest, or race at less favorable distances while awaiting another meet. Alert handicappers also eagerly await the appearance of such horses at a later meet.

Experienced handicappers are also aware that horses that tire badly at sprint distances often carry their speed much farther in a route. The slower route pace gives the horse a chance to relax and settle into stride. Possibly, the horse may never have raced as far. Equally as likely, the horse may never have been asked to race as slowly in the early stages of a race. Such was the case with Count Advocate on February 24. After weakening at six panels, he was able to get a clear lead at the route distance, set a leisurely pace, then have enough left to pull away when challenged in the stretch. In effect, he had turned the route into a four-furlong sprint. He returned $12.80 to those who were aware of the possibility and not afraid to support a horse that was stretching out after a tiring performance at a shorter distance.

Count Advocate — B. c. 4, by Turn and Count—Lucky Sari, by Advocator
$8,000 Br.—Bricken Mrs J & Tantivy Inc (NY)
Own.—Brennan Robert — Tr.—Coletti Edward J
113 — Lifetime 12 3 1 1 $26,370 — 1983 3 1 1 0 $7,680 — 1982 6 1 0 0 $5,610

24Feb83- 9Aqu	fst	1^{70}	⊡:48	1:13⅘	1:45⅗	Clm 8000	5	1	1^{5}	$1^{1\frac{1}{2}}$	$1^{\frac{1}{2}}$	$1^{1\frac{1}{2}}$	Hernandez R	b 113	5.40	74-24	Count Advocate $113^{1\frac{1}{2}}$ Click Off$113^{1\frac{1}{2}}$KingofClassics$112^{3\frac{1}{2}}$	Driving	10
10Feb83- 9Aqu	fst	6f	⊡:23	:47⅕	1:12⅗	Clm 8500	5	2	$2^{\frac{1}{2}}$	$3^{1\frac{1}{2}}$	$4^{2\frac{1}{4}}$	$5^{2\frac{3}{4}}$	Cordero A Jr	b 117	*2.30	78-18	RomnSpry117^{nk}MickeyRooney$110^{2\frac{1}{4}}$SouthrnPrinc108^{nk}	Weakened	12
30Jan83- 3Aqu	fst	6f	⊡:23	:46⅖	1:13	Clm 8500	3	9	$7^{7\frac{1}{2}}$	$5^{6\frac{1}{2}}$	3^{3}	2^{1}	Hernandez R	b 117	16.60	78-20	Total Run 117^{1} Count Advocate $117^{\frac{1}{2}}$ Saltseller $113^{\frac{1}{2}}$	Rallied	14
26Sep82- 3FL	fst	6f	:22⅗	:46	1:12	3↑ⓈClm 10000	3	8	$7^{7\frac{1}{2}}$	8^{11}	8^{11}	$7^{6\frac{3}{4}}$	Laiz G	113	3.80	82-14	Bout 119no Giovanni'sExpress$113^{\frac{3}{4}}$Sportman'sPrince113^{no}	Outrun	8
29Aug82- 9FL	fst	1^{70}	:48	1:13	1:44⅕	3↑ⓈAlw 9900	1	3	5^{4}	$5^{4\frac{1}{4}}$	6^{6}	$6^{4\frac{3}{4}}$	Whitley K	115	9.60	75-18	Stans Choice $119^{\frac{1}{2}}$ Starkly Babe $113^{\frac{1}{2}}$ Mister Kite 115^{1}	Tired	7
20Aug82- 8FL	sly	6f	:23	:46⅗	1:11⅘	3↑ⓈAlw 9600	9	2	$4^{1\frac{1}{2}}$	$6^{4\frac{1}{2}}$	$7^{5\frac{3}{4}}$	$6^{9\frac{3}{4}}$	Laiz G	114	4.10	80-24	Dynasty Doll 109^{3} Bold Arrow 115^{1} Starkly Babe $113^{\frac{1}{2}}$	Early foot	9
1Aug82-10FL	fst	6f	:22⅕	:45⅗	1:12⅖	3↑ⓈAlw 8800	2	5	3^{3}	3^{2}	3^{1}	$1^{\frac{3}{4}}$	Laiz G	113	*1.90	87-15	Count Advocate $113^{\frac{3}{4}}$ Mister Kite$114^{\frac{1}{2}}$SterlingDisplay114^{1}	Driving	11
7Jly82- 6Mth	fst	6f	:22⅖	:45	1:10⅖	Clm 35000	7	3	3^{5}	$4^{6\frac{1}{2}}$	$4^{5\frac{1}{2}}$	$5^{4\frac{1}{2}}$	Gonzalez B	116	18.80	83-16	Old King Cole $111^{4\frac{1}{2}}$ Tech 116no Dale's Gros 107no	Tired	7
29Jun82- 8Mth	fst	6f	:22⅖	:45⅕	1:10	3↑Alw 10000	4	3	5^{2}	7^{11}	7^{12}	$6^{8\frac{3}{4}}$	Gonzalez B	109	10.20	81-12	Over Deposited 116^{2} Silver Salt 112^{5} MickeyRooney111^{no}	Outrun	7
10Dec81- 5Aqu	fst	$1\frac{1}{16}$	⊡:48⅖	1:13⅗	1:46⅖	ⓈAlw 19000	3	1	1^{hd}	1^{hd}	1^{hd}	3^{4}	Verge M E[5]	114	7.10	78-18	PerfectCut117^{4}FadedPoster117^{hd}CountAdvocate$114^{5\frac{3}{4}}$	Weakened	10

LATEST WORKOUTS ●Jan 22 Aqu ⊡ 6f fst 1:16⅗ b Jan 14 Aqu ⊡ 5f fst 1:03⅗ bg

Horses dropping back from routes to a sprint have a severe handicap, especially those unable to contest the early lead (within one length of the leader, if not leading) in their most recent route. Such horses are perhaps the worst bets in all racing.

	NH	*WPCT*	*I.V.*	*$NET*
Route (without speed) to sprint	869	4.7%	0.42	$0.86

Horses dropping back to a sprint after showing speed for a half mile or six furlongs in a recent route are at far less of a disadvantage. An analysis of pace often points out those capable of winning at a sprint distance. (This point will be discussed in Chapter 10.) We point out, however, that a front-running router will usually have to race from behind in sprints, his early speed having been dulled somewhat by the slower route pace to which it has become accustomed.

Statistical studies done since *Winning at the Races* appeared have revealed that a one-race (conditioning) experiment at the opposite distance is especially useless, probably serving to confuse a horse more than anything else. When returned to its normal distance, it fares poorly. Several of the trainers who responded to our questionnaire agreed, adding that a competent conditioner can train a horse up to a specific race, without the need for confusing conditioning efforts at unexpected distances.

	NH	WPCT	I.V.	$NET
Sprint to route, back to sprint	474	6.1%	0.55	$0.72
Route to sprint, back to route	213	8.5%	0.68	$0.89

Some trainers, however, are successful with one or the other of these conditioning moves. It pays to find out who they are. Our research, supported by that of Henry Kuck, has indicated very strongly, on the other hand, that the best preparation for a route attempt comes from two sprints. Results are all the better if the horse had previously demonstrated ability at route distances, and had not raced all that well in its sprint preps, thereby disguising its fitness, and hopefully increasing its odds. Count Advocate (above) is just such an example. The pattern he demonstrates is quite effective—a strong rally in the first sprint, then a speed sharpener in the final tuneup.

	NH	WPCT	I.V.	$NET
Two Sprints, then a Route	347	13.8%	1.12	$1.96

☐ CLASS CHANGES ☐

Thoroughbreds change classification frequently. Especially the claiming animal. A horse on the rise may be a sharp, improving animal whose trainer feels it deserves the chance to prove its mettle against better competition than it has been facing. Or the rise in class could mean the horse is not at its best, and is being raced into condition at a level where it is not likely to be claimed. Or that the horse has been entered at the racing secretary's request, to help fill a race. A drop in class could spotlight a horse brought to the peak of condition against better competition, and that is now entered where it is likely to win. Or it could signify a horse gone off form, or suffering from a slight injury, whose trainer has neither the time nor the patience to rest the animal.

Most horses dropping in class are seeking their proper level. Those dropping sharply, however, are probably hurting and not worth betting, especially at the low odds likely. Beware the horse that drops in class without showing improved form, then drops again. Most likely, the horse has a physical problem that continued racing will not solve, regardless of the level of competition to which it is dropped.

Claiming horses that drop in class after winning should be regarded with extreme caution. They are likely to be favored, and even more likely to have serious physical problems. Sound horses are not devalued when in form.

Claiming horses that drop in class upon returning from a layoff also should be regarded suspiciously. If all is well, a trainer is far more likely to race a horse into shape above its previous class, before dropping it back to its proper level when set for a top effort. Such horses either win off the layoff, or will be forced to drop considerably before finding the proper level for their current ability.

Handicappers should also proceed cautiously when dealing with the infrequent starter, especially one dropping in class. Or the horse dropping in class after a two- or three-week layoff, with no workouts showing during that period. Its lack of activity hints of physical problems, and the drop in class suggests very strongly that these problems have worsened.

A drop in class is "believable" only if the animal had been more or less uncompetitive recently at higher class levels. It has long been suspected that a horse dropping in class after being close (within two lengths) at some call in its last race is loaded for bear. Not exactly true, according to our research, but if play is restricted to sprinters that have won at least once in their last ten starts and are returning within ten days of their most recent start—as some assurance of fitness—then the statistics are promising:

NH	NW	WPCT	MPCT	I.V.	$NET
136	34	25.0%	47.8%	2.27	$2.25

Mugsy's Boss is a case in point. He raced within two lengths of the early lead on December 28, prior to dropping a class in the maiden ranks and winning at $130.60 on January 21. In fact, the horse nearly qualified for the "carried speed farther" angle as well (see Chapter 3).

On the other hand, if a horse races unsuccessfully above its head too often, it can become frustrated and discouraged, and will give no effort when dropped back to its proper classification.

"Back class" refers to the once-classier animal now competing against rivals it would have annihilated in its perhaps not-so-distant past. The horse has suffered, perhaps in slow, painful stages, through a significant drop in class (value). But should it recapture its form (and health) at some point, it is capable of moving right back up the class ladder, perhaps all the way back to its former level. Injury can cause the initial drop in class, perhaps in combination with a second-rate trainer. Should the animal find its way into a better barn, its chances of rising again are magnified considerably.

Chapter 8

COMPARATIVE HANDICAPPING

The transitive law is usually encountered for the first time when studying high school algebra. "If A is greater than B, and B is greater than C, then A is greater than C," it says. The transitive law finds no more frequent use than at the racetrack. "If horse A beat horse B, which in turn had beaten horse C, then surely horse A will beat horse C in today's race," handicappers reason. They are wrong as often as right. There is no ironclad transitive law at the races. Even if one horse beat another last week, there is no guarantee it will do so again today.

Handicappers are forever trying to surmise the pecking order among horses. While in the broad sense there is such a thing, it nevertheless remains a fact that horses of approximately the same class will often take turns beating each other over the course of a meeting. Whether this can be attributed to trips, trainer intent, or simply variations in the form cycle, the handicapper must proceed cautiously. When a field like this gathers, the wise handicapper often turns to the "stranger" in the field, the horse dropping down from a higher classification, shipping in from a neighboring track, or freshened recently. It would prove far too difficult to try to separate the "regulars," one from the other. They look too much alike. "Strangers" are unknown quantities, at least to some extent, and often go postward at decent odds as a result. If a reasonable case can be made for one of them, they may be the player's only possible recourse in a field filled with "look-alikes."

Handicappers who attempt to classify horses according to how they fared in previous encounters, or against common opponents, are engaging in what is termed "comparative handicapping." For them, the most significant part of the past performances is the company line which appears at the right-hand side of each running line.

Subordinate — Dk. b. or br. g. 7, by Insubordination—Steel Edge, by Nashua
Own.—Davis A — $45,000 — Br.—Farnsworth Farm (Fla) — Tr.—Moschera Gasper S — **113**

Lifetime						
74 22 14 13	1983	4	1	0	2	$17,040
$323,185	1982	20	6	1	4	$81,120
	Turf	3	0	0	1	$1,560

9Mar83- 3Aqu	gd	6f	⊡:23⅖	:47	1:10⅗	Clm 50000	7	2	$1^{1\frac{1}{2}}$	2^{hd}	3^{nk}	3^{1}	Cordero A Jr	118	*2.70	90-09	Puritan Chief 117^{nk} Jeffery C. $113^{\frac{3}{4}}$ Subordinate 118^{hd}	Weakened	9
23Feb83- 3Aqu	fst	6f	⊡:22⅘	:46⅖	1:11⅗	Clm 50000	1	5	1^{1}	1^{hd}	$1^{\frac{1}{2}}$	$3^{\frac{1}{2}}$	Cordero A Jr	117	*2.60	85-21	[D]Shamstar $112^{\frac{1}{2}}$ Surf Club 113^{hd} Subordinate 117^{1}	Weakened	10
27Jan83- 7Aqu	fst	1⅛	⊡:47⅘	1:13⅕	1:50⅗	Clm 50000	4	2	$2^{\frac{1}{2}}$	1^{hd}	$3^{3\frac{1}{2}}$	4^{10}	Asmussen S M^{5}	114	2.50[D]	83-19	To Erin $108^{8\frac{1}{2}}$ Rain Prince $108^{1\frac{3}{4}}$ Might Be Home 108^{hd}	Bore out	6
27Jan83-Disqualified and placed fifth																			
3Jan83- 6Aqu	fst	$1\frac{3}{16}$	⊡:48⅘	1:14	2:01	Clm 50000	5	2	2^{hd}	$2^{\frac{1}{2}}$	1^{hd}	2^{hd}	Alvarado R Jr^{5}	114	*.90	73-25	[D]Prete Khale117^{hd}Subordinate$114^{2\frac{1}{4}}$MightBeHome109^{4}	Impeded	6
3Jan83-Placed first through disqualification.																			
19Dec82- 1Aqu	fst	$1\frac{1}{16}$	⊡:49	1:13⅘	1:45⅘	3↑ Clm 45000	4	1	$1^{1\frac{1}{2}}$	1^{4}	1^{6}	$1^{3\frac{1}{2}}$	Alvarado R Jr^{5}	108	5.40	84-23	Subordinte$108^{3\frac{1}{2}}$GrndFelice$117^{2\frac{3}{4}}$NorthernRegnt$113^{3\frac{3}{4}}$	Ridden out	6
12Nov82- 5Aqu	fst	7f	:22⅘	:45⅕	1:23⅖	3↑ Clm 50000	1	5	$1^{\frac{1}{2}}$	$3^{\frac{1}{2}}$	5^{6}	$6^{4\frac{1}{2}}$	Alvarado R Jr^{5}	112	6.50	79-21	Surf Club 113no Crockford Lad $117^{\frac{3}{4}}$ Northern Regent113^{nk}	Tired	8
27Oct82- 8Aqu	fst	6f	:21⅘	:44⅗	1:09⅕	3↑ Alw 32000	3	5	4^{6}	5^{8}	$5^{7\frac{1}{2}}$	5^{10}	Migliore R	115	5.60	85-17	Havagreatdate 115^{3} Mayanesian $105^{\frac{3}{4}}$ Cut High $115^{2\frac{1}{2}}$	Fell back	5
11Oct82- 4Bel	fst	6f	:22⅗	:46⅕	1:12	3↑ Clm.c-50000	2	3	$3^{4\frac{1}{2}}$	3^{7}	$3^{6\frac{1}{2}}$	4^{7}	Miceli M	117	*1.70	75-28	Speedy Reality $109^{5\frac{3}{4}}$ TermPaper117^{no}PrivateSun$114^{1\frac{1}{4}}$	No excuse	8
9Sep82- 6Med	fst	6f	:23	:47	1:12⅕	3↑ Alw 18000	1	5	4^{3}	4^{2}	$3^{4\frac{1}{2}}$	$3^{2\frac{1}{4}}$	Miceli M	115	*.70	80-17	IrishSwords115^{nk}Can'tholdmebck115^{2}Subordinte115^{9}	Bobbled st.	5
1Sep82- 7Bel	fst	6f	:22⅘	:45⅕	1:08⅘	3↑ Alw 32000	5	2	2^{1}	2^{4}	$3^{6\frac{1}{2}}$	$3^{7\frac{1}{2}}$	Migliore R	115	*1.40e	90-13	Chan Balum $111^{4\frac{1}{2}}$ Prosper 115^{3} Subordinate $115^{2\frac{3}{4}}$	Weakened	5

LATEST WORKOUTS Feb 15 Bel tr.t 4f fst :46⅗ h Jan 24 Bel tr.t 4f sly :48⅕ h

The company line identifies the horses that (originally) finished first, second, and third in a race, the weight each carried, and the margins between them. The top race in the past performances of Subordinate was won by Puritan Chief while carrying 117 pounds. He finished a neck ahead of second-place finisher Jeffery C., who carried 113 pounds while finishing ¾ of a length ahead of Subordinate, who finished third on that occasion. Subordinate carried 118 pounds, and finished a head in front of the horse (not identified) that picked up fourth money.

The symbol [D] is used to designate disqualified horses. If appearing before the name of a horse in the company lines, it means that horse was disqualified from its original finish position as shown. Prete Khale and Shamstar, winners of the January 3 and February 23 races appearing in Subordinate's past performances, were subsequently disqualified. The disqualification of Prete Khale changed Subordinate's official placing in the race, and so a comment appears below the line for that race. Shamstar was placed second, not affecting Subordinate's placing, so no such comment appears below that line. Finally, Subordinate himself was disqualified from his fourth place finish on January 27. Since his name does not appear in the company line for that race (he did not finish among the first three), it cannot be preceded by a [D]. However, the symbol [D] nonetheless appears after Subordinate's odds for that race, which is standard procedure regardless of the disqualified horse's finishing position.

When a horse finishes in a dead heat with another, the symbol [DH] is placed before the names of both, and a comment is placed below the past performance line. Evasive John, for example, finished on even terms with Rain Prince on December 11, 1981. Note that the margin between Evasive John, listed first because he got to the lead first, and Rain Prince is recorded as seven and three-fourths lengths, as is Evasive John's margin of victory. Careless handicappers may overlook the footnote, and credit the horse with a far more impressive performance than he actually gave.

Evasive John — Ch. g. 7, by Prince John—Evasive, by Buckpasser — $250,000 — Br.—Volkert D G (Ky) — Tr.—Nocella Vincent — Own.—Daren J — 112 — Lifetime 38 8 5 8 $125,450 — 1983 5 2 1 1 $35,760 — 1982 3 1 0 0 $9,600 — Turf 10 1 1 2 $16,620

14Feb83- 6Aqu	fst	170	⊡:50 1:14⅗ 1:42⅗	Alw 27000	4 6 4^{3} 5^{3} $5^{\frac34}$ $1^{1\frac12}$	Samyn J L	117	3.90	89–13 EvsiveJohn117$^{1\frac12}$CleverShot112^{nk}DetrmindBiddr119^{1}	Going away	6
5Feb83- 8Aqu	fst	1⅛	⊡:46⅘ 1:11⅖ 1:51	3+Stymie H	6 7 $7^{6\frac12}$ $7^{6\frac34}$ $7^{9\frac14}$ 7^{11}	Graell A	108	9.40	80–20 Sing Sing 120$^{\frac12}$ Lark Oscillation 113$^{1\frac14}$ Fort Monroe 112$^{2\frac34}$	Trailed	7
28Jan83- 7Aqu	fst	1 1/16	⊡:49⅗ 1:14⅗ 1:45⅗	Clm 75000	1 5 $5^{2\frac12}$ $4^{2\frac14}$ 3^{nk} 2no	Alvarado R Jr^{5}	112	*1.60	85–25 Deedee's Deal 117no Evasive John 112$^{1\frac34}$ Tarberry 115^{1}	Steadied	6
19Jan83- 1Aqu	fst	1⅛	⊡:48⅕ 1:13 1:52⅖	Alw 29000	2 5 3^{3} $3^{\frac12}$ 2^{hd} 1^{2}	Alvarado R Jr^{5}	112	7.00[D]	84–24 [D]Evasive John 112^{2} Grand Felice 117$^{\frac34}$ John's Gold 117^{4}	Bore in	6
19Jan83-Disqualified and placed third											
6Jan83- 9Aqu	sly	1¼	⊡:46⅘ 1:38⅗ 2:04⅗	Clm 32500	3 4 4^{9} 1^{1} 1^{2} $1^{2\frac14}$	Alvarado R Jr^{5}	110	*1.50	95–17 EvasiveJohn110$^{2\frac14}$Starhitch112$^{8\frac34}$SurrenderGround114$^{1\frac14}$	Drew out	8
24Dec82- 5Aqu	fst	170	⊡:49 1:14 1:44	3+Clm 25000	1 5 4^{2} 4^{2} 1^{1} $1^{5\frac12}$	Alvarado R Jr^{5}	112	*2.50	82–27 Evasive John112$^{5\frac12}$OurCelticHeir119^{hd}Mr.Nicefield115^{no}	Drew out	8
4Dec82- 9Aqu	gd	1 1/16	⊡:48 1:12⅗ 1:45⅕	3+Clm 30000	8 6 $4^{3\frac12}$ $2^{3\frac12}$ $3^{5\frac12}$ $5^{5\frac12}$	Bailey J D	117	3.50	82–15 LetterFromLucy115$^{2\frac14}$PrincelyHeir115^{2}DedictdBoy117^{1}	Weakened	10
25Nov82- 5Aqu	fst	7f	:23⅖ :46⅖ 1:24⅕	3+Clm 32500	7 11 $10^{5\frac34}$ 9^{6} $9^{7\frac14}$ $7^{6\frac14}$	Maple E	115	22.50	74–26 Was He Fuzzy 119no Raise ABuck115$^{1\frac12}$CourtWise117$^{1\frac12}$	No factor	13
24Dec81- 7Aqu	fst	170	⊡:48 1:12 1:42⅗	3+Alw 22000	7 5 $6^{2\frac34}$ $5^{3\frac34}$ $5^{3\frac12}$ $4^{3\frac34}$	Borden D A	117	5.40	85–22 Deedee's Deal 117^{nk} King Neptune 117$^{3\frac12}$ Palace 117no	Evenly	7
11Dec81- 6Aqu	fst	1⅛	⊡:48⅕ 1:13 1:51⅖	3+Clm 37500	3 8 8^{7} 4^{2} 2^{hd} $1^{7\frac34}$	Maple E	115^{4}	7.30	89–16 [DH]EvasiveJohn115$^{7\frac34}$[DH]RinPrince117$^{7\frac34}$PerfectBidder108^{3}	Driving	10
11Dec81-Dead heat											

At times, a horse may be disqualified "after the fact," when found positive for some prohibited drug. Although too late to revise the betting payoffs, the purse monies can be redistributed. Such was the fate of Copelan in an allowance race at Belmont on July 31, 1982.

Copelan — B. c. 3, by Tri Jet—Susan's Girl, by Quadrangle — Br.—Hooper F W (Fla) — Tr.—Griffin Mitchell — Own.—Hooper F W — 122 — Lifetime 10 7 0 0 $500,333 — 1983 1 1 0 0 $44,888 — 1982 9 6 0 0 $455,445

21Feb83-10GP	fst	1 1/16	:47⅘ 1:12 1:43⅗	Ftn Youth	8 1 $1^{\frac12}$ 1^{3} $1^{\frac12}$ $1^{2\frac14}$	Pincay L Jr	122	*1.10	83–24 Copelan 122$^{2\frac14}$ Current Hope 117$^{1\frac12}$ Blink 112$^{3\frac12}$	Ridden out	8
21Feb83-Run in two divisions 9th & 10th races											
12Dec82- 8Hol	fst	1 1/16	:45⅘ 1:10⅕ 1:41⅘	Hol Fut'y	2 7 5^{4} $5^{6\frac34}$ 5^{10} 5^{16}	Bailey J D	121	*1.50	70–20 Roving Boy 121^{nk} Desert Wine 121^{2} Fifth Division121^{4}	No excuse	9
27Nov82- 8Hol	fst	7f	:21⅘ :43⅘ 1:21⅖	Prevue	6 3 $3^{2\frac12}$ 2^{hd} $1^{\frac12}$ $1^{1\frac12}$	Bailey J D	122	*.80	90–14 Copelan 122$^{1\frac12}$ R. Awacs 115$^{1\frac12}$ Desert Wine 122^{2}	Driving	8
4Nov82- 6Med	fst	1 1/16	:45⅘ 1:09⅗ 1:43⅖	Yng Amer'a	9 2 $2^{\frac12}$ $2^{1\frac12}$ $3^{4\frac12}$ $4^{6\frac34}$	Bailey J D	122	*.40	85–14 Slewpy 119$^{3\frac14}$ Bet Big 122^{1} El Cubanaso 119$^{2\frac12}$	Tired	11
9Oct82- 7Bel	fst	1	:45⅖ 1:10⅖ 1:37⅘	Champagne	9 3 3^{1} $1^{1\frac12}$ 1^{5} $1^{6\frac12}$	Bailey J D	122	*.80	76–25 Copelan 122$^{6\frac12}$ Pappa Riccio 122^{hd} El Cubanaso 122$^{3\frac14}$	Ridden out	13
12Sep82- 8Bel	fst	7f	:23 :46⅕ 1:24⅕	Bel Fut'y	3 6 3^{1} 1^{hd} $1^{2\frac12}$ $1^{4\frac34}$	Bailey J D	122	*.50	81–19 Copelan 122$^{4\frac34}$ Satan's Charger 122$^{\frac12}$ Pax InBello122$^{1\frac34}$	Ridden out	6
28Aug82- 8Sar	fst	6½f	:22⅕ :44⅘ 1:16⅗	Hopeful	8 3 1^{hd} 2^{hd} $1^{1\frac12}$ $1^{3\frac14}$	Bailey J D	122	3.30	89–13 Copelan 122$^{3\frac14}$ Victorious 122$^{\frac12}$ Aloha Hawaii 122$^{\frac12}$	Ridden out	9
18Aug82- 8Sar	fst	6f	:22 :44⅗ 1:10⅖	Sanford	1 2 1^{1} 1^{hd} 1^{2} $1^{1\frac12}$	Bailey J D	115	2.20	88–15 Copelan 115$^{1\frac12}$ Smart Style 115$^{3\frac12}$ Safe Ground 117$^{1\frac34}$	Driving	5
31Jly82- 5Bel	fst	6f	:22⅗ :45⅘ 1:10⅘	Alw 19000	4 2 1^{hd} 2^{hd} $1^{1\frac12}$ 1^{2}	Bailey J D	119	9.50	88–15 Copelan 119^{2} Nearice 119$^{1\frac14}$ Northern Ice 117$^{1\frac34}$	Ridden Out	7
31Jly82-Disqualified from purse money											
13Jly82- 6Bel	fst	5½f	:22⅘ :46⅘ 1:05⅘	Md Sp Wt	1 1 $1^{2\frac12}$ 1^{3} 1^{2} $1^{\frac12}$	Migliore R	118	3.00	86–22 Copelan 118$^{\frac12}$ Rising Raja 118$^{5\frac34}$ Torpedo Los 118^{1}	Driving	10

LATEST WORKOUTS ●Mar 3 Hia 4f fst :46⅖ h — Feb 19 Hia 2f fst :24 bg — Feb 12 GP 1 fst 1:36⅖ h

Note the comment placed in the *Form* beneath the running line for that race. Note also the comment in the past performances of Northern Ice for the same race, in which he was awarded second money upon the disqualification of Copelan.

Northern Ice — Ch. c. 3, by Fire Dancer—Full Heart, by Vertex — Br.—Shur-Win Venture (Fla) — Tr.—Bailie Sally A — Own.—Aisco Stables — 122 — Lifetime 14 3 5 2 $80,779 — 1983 3 0 1 1 $14,372 — 1982 11 3 4 1 $66,407

26Mar83- 9Lat	fst	1 1/16	:46⅕ 1:10⅗ 1:42⅖	Spiral	6 4 $5^{6\frac12}$ 5^{3} 9^{17} 9^{23}	Graell A	120	11.10	75–24 Marfa 120^{8} Noble Home 120$^{5\frac12}$ Hail To Rome 120no	Fell back	12
26Mar83-Daily Racing Form Time 1:44 1/5											
5Mar83- 8Aqu	fst	6f	⊡:22⅗ :46 1:10⅕	Swift	3 5 5^{4} $5^{1\frac34}$ 3^{3} $3^{3\frac14}$	Graell A	120	*1.70	90–16 Chas Conerly 115$^{1\frac12}$TwoDavids120$^{1\frac34}$NorthernIce120$^{5\frac14}$	Evenly late	7
23Feb83- 8Aqu	fst	6f	⊡:22⅗ :46⅗ 1:12⅕	Alw 35000	1 3 $6^{7\frac12}$ 4^{6} 3^{2} 2^{nk}	Graell A	122	*2.20	83–21 Irish Rye 110^{nk} Northern Ice 122$^{3\frac14}$ King's Swan 117$^{1\frac14}$	In close	6
4Nov82- 6Med	fst	1 1/16	:45⅘ 1:09⅗ 1:43⅖	Yng Amer'a	8 9 10^{16} 9^{13} 9^{16} 9^{16}	Samyn J L	119	89.40	76–14 Slewpy 119$^{3\frac14}$ Bet Big 122^{1} El Cubanaso 119$^{2\frac12}$	No menace	11
11Oct82- 8Bow	fst	7f	:22⅗ :45⅘ 1:24⅘	Marl Nrsry	1 6 6^{5} 5^{3} $1^{1\frac12}$ $1^{\frac12}$	Passmore W J	119	4.90	81–24 Northern Ice 119$^{\frac12}$ Gaylord's Carousel 116$^{1\frac14}$ Aurbar 115^{7}	Driving	8
11Oct82-Run in two divisions 7th & 8th races											
12Sep82- 8Bel	fst	7f	:23 :46⅕ 1:24⅕	Bel Fut'y	2 1 2^{1} $4^{2\frac12}$ 6^{8} 6^{12}	MacBeth D	122	35.00	69–19 Copelan 122$^{4\frac34}$ Satan's Charger 122$^{\frac12}$ Pax In Bello 122$^{1\frac34}$	Tired	6
25Aug82- 6Sar	sly	6f	:21⅘ :45⅗ 1:12	Alw 19000	8 2 $6^{2\frac14}$ 3^{2} 1^{hd} $1^{\frac12}$	Velasquez J	117	4.30	80–17 Northern Ice 117$^{\frac12}$ Q. Naskra 122no Thalassocrat 119$^{2\frac34}$	Stiff drive	8
9Aug82- 8Sar	my	6f	:22 :45⅗ 1:10⅗	Sar Special	3 5 $4^{3\frac12}$ 3^{3} $5^{4\frac14}$ $5^{7\frac34}$	McCarron G	117	15.00	79–16 Victorious122$^{\frac12}$PppRiccio124^{4}SfeGround119$^{1\frac34}$	Lacked a response	7
31Jly82- 5Bel	fst	6f	:22⅗ :45⅘ 1:10⅘	Alw 19000	2 5 4^{3} $4^{2\frac12}$ $4^{3\frac12}$ $3^{3\frac14}$	McCarron G	117	3.40	85–15 Copelan 119^{2} Nearice 119$^{1\frac14}$ Northern Ice 117$^{1\frac34}$	Lacked Rally	7
31Jly82-Awarded second purse money											

LATEST WORKOUTS Apr 5 Bel tr.t 5f fst 1:02⅗ b — Mar 25 Lat 3f fst :36⅕ h — ●Mar 16 Bel tr.t 1 fst 1:41⅖ h — Mar 11 Bel tr.t 5f sly 1:01⅕ b (d)

Backers of Copelan were not asked to refund their $21.00 win payoff, however.

CASE STUDY: HONEST GAL

It is important to pay close attention to the margins between each of the first four finishers. Unusually large margins can be quite significant. Take a look at the past performances of Honest Gal, a lightly raced juvenile filly entered in a minor stakes event at Monmouth Park on September 4, 1982. At first glance, she might not appear to be of stakes quality. Although impressive when winning her maiden race by a widening ten lengths, she was all-out to win in allowance company two weeks later. Honest Gal's performance in that allowance event might be far better than appears at first glance. There are three points a clever handicapper would note. Honest Gal flashed improved early speed on August 16, for one thing. She was in close contention at the top of the stretch, not back in the middle of the pack, several lengths out of it, as she was in her debut. Also, Honest Gal proved herself a game animal on August 16, a trait that went untested in her debut. After moving to within half-a-length of the lead at the top of the stretch, she fell back somewhat in midstretch before coming on again to edge her rival. Finally, and this speaks to the point at hand, the second-place filly, Am Capable, finished fourteen lengths ahead of the third filly, a quite considerable distance. Although Honest Gal's margin of victory was merely a nose, she did trounce six other "allowance" fillies by open daylight.

The comparative handicapper would now ask "Who is Am Capable? What had she accomplished prior to meeting Honest Gal?" (Am Capable had won her debut in MSW company at Laurel before tiring in an NW1 race at Monmouth, finishing a well-beaten third, thirteen lengths behind the winner, in a small field of five.) He would also be interested in Singadon (a maiden winner at Atlantic City in her prior start), and the fillies that finished off the board behind Honest Gal. Had any of them distinguished themselves beforehand?

With Honest Gal heavily backed at 1–2 odds on August 16, one might have suspected she had little opposition that day. On the other hand, she was a fashionably bred filly from a top barn that had won her only start by ten lengths, while favored on that occasion. She was as likely a candidate as any to be 1–2 next time out, regardless of possible opposition. In this case, comparative handicapping did nothing to en-

Honest Gal — B. f. 2, by Honest Pleasure—Regal Gal, by Viceregal — Br.—Cox E A (Ky) — Tr.—Delp Grover G — **115** — Lifetime 2 2 0 0 $11,100 — 1982 2 2 0 0 $11,100
Own.—Windfields Farm

16Aug82- 6Mth	fst	6f	:22⅗	:45⅖	1:11	ⒻAlw 10000	4	3	3³	2½	2¹½	1no	Saumell L	117	*.50	85-23	Honest Gal 117no Am Capable 115^14 Singadon 113½	Came again 8
30Jly82- 4Mth	fst	5½f	:22⅘	:46⅗	1:05⅗	ⒻMd Sp Wt	5	5	7⁶½	5³	2^hd	1^10	Saumell L	117	*2.10	87-20	Honest Gal 117^10 SauceOfLife112^nk Mommy'sGirl117½	Ridden out 9

LATEST WORKOUTS ●Aug 30 Mth 4f fst :47⅗ h Aug 26 Mth 5f fst 1:01⅘ b Aug 15 Mth 3f fst :37⅖ b Aug 11 Mth 4f fst :48⅘ b

hance Honest Gal's credentials. Neither Am Capable nor Singadon, to that point, had accomplished more than a modest maiden victory. Perhaps Honest Gal's maiden win had come at the expense of a weak field.

Honest Gal was off the board in the Monmouth stakes race.

Comparative handicapping is far from foolproof. Comparing two horses, based on previous races together or against common opponents, does give some measure of the relative abilities of the two horses. For these comparisons to be accurate and reliable, however, they must take into consideration the circumstances of each horse involved in the comparison. Where was it in its form cycle? Was it at its best on the day in question? What kind of trip did it have? Did it take advantage of a track bias? Was it the victim of a track bias, or poor racing luck? Any of the above could distort what appears so clear-cut on paper: that one horse was x lengths better than another on a given day. Just because horse A defeated horse B in a recent race does not imply that horse A is the better of the two. It doesn't even mean that horse A's performance was the better of the two. Horse A may have romped after setting an uncontested pace, leaving stretch runner horse B little chance to catch up. Or horse B may have finished off the board, a few lengths behind horse A. But if horse B had been racing for the first time in three months, or had been forced very wide on the turn, checked in midstretch behind a wall of horses, or weakened from a suicidal speed duel, who is to say that it was not the circumstances that accounted for the order of the finish, or the margins between the two horses. Given a different set of circumstances, their placings easily might be reversed.

Never forget that each race presents its contestants with a new set of circumstances relative to track conditions, pace, fitness, etc. The handicapper must decide who will be favored by the present conditions, and to do so requires knowledge of circumstances prevalent in previous races.

Consider the following situation involving a stretch-runner. The last time out, he rallied nicely, only to be beaten two lengths by a horse that had been able to set a leisurely pace. The time before that, he had been victimized in exactly the same manner by another front-running winner. Today, he faces both of his recent conquerors, and figures off recent form to be third choice. Yet today, the race sets up in his favor, with the two speed horses possibly wearing each other out in a duel for the early lead. In this situation comparative handicapping would only lead the player astray.

CASE STUDY: LITUYA BAY VS. NATIONAL BANNER

The juvenile fillies Lituya Bay and National Banner were meeting for the third time on grass when they were entered in a mile "nonwinners of one" allowance race at Belmont on September 18, 1982. Their first two encounters proved inconclusive, with each filly gaining the upper hand on one occasion. Was there a reason to prefer one over the other in their upcoming matchup? The two fillies met for the first time August 11 at Saratoga, at a mile over that track's inner grass course. That type of race at Saratoga tends to favor inside speed, a situation that Lituya Bay fully exploited. National Banner broke from a disadvantageous outside post position (post 9), and chased Lituya Bay throughout. Hers was a promising effort to a more seasoned rival, and was followed by an easy front-running score over the same course August 20, setting the stage for their second meeting, in the Evening Out Stakes at Belmont.

The Evening Out presented a completely different situation. Lituya Bay faced considerable contention for the early lead, most notably from National Banner's highly regarded stablemate Bemissed. In deference to Bemissed's speed, trainer Woody Stephens used this occasion to test National Banner's ability to rate (race from behind). She adapted nicely to this style, catching Bemissed right at the wire for second money. Lituya Bay challenged repeatedly for the lead for seven furlongs, before weakening somewhat in the late stages of the race. She finished a decent fourth.

Both fillies worked smartly for their September 18 engagement. National Banner was the public choice, at 6-5. Yet Lituya Bay had the advantage on this occasion, and should have been favored to reverse the result of September 3. Lituya Bay figured to be alone on the early lead, as had happened at Saratoga on August 11. It was unlikely that National Banner would look to contest the early pace. Well-bred young Thoroughbreds from top barns that adapt nicely to rating tactics generally

Lituya Bay — Own.—Jones A U — Ch. f. 2, by Empery—Reason to Please, by Boldnesian — Br.—Jones Aaron U (Ky) — Tr.—Barrera Lazaro S — **116** — Lifetime 5 1 2 0 $22,337 — 1982 5 1 2 0 $22,337 — Turf 2 1 0 0 $14,262

3Sep82- 8Bel	yl	1	Ⓣ:47⅘ 1:12⅖ 1:38⅕	ⒻEvening Out	8	2	21½	42	32½	45¾	Cordero A Jr	112	4.10	68-26	Cryptic 1143½ National Banner 112hd Bemissed 1122¼	Weakened	11
11Aug82- 4Sar	gd	1	Ⓣ:48⅕ 1:13⅕ 1:39	ⒻMd Sp Wt	4	1	11	11½	14	13¾	Cordero A Jr	117	*2.20	81-18	Lituya Bay 1173¾ National Banner 1171½Bammer1173½	Ridden out	9
18Jly82- 4Hol	fst	6f	:22⅕ :44⅘ 1:09⅘	ⒻMd Sp Wt	6	1	32	23	22½	21½	McCarron C J	116	2.20	86-12	Ruling Diplomat 1161½ Lituya Bay 11612 Hold The Hula 1161½		9
26Jun82- 6Hol	fst	5½f	:22⅗ :45⅖ 1:04⅖	ⒻMd Sp Wt	6	2	32	53½	55½	44¾	Guerra W A	116	*.90	84-10	Body Talk 1163 Known To Win 116¾ Ruling Diplomat 1161		8
11Jun82- 4Hol	fst	5f	:21⅘ :44⅗ :57⅖	ⒻMd Sp Wt	6	7	34	34½	25	22½	Guerra W A	116	2.50	89-13	Barzell 1162½ Lituya Bay 1164 Body Talk 1161		10

LATEST WORKOUTS Sep 11 Bel 4f fst :46⅖ h Aug 26 Sar tr.t 5f fst 1:02 b Aug 19 Sar tr.t 4f fst :49⅘ b ● Aug 8 Sar tr.t 5f fst 1:02⅕ b

National Banner — Own.—Hurstland Farm — B. f. 2, by Hoist The Flag—Clever Bird, by Swoon's Son — Br.—Nuckols Bros (Ky) — Tr.—Stephens Woodford C — **118** — Lifetime 4 1 2 1 $29,494 — 1982 4 1 2 1 $29,494 — Turf 3 1 2 0 $27,454

3Sep82- 8Bel	yl	1	Ⓣ:47⅘ 1:12⅖ 1:38⅕	ⒻEvening Out	6	7	87½	75½	45½	23½	Velasquez J	112	*.90e	70-26	Cryptic 1143½ National Banner 112hd Bemissed 1122¼	Rallied	11
20Aug82- 9Sar	fm	1	Ⓣ:47⅘ 1:12⅗ 1:38⅖	ⒻMd Sp Wt	8	2	1hd	12	12	15¾	Maple E	117	*.90	84-11	NationalBanner1175¾BirchBrk117¾ImperiousMiss1176	Ridden out	10
11Aug82- 4Sar	gd	1	Ⓣ:48⅕ 1:13⅕ 1:39	ⒻMd Sp Wt	9	2	21	21½	24	23¾	Maple E	117	3.10	78-18	Lituya Bay 1173¾ National Banner 1171½ Bammer 1173½	2nd best	9
31Jly82- 4Bel	fst	5½f	:23⅕ :47⅖ 1:06⅖	ⒻMd Sp Wt	6	7	57	57½	47½	34½	Bailey J D	117	5.00	78-15	Tarquinia 1173¼ Cajun Best 1171¼ NationalBanner1172	Off slowly	7

LATEST WORKOUTS Sep 15 Bel 6f fst 1:12⅗ h Sep 11 Bel 5f fst 1:01⅗ h Sep 2 Bel 3f sly :35⅗ h Aug 29 Sar 6f fst 1:13⅘ h can be expected to continue racing under restraint in the early stages. Learning to rate is part of their educational process, and this is exactly what did happen. Lituya Bay set her own pace, then had plenty in reserve to thwart National Banner's challenge at the top of the stretch and draw off to win rather easily. She returned $7.00 as second choice in what on paper shaped up as a two-filly race. National Banner, her challenge turned back, faded late to finish third. Singadon, a daughter of the relatively obscure grass sire Ramsinga, rallied to split the favored-exacta horses.

CASE STUDY: MISS DUTCHESS

Handicappers often attempt to judge class, especially among allowance horses, by recognizing the names of their opponents. It is quite useful to know that an animal competing successfully in allowance contests has been doing so against stakes horses, especially if none of its key rivals can boast of such credentials. Such was the case with Miss Dutchess. In her second start of the year, she was a fast-closing second to the multiple-stakes-winner Captivating Grace, then came back to defeat the top-class stakes winners Sprouted Rye and Mochila. Entered once again at seven furlongs on April 30, she faced no rival with comparable credentials. Co-favorite Micktom, Wancha, and Liz Matizz were refugees from the claiming ranks. (Liz Matizz had recently placed in a restricted stakes at Aqueduct, in a field that in no way was comparable to those in which Miss Dutchess had been competing.) Venus Star had won her last two races in restricted allowance company, and was moving up considerably. Debonair Dancer, who was stakes-placed out of town at least four times, was returning from a three-month layoff at a distance short of her best trip. At 2–1 in this small field of six, Miss Dutchess was a considerable overlay. She won going away.

Miss Dutchess — **Ch. m. 5, by Duke Tom—Miss Kingwood, by Crewman**
Own.—Joia Stable — **Br.—Del Presto A (NJ)** — **Tr.—Baeza Braulio** — **121**

	Lifetime				
33 7 7 6	1983	3 1 1 1	$32,900
$119,992	1982	15 2 3 3	$43,807
	Turf	1 0 0 0	

14Apr83- 8Aqu	fst	7f	:23	:46⅕	1:23⅘	3↑ⒻHandicap	1	4	43½	42½	31½	11½	Santiago A	b 116	7.00	82-25	Miss Dutchess 1161½ Sprouted Rye 1221½ Mochila 120nk	Driving	4
5Apr83- 8Aqu	fst	6f	:22⅖	:46	1:11⅕	3↑ⒻHandicap	4	2	43½	44½	33½	22	Santiago A	b 117	7.60	83-22	CaptivatingGrce1122MissDutchess1171¼HurricneCrol1152¾	Rallied	5
25Mar83- 8Aqu	fst	7f	:23⅘	:48⅖	1:25⅗	ⒻAlw 35000	3	5	2hd	42	66	37½	Santiago A	b 115	20.80	65-36	Sweet Laughter1126DamLittle1151½MissDutchess115hd	Weakened	9
30Oct82- 6Med	fst	6f	:22	:45	1:10⅕	3↑ⒻAlw 25000	10	1	54½	812	816	715	Tejeira J	b 116	29.60	77-13	Class Night 1148 Pebble Patter 114noJet'sDelta1141½	Early speed	10
18Sep82- 7Med	fst	6f	:22⅖	:46⅗	1:12⅗	3↑ⒻStarlight	2	2	32	59	56½	54½	MacBeth D	b 119	4.40	75-19	Joyous Time 115no Maddy's Tune 1151¼ Pert 1111¼	Tired	5
18Sep82-Run in Two Divisions: 7th & 9th Races																			
7Sep82- 6Med	fst	6f	:22⅖	:45⅗	1:10⅘	3↑ⒻAlw 20000	3	3	11	1hd	21½	34½	MacBeth D	b 114	4.10	84-13	Sword of Song1141½Coprincess1143MissDutchess1141¼	Weakened	6
31Aug82- 9Mth	fst	6f	:22⅖	:45	1:09⅗	3↑ⒻⓈFairHavenH	3	8	87½	814	816	820	Verge M E	b 122	5.10	72-16	Tiara Rose 1182 Hill Billy Dancer 1173 Special Mah 117½	Trailed	8
31Jly82- 4Mth	fst	6f	:22	:44⅘	1:10⅖	3↑ⒻAlw 14000	3	5	21	21½	1½	21¼	Verge M E5	b 114	3.80	87-08	Phob'sPhncy1221¼MssDtchss1141½Hgly'sPnt1171½	Couldn't resist	11
25Jly82- 1Bel	fst	6f	:23⅘	:47⅕	1:11	3↑ⒻAlw 32000	1	1	1½	21½	34	48¾	Brumfield D	b 115	9.90	78-21	Nancy Huang 1121¾ Expressive Dance1151SproutedRye1176	Tired	4
10Jly82- 6Mth	fst	6f	:22⅖	:45	1:10⅕	3↑ⒻⓈAlw 17000	5	1	1hd	1hd	1hd	33¾	Tejeira J	b 119	3.00	85-12	Paris Press 1151¼ Al's Annie 1162½ Miss Dutchess1195	Weakened	7

LATEST WORKOUTS **Mar 21 Bel tr.t 4f fst :47⅖ hg** **Mar 15 Bel tr.t 4f fst :48⅖ h** **Mar 10 Bel tr.t 1 sly 1:47⅖ b**

Liz Matizz — Own.—Tresvant Stable

B. m. 5, by Double Warrant—Self Honor, by Hedevar
Br.—Bazo & Callar (Md)
Tr.—Sedlacek Sue

1125 — Lifetime 52 8 12 6 $118,883 — 1983 8 0 2 1 $16,044 — 1982 27 2 6 3 $65,219 — Turf 3 0 1 0 $3,045

20Apr83- 8Aqu gd	1	:45⅗ 1:10 1:35⅘	3↑ Ⓕ Alw 37000	2 2 3^{2} 2^{4} $2^{2\frac{1}{2}}$ $2^{1\frac{3}{4}}$	Davis R G5	114	4.90	85-19	Wancha $107^{1\frac{3}{4}}$ Liz Matizz $114^{1\frac{3}{4}}$ Prime Prospect $121^{1\frac{1}{2}}$	2nd best	5
10Apr83- 6Aqu sly	6f	:22⅖ :45⅘ 1:11⅘	3↑ Ⓕ Miss Disco	8 8 8^{11} 8^{10} $5^{6\frac{1}{2}}$ $3^{1\frac{1}{2}}$	Davis R G	119	16.20	80-23	Rosa D'Argent $119^{\frac{1}{2}}$ Chime 119^{1} Liz Matizz 119no	Rallied	8
26Mar83- 3Aqu fst	7f	:23⅗ :47⅗ 1:24⅗	Ⓕ Clm c-50000	4 5 $5^{5\frac{1}{2}}$ $5^{3\frac{3}{4}}$ 3^{9} $2^{7\frac{3}{4}}$	McCarron G	117	6.30	70-19	Minor's Gift $117^{7\frac{3}{4}}$ Liz Matizz $117^{\frac{3}{4}}$ Sharonna $113^{3\frac{1}{4}}$	Wide	7
20Mar83- 7Aqu fst	7f	:22⅘ :45⅘ 1:24⅘	3↑ Ⓕ Alw 25000	2 6 7^{15} 7^{17} 7^{10} 6^{6}	McCarron G	121	15.50	71-27	RegalValley$111^{\frac{1}{2}}$QuickQuckQuick$113^{1\frac{3}{4}}$MkesRoylSense$112^{\frac{3}{4}}$	Outrun	8
11Mar83- 1Aqu sly	6f	⊡:23⅕ :46⅖ 1:10⅖	3↑ Ⓕ Alw 25000	6 2 5^{11} 5^{12} 6^{16} 5^{13}	McCarron G	121	10.30	79-11	Better Bourbon $110^{5\frac{3}{4}}$ Annulus $121^{\frac{3}{4}}$ Cobitony 107^{2}	Outrun	6
5Feb83- 9Aqu fst	6f	⊡:23 :47⅕ 1:13	Ⓕ Alw 25000	4 6 10^{11} $9^{8\frac{1}{4}}$ $8^{8\frac{1}{4}}$ $8^{6\frac{1}{2}}$	McCarron G	117	7.60	72-20	Maggie Gold $117^{\frac{1}{2}}$ Irish Toy $112^{\frac{3}{4}}$ Princess Ebony 117^{nk}	Outrun	10
24Jan83- 7Aqu sly	6f	⊡:22⅘ :46 1:11	Ⓕ Alw 25000	7 8 $8^{9\frac{3}{4}}$ $8^{7\frac{3}{4}}$ $6^{8\frac{1}{2}}$ 6^{11}	McCarron G	117	6.20	78-15	Miss Actress 117^{6} Swift And Sudden 119^{1}SingingOak117^{2}	Outrun	8
8Jan83- 8Aqu fst	6f	⊡:22⅖ :45⅗ 1:11	3↑ Ⓕ Int'borough H	5 6 6^{18} 6^{14} 6^{16} 5^{13}	Beitia E	b 111	18.00	76-16	JonsTimMchin$116^{8\frac{1}{2}}$Stllrtt$112^{1\frac{1}{4}}$LdyLothrio$108^{3\frac{1}{2}}$	Showed Nothing	6
22Dec82- 7Aqu fst	6f	⊡:23 :46⅘ 1:12⅗	3↑ Ⓕ Alw 37000	5 8 $8^{8\frac{1}{4}}$ 8^{11} $7^{7\frac{1}{4}}$ $7^{6\frac{1}{4}}$	Beitia E	115	8.80	75-22	ChristmsBonus$115^{1\frac{3}{4}}$ExplosivKingdom110^{1}PoltRbuff113^{nk}	Outrun	8
9Dec82- 8Med fst	1 1/16	:48⅕ 1:13⅖ 1:46⅕	3↑ Ⓕ Meadowlark	2 7 $7^{8\frac{1}{2}}$ $8^{6\frac{1}{4}}$ 7^{10} 6^{13}	Alvarado R Jr	113	6.10	65-23	Josalee 113^{2} Lonely Balladier $115^{1\frac{1}{2}}$ Dareport 115^{hd}	No menace	9

Debonair Dancer — Own.—Marablue Farm

B. m. 5, by Staff Writer—In The Bag, by Lucky Debonair
Br.—Marablue Farm & Training Center (Fla)
Tr.—Hernandez Ramon M

1107 — Lifetime 26 5 5 5 $122,125 — 1983 2 0 1 1 $14,276 — 1982 11 0 2 2 $32,631 — Turf 1 0 0 0

22Jan83- 6Aqu fst	1 1/16	⊡:46⅘ 1:11 1:43⅖	3↑ Ⓕ Affectnly H	3 2 3^{2} $4^{2\frac{1}{2}}$ 4^{3} 3^{2}	Graell A	113	9.80	94-07	Adept 108^{1} Princess Oola 118^{1} Debonair Dancer $113^{\frac{3}{4}}$	Evenly	7
22Jan83-Run in Two Divisions 6th & 7th Races											
3Jan83- 8Aqu fst	1 70	⊡:50⅕ 1:15⅗ 1:45⅗	Ⓕ Alw 35000	3 1 1^{hd} $1^{\frac{1}{2}}$ 2^{2} 2^{1}	Graell A	117	2.30	73-25	Halo Again117^{1}DebonairDancer117^{hd}HarlemQueen$112^{1\frac{1}{2}}$	Game try	7
18Dec82- 8Key fst	1 1/16	:47⅖ 1:12⅕ 1:44⅖	3↑ Ⓕ WhitemarshH	3 1 1^{hd} 1^{hd} $2^{\frac{1}{2}}$ 2^{nk}	Graell A	113	6.30	82-18	PrincessOola117^{nk}DebonairDancer$113^{2\frac{1}{2}}$LonelyBalldier116^{2}	Sharp	14
10Dec82- 7Aqu fst	1 70	⊡:47⅕ 1:12⅗ 1:44	3↑ Ⓕ Alw 40000	4 2 2^{8} 3^{7} $4^{5\frac{1}{2}}$ $4^{1\frac{3}{4}}$	Graell A	115	12.80	80-24	Patella $117^{1\frac{3}{4}}$ Fancy Naskra 115no Christmas Bonus 115^{hd}	No rlly	6
25Nov82- 8Key fst	1 70	:46⅗ 1:12⅖ 1:44⅕	3↑ Ⓕ Heirloom	1 2 2^{3} $2^{1\frac{1}{2}}$ 2^{hd} 2no	Graell A	113	5.20	79-29	DestryAgain113^{no}DebonirDncer$113^{\frac{1}{2}}$FrenchFlick$117^{1\frac{1}{2}}$	Just missed	11
11Nov82- 8Key fst	1 70	:46⅘ 1:11⅘ 1:43⅗	3↑ Ⓕ Alw 15000	1 3 4^{5} 5^{12} 5^{15} 5^{10}	Smith T R III	112	2.80	72-25	QuickPick$112^{1\frac{1}{2}}$KaylemHo111^{nk}UtmostCelerity$122^{1\frac{1}{4}}$	Unruly early	5
18Oct82- 8Bow fst	1 1/16	:46⅗ 1:11⅘ 1:44⅕	3↑ Ⓕ Tosmah H	10 2 2^{6} 2^{hd} 1^{hd} $3^{1\frac{1}{2}}$	Cintron J O	111	117.70	83-23	Lady Dean 123^{1} Zvetlana $115^{\frac{1}{2}}$ Debonair Dancer 111^{4}	Weakened	11
1Oct82- 6Med fst	1 70	:46⅗ 1:12 1:41⅗	3↑ Ⓕ Alw 20000	4 2 2^{3} 1^{hd} 4^{3} $4^{6\frac{3}{4}}$	Melendez J D7	107	2.90	86-16	SportingLassie111^{2}DanceTroupe$119^{\frac{3}{4}}$HereComesMyBby117^{4}	Tired	7
12Sep82- 7Bel fst	7f	:23⅕ :46⅖ 1:23⅕	3↑ Ⓕ Alw 32000	2 4 2^{hd} $2^{1\frac{1}{2}}$ 3^{5} 4^{11}	Samyn J L	115	16.80	75-19	Mochila $112^{5\frac{1}{4}}$ Michelle Mon Amour $111^{3\frac{1}{2}}$ Dam Little 104^{2}	Tired	7
10Aug82- 7Sar gd	7f	:22⅘ :45 1:22⅕	3↑ Ⓕ Alw 27000	7 1 $3^{1\frac{1}{2}}$ $3^{2\frac{1}{2}}$ 4^{6} $5^{8\frac{3}{4}}$	Samyn J L	117	*2.40	82-19	Chilling Thought $112^{2\frac{1}{2}}$ MichelleMonAmour$112^{\frac{3}{4}}$Norsan112^{4}	Tired	7

LATEST WORKOUTS ●Apr 19 Bel tr.t 5f sly 1:01⅗ h   Apr 13 Bel tr.t 5f fst 1:01 h   Apr 6 Bel tr.t 4f fst :49 b   Mar 31 Bel tr.t 4f fst :50 b

CASE STUDY: 1983 KENTUCKY DERBY

Aside from standard considerations regarding current fitness, racing fans usually turn to comparative handicapping when analyzing the field for the Kentucky Derby. Analysis based on speed handicapping would be difficult—the average fan does not have access to accurate figures from the myriad of tracks at which the Derby contenders have prepped, nor the sophistication to properly handle the *Form* speed ratings and track variants.

The 1983 Derby presented a difficult puzzle for comparative handicappers to solve. A crucial clue came just an hour before post time. The Flamingo Stakes at Hialeah provided links between most of the major contenders. In that race, eleven horses finished within five lengths of each other, including six that were to compete in the Derby five weeks later. Play Fellow, who finished tenth, four lengths in arrears, came out of that race to edge West Coast leader Marfa in the Blue Grass Stakes at Keeneland. Stablemates Country Pine and High Honors, eighth and eleventh respectively, narrowly missed in separate divisions of the Wood Memorial at Aqueduct. It appeared that the country's three-year-olds were fairly evenly matched. This, of course made the Flamingo-winner Current Hope and runnerup Chumming look all the better. But Current Hope failed to race in the five weeks between the Flamingo and Derby, raising suspicions about his fitness. And Chumming raced dismally in the Derby Trial at Churchill Downs a week before the Derby, after traveling from Florida to Arkansas to New York before arriving in Kentucky. Possibly, he was a tired horse.

The missing link concerned Derby co-favorite Sunny's Halo, the Arkansas Derby winner and choice of the majority of speed handicappers. John Pricci, Newsday's outstanding selector and a devotee of the speed handicapping concepts described in Chapter 9, rated Sunny's Halo's Arkansas Derby at 119, four lengths superior to the best figure from any of the other major Derby preps. Others, however, questioned Sunny's Halo's class. What had he beaten at Oaklawn? As a juvenile, Sunny's Halo was the undisputed champion of Canada, but failed each time he raced in the States. Was he simply beating Canadian-caliber horses in Arkansas? The final clue came from the Twin Spires purse, the co-feature at Churchill Down on Derby Day, a consolation prize, as it were, for horses unable to get into the Derby. When Le Cou Cou, twice soundly beaten by Sunny's Halo at Oaklawn, ran High Honors to a neck decision, and then was placed first via disqualification, it became apparent that the three-year-old Sunny's Halo was a much improved animal, certainly not outclassed, and likely a few lengths the best in the twenty-horse field.

☐ THE KEY RACE ☐

The premier weapon in the comparative handicapper's arsenal is the "key race." This concept has been around for years, and has been discussed by several authors, most notably Andy Beyer and Steve Davidowitz. All have tended to look at the key race from the same viewpoint. We shall discuss this, as well as a second approach to the key race. Stripped to its bare essentials, the key race concept works on the simple premise that if two horses raced competitively with each other, and one came back to win its next start, then naturally the other would also do well next out. Things would look especially promising for the latter had the former moved up in class while winning its subsequent start.

CASE STUDY: SCREEN TREND, ALL OF A SUDDEN, AND MEGATURN

New Yorkers were treated to twin maiden events for three-year-olds on March 3, 1983 at Aqueduct. Together, they proved a comparative handicapper's delight. The first division was won by Screen Trend in a rousing photo finish from All Of A Sudden. The second division went to Megaturn, a hot tip at the track making his first start. Screen Trend's final time was eight lengths the faster of the two, and exceptionally fast for the class. Visually, though, Megaturn was far more impressive. The strapping son of Best Turn changed course sharply in upper stretch, then accelerated dramatically to win going away. So impressive was his performance, in fact, that this writer went on record after the race predicting that, despite what the figures said, Megaturn would defeat either Screen Trend or All Of A Sudden, should they meet in the near future.

On March 13, All Of A Sudden won a maiden race at Aqueduct by seven lengths, and in the process confirmed the figure from his encounter with Screen Trend. Comparative (and speed) handicappers now knew that Screen Trend was genuine, and were not surprised when he ran off with a mile NW1 contest at Aqueduct on March 21, improving on his previous speed figure by a few lengths. Screen Trend's performance made All Of A Sudden look solid in his first allowance attempt on March 27, yet he lost—to our friend Megaturn, of course, who also was making his debut in allowance company. We emphasize that this was not a case of All Of A Sudden failing to run to his figures. On the contrary, Megaturn improved some fourteen lengths. Those who had witnessed his first race were not the least surprised.

Interestingly, Model Flight, second to Megaturn on March 3, earned a speed figure competitive with Screen Trend and All Of A Sudden while winning his next start. And Chaudierre, second to Model Flight on that occasion, came right back to win. From the viewpoint of comparative handicapping, there was indeed a case for Megaturn.

Screen Trend B. c. 3, by Silent Screen—Falling Evidence, by Prove It
Own.—Rafsky J K Br.—Rolling Mill Farm (Md) Tr.—Donato Robert A **114** Lifetime 3 2 1 0 $27,360 1983 3 2 1 0 $27,360 1982 0 M 0 0

21Mar83- 7Aqu sly 1 :45⅕ 1:10 1:36⅗ Alw 21000 3 2 1^{1} 1^{5} 1^{6} 1^{10} Beitia E 117 *1.00 83-26 ScreenTrend117^{10}DerRichrd117$^{1\frac{1}{4}}$KeyToThOrint117$^{3\frac{1}{2}}$ Ridden out 8
3Mar83- 4Aqu fst 6f ⊡:23⅘ :47⅘ 1:11⅕ Md Sp Wt 11 1 2$^{1\frac{1}{2}}$ 1^{hd} 1^{hd} 1^{nk} Beitia E 122 *1.20 88-21 Screen Trend122^{nk}AllOfASudden122$^{5\frac{3}{4}}$ScarletHobeau122^{3} Driving 11
14Feb83- 4Aqu fst 6f ⊡:23 :46⅖ 1:11⅗ Md Sp Wt 12 9 3^{1} 2^{hd} 1^{1} 2½ Beitia E 122 14.10 85-13 Quati Gold 122½ Screen Trend122$^{3\frac{1}{2}}$AtomSmasher122½ Just failed 14
LATEST WORKOUTS Mar 28 Aqu 3f sly :36⅗ h (d) ●Mar 10 Aqu ⊡ 6f sly 1:11⅖ h (d) ●Feb 25 Aqu ⊡ 5f fst 1:01⅕ h ●Feb 8 Aqu ⊡ 4f fst :48⅗ h

All Of A Sudden Ro. c. 3, by Ramsinga—Sudden Snow, by Tudor Grey
Own.—Freeark R H Br.—Freeark R H (Ill) Tr.—Pascuma Warren J **119** Lifetime 6 1 2 1 $22,420 1983 5 1 2 1 $22,420 1982 1 M 0 0

28Mar83- 7Aqu my 7f :22⅕ :45 1:22⅗ Alw 20000 6 3 3$^{1\frac{1}{2}}$ 2½ 2½ 3^{3} Smith A Jr b 122 *1.00 85-14 Megaturn 122$^{1\frac{3}{4}}$ Very Funny 117$^{1\frac{1}{4}}$ AllOfASudden122$^{1\frac{1}{2}}$ Weakened 7
13Mar83- 4Aqu fst 6f ⊡:23 :46⅘ 1:10⅖ Md Sp Wt 4 7 3^{1} 3^{nk} 1$^{2\frac{1}{2}}$ 1^{7} Smith A Jr b 122 *.60 92-08 All OfASudden122^{7}VagueReality117^{3}BonApetite122^{nk} Ridden out 14
3Mar83- 4Aqu fst 6f ⊡:23⅘ :47⅘ 1:11⅕ Md Sp Wt 8 5 4^{3} 3^{nk} 2^{hd} 2^{nk} Smith A Jr 122 2.70 88-21 Screen Trend 122^{nk} AllOfASudden122$^{5\frac{3}{4}}$ScarletHobeau122^{3} Sharp 11
14Feb83- 4Aqu fst 6f ⊡:23 :46⅖ 1:11⅗ Md Sp Wt 14 8 5$^{1\frac{3}{4}}$ 3½ 4$^{2\frac{1}{2}}$ 4$^{4\frac{1}{2}}$ Alvarado R Jr 122 2.50 81-13 Quati Gold 122½ Screen Trend 122$^{3\frac{1}{2}}$ AtomSmasher122½ Wide, str 14
7Jan83- 4Aqu gd 6f ⊡:22⅖ :45⅘ 1:11⅖ Md Sp Wt 7 4 5^{7} 5^{4} 3^{nk} 2^{nk} Alvarado R Jr^{5} 117 26.70 87-16 BelieveTheQueen122^{nk}AllOfASudden117$^{1\frac{1}{4}}$AtomSmshr122$^{3\frac{3}{4}}$ Wide 10
13Aug82- 1AP fst 5½f :22⅕ :46 1:05⅘ ⓈMd Sp Wt 11 9 7$^{7\frac{3}{4}}$ 5$^{9\frac{1}{2}}$ 6^{11} 8^{14} Evans R D 122 3.70 72-18 Group Shoot 122^{5} Whispering Faith 122$^{1\frac{1}{4}}$ Via Lusso 122$^{2\frac{1}{4}}$ 12
LATEST WORKOUTS Mar 26 Bel tr.t 4f fst :48⅖ h ●Mar 20 Bel tr.t 4f my :45⅗ h ●Mar 10 Bel tr.t 5f sly :59⅘ h ●Feb 28 Bel tr.t 4f fst :47 h

Megaturn Dk. b. or br. c. 3, by Best Turn—Good Taste, by Vertex
Own.—Peace J H Br.—Welcome Farm & Winn (Pa) Tr.—Nieminski Richard **119** Lifetime 2 2 0 0 $22,800 1983 2 2 0 0 $22,800 1982 0 M 0 0

28Mar83- 7Aqu my 7f :22⅕ :45 1:22⅗ Alw 20000 4 4 6$^{5\frac{1}{2}}$ 6$^{8\frac{1}{2}}$ 3^{2} 1$^{1\frac{3}{4}}$ Hernandez R 122 3.50 88-14 Megaturn 122$^{1\frac{3}{4}}$ Very Funny 117$^{1\frac{1}{4}}$AllOfASudden122$^{1\frac{1}{2}}$ Drew clear 7
3Mar83- 6Aqu fst 6f ⊡:23⅕ :47⅗ 1:12⅘ Md Sp Wt 4 7 5$^{3\frac{1}{2}}$ 5$^{4\frac{1}{2}}$ 3^{3} 1^{3} Hernandez R 122 2.90 80-21 Megturn122^{3}DrssForSuccss122^{1}ModlFlight122^{nk} Greenly, driving 10
LATEST WORKOUTS Apr 13 Bel tr.t 4f fst :47⅘ b Mar 21 Bel tr.t 4f fst :47⅗ h Feb 26 Bel tr.t 4f fst :49⅘ h Feb 19 Bel tr.t 3f fst :36⅕ h

Of course, one horse may have been on the improving side of its form cycle and the other on (or about to be on) the down side when they met. A close encounter with a horse on the upgrade will not likely change the direction of the deteriorating horse's cycle.

Overall, however, the key-race concept has proven quite productive over the years, and promises to remain profitable. The reason is obvious. The *Racing Form* does not use an asterisk, or any such symbol, to denote key races. The individual handicapper must do the work, identifying key races for himself. Such diligent effort is usually rewarded, at least often enough, and frequently at surprisingly delicious odds. Anything one can learn that remains unknown to the masses is bound to be helpful.

The two examples that follow present contrasting approaches to the key-race concept. One, the traditional approach, waits for two or three horses to come out of a race and run especially well, before declaring the race a key race. Those horses that finished ahead of, or close to, the ones that subsequently ran well would be watched closely in their next start. The other approach anticipates what may become a key race simply by noting beforehand the race's unusual depth of competition. Both approaches attempt to identify fields that were especially strong for their classification, then cash in when horses from these fields return under reasonably similar conditions.

The traditional concept identifies key races on the basis of how well their contestants perform in their next start. Is it not just as valid to make such a decree based on how those same horses had performed in their prior start? Should a race feature four horses coming off wins and three others that were second last time, some fit horses will run well, yet finish out of the money. Their form will be disguised. Their most recent race appears only fair (at best) on paper. Few will know or recall that their performance took place in an exceptionally strong field.

CASE STUDY: THE DOODLE RACE

Although away from the races nearly six weeks (not so negative a sign, actually, knowing her trainer's reputation) when entered in the Boiling Springs Handicap at the Meadowlands September 11, 1982, Doodle was made second choice to the season's leading three-year-old grass filly, Larida. Doodle had proven ability in middle-distance grass competition, and Laffit Pincay in the irons. Most significantly, she was coming from a powerful key race. The second and third finishers behind Doodle in that August 4 allowance event at Saratoga had come back to win stakes races in their next start. The three-year-old Immense captured the Little Silver Handicap over Monmouth's grass course August 17. And the older filly Hush Dear came back August 19 to defeat some of the premier grass fillies in the East in Saratoga's prestigious Diana Handicap. Hush Dear's victory came at the direct expense of Larida, who had raced uncontested on the lead through midstretch. After the results of these two stakes became known, key-race advocates eagerly awaited the return of Doodle.

This example presents the essence of the traditional "key race" concept. It also highlights the realities of racing. Things do not always work out exactly as expected. Perhaps Doodle's six-week layoff between races hurt. Or possibly Larida's exceptionally fast six-furlong pace in the Diana (something pace handicappers would have noticed) cost her in the late stages of that race, allowing Hush Dear to pass her. With an easier pace, Larida may easily have held off Hush Dear, and consequently appeared superior (on paper) to Doodle. Apparently, many present at the Meadowlands that evening felt this to be the case, favoring Larida over Doodle. They were correct, with Larida returning a two-length victress. Another factor contributing to Doodle's defeat was the fact that she was forced into the role of "watchdog." She had to contest the early lead to guarantee that Larida did not coast on a slow pace. The change in tactics—running on the front end—did not help Doodle. (We will discuss the "watchdog" concept in more detail in Chapter 11.)

And now, for the contrasting example:

CASE STUDY: THE LAMEROK RACE

The ninth race at Belmont on Marlboro Day (September 18, 1982) had the looks of a potential key race. Six of the nine starters (Ol' Reliable was scratched) appeared solid contenders. Only Grandange could be thrown out. Let's look at the contenders, one at a time, in post-position order. Note that the race was at a mile and a sixteenth on the grass for "nonwinners of two other than maiden, claiming, or starter."

Belmont race 9 past performance chart for the one-and-one-sixteenth-mile turf allowance, showing horses Lamerok, Pin Puller, and Ol' Reliable with their past performance lines and latest workouts.

Lord Lister

B. c. 3, by Sir Lister—Negation, by Mongo
Br.—Whitmore Mrs H P (Md)
Own.—Whitmore Mrs H P
Tr.—Hirsch William J Jr

						Lifetime	1982	10	1	6	3	$76,997
				113		12 2 6 3	1981	2	1	0	0	$9,360
						$86,357	Turf	3	0	3	0	$13,860

6Sep82- 8Bel fst 1 :45½ 1:10½ 1:35¾ 3↑Alw H Jerome H 5 6 52½ 42 57 38¾ Graell A 107 15.60 79–17 Fit to Fight 112⁶ John's Gold 115²½ Lord Lister 107¹ Wide 6
29Aug82- 9Sar fm 1⅛ ⊕:48½ 1:12 1:48¾ 3↑Alw 21000 3 3 32 32 2½ 2ⁿᵒ Maple E 112 *2.00 85–08 Forkali 122ⁿᵒ Lord Lister 112⁶½ Broadly 117⁴ Just missed 10
14Aug82-10Suf fst 1⁷⁰ :46½ 1:10½ 1:41½ Yankee H 5 6 66½ 43½ 52½ 33½ Graell A 110 17.90 90–17 Timely Writer 125½SalemEndRoad110³LordLister110¹½ Lugged in 8
6Aug82- 5Sar fm 1⅛ ⊕:50 1:14 1:43¾ 3↑Alw 21000 2 2 21 1ʰᵈ 1ʰᵈ 2½ Maple E 112 3.10 77–20 Thunder Puddles 112½ LordLister110²HouseSpeaker112½ Gamely 9
25Jly82- 8Bel fst 1 :46½ 1:11½ 1:37 Jamaica H 4 3 31 32 25 29¾ Maple E 111 9.30 71–21 John's Gold 113⁹¾ Lord Lister 111²½ Estoril 114⁵½ Best of others 5
10Jly82- 8Key fst 1⅛ :46½ 1:10½ 1:42½ Devon 5 5 33 31½ 2½ 21½ Smith T R III 117 5.80 88–19 Star Choice 117¹½ Lord Lister117²ThunderRunner115⁶½ Game try 10
20Jun82- 7Bel gd 1 ⊕:48 1:12 1:39 3↑Alw 21000 6 4 41½ 21 2½ 2 Cordero A Jr 112 4.36 69–33 Heroic Spirit 109½ Lord Lister 112ⁿᵏ Piling 117ʰᵈ Gamely 9
5Jun82- 3Bel gd 8f :22½ :46 1:10 3↑Alw 20000 2 5 41½ 54 32 22½ Shoemaker W 109 2.80 90–11 FittoFight113²½LordLister109ʰᵈAccomplishment112²½ In close st. 6
27May82- 8Bel fst 6f :22½ :45½ 1:09½ 3↑Alw 20000 1 7 78½ 55½ 54½ 32½ Maple E 117 11.00 92–18 T. Dykes 114² Accomplishment 112½ Lord Lister 112½ Mild rally 9
6Jan82- 7Aqu fst 1⅛ □:49½ 1:13¾ 1:45¾ Alw 17000 1 1 1½ 1½ 1½ 1½ Venezia M 117 *2.10 86–16 Lord Lister 117¹½ Brae Axe 117¹½ What A Charger 117¹ Driving 7
LATEST WORKOUTS Sep 17 Bel 3f fst :37 b ● Sep 13 Bel 4f fst :50 b Sep 5 Bel 3f fst :36¾ h Aug 28 Sar 3f fst :36½ h

Groomed

B. c. 3, by Naskra—Misty Bride, by Hethersett
Br.—Meadowhill (Ky)
Own.—Meadowhill
Tr.—Johnson Philip G

						Lifetime	1982	8	2	1	2	$32,280
				113		9 2 2 2	1981	1	M	1	0	$3,080
						$35,360	Turf	5	1	1	1	$20,400

15Aug82- 5Sar fm 1⅛ ⊤:48½ 1:11½ 1:36½ 3↑Alw 21000 7 6 65 53½ 31 31½ Samyn J L b 112 3.20 90–07 Who'sForDinner114¹½Sprink117ⁿᵒGroomed112¹½ Altered course 10
8Jly82- 8Bel fm 1⅛ ⊤:45½ 1:09½ 1:40½ 3↑Alw 21000 8 7 73¾ 74 43½ 22½ Samyn J L b 111 16.80 91–12 Runaway Groom113²½Groomed111¼RedBrigade113½ Unruly, wide 11
1Jly82- 7Bel fm 1¼ ⊤:48½ 1:38½2:03½ 3↑Alw 21000 3 3 42½ 54½ 61½ 61⁷ Samyn J L b 111 2.80 61–20 Rivertot 117½ Shoen 117¼ Lejoli 112ⁿᵒ Tired 6
20Jun82- 7Bel gd 1 ⊕:48 1:14 1:39 3↑Alw 21000 8 8 62½ 1½ 2ʰᵈ 41 Samyn J L b 111 3.00e 69–33 Heroic Spirit 109½ Lord Lister 110ⁿᵏ Piling 117ʰᵈ Weakened 9
29May82- 5Bel fm 1 ⊤:47¼ 1:12 1:37¾ 3↑Alw 20000 10 4 32 3½ 31 1ⁿᵏ Samyn J L b 108 5.30 78–18 Groomed 108ⁿᵏ Hunter Hawk 113² Honed Edge 108¹½ Driving 11
20May82- 7Bel fst 1⅛ :47½ 1:11½ 1:43¾ 3↑Alw 20000 7 3 3ʰᵏ 2ʰᵈ 44½ 58¾ Samyn J L b 108 *2.20e 75–18 Main Top 113⁴½ Play For Love 108ⁿᵏ FastReason112²½ Weakened 7
10May82- 7Aqu fst 6f :23 :47 1:12¾ Md Sp Wt 5 5 45½ 36½ 23 1ʰᵈ Samyn J L b 122 *.80e 79–29 Groomed 122ʰᵈ Fortuis 122²½ Arctic Avenger 122³ Lasted 10
13Mar82- 4Aqu fst 6f □:22½ :45½ 1:10½ Md Sp Wt 9 4 32 32½ 34 25½ Skinner K 122 *1.40 82–17 Jordana'sCount122²²PamsMcAllister122⁴Groomed122½ Drifted out 14
28Dec81- 6Aqu gd 6f :23 :46½ 1:11½ Md Sp Wt 9 3 31 2ʰᵈ 22 25½ Samyn J L b 122 *1.00 82–18 HollywoodHndrson118⁵½Gold113² FstGold113² Best of others 9
LATEST WORKOUTS Sep 15 Bel 4f fst :47¾ h ● Sep 10 Bel 6f fst 1:11¾ h Sep 5 Bel tr.t 4f fst :48½ h Aug 31 Bel 5f fst 1:00¾ h

Natomas Breeze

Ch. h. 5, by Secretariat—Spanish Breeze, by Windy City II
Br.—Grosse Pointe Stud Farm (Ky)
Own.—Badgett B
Tr.—Murty Wayne

						Lifetime	1982	4	0	1	1	$8,670
				117		20 2 4 3	1981	15	2	3	2	$45,330
						$54,000	Turf	5	1	1	0	$39,220

20Aug82- 7Sar fm 1⅛ ⊤:50 2:04½2:28¾ 3↑Alw 21000 5 7 78½ 43 45 27½ Migliore R 117 6.00 91–11 Half Iced 112²¾ Natomas Breeze 117ⁿᵏ Lamerok 114ʰᵈ Rallied 8
6Aug82- 8Sar fm 1⅛ ⊕:48½ 1:12½ 1:43¾ 3↑Alw 21000 7 8 86 55½ 54 5¾ Migliore R 117 16.80 74–20 World Leader 117¹ Pinstripe 112ʰᵏ Secret Cipher112ⁿᵏ No factor 9
16Jan82- 5SA fm 1⅛ ⊤:47½ 1:36½ 2:02 Alw 27000 9 10 10¹¹ 76 78½ 78¾ Toro F 115 *2.70 68–23 Sunshine Swag 114¹ Princely Verdict 120ⁿᵏ Full Payment 121¹½ 11
2Jan82- 9SA hy 1½ :48½ 1:14 1:53½ Alw 27000 8 5 59 46½ 49 36 McHargue D G 117 4.00 54–37 Caesar's Profile 121²½ Western 118½ Natomas Breeze 117²½ 8
26Dec81- 6SA fst 1⅛ :46½ 1:10½ 1:42 3↑Alw 25000 5 6 69½ 68½ 55 36¼ Shoemaker W 117 9.30 85–10 Mehmet 114²½ Full Payment 119²½ Natomas Breeze 117¹ 7
27Nov81- 3Aqu fst 1⅛ :48½ 1:12½ 1:50½ 3↑Alw 18000 3 7 712 710 47½ 49 Cordero A Jr 117 7.00 72–26 Castle Knight 115²½ Piling 115¹¼ LetterFromLucy115¹ No factor 7
12Nov81- 7Aqu fm 1⅛ ⊕:47½ 1:41¾2:20¾ 3↑Alw 18000 8 8 83½ 42½ 45½ 21½ Migliore R5 112 *1.10 66–29 ComeRainorShine117¼NatomsBreeze112½TheMessnger117¾ Wide 9
20Oct81- 8Lrl fm 1½ ⊕:48¾ 2:03½2:29½ 3↑Turf Cup H 4 14 14⁸12¹10⁹²10¹⁷ 8¹¹ Vasquez J 113 8.00f 62–23 Change the Patch 112ⁿᵒMajesty'sWorld110¾ASureHit111¹ Outrun 15
5Oct81- 7Bel fm 1¼ ⊤:47½ 1:36½ 2:00¾ 3↑Alw 25000 2 7 71 53¾ 3½ 2ⁿᵒ Vasquez J 119 5.80 91–13 ChangethePtch114ⁿᵒNtomsBreeze119¾NephewScott117½ Sharp 7
26Sep81- 7Bel fm 1⅛ :46½ 1:09½ 1:43½ 3↑Alw 21000 1 8 81² 89 79½ 49½ Migliore R5 117 6.60 89–09 Silent Sunrise 117½ Reactant 117ⁿᵏ Erin's Tiger 114⁴ Rallied 8
LATEST WORKOUTS Aug 17 Bel tr.t 1 fst 1:42¾ h ● Aug 4 Bel tr.t 4f fst :48½ h Jly 26 Bel 3f fst :37¾ bg ●Jly 21 Bel tr.t 6f gd 1:15 b (d)

Eyepleaser

Dk. b. or br. c. 3, by Verbatim—Betsy Be Good, by Pretendre
Br.—Gentry T (Ky)
Own.—Hunt N B
Tr.—Wright Frank I

						Lifetime	1982	9	2	1	0	$28,500
				115		13 2 2 0	1981	4	M	1	0	$5,067
						$33,567	Turf	7	2	2	0	$31,827

29Aug82- 9Sar fm 1⅛ ⊕:48½ 1:12 1:48¾ 3↑Alw 21000 7 2 2½ 21½ 46½ 6¹¹ Montoya D 117 4.30 74–08 Forkali 122ⁿᵒ Lord Lister 112⁶½ Broadly 117⁴ Used up 10
6Aug82- 9Sar fm 1⅛ ⊕:49 1:12½ 1:55¾ 3↑Alw 20000 5 6 42 32 1ʰᵈ 12½ Montoya D 112 13.40 87–20 Eyepleaser 112²½ Silver Tom 117ⁿᵏ Condition Red 112²½ Driving 11
17Jly82- 4Bel fm 1 ⊕:45½ 1:11¼ 1:36½ 3↑Md Sp Wt 3 4 43 43 41 1ⁿᵒ Cintron J O 116 *.90 84–12 Eyepleaser 116ⁿᵒ Beau Bidder 116ⁿᵏ Disco Dad 116¹½ Driving 8
26Jun82- 9Bel fm 1⅛ ⊕:45½ 1:10½ 1:42½ 3↑Md Sp Wt 2 4 42 32½ 22 2ʰᵈ Cintron J O 116 18.80 85–16 Lamerok 114ʰᵈ Eyepleaser 114⁷½ Beau Bidder 114¹ Checked 10
21Jun82- 6Bel fst 1 :47½ 1:11½ 1:36½ 3↑Md Sp Wt 10 6 75½ 89½ 10¹⁵ 8¹⁶ Venezia M 114 29.40 66–14 Cintula 114½ Trenchant 114½ Fulton 114⁵¼ Outrun 10
4Mar82- 4Aqu fst 6f □:23 :46¾ 1:11½ Md Sp Wt 11 5 44½ 56½ 610 715 Venezia M b 122 37.40 75–15 Air Forbes Won 122⁷½SilverPike122ⁿᵒElevatorShoes122ⁿᵒ Outrun 12
15Feb82- 4Aqu fst 1⅛ ⊕:48½ 1:13½ 1:46½ Md Sp Wt 1 5 44½ 56½ 610 715 Venezia M b 122 7.40 65–14 A Real Leader 122²½ Private Sun 117²½ SenateSeat122½ Gave way 11
28Jan82- 6Aqu fst 1⅛ ⊕:47½ 1:12½ 1:45¾ Md Sp Wt 12 3 2ʰᵈ 42 44½ 45½ MacBeth D b 122 8.90 80–12 Intervening Hero122½PrivateSun117¹AReaLeader122⁴ Weakened 12
7Jan82- 4Aqu fst 1⅛ □:47¾ 1:13 Md Sp Wt 5 9 74² 64 52½ 45 Martens G b 122 10.10 70–17 ProspectNorth122⁴½TrafficOrdinance117²½IvanLendl122¹½ Rallied 10
28Dec81- 6Aqu gd 6f □:23 :46¾ 1:11½ Md Sp Wt 8 4 63½ 74½ 68½ 51² Santiago A 118 45.50 76–18 Hollywood Hendrson 118⁵½ Groomed 118³½ Fast Gold113² Evenly 12
LATEST WORKOUTS Sep 9 Bel 3f fst :36 h ● Aug 23 Sar ⊕ 6f fm 1:12½ h Aug 14 Sar 3f fst :36¾ h Aug 2 Bel 4f fst :49 b

Broadly

B. c. 3, by Tentam—Broadside, by Stage Door Johnny
Br.—Greentree Stud Inc (Ky)
Own.—Greentree Stable
Tr.—Reinacher Robert Jr

						Lifetime	1982	5	2	0	2	$27,360
				115		6 2 0 2	1981	1	M	0	0	
						$27,360	Turf	2	1	0	1	$14,520

29Aug82- 9Sar fm 1⅛ ⊕:48½ 1:12 1:48¾ 3↑Alw 21000 5 10 10¹²10⁹½ 66¾ 36½ Fell J 117 8.90 79–08 Forkali 122ⁿᵒ Lord Lister 112⁶½ Broadly 117⁴ Rallied 10
13Aug82- 2Sar fm 1⅛ ⊕:47 1:12 1:44½ 3↑Alw 20000 9 10 87 77½ 53½ 11½ Fell J 117 10.10 76–16 Broadly 113½ □Strivor 112ʰᵈ Bandwagon 117¹½ Driving 10
28Jun82- 1Bel fm 1⅛ :46½ 1:10¾ 1:49½ 3↑Alw 20000 3 7 710 88½ 81³ 81² Fell J 114 *2.80 69–17 Tayfun 113¾ Pirouette 117¹ The Time Is Now 113ⁿᵏ Outrun 8
13Jun82- 2Bel gd 1⅛ ⊕:46½ 1:11 1:43¾ 3↑Md Sp Wt 2 2 21 2ʰᵈ 11 11 Fell J 114 *1.00 84–13 Broadly 114¹ I'm A Lyre 114⁸½ Twelve Tone 114⁴ Ridden out 7
29May82- 9Bel gd 7f :23½ :46 1:23¾ 3↑Md Sp Wt 1 8 77 65½ 33½ 22¾ Fell J 122 *2.60 81–13 Bambolino 122¾ Courage In Gold 122²½ Broadly 122⁵½ Rallied 8
17Sep81- 6Bel my 7f :22½ :46½ 1:25½ Md Sp Wt 7 6 87½ 79½ 54½ 54¾ MacBeth D 118 11.60 74–15 Bud's Majestic 118³¾TidesOfChange113½Bambolino118¾ No factor 8
LATEST WORKOUTS Sep 14 Bel 6f fst 1:14½ b ● Sep 6 Bel 5f fst 1:01¾ b Aug 24 Sar 6f fst 1:14 b Aug 21 Sar 4f fst :53½ b

Muskoka Wyck

B. c. 3, by Tentam—Lachesis, by Iron Ruler
Br.—Mandyl Farm (Md)
Own.—Rokeby Stables
Tr.—Miller Mack

						Lifetime	1982	5	2	2	1	$32,830
				113		7 2 3 1	1981	2	M	1	0	$3,740
						$36,570						

2Sep82- 7Bel sly 7f :22½ :45 1:22½ 3↑Alw 20000 1 3 1½ 1½ 12 24½ Fell J b 113 *1.50 87–19 PuritanChief119⁴½MuskokWyck113ʰᵈShiftySheik113⁴½ Weakened 7
22Aug82- 6Sar fst 6f :22½ :45½ 1:09½ 3↑Alw 20000 7 6 41½ 31 33 36½ Fell J b 112 *.80 89–12 TheTimeIsNow117²JetStm113ⁿᵒMuskokWyck113¾ Lacked a rally 7
3Jly82- 8Del fst 6f :22 :45½ 1:10½ 3↑Alw 20000 7 3 41½ 32½ 21½ Molina V H b 119 3.00 85–21 Tiny Rollick 112½ Muskoka Wyck 119¹½Wyetown112ⁿᵏ Game try 8
12Jun82- 6Bel fst 6f :22½ :45½ 1:10½ 3↑Alw 19000 4 7 21 21 21 1ⁿᵏ Fell J 114 *1.10 91–14 Muskoka Wyck 114ⁿᵏ ExclusiveOne114²½ Tory Willow111⁴½ Driving 7
2Jun82- 3Bel fst 6f :23½ :46½ 1:09½ 3↑Md Sp Wt 5 2 65 52½ 41½ 1ⁿᵒ Fell J b 114 5.40 90–14 MuskokaWyck114ⁿᵒ ExclusiveOne114²½HoldYourSnapper118¹ Gamely 12
40ct81- 2Bel fst 6f :22½ :46½ 1:12 3↑Md Sp Wt 6 7 21½ 1½ 11 2ʰᵈ Donahue G W5 113 *2.80 81–25 Bronze Cup118¾MuskokaWyck113²HoldYourSnapper118¹ Gamely 12
25Sep81- 5Bel fst 6f :22½ :46½ 1:10½ Md Sp Wt 11 13 76 86½ 611 5¹⁵ Donahue G W5 118 11.10 74–18 Guyana 118ⁿᵒ Distinctive Pro 118⁴ Joy's Nest 113²½ Off slowly 13
LATEST WORKOUTS Sep 17 Bel 3f fst :36½ h ● Sep 13 Bel 6f fst 1:12¾ h Sep 8 Bel 4f fst :48½ h Aug 31 Bel 3f fst :35½ h

Grandange

Ch. c. 4, by Son Ange—Floragranda, by Grand Central
Br.—R & G Thorobreds (Ky)
Own.—Corrado F L
Tr.—Hernandez Ramon M

						Lifetime	1982	3	0	0	2	$1,120
				107¹⁰		8 2 1 2	1981	5	2	1	0	$10,462
						$11,582						

5Sep82- 1Bel fst 1 □:23½ :46½ 1:11¾ 3↑Clm 18000 6 1 51½ 76 86½ 86¼ Alvarado R Jr7 106 19.20 76–18 NonRecours113²½BusyHilrious117²½BigSport108ʰᵈ Unruly pre-st. 12
27Jun82- 7FL fst 1 :48½ 1:13½ 1:40½ 3↑Alw 6200 5 2 74¾ 22 23 33½ Reynolds R L 115 3.00 77–23 Dr. Dodd 113½ Holiday Chip 113² Grandange 115½ Drifted out 6
13Jun82- 9FL fst 6f :23 :47 1:12½ 3↑Alw 5000 5 3 2ʰᵈ 32½ 42½ 32 Reynolds R L 113 22.70 83–16 Jodhpur 115² Mister Kite 114ⁿᵒ Grandange 113¼ Weakened 11
12Sep81- 1Bel fst 1 :47½ 1:13½ 1:39½ Clm 12000 4 1 21 2½ 12 12½ McCarron G 113 5.70 72–26 Grandange 113²½ L'Arabique 117ⁿᵏ Proud Pic 117ⁿᵒ Ridden out 9
12Aug81- 7FL fst 6f :22 :46½ 1:13¾ 3↑Alw 4600 4 3 32½ 33½ 33 22½ Reynolds R L 115 17.30 77–23 Enthusiasm 110²½ Grandange 115² Sky High Bid 108³ Rallied 8
25Jly81- 4FL fst 1⁷⁰ :48½ 1:14½ 1:46 3↑Md Sp Wt 7 2 1ʰᵈ 11½ 14 17½ Reynolds R L 115 6.70 71–21 Grandange 115⁷½ Roi De Pique 116½ Beasty Tales 114²½ Driving 7
8Jly81- 4FL fst 6f :23 :46½ 1:13¾ 3↑Md Sp Wt 2 8 54½ 56 44 98 Reynolds R L 115 17.60 72–22 Dockwalloper 122½ Exclusive Needle110⁶BeastyTales115²½ Evenly 9
1Jly81- 5FL fst 5½f □:23½ :47½ 1:07¾ 3↑Md Sp Wt 2 9 914 815 711 68¾ Reynolds R L 115 21.50 76–25 Walloon Lake110³ExclusiveNeedle110⁶Dockwalloper122¹ Outrun 9
LATEST WORKOUTS Sep 11 Bel tr.t 4f fst :49 b Sep 3 Bel tr.t 3f sly :38¾ b ●Aug 23 Bel tr.t 4f fst :48½ h

LAMEROK: This son of Round Table from an Exclusive Native mare (strong grass bloodlines) won his first two grass tries, then finished a gutsy second to the classy Majesty's Prince in the Lexington. Although his last two starts hint of deteriorating form, perhaps the drop in class and the shorter distance will be more to this front-runner's liking.

PIN PULLER: As a rule, Chester Ross does not train the kind of stock worth taking to Saratoga. Instead, he sent Pin Puller to Monmouth Park, where the colt broke its maiden on grass, then finished a fast-closing third in that track's grassy Choice Handicap. Returned to his home base at Belmont, Pin Puller was an impressive winner in "nonwinners of one" company, and now was taking the mandatory step up the allowance ladder.

LORD LISTER: This colt had started three times on grass, and finished second on each occasion. Particularly noteworthy was his close finish to Thunder Puddles, who since had won two stakes on grass. Lord Lister's recent dirt efforts were in stakes competition, and resulted in commendable efforts behind the likes of Timely Writer and Fit to Fight.

GROOMED: Although away from the races five weeks, this colt was the betting favorite, based no doubt on his most recent start. The first two finishers in that race had since done very well, Who's For Dinner running third in the Rutgers, and Sprink winning the Brighton Beach Handicap, in their next starts. Prior to that race, Groomed had finished a solid second to the eventual Travers winner Runaway Groom, despite racing wide. His workouts in preparation for today's race were top-notch.

NATOMAS BREEZE: This late-running five-year-old son of Secretariat had edged Lamerok in his latest, but the shorter distance today did not appear in his favor. Not a likely contender, but a late threat to be in the money.

EYEPLEASER: This one appeared to have gone off form, after consecutive wins on the grass. He had, however, narrowly missed to Lamerok in a maiden event June 26. Compared to some of the contenders already seen, Eyepleaser seemed to lack class. Consequently, not a likely contender, even if he was fit.

BROADLY: Another late-rallier who might not appreciate the mile-and-a-sixteenth distance, this son of Tentam and a Stage Door Johnny mare won his grass debut, then rallied late despite an extremely wide trip when third recently. He might not get up at this distance, but he's a solid late threat to be in the money.

MUSKOWA WYCK: This is the mystery horse in the race, and likely to be a key factor in its outcome. A son of Tentam, who won Grade I stakes on the grass, and from the grass-oriented Mack Miller barn, Muskoka Wyck had to be reckoned with in his grass debut. If he took a liking to the grass, he most likely would set a fast pace, and make things difficult for Lamerok, at the very least. An unknown quantity, but a definite threat to lead all the way, or possibly set things up for the late closers.

To summarize, then, the first four horses were of stakes quality, both of the next pair had been competitive with Lamerok, and the last two were promising animals normally among the choices in a race of this classification. Quite a power-packed field for a restricted allowance race!

Long before this field reached the starting gate, clever handicappers would have realized that at least three (probably) sharp horses would finish out of the money—at least three horses with hidden form worthy of serious consideration next time they ran (two of them, it was hoped, at longer distances). And the first three finishers would be given extra credit for having done so well in such a strong "nonwinners of two" field. As things turned out, Muskoka Wyck did not take to the grass at all, allowing Lamerok to have things his own way on the lead, then draw clear impressively through the lane. Lord Lister ran his usual second, and both Broadly and Natomas Breeze rallied nicely, for third and fourth. Pin Puller ran an even fifth, while Groomed hung after bidding mildly and Eyepleaser tired from his early efforts. Speed figures for the race were above-average all the way—both pace and final time figures running two points faster than par for the classification.

Comparative handicappers would have eagerly awaited the return of each of these horses, suspecting that several would run well. Unfortunately, things did not work out as planned. For one thing, the weatherman failed to cooperate. Lord Lister, Broadly, Natomas Breeze, and Pin Puller all returned on schedule, entered in a mile and a quarter grass event September 27 at Belmont. Heavy rains, however, forced the race onto the wet main track. All bets were off (these were grass horses, remember), and thankfully so, as only Lord Lister hit the board. Pin Puller returned October 11 at the Meadowlands, in a mile and a sixteenth grass allowance. He won going away, and returned a liberal $8.20, and then repeated a month later in NW3 company, paying $4.40 this time. Groomed disappeared until late October, only to reappear in a dirt race, in which he finished last. Muskoka Wyck was tried twice (without success) at route distances on the main track before returning (successfully) to the sprint distances he clearly preferred. Eyepleaser returned in a grass contest, a seven-furlong sprint that proved short of his best distance.

This race was purposely chosen because it fulfilled the requirements for a potential key race, yet also makes another important point. Most of the horses in the September 18 field failed to reproduce their good form (going in) in their subsequent starts because they were entered in what turned out to be unsuitable spots. Only one was bettable in a follow-up start. Only one raced in a grass route within six weeks of September 18.

Oh yes, there is the race winner, Lamerok, to report on. He did race on the grass in his next start, at a mile and an eighth, in a stakes race, the Volante Handicap at Santa Anita. And he won, needless to say! Most New Yorkers awaiting Lamerok's next start were taken by surprise, unaware the horse had been shipped across the country. Nobody ever said this game was fair! Luckily for New Yorkers, Lamerok paid just $7.20.

The key-race concept is especially useful with maiden races, and with grass races for three-year-olds early in the season. In both cases, the form of the contestants is often clouded due to lack of racing experience, or experience on the grass course. Some of these fields attract an overflow of talented runners, many of whom will look only average on paper, until others from the same field prove their worth in subsequent starts. With maiden races on the dirt, speed figures often point to the same races, and horses. But on the grass, where figures are less reliable, the key race is a powerful weapon.

□ CONCLUSION □

It is wise to make note that a horse earned an especially big figure, had a bad trip, ran against a track bias, or participated in a key race in its latest start. Then await that horse's next appearance. Yet the handicapper must not fall into the trap of feeling "obliged" to bet the horse when it does reappear. If the horse is not properly placed, must race against a track bias, or if the odds are unacceptable, the smart player will pass. All handicappers, regardless of their persuasion (speed, trip, class), face this situation on a daily basis, and must acquire the patience to await a better spot for the horse, or a better betting opportunity. They should not be psychologically deflated should the horse win, without their betting support.

Chapter 9

SPEED AND PACE FIGURES

Speed handicapping is the attempt to analyze a horse's ability and (early) speed potential in a quantitative manner, by means of precise numerical ratings. These ratings, called "speed figures," allow accurate comparisons of races run on different days over different distances at different tracks. Speed handicapping became immensely popular during the latter half of the 1970s. Books such as my own *Winning at the Races*, Andrew Beyer's *Picking Winners*, and Gordon Jones' *Gordon Jones To Win!* created legions of speed handicappers. So many, in fact, that the obvious "figure horse" routinely becomes the betting favorite nowadays. As a result, speed handicappers of the 1980s must go beyond speed figures that rate only the final time of races, if they wish to remain ahead of the game. While such figures remain quite helpful, they become more useful and meaningful when seen in the context of the total race. They are best interpreted when viewed side-by-side with figures that rate the pace of the race.

Many successful players of the 1980s focus their handicapping technique on the relationship between speed figures and trips. A significant part of trip handicapping is the pace trip, best revealed through pace figures. When these are placed out front of traditional speed figures for the race, they reveal how the race was run, and make the final figures all the more meaningful. In addition, many profitable winners are spotlighted by internal pace figures from their most recent race. For these reasons, we shall supplement our discussion of speed figures with a parallel development of pace figures. We can assure the reader that the extra time spent will be well worth the effort.

□ RACE TIMES □

We shall begin our discussion of speed figures with a look at what can be found in the *Daily Racing Form* relating to this topic. First, there are the actual running times of the races included in a given horse's past performances—fractional times for the pacesetters at the first and second calls, and the final time of the race winner. Quarter- and half-mile fractional times are given for sprints, and half-mile and six-furlong fractionals for standard middle-distance routes (see Chapter 3).

Tuckahoe Glory — Ch. f. 3, by Explodent—Fame and Glory, by Francis S — $5,000 — Br.—O'Farrell M & Nancy (Fla) — Tr.—Smith Hamilton A — 107^{5}

Own.—Medico L G

	St.	1st	2nd	3rd	Amt.
1979	13	2	0	2	$10,950
1978	13	2	2	2	$16,175

28Jun79- 2Pim	fst	6f	:23⅕	:46⅘	1:12⅕	ⒻClm 8500	6	7	9^{12}	9^{14}	9^{11}	10^{10}	Lindberg G	b 114	37.00	75-15	Rejuvavate 114^{2} DottiesProspect109^{1}SassySneakers115^{no}	Outrun 10
30May79- 9Pim	fst	1$\frac{1}{16}$	:47⅖	1:12⅕	1:45⅖	Clm c-6500	4	4	$4^{1\frac{1}{2}}$	$5^{5\frac{1}{2}}$	$6^{7\frac{1}{2}}$	8^{10}	Miceli M	b 109	17.70	68-16	Umpy Dan 114^{1} Mr. Josh P. 114^{1} Poggio Road 107$^{3\frac{1}{2}}$	Tired 12
18May79- 4Pim	fst	1$\frac{1}{16}$	:48⅕	1:14⅕	1:47⅖	Clm 6500	5	4	4^{5}	$5^{2\frac{1}{4}}$	$7^{8\frac{1}{2}}$	$8^{8\frac{1}{4}}$	Pino M G^{5}	b 106	5.50	60-21	Asli Han 109$^{\frac{3}{4}}$ Bounty Boy 119^{2} Miss Satin 105^{hd}	Wide 8
25Apr79- 5Pim	fst	1$\frac{1}{16}$	:48⅕	1:14⅗	1:48⅘	Clm 6500	7	6	5^{4}	4^{4}	4^{4}	$3^{2\frac{1}{4}}$	Baker C J^{5}	b 108	4.10	59-21	Pioneer Pop 107^{nk} SurfSoldier109^{2}TuckahoeGlory108^{2}	No excuse 9
18Apr79- 5Pim	fst	6f	:24⅖	:48⅘	1:14	ⒻClm 6500	10	1	$7^{6\frac{1}{4}}$	$5^{4\frac{1}{2}}$	$3^{3\frac{1}{2}}$	$3^{2\frac{3}{4}}$	Mackaben B W^{5}	b 112	5.60	73-27	CornishHussy114^{nk}MureenMichl109$^{2\frac{1}{2}}$TuckhoGlory112^{1}	Mild rally 10
9Apr79- 2Pim	sly	6f	:23⅗	:47⅘	1:14	ⒻClm c-5000	3	7	$8^{5\frac{1}{4}}$	$6^{6\frac{1}{2}}$	$5^{7\frac{1}{2}}$	$4^{3\frac{1}{2}}$	Bracciale V Jr	b 117	*2.80	72-26	Leisure Dancer 102$^{1\frac{1}{2}}$ Aunt Puddin 112no Best Luck 112^{2}	Rallied 11
3Apr79- 6Pim	sly	6f	:23⅘	:48⅗	1:15⅗	ⒻClm 7500	3	7	$8^{8\frac{3}{4}}$	$7^{7\frac{3}{4}}$	$5^{8\frac{3}{4}}$	$5^{3\frac{1}{2}}$	Osani J R Jr^{7}	b 110	10.60	64-28	ShortyQueen114$^{\frac{1}{2}}$DottiesProspect115^{2}SweetEllieDee114^{no}	Outrun 8
13Mar79- 6Bow	fst	6f	:23⅗	:47⅗	1:13⅖	ⒻClm 8500	6	7	8^{8}	8^{12}	7^{11}	7^{9}	Miceli M	b 119	9.20	64-29	Gyro Lite 114$^{2\frac{3}{4}}$ Dotties Prospect 109^{nk} Can CanBelle114^{2}	Outrun 8
6Mar79- 7Bow	my	6f	:23	:47	1:14	ⒻClm 9500	2	6	$6^{5\frac{1}{2}}$	7^{12}	6^{12}	6^{13}	Miceli M	b 112	7.20	57-32	Mrs. Secret 114$^{\frac{1}{2}}$ Sut 114^{2} Coming Out 112^{1}	Outrun 7
1Mar79- 5Bow	fst	6f	:23⅘	:48⅗	1:15⅗	ⒻClm 7500	2	6	$5^{1\frac{3}{4}}$	6^{4}	$3^{3\frac{1}{2}}$	$1^{2\frac{1}{2}}$	Miceli M	b 115	6.70	62-33	Tuckahoe Glory 115$^{2\frac{1}{2}}$MarisaLee115^{hd}LittleIodine105^{1}	Drew clear 7

LATEST WORKOUTS Jly 18 Del 4f fst :50⅖ b

Note that times are recorded to the nearest fifth of a second, and so contain a built-in roundoff error of as much as one-tenth of a second, the equivalent of half a length. Closer precision cannot be expected. To determine the time of a horse not in the lead at a particular call, simply add one fifth of a second for each length behind the leader. Though not completely accurate, this avoids much wasted effort involving fractional arithmetic. A horse averages closer to six lengths per second—more, actually, in the early stages of a race, when it is traveling its fastest, and somewhat less at the finish, as it slows down. Consequently, lengths behind mean one thing at the first call, and quite another at the wire. There is really no need for the precise ratings of horses that lost or trailed early by wide margins. A horse's ability should be measured by figures earned when it performed well, not when slaughtered. Horses that trail early will not enter into any analysis of pace, so their pace figures are practically useless.

□ SPEED RATINGS AND TRACK VARIANTS □

Few handicappers use official running times as the basis for their speed analysis. Many glance at fractional times to help visualize the probable pace, but are as likely to be deceived as not. One's first attempts at speed handicapping usually are based on the two numbers found toward the right-hand side of the past performance lines—the speed rating and the track variant.

Promising Forecast B. f. 3, by Explodent—Stormy Pursuit, by Tropical Breeze

But both the speed rating and the track variant have serious flaws which render them almost useless to serious speed handicappers. Very few successful speed handicappers do not make their own figures. While this entails a considerable amount of work, it definitely has its rewards. Speed handicappers live for situations where their figures differ significantly from the numbers found in the *Form*. Daily variants calculated as described in this chapter differ from the *Form* variant by an average of two points, yet in one instance the two may agree, while in another the difference may be four points or even more. It is these latter situations that speed handicappers watch for, and exploit.

Speed Ratings

A speed rating is calculated by comparing the official running time of a race with the track record for the distance in effect at the beginning of the meet. Each record is assigned the rating one hundred, and then one point is subtracted for each fifth of a second slower than the record, with the result being the speed rating for the race. For example, a six-furlong race run in 1:11.2, sixteen fifths slower than the 1:08.1 track record, is rated 84, which is sixteen points below 100.

The *Form* speed rating has three flaws: First, should a track record be broken during one meeting, the value of race times will change from that meeting to the next. What had been an 84 (sixteen points slower than the old record) will then become 82 (eighteen points behind the new record), should the new record be two fifths faster than the old one. Those unaware of the change will make errors when comparing speed ratings from the two meetings. Second, there is no guarantee that the various records at a given track are equal. One may have been set by a superstar, another by a moderate field of allowance or claiming horses.

The average horse will find it much easier to approach the latter record, and so will earn higher speed ratings at that distance than at the one with the superior record. As a consequence, horses coming out of races at the latter distance will look better on paper than those that had recently raced at the former distance, against the tougher record. Superior track records which tend to distort figures can be found across the country. There is Aqueduct's seven-furlong standard, set by the incomparable Dr. Fager, Belmont's mile and a half standard, set by Secretariat in his superb Belmont Stakes, the exceptionally fast seven-furlong records at Hialeah and Hollywood, the misleading mile and an eighth record at Santa Anita, and so on. Finally, average horses are able to run closer to sprint records. As the distances lengthen, the spread between average times and the track records grows. Speed ratings earned at route distances generally fall considerably short of those recorded at shorter distances. This works to the advantage of the unsuspecting novice, helping downgrade the chances (figures) of routers entered in sprints, while upgrading those of sprinters trying to route.

Track Variants

The track variant was designed to represent numerically the speed of the racing surface on a given day. Unfortunately, it is just as sensitive to the caliber of horses competing on the day's program, and consequently falls short of its objective. The *Form's* track variant is simply the average of the day's deviations from the track records. If, for example, the day's nine races were 24, 20, 18, 21, 17, 15, 16, 10, and 20 fifths slower than their respective records, then the *Form's* variant would equal 18, the (approximate) average of these nine numbers.

However, on one day, a terrible card including races for the cheapest claimers on the grounds, a few maiden claiming events, perhaps topped by a couple of weak restricted allowance races, might have resulted in a track variant of 25. The next day, likely a Saturday, may have seen a sparkling card filled with allowance events and topped by a major stakes contest, and a variant of just 15. Yet the racing surface and weather conditions may have been identical over the two-day period. The high caliber of horses racing on Saturday were able to get much closer to the track records, as expected, with the result being a much lower variant that day. Therein lies the problem with the *Form's* track variant. The casual speed handicapper cannot tell how much of the variant reflects track conditions, and how much is due to the horses racing that day. Put another way, the serious speed handicapper must determine how much of a horse's running time is due to its performance, and how much can be attributed to the condition of the racing surface.

To be successful, speed handicappers must do better than the speed rating and track variant appearing in the *Form*. Yet it would seem wise not to stray too far afield. When dealing with shippers, it is often necessary to rely on the numbers found in the *Form*. They are the only available measure of the stranger's speed. So speed figures compatible with the *Form* speed rating and track variant, yet more accurate, would represent the best of all possible worlds.

For the remainder of this chapter, we are going to describe the process of creating speed figures. We shall segment that process into three phases:

(1) Determining how fast the races on a day's program should have been run.
(2) Calculating the true speed of the racing surface that day. This is done by comparing actual running times with those anticipated.
(3) Creating the actual speed figures for the day's races. This is done by adjusting certain base figures to account for track speed.

☐ PAR TIMES TABLES ☐

The first phase of our process demands that we know how fast each race scheduled for the day should be run, under normal conditions. This is usually done by referencing a table of "par times," like the one for Santa Anita below.

Par tables for other tracks can be constructed following the same basic patterns found in the Santa Anita table. The relationships between claiming pars are fairly constant from one track to another, but where the allowance pars fit in varies. For more details, the reader is referred to Chapter 16 of *Winning at the Races*.

The reader interested in purchasing additional par tables is invited to write to the author in care of the Mathematics Department at Adelphi University, Garden City, NY, 11530.

SANTA ANITA

Class	**	Pace	6F	6½	7F	**	Half	¾	1M	1¹⁄₁₆	1⅛M
STAKES	**	44.0	108.2	114.4	121.1	**	45.8	110.1	134.4	141.2	147.4
CLF	**	44.2	108.4	115.1	121.3	**	45.9	110.3	135.1	141.4	148.1
NW3	**	44.3	109.0	115.2	122.0	**	46.0	110.5	135.3	142.1	148.4
NW2	**	44.4	109.1	115.3	122.1	**	46.1	110.7	136.0	142.3	149.1
NW1	**	44.6	109.3	116.0	122.3	**	46.2	110.9	136.2	143.0	149.3
MSW	**	44.8	110.0	116.2	123.0	**	46.3	111.2	137.0	143.3	150.1

Class	**	Pace	6F	6½	7F	**	Half	¾	1M	1¹⁄₁₆	1⅛M
$50,000	**	44.4	109.1	115.3	122.0	**	46.0	110.5	135.3	142.1	148.3
$35,000	**	44.5	109.2	115.4	122.2	**	46.1	110.7	136.0	142.3	149.0
$25,000	**	44.6	109.3	116.0	122.3	**	46.2	110.9	136.2	143.0	149.2
$20,000	**	44.7	109.4	116.1	122.4	**	46.2	111.0	136.3	143.1	149.4
$16,000	**	44.8	110.0	116.2	123.0	**	46.3	111.2	137.0	143.3	150.1
$13,000	**	44.9	110.1	116.3	123.1	**	46.4	111.3	137.1	143.4	150.2
$10,000	**	45.0	110.2	116.4	123.2	**	46.4	111.4	137.2	144.0	150.3
$ 8,500	**	45.1	110.3	117.0	123.3	**	46.5	111.5	137.3	144.1	150.4
$ 7,500	**	45.2	110.4	117.1	123.4	**	46.5	111.6	137.4	144.2	151.0
$ 6,500	**	45.3	111.0	117.2	124.0	**	46.6	111.7	138.0	144.3	151.1

Two-year-old MSW par = 110.2 (Oak Tree)

Distance	SR Adjustment	SR + TV Adjustment	Record
5½f	+9	−7	102.1
6f	+14	−2	107.3
6½f	+14	−2	114.0
7f	+17	+1	120.0
1m	+19	+3	133.3
1¹⁄₁₆m	+19	+3	140.1
1⅛m	+24	+8	145.4
1¼m	+32	+16	157.4

PAR VARIANT = 16

If pace figures are to be part of our methodology, we encounter an immediate numerical problem. There is a "telescoping effect" relating final time to pace that must be considered. Differences in final time usually are only half as large at the pace call. For example, if one sprint was run two fifths faster than another, chances are it was only one fifth faster after half a mile. If one route was four fifths faster than another, the difference was likely only two fifths after six furlongs, and just one fifth after half a mile.

These are facts that have been verified over thousands of races. Yet the average final times for adjacent classes usually differ by just a fifth of a second. Consequently, to accurately assess class differences, pace figures should be calculated in tenths of seconds. Indeed, half-mile pace figures for routes should be measured in twentieths of a second. We have compromised somewhat. Some readers will find it difficult to work in fifths of a second when dealing with final time while at the same time working in tenths when analyzing pace. Yet this is a necessary evil. On the other hand, we have refrained from working in twentieths when dealing with the half-mile pace in routes. Appropriate adjustments for this will be dealt with later.

Let us turn now to the par times table for Santa Anita. It contains the par (or normal) times for all classes at all distances frequently run at this Southern California paradise. These are the average times each grade of horse will run the distance under normal circumstances. The par times are for the winners (leaders) of dirt races involving male Thoroughbreds aged four years and up. Par times are omitted for marathon routes, grass races, state-bred contests, and starter races. Standard adjustments to these basic times yield pars for races restricted to three-year-olds, two-year-olds, fillies and mares, and for claiming races restricted to limited winners, including maiden claimers. The following tables detail these adjustments.

☐ TABLES OF PAR TIME ADJUSTMENTS ☐

THREE-YEAR-OLDS: Early in the year, par times for three-year-old races are as much as nine fifths slower than those for older runners of the same sex and class. The following table shows those differences in fifths of a second, and the dates on which they change.

	6f	6½f	7f	1m	1¹⁄₁₆m	1⅛m	
+9						Jan. 1	+9
+8						Feb. 1	+8
+7					Jan. 1	Mar. 15	+7
+6					Feb. 15	May 1	+6
+5				Jan. 1	Apr. 15	June 1	+5
+4		Jan. 1	Jan. 1	Apr. 15	June 1	July 1	+4
+3	Jan. 1	Feb. 1	Mar. 15	June 1	July 1	Aug. 1	+3
+2	Apr. 15	June 1	June 15	July 15	Aug. 15	Sept. 15	+2
+1	July 1	Aug. 1	Aug. 15	Sept. 15	Oct. 15	Dec. 1	+1
0	Nov. 1	Dec. 1	Dec. 15	—	—	—	0

At six furlongs, for example, three-year-old pars tend to run three fifths slower during the period January 1 to April 15. The difference reduces to two fifths slower from April 15 to July 1, then to one fifth slower from July 1 to November 1, and finally to no difference for the rest of the year.

TWO-YEAR-OLDS: Par times for two-year-olds are also seasonal. The table below divides the year into four seasons to give precise differences between both open and maiden-claiming sprints for two-year-olds and races of similar class and sex for older horses:

Maiden Claiming	Season	Open Claiming
+12	Thru June	+10
+11	July/August	+9
+10	Sept/Oct	+7
+9	Nov/Dec	+5

The juvenile MSW par for six furlongs at Santa Anita is listed at the bottom of the table. It is for the October part of the Oak Tree meeting. The MSW par for other seasons can be obtained by making a one-fifth adjustment per season, the pars being fastest in December and slowest in June. NW1 pars for two-year-olds run two fifths faster than MSW pars. Stakes races are one fifth faster than NW1 thru June, with the difference increasing by one fifth for each subsequent season until they are four fifths faster in the November to December period. Par times at five and one-half furlongs are usually six and two-fifths seconds faster than at six furlongs, and five-furlong pars another six and two-fifths faster. We refrain from offering juvenile pars for races at a mile or longer. Sufficient data have never been available to properly assess the situation.

FILLIES AND MARES: The normal times for sprints restricted to females are two-fifths slower than the times for males of the same class and age group. In races at a mile or longer, the times for females are three-fifths slower.

MAIDEN CLAIMERS: Maiden-claiming sprint par times are a full second slower than those of straight (nonmaiden) claimers for horses of the same age, sex, and claiming price at the same distance. Maiden claimers at a mile or longer normally are seven-fifths slower than comparable straight claimers at the same distance.

RESTRICTED CLAIMERS: Some tracks offer competition among claiming horses that have yet to win a specific number of races in their lifetimes. Races open to any horse entered at that claiming price call for the regular par times for the age and sex. Races for limited winners are slower:

	Sprints	Routes
Nonwinners of 3	+1	+2
Nonwinners of 2	+2	+3
Nonwinners of 1	+3	+5
Maiden-claimers	+5	+7

AN EXAMPLE: What is the par time for the winner of a $25,000 maiden-claiming race for three-year-old fillies at six furlongs during January at Santa Anita?

Par time for older $25,000 males	109.3
January, three-year-olds, six furlongs	+3
Maidens	+5
Fillies	+2
Par time	111.3

Note that there is no standard adjustment for races restricted to horses bred in a particular state. What may be true in New York will not necessarily hold in California, Maryland, or Illinois. The serious speed handicapper is best advised to determine for himself what the differences between open and state-bred races might be on his home circuit.

There is no need to adjust pace pars directly. Simply adjust the final time, as described above, and use the pace figures associated with that time. Extrapolating beyond the bottom of the Santa Anita table, for example, we find the half-mile pace par that goes with a six-furlong par of 111.3 to be 45.6. Both are found three points below the bottom line of the table.

Note that we list pace pars for two points of call in route races, as contrasted with just one for sprints. This allows measurement of prestretch moves often seen in races at longer distances. However, six-furlong final times are not meant as six-furlong pace figures for seven-furlong races. Nor are mile par times meant to be used as fractional pars for mile-and-a-sixteenth races. Notice, however, that we give one pace par per class for use at both six and seven furlongs, and one pair of pace pars for each class to be used at all route distances. One might expect the pace at seven furlongs to be somewhat slower than the pace for a comparable six-furlong race. The jockeys figure to rate a little more, hoping to conserve some energy for the longer race. But apparently, the longer run on the straightaway of the backstretch, while the horses are traveling at their highest speed, has a countering effect. At the shorter route distances, those that start close to the clubhouse turn, the horses are unable to accelerate as quickly as they do when given a longer run to that turn, balancing the effect of stronger rating tactics employed at the longer distances. Notice also that the spread from top to bottom increases as the distances lengthen. The difference between $10,000 and $50,000 claimers is six fifths at six furlongs, and ten fifths at a mile and an eighth. The spread allows separate pars at route distances for "in-between classes," such as $40,000 or $18,000 claimers. At a mile and a sixteenth at Santa Anita, these pars would be 142.2 and 143.2, respectively.

☐ ACCURATE VARIANTS ☐

An accurate variant will tell whether a track was faster or slower than normal on a particular day, and by how much. It is calculated by comparing the day's official running times with the par figures for the class, and averaging the differences. We illustrate the procedure with an actual day of racing taken from the 1983 winter meet at Santa Anita. First listed are the eligibility conditions and official running times for the races of January 6:

Race	Class	Distance	Half mile & 6f Pace		Final Time
1.	4up $10,000	1¹⁄₁₆m	46.0	110.4	143.3
2.	3yos M32,000	6½f	45.2	—	117.4
3.	3yos M32,000	6½f	44.6	—	117.1
4.	3f NW1	6f	44.0	—	108.3
5.		GRASS	RACE		
6.	4upf MSW	6f	44.6	—	110.1
7.		GRASS	RACE		
8.	4up CLF	1¹⁄₁₆m	46.4	110.6	141.0
9.	4up $40,000	6½f	44.4	—	115.3

Next, for comparison, we list the par times for these races:

Race	Half-mile Pace Par	6f Pace Par	Par Time
1.	46.4	111.4	144.0
2.	45.3	—	117.2
3.	45.3	—	117.2
4.	45.1	—	110.3
5.	GRASS	RACE	
6.	45.0	—	110.2
7.	GRASS	RACE	
8.	45.9	110.3	141.4
9.	44.5	—	115.4

Then the individual deviations from par are calculated, those for final time in fifths of a second, and those for pace in tenths:

Race No.	Half-mile Pace Deviation	6f Pace Deviation	Final Time Deviation
1.	−4	−10	−2
2.	−1	—	+2
3.	−7	—	−1
4.	−11	—	−10
5.	GRASS	RACE	
6.	−4	—	−1
7.	GRASS	RACE	
8.	+5	+3	−4
9.	−1	—	−1

Bear in mind that an actual running time slower than par is listed as a "plus," while one faster than par is recorded as a "minus." Next we list these variants in two tables, one for sprints, the other for routes. (A third table would be required at tracks like Aqueduct, Arlington, Laurel, and Ellis Park, where some route races are run around one turn, or a turn and a half, rather than the standard two turns.)

SPRINTS

Race	Half mile	Final time
2.	−1	+2
3.	−7	−1
4.	−11	−10
6.	−4	−1
9.	−1	−1
	−24/5	−11/5

ROUTES

Race	Half mile	Six furlongs	Final time
1.	−4	−10	−2
8.	+5	+3	−4
	+1/2	−7/2	−6/2

On paper, the race deviations from par averaged Fast 2 for the day's five sprints, and Fast 3 for the two routes. However, the day's racing produced one exceptionally fast time. Little Hailey, the (then) undefeated three-year-old filly who won the fourth race by several lengths, was much faster than the day's other sprints at both the pace call and the finish. She confirmed her exceptional speed in her next start, running even faster on that occasion. Clearly, she was far superior to the NW1 classification.

Disregarding the Little Hailey race, then, the other six races averaged Fast 1, which we choose to be our sprint variant for the day. The other four sprints averaged Fast 3 at the pace call, which will be used as our sprint pace variant. We could also use Fast 1 as our route variant for the day, or Fast 3, the actual average of the day's two routes. Instead, we compromise and use Fast 2. And finally, since the two routes offer contrasting evidence regarding route pace, we shall use Fast 1 (at the half) and Fast 2 (after six furlongs) as our route pace variants—these are standard with a Fast 2 for final time. However, there is no way of knowing whether the pace of the first race may have been normal for the day, and that of the eighth exceptionally slow, or the eighth normal, and the first exceptionally fast. This is a common dilemma that arises when the speed handicapper attempts to use two races to determine a variant.

Before we discuss how to use the variant to make speed figures, a few useful considerations about the variant itself are in order.

It has already been recommended that the day's individual race deviations from par be averaged, with the average becoming the day's variant. This is fine, as long as the race deviations cluster around some number, with some slightly above, and others below. On some days, however, this simply is not the case. Track speed may change during the course of a racing program if drying out after a rainstorm, or if rain begins falling during the middle of the card. Shifting winds may have the same effect, a track that appears to be fast during one part of the program, and slower for the rest. When faced with such situations, experienced speed handicappers calculate two variants for the day, one for either part of the program.

Whenever track conditions change during a program, certain questions must be asked, especially by a handicapper who was not present at the track that day. Exactly when did the conditions change? And why? Was the change gradual? Or sudden? Whatever the answers, experienced speed handicappers often find it difficult to assess the impact of the changing weather conditions, and remain a bit wary of their figures for that day.

As a rule, a slow track will produce route variants that run about 50 percent slower than sprint variants the same day. (This is not necessarily true on fast days.) For example, if sprints average slow by four fifths, routes will probably average slow by six fifths. However, there are days when the route deviations are totally out of whack with the sprint deviations, possibly because of wind conditions. Or perhaps the depth of the track's cushion around the clubhouse turn differs from the rest of the track. On such days, it is wise to calculate separate variants, one for sprints, the other for routes. At times, one race on the card will stand out as exceptionally fast or unusually slow. This could happen if the winner proved far superior to the classification in which it was competing, or because the race attracted a particularly weak group of horses. Horses getting loose on the front end often run much faster than they would if facing competition for the early lead. At times, an exceptionally fast or slow pace can have a telling effect on the final time of a race. However, the track was probably as fast for the exceptional race as it was for preceding and succeeding races. The speed handicapper is best advised to eliminate that race's deviation from par from his calculation of the daily variant. One out-of-line deviation from par, if averaged in with the others, can alter a daily variant by two or even three points. The race itself, however, can still be rated, based on the variant calculated using the day's other races.

There is an alternative that can be used when a runaway winner turns in an exceptionally fast time for its classification. That race's time can be adjusted to account for where the average race-winner would have finished—two lengths ahead of the second-place finisher. So if a horse was clocked in at a fast 1:09.2 while winning by seven lengths, the running time can be adjusted to 1:10.2. The five-tick adjustment reflects the fact that a more typical winner of the race would have finished two lengths ahead of the second horse, or five lengths behind the exceptional winner.

Windy days will always pose problems for speed handicappers, especially those who calculate pace figures as well. Unless present at the track and particularly attentive to the wind, one never knows whether or not it was blowing during the running of any given race and, if so, how strongly. Deviations from par for both pace and final time likely will be quite erratic on such days, and the resulting figures somewhat unreliable.

When one race results in an extremely fast or slow time for which there appears no simple explanation, speed handicappers proceed cautiously. They watch closely when its contestants make their next starts, and note whether they run back to their "suspicious" figure. Perhaps subsequent events will substantiate the race's figure, perhaps not. Until proven accurate, however, the figure should be disregarded, and horses evaluated on the basis of figures earned in other starts. For all the player knows, the track's electronic timer may have malfunctioned during that particular race.

During periods of unchanging weather conditions, it is possible to group several days' races together into one larger sample, and calculate one variant for the entire period. This can be done, of course, only if the individual race deviations during that period look like they all belong to one large, homogeneous sample. The variant is an average, remember, and the larger the sample of races upon which it is based, the better its accuracy.

Grouping similar days together is especially helpful when making speed figures for grass races. The two or three grass contests on a typical card are hardly enough to produce a reliable variant, but an average based on ten grass races over a four-day period would be far more reliable. Provided the weatherman cooperates, of course. Note also that the length of the grass has an effect on running times, which become slower as the grass grows longer. Knowing when the course was mowed can be invaluable information.

☐ THE PROJECTION METHOD ☐

In his classic *Picking Winners*, Andy Beyer advocates what he calls the "projection method" for calculating variants. After making figures for two or three months in the manner just described, the speed handicapper will have a good line on the horses competing on his circuit. At this stage, rather than using class pars, a race par can be "projected" based on what might have been expected of the horses that actually proved contenders in the race. The race deviation would be the difference between their expected running time and their actual running time. After the day's running times have been adjusted by a variant, it is hoped these horses (the contenders) will receive figures that look reasonable in light of their previous efforts. If not, the variant could be altered slightly to better fit the figures profiles of the "reliable" horses. In other words, if we can identify two or three horses in each race that run fairly consistent figures race after race, chances are that enough of them will run true to form, allowing the advanced speed handicapper to calculate a variant based on their performances. Otherwise, if comparisons are based on class pars alone, an unusually weak or strong field may produce a deviation from par inexplicably out of line with the day's other deviations, and distort the calculation of the day's variant. Not every race in a given classification will be run in near-par figures. Considerable deviation can be anticipated in many cases.

I endorse the projection technique, and would recommend it to anyone willing to spend the enormous amount of time it requires. It clearly will produce the most accurate variants possible. Most speed handicappers, unfortunately, simply do not have that kind of time on their hands. Many work from the result charts found in their daily newspaper, without reference at all to the past performances of the horses competing. The figures they make are quite accurate, nonetheless, and far superior to the speed rating and track variant found in the *Form*.

☐ MAKING FIGURES ☐

The goal with speed figures, remember, is compatability with the sum of the speed rating and track variant that appear in the *Form*. When confronted with a shipper, the speed handicapper usually has no alternative to the *Form*'s numbers. Compatability makes comparisons possible. Toward this end, we assign a rating of 100 to a common base—par times for older male $10,000 claimers. At the New York and Los Angeles tracks, these may be the cheapest runners on the grounds, but at many smaller tracks, a horse worth $10,000 may well be the star attraction. We choose $10,000 as a national average. Experience shows that a $10,000 horse is a $10,000 horse, wherever it goes (with some possible exceptions, as noted in Chapter 2), and this makes our figures transportable. A $10,000 horse will be rated 100 at all tracks and at all distances.

At Santa Anita, for example, the $10,000 pars (for both pace and final time) assigned the rating 100 at the sprint distances are:

$$100 = 45.0 \quad 110.2 \quad 116.4 \quad 123.2$$

and at the route distances:

$$100 = 46.4 \quad 111.4 \quad 137.2 \quad 144.0 \quad 150.3$$

For each fifth of a second faster that these standards (tenth of a second for pace), add one point to the rating. For slower races, deduct points from 100. Before rating the races on a day's card, first shift the 100-base times in accordance with the day's variant. On January 6 at Santa Anita, the track was FAST 1 for sprints (with pace FAST 3), and FAST 2 for routes (with pace FAST 1 and FAST 2). Consequently, our 100-standards for Santa Anita that day must be faster than usual, by the appropriate amounts dictated by the day's variants. For sprints, we have:

$$100 = 44.7 \quad 110.1 \quad 116.3 \quad 123.1$$

and for routes:

$$100 = 46.3 \quad 111.2 \quad 137.0 \quad 143.3 \quad 150.1$$

Comparison with these numbers will produce the ratings for the day's races. These comparisons must be made in fifths for final time, and in tenths for pace. Still, there will be a slight imbalance that should be corrected. Route pace figures at the half-mile mark must be doubled away from 100 to account for the fact that these ratings should have been measured in twentieths of a second, rather than in tenths. So, for example, a route half-mile pace figure of 104 should become 108 instead, the difference (4) above 100 being doubled. And a figure of 98 should be reduced to 96, the difference (2) below 100 doubled.

With this done, the figures will be fairly level. A $20,000 claiming route run in average time will earn figures of 104–104–104. A stakes route run in par figures will rate 112–113–113. A fast (or slow) pace or finish, and moves between the half and three-quarters, all stand out clearly.

Here, then, are the figures for the races of January 6, 1983, at Santa Anita:

Race	Half mile	Three quarters	Final Time
1.	106	108	100
2.	95	—	94
3.	101	—	97
4.	107	—	108
5.	GRASS	RACE	
6.	101	—	100
7.	GRASS	RACE	
8.	98	106	113
9.	103	—	105

We point out once again that sprint figures tend to run closer to 100 than route figures for the same caliber of horses. For example, a $50,000 claiming race at Santa Anita will rate:

sprint pace	106
six furlongs	106
six and one-half furlongs	106
seven furlongs	107
half-mile route pace	108
three-quarters route pace	109
flat mile	109
mile and a sixteenth	109
mile and an eighth	110

The increasing spread away from 100 as the distances get longer is roughly proportional to the number of furlongs traveled: six points at six furlongs will be equivalent to seven points at seven furlongs and to nine points at nine furlongs (a mile and an eighth). This should be kept in mind when comparing figures earned at different distances.

Although comparisons are possible, however, a sprinter should not have its rating projected over a distance and assumed capable of re-producing its sprint figure at a possibly unsuitable distance. Nor should a route figure be projected back to a sprint distance.

Speed figures for horses turning back from a route to a sprint may be projected based on their six-furlong pace figure from their recent route, simply by subtracting three points from that number. Statistics suggest that a horse will earn a sprint speed figure on the average three points lower than its recent six-furlong route pace figure. We emphasize, how-ever, that this is an average, and, indeed, one based on a sample with a wide variance.

Once a rating has been established for the winner of a race, simple adjustments can be made to rate the others in that field. Simply subtract one point for each length beaten, or behind. Fractional lengths must be handled carefully, however. One half or three quarters of a length must be treated as a full length, and anything less as nothing. So a loss by five and one-half lengths is treated equal to a loss by six lengths, as is one by six and one-quarter lengths.

Theoretically speaking, we should subtract two points for each length behind at pace calls (four points at the route half-mile mark), but this produces unrealistically low pace figures for horses not on the lead.

Since fields tend to spread out just as much by the first call as at the finish, we feel justified in adopting a simple point-for-a-length formula.

For example, a horse with a running line of:

$$4^3 \quad 3^{2\frac{1}{2}} \quad 2^2 \quad 2^1$$

from a route with figures 106–107–106 would itself be rated 103–104–105. There must always be some doubt about the accuracy of pace figures for other than pacesetters. Whereas margins between horses at the finish are measured quite accurately with the help of the photo finish camera, lengths behind at the fractional calls are simply the chart caller's estimate.

☐ SHIPPERS ☐

When a horse first arrives on the local circuit, the handicapper is usually at a loss for speed figures. Unless, of course, he has accurate figures for the circuit on which the horse had previously raced. Typically though, the speed handicapper must rely on the speed rating, track variant, and running times published in the *Form*. That, or ignore the horse, and possibly be forced to pass the race as a result.

We have already discussed why *Form* speed ratings need adjusting. The difference between weak and strong track records must be acknowledged, and the increasing difficulty horses have in approaching track records as the distances lengthen must be considered. To understand the basis for the numerical calculations involved in making adjustments, let us take a look at the speed-rating equivalents of the various $10,000 par times at Santa Anita:

Distance	$10,000 par	Track Record	Speed Rating
6f	110.2	107.3	86
6 ½f	116.4	114.0	86
7f	123.2	120.0	83
1m	137.2	133.3	81
1 1⁄16m	144.0	140.1	81
1 1⁄8m	150.3	145.4	76

To bring each rating up to 100, make the adjustments given below.

Distance	Speed Rating	Adjustment
6f	86	+14
6 ½f	86	+14
7f	83	+17
1m	81	+19
1 ¹⁄₁₆m	81	+19
1 ⅛m	76	+24

These adjustments bring speed ratings into line with figures produced by our previous method—a $10,000 claiming race run in average time will earn 100 regardless of the distance and track speed. If the handicapper has an accurate variant for the day, the adjusted figure just calculated could be modified further. Should the track be faster than par, speed ratings will be higher than normal, and must be reduced by the variant. On slow days, figures must be increased by the variant. For example, suppose a horse earns a speed rating of 92 at six furlongs on a Fast 2 day at Santa Anita. First add 16, the six-furlong adjustment number at Santa Anita, getting a figure of 106. Then subtract 2, the variant, giving a final figure of 104.

Adjustments similar to these for all distances at all North American tracks can be found in the "Speed Rating Adjustment Table" on pages 198 and 199. This table, and the one that follows, reflect racing through December 31, 1983. We strongly advise that both be used in conjunction with an accurate daily variant.

Handicappers are advised to make use of the *Form* track variant by adding it to the *Form* speed rating. Statistical studies have proven the result far superior to the speed rating alone. As with speed ratings, however, adjustments must be made, in this case not only to iron out differences in quality between track records, but also to account for the quality of racing at the track. The key number in our adjustment is the Par Variant for the track—16 for Santa Anita. This is the average race differential from track records over the same sample of races on which the par times were based.

Let us take a look at what happens when this average variant is added to the $10,000 par speed ratings listed above:

Distance	Par Speed Rating	Plus Par Variant
6f	86	102
6 ½f	86	102
7f	83	99
1m	81	97
1 ¹⁄₁₆m	81	97
1 ⅛m	76	92

TRACKS	4F	4.5F	5F	5.5F	6F	6.5F	7F	7.5F	1M	1-40	1-70	8.5F	9F	9.5F	10F	PV
AK-SAR-BEN	0	0	8	15	20	0	0	0	0	0	20	20	26	25	0	22
ALBUQUERQUE	0	0	6	10	12	10	16	0	17	0	22	8	22	8	16	20
AQUEDUCT(INNER)	0	0	0	10	18	0	0	0	0	0	21	0	22	23	16	19
AQUEDUCT(MAIN)	0	0	11	15	19	17	24	0	26	0	0	0	29	36	36	20
ARLINGTON	0	0	13	16	21	20	26	0	33	0	27	27	31	16	31	27
ASSINIBOIA DOWNS	0	2	10	8	8	0	8	0	11	0	10	0	10	0	0	18
ATLANTIC CITY	2	2	7	12	16	0	20	0	26	0	26	26	31	22	22	22
ATOKAD PARK	3	0	6	7	14	7	0	0	8	0	13	8	13	12	0	18
BALMORAL	0	0	0	7	13	0	0	0	10	17	20	0	0	0	0	19
BAY MEADOWS	0	0	10	10	15	0	0	0	18	0	27	0	27	13	18	21
BAY MEADOWS FAIR	0	0	10	10	15	0	0	0	18	0	18	0	21	8	18	23
BELMONT	0	0	7	11	16	14	21	0	25	0	25	21	29	10	24	17
BERKSHIRE DOWNS	0	0	24	0	0	33	0	0	0	0	0	0	0	0	0	38
DARBY DOWNS	0	0	6	7	13	0	0	0	0	0	12	20	15	0	10	19
BOWIE	6	-3	8	9	21	10	13	26	13	0	17	30	26	28	23	30
CAHOKIA DOWNS	0	0	7	7	14	13	16	0	19	0	18	0	18	15	8	16
CALDER	0	-8	-1	4	8	0	0	0	4	0	4	0	21	24	2	15
CALIENTE	12	12	4	5	9	19	17	0	10	0	9	0	8	8	15	15
CENTENNIAL	0	4	4	5	13	12	18	0	29	0	10	15	10	10	19	22
CHARLES TOWN	0	4	4	13	18	9	0	0	9	0	25	23	26	24	35	20
CHURCHILL DOWNS	0	4	5	5	0	12	15	0	12	0	8	25	24	15	0	15
COLUMBUS(NEB)	6	4	5	9	18	0	0	0	26	0	8	8	0	0	0	23
COMMODORE DOWNS	4	4	11	9	0	19	15	0	12	0	23	11	16	13	30	20
DELAWARE	0	0	9	17	18	0	0	0	26	22	26	22	23	0	30	26
DEL MAR	7	7	8	22	16	8	0	0	12	0	11	27	27	13	38	16
DETROIT	0	0	10	0	23	0	16	0	32	22	36	19	30	41	36	28
ELLIS PARK	4	0	3	15	15	9	10	0	20	0	0	11	42	13	16	20
EVANGELINE DOWNS	4	0	0	7	16	6	0	12	0	0	16	23	0	3	0	21
EXHIBITION PARK	0	0	0	10	18	13	0	0	0	23	17	20	20	0	0	23
FAIR GROUNDS	12	11	15	13	23	0	0	0	11	14	25	0	26	23	29	27
FAIRMOUNT	0	0	1	16	22	0	0	0	7	27	27	24	29	24	0	19
FINGER LAKES	0	0	18	15	10	0	0	0	17	30	33	8	8	-1	4	28
FONNER PARK	0	0	0	7	23	0	0	0	6	0	-4	0	-4	21	17	12
FORT ERIE	0	0	5	5	10	12	0	0	12	0	11	8	-10	13	11	15
FRESNO	0	0	4	4	7	0	0	0	9	0	13	9	13	7	7	16
GARDEN STATE	0	0	16	11	22	0	0	0	0	0	14	14	18	21	41	31
GOLDEN GATE	1	1	6	16	15	17	0	0	25	0	33	33	36	30	36	24
GREAT BARRINGTON	0	0	8	4	0	16	37	0	0	0	0	0	23	26	0	26
GREEN MOUNTAIN	0	14	7	0	0	0	0	0	9	8	0	0	19	0	0	17
GREENWOOD	0	0	0	0	21	17	10	0	22	0	22	19	25	24	24	23
GULFSTREAM	0	0	0	0	0	18	20	0	0	0	0	0	34	0	38	25
HAWTHORNE	3	0	0	18	18	0	22	0	0	15	0	0	37	0	42	25
HAZEL PARK	0	0	8	0	23	0	0	0	39	27	42	0	42	0	0	23
HIALEAH	8	0	11	17	15	20	0	0	0	10	24	0	0	0	30	20
HOLLYWOOD	0	0	17	17	17	22	0	0	24	0	28	28	27	0	33	20
JEFFERSON DOWNS	5	6	5	13	0	11	17	0	0	15	14	0	0	0	0	20
JUAREZ	0	0	0	20	16	7	15	22	1	0	-1	4	4	4	0	11
KEENELAND	3	3	3	16	14	17	20	0	0	0	0	0	23	27	26	18
KEYSTONE	0	0	0	3	14	13	14	13	0	0	14	0	22	24	17	19

LA MESA	-6	-3	5	7	5	0	6	3	11	0	0	0	9	14	0	0	13
LATONIA	0	0	11	13	26	27	0	0	29	0	0	0	33	33	0	0	31
LAUREL*	0	8	-1	9	17	0	16	0	21	18	19	13	23	18	0	13	21
LETHBRIDGE*	0	0	11	0	0	18	11	0	20	0	0	0	18	18	0	0	17
LINCOLN DOWNS	4	0	0	0	0	23	0	0	17	0	20	0	21	23	0	0	22
LINCOLN(NEB)	0	0	10	0	12	0	0	0	17	0	12	0	24	0	0	0	21
LONGACRES	0	0	0	6	14	12	12	0	0	0	0	0	20	19	0	17	22
LOS ALAMITOS	0	0	3	11	11	11	5	0	0	0	0	0	13	17	0	0	15
LOUISIANA DOWNS	0	0	0	5	20	21	0	0	7	0	29	0	25	21	0	30	24
MARQUIS DOWNS	0	0	4	5	7	0	5	0	0	0	0	0	-2	9	0	0	19
MARSHFIELD FAIR	0	0	7	3	0	9	0	0	0	0	0	0	-2	0	-2	29	14
MEADOWLANDS	0	0	11	10	19	0	8	0	16	0	19	0	21	30	0	29	20
MONMOUTH	0	0	7	4	17	6	0	0	22	0	20	0	23	26	21	-5	21
NARRAGANSETT	3	0	6	10	19	0	0	0	0	0	14	0	16	14	0	0	19
NORTHAMPTON FAIR*	1	0	14	4	11	6	0	0	16	0	0	0	10	0	17	18	14
NORTHLANDS	0	0	0	16	8	0	10	0	13	0	0	0	10	0	0	0	25
OAKLAWN	0	0	0	16	21	0	0	0	0	0	29	0	29	27	17	18	20
PARK JEFFERSON	0	0	12	5	7	0	10	0	20	0	7	0	8	8	24	11	21
PENN NATIONAL	0	0	15	11	16	9	0	0	0	0	22	0	28	15	29	17	24
PIMLICO	0	0	11	2	18	0	0	0	14	0	0	0	27	23	12	11	18
PLAYFAIR	0	0	0	0	10	0	0	0	0	0	0	0	8	14	0	0	17
PLEASANTON	4	0	0	11	11	9	0	0	6	0	14	0	18	21	12	17	18
POCONO DOWNS*	0	4	7	8	8	13	0	0	15	0	18	0	13	0	0	0	16
PORTLAND MEADOWS	0	4	0	14	13	0	0	0	0	0	11	0	16	19	5	6	16
POMONA	0	0	0	8	11	0	8	0	0	0	0	0	9	17	0	11	15
PRESCOTT DOWNS	3	0	0	3	4	7	0	9	2	0	0	0	9	4	0	0	12
RILLITO	0	0	11	18	22	19	0	0	0	0	27	0	31	29	21	34	31
RIVER DOWNS	0	0	17	13	21	14	0	0	29	0	27	22	25	27	23	37	29
ROCKINGHAM	5	0	0	12	11	9	0	0	12	0	13	0	13	17	0	0	27
RUIDOSO DOWNS	0	0	0	9	4	0	0	0	16	0	10	0	10	15	0	5	16
SACRAMENTO	0	0	0	8	11	0	9	0	0	0	0	0	11	0	15	10	13
SALEM	0	0	0	0	10	0	0	0	12	0	0	0	25	0	0	0	20
SANDOWN	0	1	0	9	14	14	17	0	29	0	34	0	19	24	0	32	31
SANTA ANITA	4	3	11	9	11	9	12	0	19	0	0	0	16	-1	24	4	16
SANTA FE	0	0	11	12	12	0	0	0	16	0	0	0	19	17	0	0	18
SANTA ROSA	0	0	0	7	16	16	19	0	10	0	0	0	0	23	19	26	15
SARATOGA	4	0	3	10	10	0	0	0	12	0	9	0	15	0	0	0	18
SHENENDOAH DOWNS*	4	0	0	0	14	15	0	0	17	0	25	0	18	14	0	8	19
SOLANO	4	0	0	5	9	-8	0	0	20	0	18	0	8	21	0	0	18
SPORTSMANS	0	0	0	4	3	0	2	0	10	0	8	0	8	17	0	0	19
STAMPEDE PARK	0	4	6	2	16	0	0	0	11	0	19	0	19	20	18	12	22
STOCKTON	5	0	9	10	13	13	0	18	18	0	13	16	13	16	16	24	18
SUFFOLK DOWNS	0	8	9	9	16	0	0	0	10	0	20	0	25	31	18	0	24
SUNLAND	1	0	7	9	0	0	0	0	19	0	18	0	13	18	1	21	14
THISTLEDOWN(INNER)	0	2	9	10	16	8	0	0	12	0	5	0	22	13	11	14	20
THISTLEDOWN(MAIN)	0	8	18	21	26	11	0	0	17	0	39	0	51	60	0	49	35
TIMONIUM	0	0	11	11	17	21	19	0	50	0	19	0	25	28	23	31	22
TURF PARADISE	0	5	7	7	10	0	0	0	11	0	0	0	8	10	0	0	19

TRACKS	4F	4.5F	5F	5.5F	6F	6.5F	7F	7.5F	1M	1-40	1-70	8.5F	9F	9.5F	10F	PV
AK-SAR-BEN	0	0	-14	-7	-2	0	0	0	0	0	-2	4	3	0	0	22
ALBUQUERQUE	0	0	-14	-10	-10	-4	0	0	-3	0	0	4	-12	-4	-4	20
AQUEDUCT(INNER)	0	0	0	0	-1	0	0	0	0	0	2	3	4	4	-3	19
AQUEDUCT(MAIN)	0	0	-9	-5	-3	4	0	0	-6	0	0	0	9	16	16	20
ARLINGTON	0	0	-13	0	-1	4	0	0	0	0	0	4	-11	-11	0	27
ASSINIBOIA DOWNS	0	-16	-8	-10	-10	-1	0	0	-7	0	0	-8	2	0	0	18
ATLANTIC CITY	0	-20	-15	-10	-6	-2	0	0	0	0	0	4	9	4	0	22
ATOKAD PARK	-15	0	0	-12	-11	0	0	0	-10	0	0	-5	-6	0	0	18
BALMORAL	0	0	0	-12	-6	4	0	0	0	-10	0	1	0	0	0	19
BAY MEADOWS	0	0	0	-11	-8	0	0	0	-3	0	-2	6	0	-8	-3	21
BAY MEADOWS FAIR	0	0	0	-13	-8	-5	0	0	-5	0	0	4	-2	-15	-5	23
BELMONT	0	0	-10	-6	-1	0	0	0	8	0	-2	1	12	-7	7	17
BERKSHIRE DOWNS	0	0	-14	0	-6	-5	0	0	0	0	0	4	10	0	0	38
DARBY DOWNS	0	0	-11	-12	-6	0	0	0	0	-7	0	0	-4	-9	-9	19
BOWIE	0	0	-24	-21	-9	-8	-4	0	0	0	0	-4	-4	-2	-7	30
CAHOKIA DOWNS	-10	-19	0	0	-6	-3	-3	0	-3	-1	0	2	4	0	0	16
CALDER	0	-12	-8	-13	-7	-4	-4	0	-1	0	0	1	4	0	-12	20
CALIENTE	0	-23	-16	-11	-7	0	0	0	-9	-11	0	-6	-7	-13	0	15
CENTENNIAL	0	-10	-11	-10	-6	-5	0	0	-5	-4	0	0	-5	-19	-5	15
CHARLES TOWN	0	0	0	0	-3	0	0	0	0	0	0	1	4	-7	-3	22
CHURCHILL DOWNS	0	-16	-16	-15	-8	-5	0	0	9	0	0	5	-7	-15	-15	20
COLUMBUS(NEB)	0	0	-12	-10	-6	-2	0	0	0	0	0	-7	4	0	0	15
COMMODORE DOWNS	-17	-19	-11	-11	-2	-4	0	0	-11	-12	0	-7	0	0	0	23
DELAWARE	0	0	0	0	-4	0	0	0	0	2	0	3	7	10	0	20
DEL MAR	0	0	-9	-9	-4	-8	0	0	-4	-7	0	4	-7	12	0	26
DELTA DOWNS	0	-9	-8	-13	-8	0	0	0	4	0	0	-3	0	0	0	16
DETROIT	0	0	-18	-13	-5	-5	0	0	4	-5	0	14	14	13	8	28
ELLIS PARK	0	0	-17	-13	-11	-10	0	0	4	-6	0	8	-2	-4	0	20
EVANGELINE DOWNS	0	-16	-13	-10	-5	-8	-8	0	3	-4	0	3	-14	-17	0	20
EXHIBITION PARK	0	0	0	-14	-15	0	0	0	0	0	0	4	-1	0	0	21
FAIR GROUNDS	0	0	0	0	-5	0	0	0	0	0	0	2	3	0	0	23
FAIRMOUNT	-15	-16	-12	-11	-9	0	-9	0	0	-13	-13	-5	0	0	0	27
FINGER LAKES	0	0	-18	0	-9	0	0	0	-8	-12	0	-2	-11	-20	-15	19
TAMPA BAY DOWNS	0	0	-10	-13	-5	0	0	0	0	0	0	-5	5	-7	0	28
FONNER PARK	0	0	0	0	-3	0	0	0	-4	0	0	2	5	4	-9	12
FORT ERIE	0	0	-10	-10	-6	0	0	0	0	-3	0	-3	-16	-22	-4	15
FRESNO	0	0	-11	-12	-10	0	0	0	-7	0	0	-4	3	-2	0	16
GARDEN STATE	0	0	-15	-24	-11	0	0	0	-8	0	0	2	-7	-7	-9	31
GOLDEN GATE	0	-23	-18	-13	-9	0	0	0	0	0	0	5	-2	5	-10	24
GREAT BARRINGTON	0	0	-18	-22	-11	0	0	0	1	0	0	-1	2	-6	-12	26
GREEN MOUNTAIN	0	0	-10	0	0	0	0	0	-8	0	0	0	0	0	0	17
GREENWOOD	0	-9	0	0	-6	-7	-3	-9	-1	0	0	2	11	-3	1	23
GULFSTREAM	0	-15	-13	-11	-7	-3	0	0	0	0	0	-5	9	13	13	25
HAWTHORNE	0	0	0	0	-7	-3	0	0	-4	0	0	5	12	10	17	23
HAZEL PARK	-20	0	0	-7	4	0	0	0	16	-10	4	19	0	0	0	20
HIALEAH	0	0	-12	-13	-9	4	0	0	-9	4	0	4	0	0	0	20
HOLLYWOOD	0	-14	-7	-5	-4	2	0	0	0	0	0	8	8	13	13	20
JEFFERSON DOWNS	-15	0	-15	-9	-7	-3	-5	0	-10	-12	0	-7	7	0	0	20
JUAREZ	0	0	0	-9	-4	0	0	0	4	0	0	-7	-7	0	0	11

- LA MESA
- LATONIA
- LAUREL*
- LETHBRIDGE*
- LINCOLN DOWNS
- LINCOLN(NEB)
- LONGACRES
- LOS ALAMITOS
- LOUISIANA DOWNS
- MARQUIS DOWNS
- MARSHFIELD FAIR
- MEADOWLANDS
- MONMOUTH
- NARRAGANSETT
- NORTHAMPTON FAIR*
- NORTHLANDS
- OAKLAWN
- PARK JEFFERSON
- PENN NATIONAL
- PIMLICO
- PLAYFAIR
- PLEASANTON
- POCONO DOWNS*
- PORTLAND MEADOWS
- POMONA
- PRESCOTT DOWNS
- RILLITO
- RIVER DOWNS
- ROCKINGHAM
- RUIDOSO DOWNS
- SACRAMENTO
- SALEM
- SANDOWN
- SANTA ANITA
- SANTA FE
- SANTA ROSA
- SARATOGA
- SHENENDOAH DOWNS*
- SOLANO
- SPORTSMANS
- STAMPEDE PARK
- STOCKTON
- SUFFOLK DOWNS
- SUNLAND
- THISTLEDOWN(INNER)*
- THISTLEDOWN(MAIN)*
- TIMONIUM
- TURF PARADISE
- WATERFORD
- WOODBINE
- YAKIMA MEADOWS

Since our goal is that the average $10,000 claiming race earn a figure of 100 regardless of distance, the following adjustments are called for:

Distance	Adjustment
6f	−2
6 1/2f	−2
7f	+1
1m	+3
1 1/16m	+3
1 1/8m	+8

A complete list of current SR + TV adjustments for all North American tracks can be found in the "Speed Rating + Track Variant Adjustment Table," on pages 200 and 201. The last column of the table lists the Par Variant for each track.

In practice, one does not add the track's Par Variant to *Form* speed ratings. Rather, it is the *Form's* own track variant that is added to their speed rating, and the sum must then be modified with the appropriate adjustment figure for the track and distance. For example, a horse recording a 90 speed rating for six furlongs at Santa Anita on a fourteen-variant day would be rated: $90 + 14 - 2 = 102$.

Some speed handicappers may wish to keep notebooks that record speed and pace figures for each race on each racing day of the year. Others may record simply the 100-equivalent speed and pace figures for the day.

Those with no interest in pace figures can get away with recording just one number each day, their own *Form*-like daily variant. This is obtained by making one simple adjustment to the track's Par Variant. If a track is fast on a given day, subtract the amount by which it is fast from the Par Variant. If slow, add the amount to the Par Variant. For example, on a Slow 2 (Slow 3 for routes) day at Santa Anita, the variant to be used with sprint speed ratings is $16 + 2 = 18$, and for route speed ratings $16 + 3 = 19$. This homemade daily variant can be added to the *Form* speed rating, with the sum modified by the appropriate SR + TV adjustment.

We note in passing that both adjustment tables must be kept up to date. Should a track record be broken at a particular meeting, a new adjustment will be needed for subsequent meets. To update an SR-adjustment number, simply add one point for each fifth of a second by which the new record surpasses the old one. Add the same differential to the SR + TV-adjustment number as well. For every two fifths shaved from a track's six-furlong record (or whatever sprint distance is used most frequently), one point must be added to the track's Par Variant, and all SR + TV-adjustments revised so that

$$\text{SR-adjustment} - \text{SR} + \text{TV-adjustment} = \text{Par Variant}$$

Likewise, for every four fifths knocked from the record at the track's most popular route distance.

Handicappers wishing to have approximate pace figures for shippers can project the *Form* variant down to the fractional times. For example, a daily variant of 20 at Santa Anita represents a track that was (approximately) slow by four fifths of a second (six fifths at route distances). We could then adjust our 100-line accordingly, coming up with the following:

$$100 = 45.4 \qquad 111.1 \qquad 117.3 \qquad 124.1$$

at sprint distances, and

$$100 = 46.7 \qquad 112.0 \qquad 138.3 \qquad 145.1 \qquad 151.4$$

at route distances. The sprint figures represent the line four fifths below the $10,000 line. The route figures can be found six fifths below that standard. In this way, we have allocated half the track speed differential to the pace, an educated guess that may, or may not, be accurate. We cannot overstate the importance of being able to deal accurately with shippers. They offer the speed handicapper his best opportunities to find significant overlays, provided he "knows" precisely how fast the horse can run. This is especially true with the "ad hoc" shipper discussed in Chapter 7, whose mere presence at other than its home track answers the question of stable intentions.

CASE STUDY: LANDALUCE AND PRINCESS ROONEY

During 1982, two juvenile fillies were so impressive that comparisons with the immortal Ruffian became inevitable. Both Landaluce in California and Princess Rooney on the East Coast were undefeated and virtually untested. Supporters of each were demanding a confrontation, one that would never take place. Landaluce's tragic death from a mysterious illness left the issue forever in the realm of speculation, and made comparisons between her and Ruffian all the more unavoidable. Speed handicappers, however, were able to make comparisons, not only between Landaluce and Princess Rooney, but between both of them and Ruffian as well. Below you will find the past performances of both, and their speed figures for 1982:

Landaluce — Dk. b. or br. f. 2, by Seattle Slew—Strip Poker, by Bold Bidder — Lifetime 5 5 0 0 $372,365 — 1982 5 5 0 0 $372,365

Own.—Beal & French — Br.—Spendthrift Farm & Kernan F (Ky) — Tr.—Lukas D Wayne

23Oct82- 8SA	fst	1 1/16	:45⅘	1:00⅘	1:41⅘	Ⓕ Oak Leaf	6	3	1^{hd}	1^{3}	1^{4}	1^{2}	Pincay L Jr	117	*.05	92-10	Landaluce 117^{2} SophisticatedGirl 115^{8} GranjaReina $115^{1/2}$	Ridden out	7
11Oct82- 8SA	fst	7f	:22⅖	:45	1:21⅘	Ⓕ Anoakia	8	2	3^{nk}	1^{2}	1^{8}	1^{10}	Pincay L Jr	123	*.10	91-15	Landaluce 123^{10} Rare Thrill $117^{1 1/2}$ Time Of Sale $120^{2 1/2}$	Easily	8
5Sep82- 8Dmr	fst	1	:46	1:10⅘	1:35⅗	Ⓕ Debutante	4	2	$2^{1/2}$	1^{hd}	$1^{1 1/2}$	$1^{6 1/2}$	Pincay L Jr	119	*.30	90-12	Landaluce $119^{6 1/2}$ Issues N' Answers 116^{4} Granja Reina 113^{2}	Easily	6
10Jly82- 8Hol	fst	6f	:21⅖	:43⅘	1:08	Ⓕ Hol Lassie	3	2	$2^{1/2}$	$1^{1 1/2}$	1^{9}	1^{21}	Pincay L Jr	117	*.30e	97-16	Landaluce 117^{21} Bold Out Line $115^{1 1/2}$ Barzell $119^{1/2}$	Easy score	5
3Jly82- 4Hol	fst	6f	:22	:44⅘	1:08⅕	Ⓕ Md Sp Wt	6	2	$1^{1 1/2}$	1^{3}	1^{6}	1^{7}	Pincay L Jr	117	*.80	96-10	Landaluce 117^{7} Midnight Rapture 116^{5} Miss Big Wig $116^{1 1/2}$	Easily	7

Princess Rooney — Gr. f. 3, by Verbatim—Parrish Princess, by Drone — 114 — Lifetime 6 6 0 0 $223,815 — 1982 6 6 0 0 $223,815

Own.—Tucker Paula — Br.—Roach B & T (Ky) — Tr.—Gomez Frank

23Oct82- 6Med	fst	1 1/16	:47⅕	1:11	1:43	Ⓕ Gardenia	6	1	$1^{1/2}$	1^{2}	1^{7}	1^{11}	Vasquez J	121	*.30	94-11	PrincessRooney 121^{11} ForOnc'nMyLif 118^{3} GoldSpruc 118^{12}	In Hand	7
10Oct82- 8Bel	fst	1	:46⅕	1:11⅗	1:39	Ⓕ Frizette	2	1	1^{hd}	$1^{1 1/2}$	1^{6}	1^{8}	Fell J	119	*1.30	70-29	PrincessRooney 119^{8} WinningTck $119^{3 1/2}$ WekndSurpris 119^{nk}	Handily	13
11Sep82- 9Crc	fst	7f	:22⅖	:45⅘	1:23⅘	Ⓕ Melaleuca	7	1	1^{1}	$1^{2 1/2}$	1^{8}	1^{12}	Pennisi F A	116	*.20	97-14	Princess Rooney 116^{12} Hiusoanso 114^{4} Rina's Missy 114^{6}	Easily	8
1Sep82- 9Crc	fst	7f	:22⅖	:46	1:25⅕	Ⓕ Alw 10000	1	2	$1^{1/2}$	$1^{1 1/2}$	1^{10}	1^{18}	Pennisi F A	116	*.90	90-18	PrincessRooney 116^{18} CourtUnion 116^{nk} FlwlessDimond $116^{1 1/2}$	Easily	5
7Jun82- 7Crc	fst	5f	:22⅗	:46⅗	:59⅗	Ⓕ Alw 9500	1	3	$1^{1/2}$	$1^{1 1/2}$	1^{3}	1^{4}	Pennisi F A	114	*1.20	94-15	PrincessRooney 114^{4} Ishudahdtht 107no RoylityMiss 117^{6}	Ridden out	6
22May82- 3Crc	fst	5f	:22⅘	:47	1:00⅖	Ⓕ Md Sp Wt	9	8	3^{nk}	1^{hd}	1^{2}	1^{3}	Pennisi F A	115	*2.10	90-14	Princess Rooney 115^{3} Rilia 115^{2} Marie V. 115^{1}	Driving	9

LATEST WORKOUTS Feb 22 Crc 1 fst 1:44 b (d) Feb 16 Crc 5f fst 1:04⅘ b (d) Feb 3 Crc 4f sly :50⅘ b (d) Jan 29 Crc 4f fst :49⅖ b (d)

(past performance of Landaluce and Princess Rooney)

Landaluce		*Princess Rooney*		*Ruffian*	
MSW	103	MSW	98	MSW	110
Lassie	112	NW1	104	Fashion	111
Debutante	102	NW2	106	Astoria	112
Anoakia	109	Melaleuca	111	Sorority	105
Oak Leaf	107	Frizette	106	Spinaway	109
		Gardenia	113		

THE FASTEST HORSES

With any organized sport, there will always be debates regarding the relative merits of the current year's champions *vis-à-vis* those from previous seasons. Thoroughbred racing is no different. In fact, speed handicappers have the means by which to make valid comparisons. Several years ago, I wrote a series of articles for the *American Turf Monthly* magazine presenting the results of a study of the country's important stakes events during the period 1954–1978. That study has now been extended through 1982, and the results are presented here. Grass stakes were not included in the study, due to the difficulty in calculating accurate daily variants without knowledge of weather conditions.

Most racing fans would be curious to learn the identity of the fastest horses to have raced during the period 1954–1982. This is an attempt to answer that question, but the reader can draw his own conclusions from the data. To qualify for inclusion in the following table, a horse must have won at least three of the races studied, including one (or more) at a mile or longer. We present the career-best speed figure for each horse, and the average of its three best figures. All figures have been projected to their ten-furlong equivalents, and have been adjusted to account for track speed and inflation. Only those horses whose average figure was 120 or higher appear in the table.

Here, then, are the fastest male Thoroughbreds from Native Dancer to Conquistador Cielo:

Horse	Best Figure	Average Figure
Ack Ack	124.3	124.1
Affirmed	130.0	127.3
Alydar	128.9	124.7
Arts & Letters	130.0	125.8
Bald Eagle	126.3	124.1
Bold Forbes	128.6	125.1
Bold Ruler	132.0	129.6
Buckpasser	127.0	124.6
Carry Back	128.0	125.8
Coastal	126.7	123.3
Conquistador Cielo	125.0	120.0
Damascus	132.0	130.3
Dr. Fager	130.0	128.8
Forego	125.0	124.3
Gallant Man	126.3	123.8
Gen. Duke	125.6	121.1
General Assembly	129.0	122.9
Gun Bow	132.0	129.3
Honest Pleasure	122.2	121.1
Intentionally	122.5	121.4
Kelso	129.0	127.4
Key To The Mint	125.0	123.0
Majestic Light	129.0	125.4
Majestic Prince	125.0	120.0
Nashua	124.2	123.7
Native Dancer	128.0	125.4
Northern Dancer	127.0	121.0
Riva Ridge	127.4	124.9
Round Table	131.0	128.7
Secretariat	132.0	129.7
Seattle Slew	125.0	124.0
Sensitive Prince	127.0	122.3
Spectacular Bid	130.0	128.6
Swaps	129.0	126.2
Sword Dancer	124.0	123.6
Tom Fool	129.5	127.5
Wajima	125.6	123.2
Winter's Tale	124.4	120.4

We next present the results of a similar study of the fastest fillies of the last thirty years. Our qualifying figure was lowered to 115:

Horse	Best Figure	Average Figure
Affectionately	121.4	120.1
Alma North	119.0	118.0
Bold 'N' Determined	124.4	119.9
Caesar's Wish	118.9	116.8
Cicada	120.0	116.6
Dark Mirage	118.8	116.0
Davona Dale	120.0	119.2
Desert Vixen	123.3	121.1
Double Delta	117.1	115.0
Gallant Bloom	123.2	119.6
Gamely	115.6	115.0
Genuine Risk	118.8	116.7
Glorious Song	121.1	117.7
Heavenly Cause	117.5	115.0
High Voltage	123.3	115.6
It's In The Air	120.0	118.5
Late Bloomer	121.1	116.4
Love Sign	121.1	118.6
Numbered Account	126.7	120.7
Open Fire	129.0	121.9
Optimistic Gal	122.0	118.5
Parlo	118.9	118.2
Pearl Necklace	126.3	125.2
Politely	124.0	122.4
Priceless Gem	118.5	116.6
Primonetta	117.8	115.3
Relaxing	119.0	117.4
Revidere	127.0	120.1
Ruffian	124.3	122.6
Searching	120.0	117.2
Shuvee	118.9	117.9
Silver Spoon	116.3	115.3
Straight Deal	121.0	119.2
Summer Scandal	121.1	118.9
Summer Guest	120.0	116.3
Susan's Girl	123.0	121.0
Tempted	123.8	121.8
Tosmah	118.8	116.9
Track Robbery	122.2	118.1
What A Summer	118.3	115.6

To assist handicappers in placing the outstanding performances of the day into proper perspective, here is a table of "world record" speed figures at each distance from five furlongs to a mile and a half. Divisions have been made for age and sex.

HANDICAPS AND WEIGHT-FOR-AGE RACES

	3-up		*3-up F*	
6f	Barrera	120	Gold Beauty	115
7f	Dr. Fager	121	Canadiana	
			Affectionately	
			My Juliet	115
1m	Arts & Letters	124	Pearl Necklace	121
1-1/16m	Cougar II	123	Pearl Necklace	122
1-1/8m	Secretariat	125	Numbered Account	124
1-3/16m	Riva Ridge	126	Politely	
			Gallant Bloom	122
1-1/4m	Damascus		Open Fire	
	Gun Bow	132	Revidere	127
1-1/2m	Affirmed	127		

RACES RESTRICTED TO THREE-YEAR-OLDS

	Colts		*Fillies*	
7f	Bold Forbes	120	Ruffian	
			Davona Dale	117
1m	Dr. Fager	123	Davona Dale	116
1-1/16m	Kelso	122	Sarsar	116
1-1/8m	Dr. Fager		Desert Vixen	
	Coastal	124	Miss Cavandish	120
1-3/16m	Secretariat	124		
1-1/4m	Secretariat	132	Quaze Quilt	118
1-1/2m	Secretariat	135	Ruffian	116

RACES RESTRICTED TO TWO-YEAR-OLDS

	Colts		*Fillies*	
5f	Bold Ruler		Little Tumbler	108
	Golden Joey	108		
5-1/2f	Native Prince	112	Ruffian	
			Dark Charger	112
6f	Bold Forbes	113	Heavenly Body	114
6-1/2f	Summer Tan		Priceless Gem	112
	Intentionally	114		
7f	Spectacular Bid	121	Princess Rooney	111
1m	Spectacular Bid	121	Numbered Account	114
1-1/16m	Spectacular Bid	119	Syrian Sea	
			Optimistic Gal	114
1-1/8m	Believe It	121	Bring Out The Band	
			Caesar's Wish	110

The following are the "best ever" figures for maiden races (at least over the last ten years):

Sprints	Ruffian	110 at 5-1/2 furlongs (1975)
Routes	Au Point	115 at one mile (1983)
Turf	Shredder	117 at 1-1/8 miles (1975)

And finally, the figures for Secretariat over his Triple Crown races, in which the son of Bold Ruler established the standard for each race (if one is willing to accept the unofficial, though very plausible, time for the Preakness):

Kentucky Derby	132
Preakness	124
Belmont	135

Chapter 10

FIGURE HANDICAPPING

It is useful to know that a relatively slow running time (or low speed rating) is actually better than a faster time (higher speed rating) from another day. Accurate speed figures make such revelations possible. Speed figures tell how fast a horse ran on previous occasions. What they imply about today's race, possibly at a different track or over a radically different distance, is debatable. As a general rule, the race goes to the fastest horse, provided it is qualified on other grounds. Speed handicappers are best able to judge how fast a horse is capable of running, but they constantly must be aware that their figures measure how fast a horse ran on previous occasions, and not necessarily how fast it will run today. Form must be considered, and the trainer is also an important part of the equation.

Good figures do not imply a fit horse, no more so than does a bad trip last time out, or recent participation in a key race. A horse may be exhausted from efforts given earning those sterling figures. Another may be about to come into form, yet recent poor figures will downgrade its chances, at least in the eyes of dyed-in-the-wool speed handicappers.

On the other hand, erratic figures, strange fluctuations in form, or the apparent lack of a form cycle, may not be as confusing as they seem on paper. Trips, especially the pace trip, can confound a horse's form as revealed in its figures. Pace figures often shed considerable light on a horse's overall figure profile, explaining a good figure one day, and excusing a disappointing performance another day. They paint a picture of how previous races were run, and how today's race is likely to be run.

Comprehensive speed handicapping has its cost, however. The effort expended jotting down speed figures for each contestant takes time.

Time that may have been better spent in analyses of a more qualitative nature. One can become so engrossed with figures that little time is left for other equally important considerations. Handicappers are best advised to precede their speed analysis with other considerations that will identify the contenders, and then use the figures to separate the contenders. In this way, much wasted effort can be eliminated. There will be no need to quantitatively evaluate the noncontenders.

Supplementing the speed analysis of the contenders will be a numerical evaluation of the probable pace. Pace figures should be noted for those horses likely to contest the issue in the early stages. Perhaps one horse will stand out, making that horse worthy of special consideration. Or possibly two or three will appear likely to contest a rapid pace that could have a telling effect on all in the late stages. Perhaps a lone speed horse will emerge as the result of the late scratch of its chief rival for the early lead. This happens regularly, and the handicapper prepared to assess the true significance of the scratch will benefit most. Even then, some races will not be amenable to solution via speed figures. In some instances, the contenders will rate too close to separate. Other times, the figures will be too erratic to properly rate the horses.

No matter how accurately a speed handicapper is able to measure daily track variants, it nevertheless remains true that trips affect a horse's figures. When two horses race within one point (length) of each other, the experienced speed handicapper realizes that it would be foolish to conclude that he has discovered a measurable difference between the two animals.

□ RATING HORSES □

How does one establish a horse's rating? How many races should be used to create the rating? Which races? Can all figures be accepted at face value? Clearly a rating based on the average of two or three figures would be superior to one based on a single race. Any individual speed figure can be misleading, or slightly inaccurate. The determination of a daily variant often demands some judgment on how to best interpret the day's results. Such judgments may later be proven incorrect, leaving all figures for that day slightly off the mark. The effect of such inaccuracies would be diminished to an extent if the figure were only part of an average, rather than the sole basis of a rating.

Rating a horse solely on the basis of its last figure, or its best figure, can be hazardous. If a horse's last figure was its best ever, that was the time to have bet the horse. That figure may not be the best estimate of

how fast it will run today. Most likely, it will not repeat that performance, much less improve upon it. Unless, of course, the animal is a
lightly raced young horse obviously on its way to better things. Out of
curiosity, I asked the computer to search for horses whose last figure (a
modified *Form* speed rating plus track variant) was the best of those
found in its past performances. The results were among the worst found
in studies of speed figures:

NH	NW	WPCT	MPCT	I.V.	$NET
578	81	14.0%	37.5%	1.26	$1.21

There is no practical application intended here. We present these statistics to prove a point—handicappers should be suspicious of horses
whose last race was uncharacteristically good. It may be an aberration,
or the horse may have worn itself out in the process.

Which races in a horse's past performances should be used for rating
purposes? In accordance with the suggestion to rate only contenders, it
seems fitting to recommend the use of a horse's two or three most recent
good efforts. The rating will then provide a good reflection of the horse's
capabilities when at or near its best. Of course, two corollary questions
must be considered. If a horse has been racing well of late, how long is it
likely to maintain its recent peak figures? And for the erratic animal,
how frequently does it throw its best figure? Figures earned when completely outrun are useless. Those earned when carried along to a good
figure while noncompetitive in better company can be deceptive.

Some writers warn against using speed figures more than thirty days
old. I disagree—how else can a freshened horse be rated? Numerous
good bets on such horses will be missed if one follows this advice and
refuses to accept figures earned prior to the recent layoff.

There are times when an exceptionally "big" figure can be misleading. When a horse gets free on the early lead and runs away from its
field, with plenty apparently in reserve, it likely will have run faster
than if pushed throughout in a more competitive contest. It is not likely
to run back to that figure. All the more so had the horse been racing over
a surface biased in favor of early speed types, such as a sloppy track or a
track showing a strong rail bias. Figures earned in such situations
should be discounted somewhat. Averaging them with two other, more
representative figures helps dampen their effect on the horse's final
rating.

CASE STUDY: AU POINT

When Au Point broke his maiden in sensational style on May 4, 1983, I was not overly impressed. Although his pace and speed figures (122–116–115) proved to be the fastest ever for a maiden dirt route, Au Point had gotten loose on the lead over a wet-fast track that was favoring early speed. Visually, he never gave the impression of an exceptional horse in the process of running a mile in 1:34.2. My reaction was "He'll make a great textbook example when he falls apart in his next start." His faltering performance on April 15, in the second start of his career, had left me skeptical.

Au Point came back on May 22 to duplicate his previous effort. Although not running quite as fast at any stage of the race (114–112–111), he was able to get clear early and win off by himself, once again over a wet-fast track favoring early speed. This time, I felt that he looked like a superior racehorse as well.

Au Point's acid test came on June 2 at a mile-and-an-eighth. The colt skipped a class to contest this NW3 race, which was meant to be his final prep for the Belmont Stakes. On this day, the track was fast and unbiased. The pace was slow (110–105–110), yet contested, and Au Point backed off.

Au Point * B. c. 3, by Lyphard—Quillo Queen, by Princequillo
Own.—Snowberry Farm Br.—Gaines & Hunt (Ky) Tr.—Maloney James W
126 Lifetime 5 2 1 1 $31,740 — 1983 5 2 1 1 $31,740 — 1982 0 M 0 0

2Jun83- 8Bel	fst	$1\frac{1}{8}$	:46⅖	1.11⅗	1:50	3↑Alw 27000	1	2	$2^{1\frac{1}{2}}$	1^{hd}	4^{8}	4^{12}	Samyn J L	111	*.40	65-20	Lord Lister 117^{hd} Late Act $119^{2\frac{1}{2}}$ Count Normandy 119^{9}	Tired 5
22May83- 1Bel	my	$1\frac{1}{16}$	:45⅖	1:09⅕	1:41	3↑Alw 21000	3	1	$1^{1\frac{1}{2}}$	1^{6}	1^{8}	1^{11}	Samyn J L	113	*.90	97-14	Au Point 113^{11} New Discovery 119^{1} Huckster 111^{1}	Easily 7
4May83- 2Aqu	my	1	:45	1:09⅗	1:34⅖	Md Sp Wt	1	1	$1^{1\frac{1}{2}}$	1^{5}	1^{6}	1^{8}	Samyn J L	122	*1.10	94-18	Au Point 122^{8} TampaTown $122^{5\frac{1}{4}}$ SweetAffiliation $122^{1\frac{3}{4}}$	Ridden out 6
15Apr83- 6Aqu	fst	7f	:22⅘	:45⅘	1:24⅕	Md Sp Wt	3	4	2^{hd}	$1^{\frac{1}{2}}$	$2^{\frac{1}{2}}$	$3^{3\frac{3}{4}}$	Hernandez R	122	2.20	76-29	Intention $122^{1\frac{1}{2}}$ Par Mania $122^{2\frac{1}{4}}$ Au Point $122^{\frac{1}{2}}$	Weakened 10
7Apr83- 6Aqu	fst	6f	:23	:46⅖	1:12⅕	Md Sp Wt	11	5	3^{1}	1^{hd}	2^{hd}	2no	Hernandez R	122	4.00	80-25	Top Hat 122no Au Point 122^{nk} Vague Reality $117^{\frac{1}{2}}$	Sharp 11

LATEST WORKOUTS ●Jun 9 Bel 3f fst :34⅗ h   May 28 Bel 5f fst 1:00⅕ b   May 19 Bel (T) 4f fm :49⅖ b (d)   May 16 Bel 4f fst :47⅖ h

After gaining everlasting fame for his impression of a ping-pong ball at the head of the stretch in the Belmont Stakes, Au Point revealed his true colors in the Dwyer on July 2. Allowed to set an uncontested, though torrid, pace, the colt refused to give up in the stretch, winning while posting figures of 130–123–113. Obviously, Au Point was a colt for whom the figures did not matter. The key to his performance revolved around whether or not he would be able to get loose on the early lead.

Au Point is not unusual in this respect. Many horses "get brave" when clear on the lead, but fold up when collared. The point is that there is more to pace than fractional times and pace figures. There is also the matter of pressure applied by rival speed horses. Does the horse have the courage to respond to a challenge? Some, like Au Point, don't.

High figures earned against cheaper competition should also be downgraded somewhat. Perhaps the best way to build class into the figures is to make each race's rating the average of its actual speed figure and the par figure for the classification. For example, a race earning a figure of 108 against a 104 par would be rated 106, the average of 104 and 108—or 212, their total. These modified figures give the speed handicapper a better line on how far an impressive recent winner can move up in class, or at what level a recently unsuccessful runner might best fit.

Others prefer proper interpretation to numerical quantification. Against whom did the horse earn its figure? The speed handicapper often finds himself comparing two horses with equal figures from their latest race. But if one earned its figure against some of the fastest horses on the grounds, while the other did so against questionable opposition, the choice is obvious.

Fast pace figures are more significant when a horse then drops in class, or at most remains in the same classification. Horses often run big pace numbers, then move up in class and fall apart when challenged on a slower pace by a classier animal. The better horse is able to run more effortlessly on the lead, regardless of the pace, discouraging its cheaper rival. I have been told by a prominent New York veterinarian that one horse is well aware of its superiority over another, and can transmit this message with a simple flick of its ears, causing the lesser horse to give up the chase.

CASE STUDY: BEAU BIDDER

Beau Bidder provides an excellent example of the type of horse that blind adherence to speed figures might recommend, but sensible handicapping principles would discard. He was entered in the Roamer Handicap at Aqueduct, a mile and three-sixteenths contest on December 18, 1982.

Beau Bidder's last performance earned a 110 figure, seven points faster than par for its NW1 classification, and equal to par for a three-year-old stakes at that time of year. The figure made Beau Bidder appear competitive in the Roamer field, although three points behind the 113 earned by 4–5 favorite Dew Line in the recent Discovery Handicap. The figure was also five points higher than anything Beau Bidder had thrown before. If one wished to bet against the odds-on favorite, the figures pointed to Beau Bidder. In fact, his 110 figure appeared authentic. Runnerup Swallanga had returned in the same classification and finished within one length while repeating his figure. Pace analysts also may have considered Beau Bidder. There was only one other speed type in the field—a claiming refugee from the Meadowlands. "Horses for courses" advocates also might have found Beau Bidder an attractive proposition. His big race had come in his first start over Aqueduct's inner dirt course, and they might have anticipated his becoming another "winter-course specialist."

There were three major problems one would have had to resolve, however, before taking this horse seriously in stakes company, no matter how weak the field might have seemed. First of all, Beau Bidder did not make a habit of winning. He had returned victorious on only two occasions in seventeen career starts. Next, his big win may have been assisted by a soft pace. The figures for his December 9 race read 104–105–110. Beau Bidder would likely encounter stiffer competition for the early lead in the Roamer, if not at the half, then certainly by the three quarters. This, in turn, would likely decrease his final speed figure to a less impressive level. Finally, the entire appeal of Beau Bidder came from one race. To properly assess the horse's ability, one or two other recent routes should be averaged with his December 9 figures. His appeal would lessen considerably as a result.

Beau Bidder performed in the Roamer as seasoned handicappers might have expected. He challenged a faster pace, then faded out of the picture, finishing last. Dew Line rallied to win the race, rather unimpressively. The figures for the race were dismal: 114–110–104.

Beau Bidder — Dk. b. or br. c. 3, by Raise A Bid—Beau Edie, by Beau Brummel
Own.—Marablue Farm — Br.—Marablue Farm (Fla) — Tr.—Hernandez Ramon M
109 — Lifetime 17 2 3 4 $49,029 — 1982 17 2 3 4 $49,029 — 1981 0 M 0 0 — Turf 8 1 3 1 $25,940

9Dec82- 1Aqu fst 1⅛ [•]:48⅕ 1:14⅖ 1:54⅕ 3↑ Alw 22000 4 1 11 21 11 12¾ Hernandez R 115 *2.50 75-30 Beau Bidder 1152¾ Swallanga 1177¾ Sestrel 1202½ Driving 6
28Nov82- 7Aqu fst 1 :48⅕ 1:13 1:37⅘ 3↑ Alw 20000 4 3 32 43 44½ 46¾ Hernandez R 115 3.90 70-28 High Gold 115no Chapter One 1153½ Asticou 1153½ Tired 7
13Nov82- 8Key fst 1 1/16 :46⅗ 1:11⅖ 1:43 Minuteman H 3 3 62¼ 31 32½ 45½ Smith T R III 112 8.80 83-20 VgbondSergent113noJ.P.'sNewBdge1145ThunderRunnr118½ Tired 8
27Oct82- 3Aqu fst 7f :23⅗ :46⅗ 1:22⅕ 3↑ Alw 19000 2 5 65½ 62¼ 24 37 Alvarado R Jr5 109 5.30 83-17 Determined Bidder 1146¼ Cintula 114¾ BeauBidder1093¾ Checked 8
16Oct82- 5Aqu fst 1 :48 1:12⅗ 1:37⅘ 3↑ Alw 20000 1 1 1½ 1hd 1hd 33 Hernandez R 114 21.60 74-26 NathnDetroit114¾ReservtionAgent1142¼BeuBidder1141 Weakened 8
17Sep82- 1Bel fm 1¼ [T]:49⅘ 1:40⅗ 2:04⅘ Clm 70000 3 1 13 1½ 1½ 2hd Cordero A Jr 113 6.00 70-22 Hail Victorious 117hd Beau Bidder 1131 SparkyRidge1134 Gamely 6
5Sep82- 3Bel fm 1¼ [T]:48 1:37⅘ 2:01⅗ Clm 90000 6 4 55¾ 42½ 49 615 Hernandez C 118 18.80 71-13 Uncle Jeff 118½ Ten Below 12211 Sparky Ridge 112¾ Tired 7
22Aug82- 7Sar fm 1 1/16 [T]:47⅗ 1:11⅖ 1:42⅖ 3↑ Alw 20000 2 7 56 45½ 57 67¾ Hernandez C 117 11.10 90-11 Forkali 117no Fortuis 112nk Bandwagon 1172 Lacked a response 10
12Aug82- 3Sar fm 1 1/16 (T):48⅕ 1:13⅖ 1:45⅖ 3↑ Md Sp Wt 9 8 69½ 44½ 2hd 11¾ Hernandez C 117 *2.40e 70-25 Beau Bidder1171¾Urbanized1174WingedUniverse117no Drew clear 12
30Jly82- 1Bel yl 1⅜ [T]:52⅖ 1:43⅗ 2:21 3↑ Md Sp Wt 1 3 34 32 31½ 42 Maple E 116 2.60[D] 50-48 Luckington 116nk Disco Dad 116¾ Flaming Pirate 1161 Bore out 7
30Jly82-Disqualified and placed fifth
LATEST WORKOUTS Nov 9 Bel tr.t 6f fst 1:17⅘ b Nov 5 Bel tr.t 4f sly :52 b

Dew Line — B. c. 3, by Cannonade—Cold Hearted, by The Axe II
Own.—Ryehill Farm — Br.—Ryehill Farm (Ky) — Tr.—Cantey Joseph B
112 — Lifetime 21 4 6 3 $166,933 — 1982 17 3 5 3 $152,993 — 1981 4 1 1 0 $13,940 — Turf 7 1 2 1 $60,690

20Nov82- 8Lrl yl 1 1/16 (T):49⅕ 1:15⅕ 1:46⅗ Japan Asoc H 13 13 129¼ 129¾ 1315 1215 McCarron G b 117 *1.70 55-30 Northrop 1144 A Magic Spray 1131 Pin Puller 113nk Dull try 14
13Nov82- 6Aqu my 1 3/16 :49 1:39⅖ 2:11 3↑ Handicap 6 2 21 11½ 2½ 21¼ Maple E b 113 *.80 83-25 Piling 1151¼ Dew Line 113¾ Worthy Too 1141¾ Weakened 6
6Nov82- 8Aqu fst 1⅛ :50 1:14 1:50⅘ Discovery H 3 5 511 44 32 2¾ McCarron G 113 3.50 30-17 Trenchant 113¾ Dew Line 113¾ Exclusive Era 1121¼ Gaining 5
28Oct82- 6Med yl 1 1/16 (T):48⅕ 1:12⅗ 1:44⅗ 3↑ Cliff Hngr H 6 7 78¼ 76¾ 47 33½ Maple E 114 2.80 75-22 Erin's Tiger 1142½ Santo's Joe 1161 Dew Line 1146 Late gain 8
28Oct82-Run in Two Divisions: 6th & 8th Races
9Oct82- 8Bow fst 1⅛ :47⅖ 1:11⅗ 1:50⅗ Gov's Cup H 6 12 1118 1116 54½ 41½ Kaenel J L 114 6.70 90-17 Trenchant 108nk Semaj 106nk Royal Roberto 1181 Wide, rallied 14
25Sep82-10LaD fst 1¼ :46⅘ 1:36 2:01⅗ Super Derby 3 8 77½ 98½ 97½ 97½ Maple E 126 19.00 100-06 Reinvested 126no El Baba1261½DropYourD:awers1262 Never close 10
6Sep82- 8AP fm 1½ (T):51 2:06⅖ 2:31⅕ Secretariat 4 6 56 1hd 21½ 23 Kaenel J L 114 2.80 80-19 Half Iced 1143 Dew Line 1142½ Continuing 1142¾ Weakened 8
1Aug82- 8Bel fm 1¼ [T]:48⅗ 1:37⅕ 2:01⅘ Lexington 3 3 42½ 41¾ 3nk 11 Maple E 117 2.60[D] 85-20 [D]Dew Line 1171 Royal Roberto 1261½[D]Reinvested1261¾ Bore out 6
1Aug82-Disqualified and placed fifth
1Aug82-Run in Two Divisions 6th & 8th Races
10Jly82- 8AP sly 1¼ :47⅘ 1:38⅗ 2:05⅗ Amer Derby 4 4 44½ 21 2hd 2no MacBeth D 114 2.20 69-28 Wolfie's Rascal 123no Dew Line 1147 NorthernMajesty120½ Sharp 8
LATEST WORKOUTS Dec 15 Bel tr.t 1 fst 1:44⅘ b Dec 8 Bel tr.t 5f fst 1:02⅖ b Nov 30 Bel tr.t 5f gd 1:01 b Oct 25 Bel 6f fst 1:15 b

Freshened horses rounding into form may have their most recent figure upgraded by using lengths behind at the stretch call as a substitute for actual beaten lengths. For example, a fresh horse rated 101 on the basis of running line:

$$2^2 \quad 2^1 \quad 3^1 \quad 4^4$$

would be upgraded three points (the difference between four beaten lengths and the one length behind at the stretch call) to 104.

The chances of first-time starters can best be assessed by considering the figures of the logical contenders that have already started. If these have all fallen well below par for the race—say five points or more—it is reasonable to assume the contest could easily go to a first-time starter.

☐ DOUBLE-ADVANTAGE HORSES ☐

Several writers of late, most notably Andrew Beyer and William Scott, have advocated the chances of the "double advantage" horse. This is the animal whose two rated races are both better than the best recent figure of each of its opponents. Statistics prove their point.

Only once in every eight races does one find a horse with such an advantage over its rivals. The figures below are for horses whose latest two figures both were better than the best each opponent had to offer from its latest two starts:

NH	NW	WPCT	MPCT	I.V.	$NET
120	37	30.8%	55.0%	2.78	$2.74

☐ PACE ANALYSIS ☐

I have always found speed figures most reliable when dealing with classier horses, especially with juveniles. When appraising claiming animals, however, pace figures become more useful, helping to explain the apparent ups and downs in form so typical of lower-class animals.

The importance of pace analysis seems to have been stressed more years ago than it is today. Tom Ainslie's *The Compleat Horseplayer* (published in 1966) and Ray Taulbot's *Thoroughbred Horse Racing— Playing for Profit* (1959) laid the groundwork for what we are about to discuss. Taulbot contended that a horse's class and present fitness can best be seen in the rate of pace, and the manner in which the horse deals with it. Taulbot believed that a horse's best race (and figure) came when it raced on or close to the lead.

We shall work on the premise that a horse has just so much energy available, and this is reflected in the total of its speed and pace figures. This total remains fairly constant while a horse is racing in good form. (In actuality, statistical studies suggest that a horse's speed and pace figures each are subject to a variation of 1–2 points from race to race during periods of relatively stable form. This can likely be attributed to trips—how far the horse raced from the rail, how alertly it broke from the gate, racing luck, and so on. Consequently, a sprinter's total figure can be expected to vary about three points from one race to the next, and a router's figure by five points.) From our premise, it follows that energy expended early will not be available late. Higher-than-usual pace figures result in lower-than-normal speed figures. Lower pace figures, on the other hand, result in higher speed figures. Should a horse run two fifths (four tenths) faster than accustomed early, it likely will finish four fifths slower than usual.

What has just been said relates mostly to horses likely to be involved in the early pace. We do not advocate rating horses by adding their speed and pace figures. Closers would never come out on top that way. We do recommend using this approach for early speed types, however, projecting their speed figure based on the estimated pace figure they are likely to run in the presence (or absence) of other speed types in the field. For example, should a horse figure to run a 205 pace and speed total, and be forced to a 105 pace number, its final speed figure could be projected at 100, the difference between 205 and 105. Once projected speed figures have been established for the pacesetters, the chances of the stretch-runners can be assessed. Is the race set up for them? Do any of them have the figures to catch the speed?

☐ THE SHAPE OF THINGS ☐

During the Speed Handicapping Symposium at Handicapping Expo '83, Andy Beyer asked me what I do with my pace and speed figures. Although it drew a few laughs, my answer "I look at them" was not meant to be facetious. The combined pace and speed figures have both a predictive and interpretive function. We have just finished discussing the former, but it was to the latter that my comment was directed. To better understand a horse's recent performance lines, it is necessary to take a look at the pace with which it was confronted, and how it dealt with that pace. How did those races "shape up," from the viewpoint of pace?

Looking at pace and speed figures, there are basically nine different "race shapes." The pace may have been nearly average, or significantly faster or slower than normal. The overall race time offers the same three possibilities, each in conjunction with one of the pace types. We shall discuss each "shape" individually, using sprint figures for simplicity. Assume a race par figure of 105.

AVERAGE-AVERAGE (105–105): A completely average race for the class. Favors no particular running style.

AVERAGE-FAST (105–108): An average pace leading to an above-average speed figure. Usually the result of a strong front-running performance.

AVERAGE-SLOW (105–102): An average pace that fell apart, with nothing able to rally in the stretch and sustain the figure. A rallying performance here can be deceptive, not as good as it might appear.

FAST-FAST (108–107): The most impressive "race shape." Anything close at the wire has raced exceptionally well.

FAST-AVERAGE (108–105): An above-average performance if by a front-runner. If won from behind, the winner was taking advantage of an exceptionally quick pace.

FAST-SLOW (108–102): An above-average pace that had a telling effect. Not a bad performance if won in front, but exceptionally weak if the winner ran late.

SLOW-FAST (102–108): An exceptionally strong performance by a relatively fresh horse that got away with leisurely fractions. Especially impressive if won from behind.

SLOW-AVERAGE (102–105): The winner was able to finish strongly and record an average figure despite a slow pace. Usually won by a front-runner, this type of race is most powerful when won by a stretch-runner.

SLOW-SLOW (102–102): A complete washout, with nothing in the field able to run early or late. Most unimpressive are front-runners unable to capitalize on an advantageous slow pace.

With two pace figures complementing the speed figure, route races are more complex. But the basic point has been made. Slow-pace races are usually won on the front-end, but are more impressive when won from behind by a horse overcoming its tactical disadvantage. On the other hand, fast-pace races can be won from behind, but are more impressive if won up front by a speedball refusing to surrender.

In this same vein, we recommend that closers not be "blamed" for slow speed figures if able to get up in a slow-paced race. They cannot be faulted for the pace. They begin their move at a certain point, regardless of pace, that will hopefully bring them to the front inside the last sixteenth.

The eighth race at Santa Anita on January 6, 1983 (see Chapter 9) was won in fast time despite exceptionally slow pace figures. Surprisingly, this classified route was won by the late-charging Kangaroo Court, who came back in his next start to win a seven-furlong stakes at Santa Anita. Figure profiles of this type are rare indeed.

CASE STUDY: KING BELGIAN

Route races offer at least one interesting shape not seen in sprints—the race that quickens noticeably from the first pace call to the second. Horses able to gain ground during this phase of such a race are doing some serious running. A strong "middle move" is an excellent indicator of impending success.

On paper, King Belgian's performance on May 11 hardly appears formidable. However, a look at the figures and trips reveals the opposite to be true. The race figures were 104–106–108, above average for the classification. And as the pace quickened from the half to the three quarters, King Belgian gained three lengths while racing on the far outside. Then, after losing some of his momentum entering the stretch, the gelding gained two lengths and passed three horses in the final furlong, again as the pace quickened. He ended up losing the race by less than four lengths. Everything considered, it was not a bad performance, and set the horse up for a smashing win at 4–1 odds on May 21.

King Belgian — B. g. 5, by Wardlaw—Honest Amber, by Amber Morn
Own.—Tresvant Stable — **$18,000** Br.—Lasater Farm (Fla) — Tr.—Sedlacek Sue — **108**5

Lifetime	1983	9	2	0	0	$16,260
51 7 8 5	1982	23	3	3	2	$33,540
$82,475	Turf	2	0	0	0	

11May83- 9Aqu fst 1⅛	:49⅕ 1:14⅕ 1:52	Clm 20000	8	7	86¾	73¾	86	53¾	Murphy D J7	b 110•	16.40	71-30	FriendlyLetters1122½ColdTrilin'117½ThundrBring108¾	Raced Wide	10
11May83-Dead heat															
28Apr83- 3Aqu fst 1⅛	:48⅘ 1:13 1:51⅖	Clm 18000	3	2	2hd	1hd	2hd	43	Thibeau R J5	b 108	12.90	75-16	Cartucho 117½ Friendly Letters 117½ Hot Words 1171	Weakened	8
16Apr83- 9Aqu sly 1	:48⅖ 1:14⅕ 1:39⅗	Clm 20000	4	5	31½	57	47½	46	Davis R G5	b 108	6.00	62-26	NeedAPenny1122¾SeldConqust113nk DlingDiplomt1173	Weakened	8
9Apr83- 2Aqu my 1 3/16	:47⅕ 1:12⅕ 1:59	Clm 16000	9	4	11½	12	14	12¾	Davis R G5	b 112	20.90	67-26	KingBelgin1122¾[DH]PerfectBidder112[DH]TheMngler117nk	Drew off	9
31Mar83- 2Aqu fst 7f	:23⅕ :46⅕ 1:24⅕	Clm c-12500	11	14	1313	1111	69	78¾	Beitia E	b 119	6.40	71-21	SpartnMonk1173½AnotherRodger1101¾ComeUpPence112½	Outrun	14
18Mar83- 5Aqu sly 1	:47⅘ 1:12⅘ 1:38⅘	Clm 18000	11	11	85¼	811	811	1015	Beitia E	b 113	15.90	57-27	WhtAChrger1083ReverseDecision117½EdgOfWisdom1124¾	Outrun	14
12Mar83- 9Aqu sly 6f [•]	:23 :46⅘ 1:11⅗	Clm 20000	2	10	1010	108	87¾	86½	Beitia E	b 117	14.10	79-15	Snowgun 1171¾ Cold Trailin' 1171¾ Tiempo 1101	Outrun	10
23Feb83- 1Aqu fst 6f [•]	:22⅘ :46⅘ 1:12⅖	Clm 16000	12	10	95¾	86	51¼	11	Beitia E	b 117	19.30f	82-21	King Belgian 1171HerefordMan117hdAnotherRodger117hd	Driving	12
19Jan83- 5Aqu fst 1⅛ [•]	:47⅗ 1:13⅕ 1:53	Clm 16000	10	9	66	64¼	814	917	Beitia E	b 117	33.90	64-24	Recidian 112½ Sir Sizzling Nehoc 1136 Tantivy 115¾	Mild bid	11
28Dec82- 9Aqu fst 1 3/16 [•]	:48⅗ 1:14 2:00⅗	3 • Clm 20000	9	6	78½	85½	87	813	Migliore R	b 117	27.90	62-22	Gig'sLittleTiger1122BraveTheReef1172¾PerfectBidder108nk	Outrun	10

CASE STUDY: MY LIPHARD

The fourth race at Belmont September 4, 1982, a maiden special event for older horses, presented a typical handicapping problem. On speed figures alone, My Liphard stood over his field. The 103 he earned in his most recent start was four lengths faster than anything his chief rivals, Cricket Drummer and October Wind, had ever achieved. Pace figures, however, made his task appear far more difficult.

My Liphard earned his top figure with a front-running effort at seven furlongs. The pace was quite slow (98), yet he nonetheless gave way in the late stages. Obviously improving, the Laz Barrera-trained son of Lyphard could. be expected to improve his 201 total figure. How he would distribute this total was the question. In his prior start, he set a blistering pace (106), then fell apart in the last eighth-mile, losing thirteen lengths in a race rated 106–101.

Complicating My Liphard's life was Cricket Drummer, his main rival for the early lead. He had set a fast pace (105) in his latest start, before faltering to a not-so-bad 98 figure. If forced to a 105 pace, My Liphard figured to slow down to a 96 at the wire.

A suicidal speed duel would benefit October Wind, who had rallied in just such a race August 27 at Saratoga, passing Cricket Drummer in the lane. Yet his performance was hardly earthshaking. He had rallied in a 105–100 race, which is no great feat, and he had never come within three points of the MSW par figure.

Track bias would play a predominant role in the outcome of this race, and also in the prerace selection of its winner. Over a speed-favoring track that would later in the day assist Island Whirl to his impressive victory in the Woodward, October Wind could be eliminated. The choice was therefore between the two front-runners, My Liphard at 6–5 and Cricket Drummer at 4–1.

In light of a strong track bias at Saratoga August 18, My Liphard's performance increases in magnitude. Only two of fourteen dirt races run at the Spa between August 17 and August 19 were won by horses among the first three at the first call—far below average. For a horse that appeared ready for six furlongs at best, My Liphard's strong front-running effort at seven furlongs now looks quite impressive. Were it not for the bias, he likely would have won at seven furlongs that day. And now he was set to run just six furlongs, with a speed bias in his favor. Add to this the fact that he easily outran Cricket Drummer for the early lead on August 10, and My Liphard at least becomes the logical selection, even if unappetizing at the odds.

My Liphard did, in fact, go wire-to-wire, besting Cricket Drummer by a length. The latter ran second most of the trip. October Wind never entered contention. The race figures were 101–102.

My Liphard B. c. 3, by Lyphard—Dawn's Cove, by Donut King
Own.—Miglietti Br.—Winchell V H Jr (Ky) Tr.—Barrera Lazaro S 118
Lifetime 3 0 1 0 $3,860 — 1982 3 M 1 0 $3,860 — 1981 0 M 0 0
18Aug82- 4Sar fst 7f :22⅘ :45⅘ 1:23⅕ 3+Md Sp Wt 6 3 11 13 13 21¼ Cordero A Jr 117 6.30 85-15 Trenchant 1171¼ My Liphard 1176¾ Mi Negro 1173¾ Weakened 11
10Aug82- 6Sar gd 6f :22 :45 1:10⅗ 3+Md Sp Wt 4 1 12 1hd 1hd 513 Hernandez R 117 6.80 74-19 HonestTreasure1173Arawak1124¾CricketDrummer107nk Gave way 9
25Jan82- 6Hia fst 6f :22⅘ :45⅗ 1:11⅗ Md Sp Wt 6 9 97¼ 75¾12201219 Migliore R3 117 8.70 66-21 Main Top 1204 Songburst 1201 Chattering 1201 Forced wide 12
LATEST WORKOUTS ●Aug 7 Sar 5f fst :59⅘ hg Aug 1 Sar tr.t 5f fst 1:01 b Jly 26 Sar 4f fst :48⅘ h

Cricket Drummer B. c. 3, by What a Pleasure—Laughing Bridge, by Hilarious
Own.—Russell R Br.—Hellman Acres Inc (Fla) Tr.—Kelly Thomas J 118
Lifetime 7 0 1 1 $4,830 — 1982 4 M 0 1 $2,280 — 1981 3 M 1 0 $2,550
27Aug82- 5Sar fst 6½f :22⅘ :45⅗ 1:18 3+Md Sp Wt 7 3 1½ 1½ 1½ 52¼ Velasquez J b 117 4.10 80-14 HenryWilliams122nkHveANiceDy117½OctoberWind117nk Gave way 11
27Aug82-Dead heat
10Aug82- 6Sar gd 6f :22 :45 1:10⅗ 3+Md Sp Wt 2 7 45½ 47 54½ 37¾ AntongrgWA10 b 107 11.50 79-19 Honest Treasure 1173 Arawak 1124¾ Cricket Drummer107nk Wide 9
23Jan82- 3Hia fst 7f :22⅗ :45⅕ 1:26 Md Sp Wt 11 1 1hd 13 11191121 Bailey J D b 120 9.00 52-19 RoiMusiqu120noTwo'sNotEnough1201½I'mPurGold1202½ Stopped 12
8Jan82- 6Hia fst 6f :21⅘ :45⅖ 1:11 Md Sp Wt 10 3 1hd 15 21½ 713 Bailey J D b 120 2.90 75-15 Star Choice 1205 Crafty Mac 1202 Fastness 1201 Gave way 11
19Dec81- 3Crc fst 7f :22⅘ :46⅕ 1:25 Md Sp Wt 4 3 1½ 15 11 25 Bailey J D 119 10.60 86-12 North Cat 1195 CricketDrummer1191½Greers'Leader1195 2nd best 12
15Dec81- 4Crc fst 6f :22⅗ :46⅗ 1:13⅗ Md Sp Wt 4 5 2½ 1½ 11½ 69¼ Bailey J D 119 3.90 75-18 Catch Villa 119½ Star Choice 1191 Lederhosen 1195 Faltered 10
14Nov81- 4Aqu fst 6f :23 :46⅗ 1:13⅖ Md Sp Wt 7 4 12 16 15 3nk Hernandez R 118 *1.90 D 74-22 Jacart118hdWhatAChrger113hd D CricketDrummer118½ Drifted out 10
14Nov81-Disqualified and placed fourth
LATEST WORKOUTS Aug 25 Sar 3f fst :36 h Aug 18 Sar 5f fst :59⅕ h Aug 1 Mth 4f fst :48⅗ h ●Jly 23 Mth 4f fst :47 h

October Wind B. c. 3, by Raja Baba—Olden, by Olden Times
Own.—Augustin Stables Br.—Bayard & Farish III (Ky) Tr.—Sheppard Jonathan E 118
Lifetime 3 0 0 1 $2,490 — 1982 3 M 0 1 $2,490 — 1981 0 M 0 0
27Aug82- 5Sar fst 6½f :22⅘ :45⅗ 1:18 3+Md Sp Wt 4 7 54½ 33½ 32½ 3¾ Miranda J b 117 21.00 81-14 HenryWillims122nkHveANiceDy117½OctobrWind117nk Raced wide 11
10Aug82- 6Sar gd 6f :22 :45 1:10⅗ 3+Md Sp Wt 3 5 810 814 612 615 Alvarado R Jr7 110 6.00 72-19 Honest Treasure 1173 Arawak 1124¾CricketDrummer107nk Outrun 9
22Jly82- 5Del fst 6f :22⅗ :46⅕ 1:11⅘ 3+Md Sp Wt 11 1 51½ 32½ 24 43 Dufton E 115 5.50 79-19 Parting Crack 1053SunriseBound115noMostlyBad115hd Weakened 12
LATEST WORKOUTS Aug 19 Sar 4f fst :47⅖ h Aug 7 Sar 5f fst 1:00 h Jly 19 Del 4f fst :48⅘ b Jly 5 Del 5f fst 1:02⅖ b

The classic example found in the Ainslie and Taulbot books deals with two races run in the identical speed figure, but with one having a faster pace than the other. For example,

108–106 vs. 104–106

Which was the better race? Obviously, the first. Its pace figure was higher, and so the total of its pace and speed figures was higher.

Suppose that both races were won on the front end, and that the winners now were about to meet at approximately the same distance. The winner of the first race could slow down a few ticks early and still lead, while conserving energy and improving its final figure. Remember, we assume the sum of the two figures remains constant. The winner of the second race, however, would have to run faster early to keep in touch with the lead, and would consequently slow down to a slower final figure. In other words, the first horse might be able to run 106–108, while the second would record figures of 106–104. The two horses would battle for the early lead, with the former better able to cope with the pace, then draw out to a four-length margin at the wire.

CASE STUDY: THE 1982 MATRON

When Share The Fantasy and Weekend Surprise met in the 1982 Matron Stakes at Belmont, they were renewing an argument that had raged throughout the preceding Saratoga meet. Share The Fantasy was the speed type, Weekend Surprise the stretch runner. When they first met in the Schuylerville Stakes, conditions favored Weekend Surprise. On a speed-killing track, Share The Fantasy set a blistering pace, only to be caught in the late stages by the onrushing daughter of Secretariat. Share The Fantasy's figures for the race read 105–100. Weekend Surprise's winning figure was a 101.

On an unbiased track for the Spinaway, Share The Fantasy rated off a relatively mild pace, then exploded in the stretch. Her figures now looked like 100–106, the reverse of her previous numbers. Weekend Surprise earned a 99 for her uninspiring effort. The figures for these two fillies were fairly constant. Share The Fantasy's totals were 205 and 206, while Weekend Surprise rated 101 and 99. In fact, the latter's effort before her two Saratoga stakes rated 100.

One could predict fairly confidently that Weekend Surprise would run approximately 100 in the Matron. But what of Share The Fantasy? Her final figure depended to a great extent on her pace figure.

Complicating the picture was Wings of Jove, a filly that had run close to the front while winning the recent Astarita Stakes, earning figures 102–103 for the effort. Her 205 total placed her right there with Share The Fantasy.

If Share The Fantasy rated, as she did so well in the Spinaway, she might find it difficult catching Wings Of Jove, especially on a track favoring early speed. On the other hand, if the two dueled for the early lead without setting too fast a pace, the figures predicted they would be hard to separate at the wire, and probably a couple of lengths clear of Weekend Surprise. The latter's only chance appeared to be a suicidal speed duel up front.

As things worked out, Share The Fantasy chose to allow Wings Of Jove to set her own pace, and was unable to catch her. Weekend Surprise rallied nicely for third. The race figures: 103–103.

☐ THE KEY RACE, REVISITED ☐

In Chapter 8, we discussed the key-race concept at some length. What we presented there was pure conjecture, with no statistics proving its value to handicappers, and no detailed set of rules defining its application. When does a race become a key race? How many of its contestants must come back and run well before a race earns such a designation? And which horses should be bet? If the first, third, and fifth finishers come back to win, obviously the second and fourth are worth following. But what of those sixth or worse?

I have found the key-race concept to be an invaluable handicapping weapon over the years, as have numerous others including Andy Beyer, Steve Davidowitz, and John Pricci, to mention just three of the game's leading authorities.

We are now going to define a new key-race concept, one based on pace figures. The method is simple to apply, if one bothers to make pace figures, and the results thus far have been quite good. A key-race sprint is one in which the pace figure was at least four tenths (points) faster than par. For routes, both pace figures must satisfy this requirement, with the half-mile figure, therefore, being eight points faster than par. Eligible horses are those first, second, or third at the first call in such races, excepting those five lengths (or more) in arrears at that stage of the race. Horses remain eligible for one month after participating in such a race.

We tracked this system in New York from the beginning of 1983 through the end of the summer meeting at Belmont. Here are the results:

Number of bets	432
Number of winners	102
Win percentage	23.6%
Average Payoff	$2.66
Number placed 1–2	172
Place percentage	39.8%
Average Place Payoff	$2.12

These results are all the more amazing when one realizes that no attention was paid to where a key-race horse raced next. Changes in distance, surface, or class were not considered. How the horse finished in the key race was of no matter. The horse was bet, with no questions asked, provided that it raced back within the month. All other handicapping considerations were suspended.

How does one explain the success of this system? Contesting a brusque pace can have two notable effects: It can sharpen a horse's form and help bring the animal to a peak of fitness. Or it can result in a deceptively poor performance (finish), disguising the horse's form, with the result being better odds next time the horse races. The two combine often enough to produce a good percentage of winners at attractive odds.

CASE STUDY: INFINITE SAGA

Infinite Saga embodied the essentials of the key race to their fullest when entered in a seven-furlong sprint at Aqueduct on March 31, 1983. In his previous start on March 6, the fleet gelding had participated in a classic key race. The pace on that occasion had been exceptionally quick, qualifying the race under our standards. Both the winner, Rapido's Repeat, and the fourth-finisher, Peregrine Power, had returned to win in the same company. And third-place finisher Ruler Come Back had since finished second to Dancer's Melody, a horse on its way to allowance company. The March 6 race was truly a key race in both senses of the term.

Also working in Infinite Saga's favor was the seven-furlong distance of the March 31 race. Although the horse had a history of tiring at six panels, he was likely to find the pace at the longer distance more to his liking. On March 31, Infinite Saga was to meet no rival with "six-furlong" early speed, assuring him a clear lead, as long as he broke alertly. And this is exactly what happened, as Infinite Saga opened a long lead on the backstretch, then coasted to an easy win. The only surprise was the payoff—a more-than-liberal $40.20!

There are two lessons to be learned from Infinite Saga. One is the power of the key-race concepts. And the other is the advantageous position in which a horse with six-furlong speed often finds itself when stretching out to seven furlongs.

CASE STUDY: NORTHERN MAGUS

Speed horses often signal impending improvement in form with an exceptional pace figure. Such was the case with Northern Magus, entered against eight other four-year-olds in a six-furlong NW1 allowance at Aqueduct on February 6, 1983. Northern Magus set a blistering pace on January 27, his first start in over four months. Speed figures for that race were 113–105, giving Northern Magus a final figure of 101, and a pace-speed total of 214, well above par for the classification. If Northern Magus only apportioned his energy more wisely in his next start . . .

Working in Northern Magus' favor February 6 was the fact that he was the lone speed in his field. Allowed to slow the pace to a moderately fast 106, Northern Magus kept right on going, recording the exceptional speed figure of 109 for his seven-length win. His pace-speed total for this race was 215, just one point higher than his previous effort. Northern Magus paid $14.80 while reversing over the horses that had finished second, third, and fourth ahead of him in the January 27 race. Speed handicapping alone, without an assist from pace figures, would not have pointed to this logical horse.

CASE STUDY: ABLE MONEY

Sharp early speed is an especially good sign with freshened horses just off a layoff. Able Money was making her first start after an eight-week layoff when she pushed Far Flying to exceptionally fast pace and speed figures on April 16. The conditioning gained from that race helped Able Money come back and upset a good field in the Prioress Stakes on May 1 at a $63.20 parimutuel, and then repeat in the Comely Stakes two weeks later at $8.80. Able Money earned a speed figure of 103 in both stakes, one point slower than her maiden voyage, the race that spotlighted her ability in the first place.

Able Money — Dk. b. or br. f. 3, by Distinctive—Able Maid, by Good Behaving
Br.—Miranda & Sierra (Fla)
Tr.—Russo Anthony J
Own.—Donnelly Faith
112
Lifetime 2 1 1 0 $15,200 | 1983 2 1 1 0 $15,200 | 1982 0 M 0 0

16Apr83- 5Aqu sly 7f	:23⅗ :47⅗ 1:24⅘	ⒻAlw 20000	4 3 2½ 2^{2} 2^{8} 2^{14}	Smith A Jr	116	*1.70	63-26	Far Flying 118^{14} Able Money 116½ Ida Lewis 118¾	No match	6
20Feb83- 6Aqu fst 6f	⊡:22⅘ :46⅘ 1:11⅘	ⒻMd Sp Wt	11 6 2^{2} 1½ 1^{5} 16¾	Smith A Jr	121	17.60	85-20	AbleMoney$121^{6¾}$ShwneeCreek$121^{1¾}$HighSchemes114¾	Ridden out	14

LATEST WORKOUTS Apr 28 Bel 3f fst :36 h | Apr 23 Bel 6f fst 1:14⅗ h | Apr 14 Bel tr.t 4f fst :50 b | Apr 6 Bel tr.t 6f fst 1:20 b

CASE STUDY: GRAND FELICE AND DR. FARR

In Chapter 7, we discussed the merits of the horse dropping in class after being close at some call in its previous race. Grand Felice was such an example when entered in a classified allowance route at Aqueduct on March 2, 1983. The five-year-old had chased the pace for seven furlongs in the Grey Lag Handicap, and now was dropping to a more suitable level. His presence in the Grey Lag suggested his connections considered him a fit horse, something his prior sprint had not revealed. These two clues alone made Grand Felice worth considering. The exceptionally fast pace of the Grey Lag cinched the case. Grand Felice led the allowance field wire-to-wire on March 2, and paid an amazing $40.20 for his efforts.

Grand Felice — Ch. h. 5, by Full Pocket—Julie Tim, by Blade
Br.—Nuckols Bros (Ky)
Tr.—Wright Floyd
Own.—O'Connor R F
117
Lifetime 34 5 13 1 $78.453 | 1983 4 1 1 0 $23,780 | 1982 16 2 3 1 $39,140 | Turf 13 1 9 0 $5,933

21Feb83- 8Aqu fst 1⅛	⊡:46⅘ 1:11 1:50⅕	3+Grey Lag H	6 3 3^{1} 3^{2} 89¾ 9^{13}	Faine C		112	41.20	82-22	Sing Sing 122½ Fabulous Find 115¾ Lark Oscillation 113^{1}	Tired	9
14Feb83- 7Aqu fst 6f	⊡:22⅘ :46⅕ 1:10⅘	Alw 35000	8 6 74¼ 72¼ 65½ 6^{4}	Faine C		117	18.30	86-13	Main Stem 110no With Caution $119^{2¼}$ MortgageMan117^{hd}	Outrun	8
19Jan83- 1Aqu fst 1⅛	⊡:48⅕ 1:13 1:52⅖	Alw 29000	1 1 2^{hd} 1^{hd} 1^{hd} 2^{2}	Faine C		117	7.40	82-24	ⒹEvasive John 112^{2} Grand Felice 117¾ John's Gold 117^{4}	Tired	6
19Jan83-Placed first through disqualification											
9Jan83- 9Aqu fst 170	⊡:48⅕ 1:12⅗ 1:42	Alw 29000	1 2 2^{hd} 1^{hd} 1^{hd} 2^{hd}	Faine C		117	16.60	92-17	Tarberry 112^{hd} Grand Felice $117^{1½}$ ClimbingHigh$119^{1½}$	Just failed	10
30Dec82- 8Aqu fst 6f	⊡:23 :46⅖ 1:11⅗	3+Alw 27000	7 2 4^{3} 5^{5} 56½ 5^{4}	Faine C		117	16.10	82-24	Lost Creek 115no Mr, Howard $114^{1¾}$ King Naskra $115^{1¾}$	Tired	7
19Dec82- 1Aqu fst 1 1/16	⊡:49 1:13⅘ 1:45⅘	3+Clm c-47500	2 3 31½ 34½ 2^{6} 23½	Miceli M		117	*2.50	80-23	Subordinte$108^{3½}$GrndFelic$117^{2¾}$NorthrnRgnt$113^{3¾}$	Best of others	6
10Dec82- 1Aqu fst 1⅛	⊡:48⅕ 1:13⅘ 1:52⅘	3+Clm 45000	5 5 53½ 53¾ 11½ 12¾	Miceli M^{3}		113	6.80	82-24	GrndFelice$113^{2¾}$CmpusCpers117^{nk}CremeDeLFete113¾	Drew clear	7
26Nov82- 8Med fst 1 1/16	:47⅘ 1:12⅕ 1:45⅕	3+Alw 16000	3 2 21½ 2^{2} 44½ 44½	Miceli M	b	116	7.20	78-21	Class Hero $113^{1¼}$ Wind Jet 116^{3} Big Greg 116^{nk}	Tired	7
12Nov82- 5Aqu fst 7f	:22⅘ :45⅕ 1:23⅖	3+Clm 50000	6 3 5^{3} 4^{3} 77¾ 85¼	Miceli M	b	117	10.70	79-21	Surf Club 113no Crockford Lad 117¾ Northern Regent113^{nk}	Tired	8
28Oct82- 7Aqu fst 1	:45⅖ 1:09⅕ 1:34⅖	3+Alw 25000	4 4 33½ 4^{7} 59½ 5^{9}	Miceli M		117	14.10	85-14	Citius $114^{1¼}$ King Neptune 117^{3} Hominy Hill $114^{3½}$	Tired	7

LATEST WORKOUTS Feb 2 Bel tr.t 4f fst :49 b

Dr. Farr, whose past performances appear on page 71, was a similar case, dropping one class after chasing an exceptionally fast (for the class) pace. He returned a modest $79.00!

CASE STUDY: STONEY LONESOME AND EARLY RISING

Our key-race concept did no better than hold its own at the summer meet at Belmont in 1983. The mixture of grass and dirt races, marathons, one-turn routes, and overall conditions unfavorable to early speed helped produce the sub-par results. But when exceptional pace figures point out a grass-bred horse moving to the turf for the first time, one potent angle seems to reinforce the other. This is especially true during the summer months, when grass courses are most conducive to early speed.

Two examples from the summer 1983 meeting at Belmont come quickly to mind. Stoney Lonesome, a son of Caro from a Prince John mare, flashed exceptional speed in his seasonal debut, then came back seven days later to score in his grass debut at a $15.60 mutuel.

Stoney Lonesome — Dk. b. or br. c. 3, by Caro—Princess Red Wing, by Prince John
Br.—Morrisania Oaks Farm (Ky)
Own.—Clark S C Jr — Tr.—Watters Sidney Jr — **108**
Lifetime 6 1 3 1 $25,380 — 1983 1 0 0 0 — 1982 5 1 3 1 $25,380

12May83- 1Aqu fst 7f	:23 :46 3/5 1:23 1/5	Alw 20000	6 2 1 1 3nk 7 12 7 22	Vasquez J	b 117	4.50	63-20	Silent Landing 117 3/4 Potentiate 117 8 3/4 Interbanking117 1 1/4	Stopped	7
11Dec82- 5Aqu fst 1 1/8 [•]	:49 1/5 1:14 2/5 1:53 3/5	Alw 22000	3 1 1 1 1 1/2 1hd 2 1/2	Cordero A Jr	b 117	2.10	77-20	MomentofJoy117 1/2 StoneyLonesome117nk LawTlk117no	Just failed	8
29Nov82- 4Aqu my 1	:46 3/5 1:11 2/5 1:36 4/5	Md Sp Wt	6 2 1hd 2 1/2 1 1 1/2 1 1 1/4	Bailey J D	b 118	*2.30	82-24	Stoney Lonesome 118 1 1/4 TampaTown118 1 1/4 Chaudiere113nk	Driving	9
12Nov82- 2Aqu fst 1	:45 4/5 1:11 1/5 1:38 2/5	Md Sp Wt	1 3 2 1/2 3 2 2 1 2 2 1/2	Bailey J D	118	1.80	71-21	MomentofJoy118 2 1/2 StonyLonsom118 3/4 Lt'sGtPhysicl113hd	Steadied	12
4Nov82- 6Aqu fst 6f	:22 2/5 :45 4/5 1:12 2/5	Md Sp Wt	1 6 2 1 4 3 1/4 3 2 1/2 2 3/4	Bailey J D	118	*1.00	78-24	Structure 118 3/4 Stoney Lonesome 118 1 3/4 Quati Gold 118nk	Gamely	9
21Oct82- 9Aqu fst 6f	:22 2/5 :46 1/5 1:11 1/5	Md Sp Wt	5 9 5 6 1/2 3 8 4 11 3 5 3/4	Bailey J D	118	2.50	79-24	Fibk118 5 BoundingBsque118 3/4 StoneyLonesome118 1 1/2	Lacked room	10

LATEST WORKOUTS — May 11 Bel 3f fst :35 hg — Apr 28 Bel 6f fst 1:15 h — Apr 23 Bel 6f fst 1:13 2/5 h — Apr 18 Bel tr.t 5f fst 1:00 3/5 h

Copyright © 1984, by DAILY RACING FORM, INC. Reprinted with permission of copyright owner.

And Early Rising, a daughter of Grey Dawn and a Tom Rolfe mare, from the grass-oriented Rokeby stable, first showed signs of life chasing a fast pace on June 19, then followed up at $31.80 in her grass debut.

Early Rising — Dk. b. or br. f. 3, by Grey Dawn II—Gliding By, by Tom Rolfe
Br.—Mellon P (Va)
Own.—Rokeby Stable — Tr.—Miller Mack — **116**
Lifetime 4 0 0 0 — 1983 4 M 0 0 — 1982 0 M 0 0

19Jun83- 6Bel fst 1 1/16	:46 1:11 2/5 1:44 4/5	3+ (F)Md Sp Wt	2 3 3 4 1/2 4 6 1/2 4 5 1/2 5 8 1/2	MacBeth D	b 114	20.50	69-15	Betty's Bullet 114 3 1/2 Nonchalance 114 1 1/2 CountessCork117 1 1/4	Tired	7
9Jun83- 6Bel fst 7f	:22 3/5 :46 1/5 1:24 2/5	(F)Md Sp Wt	3 8 6 5 3/4 4 2 1/2 4 7 1/2 6 11	MacBeth D	b 121	26.80	69-17	Little Thief 121 1/2 Irish Liberal 116 8 Nonchalance 121 1/2	Tired	14
30May83- 6Bel my 6f	:22 1/5 :45 3/5 1:11 3/5	(F)Md Sp Wt	13 11 12 12 13 18 13 17 12 13	Bailey J D	121	6.30	71-11	Smuggled 121hd Parisian Print 121 1 3/4 Sauce OfLife121 3/4	Very wide	13
22May83- 6Bel my 6f	:22 3/5 :46 1:11	3+ (F)Md Sp Wt	10 9 8 9 1/4 8 7 1/2 7 8 1/2 5 10	Bailey J D	113	*1.80	77-14	Chic Belle 106 2 3/4 Beneficence 113 2 3/4 Sauce Of Life108 2 3/4	No threat	10

LATEST WORKOUTS — Jly 12 Bel 4f fst :48 1/5 h — Jly 1 Bel 4f fst :48 3/5 h — Jun 25 Bel 4f fst :48 3/5 h — Jun 16 Bel 4f fst :50 b

Copyright © 1984, by DAILY RACING FORM, INC. Reprinted with permission of copyright owner.

Interestingly, both horses were bred top and bottom for grass.

A horse that sets or closely presses the pace in a key-race route, before tiring through the stretch, has the figures to turn back to a sprint distance and win. Reducing the animal's six-furlong pace figure by three points (the average reduction mentioned in Chapter 9) gives the animal a figure still at least one point better than par for its previous classification. If the horse is properly placed in the sprint, it should be a solid contender.

As plausible as the preceding paragraph may sound, we found little evidence in our study of key-race participants turning back successfully from a route to a sprint. At this stage, I would have to say that there is insufficient evidence to make a definitive statement, one way or the other.

Handicappers not wishing to calculate pace figures can nevertheless profit from this methodology. Basic to its success is the value of high early speed as a tightener. The problem then becomes one of correctly identifying exceptional pace without figures.

Chapter 11

TRIP HANDICAPPING

My early years at the racetrack coincided with the halcyon days of Dr. Fager and the exciting three-year-olds of 1969, possibly the most talented (and rewarding) horses of recent years.

When Dr. Fager's first foals reached racing age, I followed their progress with great interest and enthusiasm, eagerly anticipating the second coming of the fastest horse I had ever seen. When his daughter Lady Love appeared in the entries for the 1973 Acorn Stakes, the first jewel of New York's Triple Crown for fillies, I attended and watched her closely. After she made a sweeping run three-wide around the turn to reach contention, only to hang through the late stages, I had been set up for the worst "beat" of my handicapping career.

During the ensuing two weeks preceding the Mother Goose Stakes, the second race in the series, I was on edge, anticipating Dr. Fager's first stakes winner, not to mention cashing a prime bet. I carried the wishes (and funds) of several friends to Belmont that day, and was astonished to find Lady Love offered at odds of 17–1. The track was sloppy, yet by the top of the stretch, Lady Love's inside rally had carried her into second place, with only the front-running Acorn winner, Windy's Daughter, to catch. I remember yelling "Get her off the rail," but jockey Eddie Maple didn't hear me. Lady Love gained with every stride, cutting into the tiring Windy's Daughter's lead relentlessly, and finally passed her rival one jump beyond the wire. The photo-finish camera gave the verdict to Windy's Daughter, by a diminishing nose. I'll always wonder what might have happened had Maple taken Lady Love to the outside for the stretch drive.

229

Lady Love
Own.—Rice Ada L

B. f. 3, by Dr Fager—Fresh As Fresh, by Count Fleet
Br.—Danada Farm (Ky)
Tr.—Catrone F

111

	St.	1st	2nd	3rd	Amt.
1973	9	2	2	2	$49,975
1972	1	M	0	0	

16Jun73- 7Bel	fst	1½	:47⅗	1:11⅖	2:27⅘	(F)Cc Am Oaks	11	5	4^{4}	2^{2}	$3^{1\frac{1}{2}}$	$3^{1\frac{3}{4}}$	Maple E	121	3.30	92-07	Magazine $121^{1\frac{1}{2}}$ Bag Of Tunes 121^{nk} Lady Love 121no	Lugged in 13
26May73- 7Bel	gd	1⅛	:44⅗	1:08⅘	1:48⅖	(F)Mother Goose	8	6	$6^{5\frac{1}{4}}$	2^{2}	$2^{1\frac{1}{2}}$	2no	Maple E	121	15.70	89-12	Windy's Daughter 121no Lady Love 121^{5} North Broadway 121^{hd}	Sharp 10
12May73- 7Aqu	fst	1	:45⅗	1:09⅘	1:35⅖	(F)Acorn	5	7	4^{4}	3^{2}	3^{2}	$4^{1\frac{3}{4}}$	Maple E	121	21.20	88-09	Windy's Daughter 121^{1} Poker Night $121^{\frac{3}{4}}$ Voler 121^{hd}	Weakened 11
2May73- 7Aqu	fst	7f	:22⅗	:45⅖	1:22⅘	(F)Comely	5	11	$8^{5\frac{1}{2}}$	$8^{6\frac{3}{4}}$	$4^{5\frac{1}{2}}$	$4^{3\frac{3}{4}}$	Maple E	113	30.10	83-18	Java Moon $116^{1\frac{1}{2}}$ Windy's Daughter 121^{nk} Voler 116^{2}	Rallied 11
20Apr73- 7Aqu	fst	6f	:22⅗	:45⅖	1:10⅕	(F)Prioress	5	9	8^{6}	7^{6}	$7^{7\frac{3}{4}}$	$6^{7\frac{3}{4}}$	Castaneda M	115	15.20	84-18	Windy's Daughter $121^{1\frac{1}{2}}$ Voler 115^{1} Waltz Fan 115^{2}	Off slowly 9
6Apr73- 5Aqu	fst	7f	:23	:46⅕	1:23	3↑ (F)Allowance	5	3	1^{hd}	1^{hd}	2^{hd}	$1^{1\frac{1}{2}}$	Turcotte R	114	2.10	86-16	Lady Love $114^{1\frac{1}{2}}$ Protesting Bid 114^{2} Tommy's Girl $114^{2\frac{1}{2}}$	Driving 7
16Mar73- 4Aqu	fst	6½f	:23	:45⅘	1:17⅕	(F)Md Sp Wt	1	5	$2^{\frac{1}{2}}$	1^{hd}	1^{hd}	1^{4}	Baeza B	122	3.90	91-14	Lady Love 122^{4} In Prosperity $122^{5\frac{1}{2}}$ All Or None $122^{3\frac{1}{2}}$	Ridden out 7
21Feb73- 1Hia	fst	7f	:23⅘	:47⅖	1:25⅘	(F)Md Sp Wt	5	9	$8^{5\frac{3}{4}}$	$6^{5\frac{3}{4}}$	$4^{2\frac{1}{2}}$	$3^{1\frac{3}{4}}$	Vasquez J	121	2.50	76-14	Millinery Lady $121^{1\frac{1}{2}}$ Happy Chile 121^{nk} Lady Love 121^{3}	Rallied 12
1Feb73- 1Hia	fst	7f	:23⅗	:47	1:25	(F)Md Sp Wt	10	6	$7^{4\frac{1}{4}}$	$5^{3\frac{1}{2}}$	3^{4}	2^{4}	Baltazar C	121	*2.50	78-16	Tantura 121^{4} Lady Love 121^{2} Ride The High Wind 121^{1}	Gamely 11
28Nov72- 3Aqu	fst	6f	:22⅕	:46	1:12⅖	(F)Md Sp Wt	3	14	14^{11}	12^{12}	$9^{9\frac{1}{4}}$	$7^{9\frac{1}{2}}$	Maple E	120	8.00	71-19	Yofit $120^{1\frac{1}{4}}$ Play It Cool $120^{2\frac{1}{2}}$ Don't Get Caught $120^{1\frac{1}{2}}$	Sluggish 14

LATEST WORKOUTS Jly 2 Aqu 5f fst 1:01 h Jun 28 Aqu 1 fst 1:43⅘ h Jun 24 Aqu 5f sly 1:03⅘ b Jun 13 Aqu 5f fst 1:02 h

The point of this story is simple: Trip handicapping was alive and well in 1973, and no doubt much earlier. I myself, and those with whom I attended the races, were attuned to outside trips that fizzled, the "bid, but hung" angle, and track biases, such as those against rail horses on wet Belmont or Saratoga strips, and those caused by wind conditions at Aqueduct, exactly the factors that made Lady Love an intriguing bet, and ultimately defeated her.

Trip handicapping has grown in popularity with the coming of the electronic age. Before the 1970s, handicappers had but one chance to view the proceedings—during the actual running of the race. Nowadays, the stretch run is shown thirty seconds after the race. The entire race is replayed after the result is made official, then again the next morning. In many areas, cable television provides a third replay of the race tape. Trip handicappers have ample opportunity to make their notes for each race as complete as possible, and trip handicapping has become more accessible to the average once-a-week fan.

There are two aspects of trip handicapping, one dealing with the recognition and exploitation of track biases, and the other with the observation of bad trips and aborted moves. Trips must be evaluated in context. Track conditions and existing biases tell whether a particular trip placed a horse at a disadvantage, or aided its cause. The trip handicapper, with his detailed trip notes, is best capable of making such judgments.

We emphasize that the final result of a race—finish positions, beaten lengths, speed figures—don't tell the complete story. How the race was run often is equally as important. The best horse doesn't have to win—it may be victimized by the existing conditions, and finish off the board.

A Thoroughbred's form cycle may appear to be up and down from one race to the next. Part of this is due to its physical condition, but much of it can be attributed to trips. Trainers responding to our questionnaire indicated that the average horse can hold its top form for eight weeks, during which it may race four or five times. A horse can no longer be summarily dismissed simply because its most recent race or two appear below par. Those efforts may be excusable because of trips—an unsuitable pace, a track bias, or simply the more traditional "traffic problems." It is the handicapper's responsibility to uncover how much of the running lines reflect performance (class, ability, fitness), and how much the influence of the trip. Trip handicappers are best able to make such assessments. Without trip notes, one simply doesn't know.

CASE STUDY: MAYBE MORGEN

Trip handicapping is especially effective with grass races, where sharp turns, narrow courses, and full fields result in a higher-than-normal incidence of traffic problems. An inside trip is almost mandatory on most grass courses. Horses racing on the outside around a turn not only lose ground but momentum as well.

Maybe Morgen was a prime example when entered in a $50,000 claiming event at Belmont on May 25, 1983. In her turf debut over the sharply turning grass course at Aqueduct, the daughter of Dewan raced four or five horses wide throughout, then made a nice move around rivals on the turn, only to falter in the stretch against good allowance fillies. Maybe Morgen proved that she could handle grass on that occasion, and when given a second chance against more suitable opposition, also proved a punctual favorite. New York's trip handicappers were out in force that day. Maybe Morgen returned just $7.40.

Maybe Morgen — B. f. 3, by Dewan—Pago Dancer, by Pago Pago — **$47,500** — Br.—Kilroy & Rogers Jr (Ky) — Tr.—DeStasio Richard T — **114**
Own.—Fried A Jr

Lifetime	1983	6 1 0 2	$10,530	
12 1 0 3	1982	6 M 0 1	$1,920	
$12,450	Turf	1 0 0 0		

11May83- 5Aqu	fm	1 1/16	Ⓣ:47	1:12	1:43	3↑ⒻAlw 21000	4	7	6^{11}	$4^{3\frac12}$	6^9	6^{14}	Graell A	b 110	28.80	76-10	Spit Curl 111^1 Rose of Montreaux $121^{\frac12}$ Mamamia $121^{5\frac34}$	Bore out	10
22Apr83- 2Aqu	fst	1	:47	1:11 4/5	1:38	ⒻMd 30000	5	1	$1^{2\frac12}$	$1^{3\frac12}$	1^2	$1^{2\frac34}$	Vasquez J	b 119	3.60	76-16	Maybe Morgen $119^{2\frac34}$ Outboard $121^{2\frac34}$ HatchRose121^1	Ridden out	8
23Mar83- 2Aqu	fst	7f	:22 4/5	:47	1:26 3/5	ⒻMd 25000	2	14	$7^{4\frac12}$	5^3	$5^{4\frac34}$	3^7	Velasquez J	b 121	2.60	61-28	BellCrmel121^5ARreGift117^2MybeMorgen121^{nk}	Stumbled st, wide	14
3Mar83- 2Aqu	fst	1 1/16	⊡:48	1:14 1/5	1:48	ⒻMd 35000	6	5	$4^{7\frac12}$	4^6	4^7	$5^{9\frac12}$	Asmussen S M5	b 116	6.10	63-21	CosmicSeaQueen$119^{\frac34}$PourL'Oiseau$116^{\frac34}$Pentecost$121^{7\frac34}$	No threat	12
6Feb83- 4Aqu	fst	1 1/16	⊡:49 1/5	1:15	1:49	ⒻMd 45000	4	6	$5^{4\frac12}$	4^4	$4^{6\frac12}$	$3^{3\frac12}$	Asmussen S M5	b 112	8.90	64-22	Bon Eglogue 121^{nk} Pour L'Oiseau$112^{3\frac14}$MaybeMorgen112^1	Rallied	8
29Jan83- 9Aqu	fst	6f	⊡:22 4/5	:47	1:13 1/5	ⒻMd 45000	2	10	$7^{6\frac12}$	$5^{5\frac14}$	$5^{3\frac12}$	$4^{4\frac34}$	Asmussen S M5	b 112	16.20	73-20	Real Jenny 117^1 PourL'Oiseau$112^{1\frac14}$MinuteByMinute$117^{2\frac12}$	Evenly	12
31Dec82- 3Aqu	fst	6f	⊡:23 4/5	:48 3/5	1:15 4/5	ⒻMd 35000	5	7	$7^{4\frac34}$	7^9	$8^{4\frac34}$	4^3	Asmussen S M7	b 110	7.30	62-25	ⒹLizzy'sGal$108^{2\frac14}$Marci'sBnquet$117^{\frac34}$CrftySenorit113^{hd}	Carried in	12
31Dec82-Placed third through disqualification																			
10Dec82- 4Aqu	fst	1 70	⊡:49 1/5	1:15 2/5	1:47 3/5	ⒻMd 35000	10	8	5^6	4^3	$5^{3\frac12}$	$5^{5\frac14}$	Asmussen S M7	b 110	10.50	59-24	Epanoui $113^{\frac12}$ First Excuse 117^1 Bon Eglogue $113^{\frac12}$	Lacked bid	10
28Nov82- 3Aqu	fst	7f	:23	:46 4/5	1:27 3/5	ⒻMd 35000	12	5	$5^{4\frac34}$	$3^{1\frac12}$	3^3	$4^{3\frac14}$	Asmussen S M7	b 110	15.70	60-28	Knotty Blue 113^{nk} Bravest Girl 112^3 More Ciao 109^{hd}	Weakened	13
24Sep82- 4Bel	fst	6f	:22 4/5	:47 3/5	1:13 1/5	ⒻMd 50000	6	9	$7^{6\frac14}$	$7^{4\frac12}$	9^9	9^{12}	MacBeth D	b 117	16.40	64-22	GarrulousGal$117^{3\frac14}$FirstExcuse$114^{1\frac14}$GetOffMyCse$117^{1\frac34}$	No factor	12

LATEST WORKOUTS May 21 Bel tr.t 4f my :51 4/5 b May 9 Bel tr.t 3f fst :36 4/5 b May 2 Bel tr.t 4f fst :49 h Apr 16 Bel tr.t 5f fst 1:03 2/5 b

□ THE WATCHDOG □

At times, a race (usually a route) will shape up with one confirmed front runner, a second horse that could run on the lead, but would rather stalk the pace, and several closers. Should the speed horse pose a serious threat to lead all the way, the second horse is in a difficult position. In effect, it must play "watchdog" for the rest of the field. It cannot afford to allow the speed horse to coast on an easy lead, or else no one would stand much chance of catching it. Nor can it afford to challenge that one too early, and thereby compromise its own chances, not to mention those of the speed horse, while setting things up for one of the late runners.

It takes a good horse running a strong race to overcome the watchdog trip, not to mention a finely judged ride. As a general rule, watchdogs should be bet against, but without knowing beforehand the eventual tactics of the watchdog, it is difficult to decide whether to bet the speed horse on the front end, or one of the ralliers from behind.

Princess Rooney found herself in such a situation in the 1983 Acorn Stakes at Belmont Park. Able to set the pace, rate on the lead, on sit in behind the leaders, the unbeaten daughter of Verbatim was to face Ski Goggle, an undefeated filly who had never been headed. Unless one of the other entrants challenged Ski Goggle for the lead, which was unlikely, Princess Rooney would be forced to play watchdog. This is exactly what did happen, with Princess Rooney choosing to rate behind Ski Goggle (or not being able to match strides with her rival). Ski Goggle, alone on the lead, never looked back. By conserving her energy early, Princess Rooney was able to maintain second position throughout the race.

Princess Rooney
Own.—Tucker Paula

Gr. f. 3, by Verbatim—Parrish Princess, by Drone
Br.—Roach B & T (Ky)
Tr.—Gomez Frank

121

Lifetime						
10 10 0 0	1983	4	4	0	0	$227,301
$451,116	1982	6	6	0	0	$223,815

6May83- 8CD	fst	1⅛	:47	1:12	1:50⅘	ⒻKy. Oaks	1	1	1^{1}	1^{1}	$1^{1\frac{1}{2}}$	$1^{1\frac{1}{4}}$	Vasquez J	121	*.20	88-15	Princess Rooney $121^{1\frac{1}{4}}$ Bright Crocus 121^{2} Bemissed$121^{\frac{1}{2}}$	Driving	7
23Apr83- 7Kee	sly	1 1/16	:46⅗	1:11⅗	1:45⅖	ⒻAshland	4	2	1^{hd}	1^{hd}	$1^{2\frac{1}{2}}$	$1^{9\frac{1}{2}}$	Vasquez J	121	*.20	79-24	Princess Rooney $121^{9\frac{1}{2}}$ Shamivor114^{9}Decision$116^{7\frac{1}{2}}$	Drifted, clear	6
13Apr83- 7Kee	fst	*7f			1:27⅖	ⒻAlw 28000	8	1	2^{1}	2^{hd}	1^{3}	1^{10}	Vasquez J	123	*.30	86-21	Princess Rooney 123^{10} Fiesty Belle$114^{3\frac{1}{2}}$SilveredSilk113^{1}	Handily	8
5Mar83- 7GP	fst	7f	:22⅕	:45	1:23⅘	Alw 30000	2	8	$3^{1\frac{1}{2}}$	$3^{\frac{1}{2}}$	$1^{\frac{1}{2}}$	$1^{\frac{1}{2}}$	Vasquez J	114	*.20	85-19	PrincessRooney$114^{\frac{1}{2}}$Morgnmorgnmorgn$115^{2\frac{1}{4}}$Alchise$115^{2\frac{3}{4}}$	Driving	8
23Oct82- 6Med	fst	1 1/16	:47⅕	1:11	1:43	ⒻGardenia	6	1	$1^{\frac{1}{2}}$	1^{2}	1^{7}	1^{11}	Vasquez J	121	*.30	94-11	PrincessRooney121^{11}ForOnc'nMyLif118^{3}GoldSpruc118^{12}	In Hand	7
10Oct82- 8Bel	fst	1	:46⅕	1:11⅗	1:39	ⒻFrizette	2	1	1^{hd}	$1^{1\frac{1}{2}}$	1^{6}	1^{8}	Fell J	119	*1.30	70-29	PrincessRooney119^{8}WinningTck$119^{3\frac{1}{2}}$WekndSurpris119^{nk}	Handily	13
11Sep82- 9Crc	fst	7f	:22⅖	:45⅘	1:23⅘	ⒻMelaleuca	7	1	1^{1}	$1^{2\frac{1}{2}}$	1^{8}	1^{12}	Pennisi F A	116	*.20	97-14	Princess Rooney 116^{12} Hiusoanso 114^{4} Rina's Missy 114^{6}	Easily	8
1Sep82- 9Crc	fst	7f	:22⅖	:46	1:25⅕	ⒻAlw 10000	1	2	$1^{\frac{1}{2}}$	$1^{1\frac{1}{2}}$	1^{10}	1^{18}	Pennisi F A	116	*.90	90-18	PrincessRooney116^{18}CourtUnion116^{nk}FlwlessDimond$116^{1\frac{1}{4}}$	Easily	5
7Jun82- 7Crc	fst	5f	:22⅗	:46⅗	:59⅗	ⒻAlw 9500	1	3	$1^{\frac{1}{2}}$	$1^{1\frac{1}{2}}$	1^{3}	1^{4}	Pennisi F A	114	*1.20	94-15	PrincessRooney114^{4}Ishudahdtht107^{no}RoylityMiss117^{6}	Ridden out	6
22May82- 3Crc	fst	5f	:22⅘	:47	1:00⅖	ⒻMd Sp Wt	9	8	3^{nk}	1^{hd}	1^{2}	1^{3}	Pennisi F A	115	*2.10	90-14	Princess Rooney 115^{3} Rilia 115^{2} Marie V. 115^{1}	Driving	9

LATEST WORKOUTS May 24 Bel 5f fst :58⅘ h ●May 17 Bel 4f sly :47⅗ b (d) May 2 CD 6f gd 1:16 b Apr 21 Kee 5f fst 1:00⅖ b

Ski Goggle *
Own.—Yoshida Zenya

Gr. f. 3, by Royal Ski—Mississippi Siren, by Delta Judge
Br.—Fountainbleau Farm (Ky)
Tr.—Doyle A T

121

Lifetime						
4 4 0 0	1983	4	4	0	0	$91,050
$91,050	1982	0	M	0	0	

4May83- 8Hol	fst	7f	:22⅕	:45	1:23⅖	ⒻRailbird	5	3	1^{1}	$1^{1\frac{1}{2}}$	$1^{2\frac{1}{2}}$	$1^{2\frac{1}{2}}$	McCarron C J	122	*.80	80-27	Ski Goggle $122^{2\frac{1}{2}}$ Madam Forbes $115^{2\frac{1}{2}}$ Gatita 117^{2}	Easily	9
16Feb83- 8SA	fst	1 1/16	:46	1:10⅖	1:41⅗	ⒻSanta Ysabel	1	1	$1^{1\frac{1}{2}}$	$1^{1\frac{1}{2}}$	1^{3}	$1^{5\frac{1}{2}}$	McCarron C J	115	*.90	93-14	Ski Goggle $115^{5\frac{1}{2}}$ Sophisticated Girl 116^{2}SaucyBobbie$115^{\frac{3}{4}}$	Easily	7
3Feb83- 5SA	my	6½f	:21⅗	:44⅗	1:16⅖	ⒻAlw 19000	5	3	$1^{1\frac{1}{2}}$	$1^{2\frac{1}{2}}$	1^{6}	1^{11}	McCarron C J	120	*.50	88-23	Ski Goggle 120^{11} Princess Lurullah $115^{1\frac{1}{2}}$ DH Infantes 117	Easily	9
22Jan83- 3SA	sly	6½f	:21⅗	:44⅘	1:16	ⒻMd Sp Wt	9	3	$1^{1\frac{1}{2}}$	$1^{2\frac{1}{2}}$	1^{5}	1^{12}	McCarron C J	117	*1.50	90-19	Ski Goggle 117^{12} Gentle J. O. 117^{1} Athar 117^{6}	Easily	11

LATEST WORKOUTS May 26 Bel 3f fst :36⅖ h May 21 Hol 4f fst :47⅗ h ●May 16 Hol 6f fst 1:10⅘ h May 11 Hol 6f fst 1:15⅗ h

Unfortunately, injuries to both fillies prevented a rematch in the Mother Goose three weeks later. One might guess that Princess Rooney would have attempted to use different tactics on that occasion.

When a race shapes up as having a lone speed horse, one of the other contestants may be forced into the role of watchdog (unless, of course, the front-runner is "cheap speed" almost certain to stop in the stretch). This is especially true in stakes races, where prerace publicity will likely bring the situation to the attention of all concerned. At times, one of the trainers may decide to enter a stablemate to act as watchdog (or rabbit), and help guarantee an honest pace for its more highly regarded running mate.

Probably the most celebrated example of the watchdog situation came in the 1968 Suburban Handicap, the third in a series of four matchups between all-time greats Dr. Fager and Damascus. With the scratch of Hedevar, who had been entered to set the pace for Damascus (and exploit Dr. Fager's volatile nature), Dr. Fager became the lone speed horse in the field. Damascus' connections realized that their only chance for victory lay in challenging Dr. Fager early. With the most (prestige) to lose, Damascus was forced into the role of watchdog. But the unusual tactics—racing on the front end—did not suit Damascus, who faded to third, while Dr. Fager drew off to the definitive victory in their series.

When a stretch-runner is forced to adopt front-running tactics, the results are usually predictable. Forced into action at a time when it is usually just getting the feel of the track, the horse will be run off its feet, and consequently not have its usual punch in the stretch.

A trainer wishing to "disguise" a horse's form ("stiff the horse," to use the more common terminology) need only instruct his jockey to race the horse over the worst part of the track. Or to race it against its usual style, by placing a stretch-runner on the early lead, or rating a speedball off the pace. The sharp trip handicapper would be the first to suspect chicanery.

☐ THE TROUBLE LINES ☐

The casual handicapper, with little (if any) time for serious trip handicapping, must rely on the "trouble lines" that appear at the right-hand side of the past performances.

Marfa * Gr. c. 3, by Foolish Pleasure—Gray Matter, by Stratmat
Own.—Beal & French Jr & Lukas Br.—Gentry T (Ky) Tr.—Lukas D Wayne
126 Lifetime 12 3 3 1 $386,944 | 1983 10 3 3 0 $384,544 | 1982 2 M 0 1 $2,400

7May83- 8CD	fst	1¼	:47⅕ 1:36⅘ 2:02⅕	Ky Derby	18	13	1415	85¾	43	53½	Velasquez J	b 126	*2.40e	82-10	Sunny's Halo 1262DesertWine126nkCaveat1261	Lckd suffient resp 20
28Apr83- 7Kee	sly	1⅛	:46⅘ 1:11 1:49⅖	Blue Grass	7	9	69½	56	2hd	2no	Velasquez J	b 121	*1.50[D]	90-16	Play Fellow 121no[D]Marfa1217½DesertWine1211	Bore in upper str 12
28Apr83-Disqualified and placed fourth																
10Apr83- 4SA	fst	1⅛	:46 1:10⅖ 1:49⅖	S A Derby	7	8	78¼	65½	31½	13	Velasquez J	b 120	3.60e	82-19	Marfa 1203 My Habitony 1202½ Naevus 1201¼	Drew off 10
26Mar83- 9Lat	fst	1 1/16	:46⅕ 1:10⅗ 1:42⅖	Spiral	10	6	46	31½	1hd	18	Velasquez J	b 120	*3.40	98-24	Marfa 1208 Noble Home 1205½ Hail To Rome 120no	Bore in, clear 12
26Mar83-Daily Racing Form Time 1:44 1/5																
16Mar83- 8SA	fst	1 1/16	:46⅕ 1:10⅘ 1:42⅗	S Catalina	7	6	84¾	84½	56½	45½	Pincay L Jr	b 117	*2.10	82-17	FstPssge1162½Hyperboren114hdMyHbitony1143	Forced wide turn 8
6Mar83- 5SA	fst	1 1/16	:46 1:10⅘ 1:43⅗	Alw 20000	7	7	76¾	54¼	2hd	2nk	Toro F	120	5.40	83-17	SilentFox117nkMarf1201½LouisvilleSummit119¾	Broke slowly,wide 9
13Feb83- 6SA	fst	1 1/16	:46⅗ 1:11⅖ 1:43⅖	Md Sp Wt	10	8	43	11	15	13½	Toro F	b 118	4.00	84-12	Marfa 1183½ Blue Seas 1184½ Gato Montes 1182½	Ridden out 12
30Jan83- 4SA	gd	7f	:22⅕ :45⅕ 1:24⅘	Md Sp Wt	4	6	35	31½	2½	2no	Toro F	b 118	2.20	76-22	Added Feature 118no Marfa 1187½ Flint Fire 1184	Sharp try 7
9Jan83- 6SA	fst	1 1/16	:46⅕ 1:10⅘ 1:41⅘	Md Sp Wt	8	7	66½	53½	55½	56	Toro F	b 118	3.20	86-09	Major Henry 118hd Fast Screen 1133 Blue Seas 1184	No rally 8
1Jan83- 4SA	fst	6f	:21⅗ :44⅘ 1:09⅘	Md Sp Wt	3	6	912	911	75¼	22	Pincay L Jr	b 118	7.30	87-11	Fast Passage 1182 Marfa 118½ Viron 118nk	Rallied 10
7Nov82- 6Hol	fst	1 1/16	:47⅕ 1:11⅘ 1:44	Md Sp Wt	2	5	52¼	31½	32	34½	Pincay L J	b 118	7.50	70-20	Eminent Lad 1183½ Right On Center 1181 Marfa 1183½	Mild bid 10
17Oct82- 6SA	fst	1 1/16	:46⅕ 1:10⅘ 1:42⅖	Md Sp Wt	7	5	51¾	53¾	710	825	Pincay L Jr	b 117	4.60	64-09	Fifth Division 1177 Something Beyond 1171¼Estupendo1173	Tired 10

LATEST WORKOUTS May 18 Pim 4f fst :46⅖ h Apr 22 Kee 5f fst 1:00⅕ b Apr 4 SA 5f fst 1:01⅗ h

The vast majority of handicappers get no deeper into trip handicapping than what they read in the *Form,* yet they seem to attach some sort of mystical significance to these remarks, almost as if they expect the fates to smile on a horse slighted last time, assuring it a perfect trip this time. There is no such guarantee. The horse may encounter trouble again. It may not even race well, yet, most likely it will be overbet.

CASE STUDY: FIT TO FIGHT

When Fit To Fight returned to the races with a smashing win over an outstanding allowance field on April 22, 1983, many New Yorkers felt that this was the horse to beat in the Metropolitan Handicap later in May. They made the four-year-old their 2–1 favorite for the Carter Handicap, only to watch in dismay as the horse was blocked behind a wall of horses through half the stretch run. One thing was certain following the Carter—Fit To Fight would not be a value bet in the Metropolitan. Those who supported him in the Carter would be back in the Met, convinced they were right. Those who hadn't, but had witnessed his problems, might jump on the bandwagon. Fit To Fight was certain to be an underlaid favorite for the Metropolitan Handicap. Realizing this, and not wishing to bet against the horse, I passed on the Met, and took my daughter horseback riding instead. A late afternoon thunderstorm changed the picture, however. The Met was run over a sloppy track, conditions Fit To Fight had never faced. A small wager against the favorite would have been in order, and the logical play turned out to be the eventual upsetter. Star Choice, a son of mud sire In Reality, had performed well in the slop the previous season at Monmouth, and was rounding into top form for John Veitch. He won rather easily, and returned $36.00 to those who adapted to the changing conditions. Fit To Fight never got into contention.

Fit to Fight — B. c. 4, by Chieftain—Hasty Queen II, by One Count — Br.—Congleton & Courtney (Ky) — Tr.—Miller Mack — **115** — Lifetime 11 7 0 2 $227,016 — 1983 2 1 0 1 $34,560 — 1982 6 4 0 1 $173,436

Own.—Rokeby Stable

7May83- 8Aqu	fst	7f	:22⅖	:44⅗	1:22⅘	3↑ Carter H	2	8	7 3¾	6 4½	7 1¾	3 3	McCarron G	116	*1.50	84-19	Vittorioso 113nk Sing Sing 122 2¾ Fit to Fight 116¾	Blocked	9
22Apr83- 8Aqu	fst	6f	:22⅖	:45⅗	1:09⅖	3↑ Alw 35000	4	9	4 3	4 2½	1hd	1 1½	Bailey J D	121	4.40	94-16	Fit to Fight 121 1½ Star Gallant 121 3½ Sepulveda 119nk	Drew clear	11
30Oct82- 8Aqu	fst	1⅛	:47⅘	1:11⅗	1:49⅗	3↑ Stuyvesant H	3	2	2½	2 1	3 3½	3 4	Bailey J D	118	2.40	83-16	Engine One 123 2 Bar Dexter 112 2 Fit to Fight 118 2	Weakened	6
30Sep82- 6Med	fst	1⅛	:47⅗	1:11⅖	1:49	Pegasus H	1	2	3 1½	3 3	6 8½	4 8¼	Bailey J D	118	*1.30	80-15	Fast Gold 110 3¼ Muttering 120 2 Exclusive One 116 3	Weakened	8
6Sep82- 8Bel	fst	1	:45⅘	1:10⅕	1:35⅖	Jerome H	1	2	1hd	1½	1 3½	1 6	Bailey J D	112	1.60	88-17	Fit to Fight 112 6 John's Gold 115 2¾ Lord Lister 107 1	Ridden out	6
19Aug82- 7Sar	fst	6f	:22	:45	1:09⅖	3↑ Alw 32000	1	4	4 5	3 2	2 1½	1¾	Fell J	117	*1.60	93-17	Fit to Fight 117¾ Hat Room 115 1¼ Ring of Light 119 1	Driving	6
7Aug82- 5Sar	fst	6½f	:22⅗	:45⅕	1:16⅖	3↑ Alw 23000	3	10	7 5	4 3	1hd	1¾	Fell J	112	*.80	90-14	Fit to Fight 112¾ Jet Steam 112no GrandCourant117no	Ridden out	11
5Jun82- 3Bel	gd	6f	:22⅘	:46	1:10	3↑ Alw 20000	4	2	5 2¼	2 1½	2hd	1 2¼	Fell J	113	*1.40	92-11	FittoFight113 2¼LordLister109hdAccomplishment112 2¾	Ridden out	6
26Nov81- 5Aqu	fst	7f	:23⅖	:46⅗	1:24	Alw 16000	6	3	6 3¾	3½	1hd	1nk	Fell J	122	*1.50	81-21	Fit to Fight 122nk Cut Away 117 1½ Richness 119½	Driving	10
6Nov81- 6Aqu	gd	7f	:22⅗	:45⅘	1:23⅖	Md Sp Wt	6	1	4 2½	3 2	1 1½	1 8½	Fell J	118	*1.10	84-21	FittoFight118 8½DeterminedBiddr118nkWhtAChrgr113 2	Ridden out	7

LATEST WORKOUTS ●May 26 Bel 7f fst 1:27⅖ h   May 4 Bel 5f sly 1:02 b   Apr 29 Bel 4f fst :49⅖ b   Apr 20 Bel tr.t 4f sly :47⅕ h

The role bloodlines played in the outcome of the Metropolitan was underlined a few weeks later when Star Choice made his next start.

Star Choice — B. c. 4, by In Reality—Some Swinger, by Tirreno
Br.—Frances A Genter Stable (Fla)
Own.—Genter Frances A — Tr.—Veitch John M — 113
Lifetime 15 7 4 1 $127,881 — 1983 4 1 1 0 $36,436 — 1982 9 6 1 1 $88,115

15May83-	1Aqu	fst	1	:46	1:09⅘	1:35	3↑ Handicap	5	3	3^{2}	2½	2^{2}	2^{2½}	Velasquez J	b 115	*1.70	88-18	West On Broad 109^{2½} StarChoice115^{1¾}OtterSlide113^{nk}	Bid,evenly	6
15Apr83-	9OP	fst	1 1/16	:47⅕	1:11⅗	1:43	Oaklawn H	6	4	4^{15}	4^{13}	4^{8}	4^{5½}	Velasquez J	116	4.90	87-16	Bold Style 113½ Eminency 123^{3½} Listcapade 123^{1½}	Evenly	8
26Mar83-	8Aqu	fst	1	:45⅖	1:09⅗	1:35⅕	3↑ Westchester	2	6	7^{7½}	4^{5}	4^{5}	4^{4}	Brumfield D	116	2.50	86-19	Singh Tu 109½MasterDigby114¾FabulousFind114^{2¾}	Lacked a rally	10
10Mar83-	9Hia	fst	6f	:22⅖	:45⅖	1:10	Alw 14000	2	6	6^{2¾}	5^{3½}	3^{1}	1^{hd}	Brumfield D	119	*1.20	93-17	Star Choice 119^{hd} Bill Wheeler 122½ Spirited Boy 122^{hd}	Driving	7
17Jly82-	6Atl	fst	1⅛	:46	1:10	1:49⅗	Jersey Dby	2	4	3^{9}	3^{6}	3^{1}	2no	Thomas D B	116	4.50	90-16	Aloma's Ruler 126no StarChoice116^{2}SpanishDrums126^{1}	Came out	6
10Jly82-	8Key	fst	1 1/16	:46⅖	1:10⅘	1:42⅘	Devon	1	9	9^{9¾}	5^{5}	3^{1½}	1^{1½}	Thomas D B	117	*1.70	90-19	Star Choice 117^{1½}LordLister117^{2}ThunderRunner115^{6½}	Drew clear	10
26Jun82-	6Mth	fst	1 1/16	:47⅗	1:11⅕	1:42⅗	3↑ Alw 16000	3	5	3^{5}	4^{1¾}	3^{1}	1^{hd}	Fann B	110	*.80	92-12	Star Choice 110^{hd} CenturyBanker119^{2}DynamicMove115^{2½}	Driving	6
7Jun82-	7Mth	sly	170	:46⅘	1:11⅖	1:41⅕	3↑ Alw 12500	1	5	3^{2½}	3^{1}	1^{2}	1^{4}	Fann B	111	*.60	90-20	Star Choice 111^{4} Spellbounder107^{7}CannonRoyal114^{6½}	Ridden out	6
10May82-	7Mth	fst	170	:47⅕	1:12⅘	1:43⅗	3↑ Alw 10500	3	4.	4^{6¼}	1^{hd}	1^{1½}	1^{8}	Fann B	109	*.90	78-26	Star Choice 109^{8} Sal's Gomvate 119¾ T. V. Table121^{hd}	Drew clear	6
22Feb82-	3Hia	fst	1 1/16	:48⅖	1:13⅕	1:44⅘	Alw 14000	3	3	3^{1½}	2½	1½	1^{1}.	Vasquez J	116	1.80	79-20	Star Choice 116^{1} Reinvested 118^{10} Pavarotti 116^{5½}	Driving	7

LATEST WORKOUTS May 26 Bel 4f fst :49⅕ b — May 14 Bel 3f fst :35 b — ●May 9 Bel 6f fst 1:11⅗ h — May 3 Bel 5f fst 1:00⅖ b

Copyright © 1984, by DAILY RACING FORM, INC. Reprinted with permission of copyright owner.

Over a dry Belmont strip, the Met winner finished a fading fifth in a field of six classified allowance routers.

CASE STUDY: CHRISTY'S RIDGE

Seldom has there been a more flagrant example of a crowd jumping all over a horse with a trouble line in its most recent start than in the case of Christy's Ridge at Aqueduct on March 13, 1983. But then, few trouble lines have received as much media coverage.

On March 2, Christy's Ridge was moving to the leader on the rail in midstretch when *that* horse (Delta Leader) lugged in. Christy's Ridge was forced to check sharply, stumbled, and threw jockey Alfredo Smith. But, in an amazing display of horsemanship, Smith landed on the inner rail, regained his balance, leaped back in the saddle, and finished the race. The *Daily Racing Form* reported simply "impeded." The incident received coverage from the network news shows that evening, completely eliminating any chance aware race-watchers would get a fair price on the horse in its next start.

Christy's Ridge — Ch. h. 5, by Riva Ridge—Rubye Brooks, by Bold Hour
$8,500 Br.—Oxford Stable (Ky)
Own.--Flying Zee Stable — Tr.—Martin Jose — 117
Lifetime 29 1 3 3 $21,660 — 1983 3 0 0 0 $630 — 1982 8 1 0 0 $8,400 — Turf 1 0 0 0

2Mar83-	9Aqu	fst	1⅛	⊡:47⅖	1:12⅘	1:52⅖	Clm 10000	5	9	8^{8½}	5^{4½}	8^{6½}	9^{17}	Smith A Jr	117	9.50	67-12	Come Up Pence117^{hd}GoingOrange119^{hd}IndigoStar108^{nk}	Impeded	11
2Mar83-Placed eighth through disqualification																				
26Feb83-	9Aqu	fst	6f	⊡:23⅕	:47⅘	1:13⅕	Clm 10000	4	9	11^{10}	9^{5¾}	6^{6¾}	4^{7¼}	Smith A Jr	117	13.80	71-25	FoxmoorFlight117½Rapido'sRepeat112^{2¾}AMnShort112^{4}	Hung late	12
10Feb83-	9Aqu	fst	6f	⊡:23	:47⅕	1:12⅗	Clm c-8000	9	10	10^{6¾}	10^{5¾}	6^{3¾}	6^{3¾}	Molina V H	113	35.50	77-18	RomnSpry117^{nk}MickeyRooney110^{2¼}SouthrnPrinc108^{nk}	No threat	12
31Dec82-	9Aqu	fst	6f	⊡:23⅖	:47⅘	1:12⅖	3↑ Clm 10500	3	8	6^{3½}	7^{5½}	6^{8}	6^{13}	Garramone A	b 113	10.90	69-25	Sir Sizzling Nehoc117^{2}Imaromeo119^{6}CounterAttack117^{1}	No rally	9
22Dec82-	9Aqu	fst	6f	⊡:23⅕	:47⅗	1:13⅘	3↑ Clm 10500	9	9	8^{7½}	10^{10}	10^{11}	5^{4¾}	Garramone A	b 113	25.40	70-22	Counselor George117^{hd}Michael'sEdge117^{2½}PokieJoe119^{1¾}	Rallied	11
13Dec82-	9Aqu	fst	6f	⊡:23	:47	1:13	Clm 12500	1	8	9^{9¼}	10^{12}	8^{14}	7^{9¾}	Attanasio R	117	9.70	69-22	Big Beau Ridge 114no Implosion 117^{4½} Ted Brown 114¾	Outrun	10
4Dec82-	1Aqu	gd	1 1/16	⊡:47⅘	1:12⅖	1:44⅗	3↑ Clm 20000	3	5	6^{11}	6^{6½}	7^{12}	7^{11}	Attanasio R	117	12.30	79-15	Our Celtic Heir 119^{6} Roman Chef 108^{nk} DaringBet117½	No factor	7
13Nov82-	9Aqu	gd	1	:47⅕	1:12⅕	1:37⅕	3↑ Clm 35000	5	5	5^{2¼}	7^{8}	7^{15}	7^{19}	Molina V H	b 117	25.30	61-20	Solid Credit 113^{2} Creme De La Fete 117^{2} Kan Reason117^{nk}	Tired	8
7Nov82-	1Aqu	fst	1	:47⅕	1:12⅖	1:37⅖	3↑ Alw 20000	4	2	6^{2¾}	6^{6½}	6^{14}	6^{18}	Beitia E	117	16.00	61-19	LuckySpruce115^{2}KingMoshoeshoe115½CareTaker115^{11}	Early foot	6
27Oct82-	3Aqu	fst	7f	:23⅗	:46⅗	1:22⅕	3↑ Alw 19000	1	7	8^{17}	8^{20}	8^{19}	7^{18}	Beitia E	117	29.60	72-17	Determined Bidder 114^{6½} Cintula 114¾ Beau Bidder 109^{3¾}	Outrun	8

LATEST WORKOUTS Mar 10 Bel tr.t 4f sly :49⅕ b — Feb 6 Bel tr.t 4f fst :49⅗ h — Feb 1 Bel tr.t 4f fst :48 h

Copyright © 1984, by DAILY RACING FORM, INC. Reprinted with permission of copyright owner.

Was Christy's Ridge worth 3–1 on March 13? Considering his overall record of futility and/or disinterest, there was every reason to suspect the horse would just trail along once again. That the horse was able to win going away, then repeat in $16,000 company, is a tribute to the talent and astuteness of trainer Jose Martin, who spotted something in this unimpressive horse that was not apparent on paper, claimed it, and then turned the horse around. If anything, it was this aspect of the horse's profile that warranted support, although perhaps not at odds as low as three to one.

The trouble comment that appears in the past performances is a condensation of what appears in the result chart (see Chapter 12). It is often just a vague word or standard short phrase. Frequently, much of what appears in the result chart does not make the past performances. Even more frequently, much of what happens in the running of a race fails to make the result chart. This is precisely what trip handicappers count on—why they exist, and why they prosper.

The problems of Marfa in the prep races leading up to the 1983 Kentucky Derby received considerable press coverage, yet the *Form* comments hardly do them justice. The simple comment "bore in upper stretch" says nothing of the severe mugging inflicted upon both Desert Wine and Copelan in the Blue Grass. Nor does the comment "bore in, clear" reveal the difficulty jockey Velasquez had in keeping Marfa from forcing Noble Home over the inner rail in the Latonia Spiral. And finally, the comment "forced wide turn" fails to report the severity of the incident, how much it cost Marfa in the Santa Catalina.

Note that the trouble comment is not a standard part of the running lines in Western editions of the *Form*. Trouble comments appear beneath the running line only when particularly noteworthy (see Appendix A). West coast editions of the *Form* also publish a separate "Horses In Trouble" column, which basically reproduces result-chart comments for all horses entered that day which had encountered trouble of some sort in their most recent start. However, no mention is made of trouble encountered in previous races.

The *Form* trouble comments fall into four broad categories:

(1) Those relating to the *Start* of the race. The comment may read simply "Bad Start," "Poor Start," or "Slow Start." Or the slightly different "Stumbled Start," "Broke In Air," "Propped," or "Reared At Start," which offer some explanation of the problem. Or possibly "Unruly Start," signifying reluctance to enter the starting gate, or "Dwelt Start," meaning the horse refused to leave the starting gate, or its vicinity. Trip handicappers can assess, in lengths, what the poor start may have cost the horse.

(2) Those describing *Traffic* problems that may have occurred during the running of the race. "Brushed," "Bumped," and "Roughed," imply physical contact. The progressively worse "In Close,"

"Steadied," "Lacked Room," "Impeded," "Forced Wide," "Forced Out," "Blocked," "Checked," and "Taken Up," indicate that the horse's forward progress was impaired. Again, the trip handicapper is best able to assess the damage, and to observe the horse and rider's reaction once clear of the trouble, and the horse's run prior to the incident.

(3) Those describing the *Finish* of the race. The term "Driving" means the rider kept the horse under steady pressure with both whip and hands. "All Out" is slightly stronger, implying the horse gave its all, and was exhausted at the finish. The terms "Ridden Out," "Handily," and "Easily," all signify a horse hand-ridden to the finish, with the vigor of the ride decreasing from first to last mentioned.

(4) Those denoting *Physical* problems. The terms "Lugged In" and "Lugged Out," "Bore In" and "Bore Out," refer to a tiring, and probably hurting, horse unable to keep a straight course through the stretch. Even the strongest riders find it difficult to ride such horses effectively. A horse with a tendency to lug in is a risky bet when breaking from an outside post, with several horses between it and the rail, its likely destination. Horses that lug in are not necessarily hurting—many simply need the security of racing along the rail. They are safer betting propositions when breaking near the wood. Other horses are timid, and don't give their best when asked to race inside rival horses. Likewise, a lug-out horse is better situated if starting on the outside. Lug-outs, though, are more likely to have physical problems than lug-ins. A horse "Eased" finished the course, but well behind its field, while one "Pulled Up" was unable to finish. "Broke Down" refers to a horse incapable of finishing because of a severe injury, probably a broken bone. Less severe injuries may be termed "Lame." "Fell" means the horse fell during the running, possibly because of injury, possibly because of traffic problems. "Clipped Heels" means the horse stumbled over another's heels. A horse slowed to a walk after bleeding through its nostrils is said to have "Bled."

Many horses bleed, and quit badly as a result, yet their trouble line makes no mention of the problem. After treatment with the drug Lasix, many of these horses return to the races with normal performances, as if their previous race had never happened, and unsuspecting players curse the unforeseen and inexplicable form reversal.

Injured horses generally take time before returning to competition. If a horse was eased in its most recent start, and is now returning to the racing wars a week or two later, chances are its problem was not physical at all. Remember that the track veterinarian must OK each horse before it is allowed to race.

Counter Espionage was pulled up (why, we don't know) in his most recent start, but was back at the races six days later, winning easily with a powerful late rush. In his case, however, two sharp drops in class, from $50,000 to $16,000 on December 6, then from $16,000 to $7,500 on January 1, combined with the "nonperformance" on January 1, were sufficient to make cautious players wary of the horse, even though he had worked four furlongs two days after being pulled up. Although a winner on January 7, Counter Espionage has not been seen since (as of this writing, seven months later).

Counter Espionage — B. h. 5, by Avatar—Scheming, by Drone — **$8,500** Br.—Brant P M (Ky) Tr.—Martin Frank — **117**
Own.—Brant P

	Lifetime				
24 3 4 6					
$65,080					
1983	1	0	0	0	
1982	5	0	1	0	$4,440
Turf	1	0	0	0	

1Jan83- 2Aqu	fst	1⅛	⊡:49⅕	1:15⅖	1:57⅖	Clm 7500	5	6	—	—	—	--	Prough J D^{5}	112	*1.40	— —	Paris Station 113^{3½} Judger Verdict 117^{2} Powhite 112^{3¼}	Pulled up	8
22Dec82- 2Aqu	fst	1$\frac{1}{16}$	⊡:48⅘	1:14⅖	1:47⅖	3↑Clm 16000	5	8	8^{6¾}	6^{6}	4^{6}	7^{9¾}	Vergara O	b 117	*4.00	66-22	Charlie's Star 112^{4} Recidian 117¾ Soudan 117^{2}	Outrun	12
15Dec82- 2Aqu	fst	6f	⊡:23	:46⅖	1:12⅖	3↑Clm 16000	6	3	3^{1}	2^{3}	2^{3}	4^{4½}	Graell A	b 117	*1.20	77-25	Need A Penny117^{nk}MoonGlider117^{3}OscarMyLove115^{1¼}	Weakened	8
6Dec82- 9Aqu	my	6f	⊡:22⅖	:46	1:11⅗	3↑Clm 16000	10	1	2^{1}	2^{½}	2^{hd}	2^{hd}	Graeil A	b 117	4.90	86-15	RoyalMnner119^{hd}CounterEspionge117^{2½}CounterAttck117^{1¼}	Sharp	10
29Sep82- 5Bel	fst	7f	:23⅗	:46⅕	1:22⅘	3↑Clm 50000	8	3	7^{5}	6^{5¾}	6^{9½}	7^{11}	Cordero A Jr	b 117	*2.50	77-18	Crockford Lad 113no Private Sun102^{5¼}NorthernRegent115^{3}	Wide	8
17Sep82- 6Bel	fst	6f	:22⅘	:45⅖	1:09⅘	3↑Clm 50000	3	3	6^{11}	6^{11}	5^{8½}	4^{6¼}	Cordero A Jr	b 117	7.20	87-15	WstgtBrunswick110^{4¼}Fnny'sFox117^{1¼}NorthrnRgnt117¾	No factor	7
11Dec81- 7Aqu	fst	1$\frac{1}{16}$	⊡:47⅕	1:12⅕	1:43⅘	3↑Alw 22000	7	4	3^{4}	2^{1}	1^{hd}	2^{½}	Maple E	b 115	7.00 [D]	94-16	CstleKnight117^{½}[D]CounterEspionge115^{1½}Deedee'sDel117^{½}	Bore in	12
11Dec81-Disqualified and placed third																			
30Nov81- 8Aqu	fst	1	47⅗	1:12	1:36⅗	3↑Alw 22000	3	5	3^{1}	3^{5½}	2^{10}	2^{17}	Cordero A Jr	115	2.20	66-30	JohnCsey112^{17}CounterEspiong115^{½}Buckspishr117^{1¼}	Second best	6
23Nov81- 7Aqu	fst	7f	:23⅕	:46	1:24	3↑Alw 22000	1	7	7^{7}	7^{7½}	5^{3¾}	3^{1¾}	Maple E	115	5.40	79-23	In From Dixie 117^{1¾}Gerontas117^{hd}CounterEspionage115^{nk}	Rallied	9

LATEST WORKOUTS Jan 3 Bel tr.t 4f fst :49⅘ b — Nov 29 Bel tr.t 4f sly :51⅘ b (d) — Nov 23 Bel tr.t 4f fst :48⅘ b — Nov 18 Bel tr.t 3f fst :39 b

□ RACE WATCHING □

The trip handicapper attempts to substitute his own visual impressions of how the race was run for the comments appearing in the *Form*. He tries to watch as much of the race as possible, as many times as possible. He must overcome the temptation to watch just the horse he bet. Watching his horse won't help it win, but will distract the player from seeing all the horses. During the live running of a race, the trip handicapper makes a special effort to observe the horses toward the rear of the field—these often cannot be seen on the replay.

Shortly after arriving at the track, the trip handicapper will note the prevailing track and weather conditions. Of special interest will be the wind, its velocity, and its direction. A strong wind blowing against the horses in the backstretch will severely compromise the chances of the front-runners, who must break the wind. A tail wind on the backstretch will help the speed horses. When the field fans out for the stretch run, few contenders will have "cover" from the wind. A strong wind can be especially telling in sprint races. In the standard two-turn route, the effect of the wind tends to balance out. In fact, a strong wind blowing from right to left that normally favors speed types in sprints can retard the quick getaway of front-runners in routes. They must overcome both the wind and inertia to get into high gear quickly. However, a quick getaway under such conditions tires a horse. Since many jockeys realize this, they will try to rate their horse, and consequently bunch the field at the clubhouse turn, causing traffic problems. For that matter, a strong wind blowing into the face of a stretch-runner at the point where it is about to make its move produces the same negative effect—the horse has difficulty getting into high gear.

CASE STUDY: DEDICATA

The speakers and participants at Handicapping Expo '83, the first national conference on handicapping, spent a cold and wet afternoon at Santa Anita on Wednesday, February 2, 1983. The most controversial horse of the day, and the conference consensus's best bet, was a lightly raced three-year-old colt named Dedicata, who was entered in an NW2 allowance event at a flat mile. The consensus opinion was that Dedicata would control the pace rather easily, and also be aided by the sloppy track conditions. He was the only front-runner in the field of seven, and figured to be several lengths clear in the early stages.

New York-based Paul Mellos, a noted trip handicapper, cast a dissenting vote, warning that Dedicata's early charge to the lead would be hampered by the strong wind blowing at the horses as they raced to the clubhouse turn. Yet Dedicata had no real competition for the early lead. . . .

A second dissenting vote was cast by Dr. Steven Roman, the acclaimed bloodlines expert. Roman calculated Dedicata's dosage index to be an astronomical 23.0, suggesting that the horse, who was closely inbred to Bold Ruler, had little inherent potential for distance racing. Yet Dedicata figured to slow the pace down, and turn the mile race into a half-mile dash. . . .

As things turned out, Mellos and Roman were correct. Dedicata never got clear in the early stages, and then faltered when the real running began.

The horse that won the race, Fast Screen, proved to be an interesting study. The recent maiden graduate, who showed a distinct preference for distance racing, was jumping a class, skipping "nonwinners of one" and moving right into "nonwinners of two." Why had his trainer made this move? Did he have that much confidence in his horse? Or was he asked to enter to help fill the race? Whatever the case, the horse deserved special scrutiny.

A "nonwinners of one" allowance route that Fast Screen might have entered came up the following Sunday. Major Henry, who had beaten

Fast Screen on January 9, came back in that contest, and finished a dismal sixth. On that same day, Preprint, who had finished second when Fast Screen broke his maiden, ran sixth in a maiden route. It was not a good day for comparative handicappers. Their recent close encounters with Fast Screen did nothing for Major Henry and Preprint.

An interesting postscript: Dedicata came back to win the six-furlong Bolsa Chica Stakes at Santa Anita in his next start, lending further credence to Roman's dosage index theory. Dedicata failed on February 2 because he was unable to handle the mile distance, and not because he lacked class, or his form was deteriorating.

Dedicata		Ch. c. 3, by Destroyer—Wild Courage, by Bold Lad			
		Br.—Opstein K (Fla)	1983	2 1 1 0	$14,250
Own.—Opstein K	114	Tr.—Van Berg Jack C	1982	1 1 0 0	$8,250
		Lifetime 3 2 1 0 $22,500			

22Jan83-7SA	6½f :22 :45 1:18 sy	3½ 118	2hd 21 2½ 12½	Romero R P4	Aw19000 80	Dedicata, Upper Rullah, Grenoble 7
8Jan83-2SA	6f :21² :44¹ 1:09 ft	5½ 120	6⁵ 5⁶ 3⁴ 2⁶	Black K¹	Aw19000 87	Naevus, Dedicata, Pre Book 11
11Dec82-6Hol	6f :22¹ :45¹ 1:10¹ft	3½ 118	1hd 2hd 2hd 1hd	Black K²	Mdn 86	Dedicata,DrumScore,TempestWys 11

Jan 30 SA 4f gd :49¹ h   Jan 6 SA 4f ft :52 h   Dec 8 Hol 6f ft 1:12² hg   Dec 2 Hol 6f ft 1:12³ hg

Fast Screen		Ch. c. 3, by Silent Screen—Cerisette, by My Babu			
		Br.—Hill'n Dale Farm (Ill)	1983	2 1 1 0	$13,500
Own.—Longden & Carr Stables	1095	Tr.—Longden John	1982	2 M 0 0	$425
		Lifetime 4 1 1 0 $13,925			

23Jan83-3SA	1₁₆ :48¹ 1:13² 1:46⁴m	*4-5 1135	62½ 42½ 21½ 11	Steiner J J5	Mdn 67	Fast Screen, Preprint, Lucky Key 7
9Jan83-6SA	1₁₆ :46¹ 1:10⁴ 1:41⁴ft	6 1135	4⁵ 6⁴½ 3³ 2hd	Steiner J J¹	Mdn 92	Major Henry, Fast Screen,BlueSeas 8
28Dec82-6SA	6f :21² :44¹ 1:09 ft	28 1135	12¹⁸12¹²1⁷ 9¹³ 68½	Steiner J J¹	Mdn 85	DrumScore,Trento,BroadwayHarry 12
20Oct82-6SA	6f :21³ :44⁴ 1:10¹ft	24 118	10⁸ 10¹² 6⁹ 59½	Campas R¹⁰	Mdn 78	Mezzo, Gold Ruler, Elegant Gold 12

Jan 30 SA 6f gd 1:14 h   Jan 21 SA 4f ft :48⁴ h   ●Jan 15 SA 7f ft 1:25¹ h   Jan 4 SA 5f ft 1:00 h

Effective race watchers prepare themselves beforehand by analyzing the past performances so that they might know what to expect when the gates open. Which horses will try for the early lead? Are there impetuous speed types in the race, horses that must have the early lead at any cost? Which horses will be inside? Will they be able to stay there? Or will the jockey be forced to the outside before the horse will run? Some horses have a fear of racing inside others, and only do their best when placed outside. It is helpful to be aware of such horses, so that their progress can be watched with full understanding. If aware of a horse's preferences, the trip handicapper can spot problems quickly, as well as any unnecessary use of the horse. He will be able to note horses raced against their usual style, frequently the sign of an improving horse, one prepping for a future engagement, or simply a victim of a poor ride.

Although watching the entire race, trip handicappers pay particular attention to five points along the way:

(1) The Start: A horse can quickly lose several lengths (or more) if not prepared for the start. The break from the gate is especially critical for speed types, especially those that must grab the lead at any

expense, and for rail horses, who don't want too many rivals cross-ing in front of them, pinching them back and possibly out of con-tention. A good start is especially critical on a track favoring speed on the rail. Whichever horse breaks the quickest and gets the rail often proves the winner. A handicapper may find it fairly easy to determine that the horses breaking from posts two and five are the speed of a race, and then prefer the "two" because it figures to get the rail trip. But that reasoning would have been in vain should the "five" break faster, cross over, and take the rail before the "two" gets into high gear. The trip handicapper watches the break very closely, identifies those horses breaking slowly or more slowly than expected, then attempts to assess how much (lengths, posi-tion) their poor start cost. He makes special note of their progress, noting if they were rushed hard to get back into contention, or if they did any running later in the race.

(2) Going to the Turn: Were the early leaders running easily, well within themselves, under a rating ride? Or were they being used up in the pace? Was the jockey high in the saddle, strangling the horse, trying to slow it down? Or was he pushing hard, possibly even using his whip at this early stage? A horse pushed hard early that tires late may have a valid excuse while a horse that tires after running easily on the lead does not. How did the leaders get to the first call? Did they break alertly? Or were they forced to rush up quickly after breaking midpack, or worse?

How well situated were the horses expected to rally? Which horses had to check at this stage of the race, waiting for racing room? Did any of the closers start their move too soon—and later run out of gas in midstretch (often the sign of a prep race or of a poorly timed ride)? At times, another horse making its move can force a rider to move his own horse prematurely. That, or forfeit position.

(3) Midway on the Turn: Each horse-width away from the rail is termed a "path." The rail position is called the "1-path," the sec-ond horse out is said to be in the "2-path," and so on. The trip handicapper notes the path of each horse at this crucial juncture in the race, and records it in his program. Horses in the "4-path," or wider, are severely disadvantaged. They are worth noting, and pos-sibly worth following, especially if they remain competitive in the stretch despite their bad trip. (Similar comments apply to the first, or clubhouse, turn in the standard two-turn route, or two-turn sprints at the bullrings.)

(4) At the Head of the Stretch: Or "Entering," in the jargon of trip

handicappers. Once again, the trip handicapper notes the path of each horse in his program. The notation "1–3" means the horse was on the rail midway around the turn, then swung out around two horses, into the "3-path," entering the stretch. Normally, a stretch-runner will find itself in the 2- or 3-path around the turn, then wider entering the stretch. An abrupt change, say a "2–6" trip, suggests a poor ride. The horse was angled out too sharply, and probably lost some momentum as a result.

(5) At the Finish: The trip handicapper makes his own judgment about how each horse finished. He observes which jockeys were using their whips, which were vigorously hand-riding, and which were not seriously persevering with their mounts in the late stages. How were the closers moving, relative to each other? If two were running equally fast in the late stages, their positions easily could be reversed next time out should their trips be different. Keen race watchers also observe which horses were blowing especially hard after their race. Fit, seasoned horses that come back blowing noticeably may be revealing overexertion, the tapping of their energy reserves, and impending poor form. For a freshened horse, however, a fatiguing race or workout may be just what the doctor ordered, advancing the horse's conditioning to a winning peak.

Seasoned race watchers pay close attention to the trailers during the stretch run, to observe what they probably will not see on the television replays. At times, horses at the back of the pack work out from the top of the stretch well past the finish line, a move usually not seen by the stewards, nor timed by the clockers. The typical stretch-runner begins its move at the three-eighths pole, not at the three-sixteenths, so it is important to note when a jockey first cocks his whip and asks his horse to run. Horses working through the stretch probably will pass the entire field—most of them after the finish line—and not be pulled up possibly until reaching the backstretch. They will be the last to report back to the weigh-in stand, and probably will not be blowing very hard. These hidden workouts usually take place in sprint races, and set the horse up nicely for a future route engagement, and the past performance line seldom even hints of this training move.

Professional trip handicappers have their own jargon, a form of shorthand notation they use to mark their programs and record their trip notes for each race. We shall not attempt to explain it here. Whether the individual player adopts that notation, or creates his own, is not the point. What is important is that the player begins to watch races closely, as many times as possible, and records notes on what he saw for future reference.

□ TRACK BIASES □

Trip handicappers are always on the alert for the development or continuation of a track bias. A bias can assist horses racing along the rail, or impede their progress. It can work in favor of early speed types, or make it impossible for them to win. A positive rail bias favors horses able to stay on, or near, the wood for most of the trip. To be successful on such a track, the stretch-runner must get a clear trip along the rail down the backstretch and around the turn, before coming out into the "2-path" in the stretch, if unable to get through along the inside. A successful outside rally on a positive rail track represents a superlative effort. The typical outside move, however, will fall short, and possibly spotlight a horse worth following.

CASE STUDY: PRINCELY HEIR

Princely Heir's performance at Aqueduct on December 4, 1982, was every trip handicapper's dream. Racing on a track exhibiting a strong rail bias, Princely Heir moved up menacingly along the inside on the backstretch, only to be checked sharply when Dedicated Boy fell back suddenly. Once clear, Princely Heir moved to the outside around the turn, then rallied strongly down the middle of the track, against the bias. His performance was truly outstanding. Yet the result chart for the race made no mention of his problem on the backside, nor of the track bias.

NINTH RACE
Aqueduct
DECEMBER 4, 1982

$1\frac{1}{16}$ MILES.(INNER DIRT). ($1.42\frac{3}{5}$) CLAIMING. Purse $17,000. 3-year-olds and upward. Weight, 3-year-olds, 120 lbs. Older, 122 lbs. Non-winners of two races at a mile or over since November 1 allwoed 3 lbs. Of such a race since then, 5 lbs. Claiming price $30,000 for each $2,500 to $25,000, 2 lbs. (Races when entered to be claimed for $20,000 or less not considered.)

Value of race $17,000, value to winner $10,200, second $3,740, third $2,040, fourth $1,020. Mutuel pool $150,006, OTB pool $303,127. Triple Pool $279,547. OTB Triple Pool $512,304.

Last Raced	Horse	Eqt.A.Wt	PP	St	¼	½	¾	Str	Fin	Jockey	Cl'g Pr	Odds $1
21Nov82 ^{5}Aqu^{2}	Letter From Lucy	b 4 115	6	3	1^{hd}	1^{1}	$1^{3\frac{1}{2}}$	1^{4}	$1^{2\frac{1}{4}}$	MacBeth D	27500	3.10
25Nov82 ^{5}Aqu^{10}	Princely Heir	6 115	2	5	4^{1}	$5^{2\frac{1}{2}}$	$4^{\frac{1}{2}}$	$2^{1\frac{1}{2}}$	2^{2}	Santagata N	27500	9.20
13Nov82 ^{9}Aqu^{5}	Dedicated Boy	b 5 117	1	1	2^{4}	2^{2}	$5^{2\frac{1}{2}}$	5^{1}	3^{1}	Miceli M	30000	8.50
24Nov82 ^{1}Aqu^{4}	Pumas Pride	4 117	5	10	10	10	9^{3}	6^{1}	4no	Vergara O	30000	21.90
25Nov82 ^{5}Aqu^{7}	Evasive John	6 117	8	6	$6^{2\frac{1}{2}}$	$4^{\frac{1}{2}}$	2^{hd}	3^{hd}	$5^{1\frac{1}{4}}$	Bailey J D	30000	3.50
15Nov82 ^{7}Aqu^{7}	Inpenetrable	b 4 117	9	4	$3^{1\frac{1}{2}}$	$3^{\frac{1}{2}}$	3^{2}	$4^{1\frac{1}{2}}$	6^{2}	Maple E†	30000	5.90
10Oct82 ^{1}Bel^{2}	Insense Plaisir	4 117	4	7	8^{1}	9^{5}	$7^{1\frac{1}{2}}$	$7^{1\frac{1}{2}}$	7^{1}	Miranda J	30000	9.50
25Nov82 ^{5}Aqu^{9}	Edge Of Wisdom	b 4 117	7	9	9^{8}	8^{1}	6^{hd}	8^{5}	8^{5}	McCarron G	30000	8.50
11Nov82 ^{1}Aqu^{5}	Osage Chief	b 4 113	3	2	5^{hd}	$7^{\frac{1}{2}}$	10	10	$9^{3\frac{1}{2}}$	Venezia M	25000	11.30
21Nov82 ^{5}Aqu^{3}	King Belgian	b 4 117	10	8	$7^{1\frac{1}{2}}$	6^{2}	$8^{\frac{1}{2}}$	9^{hd}	10	Beitia E	30000	21.30

OFF AT 4:14, Start good, Won driving. Time, :24, :48, $1:12\frac{3}{5}$, $1:38\frac{2}{5}$, $1:45\frac{1}{5}$ Track good.

$2 Mutuel Prices:

6-(F)-LETTER FROM LUCY	8.20	4.40	4.00
2-(B)-PRINCELY HEIR		9.60	5.00
1-(A)-DEDICATED BOY			6.20

$2 TRIPLE 6-2-1 PAID $668.00.

B. c, by Roberto—Lucy Letters, by Arts and Letters. Trainer Lake Robert P. Bred by Forest Retreat Farms Inc (Ky).

LETTER FROM LUCY contested the early pace outside DEDICATED BOY, opened a clear lead nearing the second turn and was not menaced while kept to urging. PRINCELY HEIR launched a bid from the outside approaching the stretch and finished with good energy. DEDICATED BOY saved ground contesting the early pace, fell back nearing the second turn but came again late on the outside. PUMAS PRIDE rallied belatedly along the inside. EVASIVE JOHN made a run from the outside leaving the backstretch but weakened soon after entering the stretch. IMPENETRABLE, a forward factor racing off the rail, tired approaching the stretch. EDGE OF WISDOM failed to threat. OSAGE CHIEF was through early.

Owners— 1, Wildman Jody; 2, Feldman Marian S; 3, Old Glory Stable; 4, Shapoff E L; 5, Daren J; 6, Sommer Viola; -7, Sasso L P; 8, Kelley Mrs W A; 9, Faherty J F; 10, Falcone M J.

Trainers— 1, Lake Robert P; 2, Pascuma James J Jr; 3, DeBonis Robert; 4, Shapoff Stanley R; 5, Nocella Vincent; 6, Martin Frank; 7, Preger Mitchell C; 8, Daggett Michael H; 9, Russo Anthony J; 10, Van Wert Robert G.

† Apprentice allowance waived: Inpenetrable 5 pounds. Corrected weight: Inpenetrable 112 pounds.

Scratched—Big Expectation (24Nov82 9Aqu8); Together Again (15Nov82 7Aqu6); Tiempo (3Dec82 9Aqu4); Hangover Yank (22Nov82 1Aqu5).

Attendance 21,141. Total Mutuel Pool $3,853,699. Total OTB Pool $4,109,773. $2 Daily Double 4–6 Paid $37.20. DD Pool $313,501. OTB DD Pool $413,440.

New York's trip handicappers never had the opportunity to "cash in" on this horse. Princely Heir raced later that month at the Meadowlands, and once again was forced to check sharply on the backstretch before rallying to finish second. Then he did not race again until late in 1983. It was not surprising to learn that Princely Heir also had traffic problems in his race prior to the December 4 contest. Some horses simply are prone to trouble, not being quick enough to avoid it. They are usually slow out of the gate, and as a general rule are poor betting risks.

A positive rail bias usually favors the speed horse able to break alertly and establish position along the rail. Sloppy conditions also produce a speed bias, as a rule, as does a tail wind on the backstretch. When such a bias exists, even the most fainthearted of quitters becomes a threat to go all the way. The horse usually gasping for oxygen after six furlongs may stretch out successfully to seven furlongs or longer.

When a strong wind blows up the backstretch, into the faces of the front-runners, it may appear that a positive rail bias exists, favoring closers in this situation. The horses that do best are those with "cover" from the wind, in many cases horses racing off the pace, along the inside. Many of these stay on or near the rail the entire trip. Others come out around the turn or in the stretch, where the effect of the wind lessens or diminishes. A negative rail bias produces the opposite effect. Since speed horses tend to race near the rail, this type of bias tends to favor stretch-runners, particularly those able to get position in the middle of the track. The horse most hurt by these conditions is the speed type likely to be trapped down on the rail all the way, unless able to rush clear early and angle out to the better part of the track. The primary questions to ask when handicapping on such a track are "Who will be able to escape the rail? Who will be trapped on the inside?"

At some tracks, a negative rail bias results from wet conditions. Many tracks are banked slightly, and the inner part of the surface gets the drainage, and dries out slower after the rains have stopped. Belmont and Saratoga are two notable examples. Drying-out conditions, as well as the cuppy track that often occurs toward the end of a prolonged meeting, can produce a negative rail bias, or simply a surface favoring stretch-runners. A strong wind blowing into the faces of the front-runners on the backstretch also will produce a track biased in favor of late closers.

Grass courses have their biases, too. Whether due to the amount of rainfall recently, the length of the grass, or simply the design of the course, they can be as powerful as their counterparts on the dirt courses. During midsummer, after a hot dry spell has baked the course, an early speed bias usually results. The course resembles a concrete highway, and most races are won wire-to-wire.

CASE STUDY: TOLD

Most handicappers realize that a hard grass course is the most conducive of all for early speed types. Yet the opposite extreme, a soggy course, can produce the same effect—a steady stream of front-running winners. The course is so tiring that the entire field is drained by the time they reach the stretch, and the front-runner is able to maintain its lead.

The second race at Aqueduct on October 29, 1979, was a grass handicap surprisingly not taken off a damp course. After several scratches, the stakes-winning three-year-old Told stood out as the lone speed in the field. Yet the son of Tell was dismissed at 7–1, most likely because of the softened condition of the course. After controlling the pace, Told was able to withstand an early challenge from Great Neck, and score a narrow decision. None of the stretch runners ever threatened, all so leg-weary they lost the desire to make an effort to catch up.

There is still another type of bias that surfaces on occasion. On some days, it may seem that the horses in the inner post positions are all breaking slowly, race after race. Or perhaps it is the outer posts that are so affected. This phenomenon is not due to mechanical difficulties with the starting gate. Rather, track maintenance may have left a certain part of the track deeper than normal—the rail in the backstretch chute, for example, where six- and seven-furlong races begin. This impedes the getaway of horses starting over that part of the track.

Under normal circumstances, a racing surface is not biased. At some tracks, however, a bias can be expected. Gulfstream Park quite strongly favors early speed types. Pimlico is famous for its positive rail bias. Del Mar and the Meadowlands often favor inside speed.

After two months' continuous use, Belmont often becomes cuppy during the latter half of July, producing negative rail conditions that favor closers. If relatively dry, Saratoga tends to favor speed on the rail. Then, during the fall, Belmont seems to favor stretch-runners, as a rule. This swing back and forth, from closers to speed, then back to closers again, can confuse the average fan no end. Yet it very definitely works to the advantage of trip handicappers aware of what is happening. It is also one of the primary reasons why Saratoga is known as the "Graveyard of Favorites." Favoritism at Saratoga is often based on form exhibited during the late stages of the Belmont meeting, over track conditions completely opposite to those likely at Saratoga. Trip handicappers in New York prepare for the changes. Toward the end of July, they watch for speed horses that fade on a dead rail, expecting a form reversal once they get to Saratoga. And during the last two weeks of that meet, they look for closers attempting to rally wide over a track likely to be favoring inside speed, giving them extra credit when next entered at Belmont in September. Indeed, trip handicappers at the New York tracks eagerly anticipate these biases, realizing that they will provide some of their better betting opportunities of the year.

CASE STUDY: TIMELESS RIDE

New York trip handicappers were able to collect an immediate dividend on a strong negative rail bias the last two weeks at Belmont when Saratoga opened on July 27, 1983. Timeless Ride had run a "monster race" against the bias in his Belmont finale, battling for the early lead with the fleet Bright Search while trapped on the rail. That he surrendered only to Lordly Love, a recent claim making his first start for Oscar Barrera, made his performance appear exceptional by trip handicapping standards. Those who loved Timeless Ride at Saratoga—Andy Beyer among them—probably were unaware of the full power of his performance on July 20 at Belmont, something pace figures revealed quite emphatically. Despite racing against the bias that day, Timeless Ride set a blistering pace (114, compared to a race par of only 105), and still was able to hold off the challenges of all but one horse in a race run in a respectable 106 figure.

At Saratoga, the fates smiled on Timeless Ride. Despite breaking from the far outside, he was able to sit a good trip right behind the pace, then take the lead in midstretch. He returned a liberal $9.40, despite his appeal to the trip handicappers, and a slight drop in class. As things worked out, the bias at Saratoga favored outside speed during the first few days of the 1983 meeting.

Timeless Ride — B. g. 6, by Timeless Moment—Child Bride, by Jaipur
$25,000 Br.—Mangurian H T Jr (Fla)
Tr.—Root Richard R
Own.—Mangurian H T Jr — **117**

Lifetime						
27 4 5 4	1983	5	1	1	1	$12,805
$46,135	1982	7	0	2	0	$7,130
	Turf	3	0	0	0	$160

20Jly83- 3Bel	gd	6f	:22⅖	:45⅗	1:11⅖	Clm 35000	1	2	1½	2^{hd}	1½	$2^{3\frac{1}{2}}$	Velasquez J	b 117	7.30	81-25	Lordly Love $115^{3\frac{1}{2}}$ Timeless Ride 117^{hd} Jeffery C. $117^{\frac{3}{4}}$	Weakened	8
13Jly83- 2Bel	fst	7f	:23⅕	:46⅗	1:24⅗	Clm 25000	7	2	3^{1}	$3^{1\frac{1}{2}}$	1½	$3^{1\frac{3}{4}}$	Velasquez J	b 117	16.10	77-24	DelingDiplomt117^{nk}Fnny'sFox$112^{1\frac{1}{2}}$TimelessRide117^{nk}	Wide early	12
30Jun83- 7Crc	fst	6½f	:22⅗	:45⅗	1:19	3↑Clm 37500	6	2	1½	4^{nk}	7^{8}	7^{14}	Olivera M F7	b 112	6.60	76-14	Raise A Line 119^{nk} Big Win 117^{3} Gloversville $114^{\frac{1}{2}}$	Tired	7
11Jun83- 7Crc	fst	6½f	:22⅗	:46	1:19	3↑Alw 14000	4	3	2^{hd}	2^{hd}	5^{5}	6^{10}	Olivera M F7	b 109	9.30	80-20	CommndAttnton116^{nk}InAllHnsty121^{2}ChnLnk'sDrm109^{3}	Gave way	7
3Jun83- 9Crc	fst	6f	:22⅖	:45⅘	1:12⅕	3↑Alw 12000	5	2	2^{hd}	1½	1½	1no	Olivera M F7	b 110	7.40	91-17	TimelessRide110^{no}MyBestChoice114^{nk}GallantPrelude$117^{\frac{3}{4}}$	Driving	8
24Apr82- 7GP	sly	6f	:22	:45	1:10⅕	Alw 18000	4	2	2½	2^{hd}	3^{2}	$2^{3\frac{1}{2}}$	Cardone E	b 115	5.50	84-19	Ruler'sDancer$113^{3\frac{1}{2}}$TimelessRide115^{nk}Satan'sParade117^{hd}	Gamely	8
10Apr82- 9GP	fm	1½ Ⓣ	:47	2:01⅗	2:26	3↑Pan Amer'n H	5	1	1^{1}	16^{22}	16^{41}	16^{43}	Cardone E	b 106	3.00e	51-09	Robsphere 117^{hd} Come Rain or Shine $110^{\frac{1}{2}}$TheBart126^{no}	Stopped	16
23Mar82- 7GP	fst	6f	:22⅖	:45⅖	1:11	Alw 14000	3	1	1^{hd}	2^{1}	2½	2½	Cardone E	b 117	7.50	83-21	Satan's Parade $117^{\frac{1}{2}}$ Timeless Ride$117^{1\frac{1}{4}}$SnobNative117^{nk}	Gamely	8
3Mar82- 9Hia	gd	1⅛ Ⓣ			1:46⅖	3↑Ⓢ Ocala H	3	1	2^{hd}	3^{2}	11^{21}	11^{30}	Cardone E	b 111	*.50e	75-04	Robsphere $122^{3\frac{3}{4}}$ Some One Frisky 116^{1} Big Ding 114^{3}	Bore out	11
9Feb82- 9Hia	fst	7f	:22⅗	:45	1:23⅘	Alw 15000	5	1	1½	2^{hd}	$5^{2\frac{1}{4}}$	$8^{8\frac{1}{2}}$	Velasquez J	b 116	8.10	75-18	Flying Trap 119no Snob Native 116^{nk} Green Path 118^{3}	Faltered	9

LATEST WORKOUTS ●Jly 10 Bel 3f fst :35⅕ h Jly 5 Crc 4f fst :49 h Jun 25 Crc 6f sly 1:20 b

When a track bias does exist, whether it be a wind-induced affair lasting one day, or a blockbuster lasting three weeks, the trip handicapper must be ready to exploit it. Early recognition of the bias is critical. While the bias exists, he must focus his attention only on those horses likely to be aided by the conditions. When the bias is especially strong, this may be all the handicapping necessary.

When evaluating the merits of horses that had raced while the bias existed, the handicapper must proceed cautiously. A performance assisted by the bias will look better, on paper, than it actually was, and the horse will be an underlay in its next start. On the other hand, a horse that raced against the bias may appear off form, and start at rather attractive odds. A strong effort against the bias can be considered a "winning" effort, but with the horse escaping the usual penalties, such as additional weight or a forced rise in class. However, the handicapper must be careful that the effort didn't overly tire the horse.

CASE STUDY: THUNDER BRIDGE

We have already met Thunder Bridge, Oscar Barrera's miracle claim, in Chapter 7. When the roan was entered in a turf allowance at Saratoga on July 27, 1983, handicappers had to be concerned with his absence of form on the grass. His one previous attempt on that surface resulted in an out-of-the-money finish. Form handicappers also had reason to be worried. Was the five-year-old possibly entering the downside of his form cycle? His latest race seemed far inferior to his first two performances in Barrera's silks. Trip handicappers knew differently, however, but they had an even greater dilemma. On July 22, Thunder Bridge had battled a strong negative rail bias, fighting off the challenge of race co-favorite King's Glory around the turn, then a challenge from Smart Style through the stretch, without being able to escape from the rail. He had little left to repulse Silver Express' late challenge when the eventual winner, taking full advantage of the bias, charged down the middle of the track. Considering the track conditions and the way the race was run, Thunder Bridge's performance was every bit as impressive as his two daylight victories. He was lengths the best on July 22.

If Thunder Bridge was about to go downhill, the clue did not appear in his past performance lines, as casual observers might have thought. How taxing was his all-out effort against the bias? That was the relevant question. His poor performance on the grass July 27 failed to answer that question. But an atypical (for Barrera) seventeen-day layoff following that race suggested in no uncertain terms that the July 22 race did have a telling effect on the horse's condition.

CASE STUDY: LAST TURN

Trip handicappers look especially for horses that showed life against a bias, but were unable to do their best. When dropped into the high-rent claiming ranks on July 23, Last Turn was coming off two attempts against strong biases. On June 29, he was "off slowly," then offered a "mild late response" while attempting to rally along a negative rail. Then on July 8, the gelding was pushed early on the far outside, racing against his usual style over a track strongly biased in favor of early speed types, and tired badly as a result.

Track bias considerations allowed trip handicappers to forgive Last Turn his last two performances, and possibly read a little life into them. When he found a track favoring his usual running style on July 23, Last Turn was confidently taken into the 6-path for his strong looping move on the turn, then drew off through the stretch. He lit up the board to the tune of $35.40. Trip handicapping was the crucial tool in finding something positive in this horse's recent record.

Last Turn — B. g. 3, by Turn and Count—Miss Marked, by Raise a Cup — $70,000 — Br.—New Haven Farm (Ky) — Tr.—Schaeffer Stephen — Own.—Spiegel R — 113

Lifetime 24 3 4 1 $66,348 — 1983 12 1 2 1 $36,288 — 1982 12 2 2 0 $30,060 — Turf 2 0 0 0

8Jly83- 8Bel	fst	7f		:23⅕	:46⅕	1:24⅕	3↑Alw 22000	8	5	7^{5}	8^{10}	8^{19}	8^{17}	Santagata N	b	111	46.80	64-18	APhenomenon116$^{2\frac{1}{4}}$FifthDivision112^{nk}ScrenTrnd113$^{\frac{1}{2}}$	Wide, tired	8
29Jun83- 5Bel	fst	6f		:22⅗	:45⅗	1:10⅗	3↑Alw 22000	2	9	$9^{9\frac{1}{4}}$	$8^{6\frac{1}{2}}$	6^{6}	$5^{4\frac{1}{2}}$	Santagata N	b	110	34.60	84-15	AgileShoebill112$^{\frac{3}{4}}$HeldBlmeless111$^{1\frac{3}{4}}$SilentLnding109$^{1\frac{1}{4}}$	Off slowly	9
11Jun83- 7Bel	fst	1⅛		:46⅕	1:09⅘	1:48⅗	Colin	7	6	$8^{3\frac{3}{4}}$	8^{8}	8^{12}	$8^{8\frac{1}{2}}$	Migliore R	b	119	76.60	75-14	I Enclose 126no Potentiate 119^{1} Intention 119$^{\frac{1}{2}}$	Outrun	10
6Jun83- 7Bel	gd	1 1/16	[T]	:47⅘	1:12⅕	1:44	3↑Alw 23000	4	5	$5^{7\frac{1}{2}}$	8^{13}	8^{19}	8^{23}	Migliore R		110	37.90	58-31	Tough Mickey 114$^{2\frac{3}{4}}$ Saronic 117^{2} James Boswell 117^{1}	Tired	8
21May83- 3Bel	gd	1 1/16		:44⅘	1:08⅘	1:41	3↑Alw 23000	6	5	$6^{6\frac{1}{2}}$	$6^{7\frac{1}{2}}$	$5^{9\frac{1}{2}}$	$6^{7\frac{3}{4}}$	Migliore R	b	110	13.60	89-07	Ardent Bid 116$^{\frac{3}{4}}$ James Boswell 119^{2} RockyMarriage113$^{4\frac{3}{4}}$	Outrun	12
13Apr83- 1Aqu	fst	1⅛		:48⅗	1:12⅗	1:50⅘	Alw 23000	5	4	$3^{1\frac{1}{2}}$	4^{4}	5^{12}	5^{13}	Fell J	b	117	7.60	68-19	Slew O' Gold 117$^{7\frac{3}{4}}$ Law Talk 117$^{1\frac{1}{4}}$ El Cubano 117$^{\frac{3}{4}}$	Tired	6
1Apr83- 6Aqu	fst	1		:46⅘	1:12⅗	1:38	Alw 23000	3	6	$6^{9\frac{1}{4}}$	6^{11}	$5^{8\frac{1}{2}}$	$5^{6\frac{3}{4}}$	Fell J	b	117	*2.10	69-30	Bala Gala 117^{2} Esprit De Romeo 117^{no}Minabchar119$^{4\frac{3}{4}}$	No factor	7
24Mar83- 8Aqu	fst	1⅛		:48⅖	1:13⅗	1:52⅖	Handicap	3	6	$6^{5\frac{1}{4}}$	$5^{2\frac{1}{2}}$	2^{1}	2^{nk}	Smith A Jr	b	112	3.80	73-26	Aztec Red 114^{nk} LastTurn112$^{1\frac{1}{2}}$DoubleExplosion111^{4}	Just missed	6
7Mar83- 8Aqu	my	170	[•]	:48⅖	1:14	1:42⅘	Alw 23000	1	4	$4^{4\frac{1}{2}}$	$4^{1\frac{1}{2}}$	3^{2}	3^{1}	Migliore R	b	117	3.30	87-16	King's Swan 117^{1} Proud Capital 117no Last Turn 117$^{1\frac{1}{4}}$	Evenly	6
14Feb83- 8Aqu	fst	1 1/16	[•]	:47⅖	1:12	1:44⅕	Whirlaway	5	5	$5^{2\frac{1}{2}}$	$5^{3\frac{3}{4}}$	$6^{7\frac{1}{4}}$	5^{7}	Migliore R	b	117	6.90	85-13	ButWhoKnows119$^{1\frac{1}{2}}$MchoDuck117$^{1\frac{3}{4}}$EspritDeRomeo117$^{1\frac{3}{4}}$	Outrun	7

LATEST WORKOUTS Jly 18 Bel tr.t 4f fst :48⅗ h — Jun 27 Bel tr.t 3f fst :36⅖ b — Jun 21 Bel tr.t 5f my 1:02⅕ b — ●Jun 1 Bel 6f fst 1:11⅖ h

CASE STUDY: TEN BORE

Trip handicappers tend to bet against horses that are coming off perfect trips aided by a track bias. The perfect trip likely will not happen again, yet the horse will be overbet by those unaware of its previous circumstances. They especially downgrade their appraisal of horses that failed to take advantage of a bias.

A reluctant animal like Ten Bore, for example, would be identified quite clearly as a horse unwilling to win after it failed to hold its lead on a track exhibiting a strong speed bias on March 11.

Ten Bore — B. h. 5, by Tentam—Janet's Charge, by I'm For More — $70,000 — Br.—Sharp Bayard (Md) — Tr.—DeBonis Robert — Own.—Shapiro T — 113

Lifetime 40 6 9 10 $135,957 — 1983 6 0 2 3 $23,980 — 1982 13 2 0 3 $36,451 — Turf 3 1 1 0 $19,000

11Mar83- 8Aqu	sly	170	[•]	:46⅗	1:11⅕	1:40⅗	Alw 37000	2	1	1^{5}	1^{5}	1^{3}	2^{hd}	Cordero A Jr		115	2.40	99-11	Skin Dancer 115^{hd} Ten Bore 115^{2} Rain Prince 110$^{\frac{1}{2}}$	Just failed	7
27Feb83- 7Aqu	fst	1 1/16	[•]	:47	1:12	1:45⅕	Clm 70000	1	1	1^{3}	1^{2}	1^{2}	$3^{2\frac{1}{4}}$	Cordero A Jr		113	4.90	85-20	Irish Waters 108^{1} Rain Prince 108$^{1\frac{1}{4}}$ Ten Bore 113$^{\frac{1}{2}}$	Weakened	10
17Feb83- 8Aqu	fst	6f	[•]	:22⅗	:46⅕	1:11⅖	Alw 35000	4	1	1^{hd}	$2^{\frac{1}{2}}$	3^{nk}	$3^{3\frac{1}{4}}$	Cordero A Jr		117	2.90	84-17	Space Mountain 112$^{1\frac{3}{4}}$ I'mSoMerry108$^{1\frac{1}{2}}$TenBore117$^{1\frac{1}{2}}$	Weakened	7
7Feb83- 7Aqu	my	1⅛	[•]	:46⅗	1:11⅖	1:51⅕	Clm 70000	6	1	$1^{1\frac{1}{2}}$	1^{hd}	$2^{\frac{1}{2}}$	$2^{2\frac{3}{4}}$	Cordero A Jr		113	3.20	87-17	Direct Answer 115$^{2\frac{3}{4}}$ Ten Bore 113no To Erin 108^{6}	Game try	6
31Jan83- 5Aqu	fst	6f	[•]	:22⅕	:45⅖	1:10⅕	Clm 70000	3	6	6^{5}	5^{5}	6^{10}	$5^{6\frac{1}{2}}$	McCarron G		113	6.80	86-15	KentuckyEdd108$^{2\frac{3}{4}}$HappyHooligan113$^{1\frac{1}{2}}$CrockfordLd113$^{1\frac{1}{4}}$	Outrun	6
16Jan83- 2Aqu	sly	170	[•]	:47	1:12⅘	1:43⅗	Clm 75000	7	1	1^{5}	$1^{1\frac{1}{2}}$	3^{2}	$3^{4\frac{1}{2}}$	Davis R G^{5}		109	13.10	79-20	LarkOscilltion116$^{\frac{1}{2}}$AccountReceivble112^{4}TenBore109$^{6\frac{1}{2}}$	Gave way	10
11Dec82- 7Aqu	fst	170	[•]	:46⅘	1:12⅕	1:43	3↑Alw 40000	1	1	1^{3}	$1^{1\frac{1}{2}}$	2^{3}	6^{10}	Miranda J		117	19.00	77-20	Stiff Sentence 122$^{2\frac{3}{4}}$ Waj. Jr. 110$^{2\frac{1}{2}}$ AccountReceivable115^{2}	Tired	8
5Dec82- 3Aqu	gd	170	[•]	:46⅖	1:11	1:41⅖	3↑Clm 70000	4	1	1^{4}	1^{5}	2^{hd}	$2^{3\frac{3}{4}}$	Miranda J		113	20.50	91-16	[D]Waj. Jr. 108$^{3\frac{3}{4}}$ Ten Bore 113^{2} Gauguin Native 108$^{1\frac{1}{2}}$	Impeded	9
5Dec82-Placed first through disqualification																					
25Oct82- 8Lrl	sly	1		:47⅖	1:13⅕	1:39	3↑Alw 20000	1	1	$2^{\frac{1}{2}}$	3^{4}	$6^{7\frac{3}{4}}$	7^{13}	Nicol P A Jr^{5}	b	110	12.30	64-32	Mile High Club 115$^{1\frac{1}{2}}$ Peace ForPeace117^{8}IssueJoined119^{nk}	Tired	8
2Oct82- 8Bow	fst	1 1/16		:47⅕	1:11⅗	1:43⅘	3↑P M Burch	7	1	1^{2}	1^{4}	3^{1}	$6^{7\frac{3}{4}}$	Delgado A		109	42.50	79-21	Blackie Daw 113^{1} Sunny Winters 113$^{3\frac{1}{2}}$ Zvetlana 108$^{2\frac{3}{4}}$	Tired	11

LATEST WORKOUTS Mar 23 Bel tr.t 5f fst 1:02⅖ h — Mar 7 Bel tr.t 3f sly :37⅕ b — Feb 25 Bel tr.t 5f fst 1:05 b — Jan 29 Bel tr.t 3f fst :37⅗ b

Biased racetracks can easily confuse one's judgment concerning a horse's true distance capabilities. A six-furlong type may last a mile if given the right circumstances, such as a strong early speed bias, or a race totally devoid of other speed types. A router may surprise at six furlongs on a day when strong winds make things difficult for front-runners. Keen observers, nevertheless, still consider such horses suspect at the distance, even though their past performances may clearly show a victory. The trip handicapper must avoid one other pitfall as well. Just because a horse was victimized by a poor trip last time does not mean it will run well this time. Not even recent winners are guaranteed to repeat their good performance. Nor are they assured the horse will get a good trip this time. Some horses are chronic "bad trippers." They simply aren't quick enough to stay out of trouble, or take advantage when room opens on the inside.

One final word of warning: Do not jump to conclusions about the existence of a track bias. Don't conclude "dead rail" after watching one or two races, unless you know there was a dead rail the previous day. Trips must be interpreted in light of previous form. Three races in a row may witness front-runners quitting on the rail, yet this would be useless information should all three have figured to falter, based on their recent records. Statisticians would laugh at us for making conclusions about biases or variants on the basis of samples as small as nine races!

Many trainers and riders simply aren't aware of, or don't believe in, track biases. Trip handicappers must learn which are alert, and use them as their guideposts. When New Yorkers observe Angel Cordero looping his field at Belmont in the first two races, they immediately suspect that a negative rail bias exists. Each circuit has its Cordero, the jockey quick to spot and exploit a track bias.

Knowledge of a rider's style can also be helpful to trip handicappers. Some riders are daring, and look for the opening on the inside at every opportunity. Others with age become more cautious, and tend to stay outside. During periods of track bias, these riders blow hot and cold, probably unaware of the effect the bias has on their performance. The trip handicapper aware of their preference will have a good idea where their horses will be on the racetrack, and can bet with or against them with confidence when a bias exists.

Post position surveys, as they appear in many track programs, can help identify a bias, but the player must proceed cautiously. Post position surveys can be misleading unless split by distance—there may be a bias at the route distances that doesn't show up for the sprints. And track biases can be fleeting things, present one week, gone the next. So if the survey covers too many weeks, what has been happening of late will not be revealed. Everything considered, therefore, post position surveys are no substitute for personal observation.

Many players with whom I have talked or corresponded resent the fact that track maintenance can manicure a racing surface so as to produce a bias. Some feel this is being done to foil the more sophisticated players in the crowd. Others feel that racing surfaces are toyed with to help certain "insiders" cash a few bets at the expense of an unsuspecting public. Actually, the tracks could not care less about who wins and who loses. They get their cut regardless. And many biases develop naturally, and not at the instigation of the track maintenance workers. For that matter, track biases play into the hands of the sharp, observant player. They provide him with an edge over a largely unobservant crowd. Indeed, track biases are the trip handicapper's best friend.

☐ APPLICATION TO SPEED HANDICAPPING ☐

Trip handicapping allows the speed handicapper to place his figures in proper context. Did a horse earn its recent figure under very favorable circumstances? Or did it have to overcome a certain amount of adversity? Was a good figure earned with the help of a perfect trip, possibly aided by a track bias? Or was a lesser figure the result of a good effort against a bias, or trying to overcome a bad trip?

The speed handicapper who also dabbles in trip handicapping will be able to answer these questions, and will have a better feel for his figures as a result. He may wish to adjust his figures to account for trips. He would then have to judge what a slow start, a track bias, or traffic problems equate to in lengths lost. Adjusting for paths is easier, because each path from the rail is worth one length around a full turn. With these adjustments built into his figures, and daily variants based on projected race pars, the speed handicapper can come closest to determining the day's true variant.

With the aid of pace figures, the trip handicapper can visualize how a race should be run beforehand, and spot track biases quickly as a result. Which horses will set the pace? Who will be the inside speed? The outside speed? If the inside speed horses are consistently beating their rivals on the outside, one would suspect the presence of a positive rail bias. On the other hand, if the inside speed horses are consistently having difficulty getting to the lead, one would deduce the opposite, that a negative rail bias is in operation.

☐ **CONCLUSION** ☐

Trip handicapping is the attempt to bring the one-dimensional past performance lines to life, supplementing those numbers with a visual impression of what actually transpired during the running of a horse's recent races. It is the attempt to uncover performances that are actually better than they appear in black and white, and those which are less impressive than they seem on paper. The information trip handicappers possess cannot be found in the *Form*, and consequently can prove invaluable to those who bother to watch races closely. And while trip handicappers have no more guarantee than anyone else that their selections will perform to expectations, they often have disguised form on their side, assuring them the decent odds on which long-range profits are built. That will continue until trip handicapping attains the level of popularity that speed handicapping now enjoys.

Trip handicapping is the latest trend, developed to help the serious player better cope with the ever-growing sophistication of racetrack audiences. Whether an individual handicapper decides to incorporate it into his everyday routine, or finds it out of reach, there is a veiled lesson for all. We should learn to be more forgiving of an apparent poor performance, and more suspicious of an uncharacteristically good performance, unless we know its context. There may be more to the story than the *Form* reports.

Chapter 12

THE RESULT CHARTS

The information printed in *Daily Racing Form* past per-formances does not materialize out of thin air. It is extracted from a vast data bank stored in the *Form*'s computer. Each night, that data bank is updated to include the results of the day's racing. The update proceeds from the result charts, which are created at the track daily by the *Form*'s "trackman," who gives a horse-by-horse call of the race to his assistant. These charts are published a day or two later in the *Form*, and are the source for the charts that appear in most daily newspapers. Much of the information found in the result charts is transcribed directly into the past performances of the individual horses that participated in the race. But there is enough significant information that is not carried over that serious handicappers save result charts for future reference.

Class handicappers will find exact eligibility conditions reproduced, precisely as they appeared in the condition book or at the head of the past performances. Should a handicapper need to know the exact condi-tions of eligibility for a classified allowance race run two weeks pre-viously, he need only refer back to the result chart for that race and he will have the desired information, which most of the crowd will not share. (See the Eighth Race at Aqueduct on page 254.)

Key-race advocates find reference to each horse's previous start—the date and track, with race number preceding the track name, and finish position following. Main Stem, for example, last raced in the eighth at Aqueduct on March 12, finishing fifth. Should the horse run especially well in today's race, a simple check next to its name in the result chart of its previous race will help identify key races quickly. These checks add invaluable information to the result charts. They quickly point out above-average fields within a given classification.

EIGHTH RACE
Aqueduct
MARCH 31, 1983

6 FURLONGS. (1.08⅕) ALLOWANCE. Purse $35,000. 4-year-olds and upward which have not won two races of $12,500 since November 1. Weight, 122 lbs. Non-winners of three races of $15,000 in 1982–83 allowed 3 lbs. Of two such ra ces since August 1, 5 lbs. OF such a race since January 1, 5 lbs. (Maiden, claiming and state-bred races not considered.)

Value of race $35,000, value to winner $21,000, second $7,700, third $4,200, fourth $2,100. Mutuel pool $128,364, Minus show pool $2,549.15, OTB pool $115,890.

Last Raced	Horse	Eqt.A.Wt	PP	St	¼	½	Str	Fin	Jockey	Odds $1
12Mar83 ^{8}Aqu^{5}	Main Stem	b 5 112	1	5	3^{2}	2^{hd}	1½	1^{hd}	Davis R G^{5}	a-4.80
19Dec82 ^{8}Aqu^{2}	Maudlin	5 112	3	3	$4^{1\frac{1}{2}}$	$4^{1\frac{1}{2}}$	2^{2}	$2^{3\frac{1}{2}}$	Bernhardt E J Jr^{10}	b-.60
18Mar83 ^{8}Aqu^{3}	And More	5 117	5	1	5^{4}	5^{6}	5^{4}	3¾	Bush W V	3.90
12Mar83 ^{8}Aqu^{4}	Romaldo	b 5 117	4	4	2^{hd}	3^{2}	3½	$4^{1\frac{3}{4}}$	McCarron G	a-4.80
11Dec82 ^{8}Aqu^{4}	Fast Gold	4 122	2	7	7	6½	$6^{3\frac{1}{2}}$	5^{2}	Samyn J L	9.50
1Mar83 ^{9}GP^{5}	Mayanesian	b 4 115	6	2	1^{4}	$1^{2\frac{1}{2}}$	4^{hd}	6^{3}	Smith A Jr	9.50
30Sep82 ^{6}Med^{2}	Muttering	4 122	7	6	$6^{1\frac{1}{2}}$	7	7	7	Cordero A Jr	b-.60

a-Coupled: Main Stem and Romaldo; b-Maudlin and Muttering.

OFF AT 4:27 Start good, Won driving. Time, :22⅖, :45⅗, 1:10 Track fast.

$2 Mutuel Prices:

1-(A)-MAIN STEM (a-entry)	11.60	3.00	2.10
2-(C)-MAUDLIN (b-entry)		2.20	2.10
4-(E)-AND MORE			2.10

Ch. h, by Clem—Whale Tail, by Knave. Trainer Sedlacek Sue. Bred by Willwerth G & Sandra (Va).

MAIN STEM raced forwardly while saving ground, caught MAYANAESIAN soon after entering the stretch, responded readily when challenged by MAUDLIN and outfinished that rival under pressure. MAUDLIN, unhurried early moved outside approaching the stretch, engaged MAIN STEM with a furlong to go and narrowly missed. AND MORE finished willingly from the outside to best the others. ROMALDO raced forwardly outside MAIN STEM but weakened approaching the furlong grounds. FAST GOLD, outrun early, lacked a solid rally outside. MAYNESIAN quickly sprinted clear, saved ground making the pace to the stretch and gave way. MUTTERING failed to reach contention.

Owners— 1, Tresvant Stable; 2, Tartan Stable; 3, Grusmark M E; 4, Wimpfheimer J D; 5, Aisco Stable; 6, Gordonsdale Farm; 7, Tartan Stable.

Trainers— 1, Sedlacek Sue; 2, Nerud Jan H; 3, Grusmark Karl; 4, Sedlacek Woodrow; 5, Bailie Sally A; 6, Zito Nicholas P; 7, Nerud Jan H.

FIFTH RACE
Aqueduct
APRIL 15, 1983

1 ⅛ MILES. (1.47) CLAIMING. Purse $17,500. 4-year-olds and upward, fillies and mares. Weights, 122 lbs. Non-winners of two races over a mile since March 1 allowed 3 lbs. Of such a race since then 5 lbs. Claiming Price $40,000; for each $2,500 to $35,000, 2 lbs. (Races when entered to be claimed for $30,000 or less not considered.)

Value of race $17,500, value to winner $10,500, second $3,850, third $2,100, fourth $1,050. Mutuel pool $116,870, OTB pool $132,565. Exacta Pool $206,058. OTB Exacta Pool $216,544.

Last Raced	Horse	Eqt.A.Wt	PP	St	¼	½	¾	Str	Fin	Jockey	Cl'g Pr	Odds $1
29Mar83 ^{7}Aqu^{4}	Huffy's Turn	4 110	1	4	1^{2}	1^{2}	1^{hd}	2^{2}	1¾	Davis R G^{5}	37500	3.40
19Mar83 ^{7}Aqu^{5}	Path To Memories	b 5 106	3	8	8^{2}	7½	5^{1}	3^{5}	2½	Murphy D J^{7}	35000	a-1.10
6Apr83 ^{2}Aqu^{3}	Canuschka	b 5 112	6	7	5^{3}	3½	2^{2}	1^{1}	$3^{3\frac{1}{2}}$	Alvarado R Jr^{5}	40000	6.50
6Apr83 ^{2}Aqu^{6}	Vanities Bid	b 5 113	5	1	$2^{1\frac{1}{2}}$	2½	3½	4^{3}	4^{2}	Samyn J L	35000	5.90
5Apr83 ^{7}Aqu^{2}	Exactly Tricky	7 117	8	5	6½	6^{1}	$7^{1\frac{1}{2}}$	$5^{1\frac{1}{2}}$	5^{4}	Cordero A Jr	40000	a-1.10
26Mar83 ^{3}Aqu^{4}	Salt Treaty	b 5 117	2	6	9	9	8^{6}	6^{2}	$6^{4\frac{1}{4}}$	Smith A Jr	40000	24.40
26Mar83 ^{3}Aqu^{7}	Beside the Point	5 117	7	3	4½	5^{5}	$6^{1\frac{1}{2}}$	8^{6}	$7^{1\frac{1}{2}}$	Beitia E	40000	35.20
6Apr83 ^{2}Aqu^{5}	Crafty Flyer	5 113	9	9	3^{hd}	$4^{2\frac{1}{2}}$	4^{4}	7½	$8^{4\frac{1}{2}}$	Fell J†	35000	10.10
5Apr83 ^{7}Aqu^{6}	Bottome	4 112	4	2	$7^{1\frac{1}{2}}$	$8^{1\frac{1}{2}}$	9	9	9	Clayton M D^{5}	40000	19.40

a-Coupled: Path To Memories and Exactly Tricky.

OFF AT 2:57 Start good for all but CRAFTY FLYER. Won driving. Time, :25, :49⅗, 1:14⅗, 1:40⅗, 1:54⅖ Track fast.

$2 Mutuel Prices:

2-(A)-HUFFY'S TURN	8.80	3.20	2.60
1-(C)-PATH TO MEMORIES (a-entry)		2.69	2.10
6-(G)-CANUSCHKA			2.80

$2 EXACTA 2-1 PAID $18.40.

B. f, by Turn to Mars—Huffy Lady, by Tampa Trouble. Trainer Nadler Herbert. Bred by McGarrah J (Ky).

HUFFY'S TURN made the pace under good handling, drifted out when replaced by CANUSCHKA approaching the stretch, raced wide into the stretch and responded gamely to prove best. PATH TO MEMORIES rallied along the inside leaving the far turn, came out between horses leaving the furlong grounds and finished gamely. CANUSCHKA moved to the fore along the inside on the far turn but weakened under pressure. VANITIES BID raced for forwardly until near the stretch and tired. EXACTLY TRICKY failed to be a serious factor. BESIDE THE POINT was finished early. CRAFTY FLYER sent up outside horses after breaking poorly, remained a factor for six furlongs and had nothing left.

Owners— 1, Spataro J M; 2, Weinsier Mrs R; 3, Davis A; 4, Rita B Stable; 5, Triventure Farm; 6, Sweet Meadow Farm; 7, Seven Zee Stable; 8, Briar Patch Farm; 9, Manhasset Stable.

Trainers— 1, Nadler Herbert; 2, Martin Jose; 3, Moschera Gasper S; 4, Weinstein Bruce; 5, Martin Jose; 6, Gullo Thomas J; 7, Russello Anthony; 8, Vetter Robert C; 9, Zito Nicholas P.

† **Apprentice allowance waived:** Crafty Flyer 5 pounds.

Scratched—Top Rating (29Mar83 ^{7}Aqu^{8}).

Trip handicappers find a fairly detailed description of the performances of some of the contestants. Usually included in these comments is some indication of where (inside or outside) a horse raced, and a description of any trouble it may have encountered. These comments are usually restricted to the horses that finished in the money, and any others that received a significant amount of play at the betting windows, but not every horse's progress is charted. Tripsters can also find comments about the start and finish of the race. "Start good, won driving" is the standard remark. Should the win have been accomplished handily or easily, the comment would read "won handily" or "won easily" instead. Had a horse (or horses) broken poorly, we would read "Start good for all but . . ." (See the Fifth Race at Aqueduct on page 254.)

Trip and pace handicappers occasionally are made aware of strong wind conditions that easily may have affected the outcome of the day's races. The comment "against wind in backstretch" or "with wind in backstretch" will appear beneath the running lines. The chart of Secretariat's Belmont Stakes contained such a comment. A severe thunderstorm was moving into the New York area, and the wind conditions preceding it made Secretariat's speed and pace figures all the more remarkable.

1973 Belmont Stakes Chart

EIGHTH RACE

Belmont

JUNE 9, 1973

1 ½ MILES. (2.26%) 105th Running THE BELMONT. $125,000 added. 3-year-olds. By subscription of $100 each to accompany the nomination; $250 to pass the entry box; $1,000 to start. A supplementary nomination may be made of $2,500 at the closing time of entries plus an additional $10,000 to start, with $125,000 added, of which 60% to the winner, 22% to second, 12% to third and 6% to fourth. Weights, Colts and Geldings 126 lbs. Fillies 121 lbs.

Starters to be named at the closing time of entries. The winning owner will be presented with the August Belmont Memorial Cup to be retained for one year, as well as a trophy for permanent possession and trophies will be presented to the winning trainer and jockey. Closed Thursday, February 15, 1973 with 187 Nominations.

Value of race $150,200, value to winner $90,120, second $33,044, third $18,024, fourth $9,012. Mutuel pool $519,689, OTB pool $688,460.

Last Raced		Horse	Eqt.A.Wt	PP	¼	½	1	1¼	Str	Fin	Jockey	Odds $1
19May73	⁸Pim¹	Secretariat	b 3 126	1	1ʰᵈ	1ʰᵈ	1⁷	1²⁰	1²⁸	1³¹	Turcotte R	.10
2Jun73	⁶Bel⁴	Twice A Prince	3 126	5	4⁵	4¹⁰	3ʰᵈ	2ʰᵈ	3¹²	2½	Baeza B	17.30
31May73	⁸Bel¹	My Gallant	b 3 126	3	3³	3ᴹ	4⁷	3²	2ʰᵈ	3¹⁵	Cordero A Jr	12.40
28May73	⁸GS²	Pvt. Smiles	b 3 126	2	5	5	5	5	5	4½	Gargan D	14.30
19May73	⁸Pim²	Sham	b 3 126	6	2⁵	2¹⁰	2⁷	4⁸	4¹½	5	Pincay L Jr	5.10

Time, :23%, :46½, 1:09¾, 1:34½, 1:59, 2:24, (Against wind in backstretch). Track fast.
New Track Record

$2 Mutuel Prices:

2-(A)-SECRETARIAT	2.20	2.40	—
5-(E)-TWICE A PRINCE		4.60	—

(No Show Wagering)

Ch. c, by Bold Ruler—Somethingroyal, by Princequillo. Trainer Laurin L L. Bred by Meadow Stud Inc (Va).

IN GATE AT 5:38; OFF AT 5:38, EDT. Start Good. Won Ridden out.

SECRETARIAT sent up along the inside to vie for the early lead with SHAM to the backstretch, disposed of that one after going three-quarters, drew off at will rounding the far turn and was under a hand ride from Turcotte to establish a record in a tremendous performance. TWICE A PRINCE, unable to stay with the leader early, moved through along the rail approaching the stretch and outfinished MY GALLANT for the place. The latter, void of early foot, moved with TWICE A PRINCE rounding the far turn and fought it out gamely with that one through the drive. PVT. SMILES showed nothing. SHAM alternated for the lead with SECRETARIAT to the backstretch, wasn't able to match stride with that rival after going three-quarters and stopped badly.

Owners— 1, Meadow Stable; 2, Elmendorf; 3, Appleton A I; 4, Whitney C V; 5, Sommer S.

Trainers— 1, Laurin L; 2, Campo J P; 3, Goldfine L M; 4, Poole G T; 5, Martin F.

Scratched—Knightly Dawn (28May73⁸GS¹).

Pace handicappers will find fractional times not to be found in the past performances. At some tracks, the five-furlong fractional time is given for six-furlong races. At most tracks, charts for six and one-half and seven-furlong races include the six-furlong fractional. For all route distances, the quarter-mile time is listed. And for middle-distance routes longer than a mile, the time for the first mile is reported.

SEVENTH RACE
Aqueduct
MARCH 28, 1983

7 FURLONGS. (1.20⅕) ALLOWANCE. Purse $20,000. 3–year–olds which have never won a race other than maiden or claiming. weight 122 lbs.; non–winners of a race other than claiming since March 1 allowed 3 lbs.; of such a race since Feb. 15, 5 lbs.

Value of race $20,000, value to winner $12,000, second $4,400, third $2,400, fourth $1,200. Mutuel pool $149,811, OTB pool $128,458. Track Exacta Pool $226,611. OTB Exacta Pool $224,261.

Last Raced	Horse	Eqt.A.Wt	PP	St	¼	½	Str	Fin	Jockey	Odds $1
3Mar83 ^{6}Aqu^{1}	Megaturn	3 122	4	4	6^{25}	6^{30}	$3^{1\frac{1}{2}}$	$1^{1\frac{3}{4}}$	Hernandez R	3.50
7Mar83 ^{5}GP^{2}	Very Funny	3 117	1	2	2^{hd}	4^{1}	$1^{\frac{1}{2}}$	$2^{1\frac{1}{4}}$	Velasquez J	10.50
13Mar83 ^{4}Aqu^{1}	All Of A Sudden	b 3 122	6	3	$3^{1\frac{1}{2}}$	$2^{1\frac{1}{2}}$	$2^{1\frac{1}{2}}$	$3^{1\frac{1}{2}}$	Smith A Jr	1.00
9Mar83 ^{6}Aqu^{5}	North Glade	3 119	3	6	$4^{1\frac{1}{2}}$	3^{2}	5^{1}	$4^{\frac{1}{2}}$	Beitia E	5.00
21Mar83 ^{7}Aqu^{2}	Dear Richard	b 3 117	5	5	5^{1}	$5^{3\frac{1}{2}}$	4^{hd}	$5^{2\frac{3}{4}}$	Santiago A	8.40
3Dec82 ^{7}Aqu^{7}	Fibak	b 3 117	7	1	$1^{1\frac{1}{2}}$	$1^{\frac{1}{2}}$	6	6	Miranda J	10.30
4Feb83 ^{5}Aqu^{6}	Ghent	b 3 117	2	7	7	7	—	—	Venezia M	39.10

Ghent, Distanced.
OFF AT 4:01 Start good for all but GHENT, Won ridden out. Time, :22⅕, :45, 1:10⅕, 1:22⅗ Track muddy.

$2 Mutuel Prices:			
4–(G)–MEGATURN	9.00	6.20	4.20
1–(B)–VERY FUNNY		9.40	4.80
6–(I)–ALL OF A SUDDEN			2.40

$2 EXACTA 4–1 PAID $81.00.

Dk. b. or br. c, by Best Turn—Good Taste, by Vertex. Trainer Nieminski Richard. Bred by Welcome Farm & Winn (Pa).

MEGATURN, unhurried early, rallied outside after settling into the stretch gained command approaching the sixteenth pole and drew clear under a hand ride, VERY FUNNY forced the early pace while racing slightly off the rail, fell back on the turn came again outside to gain command with a furlong to go but was no match for the winner. ALL OF A SUDDEN, a forward factor outside, challenged for command approaching the stretch but weakened soon after entering the stretch. NORTH GLADE within striking distance and saving ground early, checked behind FIBAK on the turn and fell back. DEAR RICHARD was not a serious factor. FIBAK set the pace racing slightly off the rail for just over a half and tired. GHENT broke awkwardly and was outdistanced after a half.

Owners— 1, Peace J H; 2, Jablow Andrea; 3, Freeark R H; 4, Rafsky J K; 5, Joia Stable; 6, Brant P M; 7, Garren M M.

Trainers— 1, Nieminski Richard; 2, Zito Nicholas P; 3, Pascuma Warren J; 4, Donato Robert A; 5, Baeza Braulio; 6, Jolley Leroy Jr; 7, Puentes Gilbert.

Scratched—Model Flight (16Mar83 ^{6}Aqu^{1}); Flip's Little Boy (21Mar83 ^{7}Aqu^{7}); Dependence (19Feb83 ^{5}Aqu^{5}).

The running lines in the result charts differ somewhat from their counterparts in the past performances. Instead of giving the margin behind the lead horse, they tell instead the margin ahead of the next horse. For example, the symbol 3–2 means the horse was running (finished) third, two lengths ahead of the fourth horse. It is up to the handicapper himself to calculate margins behind the lead horse.

The running lines appear under the headings:

PP	post position
St	position after start of race
¼	position after quarter mile

½	position after half mile
¾	position after three quarters (routes only)
Str	position in midstretch
Fin	position at finish

Should a horse not finish the race, dashes will appear instead of running positions and lengths behind, and a note will appear immediately below the running lines in the chart:

NINTH RACE
Aqueduct
MARCH 10, 1983

$1\frac{1}{16}$ MILES.(INNER DIRT). (1.42⅖) CLAIMING. Purse $11,000. Fillies and Mares, 4–year–olds and upward. Weight, 122 lbs. Non–winners of two races at a mile or over since February 1 allowed 3 lbs. Of such a race then 5 lbs. Claiming price $10,000; for each $500 to $9,000 2 lbs. (Races when entered to be claimed for $8,000 or less not considered.)

Value of race $11,000, value to winner $6,600, second $2,420, third $1,320, fourth $660. Mutuel pool $75,811, OTB pool $197,233. Trifecta Pool $146,713. OTB Trifecta Pool $300,649.

Last Raced	Horse	Eqt	A.Wt	PP	St	¼	½	¾	Str	Fin	Jockey	Cl'g Pr	Odds $1
28Feb83 ^{7}Aqu^{11}	Ever Higher	b	4 117	8	9	9^{2}	9^{3}	4^{4}	2^{hd}	$1^{\frac{3}{4}}$	Graell A	10000	20.10
6Mar83 ^{1}Aqu^{8}	Diamond Shamrock		5 113	7	3	1^{4}	1^{5}	1^{3}	1^{3}	2^{3}	Santagata N	9000	12.00
26Feb83 ^{5}Key^{4}	Quisqueya	b	5 113	3	4	$4^{\frac{1}{2}}$	5^{5}	3^{3}	4^{6}	$3^{\frac{3}{4}}$	Gomez E R	9000	22.00
22Feb83 ^{9}Key^{1}	Vallerina Miss	b	5 110	10	7	2^{2}	2^{4}	2^{3}	$3^{1\frac{1}{2}}$	$4^{6\frac{1}{2}}$	Alvarado R Jr^{5}	9000	3.80
24Feb83 ^{1}Aqu^{5}	Coosahatchee	b	5 117	9	6	$5^{1\frac{1}{2}}$	$4^{\frac{1}{2}}$	$5^{\frac{1}{2}}$	5^{3}	$5^{1\frac{3}{4}}$	Migliore R	10000	8.60
11Feb83 ^{1}Aqu^{1}	Double Dacquare	b	6 114	4	10	10	10	8^{2}	7^{6}	6^{5}	Powers T M^{5}	10000	6.10
28Feb83 ^{1}Aqu^{1}	Jen's Doll		4 115	1	1	$8^{1\frac{1}{2}}$	$7^{\frac{1}{2}}$	$6^{\frac{1}{2}}$	$6^{\frac{1}{2}}$	7^{5}	Smith A Jr	9500	2.50
28Feb83 ^{1}Aqu^{2}	Ultimate Step	b	4 113	6	8	$6^{\frac{1}{2}}$	6^{hd}	9	9	$8^{1\frac{3}{4}}$	Miranda J	9000	8.50
2Mar83 ^{1}Aqu^{8}	Elevenses		5 108	2	2	3^{hd}	3^{hd}	7^{3}	8^{hd}	9	Davis R G^{5}	9000	7.90
23Feb83 ^{6}Aqu^{8}	Alabama Time		4 117	5	5	7^{2}	$8^{1\frac{1}{2}}$	10	—	—	McKnight J	10000	25.00

Alabama Time, Distanced.

OFF AT 4:42. Start good, Won driving. Time, :23⅗, :47⅘, 1:13⅗, 1:41⅕, 1:48⅖ Track sloppy.

$2 Mutuel Prices:				
	9–(K)–EVER HIGHER	42.20	17.00	8.60
	8–(J)–DIAMOND SHAMROCK		12.40	8.40
	5–(E)–QUISQUEYA			9.60

$2 TRIFECTA 9–8–5 PAID $7,456.00.

B. f, by Take Your Place—Lady Everest, by Fathers Image. Trainer Alvarez H G. Bred by Mountan P C (NY).

EVER HIGHER without early speed, commenced a rally leaving backstretch, came outside late and wore down DIAMOND SHAMROCK in final strides. Latter drew out to long lead in early stages, settled into stretch well in front, but could not hold off winner. QUISQUEYA forwardly placed early, lacked a rally. VALLERINA MISS raced nearest leader to stretch and weakened while saving ground. COOSAHATCHEE had no rally. DOUBLE DACQUARE far back early, showed little. JEN'S DOLL was outrun. ULTIMATE STEP had no speed. ELEVENSES had some early foot and gave way. ALABAMA TIME lost contace with his field.

Owners— 1, Bellrose Farm; 2, Quindecima Stable; 3, Sech S; 4, Lane G E; 5, Nicodemo N; 6, Girdner Kay C; 7, Sweet Meadow Farm; 8, Sorhagen Angela; 9, Laranda Stable; 10, Venable Martha B.

Trainers— 1, Alvarez H G; 2, Pascuma James J Jr; 3, Sech Stephen; 4, Sedlacek Michael C; 5, O'Brien Colum; 6, Lake Robert P; 7, Gullo Thomas J; 8, Pinero A; 9, STAKLOSA RICHARD; 10, Arnold George R II.

Scratched—Dancing Swan (2Mar83 ^{1}Aqu^{3}); Caribbinn (6Mar83 ^{1}Aqu^{4}); Lady Clown (28Feb83 ^{1}Aqu^{3}).

Also appearing on each line are the horse's age (A), weight carried (Wt), jockey (with apprentice allowance taken), and claiming price (Cl'g pr).

The name of a horse disqualified will be preceded by the symbol [D], with a relevant comment appearing beneath the running lines. The names of horses finishing in a dead heat will be preceded by the symbol [DH].

THIRD RACE
Aqueduct
MARCH 10, 1983

1 ¹⁄₁₆ MILES.(INNER DIRT). (1.42⅖) CLAIMING. Purse $12,500. 4–year–olds and up-
ward. Weight, 122 lbs. Non–winners of two races at a mile or over since February 1
allowed 3 lbs. Of such a race since then 5 lbs. Claiming price $16,000; for each $1,000 to
$14,000 allowed 2 lbs. (Races when entered to be claimed for $12,500 or less not considered.)

Value of race $12,500, value to winner $7,500, second $2,750, third $1,500, fourths $375 each. Mutuel pool $89,570, OTB
pool $146,483. Track Exacta Pool $162,782. OTB Exacta Pool $239,289.

Last Raced	Horse	Eqt.A.Wt	PP	St	¼	½	¾	Str	Fin	Jockey	Cl'g Pr	Odds $1
25Feb83 3Aqu¹	On The Charles	4 106	4	1	5½	5²	3½	1½	11½	Messina R⁷	14000	14.30
2Mar83 5Aqu¹⁰	Ben Marino	b 5 117	3	10	10¹	11²	11³	7½	2½	Diaz J R	16000	29.00
9Feb83 6Aqu¹⁰	Rout	4 113	1	8	7¹½	7½	7²	4²	3¾	Graell A	14000	
28Feb83 9Aqu³	ⒹJoycapade	b 5 117	5	12	12	12	9³	5ʰᵈ	4ⁿᵏ	Santagata N	16000	8.10
7Mar83 3Aqu¹	ⒹⒽKing of Classics	b 8 108	7	2	42½	31½	1¹	2½	5	Davis R G⁵	14000	8.80
2Mar83 9Aqu⁹	ⒹⒽCommanche Brave	b 4 113	8	4	1ʰᵈ	2ʰᵈ	21½	3³	5ⁿᵏ	Gomez E R	14000	19.30
28Feb83 9Aqu⁴	So Awesome	4 117	2	9	9²	91½	5¹	6½	74¾	Gonzalez M A	16000	30.60
7Feb83¹⁰GP⁴	Bold Blue Star	b 5 112	11	11	11²	8½	8½	8⁴	81½	Alvarado R Jr⁵	16000	16.40
23Feb83 1Aqu⁶	Prather's Image	b 5 117	6	6	8ʰᵈ	10ʰᵈ	10¹	9²	94½	Miranda J	16000	6.60
2Mar83 5Aqu¹¹	Oil Can Harry	b 4 117	10	7	6⁴	6⁴	6½	10½	104½	Samyn J L	16000	12.80
6Mar83 2Aqu⁶	Christopher Star	4 113	12	5	2ʰᵈ	1ʰᵈ	4²	11⁵	11⁴	Lovato F Jr	14000	20.40
21Jan83 9Aqu⁷	Our Celtic Heir	5 117	9	3	3³	41½	12	12	12	Smith A Jr	16000	1.10

Ⓓ–Joycapade Disqualified and placed twelfth.
ⒹⒽ–Dead heat.
OFF AT 1:58. Start good for all but JOYCAPADE and BOLD BLUE STAR. Won driving. Time, :23⅕, :47⅕, 1:12⅗,
1:39⅗, 1:46⅖ Track sloppy.

$2 Mutuel Prices:	4–(E)–ON THE CHARLES	30.60	15.60	8.60
	3–(D)–BEN MARINO		25.00	10.20
	1–(A)–ROUT			19.60

$2 EXACTA 4–3 PAID $852.80.

Gr. g, by Upper Case—Collegiate Style, by Quadrangle. Trainer Ferraro James W. Bred by Kinsman Stud Farm
(Fla).

ON THE CHARLES saved ground to the stretch turn, eased out for running room, rallied and held in a drive.
BEN MARINO, without any speed, worked his way between horses in the early stretch, angled out and closed
strongly. ROUT came to the outside for the drive and finished with good energy. JOYCAPADE dwelt at the start,
moved up between horses in the drive, came over on SO AWESOME late and was not a threat. After a stewards
inquiry, JOYCAPADE was disqualified from fourth and placed 12th. KING OF THE CLASSICS moved quickly
to circle horses on the far turn, took a short lead, gave way and finished in a dead heat with COMMANCHE
BRAVE. COMMANCHE BRAVE, well placed from the start, tired late. SO AWESOME was beaten when bothered
late. BOLD BLUE STAR went in the air at the break and lost all chance. PRATHER'S IMAGE was outrun. OIL
CAN HARRY tired. CHRISTOPHER STAR, near the front early, tired badly. OUR CELTIC HEIR flashed brief
speed and stopped.

Owners— 1, Carrington Mary M; 2, Old Star Stable; 3, Cohen M; 4, Kerr Mrs D K; 5, Barrera O S; 6,
Lacatena F P; 7, Mitchell Nancy; 8, Lane G E; 9, Giorgio R; 10, Bus Boys Stable; 11, Garren M M; 12, Rogers
Barbara D.

Trainers— 1, Ferraro James W; 2, Sherwood Colin G; 3, Schaeffer Stephen; 4, Nieminski Richard; 5,
Barrera Oscar S; 6, Delvecchio Dominick; 7, Benshoft Ronald L; 8, Sedlacek Michael C; 9, O'Connell Richard;
10, Nocella Vincent; 11, Puentes Gilbert; 12, Pascuma Warren J.

Prather's Image was claimed by Brill Sandra; trainer, Pagano Frank X Jr; Our Celtic Heir was claimed by Panta
Stable; trainer, Barrera Luis.

Scratched—Solid Gold Soul (15Jan83 1Aqu⁵); Shanty To Castle (23Feb83 2Aqu³); Another Rodger (6Mar83
2Aqu⁷); Alturas (23Feb83 1Aqu¹⁰); Quicksilver Luck (17Feb83 2Aqu¹¹); Ten Oclock Scholar (6Mar83 2Aqu¹³)

Appearing above the running lines is a description of the purse and
its distribution among the first four (or five) finishers, together with the
pari-mutuel and exotic pool totals.

To the right of the running lines are the final odds for each horse. A
pari-mutuel entry is indicated by the letter *a* appearing before the odds
of the coupled horses. Should there be two or more entries in the same
race, the letters *b*, *c*, and so on, are used to distinguish between entries.
Horses coupled in a pari-mutuel field are distinguished by the letter *f*
preceding their odds. A note explaining these symbols appears immediately below the running lines.

FOURTH RACE **6 FURLONGS.(INNER DIRT). (1.08⅘) MAIDEN SPECIAL WEIGHT. Purse $18,000.** 3-year-olds. Weight, 122 lbs.

Aqueduct

MARCH 13, 1983

Value of race $18,000, value to winner $10,800, second $3,960, third $2,160, fourth $1,080. Mutuel pool $156,485, OTB pool $122,229. Quinella Pool $253,596. OTB Quinella Pool $193,970

Last Raced	Horse	Eqt.	A.	Wt	PP	St	¼	½	Str	Fin	Jockey	Odds $1
3Mar83 ^{4}Aqu^{2}	All Of A Sudden	b	3	122	4	7	$3\frac{1}{2}$	3^{2}	$1^{2\frac{1}{2}}$	1^{7}	Smith A Jr	.60
3Mar83 ^{6}Aqu^{4}	Vague Reality	b	3	117	10	1	1^{hd}	1^{hd}	2^{4}	2^{3}	Davis R G^{5}	13.90
3Mar83 ^{6}Aqu^{5}	Bon Apetite		3	122	1	12	8^{1}	7^{1}	5^{3}	3^{nk}	Cordero A Jr	7.50
	Teriyaki Stake		3	112	7	14	7^{hd}	$4\frac{1}{2}$	$3^{1\frac{1}{2}}$	4^{nk}	Alvarado R Jr^{5}	22 20
3Mar83 ^{6}Aqu^{7}	Naskra's Gold		3	122	9	11	5^{hd}	5^{2}	$4\frac{1}{2}$	$5^{5\frac{3}{4}}$	Graell A	f-17.50
14Feb83 ^{4}Aqu^{13}	Straight Talk	b	3	122	11	10	12	11^{3}	$7\frac{1}{2}$	6^{nk}	Lovato F Jr	f-17.50
	John Favor		3	122	8	2	2^{1}	2^{hd}	6^{2}	7^{hd}	Vergara O	23.10
21Feb83 ^{6}Aqu^{10}	Proud Pauper	b	3	122	13	3	6^{1}	6^{hd}	8^{2}	$8^{2\frac{1}{2}}$	Maple E†	31.40
3Mar83 ^{4}Aqu^{5}	Go Golato		3	122	14	5	11^{hd}	10^{hd}	9^{5}	9^{4}	McCarron G	a-24.10
	My Man Scott		3	122	6	13	$13^{2\frac{1}{2}}$	12^{5}	$11^{1\frac{1}{2}}$	$10^{\frac{3}{4}}$	Miranda J	16.30
3Mar83 ^{6}Aqu^{6}	Held Blameless		3	122	12	4	$10\frac{1}{2}$	9^{hd}	10^{hd}	$11^{\frac{3}{4}}$	Gonzalez M A	a-24.10
	Star Hustler		3	122	3	8	14	14	12^{3}	$12^{5\frac{1}{4}}$	Hernandez R	56.80
23Feb83 ^{4}Aqu^{9}	Byram		3	122	5	9	$9\frac{1}{2}$	13^{1}	$13^{1\frac{1}{2}}$	$13^{6\frac{1}{2}}$	Samyn J L	56.90
	Intersection	b	3	122	2	6	$4\frac{1}{2}$	$8\frac{1}{2}$	14	14	Venezia M	11.70

a-Coupled: Go Golato and Held Blameless.
f—Mutuel field.

OFF AT 2:40 Start good, Won ridden out. Time, :23, :46⅘, 1:10⅖ Track fast.

$2 Mutuel Prices:				
	5-(D)-ALL OF A SUDDEN	3.20	2.40	2.20
	10-(J)-VAGUE REALITY		6.20	4.20
	2-(A)-BON APETITE			3.80
	$2 QUINELLA 5-10 PAID $16.00.			

Ro. c, by Ramsinga—Sudden Snow, by Tudor Grey. Trainer Pascuma Warren J. Bred by Freeark R H (Ill).

ALL OF A SUDDEN, forwardly placed early, moved quickly to gain command in the early stretch and was ridden out while widening. VAGUE REALITY moved out to a short early lead, held to the stretch, but was no match for the winner. BON APETITE, allowed to settle, bested the others in a drive. TERIYAKI STAKE lacked a closing response. NASKRA'S GOLD had no late rally. STRAIGHT TALK passed tired rivals. JOHN FAVOR prompted the pace to the stretch and weakened. GO GOLATO showed little. MY MAN SCOTT was outrun. STAR HUSTLER was never close. INTERSECTION had some early foot and stopped.

Owners— 1, Freeark R H; 2, Boyan T; 3, Buckingham Farm; 4, McNall B; 5, Pambi Stable; 6, Humphrey G W Jr; 7, DiNatle Angelo; 8, Flying Zee Stable; 9, Rosenthal Mrs M; 10, Triple Fox Stable; 11, Johnson Kathy M; 12, Schwartz B K; 13, Peace J H; 14, Greathouse D T.

Trainers— 1, Pascuma Warren J; 2, Jerkens H Allen; 3, Nesky Kenneth A; 4, Nickerson Victor J; 5, Picou James E; 6, Kay Michael; 7, Morgan Jack B; 8, Martin Jose; 9, Johnson Philip G; 10, Ramos Faustino F; 11, Johnson Philip G; 12, Kurtz Gus R; 13, Nieminski Richard; 14, Arnold George R II.

† Apprentice allowance waived: Proud Pauper 7 pounds.

Scratched—Exclusive Bear; Medal Petal (21Feb83 ^{6}Aqu^{14}); Let's Be Frank (21Feb83 ^{6}Aqu^{3}); Speke's Quest; Model Flight (3Mar83 ^{6}Aqu^{3}); Campbell Hall (5Mar83 ^{4}Aqu^{7}).

Also appearing below the running lines are the pari-mutuel prices for win, place, and show, plus the results of any exotic wagering on the race.

Directly above the race comments can be found the breeding of the winner, together with the name of its trainer and breeder. A listing of owners and trainers, in order of finish, can be found immediately below the race comments.

There is but one difference between the formats of the result charts published in the Eastern and Western editions of the *Form*. The Western editions do not include the list of trainers in order of finish.

NINTH RACE

Aqueduct

APRIL 21, 1983

6 FURLONGS. (1.08⅕) ALLOWANCE. Purse $27,000. 3-year-olds and upward. Foaled in New York state and approved by the New York State Bred Registry which have never won two races. Weight: 3-year-olds 112 lbs. Older 124 lbs. Non-winners of a race other than Claiming since April 1 allowed 3 lbs.

Value of race $27,000, value to winner $16,200, second $5,940, third $3,240, fourth $1,620. Mutuel pool $154,666, OTB pool $221,862.

Last Raced	Horse	Eqt.A.Wt PP St	¼	½	Str	Fin	Jockey	Odds $1
10Apr83 5Aqu2	D Sharp Destiny	3 111 5 6	4¹	4½	2hd	1hd	Santagata N	3.20
31Mar83 9Aqu3	Stiff Upper Lip	3 112 4 12	1²	8¹½	3¹½	2³	Velasquez J	4.60
10Apr83 5Aqu3	Quadratic's Pride	b 3 102 11 3	3½	3¹½	1hd	3¹½	Thibeau R J⁷	9.20
10Apr83 5Aqu4	J. Daniel B.	3 109 9 5	6½	6¹	4½	4½	Hernandez C	31.20
5Apr83 9Aqu1	Jaipur's Darling	3 112 8 8	11²	11²	5¹	5½	Samyn J L	4.00
26Jan83 6Aqu11	Mr. Tatt	4 116 7 10	9½	7hd	6¹½	6¹	Davis R G⁵	18.90
26Sep82 9FL1	Bix	3 107 1 4	1¹	1hd	7hd	7nk	Clayton M D⁵	5.00
1Apr83 2Aqu4	Northern Exchange	3 111 2 7	7¹	9hd	8²	8no	Lovato F Jr	12.50
1Apr83 2Aqu8	Splash Me	b 4 121 12 1	5½	5hd	9²	9²¾	Fell J	76.20
1Apr83 2Aqu6	Positively French	b 4 114 6 11	8hd	10hd	10³	10³	Murphy D J⁷	34.10
1Apr83 2Aqu10	Our Tuffy	b 4 121 10 2	2¹½	2¹	11²½	11¹½	Rogers K L†	17.10
7Apr83 7Aqu7	Philip's Daughter	4 116 3 9	10²	12	12	12	Venezia M	17.80

D-Sharp Destiny Disqualified and placed fourth.

OFF AT 5:02 Start good Won driving. Time, :22⅕, :45⅗, 1:10⅖ Track fast.

$2 Mutuel Prices:	4-(D)-STIFF UPPER LIP	11.20	6.80	5.00
	11-(K)-QUADRATIC'S PRIDE		9.20	4.80
	9-(I)-J. DANIEL B.			11.40

Stiff Upper Lip—B. g, by Upper Nile—Grinand Bearit, by Olympia. Trainer Kay Michael. Bred by Humphrey Jr & Jones B C (NY).

SHARP DESTINY, saving ground early, moved out entering the stretch coming out in front of J. DANIELS B., engaged the leaders with a furlong to go and outfinished STIFF UPPER LIP. Following a stewards inquiry and a claim of foul by the rider f J. DANIEL B. against the winner for interference just after entering the stretch, SHARP DESTINY was disqualified and placed fourth. STIFF UPPER LIP, void of early foot, rallied strongly outside into the stretch but could not get up. QUADRATIC'S PRIDE, up close and outside early, gained a narrow advantage in upper stretch but was no match for the top two in the final furlong. J. DANIEL B., between horses early, steadied when SHARP DESTINY came out entering the stretch and lacked a closing rally. JAIPUR'S DARLING passed tired horses outside. BIX saved ground in making the pace but tired entering the stretch. SPLASH ME raced outside and tired. OUR TUFFY forced the pace outside BIX for a half and tired.

Owners— 1, Chem Dance Stable; 2, Humphrey G W Jr; 3, Caronia C A; 4, Sagarin P; 5, Goldenapple Stable; 6, Headstream Stable; 7, MacMillen W Jr; 8, DiMauro S; 9, Edwards R L; 10, Daren J; 11, Tufano S; 12, Bletal Stables.

Trainers— 1, Brice Harold B Jr; 2, Kay Michael; 3, Hertler John O; 4, Walsh Thomas M; 5, Johnson Philip G; 6, Preger Mitchell C; 7, Kellman William; 8, DiMauro Stephen L; 9, Braun George E; 10, Nocella Vincent; 11 DiAngelo Joseph T; 12, Schoenborn Everett F.

Immediately above the pari-mutuel payoffs, one finds the time of the day at which the race started, and the condition of the racing surface at that time. Grass conditions will be reported as "Course Firm," or "Course Soft."

☐ EQUIPMENT ☐

Just to the right of a horse's name in the running lines, under the heading Eqt, appears (for some horses) the symbol *b* indicating that the horse was wearing blinkers. At one time, the *Form* made special note in the result charts of horses changing to or from blinkers. Although this no longer is the practice, the past performances do reveal whether or not a horse wore blinkers in its races. The symbol *b* appears immediately to the left of the weight carried whenever a horse races with blinkers. And the listing of graded entries published daily in the *Form* points out (as a footnote) all horses changing to or from blinkers for their scheduled race that day.

Victorious — Ch. c. 2, by Explodent—Paris Breeze, by Majestic Prince — Br.—O'Farrell & West & Ocala Stud Inc (FLa) — Tr.—Jacobs Eugene — **119**
Own.—Allen Herbert
Lifetime 6 3 1 0 $125,620 — 1982 6 3 1 0 $125,620

12Sep82-	8Bel	fst	7f	:23	:46⅕	1:24⅕	Futurity	1	3	11	2hd	44	57¾	Velasquez J	b	122	5.60	73-19	Copelan 1224¾ Satan's Charger 122½ Pax In Bello 1221¾	Tired	6
28Aug82-	8Sar	fst	6½f	:22⅕	:44⅘	1:16⅗	Hopeful	6	2	52¼	31½	32½	23¼	Cordero A Jr		122	*2.40	86-13	Copelan 1223¼ Victorious 122½ Aloha Hawaii 122½	Gained second	9
9Aug82-	8Sar	my	6f	:22	:45¾	1:10¾	Sar Special	1	4	54	43½	31	1¼	Cordero A Jr		122	2.20	87-16	Victorious 122½ Pappa Riccio 1244 Safe Ground 1191½	Driving	7
7Jly82-	7Bel	fst	5½f	:22⅕	:46	1:05⅗	Juvenile	6	5	45½	45	2½	1¾	Cordero A Jr		122	4.60	87-18	Victorious 122¾ Northern Ice 1151½ Laus' Cause 122¾	Ridden out	7
7Jun82-	8Bel	gd	5½f	:22	:45⅖	1:04⅖	Youthful	1	2	22	34	68½	613	Bailey J D		122	*1.10	80-13	Flying Pocket1221GreatEnding1171½Satan'sCharger1172	Stopped	6
26May82-	8Bel	fst	5½f	:22⅗	:46	1:04⅕	Flash	2	1	1½	1hd	12	14½	Bailey J D		115	5.90	94-11	Victorious1154½Satan'sCharger1191½GreatEnding119¾	Ridden out	7

LATEST WORKOUTS ●Sep 25 Bel tr.t 5f fst 1:00 h — Sep 20 Bel tr.t 5f fst 1:03 b — ●Sep 9 Bel tr.t 4f fst :46⅗ h — ●Sep 5 Bel 7f fst 1:24⅖ hg

Trainers use blinkers in an attempt to focus their charge's attention straight ahead, to keep the animal's mind on the business at hand, or perhaps simply to wake the horse up, give it a different perspective on life. Blinkers are supposed to keep a horse from looking around. They often have the added effect of increasing a horse's early speed. Note that Victorious outran Copelan in the early stages of the Belmont Futurity September 12, when blinkers were added to his equipment. Previously, in the Hopeful Stakes at Saratoga, Victorious had raced behind Copelan throughout. Of course, adding blinkers while at the same time stretching a horse out to a route distance is not a bright maneuver. If the horse has any speed whatsoever, it probably will prove unrateable on the early lead. Notice that trainer Gene Norman removed the blinkers from Explosive Wagon just prior to stretching the speedy colt out to the route distances. Without the hood, the colt was able to relax and be rated, and became the best three-year-old on the Louisiana circuit.

Explosive Wagon * — Ch. c. 3, by Explodent—Gypsy Wagon, by Conestoga — Br.—Windy City Stable (Fla) — Tr.—Norman Gene — **126**
Own.—McReynolds Peggy
Lifetime 15 9 2 2 $151,110 — 1983 6 3 0 1 $68,460 — 1982 9 6 2 1 $82,650

23Apr83-	9LaD	sl	1$\frac{1}{16}$	:48⅘	1:13⅘	1:45⅖	Hol In Dixie	2	6	4nk	1hd	14	14	Mueller C		124	*.40	85-22	ExplosiveWagon1244Emperor'sClothes1147½Hrrowgte1142	Easily	7
27Mar83-	11FG	fst	1⅛	:47⅘	1:12⅘	1:50⅗	La Derby	8	5	64½	64	54	55½	Mueller C		123	*1.20	85-20	BalboNtive118½FoundPerlHrbor1132¾Slewpv123¾	C rr'd out,1st tr	8
12Mar83-	10FG	fst	1$\frac{1}{16}$	:48⅖	1:13	1:43⅘	Handicap	2	6	51¾	31½	11½	15½	Mueller C		119	*.90	93-18	ExplosiveWgon1195½HilToRome1144½TemerityPrinc115hd	Handily	7
19Feb83-	10FG	fst	1$\frac{1}{16}$	:47⅖	1:11⅘	1:45	Lecomte H	8	7	76¾	55½	2hd	13	Mueller C		116	12.80	87-19	ExplosivWgon1163FoundPrlHrbor1164½ProntoForli1205	Drew off	11
5Feb83-	9FG	fst	6f	:21⅘	:45⅗	1:11	Blk Gold H	6	1	13	12	31	56¾	Mueller C	b	120	1.90	83-15	Pronto Forli 1174½ One For Auntie 113nk Willow Drive 1162	Tired	7
15Jan83-	9FG	fst	6f	:22	:45⅘	1:11⅕	Master Dby H	5	2	2½	1½	2hd	34	Mueller C	b	122	*.30	85-17	Pronto Forli 1141½ Willow Drive 1162½ExplosiveWagon1221	Tired	9
31Dec82-	9FG	fst	6f	:21⅗	:45⅘	1:11⅖	Sugarbowl H	3	7	64½	52¾	11½	14	Mueller C	b	119	2.60	88-22	ExplosiveWgon1194ErnstLuck114½Mindboggling1131½	Ridden out	10
12Dec82-	5FG	gd	6f	:22⅖	:46	1:12⅖	Alw 11000	2	3	1hd	1½	1hd	1½	Mueller C	b	116	*.90	83-22	Explosive Wagon 116½ Hamlet 1131½ Chance A Lot 1132½	Driving	9
17Oct82-	4LaD	fst	6½f	:22⅕	:44⅗	1:16⅕	Alw 17000	6	4	2½	2hd	1hd	18	Mueller C	b	122	*1.70	101-07	Explosive Wagon 1228 Chance A Lot 1193HailToRome1196	Easily	12
2Oct82-	9LaD	fst	6½f	:22⅗	:45⅗	1:17	Alw 18000	4	4	2½	11	13½	13	Mueller C	b	122	9.20	97-09	Explosive Wagon 1223 Wild Again 119½ Joe Joe 1192½	In hand	12
24Sep82-	6LaD	fst	6f	:23	:46⅖	1:12	Alw 14000	5	10	41¼	3nk	2½	1nk	Mueller C	b	122	*1.90	89-15	ExplosiveWgon122nkMomentofRelity1143DoubleLine114½	Driving	12
3Sep82-	9LaD	fst	6f	:23	:46⅕	1:12	Alw 14000	2	5	2½	22	22½	21	Mueller C	b	120	2.30	88-12	Chance A Lot 1171ExplosiveWagon1204½CharleyKirk1124	Gamely	10
27Aug82-	7LaD	fst	6f	:22⅖	:45⅗	1:12	Alw 15000	4	6	41½	2hd	11½	32	Perrodin E J	b	122	4.60	81-10	Mr. Storeman 119½ Soy's Hope 1171½ ExplosiveWagon1222½	Tired	10
6Aug82-	6LaD	fst	6f	:22⅗	:45⅘	1:11⅕	Alw 12500	4	9	41¾	33	34	24	Mueller C	b	120	*1.60	83-10	TemerityPrinc1204ExplosivWgon1202½SunburndBby1176½	Fair try	11
22Jly82-	5LaD	fst	6f	:22⅖	:45⅘	1:13⅕	Md Sp Wt	7	5	14	16	16	14½	Mueller C	b	120	4.10	77-16	ExplosiveWagon1204½OcenKingdom1202LndingChief1201	In hand	12

LATEST WORKOUTS ●May 5 CD 5f fst 1:00⅕ h — Apr 21 LaD 4f fst :47⅗ b — Apr 16 LaD 5f fst :58 b — Mar 25 FG 4f fst :49⅖ b

Blinkers can have the possible side effect of preventing a horse from seeing a challenger coming up on either side. For horses that bear out or in, a special partially closed blinker can be added to the right or left eye, preventing the horse from seeing, and therefore drifting, in that direction. These blinkers can be cut slightly in the back to give the horse a rear view of rivals edging up from behind.

A small study of two-year-olds changing equipment ("blinkers on" or "blinkers off") proved conclusively that the simple change of equipment was no panacea. Curiously, however, horses that had added blinkers at some point, but were now running without them, showed great promise.

	NH	NW	WPCT	MPCT	I.V.	$NET
Blinkers On	232	18	4.8%	25.0%	0.70	$0.83
Blinkers Off	36	1	2.8%	36.1%	0.25	$0.46
Blinkers On Again	30	5	16.7%	30.0%	1.50	$1.43
Blinkers Off Again	42	10	23.8%	47.6%	2.14	$3.47

These statistics bothered me, yet every time I attempted to analyze this factor, the results were similar. I began to believe that horses winning with "blinkers on" did so randomly. It was only after a recent conversation with Glenn Magnell that I saw what others had failed to explain. For most horses, the addition of blinkers is a desperation move on the part of the trainer, and is best ignored by serious handicappers. But for certain horses, it is a significant change, marking the horse as a prime betting proposition. The kind of horse we refer to is lightly raced and has shown some promise without producing the expected results as yet. The horse may have worked well in the mornings, but failed to race to its workouts in the afternoons. It may have raced unevenly, or only in spots, as if distracted by the presence of other horses and unable to concentrate on its task as well as it had in the mornings. An especially promising sign is betting action in the horse's debut, then again in its second start, even if the horse's performance first time out fell below expectations.

All of this adds up to a trainer who feels that his horse has some ability and is not satisfied with its performance to date, but feels the addition of blinkers will remedy the problem. Mayanesian was a good example. Favored in his first two starts, but speed crazy, the colt settled down somewhat at Saratoga, after blinkers had been added.

Other forms of equipment have significance too, yet no mention is made of them in the *Form*. A horse might wear "mud caulks" to gain better traction over a wet track. However, if a horse is shod for mud caulks in anticipation of rain, it would be hindered should the rains not materialize, and the track remain fast. At times, the result charts will identify horses that wore mud caulks. Note that Star Choice was one of only three horses wearing mud caulks for the 1983 Metropolitan Handicap.

EIGHTH RACE
Belmont
MAY 30, 1983

1 MILE. (1.33) 90th Running THE METROPOLITAN HANDICAP (Grade I). Purse $200,000 added. 3-year-olds and upward. By subscription of $500 each, which should accompany the nomination; $1,500 to pass the entry box, with $200,000 added. The added money and all fees to be divided 60% to the winner, 22% to second, 12% to third and 6% to fourth. Weights Wednesday, May 25. Starters to be named at the closing time of entries. Trophies will be presented to the winning owner, trainer and jockey. Closed with 39 nominations Wednesday, May 11, 1983.
Value of race $242,000, value to winner $145,200, second $53,240, third $29,040, fourth $14,520. Mutuel pool $362,822, OTB pool $212,747.

Last Raced	Horse	Eqt.	A.	Wt	PP	St	¼	½	¾	Str	Fin	Jockey	Odds $1
15May83 ^{1}Aqu^{2}	Star Choice		4	113	2	11	3½	3½	2^{3}	1^{hd}	$1^{1\frac{1}{2}}$	Velasquez J	17.00
7May83 ^{8}Aqu^{7}	Tough Critic		4	110	3	4	1½	1^{2}	$1^{1\frac{1}{2}}$	2^{5}	$2^{3\frac{3}{4}}$	MacBeth D	21.10
16May83 ^{8}Aqu^{1}	John's Gold		4	111	8	5	5½	5^{hd}	5^{2}	4½	3^{2}	Graell A	a-4.20
18May83 ^{8}Bel^{4}	Stiff Sentence	b	6	113	1	6	$2^{1\frac{1}{2}}$	4^{2}	4½	3^{hd}	4½	Fell J	31.30
18May83 ^{8}Bel^{3}	Sing Sing		5	121	6	9	$9^{1\frac{1}{2}}$	9^{3}	9^{3}	$7^{1\frac{1}{2}}$	5^{nk}	Alvarado R Jr	a-4.20
15May83 ^{1}Aqu^{1}	West On Broad	b	5	110	13	2	13	13	$11^{1\frac{1}{2}}$	10^{1}	6^{hd}	Venezia M	20.20
7May83 ^{8}Aqu^{1}	Vittorioso	b	4	115	4	13	$8^{1\frac{1}{2}}$	8^{1}	7^{3}	5^{2}	$7^{1\frac{1}{2}}$	Cordero A Jr	8.00
7May83 ^{8}Aqu^{3}	Fit to Fight		4	115	9	3	7^{hd}	6^{4}	6^{hd}	8^{1}	8no	Bailey J D	1.50
15May83 ^{1}Aqu^{3}	Otter Slide		4	110	7	7	6^{1}	7^{hd}	8½	9½	9^{1}	Samyn J L	32.60
6May83 ^{8}Aqu^{3}	Silver Supreme	b	5	115	5	12	11½	12^{5}	10^{3}	11^{6}	10^{2}	Asmussen C B	7.70
3May83 ^{8}CD^{2}	Eminency	b	5	121	12	1	4^{1}	2½	3^{2}	6½	$11^{4\frac{1}{2}}$	Maple E	14.30
8May83 ^{7}Aqu^{3}	Key Count		4	110	11	8	12^{5}	10^{hd}	$12^{1\frac{1}{2}}$	12½	12^{hd}	Smith A Jr	25.90
23Apr83 ^{7}Aqu^{1}	Bounding Basque	b	3	112	10	10	10^{1}	11½	13	13	13	McCarron G	16.10

a-Coupled: John's Gold and Sing Sing.
OFF AT 5:02 Start good for all but VITTORIOSO. Won driving. Time, :22⅗, :44⅖, 1:08⅕, 1:33⅘ Track muddy.

$2 Mutuel Prices:				
	3-(B)-STAR CHOICE	**36.00**	**16.20**	**10.20**
	4-(C)-TOUGH CRITIC		**18.40**	**9.00**
	1-(H)-JOHN'S GOLD (a-entry)			**3.60**

B. c, by In Reality—Some Swinger, by Tirreno. Trainer Veitch John M. Bred by Frances A Genter Stable (Fla).

STAR CHOICE quickly reached contention rallied from between horses on the turn, caught TOUGH CRITIC with a furlong remaining and proved clearly best. TOUGH CRITIC showed good early foot while racing well out from the rail, shook off STIFF SENTENCE nearing the turn, held a clear lead into the stretch but wasn't able to withstand the winner while besting the others. JOHN'S GOLD had no apparent excuse. STIFF SENTENCE saved ground into the stretch but lacked a late response. SING SING failed to be a serious factor. WEST ON BROAD found best stride too late. VITTORIOSO appeared unprepared for the start, rushing up along the inside on the backstretch but failed to be a serious factor. FIT TO FIGHT moved up outside horses at the turn but lacked a further response. OTTER SLIDE was finished early while racing wide. SILVER SUPREME was always outrun. EMINENCY made a run from the outside approaching the end of the backstretch but was finished leaving the turn. KEY COUNT was always outrun. BOUNDING BASQUE raced wide. STAR CHOICE, JOHN'S GOLD and SING SING raced with mud caulks.

Owners— 1, Genter Frances A; 2, Karlinsky Bette S; 3, Hobeau Farm; 4, Pen-Y-Bryn Farm; 5, Sugartown Stables; 6, Moss J A; 7, Brennan R E; 8, Rokeby Stable; 9, Rosenthal Mrs M; 10, Martin M T; 11, Happy Valley Farm; 12, Philray Stable; 13, Wimpfheimer J D.

Trainers— 1, Veitch John M; 2, Pascuma Warren J; 3, Jerkens H Allen; 4, Veitch Sylvester E; 5, Jerkens H Allen; 6, Trovato Joseph A; 7, Nobles Reynaldo H; 8, Miller Mack; 9, Johnson Philip G; 10, DeStasio Richard T; 11, Cantey Joseph B; 12, Campo John P; 13, Sedlacek Woodrow.

Overweight: Tough Critic 2 pounds; Stiff Sentence 4.

Scratched—Fortuis (25May83 ^{9}Bel^{2}); Singh Tu (18May83 ^{8}Bel^{5}).

Horses that wear steel shoes, or bar shoes, do so because they have problems with their feet. While the shoes may remedy the problem and allow the horse to race, they are a bad sign nevertheless. Steel shoes are heavier than the standard shoe, and consequently will slow the horse down somewhat. Many tracks have a "shoe board" somewhere near the paddock. It tells handicappers the type of shoe each contestant is scheduled to wear in its race that day. Make it your business to avail yourself of this service.

Many horses, including stakes runners, wear bandages on their legs. If these wraps are just on the rear legs, most likely there is no problem. Many wear back bandages because they kick themselves behind when striding, and consequently need some protection from annoying cuts. Others "run down" behind, burning their heels in the sand, and wear bandages to protect against this. A horse wearing long front bandages, however, probably has tendon or sesamoid problems, and should be regarded suspiciously, especially if the bandages are a recent addition. Small bandages on the front legs, though, are used to prevent a horse from running down, or from nicking itself while in stride. We should point out that some trainers use front bandages to fake leg problems, warning others not to bother claiming their "ailing" star runner. Others use them routinely, for protection, on most of their runners.

While discussing equipment, a comment on paddock and post parade observation would be appropriate. I recall very clearly an incident that took place at Aqueduct approximately 1970. A horse named Hans II was the odds-on favorite in a cheap claiming race, but I was certain I had detected a slight limp as the horse was led around the walking ring. I bet against Hans II with confidence, then watched as my selection won the race handily, with Hans II off the board. Several years later, I realized there was nothing wrong with Hans II that day, at least nothing my untrained eye could detect, and that, for the most part, I had been wasting my time in the paddock.

The purpose of visiting the paddock before each race is not to try to detect lameness or soreness in the contestants. Each starter must be approved by the track veterinarian before it is allowed to race, and may be scratched by the vet even at the starting gate. If there is something physically wrong with a horse, the vet will become aware of it. The average fan should not be so presumptuous to feel it is his responsibility to do the detective work. Look at the same issue from the jockey's point of view. Who is in a better position to judge a horse's physical condition just prior to a race? Should his mount show signs of physical discomfort, won't he be the first to yell "Is there a doctor in the house?" There is absolutely no reason for a jockey to keep such suspicions to himself.

He puts his life on the line every time he enters the starting gate.

The average player is best advised to use the paddock proceedings as an opportunity to note significant changes in equipment (blinkers, bits, etc.). Or to check whether a horse has a foot suitable for grass or wet-track racing. According to the trainers responding to our questionnaire, we are best-advised to make note of the sheen of the horse's coat, and how well the animal is holding its flesh, and leave the leg problems to the experts. Perhaps they can tell whether a knee or ankle is improving, or worsening. The average observer should realize that these problems did not develop overnight, and that many horses race, and win, on suspect legs as a matter of course.

Many horses reveal their uneasiness by sweating profusely in the paddock. When a normally calm horse washes out before the race, especially on a cool day, the paddock observer can confidently conclude that the horse is out of sorts and not likely to run its best race. On extremely hot days, though, most horses perspire freely. The sweat can be seen dripping off their bellies. Horses prefer cool weather. Large horses especially find it difficult to produce their best form on an extremely hot day. Horses that do overexert themselves in extreme heat are likely candidates to go off form if asked to race back too quickly.

The average player can better use time spent in the paddock by noting the mental condition and attitude of the contestants.

Bonnie Ledbetter, coauthor with Tom Ainslie of *The Body Language of Horses,* was the star of the show at the recent Handicapping Expo '83. After reading her excellent book, you will probably find yourself staring much more at the horses' ears than their feet, a thought that would have provoked laughter several years ago. But it is primarily by means of its ears that a horse reveals its feelings. With practice, the sophisticated paddock observer will become competent at tuning in on an animal's feelings simply by watching the reactions of its ears.

☐ CLAIMS ☐

Horses claimed from a race are identified toward the bottom of the chart, with the new owner and trainer mentioned. By referring to this chart, Eastern handicappers can determine from whom a horse was claimed.

In this race, Bob DeBonis claimed Minced Words from Mike Sedlacek. We deduce this from the fact that the horse finished ninth in the race, and Sedlacek was the ninth trainer listed.

THIRD RACE
Aqueduct
MARCH 25, 1983

7 FURLONGS. (1.20$\frac{1}{5}$) CLAIMING. Purse $16,500. 4-year-olds and upward. Weights, 122 lbs. Non-winners of two races since February 15 allowed 3 lbs. Of a race since then 5 lbs. Claiming Price $35,000; for each $2,500 to $30,000, 2 lbs. (Races when entered to be claimed for $25,000 or less not considered.)

Value of race $16,500, value to winner $9,900, second $3,630, third $1,980, fourth $990. Mutuel pool $106,627, OTB pool $163,013. Exacta Pool $168,959. OTB Exacta Pool $265,363.

Last Raced	Horse	Eqt.	A.	Wt	PP	St	¼	½	Str	Fin	Jockey	Cl'g Pr	Odds $1
16Mar83 ^{3}Aqu^{6}	Prete Khale	b	8	108	4	11	7$^{\frac{1}{2}}$	5$^{1\frac{1}{2}}$	1^{hd}	1^{4}	Davis R G^{5}	30000	6.30
16Mar83 ^{3}Aqu^{4}	Term Paper	b	7	112	5	7	4$^{\frac{1}{2}}$	1^{hd}	2$^{2\frac{1}{2}}$	2^{1}	Alvarado R Jr^{5}	35000	b-1.30
16Mar83 ^{3}Aqu^{12}	Rigid		5	115	6	4	8^{hd}	6^{1}	3$^{1\frac{1}{2}}$	3$^{\frac{3}{4}}$	Hernandez R	32500	9.30
10Oct82 ^{1}Bel^{10}	Sal's Son		5	108	1	9	9^{1}	8^{2}	4^{1}	4^{1}	Buscemi S^{7}	32500	29.60
16Mar83 ^{3}Aqu^{14}	Rasselas	b	5	113	9	3	11	9^{5}	5$^{\frac{1}{2}}$	5$^{5\frac{1}{4}}$	Smith A Jr	30000	a-6.20
24Feb83 ^{8}Aqu	No Heir	b	6	117	11	1	1^{hd}	4^{hd}	7^{hd}	6$^{1\frac{1}{4}}$	Cordero A Jr	35000	5.10
21Mar83 ^{5}Aqu^{9}	Firstee	b	4	115	2	8	5^{1}	7$^{\frac{1}{2}}$	9^{7}	7^{1}	Fell J	32500	a-6.20
16Mar83 ^{5}Aqu^{6}	Sonny's Hoss		5	110	3	6	3$^{1\frac{1}{2}}$	2$^{1\frac{1}{2}}$	6^{3}	8^{1}	Milo R^{7}	35000	6.50
13Mar83 ^{6}Aqu^{7}	Minced Words	b	4	112	8	2	2^{2}	3$^{\frac{1}{2}}$	8$^{\frac{1}{2}}$	9$^{3\frac{3}{4}}$	Melendez J D†^{5}	35000	b-1.30
16Feb83 ^{10}GP^{9}	Stag	b	4	117	7	10	10$^{1\frac{1}{2}}$	10^{hd}	10^{5}	10$^{7\frac{1}{4}}$	Maple E	35000	25.00
18Sep82 ^{2}Bel^{6}	Tri Irish		4	116	10	5	6^{hd}	11	11	11	Martens G	32500	40.80

a-Coupled: Rasselas and Firstee; b-Term Paper and Minced Words.

OFF AT 1:59 Start good, Won ridden out. Time, :23$\frac{4}{5}$, :48$\frac{1}{5}$, 1:13$\frac{2}{5}$, 1:25$\frac{3}{5}$ Track fast.

$2 Mutuel Prices:				
	5-(G)-PRETE KHALE	**14.60**	**5.80**	**4.20**
	2-(H)-TERM PAPER (b-entry)		**2.80**	**2.20**
	6-(I)-RIGID			**3.60**

$2 EXACTA 5-2 PAID $44.00.

B. h, by Pretense—Khalette, by Khaled. Trainer Sedlacek Sue. Bred by Asiel Mrs N I (Ky).

PRETE KHALE made a run leaving the turn, caught TERM PAPER near midstretch and drew away. The latter moved to the fore midway of the turn, opened a clear lead entering the stretch but was no match for the winner. RIGID rallied from the outside entering the stretch but failed to sustain his bid. SAL'S SON rallied along the inside near the final furlong but lacked the needed late response. RASSELAS very wide in the stretch, failed to seriously menace. NO HEIR tired. FIRSTEE was finished early. SONNY'S HOSS raced forwardly to the stretch and gave way. MINCED WORDS was used up vying for the lead. STAG raced very wide. TRI IRISH was finished early.

Owners— 1, Tresvant Stable; 2, Lane G E; 3, Christa Dee Stable; 4, Richtsmeier J; 5, Cohen R B; 6, Spiegel R; 7, Greenfair Stable; 8, Entremont; 9, Oak Manor Farm; 10, McDermott M; 11, Geoghagen R.

Trainers— 1, Sedlacek Sue; 2, Sedlacek Michael C; 3, Galluscio Dominick; 4, Coladonato Eugene J; 5, Shapoff Stanley R; 6, Schaeffer Stephen; 7, Shapoff Stanley R; 8, Baeza Braulio; 9, Sedlacek Michael C; 10, Rathburn Gordon; 11, Galimi Michael T.

† **Apprentice allowance waived:** Minced Words 2 pounds. **Corrected weight:** Term Paper 112 pounds. **Overweight:** Tri Irish 1 pound.

Minced Words was claimed by Chasrigg Stable; trainer, DeBonis Robert.

Scratched—Bit of Coral (16Mar83 ^{3}Aqu^{8}); Self Pressured (16Mar83 ^{3}Aqu^{10}); Swap for Power (5Feb83 ^{5}Aqu^{4}).

□ WEIGHT □

When a jockey is unable to make the weight assigned one of his mounts, the difference between his riding weight and the assigned weight is termed an "overweight," and is mentioned at the bottom of the result charts, following the heading "overweight." As a rule, track announcers mention the overweights when giving the day's scratches. Should the rider involved be a Pincay, a pound or two of overweight safely can be ignored, but if the rider is just a run-of-the-mill journeyman (or woman) be careful. Most likely, the slight difference in weight will not affect the horse's performance. Rather, the trainer may be signaling his overall lack of confidence in his horse's chances. Otherwise, he would have found a rider who could make the assigned weight. Many trainers believe weight is that important! Of course, overweights take on more significance the higher the weight. Most leading riders would have difficulty riding below 110 pounds. Therefore, many horses assigned weight below 110 fall into the "overweight" category, and this fact can be ignored.

Also found at the bottom of the result charts are the headings "corrected weight" and "apprentice allowance waived." With the rare exception of a clerical error, these two are usually related and concern a late rider switch involving an apprentice. Should an apprentice be replaced by a journeyman rider, the horse forfeits the apprentice allowance claimed overnight, and races at the corrected weight listed in the chart footnotes. On the other hand, should an apprentice replace a journeyman, he cannot claim his allowance, and must ride at the weight assigned the journeyman. This is listed under the heading "apprentice allowance waived." Should a five-pound apprentice replace a seven-pound "bug," the corrected weight would be noted in the chart. Had this situation been reversed, the two-pound difference would be listed under "apprentice allowance waived."

In the race above, seven-pound apprentice John Melendez replaced a five-pound boy, and five-pound apprentice Rolando Alvarado replaced a seven-pound bug.

☐ SCRATCHES ☐

The very last item found in the result chart footnotes is a listing of all horses scratched from the race. Each horse scratched is listed with the date, track, race number, and finish position from its most recent race, in standard result chart format.

SECOND RACE
Aqueduct
APRIL 8, 1983

7 FURLONGS. (1.20$\frac{1}{5}$) CLAIMING. Purse $14,500. 4–year–olds and upward. Weights, 122 lbs. Non–winners of two races since March 1, allowed 3 lbs. Of a race since then, 5 lbs. Claiming Price $25,000; for each $2,500 to $20,000, 2 lbs. (Races when entered to be claimed for $18,000 or less not considered).

Value of race $14,500, value to winner $8,700, second $3,190, third $1,740, fourth $870. Mutuel pool $87,894, OTB pool $167,356. Track Quinella Pool $149,636. OTB Quinella Pool $213,807.

Last Raced	Horse	Eqt.	A.	Wt	PP	St	¼	½	Str	Fin	Jockey	Cl'g Pr	Odds $1
5Apr83 ^{2}Aqu^{1}	Kenny J.	b	5	108	10	1	2^{hd}	$1\frac{1}{2}$	$1^{2\frac{1}{2}}$	1^{nk}	Davis R G^{5}	20000	4.60
13Mar83 ^{5}Aqu^{6}	Need A Penny	b	5	112	11	9	6^{1}	$4\frac{1}{2}$	2^{hd}	2^{1}	Alvarado R Jr^{5}	25000	4.20
31Mar83 ^{4}Aqu^{6}	Dealing Diplomat		5	115	1	7	4^{hd}	5^{5}	5^{5}	3^{hd}	MacBeth D	22500	a-7.80
24Mar83 ^{3}Aqu^{1}	Rapido's Repeat		5	117	5	5	3^{1}	3^{1}	3^{1}	$4^{2\frac{3}{4}}$	Velasquez J	25000	4.50
28Mar83 ^{3}Aqu^{4}	Cold Trailin'	b	4	117	9	3	1^{1}	2^{1}	$4\frac{1}{2}$	5^{2}	Fell J	25000	8.20
25Mar83 ^{3}Aqu^{6}	No Heir	b	6	117	7	4	$7\frac{1}{2}$	7^{2}	6^{5}	$6^{3\frac{1}{4}}$	Cordero A Jr	25000	7.10
21Mar83 ^{5}Aqu^{5}	Thunder Bridge		5	115	12	2	12^{2}	$11\frac{1}{2}$	$8\frac{1}{2}$	7^{hd}	Graell A	22500	a-7.80
25Mar83 ^{3}Aqu^{5}	Rasselas	b	5	117	4	8	10^{4}	$8\frac{1}{2}$	$7\frac{1}{2}$	$8^{2\frac{1}{4}}$	Smith A Jr	25000	8.10
7Mar83 ^{5}Aqu^{7}	Psychosis		8	110	2	13	$8\frac{1}{2}$	9^{2}	9^{3}	$9^{1\frac{3}{4}}$	Melendez J D^{5}	22500	24.10
31Mar83 ^{4}Aqu^{4}	Edge Of Wisdom	b	5	115	13	10	11^{hd}	12^{6}	10^{2}	$10^{2\frac{1}{4}}$	Migliore R†	22500	31.20
6Feb83 ^{9}Aqu^{6}	Care Taker	b	4	117	6	11	13	13	13	11^{nk}	Rogers K L	25000	f-18.70
25Mar83 ^{3}Aqu^{8}	Sonny's Hoss	b	5	110	3	12	$9\frac{1}{2}$	10^{hd}	$11\frac{1}{2}$	$12^{2\frac{1}{4}}$	Milo R^{7}	25000	17.50
28Mar83 ^{3}Aqu^{8}	Gatlinburg	b	4	117	8	6	$5^{1\frac{1}{2}}$	$6\frac{1}{2}$	$12^{1\frac{1}{2}}$	13	Santagata N	25000	f-18.70

a–Coupled: Dealing Diplomat and Thunder Bridge.
f—Mutuel field.

OFF AT 1:27. Start good, Won driving. Time, :22$\frac{3}{5}$, :45$\frac{2}{5}$, 1:09$\frac{4}{5}$, 1:22$\frac{3}{5}$ Track muddy.

$2 Mutuel Prices:

9–(L)–KENNY J.	....	11.20	5.80	4.20
10–(M)–NEED A PENNY	....		6.00	3.20
1–(A)–DEALING DIPLOMAT (a-entry) ..				4.80

$2 QUINELLA 9–10 PAID $26.00.

Dk. b. or br. g, by Droll Role—Jennie Murphy, by Royal Serenade. Trainer Barrera Oscar S. Bred by Carter Donald W (Ky).

KENNY J., prominent from the outset, drew clear while racing well out from the rail entering the stretch and lasted over NEED A PENNY. The latter rallied from the outside leaving the turn and finished gamely. DEALING DIPLOMAT, never far back, swung out near midstretch and was going well at the finish. RAPIDO'S REPEAT raced forwardly to the stretch while saving ground but wasn't good enough. COLD TRAILIN' weakened during the drive. NO HEIR failed to seriously menace. THUNDER BRIDGE raced very wide. RASSELAS was always outrun. EDGE OF WISDOM raced very wide. GATLINBURG was finished early. NEED A PENNY and COLD TRAILIN' raced with mud caulks.

Owners— 1, Barrera Oscar S; 2, Stone Arch Stables; 3, Pascuma W J; 4, Sommer Viola; 5, Triple B Stable; 6, Spiegel R; 7, Denmark Muriel; 8, Cohen R B; 9, Shahinian S A; 10, Kelley Mrs W A; 11, Otis Constance M; 12, Entremont; 13, Ricatto M.

Trainers— 1, Barrera Oscar S; 2, Sedlacek Michael C; 3, Pascuma Warren J; 4, Martin Frank; 5, Buxton Robert; 6, Schaeffer Stephen; 7, Pascuma Warren J; 8, Shapoff Stanley R; 9, Shahinian Steven A; 10, Daggett Michael H; 11, Weckerle George W Jr; 12, Baeza Braulio; 13, Ricatto Michael.

† Apprentice allowance waived: Edge Of Wisdom 5 pounds.

Scratched—What A Charger (18Mar83 5Aqu1); Sal's Son (25Mar83 3Aqu4); Might Be Home (24Feb83 3Aqu8); Bishops Pride (21Mar83 5Aqu8).

A horse will be scratched (usually) for one of five reasons. It may have come down with some physical ailment since entry time, and therefore be unable to compete. Or the trainer may have found a better spot for the horse a day or two later, and waited. Or he may have judged the competition too stiff for his charge, and chickened out for that reason. The horse may have been part of an entry, and the trainer decided that he had a better chance with the other half of the team. Finally, track conditions may have changed due to inclement weather, possibly forcing a race off the grass course. Some horses simply cannot handle wet tracks, and are routinely scratched when presented such conditions. Others are grass specialists, and are reserved for such contests. Racing secretaries with whom I have spoken estimate that approximately 75 percent of nonweather-related scratches are for physical reasons—either legs or a touch of colic, as a rule, and that the remaining 25 percent are divided evenly between instances where the trainer felt the spot came up too tough, or found a better spot a couple of days later. When a horse appears in the entries soon after being scratched, the player can rest assured that the scratch had not been for physical reasons.

CASE STUDY: ROGER'S PASS AND GOING ORANGE

Gilbert Puentes entered two horses in the second race at Aqueduct on February 5, 1983. Going Orange was the prerace favorite, having won at the mile-and-a-half distance on January 8. Roger's Pass appeared to be out for the exercise—he hadn't finished within ten lengths of the lead in any of the races appearing in his past performances. However, when Puentes scratched Going Orange, Roger's Pass warranted a closer look.

The colt had trailed along three times previously when part of an entry, but now was being asked to carry the ball by himself. There was one positive sign—Roger's Pass' previous race was easily his best of late, and the horse was being raised slightly in class. Although by no means a solid bet, he may have been worth a small wager at 22-1. He won, going away.

Generally speaking, a horse may scratch overnight for any reason whatsoever. Once the track program has been printed, however, it becomes more difficult to beg off. With the exception of stakes races, track conditions must change or a note from the vet must be presented, before a scratch will be allowed.

At some tracks, trainers may be able to scratch for no good reason from races with large fields, but usually there is little to no chance of declaring from an already small field. Tracks must consider their patrons, as well as the horseman. If there is one thing handicappers dislike, it is small and uncompetitive fields. In some states, New York included, regulations force the cancellation of exotic wagering when a field is reduced to five or fewer horses.

When a trainer is refused permission to scratch, his horse is said to be "stuck." Racing secretaries agree that the typical six-horse field includes one "stuck" horse. "Stuck" horses seldom win. Trainers estimate their win percentage at 10 percent, with grass horses forced to race in the slop especially unlikely to succeed. Unfortunately, the average racetrack does not announce which horses are "stuck" when they give the daily scratches. No more so than they announce which horses were "requested" to enter to help build a small field up to acceptable size. Otherwise, many trainers would "try" to scratch, hoping to cash a nice bet at big odds while the misled public looks elsewhere.

Contrasted with the small field is the race that draws an overflow of entries. Maiden races are the most common examples. At times a race will draw so many entries that the racing secretary will split it into two divisions, canceling at the same time another race scheduled for the same day that may have attracted only a few participants. Other times, when no other race is low on entries, or the overflow would not fill two races, we find certain horses, by the luck of the draw, placed on what is called the "also-eligible list." Should a race allow (say) twelve runners, perhaps up to eight others would be placed on this list. Should one of the first twelve scratch, one of the also-eligibles would be chosen (by lot) to replace it, taking over the outside post in the field (not the post of the horse scratched). Otherwise, the horses on the also-eligible list are all scratched.

At times, a race may attract so many entries that some do not even make the also-eligible list. These, as well as those unable to escape the also-eligible list, are given "stars." Horses with "stars" are given preference the next time a race of the same classification is drawn. Of course, should forty horses enter a given race, and only twelve race, the other twenty-eight are given "stars," and some of these may be excluded the next time around as well.

Scratched horses are listed in their original post-position order. In the Kenny J. race, for example, What A Charger was scheduled to run from post 9, Sal's Son from post 11, and Might Be Home from post 14. Bishop's Pride, Thunder Bridge, and Edge Of Wisdom were on the also-eligible list. Two of the three that were scratched came out of the race early, allowing Thunder Bridge and Edge Of Wisdom to race. The other was a late scratch, which explains why Bishop's Pride didn't get into the race. However, the result chart fails to identify which horse was the late scratch. One had to be at the track (or OTB) to know.

In some states, including New York, when part of an entry is scratched after the betting has started (in the paddock, during the post parade, or at the starting gate, to mention three possibilities), the other half of the entry is allowed to compete for the purse money, but is removed from the pari-mutuel betting pools. This is done to protect the public, which may well have wagered on the entry because of the horse that was scratched. Rather than have disgruntled customers holding "live" tickets, possibly at low odds, on the weaker half of an entry, some tracks have decided to scratch the entire entry from the betting should any part of the entry be a late scratch. Such was the case with Hopehard at Aqueduct on January 19, 1983.

Hopehard — B. g. 6, by Hard Work—Hope Against Hope, by Mt Hope
Own.—Barrera O S — $15,000 Br.—Tackett P (Ky) Tr.—Barrera Oscar S — 1105
Lifetime 68 13 6 5 $94,390 — 1983 10 3 1 4 $26,460 — 1982 21 3 3 0 $25,620 — Turf 1 0 0 0

6Apr83- 1Aqu fst 1⅛	:49 1:13⅖ 1:52⅗	Clm 18000	6	2	3½	1hd	12	32½	Alvarado R Jr5	b 108	5.60	69-22	Hail to Hardin 117hd Ben Marino 1152½Hopehard1081½	Weakened	7
20Mar83- 3Aqu fst 1⅛	:49 1:14 1:52⅘	Clm 14000	9	3	42	42½	55¼	3¾	Davis R G5	b 108	6.60	70-27	Christy's Ridge 117no Recidian 110¾ Hopehard 1081¼	Rallied	9
17Mar83- 3Aqu fst 1 5/16	:47⅘ 1:38⅘ 2:11	Hcp 7500s	8	7	56½	35½	38½	210	Smith A Jr	b 114	*1.50e	74-27	Dancer'sMelody10910Hopehard1142¾ElevtorShoes1141¾	Mate won	9
6Mar83- 9Aqu fst 1⅛ ⊡	:48⅗ 1:13⅖ 1:52	Clm 10500	3	8	74¾	41¾	1hd	12¾	Smith A Jr	b 115	7.40	86-19	Hopehard 1152¾ Castle Gem 1171¼ Sonny Booth 1122¼	Drew out	12
28Feb83- 3Aqu fst 1 3/16 ⊡	:49⅗ 1:14⅗ 2:01⅕	Hcp 7500s	2	9	1011	910	712	57	Melendez J D	b 113	9.30e	65-25	Phi Beta Key 116½ Flying Straight 1181TedBrown112nk	No factor	10
16Feb83- 3Aqu fst 1⅛ ⊡	:48 1:13⅗ 1:54⅘	Clm 10500	6	11	97¼	79¾	41½	12¾	Alvarado R Jr5	b 108	8.50	72-23	Hopehard 1082¾ Red Rang 108¾ Louhoum 115nk	Driving	11
6Feb83- 1Aqu fst 1¼ ⊡	:49⅗ 1:42⅗ 2:10	Clm c-7500	7	4	35	67	711	714	Beitia E	b 119	2.60	54-22	Pro Set 1101¼ Charlie's Loose 1102¼ Angus Lane 114½	Tired	9
19Jan83- 2Aqu fst 170 ⊡	:48⅕ 1:14⅗ 1:47⅖	Clm 7500	3	8	811	47	12	15½	Beitia E	b 117	(– –)	65-24	Hopehard 1175½ Pro Set 1121½ Pocket's Rogue 1172¼	Easily	8
19Jan83-Raced for Purse Money Only															
10Jan83- 9Aqu fst 1 1/16 ⊡	:48⅘ 1:15⅕ 1:49⅘	Clm 7500	5	8	814	58	44	42¼	Beitia E	b 117	4.10	62-23	Milliard 117no DAlturas 117nk Anjun-Sun 1172	Rallied	8
10Jan83-Placed third through disqualification															
5Jan83- 1Aqu fst 1 1/16 ⊡	:48⅖ 1:14⅖ 1:49	Clm 8000	2	7	712	69½	39	34½	Beitia E	b 113	10.90	63-24	Cornish Conqueror 1101 ParisStation1133½Hopehard1133¾	Rallied	9

LATEST WORKOUTS Mar 27 Bel tr.t 4f fst :50 b Mar 14 Bel tr.t 4f fst :50 b Mar 4 Bel tr.t 4f fst :49⅘ b Feb 26 Bel tr.t 3f fst :37⅖ h

Note the comment to this effect placed in his past performances. In this case, the weaker half of the entry was scratched, and Hopehard returned a lonesome and ignored winner. No one cashed a bet on this easy winner, who was allowed to race and win the purse, but not participate in the betting. The result chart for this race adds the missing details. Hopehard's stablemate Powhite ran off in the post parade, and subsequently was ordered to be scratched.

SECOND RACE Aqueduct JANUARY 19, 1983

1 MILE 70 YARDS.(INNER DIRT). (1.40⅖) CLAIMING. Purse $8,500. 4-year-olds and upward. Weight, 122 lbs. Non-winners of two races at a mile or over since December 15 allowed 3 lbs. Of such a race since then 5 lbs. Claiming price $7,500. (Races when entered to be claimed for $6,500 or less not considered.)

Value of race $8,500, value to winner $5,100, second $1,870, third $1,020, fourth $510. Mutuel pool $57,931, OTB pool $53,958. Quinella Pool $68,121. OTB Quinella Pool $39,489.

Last Raced	Horse	Eqt.	A.	Wt	PP	St	¼	½	¾	Str	Fin	Jockey	Cl'g Pr	Odds $1
10Jan83 9Aqu3	Hopehard	b	6	117	3	8	8	8	41	12	15½	Beitia E	7500	.00
13Jan83 3Aqu8	Pro Set	b	4	112	7	7	71½	7½	8	41	21½	Barnett W A5	7500	17.90
7Jan83 6Suf2	Pocket's Rogue		5	117	4	2	61½	61	51	64	32¼	Kaenel J L†	7500	12.20
19Dec82 2Aqu8	Follow's Finale	b	5	112	8	6	52	55	33	3hd	41	Alvarado R Jr10	7500	15.00
10Jan83 2Aqu1	Set The Charge	b	4	112	2	4	44	2hd	2hd	5½	5hd	Davis R G5	7500	.80
10Jan83 9Aqu6	Commanche Brave	b	4	110	1	1	2hd	3hd	6½	73	6¾	AntongorgiWA7	7500	7.40
2Jan83 9Aqu3	Russell Sprout	b	4	112	6	5	13½	13	14	2½	73¼	Asmussen S M5	7500	6.40
7Jan83 3Aqu6	Contorsion		4	107	5	3	32	41	71	8	8	Belmonte J E10	7500	3.90

OFF AT 12:57 EST. Start good, Won easily. Time, :23⅗, :48⅕, 1:14⅗, 1:42⅘, 1:47⅖ Track fast.

$2 Mutuel Prices:			
7-(O)-PRO SET	37.80	14.40	8.60
4-(I)-POCKET'S ROGUE		11.40	5.40
8-(K)-FOLLOW'S FINALE			7.00

$2 QUINELLA 4-7 PAID $101.80.

B. g, by Hard Work—Hope Against Hope, by Mt Hope. Trainer Sedlacek Sue. Bred by Tackett P (Ky).

HOPEHARD, running for purse money only, was reserved in the early stages, commenced a rally leaving the backsretch, circled horses into the stretch and won off with ease. PRO SET, without early speed, was carried widest of all into the stretch by POCKET'S ROGUE, rallied strongly to best the others. POCKET'S ROGUE also came wide into the stretch and finished with good energy. FOLLOW'S FINALE had no serious rally. SET THE CHARGE, well placed to the early stretch, tired. COMMANCHE BRAVE was finisehd after a half mile. RUSSELL SPROUT made the pace under a rating hold to the stretch, was put to a drive, but had little left. CONTORSION TIRED. POWHITE, A PROGRAM STARTER, UNSEATED HIS RIDER AND RAN OFF IN THE POST PARADE. HE WAS ORDERED SCRATCHED BY THE STEWARDS WITH ALL WAGERS ON HIM AND HIS ENTRYMATE HOPEHARD, BEING REFUNDED. A CONSOLATION DAILY DOUBLE WAS PAID.

Owners— 1, Tresvant Stable; 2, Ramos F F; 3, Lione A J; 4, Kerin W J; 5, Barrera O S; 6, Lacatena F P; 7, Shapiro T; 8, Gilsa Stable.

Trainers— 1, Sedlacek Sue; 2, Ramos Faustino F; 3, Lione Anthony J; 4, Hernandez Ramon M; 5, Barrera Oscar S; 6, Delvecchio Dominick; 7, DeBonis Robert; 8, Puentes Gilbert.

† **Apprentice allowance waived:** Pocket's Rogue 7 pounds. **Corrected weight:** Follow's Finale 112 pounds.

Scratched—Mikey's Charger (23Jly81 9Mth9); Powhite (1Jan83 2Aqu3); Chef De Mob (31Dec82 2Aqu9); Florida's Joy (22Dec82 9Aqu6); Emmarr's Boy (3Jan83 3Aqu5); Kinderhook (30Dec82 9Aqu9); Grandange (8Jan83 1Aqu10); Red Rang (2Jan83 2Aqu6).

The *Daily Racing Form* does not mention in the past performances that a horse has been scratched since its most recent race. The handicapper must keep notes to remain abreast of such information. The *Form* does, however, point out horses that were entered in some other race within the past two days by placing a comment under the horse's name, immediately above its running lines. Kenny J., entered in a $20,000 claiming race on May 7, had also been entered on May 5 in the ninth at Aqueduct. In fact, the *Form* tells us that Kenny J. finished eighth in that race. In this case, trainer Oscar Barrera chose to scratch the horse, and rest him until May 9, when he raced again, and won for the fourth time in 1983.

Copyright © 1984, by DAILY RACING FORM, INC. Reprinted with permission of copyright owner.

As a rule, when a horse had been entered—and scratched—from a race within two days of its scheduled engagement, it is helpful to look up the conditions of that race. Hopefully, the handicapper will gain some insight into the trainer's intentions with the horse.

It is not enough simply to look at the list of horses scratched. One must determine why a horse was taken out of a race. Should the scratch have been due to physical problems, the animal should be closely scrutinized regarding its fitness when next entered. Program scratches for other than weather-related reasons are the most critical, probably signifying physical problems. Overnight scratches remain a mystery, possibly implying physical problems, possibly not. Horses dropped precipitously in class, then scratched, should be regarded suspiciously when next entered, even if at a higher price. Horses scratched because they failed to get in from the also-eligible list should be treated as if never entered, unless their entry in the race appeared suspicious in the first place.

Chapter 13

WORKOUTS

The workouts appearing beneath a horse's past performances often shed considerable light on the horse's fitness and/or development. They usually play a key role in a trainer's preparations for a winning effort, yet at times they can be confusing and even misleading. A horse's four most recent workouts are listed, provided they had occurred within the past two months. In addition to the date, track, distance, surface conditions, and time of each workout, we find several symbols that are unique to the workout line of the past performances.

Starhitch — B. c. 4, by Political Coverup—Star Passer, by Pass Catcher
Own.—Martin Charlene — Br.—Yowell Renee (Fla) — Tr.—Martin Frank — **117**

Lifetime							
30 3 7 2	1983	6	0	5	1	$24,310
$73,950	1982	22	2	2	1	$41,840
	Turf	7	0	1	0	$9,080

29Mar83- 1Aqu	gd	1 3/16	:48	1:12⅗	1:57⅖	Clm 40000	5	3	35	23½	22½	2½	Cordero A Jr	b 117	*1.70e	74-28	Brasher Doubloon117½Starhitch1174¾LetterFromLucy1132	Rallied	8
19Mar83- 6Aqu	my	1⅛	:47⅖	1:12	1:50⅖	Alw 21000	2	6	59	57	511	213	Cordero A Jr	b 117	*.30e	70-21	Ivan Lendl 11713 Starhitch 117¾ No Fraud 1171	Mate won	6
9Mar83- 2Aqu	gd	1⅛ ⊡	:47	1:12	1:50⅕	Alw 21000	4	9	64	2hd	2½	2nk	Miranda J	b 117	3.10e	95-09	Dark 'N Bold 117nk Starhitch 1172½ Ivan Lendl 1172¾	Game try	11
26Jan83- 7Aqu	fst	1 1/16 ⊡	:47⅕	1:12	1:45⅖	Alw 21000	1	6	55	54½	33	23	Miranda J	b 117	2.90e	83-17	No Heir 1173 Starhitch 117½ Starve Easy 117nk	Gamely	10
15Jan83- 7Aqu	sly	1¼ ⊡	:48⅗	1:41	2:07⅗	Alw 22000	6	7	88	45½	310	311	Miranda J	b 117	2.20e	69-22	Masmak 1123¼ The Mangler 1107¼ Starhitch 1173	No menace	8
6Jan83- 9Aqu	sly	1¼ ⊡	:46⅘	1:38⅗	2:04⅗	Clm c-35000	6	6	616	32	22	22¼	Davis R G5	b 112	11.10	93-17	EvsivJohn1102¼Strhitch1128¾SurrndrGround1141¼	Best of others	8
30Dec82- 1Aqu	fst	1⅛ ⊡	:48⅖	1:13⅕	1:52⅖	Clm 55000	1	7	69¾	66½	66½	67	Alvarado R Jr5	b 108	2.50e	77-24	Nemrac 1171¼ Class Hero 1172¾ Four Bases 117½	No factor	7
18Dec82- 6Aqu	fst	1 1/16 ⊡	:48⅘	1:14⅖	1:46⅕	3↑ Alw 22000	1	3	32	42	43½	46½	Maple E	b 115	11.70	75-20	Cintula 115¾ Swallanga 1175½ Masmak 115nk	Tired	8
11Nov82- 3Aqu	fm	1⅛ Ⓣ	:50⅗	1:15	1:53⅗	Clm 50000	2	7	87¼	86¼	68	67	Fell J	b 117	5.00e	70-22	Four Bases 117no Flatterer 114no We Tha People117¾	No menace	8
17Oct82- 5Aqu	fst	1	:48	1:13⅕	1:38⅕	Clm 75000	5	3	69½	613	611	611	Samyn J L	112	5.40	64-27	Count Normandy1114ClassHero112nkDirectAnswer1091	Brief foot	7

LATEST WORKOUTS Mar 28 Bel tr.t 4f my :48 hg(d) ●Mar 7 Bel tr.t 4f sly :48 hg Mar 1 Bel tr.t 4f fst :51⅘ b Feb 24 Bel tr.t 3f fst :37⅖ b

The symbols *h* and *b* indicate workouts accomplished "handily" and "breezing," respectively. Starhitch's latest two works were done "handily." The preceding pair were breezes. A "handily" work represents a more serious effort than does a "breezing" workout. As a general rule of thumb, a "handily" workout can be thought of as equivalent to a "breezing" workout a full second slower.

The symbol *(d)* appearing after a workout means "dogs up." Traffic cones, similar to those seen on highways, are placed on the racing surface, protecting that part of the track nearest the rail. Horses are forced to work in the middle of the track, and consequently cover a greater distance of ground than usual. Therefore, works around the dogs will run slower than normal. Starhitch worked around dogs on March 28.

Some tracks have a special training track where horses may work, if they choose. Workouts over the training track are indicated by the symbol *tr. t.* All four of Starhitch's workouts took place over Belmont's training track. Training tracks are usually much deeper than the regular racing surface, and so can serve to help build a horse's conditioning and stamina. Training track workouts tend to run much slower than those on the regular strip.

CASE STUDY: STOLEN TITLE VS. MONTAGE

Stolen Title's workouts over the Oklahoma training track at Saratoga were excellent, and compared favorably with those turned in by 6–5 favorite Montage at Belmont, as these two juvenile fillies prepared for their racing debuts. The latter's favoritism in this maiden special event at Saratoga was due in large part to her sire, the immensely popular Alydar, whose daughter Althea five days earlier had slaughtered male rivals in the Hollywood Juvenile Championship. The fact that Stolen Title was the only other first-time starter in the twelve horse field, the first of its kind at Saratoga in 1983, receiving any attention at the betting windows, spoke volumes for her readiness. She won, paying $13.80. The conditioning she gained working over the deep training track no doubt spelled the difference.

Stolen Title	Ch. f. 2, by Nasty And Bold—Titled, by Impressive		Lifetime	1983 0 M 0 0
Own.—Rosenthal Mrs M	Br.—Rosenthal Mrs M (Ky)	**117**	0 0 0 0	
Tr.—Johnson Philip G				
LATEST WORKOUTS	● Jly 23 Sar tr.t 6f fst 1:14 h Jly 12 Sar tr.t 5f fst 1:02⅗ h	Jly 7 Sar tr.t 5f fst 1:04⅖ h		

Montage	B. f. 2, by Alydar—Katonka, by Minnesota Mac		Lifetime	1983 0 M 0 0
Own.—Happy Valley Farm	Br.—Happy Valley Farm (Fla)	**117**	0 0 0 0	
Tr.—Veitch John M				
LATEST WORKOUTS	● Jly 27 Sar 3f fst :34⅗ h Jly 18 Bel 4f fst :48⅕ hg	Jly 13 Bel 5f fst 1:02⅖ b		Jly 8 Bel 4f fst :49⅕ hg

The symbol g, if present, means the workout was from the starting gate. Starhitch's two most recent workouts were from the starting gate. Gate workouts usually begin from a standing start, while horses engaging in nongate works usually do so from a running start. Consequently, gate workouts tend to run slower than nongate works, by as much as a full second. Because numerous horses may work on any given morning, the starting gate must be placed in some out-of-the-way location. The spot usually chosen is the backstretch chute. Consequently, at most mile tracks, three- and four-furlong gate works are usually done over a straight course, making such works appear faster than they actually are.

At many tracks, a change to blinkers must be preceded by a (gate) workout during which the horse wears the new equipment. Consequently, the combination of a change to blinkers and an improved workout can point out a horse on the verge of dramatic improvement. Witty Boy, for example, improved suddenly and immediately when blinkers were added. He probably wore the hood for his work of April 13 over the deep and tiring training track at Belmont, a work considerably more impressive than its :48.3 time suggests.

Witty Boy — B. c. 3, by Anticipating—Very Witty, by Better Bee — Lifetime 4 1 0 0 $14,700 — 1983 4 1 0 0 $14,700 — 1982 0 M 0 0
Own.—Daren J — Br.—Daren J (NY) — Tr.—Nocella Vincent — 106

15Apr83- 4Aqu	fst 1	:46⅘ 1:12⅕ 1:40⅕	ⓈMd Sp Wt	10	12	9^9½	5^6½	5^1½	1¾	Samyn J L	(b)122	15.00	65-29	Witty Boy 122¾ Win 122² Loose Money 122¹¾	Driving	14
2Apr83- 4Aqu	fst 1	:47⅕ 1:12⅘ 1:39⅘	ⓈMd Sp Wt	4	9	5^6½	6^5½	7^5¾	8^4½	Santagata N	122	12.30	62-23	Kirbys' Punch 115½ Steel Pier 117^nk Young Naskra 122^hd	Outrun	12
29Mar83- 4Aqu	gd 6f	:23⅕ :47⅕ 1:13	ⓈMd Sp Wt	5	11	12^14	11^11	7^9	8^11	Velasquez J	122	21.30	65-28	Sharp Destiny 122¹¼ Jaipur'sDarling122¾GeorgeCinq122^hd	Outrun	14
14Mar83- 4Aqu	fst 6f	⊡:22⅗ :45⅘ 1:10⅘	ⓈMd Sp Wt	5	12	11^12	10^10	8^12	6^14	Buscemi S⁷	115	10.20	76-10	Megalith 115⁵¾ Pont D'Argent 122⁴ SharpDestiny122¹¼	No factor	14

LATEST WORKOUTS Apr 24 Bel tr.t 5f gd 1:01⅗ h — Apr 13 Bel tr.t 4f fst :48⅗ h — Mar 24 Bel tr.t 4f fst :50⅗ b

Likewise Prospero, who won July 21 following an uneven performance July 8 (see Chapter 12), aided no doubt by the addition of blinkers. The sharp :34.4 workout on July 15 probably came with blinkers on.

Prospero — Dk. b. or br. g. 3, by Blue Times—Play It Cool, by Impressive — Lifetime 2 0 0 0 $750 — 1983 2 M 0 0 $750 — 1982 0 M 0 0
Own.—Avonwood Stable — $35,000 — Br.—C E Mather II (Ky) — Tr.—Wright Frank I — 116

8Jly83- 2Bel	fst 6f	:22⅗ :45⅘ 1:11⅘	3↑Md 45000	1	3	3^3½	6^11	6^13	4^11	Rogers K L	112	7.50	72-18	Importunity 116³ Mock Court 116⁶¾ Piston Lift 116¾	Weakened	10
13Jun83- 3Bel	fst 6½f	:23⅕ :46⅘ 1:16⅘	3↑Md Sp Wt	2	6	2^hd	1^hd	6^6¾	6^16	Rogers K L	114	31.70	76-12	Halo's Comet 122^nk Tampa Town 114½ Antigua 114¾	Used up	6

LATEST WORKOUTS ● Jly 15 Bel 3f fst :34⅘ h — Jun 23 Bel 6f fst 1:13⅘ h — Jun 6 Bel 3f fst :36⅗ hg — Jun 2 Bel 3f fst :36⅘ hg

The symbol ● appearing before a workout is called a "bullet," and the workout termed a "bullet work." The "bullet" is used to designate the fastest work of the day at the distance. Starhitch's work on March 7 was the fastest of the day at four furlongs.

☐ THE WORKOUT TAB ☐

Each edition of the *Form* contains a complete workout tab reporting the works of the previous morning.

Since the Monday edition of the *Form* is printed earlier than usual, on Saturday afternoon, Sunday's workouts appear along with Monday's in the Tuesday *Form*. Should a horse be entered Monday and have worked the day before, its blowout will not appear in its past performances. To aid fans, some tracks post a listing of Sunday workouts each Monday. Others announce pertinent Sunday workouts when giving Monday's scratches. Some tracks do neither, leaving handicappers in the dark with respect to a potentially key piece of information. We also mention that "Early Bird" editions of the *Form* on sale at many tracks run two days behind on workouts. A blowout from the previous morning will not appear in a horse's past performances in these editions.

The workout tab supposedly contains all works at those tracks in the general area covered by that particular edition of the *Form*. Depending on the accuracy and/or honesty of the clockers, some workouts may be missed altogether, others timed (or reported) incorrectly, and in a few cases, the horse incorrectly identified. Ironically, the most impressive workouts leading up to Seattle Slew's racing debut were missed or re-

Thursday, June 9, 1983

SARATOGA – (Training) Track Fast

Three Furlongs		
Eternal Light	:37⅗	b
Gentle Knave	:37⅖	b
Her Desire	:37⅖	b
Holley Springs	:39⅗	b
Kenny's Melissa	:37	b
King of Jive	:37	b
Laughing Lover	:38	b
Refuse Defeat	:37	b
Regency Doll	:39	b
Royal Seven	:40⅘	b
September Jo	:37⅖	b
Seven Images	:37⅗	b
Siessa Bingio	:39	b
Terra Pace	:37⅘	bg
Tropical Blend	:37	b
Wandering Feet	:38	b
Yarboy	:37	b
Four Furlongs		
BePtientWithMe	:50⅘	bg
Cageycat	:52⅖	b
Dac's Prince	:50⅗	bg
Forthetimebeing	:49⅖	bg
Gene's Dream	:50⅗	bg
Haltered	:48	b
Happy Land	:48	bg
Jackson Q	:48⅖	bg
K. J. Express	:53	b
Misty Ellen	:53	bg
Notable Naskra	:48	bg
Prince Dino	:50	bg
Quarter Queen	:49	bg
Rich and Rob	:50⅘	bg
Royal Coachman	:52	b
Stoic Pride	:52⅖	b
Teason	:52	bg
ToghTddlyWnks	:51	bg
Vin Ce Vin	:50⅖	b
Five Furlongs		
Capay	1:02	b
Destinent Regent	**1:00**	**h**
Header	1:04⅖	b
Implosion	1:02⅖	b
Rocco's Girl	1:03⅗	b
Six Furlongs		
April Fools Boy	**1:15⅖**	**b**
Clue Requested	1:15⅗	b
Seven Furlongs		
Sport Time	1:30⅖	bg

BELMONT PARK – Track Fast

Three Furlongs		
Au Point	**:34⅗**	**h**
Balboa Native	:35⅖	b
Bonne Bouche	:36	h
Gold Medallion	:37⅘	b
Lunchtime	:36⅖	b
Muskoka Wyck	**:34⅗**	**h**
Prosper	:35⅘	h
Salem Trials	:36⅗	b
SharetheFantasy	:36⅗	b
Four Furlongs		
Ancient Custom	:47⅗	h
Bashert	:48⅗	h
Bet Big	**:46⅕**	**h**
Caveat	:49	b
Chic Belle	:50⅗	b
Cindy's Friend	:48	h
Cut the Music	:49⅘	b
Devil's Bag	:48⅕	hg
Eastern Prince	:49⅗	b
Errant Minstrel	:49	bg
Faraway Sound	:53	b
Firm Lady	:47⅗	h
Go Holme	:51⅘	b
Heidi's Friend	:48	h
Highland Blade	:49⅘	b
Into the Current	:52	b
LeWashingtonin	:49⅖	b
Mr. Tatt	:46⅗	h
Nafees	:48⅕	h
Nana's Boy	:50	bg
No Man's Land	:47⅘	hg
NobodyWantsMe	:47⅖	h
Nordico	:48⅖	hg
Northstation	:50	b
Pokers Judge	:49⅕	h
Quixotic Lady	:46⅗	h
Remarkable Blue	:49⅖	b
Rivator	:49⅘	b
Stark Drama	:50	b
Swale	:46⅖	h
SwornStatement	:49⅕	b
Vision	:48⅖	hg
Five Furlongs— :57⅖		
Altered Style	1:03⅘	b
Attune	1:03⅘	b
Belgard	1:01⅗	h
Bright Swan	1:02⅗	b
Counselorette	1:03⅘	b
G.i. Jane	**:59⅘**	**hg**
If Winter Comes	1:01⅗	h
MischiefBrewing	1:00⅘	hg
Ocala Joe	1:03⅘	bg
On the Turn	1:03⅘	b
Tattle Tale	1:01⅗	h
Win	1:05	b
Withdrawn	1:01⅖	h
Six Furlongs—1:08⅖		
Barbs Turn	1:14	h
Dogwood Winter	1:17	b
Keys and Keys	1:15⅕	h
Noble Pocket	**1:13⅕**	**h**
Run Amber Run	1:14⅕	h
Shamrocky	1:13⅗	h
Will's First	1:13⅗	h
1 Mile—1:33		
Country Pine	1:41⅘	b

AU POINT (3f) was under restraint. BALBOA NATIVE (3f) acts good. CAVEAT (4f) went the quarter in :25 and galloped out in 1:02.4. QUIXOTIC LADY (4f) is on the edge. G. I. JANE (5f) had good speed. WILLS FIRST (6f) turned in a good effort. COUNTRY PINE (1m) had a useful trial.

BELMONT PARK – (Training) Track Fast

Three Furlongs		
Cambalache	:36⅗	h
Carasco	:37⅖	b
Counteract	:37⅖	b
Daring Groom	:37	b
Dear Richard	:36⅕	b
Ed's Green Pens	**:35⅕**	**h**
Evoke	:39	b
Fabulous Find	:35⅖	h
I'm in Time	:35⅖	h
La Clash	:39⅕	b
Miss Dutchess	:37⅕	b
Mordida	:39	b
Noble Clansman	:39⅘	b
Ohno	:36	h
Sidewheeler	:36⅕	h
Sportingmoney	:37	b
Structure	:36	h
Wimborne Peace	:39⅘	b
Four Furlongs		
Abacerie	:52	b
Been Loved	:49	b
Bold Trumpeter	:50	b
Computer Carlos	:48	h
Contributing	:49	b
Fanny's Fox	:48⅘	h
First Class Act	:48	h
Fort More	:49⅕	b
Jan's Kinsman	:47⅗	h
Jo Nathan	:49⅗	b
Lament	:52	b
Leroy S.	:49	b
Little Blue Eyes	:50	b
Papa Bull	:49	b
Precious Pearl	:49⅗	b
Rain Prince	**:46**	**h**
Raise Trouble	:47⅘	h
RapidProspector	:50⅕	b
Return for Glory	:49	b
Royalty Prince	:51	b
Scapel	:51⅕	b
So Intent	:50	b
Thirty Flags	:50	b
Three RingCircle	:49	b
Umbriago	:50⅘	b
Wise Bold	:51⅘	b
Wright Skipper	:52	b
Yardstick	:50⅗	b
Five Furlongs		
Adam's Girl	1:03	b
Bravo Ralph	1:04⅕	b
Geraldine'sStore	1:01⅗	b
Huckster	1:01⅖	h
Jiggs Alarm	**1:00⅗**	**h**
Lady Camnelia	1:02⅗	b
Lord Grenville	1:02	b
Lovable Lady	1:01⅘	h
Naughty Nun	1:02⅗	b
Slave Doll	1:03⅘	b
Stretch Dancer	1:02	b
Swaps Hero	1:04	b
Six Furlongs		
Angies Kin	1:16	b
Bemedalled	**1:14**	**h**
I'm for Fun	1:14⅘	b
Osage Chief	1:17	b
1 Mile		
Regal Lady	1:44	b

BELMONT PARK – (Inner Turf) Course Firm (Dogs Up)

Three Furlongs

Chardonelle	**:35⅗**	**h**
Elton Song	:36⅘	h
Laugh With Me	:38⅗	b
Longwinner	:37⅕	b
Rusticlove	:38	b
Top Competitor	:36⅘	h

Four Furlongs

Bedside	:49⅗	b
Belle Glade	:50⅗	b
Chica's Prince	:49	h
Crystal Key	:48⅖	h
Daniel B.	:51	b
Defense	:48⅖	h
Futre Fun	:48⅖	h
Introduction	:50	b
Key Count	:48⅖	h
MggieMcAllister	:50⅘	b
Maidenhead	:48⅕	h
Michael'sPlesure	:48	h
Native Society	:50⅘	b
Neverknock	**:47⅘**	**h**
New Member	:48	h
NorthernRection	:48⅖	h
So Proud	:49⅗	b
Terce	:49⅖	b
Tumarshua	:48⅗	h
Twelve Tone	:53⅗	b
Vocal	:50⅖	b

Five Furlongs

All About Eve	1:03⅖	b
Bigger Enough	1:02	h
Blue Garter	1:03⅖	b
Brady	1:03⅕	b
Cashal	1:01⅖	h
Countess Cork	1:04⅗	b
Esprit de Romeo	1:01⅗	h
Gabfest	1:02	h
Hail John	1:02	h
Hones Edge	1:01⅕	h
HopefulContract	1:01⅗	h
I Take All	1:03⅘	b
Idle Gossip	1:02⅖	h
Jolly Fast	1:02⅘	b
Killmwithkindnss	1:05	b
Kilroy Hawk	1:03	b
Nice Pirate	**1:00⅖**	**h**
Pleasure On Hi	1:03⅘	b
Starack	1:02⅖	h
Starbait	1:01⅕	h
SymphonicPoem	1:01⅖	h
Thallassocrat	1:01⅘	h
Tina's Double	**1:00⅖**	**h**
Triumphal	1:04	b
WeekendWarrior	1:06⅗	b
What A Candy	1:02⅕	h

Six Furlongs

Boastful Knight	1:15⅗	b
Exuberance	1:14⅖	h
Frannies Folly	1:19	b
House Speaker	1:18⅖	h
I'm ASoutherner	1:18⅖	h
Londono	1:18	b
Puma's Pride	1:19	b
Rushing Water	1:14⅖	h
Settimino	1:16⅖	b
Speed Bus	**1:14⅕**	**h**
Torpedo Los	1:15⅕	h

Seven Furlongs

Daners Rib	1:30	b
Telly Ho	**1:29**	**b**

1 Mile

Current Charge	1:42⅗	b
Guiding Rule	1:44⅘	b
Silver Supreme	**1:42**	**b**

AQUEDUCT – (Turf) Course Firm (Dogs Up)

Three Furlongs

For Quack'sSack	:38⅖	b
Helens Champion	**:37**	**h**
Jock's Dawn	:37⅗	h
Runaway Native	:38⅗	b

Four Furlongs

Big Greg	:51⅗	b
Bim Brose Co.	:51	b
Cookies Dance	:51⅖	b
Johanna's Angel	:51	b
Lyndamar	:51	b
Only On Sundae	:51	b
Screen Trend	:50⅗	b
Super Missile	:49⅘	h
The Ghost	**:49⅖**	**h**
Valid Gal	:49⅘	h

Five Furlongs

Acquiesce	1:02⅕	h
Alturas	1:02⅕	h
Halo Dotty	1:02⅕	h
Parthia's	**1:01⅖**	**h**
Tender Heart II	1:02⅗	h

Six Furlongs

Bamboo Fan	1:20	b
Sir Mount	**1:17**	**b**

Seven Furlongs

Tyralno	**1:30**	**b**
Wolfies Rascal	1:30⅖	b

AQUEDUCT – (Inner Dirt) Track Fast

Three Furlongs

Nathan Detroit	:37	h

Four Furlongs

BelievetheDealer	:48⅕	hg
Camino Joe	:48⅗	h
Fleet Alert	:53	b
Halycon Hour	:48⅗	h
JimmySouthStrt	:49	hg
Miss Slewfonic	**:47⅖**	**h**
Palace	:50⅗	b
Princessndthepe	:50⅕	b

Five Furlongs

Brushaway	1:05⅖	b
Cobalt Sixty	1:02⅖	b
Kohala	1:03	b
Mr. Inspector	**1:02**	**h**
Raja Rock	1:02⅗	h
Root Fore	1:03⅗	b
Splits	1:03⅘	b

ported incorrectly. There was no mention of a 1:10.1 six-furlong workout at Saratoga. And a :58.2 grass work at the Spa was reported as 1:00.2 and credited to "Seattle Sue." Later on the name was corrected, but the time of the workout went into the past performances as 1:02.

Bullet workouts are highlighted in bold type. With the workout tab in front of him, the handicapper can judge the true significance of the day's best work at a distance. He will be aware of the number of horses that worked at the distance, and their identity. A maiden that worked faster than a stakes horse at a substantial distance will literally jump off the page.

When a horse travels from one part of the country to another, its workout line often remains behind. Horses that train at private training centers, rather than at the racetracks, often show no workouts at all, or possibly just the last workout in their training sequence. Many tracks require a recent public workout before allowing entry of a horse away from the races for more than a certain amount of time, usually thirty days. Some tracks actually enforce this rule! Obviously, it helps to know which trainers stable and work their horses away from the track, so that the sparse workout lines on their horses can be properly evaluated. The

Preakness winner of 1983, Deputed Testamony, for example, lived and exercised at his trainer's farm in Maryland, and seldom showed workouts in his past performances. The March 26 workout is the mandatory one, qualifying the horse as fit following his winter freshening. Without it, he would not have been allowed to race on April 4.

Deputed Testamony — **B. c. 3, by Traffic Cop—Proof Requested, by Prove It**
Own.—Sears F P — **Br.—Bonita Farm (Md)** — **Tr.—Boniface J William**

126 — Lifetime 11 6 3 0 $147,514 — **1983 4 2 1 0 $92,660** — **1982 7 4 2 0 $54,854**

14May83- 8Key	fst	1^{70}	:47	1:12⅕	1:42⅖	Keystone	2	3	$4^{¾}$	$1^{½}$	$1^{½}$	$1^{4½}$	McCauley W H	122	*.90	88-20	DptdTstmony122^{4½}ClsscStd115^{no}TwoDvds119^{4¼}	Stumbled st.clear	10
28Apr83- 7Kee	sly	1⅛	:46⅘	1:11	1:49⅖	Blue Grass	9	7	7^{10}	7^{9}	$7^{8¼}$	6^{15}	Hawley S	121	13.40	75-16	Play Fellow 121no [D]Marfa 121^{7½} Desert Wine 121^{1}	Outrun	12
16Apr83- 8Pim	fst	1$\frac{1}{16}$	:47⅗	1:12	1:42⅘	[S]Fedrco Tesio	7	5	$5^{4½}$	$3^{½}$	1^{1}	$1^{2¼}$	McCauley W H	116	*1.60e	91-17	DeputedTestamony116^{2¼}DixielandBnd122^{½}IslndChmp110^{1}	Driving	8
4Apr83- 8Key	fst	6½f	:22⅗	:45⅘	1:17⅕	Alw 17000	4	4	4^{3}	$3^{½}$	$2^{1½}$	$2^{1½}$	McCauley W H	113	4.30	85-26	TwoDvids114^{1½}DeputedTestmony113^{1¾}DixielndBnd113^{6¾}	Bobbled	6
18Dec82- 8Med	fr	1	:47⅖	1:11⅖	1:36⅕	Play Palace	4	3	$2^{1½}$	1^{1}	1^{3}	1^{4}	McCauley W H	114	*1.10	101-07	DeputdTstmony114^{4}HdofthHous112^{1¼}OpinionLdr114^{¾}	Ridden out	6
27Nov82- 8Lrl	fst	1$\frac{1}{16}$	:47⅘	1:13⅘	1:45⅕	[S]Maryland Juv	2	6	$6^{3½}$	5^{4}	$4^{2½}$	2no	Miller D A Jr	122	9.10	82-26	Dixieland Band 122no Deputed Testamony122^{1¼}Caveat122^{3¼}	Wide	9
11Nov82- 8Lrl	fst	7f	:23⅕	:46⅘	1:24⅘	Smarten	3	5	$6^{5½}$	$6^{4½}$	2^{5}	$2^{2¼}$	Pino M G	115	2.80e	85-24	SlvgConsltnt115^{2¼}DptdTstmony115^{3¾}Kng'sCorsr115^{5}	Broke right	6
29Oct82- 6Lrl	fst	1	:46⅖	1:12⅖	1:38⅖	Alw 10000	4	4	5^{11}	4^{3}	$2^{½}$	2no	Miller D A Jr	115	*1.70	80-21	[D]Princilian 119no Deputed Testamony115^{3½}Kegley115^{3¼}	Impeded	8
29Oct82-Placed first through disqualification																			
13Oct82- 3Med	sly	6f	:22⅖	:45⅘	1:11⅗	Clm 40000	7	1	2^{hd}	$2^{1½}$	2^{hd}	1^{3}	Gonzalez B	118	13.80	85-20	Deputed Testamony 118^{3} Acclimated 113^{5} AlwaysUp118^{1}	Driving	7
28Sep82- 1Key	fst	6f	:23	:47⅕	1:12⅘	Md 22500	8	3	1^{2}	1^{1}	$1^{½}$	$1^{3½}$	Wilson R	120	6.00	77-21	DputdTstmony120^{3½}Sus'sTbl120^{2¾}MontnClnsmn120^{6¼}	Ridden out	10
21Sep82- 5Bow	fst	6f	:23⅕	:46⅘	1:12⅗	Md 25000	6	7	$4^{4½}$	6^{15}	6^{11}	6^{13}	Byrnes D	120	16.10	64-27	MarchingForMargy120^{5½}Blue'sFriend120^{3½}Shekmatyr118^{nk}	Tired	11

LATEST WORKOUTS ●**Mar 26 Pim 6f fst 1:14⅖ h**

Immediately below the day's workouts at some tracks are found the "clockers' comments" regarding the performance or appearance of selected horses that worked that morning. Top stakes horses usually draw comment, as do lesser animals that may have worked especially well. The comment might state simply that a horse "appears fit," or "was impressive." The fractional times in which a stakes animal worked may be given. An equipment change may be noted. A name jockey who worked a horse may be identified. At times, the clockers' comments give a slight clue as to what the trainer tried to accomplish with the workout. The comment "finished fast" indicates the horse was rated during the early stages of its work, then finished strongly. A horse may work six furlongs in 1:14, jogging for the first two furlongs, then finishing out in :46. Another comment might report that two or three (inexperienced) horses "worked in company," or that one horse "bested" another. The trainer may have been trying to give one horse the experience of racing inside another horse or between rivals, or possibly behind others, teaching the horse how to rate, and getting the animal accustomed to having dirt kicked in its face. Or the trainer simply may have been trying to get a line on the relative ability of two or three of his young horses. Whatever the comments might reveal, that information is not carried over into the past performances. At times, this gives workout-tab collectors a big advantage over an unknowing public.

In some locales, "trial races" are held for young (usually two-year-old) horses. The end of the winter season in South Carolina is heralded by the Aiken Trials. Juveniles stabled at Saratoga during the early summer months are given a taste of actual competition at the Saratoga Trials. Although many of these races are at short distances (such as two fur-

Two Notch Road Is Aiken Trial Star

(Special to Daily Racing Form)

AIKEN, S.C.—Mrs. Willard C. Freeman's Two Notch Road took command in the stretch and scored a two-length victory in Saturday's featured City of Aiken Cup at the 41st running of the Aiken Trials.

For the first time in recent years, no one stable dominated the trials, a traditional coming-out party for untested thoroughbreds.

A crowd of more than 15,000 watched Two Notch Road, a 3-year-old filly by King's Bishop—Assemblywoman trained by Mike Freeman, outrace some fancy rivals to complete four furlongs in :48⅗ under Ken Houghton. Buckingham Farm's Gustavia was second and Mrs. H.D. Paxson's Swap Swap third in the event for maiden 3-year-old fillies.

Claiborne Farm's Fervently, trained by Steve Penrod and ridden by John McInerney, took the day's only other half-mile race, the co-featured John M. Gaver Trophy.

Fervently overtook front-runner Regal Rule to post a three-length victory in :49⅗. Quobow was third.

Buckland Farm's Northern Damsel, Kevin Hirstius up on the Ronnie Thomas-trained filly, captured the first of four quarter-mile trials for 2-year-old, finishing two lengths ahead of Lario Lace. Altmodisch was third in the trial, run in :24⅗.

In the second trial, Todahiro Hotehama's T.H. Bend edged Bwamazon Farm's Withdrawn by a half-length with Buckland Farm's Reserve Speaker third. Ricky Moss rode the winner, who raced the two furlongs in :23⅗.

The results of the trials follow:

FIRST TRIAL—1/4 MILE. (2-year-olds. Fillies)
1. Northern Damsel (Northern Jove—Damsel); K. Hirstius.
2. Lario Lace (Lothario—Ebony Necklace); T. O'Brien.
3. Altodisch (Avatar—Old Fangled); V. Walzlavick.
Time :24⅗
Also ran—Lady's Reception; Ark.

SECOND TRIAL 1/4 MILE. (2-year-olds. Colts and Geldings)
1. T. H. Ben (Full Out—Valiant Dame); R. Moss.
2. Withdrawn (To The Quick—Unsociable); K. Hirstius.
3. Reserve Speaker (Full Partner—Discourse); C. Daub.
Time :23⅗
Also Ran—Tricky Nicki, King of Wales.

THIRD TRIAL—1/4 MILE. (2-year-olds. Fillies)
1. Modicum (General Assembly—Sandstream); J. Jones.
2. Runny Nose (It's Freezing—Coraggiosio); V. Walzlavick.
3. Unnamed (Judger—Goodish); L. Jones.
Time :23
Also ran—Ageless Idea; Full Song.

FOURTH TRIAL—1/4 MILE. (2-year-olds. Colts and Geldings)
1. Unnamed (Broadway Forli—A.M. Receiver); J. Jones.
2. Tube (Full Out—Pickture Tube); V. Walzlavick.
3. Full Confidence (Full Partner—Cold Trick); K. Hirstius.
Time :23.
Also ran—Snowcot.

FIFTH TRIAL—1/2 MILE. (Maidens. 3-year-olds. Colts and Geldings)
1. Fervently (Believe It—Romanticism); J. McInerney.
2. Rega Rule (Quack—Regal Rev); V. Walzlavick.
3. Quobow (Quid Pro Quid—Belle Fiddle); M. Dowd.
Time :49⅗.
Also ran—French Sovereign; Wave The Wand.

SIXTH TRIAL—1/2 MILE. (3-year-olds. Maidens. Fillies)
1. Two Notch Road (King's Bishop—Assemblywoman); K. Houghton.
2. Gustiavia (Lyphard—Wildwook); J. Townsend.
3. Swap Swap (Quid Pro Quid—Leap Of Faith); K. Hirstius.
Time :48⅗
Also ran—Calossahatchee; Pride's Crossing.
Scratched—Honest Glow.

longs), they give fans and horsemen alike a chance to observe the horses under race conditions. The results of these trials are reported a couple of days later in the *Form*, but are not included in the horse's past performances. Serious players clip the results of the trials, and save them as they would result charts or workout tabs.

When a relatively unknown horse works well in company with an established horse of some ability, clever handicappers take notice, and eagerly await that horse's appearance in the entries. When Megaturn came to the races on March 3, 1983, his workout line was nothing out of the ordinary. But many New Yorkers were aware that the colt had worked competitively with Strike Gold as a two-year-old. Since the latter was quickly establishing a reputation as one of the country's fastest three-year-olds, the denizens of Aqueduct concluded that Megaturn was a colt of considerable talent, and bet him down to 5–2 for his debut. They were proven correct, as Megaturn's impressive stretch charge carried him to a three-length victory.

Megaturn	Dk. b. or br. c. 3, by Best Turn—Good Taste, by Vertex		Lifetime	1983 0 M 0 0
	Br.—Welcome Farm & Winn (Pa)	**122**	0 0 0 0	1982 0 M 0 0
Own.—Peace J H	Tr.—Nieminski Richard			
LATEST WORKOUTS	Feb 26 Bel tr.t 4f fst :49⅘ h Feb 19 Bel tr.t 3f fst :36½ h Feb 6 Bel tr.t 4f fst :48¾ h Jan 22 Bel tr.t 4f fst :47½ h			

For the most part, however, the workout tabs and the workout times themselves fail to reveal what the trainer was attempting to do with the work. Was he interested in developing speed? Or building stamina? Was a slow "breeze" sufficient to keep the horse fit? Did the horse work in company? Was the horse rated early, or was it pushed early, and allowed to tire? Were blinkers used for the first time? How much did the workout rider weigh? Did the horse work in the middle of the track, around imaginary dogs? Did the workout advance the horse's conditioning or help it maintain its present sharpness? Did the horse come back blowing hard, obviously tired after its exercise? As a rule, only the trainer knows the answer to many of these questions. The answers, however, affect the final time of the workout, and its intrinsic value to the horse. For these reasons, it is foolish to attempt to "rate" workout times (assign them speed figures), and then compare them with times achieved in actual competition. Nonetheless, it is wise to save the workout tabs each day, for future reference, and not only to preserve the clockers' comments, as the next example shows.

CASE STUDY: DANCE PRINCESS

Horses usually are returned to the races, or prepared for their racing debuts, with a series of (published) workouts over a period of time possibly as long as two or three months. Yet only the four most recent work-outs appear in the past performances. A key workout may not appear, having been superseded by four subsequent works. When Dance Princess came to the races on May 29, 1978, her workout line appeared nothing out of the ordinary. In actuality, it was—the filly by Northern Dancer had worked six furlongs in a sparkling 1:10.2 in early May, a workout no longer appearing in her past performances. When Dance Princess romped home an easy fourteen-length victress in 1:10.3, work-out-tab collectors rushed to the cashiers' windows and collected a very liberal $15.80.

Why the delay between the key workout and the filly's racing debut? Did the trainer feel she needed more seasoning before starting in an actual race? Or was he intentionally disguising her "form," hoping to cash a bet? We do not know, but we must also consider the further possibility that the filly had a problem that delayed her debut. In this case, not a likely one—Dance Princess' steady stream of workouts leaves little room for the treatment of a physical problem.

Dance Princess	B. f. 3, by Northern Dancer—Queen Sucree, by Ribot		St. 1st 2nd 3rd	Amt.
	Br.—Olin J M (Ky)		1978 0 M 0 0	
Own.—Mangurian H T Jr	Tr.—Root Thomas F Jr	**113**	1977 0 M 0 0	
LATEST WORKOUTS May 24 Bel 3f sly :36⅕ hg(d)	May 20 Bel 3f fst :35 hg	May 16 Bel 5f my 1:02⅗ h (d)	● May 11 Bel 6f fst 1:13⅕ h	

This same maneuver also may be used to hide an impressive grass workout for a horse set to make its grass debut. Players who save work-out tabs would be among those "in the know."

☐ SPEED, DISTANCE, AND SPACING ☐

The speed, distance, and spacing of workouts are all important, and somewhat interrelated. What exactly constitutes a fast workout? Unfortunately, there is no pat answer. As a general rule of thumb, any horse equaling or bettering the following standards can be considered to have worked fast:

3f	:36
4f	:48
5f	1:00
6f	1:13
7f	1:26
1m	1:39

At most tracks, stakes horses can be expected to (easily) better these standards. On the other hand, at most minor league tracks, these times would be unrealistically fast. The handicapper must learn for himself what is fast on his local circuit.

Generally speaking, horses that work fast can be considered fit, unless fatigued by their training regimen. Improvement in workout times often correlates with improved form in the afternoon. Some horses need hard work to stay fit, and thrive on fast workouts. Secretariat was a notable example. Others, termed "morninglories," work brilliantly in the morning, but fail to reproduce anything resembling that speed in real competition. These horses are said to have "left their race on the training track." They run faster, and their stride is smoother, when they are relaxed. When faced with competition in the afternoon, they become tense, or distracted, and unable to do their best. As we mentioned in Chapter 12, the addition of blinkers may be all that is necessary to convert a morninglory into a winner. On the other hand, many morninglories are incurable.

Notice that Recreate had two sharp half-mile workouts preceding his well-backed racing debut on June 24. Then, after showing nothing in his first two races, the colt once again worked fast for his engagement on July 16. Sharp players were not fooled this time. The three-year-old colt once again raced poorly.

Recreate	Ch. c. 3, by Unconscious—Ragtime Girl, by Francis S			Lifetime	1983	2 M 0 0
	Br.—Harbor View Farm (Ky)			2 0 0 0	1982	0 M 0 0
Own.—Harbor View Farm	Tr.—Martin Jose		**116**			

| 2Jly83- 6Bel fst 6f | .22½ .46½ 1.11¾ | 3+ Md Sp Wt | 9 9 7¹⁰ 7¹¹ 8¹¹ 7¹⁶ Graell A | 116 | 12 60 | 68-16 Will's First 116⁴½ Miami Lakes 116²¼ Avid Dancer 111¾ | Outrun 11 |
| 24Jun83- 9Bel fst 7f | .23½ .46½ 1:24 | 3+ Md Sp Wt | 1 11 6²½ 8¹¹10²¹10²³ Cordero A Jr | 114 | 4 60 | 59-20 GlintMindd114⁵½SpringCommndr122ⁿᵏIndnL114ⁿᵏ | Stumbled start 11 |

LATEST WORKOUTS ● Jly 13 Bel tr.t 4f fst :47 h   Jly 7 Bel ⊤ 4f fm :48 h (d)   Jun 22 Bel tr.t 4f fst :47¾ h   Jun 16 Bel tr.t 4f fst :47¾ h

Numerous trainers across the country make the mistake of asking too much of their horses in the morning. They put their horses through the equivalent of boot camp preparing them for the races. Their typical horse returning from a layoff, or making its racing debut, has been prepared with a series of bullet workouts at distances ranging from three furlongs up to a mile. When the horse finally gets to the races, it is a well-seasoned athlete ready to give a peak performance. Some, however, are exhausted by the time they reach the races, and never reproduce their morning form. They are not the typical morninglory, and they do not have a mental block against racing. Others last only a race or two before deteriorating form sets in, yet the bullet workouts continue between races, compounding the problem.

Handicappers must proceed cautiously when dealing with such trainers, and understand the implications of their rigid training regimen—peak performances off layoffs, and the possibility of quickly deteriorating form. Should one of their horses return to the races (debut) without the typical workout pattern, don't expect much. And when one of their animals throws in a bad race, expect more of the same.

A fast three- or four-furlong workout is relatively meaningless if turned in by a front-running sprinter. One would expect such horses to work fast over short distances. But if the same workout were recorded by a stretch-running sprinter, or a router about to turn back to a sprint distance, it would assume a much greater significance. On the other hand, a fast, short workout can put a router too much "on its toes." When High Schemes worked three panels in :33.2 for the mile and a half Coaching Club American Oaks, trainer P. G. Johnson was understandably annoyed with jockey Samyn, who had worked the filly. A horse must relax in the early stages of a race at a classic distance, and a bullet work at three furlongs can prove counterproductive. Luckily for Samyn, High Schemes ran the race of her life in the Oaks, winning by open daylight.

High Schemes — Ch. f. 3, by High Echelon—Sweetly Scheming, by Creme Dela Creme
Br.—King Mr-Mrs J Howard (Ky)
Own.—Morrisey J O Jr — Tr.—Johnson Philip G — 121
Lifetime 9 3 3 2 $90,411 — 1983 8 3 2 2 $88,211 — 1982 1 M 1 0 $2,200

18Jun83- 8Bel	fst	1⅛	:46⅖	1:10⅖	1:49⅕	ⒻMotherGoose	2	4	4 1½	2hd	2½	2 3	Samyn J L		121	6.30	78-18 Able Money 121 3 High Schemes 121 3½ Far Flying 121 3	Brushed 7
29May83- 1Bel	fst	1 1/16	:47⅗	1:11⅖	1:42⅕	3↑ⒻAlw 23000	3	4	4 2	1 1	1 4	1 6¼	Samyn J L		108	*.90	91-11 HighSchemes108 6¼Kouklamou106hdCrefulGlnce110 10	Ridden out 6
18May83- 7Bel	fst	7f	:22⅗	:45⅖	1:23	3↑ⒻAlw 22000	1	7	4 4	4 4	4 4	4 3¾	Samyn J L		109	2.70	83-15 FarFlying114 3½Poppa'sBigLil110noLadyLothrio119nk	Wide stretch 7
7May83- 7Aqu	fst	1	:45⅗	1:09⅘	1:36⅘	3↑ⒻLdy Golconda	3	3	3 1	2hd	1½	3 1½	Samyn J L	b	108	1.90	80-19 RonPromis119 1½SwiftAndSuddn119hdHighSchms108 5¾	Weakened 6
17Apr83- 8Aqu	fst	1	:46⅕	1:11⅖	1:37⅘	ⒻRare Perfume	8	5	5 5½	5 5½	4 4	2½	Clayton M D		112	*1.00e	76-23 Pretty Sensible 112½ High Schemes112hdLovinTouch115¾	Bore in 8
25Mar83- 6Aqu	fst	1⅛	:49⅘	1:16⅖	1:55⅖	ⒻAlw 21000	6	4	3 5	1hd	1 1½	1 3	Clayton M D5		116	3.30e	58-36 High Schemes 116 3 After Life 116 2¼ Cains Dusty 116 2	Driving 8
6Mar83- 6Aqu	fst	1⅛ ⊡	:49	1:14⅘	1:54	ⒻMd Sp Wt	8	4	3 2½	2½	1½	1 1¾	Clayton M D7		114	*1.50e	76-19 High Schemes 114 1¾ Cains Dusty 116 2¼ Acquiesce 121 6	Driving 9
20Feb83- 6Aqu	fst	6f ⊡	:22⅘	:46⅘	1:11⅘	ⒻMd Sp Wt	3	10	9 9½	7 10	6 11	3 8½	Clayton M D7		114	4.40	76-20 Able Money121 6¾ShawneeCreek121 1¾HighSchemes114¾	Mild rally 14
15Nov82- 3Aqu	gd	6f	:23⅕	:48	1:12⅖	ⒻMd 30000	2	13	9 8	7 5¾	2hd	2½	Clayton M D7		110	23.80	78-24 T. V. Snow 117½ High Schemes 110 5 Hello Julie 117½	Sluggish 14

LATEST WORKOUTS ●Jly 8 Bel 3f fst :33⅖ h ●Jly 2 Bel 7f fst 1:24⅘ h Jun 27 Bel 4f fst :48⅕ h Jun 11 Bel tr.t 6f fst 1:14⅘ h

A good long workout (six furlongs or more) assumes special significance in certain cases. When recorded by a six-furlong speedball, one assumes the trainer is attempting to build the horse's stamina, apparently with some success. If recorded by a horse returning from a layoff, or making its racing debut, it suggests the trainer has put a good foundation under the horse. If accompanied by a sharp, short workout and, for horses debuting, a good workout from the gate, the horse is likely to be seasoned enough to win at first asking. Such was the case with Caruso, who won his debut by seven lengths in an exceptionally strong MSW field at Santa Anita on February 2, 1983.

Caruso — Ch. c. 3, by Messenger of Song—Marlborough Set, by Acroterion
Br.—Ridder Georgia B (Cal) — 1983 0 M 0 0
Own.—Ridder Georgia B — 118 — Tr.—Campbell Gordon C — 1982 0 M 0 0
Lifetime 0 0 0 0

Jan 30 SA 4f gd :49 2 hg Jan 17 SA 7f ft 1:25 3 h Jan 11 SA 6f ft 1:13 1 h Jan 6 SA 6f ft 1:12 3 h

A very fast workout by a cheap horse, especially one entered in a maiden claiming race, can be misleading. The trainer likely has asked the horse to give its all in the morning, hoping the impressive work will catch the eye of another horseman. The trainer is setting the bait, hoping, no doubt, to have the horse claimed. If the horse were really working like a good one, why not race it in maiden special company?

Authors of handicapping books usually warn that a horse which neither races nor works for an extended period of time is probably unfit, unable to get to the track. As a general rule, they are right. Here are the statistics for horses whose last race was good, but have since been absent from the races at least seventeen days and have no published workouts:

NH	WPCT	I.V.	$NET
521	8.3%	0.74	$1.15

The usually powerful "good race last" statistics have been severely damaged. Yet horses should be viewed as individuals, not statistics. Some need frequent work to remain sharp. Others need little more than leisurely jogging each morning.

If a horse's recent record shows closely spaced races and workouts, the animal is probably fit. A horse able to work a half mile or longer between races, and within a few days of its next scheduled engagement, is likely a fit animal. The trainer is telling us as much. Otherwise, he wouldn't ask the horse for the extra effort. A horse away from the races for a few weeks, or a couple of months, can be considered fit (not necessarily sharp) if able to work out every four or five days. Since the trainer's intentions are not known to the average player, the speed and distance of the works are usually only of secondary importance.

If a horse has failed to work since its most recent start, look at its recent record. Had it previously been able to race well without workouts? Some trainers can keep a horse sharp simply by jogging it between races. They achieve good results with a minimum of timed workouts. Others accomplish the same with slow breezes. Still others have the knack of sneaking a horse past the clockers, and getting a key work into a horse without having it timed and reported. Serious players make it their business to become familiar with each individual trainer's use of workouts.

We end this chapter by emphasizing the fact that conditioning gained in actual competition is of far greater value to a horse than its morning exercise.

Chapter 14

MONEY MANAGEMENT

Good handicapping alone does not make a winning horse-player. How one bets his selections also is of considerable importance. Horseplayers operate against a house takeout far greater than what they would face in the gambling casinos, or when betting on football with their bookie. The typical North American track takes 17 percent from the win, place, and show pools, and even more from the exotic wagering pools. Yet the horseplayer has a better chance of overcoming these odds than does the casino gambler. To do so, the player must be selective in his wagering, betting only when the odds are greater than his chances of cashing the bet.

Successful players confine their betting to "overlay" situations, to use the racetrack vernacular. They cannot afford to bet "underlays," horses whose odds are much shorter than their realistic chances of winning. More often than not, one's handicapping analysis will fail to produce a definite selection. Rather, it will produce two or three horses worth further consideration. In this situation, conservative players may pass the race while others will play the overlay among the three, and still others will turn to the exotics, hoping to find a value play there.

One feels foolish getting off a winner simply because its odds were too low. To be successful, however, a handicapper must learn to accept such reversals, with a view to the long-range goal of seasonal profits. It is impossible to win at the races betting consistently with the crowd.

☐ THE ODDS ☐

Experienced handicappers realize that the odds board is underlaid at both extremes. Bettors tend to go overboard on the chances of many favorites. On the other hand, numerous players waste their money on the chances of hopeless longshots, either from ignorance, or simply to play a horse at a big price. Many horses that start at 25–1 really should be 100–1.

Most longshot winners, however, are not true longshots, in the sense that their victory came with no apparent explanation. One can usually be found after the race, yet for some reason the betting public overlooked the horse and its virtues.

A horse's odds from previous starts appear in its past performances, immediately to the right of the weight it carried in each of those races.

```
New Discovery            B. c. 4, by Arts and Letters—Synphonos, by Le Fabuleux          Lifetime      1983  1  0  0  0
                              Br.—DuPont Mrs W III (Ky)                           119   22  1  3  6    1982 10  1  2  2   $87,798
  Own.—Allen H A              Tr.—Jacobs Eugene                                           $136,954     Turf  3  0  0  1    $2,400
22Apr83- 7Aqu fst 6f     :22⅖ :45⅗ 1:10⅕      Alw 20000   2  6  69½ 611 65½ 65¾ Velasquez J  117  *2.20  84-16 Ski Jump 1102 Tory Willow 117hd Primary Care 117½   No factor 7
 1Aug82- 8Bel fm 1¼ [T]:48⅗ 1:37⅕ 2:01⅘      Lexington    4  4  53  66¾ 610 614 Vasquez J    114   6.80  71-20 [D]Dew Line 1171 Royal Roberto 1261½ [D]Reinvested 1261¾   Tired 6
     1Aug82-Run in Two Divisions 6th & 8th Races
18Jly82- 9Bel fm 1  (T):46⅕ 1:10⅖ 1:35⅗ 3↑ Alw 20000  12 10 106½ 85½ 64½ 54 Vasquez J     113  *2.50  83-19 Who's For Dinner 112½ Beagle 1071¾ James Boswell 117¾   Wide 12
 6Jly82- 1Bel fm 1 1/16 [T]:47⅗ 1:10⅘ 1:42⅕ 3↑ Alw 20000  5  5  52¼ 53½ 44 31½ Cordero A Jr  114   *.60e 88-19 Hunter Hawk 1131 Nathan Detroit 113½NewDiscovery1141   Rallied 7
 1May82- 8CD fst 1¼      :46⅕ 1:37⅕ 2:02⅖      Ky Derby     3 10 1112 1818 1811 1819 Bailey J D  126   8.90f 66-13 Gato Del Sol 1262½ Laser Light 126nk Reinvested 1262½   Far back 19
22Apr82- 7Kee fst 1⅛     :46⅗ 1:10  1:48       Blue Grass   7  9  710 814 720 725 Velasquez J  121  14.20  72-13 Linkage 1215½GatoDelSol121½WaveringMonarch1217½   No menace 9
 3Apr82- 9GP fst 1⅛      :47⅕ 1:11⅕ 1:49⅗      Fla Derby    6  5  510 510 612 513 Vasquez J    118  12.30  71-15 Timely Writer 1222 Star Gallant 1228 OurEscapade122½   No factor 7
 6Mar82-10Hia sly 1⅛     :46⅖ 1:10⅘ 1:49⅗      Flamingo    12 14  107½ 63¼ 34½ 23½ Velasquez J 122  13.50  80-17 Timely Writer 1223½ New Discovery 1221¼LeDanseur122nk   Rallied 16
13Feb82-10Hia fst 1⅛     :46⅕ 1:10⅖ 1:48⅘      Everglades   3  5  48½ 44½ 2hd 21½ Velasquez J  112   7.20  86-14 RoyalRoberto1141½NewDiscovery1122VictorianLine1194½   Brushed 8
30Jan82-10Hia fst 6f     :22⅖ :45⅘ 1:11⅖       Md Sp Wt     6  9  88½ 810 41 12½ Velasquez J   120   5.20  86-12 NewDiscovery1202½PrinceWestport1201½ToThePenny1201   Driving 12
  LATEST WORKOUTS   May 18 Bel tr.t 3f fst :36 b   May 12 Bel tr.t 5f fst :59⅘ h   ●May 7 Bel 1 fst 1:37⅗ h   May 2 Bel tr.t 1 fst 1:40⅘ h
```


Odds of 3.60 mean that the track stakes $3.60 (of the other bettors' money) for each dollar wagered on the horse. Such a horse would pay $9.20 per $2.00 bet if it were the winner, returning the player his $2.00 wager plus a $7.20 profit. Should a horse have raced as part of a stable entry, the symbol *e* would appear after its odds. New Discovery raced as part of an entry at Belmont on July 6, 1982.

In the case of overflow fields including more than twelve horses, those judged (by the track handicapper) least likely to succeed will be grouped together as an "entry" for betting purposes, and termed the "field." They usually are assigned the number twelve on the track program. Pari-mutuel fields are designated in the past performances by the symbol *f* appearing after the horse's odds. New Discovery raced as part of the "field" in the 1982 Kentucky Derby.

☐ FAVORITES ☐

If a horse had been the betting favorite in a race, an * will precede its odds. New Discovery was favored in three of his four most recent starts.

Horses that were favored last out and ran well, finishing either first, second, or third, are worth following. Those that lost as favorite do slightly better next time out, as the following statistics show:

	NH	WPCT	MPCT	I.V.	$NET
Won as favorite	312	23.1%	50.6%	2.04	$1.78
Ran second/third	253	23.3%	54.2%	2.06	$1.94

On the other hand, a horse that has been beaten frequently as favorite should be avoided. It has failed to perform as expected in the past, and likely will continue to do so in the future.

For years, favorites have been winning approximately 33 percent of their races, yet costing their backers approximately 10 percent on their investment. Is there a selective method of betting favorites that will increase the percentage of winners and turn that 10 percent loss into a betting profit? In sprint races, backing only those favorites returning within seven days of their most recent race produces just one play every six races. Yet these selections win almost 45 percent of their starts and produce a profit in excess of 20 percent.

	NH	NW	WPCT	I.V.	$NET
Sprint favorites—7 days	65	29	44.6%	4.00	$2.41

Restricting play in route races to favorites breaking from posts one through four produced more action—better than one every two races—and a win percentage of almost 40 percent, but the profit was small:

	NH	NW	WPCT	I.V.	$NET
Route favorites—posts 1–4	177	70	39.5%	3.19	$2.09

Betting favorites in the day's last race often prove to be overlays in the wagering, as the majority of the audience looks elsewhere in an attempt to get even for the day. We surveyed the results of 364 days' racing in New York, and found only 104 winning ninth-race favorites, well below average. Yet these same horses produced an average payoff of $1.93, considerably above average for favorites. The low percentage of winners probably reflects the large fields and lower-class animals that usually contest the day's nightcap in New York (and elsewhere), while the high average payoff proves our point.

CASE STUDY: CHICA'S PRINCE

When a horse with poor recent form receives surprising support at the betting windows while at the same time showing some signs of life, it is worth following in its next start. Chica's Prince was a case in point when entered in a maiden route at Aqueduct on May 11, 1983. Never bet below 20–1 previously, the three-year-old grandson of Secretariat was suddenly just 9–1 in a decent field of maidens at a distance shorter than any he had previously tried. The sign of improvement? The colt showed surprising speed, racing within two lengths of the lead for the first half mile before tiring on that occasion. When entered back at a more suitable route distance on May 11, Chica's Prince raced close to the lead throughout, and gamely held off the challenge of Sweet Affiliation.

Chica's Prince — Ch. c. 3, by Dactylographer—Chica Linda, by Grey Dawn II
Own.—Longford K Sta[ble — Br.—Royal Palm Breeders (Fla) — Tr.—Cincotta Vincent J — **113**
Lifetime 9 1 0 2 $17,100 — 1983 7 1 0 1 $14,700 — 1982 2 M 0 1 $2,400

11May83- 6Aqu fst	1⅛	:49⅘	1:15⅕	1:54⅕	Md Sp Wt	3	5	4¾	2hd	2½	1¾	Migliore R	b 122	12.10	64-30	Chica's Prince 122¾ Sweet Affiliation 1221¼ Terse 1222½	Driving	7
30Apr83- 4Aqu fst	6f	:22⅘	:46⅖	1:11⅗	Md Sp Wt	3	8	32	42½	44½	57½	Davis R G	b 122	9.10	75-22	Spring Fever 1221¾ Naskra's Gold 1223¾HailColumbus122hd	Tired	8
15Apr83- 6Aqu fst	7f	:22⅘	:45⅘	1:24⅕	Md Sp Wt	5	9	95¼	99½	814	812	Migliore R	122	23.20	68-29	Intention 1221½ Pac Mania 1222¼ Au Point 122½	Steadied	10
30Mar83- 6Aqu fst	7f	:23	:46⅖	1:25⅖	Md Sp Wt	3	12	69¼	56½	54½	3nk	Migliore R	122	78.90	74-24	Chaudiere 117hd Scarlet Hobeau 122nkChica'sPrince122nk	Rallied	13
5Mar83- 6Aqu fst	170 [•]	:49⅕	1:14⅕	1:44	Md Sp Wt	7	7	73¾	76	47½	48¼	Migliore R	122	42.60	74-16	LedTheWy1222½LordHtchet1223SweetAffilition1222¾	Lacked rally	10
24Feb83- 4Aqu fst	1⅛ [•]	:48⅕	1:13⅗	1:54⅗	Md Sp Wt	3	4	44	55¾	58½	611	Migliore R	122	44.00	62-24	Dirge 1221¼ Fast John 1221½ Lead The Way 1221¼	Tired	11
8Jan83- 4Aqu fst	1$\frac{1}{16}$ [•]	:48⅕	1:13⅘	1:46⅖	Md Sp Wt	2	7	75¼	95¾	76¼	812	Migliore R	122	37.10	69-16	Potentiate 122no Aztec Red 1224¾ North Glade 1221¾	No factor	11
31Dec82- 6Aqu fst	1⅛ [•]	:49⅘	1:15⅘	1:54	Md Sp Wt	2	4	43	32½	25	310	Migliore R	118	38.10	66-25	EspritDeRomeo1189¼Terse1131Chica'sPrince1183½	Led; weakened	7
8Dec82- 4Aqu fst	170 [•]	:47⅗	1:13	1:44	Md Sp Wt	3	8	814	815	815	722	Migliore R	118	39.40	60-21	A Native Yank 11810 Wild Chorus1183Hunter'sDawn1185¾	Outrun	10

LATEST WORKOUTS Apr 28 Bel tr.t 5f fst 1:00 h Apr 13 Bel tr.t 5f fst 1:03 b Mar 26 Bel tr.t 5f fst 1:02 b

☐ CREATING AN ODDS LINE ☐

For the most part, however, it is the odds today that concern the handicapper. Which horses are bargains (overlays)? Which are "live," clearly being bet by their stable? To answer these questions, a handicapper must be able to anticipate the odds. He must be able to create his own odds line for the race. Offered here are two approaches. One is based on good handicapping judgment. The other demands considerable research effort beforehand, and some fancy arithmetic.

Suppose that you like a certain horse. Your handicapping tells you that two of its rivals each stand a 50–50 chance of beating your selection, while none of the others in the field have any reasonable chance whatsoever. Clearly, 2–1 odds would be fair. Should your selection's form or ability be somewhat clouded, perhaps because it is moving up in class, trying grass for the first time, returning from a layoff, or being ridden by other than its regular jockey, then you might revise your estimate upward to 3–1 or 4–1, adding one point for each "cloud." In other words, for each "equal" in the field, we demand one point in the odds.

Should another rival figure to finish ahead of our selection once every three tries, we demand another half-point be added to the estimated fair odds. If once in six tries, another fifth of a point. If a seemingly superior rival may outfinish our selection three times in four, we would add three points to the odds instead of the usual one. And if uncertain that our selection will reproduce its best form, or not be suited by the conditions, we would add another point or two to the odds. Whatever the total, it represents our estimation of the minimal odds acceptable on that horse.

In a more nonintuitive vein, suppose that we have available the results of some statistical research on combinations of the major handicapping factors. And suppose further that these studies tell us that a certain horse has a 25 percent chance of winning, because horses with similar comprehensive past-performance profiles have won 25 percent of their starts. One then might say that such a horse is worth 3–1 odds, and is an overlay at anything higher. It would be better, however, to do a little more work, estimating by the same criteria the chances of all horses in the race, or at least those considered contenders. For example, suppose we have four horses with the following likelihoods of winning:

Horse	Percent
A	30%
B	25%
C	20%
D	15%
	90%

This represents a rather weak field of contenders, their combined probabilities adding up to less than 100 percent. However, relative to these opponents, Horse A's chances of winning are slightly better than the 30 percent originally calculated. Rather, that figure must be divided by the total for the race (30% / 90%), giving the horse one third of the race's total probability, making its fair odds 2–1. Likewise, revised estimates for the other three contenders can be calculated, giving the following estimate of their fair odds:

Horse	True Percent	Fair Odds
A	⅓	2–1
B	5/18	5–2
C	2/9	7–2
D	1/6	5–1

Fair odds are calculated by means of the simple formula:

$$Odds = (1.0/PCT) - 1.0$$

☐ OVERLAYS AND UNDERLAYS ☐

When a horse's odds are higher than anticipated, the bettor finds himself in an overlay situation. Nevertheless, he must still ask the question "Why is this horse not being bet?" Rather than an overlay, might the horse be an example of what is termed "ice"—a horse not being bet because insiders know the animal is not likely to reproduce its apparent good form? On the other hand, a horse may be somewhat ignored in the betting simply because its jockey and/or trainer are not fashionable, or because it has a difficult post position. Or it is pitted against an overwhelming favorite, or because it had been on the also-eligible list, and consequently escaped notice of many public (and private) handicappers.

CASE STUDY: PEREGRINE POWER

Peregrine Power repeated his victory of March 24 nine days later at Aqueduct, yet paid a generous $16.20. Why the liberal payoff?

Claimed for $12,500 by Steve Sech on February 21, the gelding rallied mildly when raised in price to $16,000, then won when (apparently) reduced to $14,000. But in actuality, the March 24 race was for $16,000 stock—two rivals in the April 2 field were coming from the same race, and had been entered for that price. So the clue that Peregrine Power was not rising in class was there in the past performances for all to see. Obviously, many missed it, possibly because the horse had been on the also-eligible list, and consequently received just a cursory glance during the early stages of their handicapping. Many thought the horse was stepping back up in class, and hence the decent odds.

The crowd instead made Ruler Come Back, an unsound and deteriorating seven-year-old with only thirty-six career starts, their 6–5 favorite, based no doubt on his recent runner-up finish to Dancer's Melody, a horse in the midst of a meteoric rise up the class ladder, from bottom-rung claimer to allowance winner. It was a mistaken case of comparative handicapping.

Speed handicappers had a better line on these two horses. Peregrine

Power's latest victory rated 103, compared to a pair of 99s for Ruler Come Back's recent performances at the $16,000 level.

Peregrine Power — B. g. 6, by Assemblyman—Halconera, by Hyphen
$16,000 Br.—Thornmar Farm (Md) Tr.—Sech Steve — **119**
Own.—Sech S
Lifetime 81 13 8 9 $123,794 — 1983 5 2 0 0 $14,52(— 1982 16 2 2 1 $21,83(— Turf 1 0 0 0 $36(

24Mar83- 1Aqu	fst	7f	:23⅖	:47⅕	1:25	Clm 14000	6	5	53¼	84¾	22	12	Migliore R	b 113	5.60	76-26	Peregrine Power 1132 Court Wise112hdSpartanMonk1171	Driving	1
6Mar83- 2Aqu	fst	6f	⊡:22⅗	:45⅘	1:11⅕	Clm 16000	4	8	97½	89	46½	43¾	Migliore R	b 117	11.90e	84-19	Rapido'sRepeat1121½InfiniteSg1121¾RulerComeBck117½	Mild bid	14
21Feb83- 2Aqu	fst	6f	⊡:23	:46⅖	1:12⅖	Clm c-12500	13	12	75¼	54½	32½	43¼	Alvarado R Jr5	b 114	*2.30	79-22	Pokie Joe 1171½ Flatbush 108½ Big Beau Ridge 1171¼	No rally	1
27Jan83- 2Aqu	fst	6f	⊡:23⅗	:47⅕	1:12⅕	Clm 10000	4	4	63¼	32	1hd	14½	Alvarado R Jr5	b 112	*2.50	83-19	PeregrinePower1124½Jon'sPoker117nkHuffwyne1101¼	Going away	
10Jan83- 1Aqu	fst	6f	⊡:23	:46⅘	1:12⅖	Clm 12500	4	7	87½	912	68½	55¾	Alvarado R Jr5	b 112	11.70	76-23	Ted Brown 1141 Delta Leader 1133¼ Spanish Beat 1171	Rallied	1
11Sep82- 2Med	fst	6f	:22⅘	:46⅕	1:11⅕ 3↑	Clm 16000	5	3	2hd	2½	45½	55¾	LizarzburuPM5	b 111	3.50	81-16	WinningMovette1162QuiteAScholr116½SpecilFlir1141¼	Weakened	1
4Sep82- 3Mth	fst	6f	:23	:46⅕	1:12⅕ 3↑	Clm 16000	7	3	65½	67	68	4½	LizarzburuPM5	b 111	2.50	78-18	Viky's Charge 114no DantzlerStreet116½ShyDom109no	Closed gap	
26Aug82- 9Sar	gd	7f	:22⅖	:45	1:23⅗ 3↑	Clm 20000	5	5	76	88½	75½	75	White J R5	b 112	3.30	79-12	OurCelticHeir117noCounterAttack117½NvyChplin117no	No Factor	1(
4Aug82- 2Sar	fst	6f	:22⅗	:46	1:10⅘ 3↑	Clm 25000	14	5	73½	85½	64¼	51½	White J R5	b 112	31.50	84-13	HappyCannibal117¾Rapido'sRepeat117½CatchMatthew119no	Wide	14
17Jly82- 6Mth	fst	6f	:22⅕	:44⅗	1:10⅖ 3↑	Alw 10000	3	7	89	814	812	58¾	LizarzburuPM5	b 111	18.50	80-13	Eaton Place 118¾ Global Jet 1163 High Gold 1143	Outrun	

LATEST WORKOUTS Apr 1 Aqu 3f fst :38⅖ b

Ruler Come Back — Gr. g. 7, by Iron Ruler—Y'All Come Back, by Carry Back
$16,000 Br.—October House Farm (Fla) Tr.—Pascuma Warren J — **117**
Own.—Pascuma M J
Lifetime 36 7 7 4 $74,160 — 1983 3 0 1 1 $3,910 — 1982 8 1 0 2 $12,960

14Mar83- 5Aqu	fst	6f	⊡:22⅗	:45⅖	1:09⅗	Clm 16000	3	3	23	21	2hd	24	Smith A Jr	b 117	*2.40	92-10	Dancer's Melody 1134 RulerComeBack1171¾Recidian112¾	Gamely	7
6Mar83- 2Aqu	fst	6f	⊡:22⅗	:45⅘	1:11⅕	Clm 16000	8	4	42	22	21	33¼	Smith A Jr	b 117	9.00	85-19	Rapido'sRepet1121½InfiniteSg1121¾RulerComeBck117½	Weakened	14
22Jan83- 2Aqu	fst	6f	⊡:23	:45⅘	1:10⅗	Clm 25000	9	4	42½	44	55	109¾	Davis R G5	b 112	12.70f	81-07	Tolerable 1171¾ Duck Call 117nk T. V. Repairman1172¼	Early foot	13
3Dec82- 9Aqu	my	6f	⊡:22⅗	:45⅗	1:11⅕ 3↑	Clm c-25000	9	9	78	56½	816	817	Alvarado R Jr5	b 112	13.00	71-13	Riva's Magic 1142¾ Rapido'sRepeat1173WorthyPiper1191¾	Outrun	10
24Apr82- 3Aqu	fst	6f	:22⅖	:45	1:10⅘	Clm 35000	8	6	4nk	76¼	813	823	Buscemi S7	b 110	19.60	64-21	Caphal 1171¼ Assension 117hd Page Six 1152¾	Done early	8
15Mar82- 5Aqu	fst	6f	⊡:22⅗	:46	1:12	Clm 35000	2	6	711	711	67	74¾	Credidio A Jr	b 117	5.40	79-22	Judge Grey 1131¼ Royal Jove 115hd ⒹCaphal 112no	Outrun	7
7Mar82- 4Aqu	sly	6f	⊡:22⅗	:46⅕	1:11	Clm 40000	8	2	32½	3nk	23	36	Miranda J	b 117	5.20	83-21	AccountReceivble1175½Clodion113½RulerComBck117hd	Weakened	8
19Feb82- 5Aqu	gd	6f	⊡:23⅖	:46⅘	1:11⅖	Clm 45000	5	1	51¼	41½	2½	42½	Taveras R	b 113	6.20	84-18	Waj. Jr. 112nk Pepper's Segundo 1172¼Assension108hd	Weakened	7
21Jan82- 5Aqu	fst	6f	⊡:23	:46⅘	1:11	Clm 45000	1	7	74¾	43½	43½	34	White J R7	b 106	5.40	85-21	Lord Boyer 1134 Fiddle Faddle117hdRulerComeBack1061¾	Rallied	9
15Jan82- 5Aqu	fst	6f	⊡:22⅘	:46⅕	1:11⅖	Clm c-35000	6	5	73¾	74	87½	129¾	MacBeth D	b 119	*2.30	77-18	HappyCannibal117nkSelfPressured117¾It'sAChallenge1171	Outrun	14

LATEST WORKOUTS Mar 28 Bel tr.t 6f my 1:17⅕ b (d) Mar 21 Bel tr.t 3f fst :37 b ●Mar 13 Bel tr.t 3f my :35 h (d) Mar 4 Bel tr.t 4f fst :49 h

The difference between "ice" and "value" is often easy to detect. When a horse's recommendations are obvious, and the horse is still not bet as heavily as expected, most likely we have an example of "ice." On the other hand, if a horse's virtues are hidden, at least partially, "value" is often attainable. A horse whose odds are lower than the handicapper's estimate is an underlay. It may also be a "live" horse, the recipient of considerable betting action from "inside" or informed sources. As a rule, insiders try to keep things quiet. They avoid making one large bet that is sure to attract the attention of board watchers. Rather, they bet steadily in smaller sums, or at the last moment. Horses backed by "inside" action tend to hold at odds much lower than anticipated, or else their odds drop dramatically near post time. Often, they are bet disproportionately in the win pool, compared to place and show. These horses are especially dangerous if they are unknown quantities such as first timers, shippers, or horses returning from layoffs, with workout lines that suggest neither ability nor readiness.

Back in the early 1970s, it seemed that every other Saturday, some horse would receive heavy, late action in the first race at Aqueduct. Then, one Saturday, the recipient of the betting action noticed the odds board on the way to the post, felt the added pressure, and refused to enter the starting gate. The horse had to be scratched, and the first-race pattern stopped!

Wise handicappers, especially those who like to watch the fluctuations of the odds board, must learn which stables bet, and which abstain, which bet early, and which late, which bet to win, and which through the exotics. And, most importantly, which bet successfully.

Over the years, handicapping experts have preached that the player will find better value in the win pool than in either place or show pools. This no longer is necessarily so. With the ever-growing popularity of exotic wagering, the place and show pools are being neglected. Overlays at times can be found, if the player takes the time to look. This is especially true in races featuring an overbet favorite that stands a good chance of running out of the money.

CASE STUDY: THE BELMONT BRIDGEJUMPER

In the spring of 1979, a three-year-old filly named Davona Dale was rewriting the record books. She won the Fantasy, Kentucky Oaks, Black-Eyed-Susan, Acorn, and Mother Goose in succession. In each, her speed figure equaled or surpassed the stakes record figure for the previous twenty-five years. Speed handicappers realized that she had entered another dimension, taking her place alongside the brilliant filly Ruffian. Now, on June 28, she was attempting the unprecedented feat of sweeping both "triple crowns" for three-year-old fillies, the Oaks series and New York's series, with a victory in Belmont's Coaching Club American Oaks. The authority of her previous victories suggested she would have little difficulty disposing of her four moderate rivals. Yet there was an unknown factor to be considered—the mile and a half distance of the Oaks, a distance Davona Dale's sire, Best Turn, might have found testing. I had not anticipated betting on the Oaks. Davona Dale was 1–5. I had come to watch a great filly in action, and applaud her accomplishment, but as I returned to my seat minutes before post time, I noticed that someone had placed a huge show bet (in the neighborhood of $50,000) on Davona Dale. The implications of this bet were quite intriguing. Should Davona Dale run out of the money—a possibility at the distance—the show payoffs on the three fillies that hit the board would be astronomical. Otherwise, all show payoffs would be the minimum $2.10, and the NYRA would have a considerable minus pool. That is exactly what happened, as Davona Dale won easily. Although I didn't have time to locate a suitable show bet on that occasion, the seed was planted. It would flower later that year.

Toward the fall of 1979, Davona Dale's early season efforts began to take their toll, and the champion was surpassed by It's In The Air, the filly that had surprised her in the Alabama at Saratoga. So impressive

Davona Dale ✻
B. f. 3, by Best Turn—Royal Entrance, by Tim Tam
Br.—Calumet Farm (Ky)
Tr.—Veitch John M
Own.—Calumet Farm
121

	St.	1st	2nd	3rd	Amt.
1979	10	8	1	0	$519,010
1978	2	2	0	0	$43,355

30Jun79- 8Bel	fst	1½	:49⅕	2:03⅘	2:30	ⒻC C A Oaks	5	5	3^{1½}	1^{2}	1^{6}	1^{8}	Velasquez J	121	*.10	70-24	Davona Dale 121^{8} Plankton 121½ Croquis 121^{14}	Ridden out	5
10Jun79- 8Bel	fst	1⅛	:45⅗	1:10	1:48⅘	ⒻMotherGoose	5	3	1^{1}	1^{1½}	1^{4}	1^{10}	Velasquez J	121	*.20	83-23	Davona Dale 121^{10} Eloquent 121^{4¾} Plankton 121^{1}	Ridden out	6
26May79- 8Bel	fst	1	:45⅖	1:10⅖	1:36	ⒻAcorn	6	3	4^{2½}	2^{hd}	1^{hd}	1^{2¼}	Velasquez J	121	*.30	88-25	Davona Dale 121^{2¼} Eloquent '21^{7¾} Plankton 121^{2¼}	Ridden out	8
18May79- 8Pim	fst	1$\frac{1}{16}$	:46⅘	1:11⅗	1:42⅗	ⒻBlk Eyed S'n	2	1	1^{1}	1^{1}	1^{2½}	1^{4¼}	Velasquez J	121	*.10	92-21	Davona Dale 121^{4¼}Phoebe'sDonkey118^{3½}Plankton121^{4}	Ridden out	6
4May79- 8CD	sly	1$\frac{1}{16}$	:48	1:13⅘	1:47⅕	ⒻKy Oaks	5	5	4^{5½}	3^{1½}	1^{hd}	1^{4½}	Velasquez J	121	*.40	72-30	Davona Dale 121^{4½} Himalayan 121^{2} Prize Spot 121½	Ridden out	6
7Apr79- 9OP	fst	1$\frac{1}{16}$	:46⅗	1:11⅗	1:44⅖	ⒻFantasy	3	5	4^{5}	2^{hd}	1^{hd}	1^{2½}	Velasquez J	121	*1.10	86-21	DavonaDale121^{2½}Cline121^{3½}VerySpecilLdy110^{6}	Stumbled st.,clear	7
17Mar79- 9FG	fst	1$\frac{1}{16}$	:48	1:13⅗	1:45	ⒻDebutante	3	3	2½	2^{hd}	1^{1½}	1^{7}	Velasquez J	121	*.30	87-21	Davona Dale121^{7}JustaReflection118^{nk}OtherShoe115^{2¼}	Ridden out	11
28Feb79- 0GP	fst	7f	:22⅕	:44⅖	1:21	ⒻBonnie Miss	3	4	2^{1½}	2½	2½	1¾	Velasquez J	122		99-17	Davona Dale 122¾ Candy Eclair122^{20}ProveMeSpecial114^{2}	Driving	4
28Feb79-Run between 7th & 8th races. No wagering																			
14Feb79- 9GP	fst	6f	:22	:44⅕	1:08⅗	ⒻSh'ley Jones	2	3	3^{4½}	2^{5}	2^{4}	2^{1¾}	Velasquez J	122	2.70	94-16	Candy Eclair 122^{1¾} Davona Dale 122^{8} Drop MeANote114^{1}	Gamely	4
13Jan79- 9Crc	fst	1$\frac{1}{16}$	:48	1:12⅘	1:44⅕	Trop Pk Dby	12	5	5^{2¼}	4^{4}	4^{6}	4^{5}	Velasquez J	114	*1.30	93-12	Bishop's Choice 111½ Lot O' Gold 119^{2} Smarten 119^{2½}	No rally	12

LATEST WORKOUTS Aug 10 Sar 3f fst :35⅖ b ●Aug 6 Sar 1 fst 1:38 b Aug 2 Sar 7f fst 1:29 b ●Jly 29 Sar 6f fst 1:13 h

was It's In The Air's victory in the Ruffian Handicap in late September that our friend the "Belmont bridgejumper" attended the subsequent Beldame Stakes at Belmont, his huge show bet in hand. He made one small miscalculation—the track was sloppy, and It's In The Air had no prior experience under such conditions. But the bet was made, nevertheless. It's In The Air figured to control the pace in the Beldame, if she liked the wet conditions. If not, anything seemed possible. Those liking the chances of Waya, the ranking older mare in the country, had two options. They could accept the 3–1 win odds, or they could divert part of their bet into the possibly lucrative show pool, on the chance that It's In The Air would dislike the sloppy conditions.

It's In the Air
B. f. 3, by Mr Prospector—A Wind Is Rising, by Francis S
Br.—Happy Valley Farm (Fla)
Tr.—Barrera Lazaro S
Own.—Harbor View Farm
118

	St.	1st	2nd	3rd	Amt.
1979	10	5	3	2	$363,390
1978	8	5	3	0	$195,665

29Sep79- 8Bel	fst	1⅛	:47⅘	1:12	1:47⅖	3↑ⒻRuffian H	4	1	1^{1}	1^{2½}	1^{5}	1^{4}	Pincay L Jr	122	3.00	90-12	It's In the Air 122^{4} Blitey 113^{5} Waya 126	Ridden out	4
12Sep79- 8Bel	fst	1	:45⅗	1:09⅗	1:34⅘	3↑ⒻMaskette	5	1	1½	2^{hd}	2^{hd}	2^{nk}	Shoemaker W	122	2.40	94-20	Blitey 112^{nk} It's In the Air 122no Pearl Necklace 125^{3½}	Game try	5
26Aug79- 9Del	gd	1⅛	:48⅖	1:12⅖	1:49⅖	ⒻDel Oaks	1	1	1½	2^{hd}	1^{1½}	1^{5}	Shoemaker W	122	*.30	90-14	It's In the Air 122^{5} Jameela 115^{1} Himalayan 114½	In hand	6
11Aug79- 8Sar	fst	1¼	:49	1:36⅘	2:01⅗	ⒻAlabama	4	1	1½	1^{1½}	1^{3}	1^{1½}	Fell J	121	3.10	94-13	It's In the Air 121^{1½} Davona Dale121^{3¾}MairzyDoates121^{2¼}	Driving	5
4Aug79- 5Sar	fst	6f	:22⅕	:45	1:09⅕	3↑ⒻAllowance	5	2	1^{1}	1^{3}	1^{5}	1^{8}	Fell J	117	*.40	94-12	It's In the Air 117^{8} English Trifle 108¾ Lucy Belle 105^{2¾}	Handily	7
15Jly79- 8Hol	fst	1⅛	:45⅗	1:09⅘	1:47⅖	3↑ⒻVanity H	1	2	2^{2½}	1^{hd}	1½	1^{nk}	Shoemaker W	113	*.90	95-12	It's In the Air 113^{nk} Country Queen 121^{hd} Innuendo 116^{9}	Driving	8
7Jly79- 8Hol	fst	1⅛	:45⅘	1:10⅕	1:48⅕	ⒻHol Oaks	2	3	2^{1}	2^{1}	2^{hd}	2^{hd}	Shoemaker W	121	*1.10	91-14	Prize Spot 121^{hd} It's In the Air 121^{6} Variety Queen 124^{1}	Sharp	7
2Jun79- 8Hol	fst	1$\frac{1}{16}$	:44⅗	1:09⅖	1:41⅕	3↑ⒻMilady H	4	2	2^{3½}	2^{hd}	1½	2½	Shoemaker W	112	2.30	88-14	Innuendo 113½ It's In the Air 112½ Country Queen 121^{3½}	Failed	9
11Mar79- 8SA	fst	1$\frac{1}{16}$	:45⅕	1:09⅖	1:41⅗	ⒻSanta Susana	7	4	4^{3}	3^{2}	3^{5½}	3^{9}	Pincay L Jr	117	1.90e	84-12	Caline 115^{1} Terlingua 115^{8} It's In the Air 117^{hd}	Checked	8
24Feb79- 8SA	fst	7f	:22	:44⅖	1:21⅕	ⒻSanta Ynez	4	5	4^{4}	2^{1½}	3^{3½}	3^{6}	Delahoussaye E	121	*1.20	91-12	Terlingua 121^{4} Caline 119^{2} It's In the Air 121^{3½}	Weakened	5

LATEST WORKOUTS Sep 26 Bel 5f fst 1:03⅕ bg Sep 20 Bel 5f fst :59⅖ b ●Sep 7 Bel tr.t 5f my :59⅘ h (d) Aug 21 Sar tr.t 4f fst :49⅗ b

***Waya ✻**
B. m. 5, by Faraway Son—War Path, by Blue Prince
Br.—Dayton Ltd (Fra)
Tr.—Whiteley David A
Own.—Brant P M
123

Turf Record									
St.	1st	2nd	3rd		St.	1st	2nd	3rd	Amt.
23	11	6	3	1979	9	4	2	2	$280,243
				1978	9	6	2	1	$359,943

29Sep79- 8Bel	fst	1⅛		:47⅘	1:12	1:47⅖	3↑ⒻRuffian H	2	4	3^{5}	3^{7½}	3^{11}	3^{9}	Velasquez J	126	2.30	81-12	It's In the Air 122^{4} Blitey 113^{5} Waya 126	Evenly	4
10Sep79- 7Bel	fm	1$\frac{1}{16}$	Ⓣ	:47	1:11	1:41⅘	3↑Allowance	1	4	4^{8½}	3^{3}	2^{2}	3^{2½}	Cordero A Jr	119	*.50	84-17	John Henry 117^{2} Silent Cal 117½ Waya 119no	Hung	4
28Jly79- 8Bel	fm	1¼	[T]	:49⅕	1:37⅗	2:01⅗	3↑ⒻShep'd BayH	10	10	10^{13}	10^{7¼}	8^{5}	7^{4¾}	Shoemaker W	130	*2.00	81-09	Terpsichorist 117no Late Bloomer 123^{2¾} Warfever 110^{nk}	Outrun	10
16Jun79- 8Bel	fm	1⅜	[T]	:48	1:35⅖	2:11⅖	3↑Bowl Green H	4	5	5^{12}	5^{7}	5^{3½}	2^{4}	Cordero A Jr	125	*.80	108-01	Overskate 117^{4} Waya 125^{hd} Bowl Game 123^{1¾}	Rallied	7
3Jun79- 6Bel	sly	1¼		:49⅘	1:39⅕	2:04⅕	Sar Cup H	5	6	6^{9}	3^{1}	1^{hd}	1no	Cordero A Jr	125	*.90	76-30	Waya 125no Late Bloomer 119^{4¾} Sten 110^{1½}	Driving	6
28Apr79- 8Aqu	sly	1⅛		:48	1:12⅖	1:50⅘	3↑ⒻTop Flight H	2	8	7^{17}	5^{7½}	2^{2}	1^{nk}	Cordero A Jr	128	*1.60	81-17	Waya 128^{nk} Pearl Necklace 120^{7} Island Kiss 112^{1}	Driving	8
25Mar79- 8SA	yl	1¼	Ⓣ	:46⅖	1:35⅘	2:01	ⒻS Barbara H	2	7	7^{13}	5^{3}	3^{1½}	1^{1¼}	Cordero A Jr	131	*.70	82-18	Waya 131^{1¼} Petron's Love 117½ Island Kiss 111¾	Easily	8
14Mar79- 8SA	sf	1⅛	Ⓣ	:47	1:11	1:48⅕	ⒻSanta Ana H	1	10	10^{11}	8^{6¼}	3^{1}	1^{3½}	Cordero A Jr	127	*1.00	86-14	Waya 127^{3½} Amazer 123¾ Shua 115^{hd}	Easily	10
10Feb79- 8SA	sf	1¼	Ⓣ	:48⅘	1:36⅘	2:03⅗	Arcadia H	8	7	7^{8¾}	4^{5}	3^{2½}	2^{1¾}	Cordero A Jr	123	*1.80	67-25	Fluorescent Light 121^{1¾} Waya 123^{nk} As de Copas 118^{1}	Gamely	9
4Nov78- 8Lrl	fm	1½	Ⓣ	:50	2:03⅗	2:27	3↑D C Inter'l	8	8	8^{11}	7^{3¼}	5^{1½}	3^{3}	Cordero A Jr	124	2.90	81-16	Mac Diarmida 120^{hd} Tiller 127^{3} Waya 124^{1½}	Lacked room	8

LATEST WORKOUTS Oct 11 Bel 4f sly :50⅖ b (d) Oct 7 Bel 4f fst :49 b Sep 28 Bel 3f fst :35⅘ b Sep 25 Bel 4f fst :47⅖ h

As things turned out, Waya's stablemate Fourdrinier showed surprise early speed to challenge It's In The Air. The 2–5 favorite, apparently not handling the footing, faded to fifth. Waya rallied to win going away, and Fourdrinier held the place. Together, they returned $8.00 to win, and $55.20 to show.

Those who reacted to the huge show bet on It's In The Air by betting Waya to show collected possibly their largest payoff of the year, on a virtual sure thing. Waya had finished out of the money only once in her American career, and her recent record showed victories in the slop over the outstanding racemares Pearl Necklace and Late Bloomer.

A similar situation arose the next year, and once again the filly involved was questionable. She was Prime Prospect, a two-year-old filly entered in the Astoria Stakes at Belmont. An impressive winner in her only start, earning a good speed figure, the daughter of Mr. Prospector looked the part of a potential division leader. The word "looked" is emphasized because in the paddock before the Astoria, she looked anything but. Nervous and overheated, she had driven her trainer, the usually intense Leroy Jolley, to laughter. Obviously, he had surrendered all hope of victory. But our friend the "bridgejumper" was not concerned. His large show bet was there, seriously tilting the show pool. Those of us returning from the paddock quickly realized that a show bonanza was imminent, and rushed to decipher the form of the other fillies. As the proven closer in the field, Demurely appeared the safest bet to finish in the money. In fact, she had finished in the money in two previous New York stakes, something none of her rivals had accomplished even once.

8 BELMONT

5½ FURLONGS. (1.03) 74th Running THE ASTORIA. $50,000 Added. 2-year-olds. Fillies. Weights, 119 lbs. By subscription of $100 each, which should accompany the nomination; $400 to pass the entry box with $50,000 added. The added money and all fees to be divided 60% to the winner, 22% to second, 12% to third and 6% to fourth. Winners of two races of $20,000 an additional 2 lbs. Non-winners of a Sweepstakes allowed, 3 lbs. Of two races other than maiden or claiming, 5 lbs. Of a race other than maiden or claiming, 7 lbs. Maidens, 9 lbs. Starters to be named at the closing time of entries. Trophies will be presented to the winning owner, trainer and jockey. Closed Wednesday, July 1, 1980 with 17 nominations.

Famous Partner — Dk. b. or br. f. 2, by Illustrious—Royal Partner, by Northern Dancer
Own.—Buckland Farm — Br.—Evans T M (Va) — Tr.—Campo John P — **112**
St. 1st 2nd 3rd Amt. — 1980 3 1 0 1 $13,070
8Jly80- 8Mth fst 5½f :22⅖ :46⅗ 1:06 ⒻColleen 1 6 45 36 47½ 517 Velasquez J b 117 1.90 68-17 Madame Premier 117nk Cavort1179BendTheTimes1152 Drifted out 6
8Jly80-Run in Two Divisions: 6th & 8th Races.
23Jun80- 4Bel fst 5½f :22⅘ :46⅗ 1:05⅖ ⒻMd Sp Wt 1 1 12 12 11½ 12 Velasquez J b 117 2.90 88-15 Famous Partner1172Shalomar1174WaywardLass1171¼ Ridden out 9
16May80- 6Aqu fst 4½f :22⅕ :46⅗ :53⅕ ⒻMd Sp Wt 10 10 1½ 12 31 Miranda J b 117 16.30 95-04 Demurely 117½ Shut Up 117½ Famous Partner 1171½ Weakened 10
LATEST WORKOUTS ●Jly 3 Bel tr.t 5f gd 1:00⅖ h — Jun 19 Bel tr.t 5f fst 1:01 h — Jun 11 Bel tr.t 4f gd :48⅘ h — May 24 Bel tr.t 5f fst 1:03 b

Demurely — B. f. 2, by Majestic Prince—A Charm, by Nashua
Own.—Phillips N F — Br.—David Mrs H N (Ky) — Tr.—Laurin Roger — **112**
St. 1st 2nd 3rd Amt. — 1980 3 1 1 1 $29,440
25Jun80- 8Bel fst 5½f :22⅗ :46⅘ 1:06⅖ ⒻFashion 7 5 54¼ 41½ 32 32½ Venezia M 116 *.30e 80-18 Sue Babe 1191 Happy One 1151½ Demurely 1163 Wide 9
4Jun80- 8Bel fst 5½f :22⅗ :45⅘ 1:04⅘ ⒻDomino 1 1 79 69 47½ 23½ Venezia M 116 1.50e 87-17 Sue Babe 1163½ Demurely 116nk Madame Premier 116½ Wide 8
16May80- 6Aqu fst 4½f :22⅕ :46⅗ :53⅕ ⒻMd Sp Wt 6 2 33½ 46½ 1½ Venezia M 117 18.90 96-04 Demurely 117½ Shut Up 117½ Famous Partner 1171½ Driving 10
LATEST WORKOUTS Jun 23 Bel 3f fst :36⅗ b — Jun 17 Bel 4f fst :49⅘ b — Jun 1 Bel 5f fst 1:01⅕ b — May 26 Bel 4f fst :50⅕ b

Cherokee Frolic — Dk. b. or br. f. 2, by Cherokee Fellow—Fauchon, by Final Ruling
Own.—Carolsteve Stable — Br.—Onett G L (Fla) — Tr.—Cole William A — **114**
St. 1st 2nd 3rd Amt. — 1980 3 3 0 0 $13,320
17Jun80- 6Crc fst 5f :22⅕ :46 :59⅗ ⒻAllowance 2 3 1½ 12 15 17½ Cohen G7 109 *.50 98-13 Cherokee Frolic 1097½ Big Dowery 1094 Color On 1124½ Easily 5
6Jun80- 6Crc fst 5f :23⅗ :47⅕ 1:00⅖ Clm c-25000 2 3 12 13 18 110 Monacelli E 111 *.30 93-15 CherokeeFrolic11110RainBouRunner1143StatelyKitty114nk Easily 5
27May80- 2Crc fst 5f :23⅘ :47⅗ 1:00 ⒻMd 12500 4 1 11½ 13 18 110 Guerra W A 115 *2.00 95-16 Cherokee Frolic11510WhatMajesty1156½SallySupper115hd Handily 9
LATEST WORKOUTS Jly 11 Bel 3f fst :38 b — Jly 7 Bel 5f fst 1:02⅘ b — Jun 25 Crc 4f fst :54 b — May 20 Crc 5f fst 1:03 bg

Prime Prospect — B. f. 2, by Mr Prospector—Square Generation, by Olden Times
Own.—Firestone Mrs B R — Br.—Jones W L Jr (Ky) — Tr.—Jolley Leroy — **112**
St. 1st 2nd 3rd Amt. — 1980 1 1 0 0 $10,200
2Jly80- 3Bel fst 5½f :22⅖ :45⅘ 1:05⅕ ⒻMd Sp Wt 1 3 21 2hd 11 11¼ Vasquez J 117 *.50 89-17 PrimeProspect1171¼QueenDesignt1123¾WywrdLss1171 Drew clear 9
LATEST WORKOUTS ●Jly 12 Bel 3f fst :34⅕ h — Jly 8 Bel 4f fst :48 b — Jly 1 Bel 3f fst :36⅘ b — ●Jun 25 Bel 5f fst :58⅖ h

Sweet Revenge — Ch. f. 2, by Raja Baba—Away, by Blue Prince
Own.—Farish W S III — Br.—Brisbine Elizabeth J (Ky) — Tr.—Carroll Del W — **112**
St. 1st 2nd 3rd Amt. — 1980 3 1 2 0 $13,032
8Jly80- 6Mth fst 5½f :23 :46 1:05⅕ ⒻColleen 4 5 31½ 33 32½ 23 Passmore W J 115 5.40 86-17 Queen Designate 1123 Sweet Revenge 1151½ Bude 1211¼ 2nd best 9
8Jly80-Run in Two DIvisions: 6th & 8th Races.
27Jun80- 5Mth fst 5½f :22⅗ :46 1:05⅕ ⒻAllowance 2 6 1½ 11 21 22 Bracciale V Jr 117 1.50 87-17 Cavort 1172 Sweet Revenge 1174 Sure Princess 1178 2nd best 6
12Jun80- 1Mth fst 5f :22⅖ :46⅕ :58⅗ ⒻMd Sp Wt 6 2 2hd 1hd 11½ 12 Bracciale V Jr 117 4.90 93-16 Sweet Revenge 1172 JeanMarie117hdAnotherChannel1173 Driving 9
LATEST WORKOUTS Jun 10 Mth 4f sly :50 bg — May 30 Key 5f fst 1:00⅘ h

Imagine the folly of making such a large wager without viewing the horse in the paddock beforehand. Indeed, of making such a bet on a young horse with so little experience. Prime Prospect ran out of the money, as expected. Unfortunately for the author, the only filly she beat was Demurely. The show payoffs were astronomical, as expected.

EIGHTH RACE
Belmont
JULY 14, 1980

5 ½ FURLONGS. (1.03) 74th Running THE ASTORIA. $50,000 Added. 2-year-olds. Fillies. Weights, 119 lbs. By subscription of $100 each, which should accompany the nomination; $400 to pass the entry box with $50,000 added. The added money and all fees to be divided 60% to the winner, 22% to second, 12% to third and 6% to fourth. Winners of two races of $20,000 an additional 2 lbs. Non-winners of a Sweepstakes allowed, 3 lbs. Of two races other than maiden or claiming, 5 lbs. Of a race other than maiden or claiming, 7 lbs. Maidens, 9 lbs. Starters to be named at the closing time of entries. Trophies will be presented to the winning owner, trainer and jockey. Closed Wednesday, July 1, 1980 with 17 nominations.
Value of race $53,700, value to winner $32,220, second $11,814, third $6,444, fourth $3,222. Mutuel pool $183,373, OTB pool $115,390.

Last Raced	Horse	Eqt.A.Wt	PP	St	¼	⅜	Str	Fin	Jockey	Odds $1
8Jly80 ^{8}Mth^{5}	Famous Partner	b 2 112	1	1	$1^{\frac{1}{2}}$	1^{2}	$1^{2\frac{1}{2}}$	1no	Velasquez J	14.20
17Jun80 ^{6}Crc^{1}	Cherokee Frolic	2 114	3	2	$2^{1\frac{1}{2}}$	2^{1}	$2^{1\frac{1}{2}}$	2^{3}	Cohen G	3.10
8Jly80 ^{6}Mth^{2}	Sweet Revenge	2 112	5	4	4^{10}	4^{8}	$3^{\frac{1}{2}}$	3^{2}	Fell J	9.90
2Jly80 ^{3}Bel^{1}	Prime Prospect	2 112	4	5	$3^{1\frac{1}{2}}$	$3^{\frac{1}{2}}$	4^{4}	$4^{\frac{1}{2}}$	Vasquez J	.50
25Jun80 ^{8}Bel^{3}	Demurely	2 112	2	3	5	5	5	5	Venezia M	5.70

OFF AT 4:43 1/2, EDT Start good, Won driving. Time, :22, :45⅕, :58, 1:05 Track fast.

$2 Mutuel Prices:				
	1-(A)-FAMOUS PARTNER	**30.40**	**10.20**	**45.00**
	3-(C)-CHEROKEE FROLIC		**5.00**	**34.60**
	5-(E)-SWEET REVENGE			**29.80**

Dk. b or Br. f, by Illustrious—Royal Partner, by Northern Dancer. Trainer Campo John P. Bred by Evans T M (Va).

FAMOUS PARTNER showed good early foot while saving ground, drew away leaving the turn and was all out to last over CHEROKEE FROLIC. The latter showed good early foot, wasn't able to stay with FAMOUS PARTNER approaching the stretch, raced greenly during the drive and finished gamely, just missing. SWEET REVENGE, wide into the stretch, lacked the needed rally. PRIME PROSPECT, hustled along early was finished leaving the turn. DEMURELY was never close.

Owners— 1, Buckland Farm; 2, Carolsteve Stable; 3, Farish W S III; 4, Firestone Mrs B R; 5, Phillips N F.

Trainers— 1, Campo John P; 2, Cole William A; 3, Carroll Del W; 4, Jolley Leroy; 5, Laurin Roger.

□ THE CHARTISTS □

In addition to making life easier for trip handicappers, the "closed-circuit era" has spawned another school of handicappers, known as the "chartists." Rather than study the *Form*, they can be found instead in front of a television screen studying possible payoffs in the exotic pools. They look for horses that are attracting more attention in those pools than their win odds would warrant—"live" horses whose connections chose to hide their wagering from obvious public viewing. Some stables wheel their horse in the exotic pools, or at least hook it up with what they consider the logical contenders. Chartists watch for their action, looking for the steady flow, or a series of spurts. One might say that the chartists are handicapping the other handicappers. In actuality, they are

THE DAILY DOUBLE

Odds	7.0	6.5	5.0	4.5	4.0	3.5	3.0	2.5	2.0	1.8	1.6	1.5	1.4	1.2	1.0	0.8	0.6	0.5	0.4	0.2
0.2	24	21	18	16	15	13	12	10	9	8	8	7	7	6	6	5	5	4	4	3
0.4	28	24	21	19	17	15	14	12	10	10	9	7	8	7	7	6	5	5	5	4
0.5	30	26	22	20	18	15	15	13	11	10	9	8	9	8	7	6	6	5	5	4
0.6	32	28	24	22	20	17	16	14	12	11	10	9	9	8	8	7	6	6	6	5
0.8	35	31	27	24	22	18	18	15	13	12	11	10	10	10	9	8	7	6	6	5
1.0	39	34	29	27	24	20	20	17	15	14	13	12	12	11	10	9	8	7	7	6
1.2	43	38	32	30	27	22	22	19	16	15	14	13	13	12	11	10	9	8	7	6
1.4	47	41	35	32	29	24	23	21	18	16	15	15	14	13	12	11	10	9	8	7
1.5	49	43	37	34	31	26	24	21	18	17	16	15	15	13	12	11	10	9	8	7
1.6	51	45	38	35	32	28	25	22	19	18	16	16	15	14	13	12	11	10	9	8
1.8	55	49	41	38	34	29	27	24	20	19	18	17	16	15	14	13	12	11	10	9
2.0	59	51	44	40	37	31	29	26	22	20	19	18	18	16	15	15	14	13	12	10
2.5	68	60	51	47	43	38	34	30	26	24	22	21	21	19	17	16	16	15	14	12
3.0	78	68	59	54	49	44	39	34	29	27	25	24	23	22	20	18	18	17	15	13
3.5	88	77	66	60	55	49	44	38	33	31	29	28	26	24	22	20	20	18	17	15
4.0	98	85	73	67	61	55	49	43	37	34	32	31	29	27	24	22	22	20	19	16
4.5	107	94	80	74	67	60	54	47	40	38	35	34	32	30	27	24	24	22	21	18
5.0	117	102	88	80	73	66	59	51	44	41	38	37	35	32	29	27	28	26	24	21
5.5	136	117	102	94	85	77	68	60	51	48	45	43	41	38	34	31	32	30	28	24
6.0	156	136	117	107	98	88	78	68	59	55	51	49	47	43	39	35	36	33	31	27
6.5	175	153	131	121	110	99	88	77	66	62	57	55	53	49	44	40	40	37	35	30
7.0	194	179	146	134	122	110	98	86	73	69	64	61	59	54	49	44	43	41	38	33
8	214	187	161	147	134	121	107	94	81	75	70	67	65	59	54	49	47	45	42	36
9	233	201	175	161	146	132	117	103	88	82	76	74	71	65	59	53	51	48	45	39
10	253	221	190	174	158	143	127	111	95	89	83	80	77	70	64	58	55	52	49	42
11	272	239	204	187	171	154	137	120	103	96	89	86	82	76	69	62	59	56	52	45
12	291	255	219	201	183	165	146	128	110	103	96	92	88	81	74	67	63	59	56	48
13	311	272	234	214	195	176	156	137	118	110	102	98	94	87	79	71	67	63	59	51
14	330	289	248	228	207	186	166	145	125	117	108	104	100	92	84	76	71	67	63	54
15	350	305	263	241	219	197	176	154	132	124	115	110	106	97	89	80	75	71	66	57
16	369	323	277	254	231	208	185	163	140	130	121	117	112	103	94	84	79	74	70	60
17	388	345	292	268	244	219	195	171	147	137	128	123	118	108	99	89	83	78	73	63
18	408	357	306	281	256	230	205	180	154	144	134	129	124	114	104	93	87	82	78	66
20	505	442	379	348	317	285	254	222	191	178	166	160	153	141	128	116	103	97	91	78
25	602	527	452	415	377	340	303	265	228	213	198	190	183	168	153	138	123	116	108	93
30	699	612	525	482	438	395	351	308	264	247	230	221	212	195	178	160	143	134	126	108
40	796	697	598	549	499	450	400	351	301	281	262	252	242	222	202	183	163	153	143	123
50	893	782	671	615	560	504	449	393	338	316	294	283	271	249	227	205	183	172	160	138
60	990	867	744	682	621	559	498	436	375	350	326	313	301	276	252	227	203	190	178	153
75	1475	1291	1108	1017	925	833	742	650	558	522	485	467	449	412	375	339	302	284	265	229

THE DAILY DOUBLE

	75.0	50.0	45.0	40.0	35.0	30.0	25.0	20.0	19.0	18.0	17.0	16.0	15.0	14.0	13.0	12.0	11.0	10.0	9.0	8.0
0.2	229	153	138	123	108	93	78	63	60	57	54	51	48	45	42	39	36	33	30	27
0.4	265	178	160	143	126	108	91	73	70	66	63	59	56	52	49	45	42	38	35	31
0.5	284	190	172	153	134	116	97	78	74	71	67	63	59	56	52	48	45	41	37	33
0.6	302	203	183	163	143	123	103	83	79	75	71	67	63	59	55	51	47	43	40	36
0.8	339	227	205	183	160	138	116	93	89	84	80	76	71	67	62	58	53	49	44	40
1.0	375	252	227	202	178	153	128	104	99	94	89	84	79	74	69	64	59	54	49	44
1.2	412	275	249	222	195	168	141	114	108	103	97	92	87	81	76	70	65	59	54	49
1.4	449	301	271	242	212	183	153	124	118	112	106	100	94	88	82	77	71	65	59	53
1.5	467	313	283	252	221	190	160	129	123	117	110	104	98	92	86	80	74	67	61	55
1.6	485	325	294	262	230	198	166	134	128	121	115	108	102	96	89	83	76	69	64	57
1.8	522	350	316	281	247	213	178	144	137	130	124	117	110	103	96	89	82	75	69	62
2.0	558	375	338	301	264	228	191	154	147	140	132	125	118	110	103	95	88	81	73	66
2.5	650	435	393	351	308	265	222	180	171	163	154	145	137	128	120	111	103	94	86	77
3.0	742	493	449	400	351	303	254	205	195	185	176	166	156	146	137	127	117	107	98	88
3.5	833	557	504	450	395	340	285	230	219	208	197	186	176	165	154	143	132	121	110	99
4.0	925	621	560	499	438	377	317	256	244	231	219	207	195	183	171	158	146	134	122	110
4.5	1017	682	615	549	482	415	348	281	268	254	241	228	214	201	187	174	161	147	134	121
5.0	1108	744	671	598	525	452	379	306	292	277	263	248	234	219	204	190	175	161	146	131
6.0	1291	867	782	697	612	527	442	357	340	323	306	289	272	255	238	221	204	187	170	153
7.0	1475	990	893	796	699	602	505	408	388	369	350	330	311	291	272	253	233	214	194	175
8.0	1658	1113	1004	895	786	677	568	459	437	415	393	371	350	328	306	284	262	241	219	197
9.0	1841	1235	1115	994	873	751	630	509	485	461	437	412	388	364	340	316	291	267	243	219
10.0	2024	1359	1226	1093	959	826	693	560	533	507	480	454	427	400	374	347	320	294	267	241
11.0	2208	1482	1337	1191	1046	901	756	611	582	553	524	495	466	437	408	378	349	320	291	262
12.0	2391	1605	1448	1290	1133	976	819	661	630	599	567	536	504	473	441	410	378	347	316	284
13.0	2574	1728	1559	1389	1220	1051	881	712	678	644	611	577	543	509	475	441	408	374	340	306
14.0	2758	1851	1670	1488	1307	1126	944	763	727	690	654	618	582	545	509	473	437	400	364	329
15.0	2941	1974	1781	1587	1394	1200	1007	814	775	736	698	659	620	582	543	504	466	427	388	350
16.0	3124	2097	1891	1686	1481	1275	1070	864	823	782	741	700	659	618	577	536	495	454	412	371
17.0	3307	2220	2002	1785	1568	1350	1133	915	872	828	785	741	698	654	611	567	524	480	437	393
18.0	3491	2343	2113	1884	1654	1425	1195	966	920	874	828	782	736	690	644	599	553	507	461	415
19.0	3674	2466	2224	1983	1741	1500	1258	1017	968	920	872	823	775	727	678	630	582	533	485	437
20.0	3857	2589	2335	2082	1828	1574	1321	1067	1017	966	915	864	814	763	712	661	611	560	509	459
25.0	4773	3201	2890	2576	2262	1949	1635	1321	1258	1195	1133	1070	1007	944	881	819	756	693	630	568
30.0	5690	3819	3445	3071	2697	2323	1949	1574	1500	1425	1350	1275	1200	1126	1051	976	901	826	751	677
35.0	6606	4434	4000	3565	3131	2697	2262	1828	1741	1654	1568	1481	1394	1307	1220	1133	1046	959	873	786
40.0	7522	5049	4555	4060	3565	3071	2576	2082	1983	1884	1785	1686	1587	1488	1389	1290	1191	1093	994	895
45.0	8438	5664	5109	4555	4000	3445	2890	2335	2224	2113	2002	1891	1781	1670	1559	1448	1337	1226	1115	1004
50.0	9355	6277	5664	5049	4434	3819	3204	2589	2466	2343	2220	2097	1974	1851	1728	1605	1482	1359	1236	1113
75.0	13936	9355	8438	7522	6606	5690	4773	3857	3674	3491	3307	3124	2941	2758	2574	2391	2208	2024	1841	1658

THE EXACTA

	7.0	6.0	5.0	4.5	4.0	3.5	3.0	2.5	2.0	1.8	1.6	1.5	1.4	1.2	1.0	0.9	0.6	0.5	0.4	0.2
0.2	8	7	6	5	5	4	4	3	3	2	2	2	0	0	0	0	0	0	0	0
0.4	12	10	9	8	7	6	6	5	4	4	4	3	3	3	3	0	0	0	0	0
0.5	14	12	10	9	8	7	7	6	5	4	4	4	4	3	3	3	0	0	0	0
0.6	15	13	12	11	10	9	8	7	6	5	5	5	4	4	4	3	0	3	0	0
0.8	19	17	14	13	12	11	10	8	7	7	6	6	6	5	5	4	4	4	4	0
1.0	23	20	17	16	14	13	11	10	9	8	7	7	7	6	6	5	4	5	5	0
1.2	27	24	20	19	17	15	13	12	10	9	9	8	8	7	7	6	5	6	5	0
1.4	31	27	23	21	19	17	15	13	11	11	10	10	9	8	8	7	6	6	6	5
1.5	33	29	25	23	20	18	16	14	12	11	11	11	10	9	8	7	6	7	6	5
1.6	35	30	26	24	22	20	17	15	13	12	11	11	10	9	9	8	7	8	7	4
1.8	39	34	29	27	24	22	19	17	14	13	12	12	11	11	10	9	8	8	7	6
2.0	43	37	32	29	27	24	21	19	16	15	14	13	13	12	11	9	8	10	9	8
2.5	52	46	39	36	33	29	26	23	20	18	17	16	16	14	13	12	10	12	11	9
3.0	62	54	46	43	39	35	31	27	23	22	20	19	19	17	15	14	12	13	13	11
3.5	72	63	54	49	45	40	36	31	27	25	23	22	22	20	18	16	14	15	14	12
4.0	81	74	61	56	51	46	41	36	31	29	26	25	24	22	20	18	16	17	16	14
4.5	91	80	68	63	57	51	46	40	34	32	30	29	27	25	23	21	18	19	19	15
5.0	101	88	76	69	63	57	50	44	38	35	33	32	30	28	25	23	20	23	21	18
6.0	120	105	90	83	75	68	60	53	45	42	39	38	36	33	30	27	24	27	25	21
7.0	140	122	105	96	87	79	70	61	53	49	46	44	42	39	35	32	28	30	28	24
8.0	159	139	119	109	100	90	80	70	60	56	52	50	48	44	40	36	32	34	32	27
9.0	178	154	134	123	112	101	90	78	67	63	58	56	54	50	45	41	36	38	35	30
10	198	173	149	136	124	112	99	87	75	70	65	62	60	55	50	45	40	41	39	33
11	217	193	163	150	136	123	109	96	82	77	71	68	66	60	55	50	44	45	42	36
12	237	207	178	163	148	134	119	104	89	83	78	75	72	66	60	54	48	49	46	39
13	256	221	192	176	160	144	129	113	97	90	84	81	78	71	65	59	52	53	49	42
14	275	241	207	190	173	155	138	121	104	97	90	87	83	77	70	63	56	56	53	45
15	295	253	221	203	185	166	148	130	111	104	97	93	89	82	75	67	60	60	56	48
16	314	275	236	216	197	177	158	138	119	111	103	99	95	87	80	72	64	64	60	51
18	334	292	251	230	209	188	168	147	126	118	110	105	101	93	85	76	68	68	63	54
20	353	305	265	243	221	199	177	155	133	125	116	112	107	98	90	81	72	71	67	57
25	372	325	280	257	233	210	187	164	141	132	122	118	113	104	94	85	76	75	70	60
30	392	343	294	270	246	221	197	173	148	138	129	118	119	109	99	90	80	94	88	76
35	423	423	367	337	306	276	246	215	185	173	161	155	148	136	124	112	100	112	105	91
40	489	513	440	404	367	331	294	258	222	207	193	185	178	163	149	134	120	131	123	106
45	586	593	513	471	428	386	343	301	258	241	224	216	207	191	174	157	140	150	140	121
50	683	683	586	537	489	441	392	344	295	276	256	247	237	218	198	179	159	168	159	136
55	780	762	659	604	550	495	441	386	332	310	288	277	267	245	223	201	179	187	175	151
60	877	853	732	671	611	550	490	429	369	344	320	308	296	272	248	223	199	280	262	226
75	974	1277	1096	1006	915	824	734	643	552	516	480	462	444	407	371	335	299			
	1459																			

THE EXACTA

Odds	75.0	50.0	45.0	40.0	35.0	30.0	25.0	20.0	19.0	18.0	17.0	16.0	15.0	14.0	13.0	12.0	11.0	10.0	9.0	8.0
0.2	77	51	46	41	36	31	26	21	20	19	18	17	16	15	14	13	12	11	10	9
0.4	113	74	68	61	53	46	38	31	30	28	27	25	24	22	21	19	18	16	15	13
0.6	131	82	79	71	62	53	45	36	34	33	31	29	27	26	24	22	20	19	17	15
0.8	150	100	91	81	71	61	51	41	39	37	35	33	31	29	27	25	23	21	19	17
1.0	186	125	113	100	88	76	64	51	49	46	44	41	39	37	34	32	29	27	24	22
1.2	223	150	135	120	106	91	76	61	58	56	53	50	47	44	41	38	35	32	29	26
1.4	260	174	157	140	123	106	89	72	68	65	61	58	54	51	48	44	41	37	34	31
1.6	296	199	179	160	140	121	101	82	78	74	70	66	62	58	54	50	47	43	39	35
1.8	315	211	190	170	149	128	108	87	83	79	74	70	66	62	58	54	49	45	41	37
2.0	333	223	202	180	158	136	114	92	87	83	79	74	70	66	61	57	52	48	44	39
2.5	370	249	224	199	175	151	126	102	97	92	87	83	78	73	68	63	58	53	48	44
3.0	406	273	246	219	192	166	139	112	107	101	96	91	85	80	75	69	64	59	53	48
3.5	498	335	301	269	236	203	170	138	131	124	118	111	105	98	92	85	79	72	65	59
4.0	590	395	357	318	279	240	202	163	155	147	140	132	124	116	109	101	93	85	78	70
4.5	681	457	412	368	323	278	233	188	179	170	161	152	143	134	125	117	108	99	90	81
5.0	773	517	468	417	366	315	264	214	203	193	183	173	163	153	142	132	122	112	102	92
6.0	865	580	523	466	410	353	296	239	228	216	205	193	182	171	159	148	137	125	114	102
7.0	956	642	579	516	453	390	327	264	252	239	227	214	201	189	176	164	151	139	126	113
8.0	1139	765	690	615	540	465	390	315	300	285	270	255	240	225	210	195	180	165	150	135
9.0	1323	889	801	714	627	540	453	366	348	331	314	296	279	261	244	227	209	192	174	157
10.0	1506	1011	912	813	714	615	516	416	397	377	357	337	317	298	278	258	238	218	199	179
11.0	1689	1134	1023	912	800	689	578	467	445	423	401	378	356	334	312	289	267	245	223	201
12.0	1872	1257	1134	1010	887	764	641	518	493	469	444	419	395	370	346	321	296	272	247	222
13.0	2056	1380	1245	1109	974	839	704	569	542	515	488	461	433	406	379	352	325	298	271	244
14.0	2239	1503	1356	1208	1061	914	767	619	590	560	531	502	472	443	413	384	354	325	295	266
15.0	2422	1626	1466	1307	1148	989	829	670	638	606	575	543	511	479	447	415	383	352	320	288
16.0	2605	1749	1577	1406	1235	1063	892	721	687	652	618	584	550	515	481	447	412	378	344	310
17.0	2789	1872	1688	1505	1322	1138	955	772	735	698	662	625	588	552	515	478	441	405	368	331
18.0	2972	1995	1799	1604	1409	1213	1018	822	783	744	705	666	627	588	549	510	471	431	392	353
19.0	3155	2116	1910	1703	1495	1288	1080	873	832	790	749	707	666	624	583	541	500	458	417	375
20.0	3338	2241	2021	1802	1582	1363	1143	924	880	836	792	748	704	660	616	572	529	485	441	397
21.0	3522	2361	2132	1901	1669	1438	1206	974	928	882	836	789	743	697	650	604	558	511	465	419
22.0	3705	2487	2243	2000	1756	1512	1269	1025	976	928	879	830	782	733	684	635	587	538	489	440
25.0	4621	3102	2798	2494	2190	1886	1583	1279	1218	1157	1096	1036	975	914	853	793	732	671	610	550
30.0	5537	3717	3353	2989	2625	2261	1893	1532	1460	1387	1314	1241	1168	1095	1023	950	877	804	731	659
35.0	6454	4332	3908	3483	3059	2635	2210	1786	1701	1616	1531	1447	1362	1277	1192	1107	1022	937	852	768
40.0	7370	4947	4463	3978	3493	3009	2524	2040	1943	1846	1749	1652	1555	1458	1361	1264	1167	1070	974	877
45.0	8286	5562	5017	4473	3928	3383	2838	2293	2184	2075	1966	1857	1748	1639	1530	1422	1313	1204	1095	986
50.0	9203	6177	5572	4967	4362	3757	3152	2547	2426	2305	2184	2063	1942	1821	1700	1579	1458	1337	1216	1095
75.0	13784	9253	8346	7440	6534	5627	4721	3815	3634	3452	3271	3090	2909	2727	2546	2365	2184	2002	1821	1640

THE QUINELLA

Odds	7.0	6.0	5.0	4.5	4.0	3.5	3.0	2.5	2.0	1.8	1.6	1.5	1.4	1.2	1.0	0.8	0.6	0.5	0.4	0.2
0.2	5				3	3	3	3	2	2										
0.4	8	5	4	4	5	4	4	3	2	2	2		0							
0.5	9	7	6	5	5	5	4	4	3	3	2		2							
0.6	10	8	7	6	6	5	5	5	3	3	3	2	2	0	0	0				
0.8	12	10	9	8	7	6	6	5	4	4	3	2	3	2	2	0		0	0	
0.9	14	12	10	9	8	7	7	6	4	5	4	2	3	2	2	2		0	0	
1.0	16	14	12	10	9	8	8	7	5	5	4	3	4	3	2	2	0	0	0	
1.2	18	15	13	12	11	9	8	7	6	6	5	4	4	3	3	2	0	0	0	0
1.4	19	16	14	13	12	10	9	8	6	6	5	4	5	4	3	3	0	2	0	0
1.5	21	17	16	14	13	11	10	9	7	7	6	5	5	4	4	3	2	2	2	0
1.6	23	19	17	16	14	12	11	9	8	8	6	5	6	5	4	3	2	2	2	0
1.8	28	20	21	19	17	15	13	11	9	9	8	6	7	6	4	4	2	2	2	0
2.0	33	24	24	22	20	17	15	13	11	10	9	7	8	7	5	5	3	3	2	2
2.5	37	28	27	25	22	20	17	15	12	11	10	9	9	8	6	5	3	3	3	2
3.0	42	32	31	28	25	22	20	17	14	13	12	10	11	9	7	6	3	4	3	2
3.5	47	36	34	31	28	25	22	19	16	14	13	11	12	10	8	7	4	5	4	2
4.0	51	40	38	34	31	27	24	21	17	16	14	12	13	12	9	8	4	5	5	2
4.5	60	45	44	40	36	32	28	24	20	19	17	14	15	14	10	9	5	6	5	3
5.0	70	52	51	47	42	37	33	28	23	21	20	16	18	16	12	10	6	8	6	4
6.0	79	60	58	53	47	42	37	32	26	24	22	19	20	18	14	12	7	9	7	4
7.0	88	68	65	59	53	47	41	35	30	27	25	21	22	20	16	13	8	10	8	5
8.0	97	76	71	65	59	52	46	39	33	30	27	24	25	22	17	15	9	11	9	5
9.0	106	84	78	71	64	57	50	43	36	33	30	26	27	24	19	17	10	12	10	6
10	116	92	85	77	70	62	54	47	39	36	33	29	29	28	21	18	11	13	11	7
11	125	100	92	83	75	67	59	50	42	39	35	31	32	30	23	20	14	15	12	8
12	134	108	98	90	81	72	63	54	45	41	38	33	34	33	25	21	15	16	13	9
13	143	114	105	96	86	77	67	58	48	44	40	36	36	35	27	23	18	17	14	10
14	152	124	112	102	92	82	72	61	51	47	43	39	39	37	30	24	19	19	15	11
15	161	132	119	108	97	87	76	65	54	50	46	41	41	39	32	26	22	21	17	12
16	171	140	126	114	103	92	80	69	57	53	48	43	44	41	34	28	23	22	18	13
17	180	149	132	120	108	97	85	73	61	56	51	48	46	43	36	29	24	23	19	15
18	189	155	139	127	114	101	89	76	64	59	53	51	48	43	38	31	26	24	20	19
20	235	205	173	157	142	126	111	95	79	73	66	63	60	54	47	40	27	30	27	23
25	281	241	207	188	169	151	132	113	95	87	79	76	72	64	56	48	40	36	32	27
30	327	283	240	219	197	175	154	132	110	101	92	88	83	74	65	56	47	42	37	30
35	372	323	274	249	225	200	175	151	126	115	105	100	95	85	75	64	53	48	42	34
40	418	363	308	280	253	225	197	169	141	130	118	113	107	95	84	72	60	54	47	38
45	464	403	342	311	280	249	219	188	157	144	131	125	119	106	93	80	67	60	53	38
75	693	602	510	465	419	373	327	280	234	215	196	187	177	158	139	120	100	89	79	57

THE QUINELLA

Odds	0.2	0.4	0.5	0.6	0.8	1.0	1.2	1.4	1.6	1.8	2.0	2.5	3.0	3.5	4.0	4.5	5.0	6.0	7.0	8.0	9.0	10.0	11.0	12.0	13.0	14.0	15.0	16.0	17.0	18.0	19.0	20.0	25.0	30.0	35.0	40.0	45.0	50.0	75.0
8.0	6	9	10	11	13	16	18	20	21	22	24	26	32	37	42	47	53	58	68	79	89	100	110	120	131	141	152	162	172	183	193	203	266	318	370	421	473	525	785
9.0	7	10	11	12	15	17	20	22	25	27	30	35	41	47	53	59	65	76	88	100	111	123	134	146	158	169	181	192	204	216	227	239	297	355	413	471	528	586	876
10.0	8	11	12	14	17	19	22	25	27	30	33	39	46	52	59	65	71	84	97	110	123	136	148	161	174	187	200	212	225	238	251	264	328	392	456	520	584	648	967
11.0	9	12	13	15	18	21	24	27	30	33	36	43	50	57	64	71	78	92	106	120	134	148	162	176	190	204	218	233	247	261	275	289	359	429	499	569	639	709	1059
12.0	9	13	15	16	20	23	26	29	33	36	39	47	54	62	70	77	85	100	116	131	146	161	176	192	207	222	237	253	268	283	298	313	389	466	542	618	694	770	1150
13.0	10	14	16	18	21	25	28	32	35	39	42	50	59	67	75	83	92	108	125	141	158	174	190	207	223	240	256	273	289	305	322	338	420	502	585	667	749	831	1241
14.0	11	15	17	19	23	27	30	34	38	41	45	54	63	72	81	90	98	116	134	152	169	187	204	222	240	257	275	293	310	328	346	363	451	539	628	716	804	892	1332
15.0	12	16	18	20	24	29	33	36	40	44	48	58	67	77	86	96	105	124	143	162	181	200	218	237	256	275	294	313	332	350	369	398	482	576	670	765	859	953	1423
16.0	12	17	19	22	26	30	35	39	43	47	51	61	72	82	92	102	112	132	152	172	192	212	233	253	273	293	313	333	353	373	393	413	513	613	713	814	914	1014	1515
17.0	13	18	21	23	28	32	37	41	46	50	54	65	76	87	97	108	119	140	161	183	204	225	247	268	289	310	332	353	374	395	417	438	544	650	756	863	969	1075	1606
18.0	14	19	22	24	29	34	39	44	48	53	57	69	80	92	103	114	126	148	171	193	216	238	261	283	305	328	350	373	395	418	440	463	575	687	799	912	1024	1136	1697
19.0	15	20	23	26	31	36	41	46	51	56	61	73	85	97	108	120	132	156	180	203	227	251	275	298	322	346	369	393	417	440	464	487	606	724	842	961	1079	1197	1788
20.0	15	21	24	27	32	38	43	48	53	59	64	76	89	101	114	127	139	164	189	214	239	264	289	313	338	363	388	413	438	463	487	512	637	761	885	1009	1134	1258	1879
25.0	19	27	30	34	40	47	54	60	66	73	79	95	111	126	142	157	173	204	235	266	297	328	359	389	420	451	482	513	544	575	606	637	791	946	1100	1254	1409	1563	2335
30.0	23	32	36	40	48	56	64	72	79	87	95	113	132	151	169	188	207	244	281	318	355	392	429	466	502	539	576	613	650	687	724	761	946	1130	1315	1499	1684	1868	2791
35.0	27	37	42	47	56	65	74	83	88	101	110	132	154	175	197	219	240	283	327	370	413	456	499	542	585	628	670	713	756	799	842	885	1100	1315	1529	1744	1959	2173	3247
40.0	30	42	48	53	64	75	85	95	105	115	126	151	175	200	225	249	274	323	372	421	471	520	569	618	667	716	765	814	863	912	961	1009	1254	1499	1744	1989	2234	2478	3702
45.0	34	47	54	60	72	84	95	107	118	130	141	169	197	225	253	280	308	363	418	473	528	584	639	694	749	804	859	914	969	1024	1079	1134	1409	1684	1959	2234	2508	2783	4158
50.0	38	53	60	67	80	93	104	117	131	144	157	186	217	247	280	311	342	403	464	525	586	648	709	770	831	892	953	1014	1075	1135	1197	1258	1563	1863	2173	2478	2783	3088	4613
75.0	57	79	89	100	120	139	158	177	196	215	234	280	327	373	419	465	510	602	693	785	876	967	1059	1150	1241	1332	1423	1515	1606	1697	1788	1879	2335	2791	3247	3702	4158	4613	6892

handicapping backstretch opinion. While there are obvious merits to the philosophy of the chartists, and the betting action they uncover can be quite revealing and useful, their methodology is very time consuming, leaving them little time for other equally important handicapping pursuits. Board-watching is relevant only in light of good handicapping and the estimated odds line such analysis produces. Chartists must also be able to factor out extraneous influences on the odds board. Popular newspaper selectors and successful tip sheets can have as much influence on the odds as backstretch opinion.

All handicappers, not just chartists, are well-advised to learn what their newspaper selectors rely on—speed figures, trips, class, whatever. When a trip handicapper picks a horse with vague form, one can easily surmise that the horse had a bad trip in its latest start. Should a speed handicapper pick the same horse, the reader can conclude that one of its recent figures was outstanding.

The vast majority of handicappers would rather spend their time at the track studying the *Form*, observing in the paddock, or socializing (i.e., bragging). Nevertheless, they often find it important to know whether a certain exotic combination represents better value than found in the win pool. To this end, we have prepared three tables, one for the daily double, a second for the exacta, and a third for the quinella. These tables relate win odds to exotic payoffs. The tables appear on the preceding pages, and are quite simple to read and use.

Suppose, for example, that you wished to play a double consisting of a 5–1 shot in the first race with a 10–1 shot in the second. Simply look across the line marked 5.00 (for 5–1) until coming to the column headed 10.00. The number you find ($161) represents fair value (at 17 percent take) for a daily double combining these two horses. If the actual payoff is significantly higher, the player has found value in the daily double. If lower, one (or possibly both) of the horses may be "live." Of course, at the time one plays the double, the eventual odds on the horse in the second race are not known. The player must use the morning line odds, or his own estimate of the second horse's fair odds, to determine if the double represents value.

When using the daily double or quinella tables, it does not matter which horse determines the line, and which the column. With the exacta table, however, odds for the win horse must be found in the column on the left, and the place horse's odds across the top of the table. A horse in the second race may appear to be attracting only lukewarm support, but a look at the double payoff may uncover the stable action. The table above can be used for this purpose, and so can a parlay analysis. Simply place the amount of the winning ticket from the first race back on the horse in the second race, and compare the potential return with the double payoff. If larger, the conclusion is that the horse was bet heavily in the double. Keep in mind that a parlay wager involves two takeouts, while when betting the double, there is just one.

□ PLAYING THE EXOTICS □

Handicappers often look to the exotic wager when their selection becomes a heavy favorite. They hope to improve their odds by combining their horse with each of the logical contenders. Others turn to the exotics simply in the hope of making a big score. As a rule, exotic payoffs involving other than the favorite and second choice tend to be significantly overlaid. Suppose, for example, that the favorite is even money, while the exacta payoffs with its three logical rivals are $12.00, $20.00, and $30.00. Rather than bet $6.00 to win, and collect $12.00 should the horse return a winner, the clever player might instead bet three $2.00 exactas. He would collect at least $12.00, and possibly as much as $30.00, which represents odds of 4–1. Unless, of course, some other horse upsets the prerace dope and runs second. Better still, the player could bet three of the $12.00 exactas, two of the $20.00 exactas, and a lone $30.00 exacta. For a total outlay of $12.00, the player would stand to collect anywhere from $30.00 to $40.00 should the exacta hit. Even money odds would have been improved to at least 3–2 and possibly as much as 5–2.

The power of this approach increases should the second choice in the wagering be overbet in the exactas, and at the same time be eliminated by the player's handicapping considerations. For example, the second choice may figure to be beaten off by the favorite after a front-end speed duel. Or it may be returning from a layoff, or figure to race against a track bias. Should this be the case, the possible exacta payoffs with the true contenders tend to run exceptionally high.

CASE STUDY: TWOSOME, MAJESTIC NORTH, AND GLAMOROUS DAISZ

There are numerous occasions when a handicapper considers a race to be a toss-up among three horses, yet the betting public makes one of them its overwhelming favorite. When three horses appear evenly matched, and well above the rest of the field, the logical bet may be an exacta box, but when one horse is bet out of proportion, the wise move may be to eliminate it and play exactas combining just the other two. Even if one's assessment of the race is correct, however, this will be a losing bet two out of every three times. More frequently, actually, when one considers the probability that the crowd might be correct in its selection of a favorite, and the possibility some other horse may surprise, and run first or second. The point is that the exacta payoff will be extremely generous should the horses played finish first and second, enough to provide a handsome profit over the long run, provided of course, that the distortion observed in the win pool carries over into the exacta pool.

The seventh race at Aqueduct on May 14, 1983, a classified allowance for fillies at a mile-and-a-sixteenth on the grass, is a case in point. The race appeared between Majestic North, Glamorous Daisz, and Twosome. The speedy Majestic North had a solid recent race over the course to recommend her, but would carry a steadying 124 pounds. Glamorous Daisz, a stakes-winner in California as a three-year-old, was making her second start, and first route attempt, of the year. And Twosome, competitive with stakes-class fillies in New York at three, was training steadily for her return to grass competition, and stood to gain from her rivals' front-running tendencies. All things considered, each of these fillies should have been bet in the 2–1 to 5–2 range. Instead, Glamorous Daisz was bet down to 9–10, while the other two were 9–2 and 5–1. When Twosome rallied to win going away, and Majestic North edged Glamorous Daisz for the place, exacta players were rewarded with a generous $44.80 payoff. Odds of 10–1 were attained in a situation warranting no more than 4–1 or 5–1.

Glamorous Daisz — B. f. 4, by Somethingfabulous—Bouquet of Roses, by Dress Up
Own.—Allen J — Br.—Ring Connie M (Cal) — Tr.—Tesher Howard M — **119**

Lifetime	1983	1	0	0	0	$640
15 4 2 5	1982	11	4	1	5	$91,400
$96,540	Turf	5	3	0	1	$56,190

2May83- 8Hia	hd	5½f Ⓣ			1:03⅖	3↑ⒻAlw 16000	7	3	9^{9}	8^{11}	$7^{9\frac{1}{4}}$	$4^{3\frac{3}{4}}$	Marquez C	b 115	*1.80	90–11	Blue Ribbon Girl $119^{\frac{3}{4}}$FlyinMimi$117^{1\frac{1}{2}}$SensitivePenny$115^{1\frac{1}{2}}$	Rallied	12
9Jly82- 8Hol	fm	1$\frac{1}{16}$ Ⓣ	:46⅗	1:10⅗	1:41	3↑ⒻC. Queen	5	2	$2^{\frac{1}{2}}$	$2^{\frac{1}{2}}$	2^{hd}	3^{nk}	Pincay L Jr	b 117	4.50	94–10	Mi Quimera 113^{hd} Pink Safir 115^{hd} Glamorus Diasz117^{1}	Willingly	8
1Jly82- 8Hol	fm	1 Ⓣ	:46⅕	1:10⅖	1:35⅕	3↑ⒻAlw 27000	2	3	$3^{2\frac{1}{2}}$	2^{1}	$1^{1\frac{1}{2}}$	$1^{1\frac{1}{4}}$	Pincay L Jr	b 117	*1.40	93–07	GlmorusDisz$117^{1\frac{1}{4}}$Aggrndizement$119^{2\frac{1}{2}}$LdyTrspss116^{hd}	Ridden out	7
12Jun82- 8GG	fm	1$\frac{1}{16}$ Ⓣ	:48⅖	1:12⅖	1:45⅖	ⒻⓈImpr'eSty'e	3	2	$1^{\frac{1}{2}}$	$1^{1\frac{1}{2}}$	$1^{1\frac{1}{2}}$	$1^{2\frac{1}{2}}$	Chapman T M	b 115	*1.00	75–21	Glamorus Diasz $115^{2\frac{1}{2}}$ Surely A Winner $115^{\frac{1}{2}}$ Buck Spring 112^{1}		9
29May82- 7Hol	fm	1$\frac{1}{16}$ Ⓣ	:47	1:11	1:41⅕	ⒻAlw 22000	8	1	$1^{1\frac{1}{2}}$	1^{1}	$1^{2\frac{1}{2}}$	1^{4}	Pincay L Jr	b 120	*1.90	93–07	Glamorus Diasz 120^{4} Break Out The Wine 114^{1} Trust Us $117^{1\frac{1}{2}}$		10
1May82- 8Hol	fst	1$\frac{1}{16}$	:47	1:11	1:42⅘	ⒻCalif Miss	6	6	6^{5}	5^{3}	$4^{6\frac{1}{2}}$	4^{6}	Olivares F	b 114	12.40	76–15	Carry A Tune 114^{2} Elusive $114^{1\frac{1}{2}}$ A Kiss For Luck $116^{2\frac{1}{2}}$	Hung	8
9Apr82- 5SA	fst	1	:46	1:10⅕	1:35⅖	ⒻAlw 21000	2	2	2^{hd}	1^{hd}	2^{hd}	$3^{1\frac{1}{4}}$	Valenzuela P A	b 120	14.50	91–13	Model Ten $117^{1\frac{1}{4}}$ Her Decision 115no Glamorus Diasz $120^{1\frac{1}{4}}$		8
27Mar82- 6SA	fst	1$\frac{1}{16}$	:46⅕	1:11⅕	1:43⅘	ⒻMd Sp Wt	5	3	$3^{1\frac{1}{2}}$	2^{hd}	1^{3}	1^{1}	Valenzuela P A	b 117	5.90	82–14	Glamorus Diasz 117^{1} Soft Song $117^{\frac{1}{2}}$ Grey Susan 117^{3}	Driving	11
14Mar82- 3SA	sly	1$\frac{1}{16}$	:47⅖	1:13⅖	1:47	ⒻMd Sp Wt	8	5	$3^{2\frac{1}{2}}$	3^{2}	$5^{3\frac{3}{4}}$	3^{3}	Valenzuela P A	b 117	5.80	63–38	Indianola $117^{2\frac{1}{4}}$ Grassy $117^{\frac{3}{4}}$ Glamorus Diasz 117^{2}		11
26Feb82- 6SA	fst	7f	:22⅕	:45⅖	1:23	ⒻⓈMd Sp Wt	2	10	$9^{4\frac{1}{4}}$	$8^{5\frac{3}{4}}$	4^{6}	$3^{5\frac{1}{4}}$	Pincay L Jr	b 117	6.80	80–15	Elusive 117^{5} That Does It 117^{nk} Glamorus Diasz $117^{1\frac{1}{2}}$		11

LATEST WORKOUTS ●Apr 26 Hia Ⓣ 4f fm :49 b (d) Apr 19 Hia Ⓣ 6f fm 1:15 b (d) Apr 12 Hia Ⓣ 6f fm 1:02⅖ b (d) Apr 2 Hia 4f fst :50 b

CASE STUDY: QUADRATIC'S PRIDE

Longshot players who like their selection's chances relative to each of its rivals except one may use the quinella (or a pair of reversed exactas) as a place bet. Suppose, for example, that you liked the chances of Quadratic's Pride, but feared the favorite, Mighty Hunter, in this race for maiden two-year-old New York-breds run at Aqueduct December 31, 1982. Consider what may have happened had you bought two $10 win tickets on Quadratic's Pride and one $10 quinella combining him with the favorite. If Quadratic's Pride won with Mighty Hunter running second (as did happen), you would have cashed all three tickets, worth a combined total of $246.00. Had Mighty Hunter failed to run second, however, you would have cashed just the win tickets, which were worth

FOURTH RACE Aqueduct DECEMBER 31, 1982

6 FURLONGS.(INNER DIRT). (1.08⅘) MAIDEN SPECIAL WEIGHT. Purse $24,000. 2-year-olds. Foaled in New York State and Approved by the New York State-Bred Registry. Weight, 118 lbs.

Value of race $24,000, value to winner $14,400, second $5,280, third $2,880, fourth $1,440. Mutuel pool $143,160, OTB pool $125,202. Quinella Pool $182,522. OTB Quinella Pool $158,053.

Last Raced	Horse	Eqt.	A.	Wt	PP	St	¼	½	Str	Fin	Jockey	Odds $1
20Dec82 ^{3}Aqu^{4}	Quadratic's Pride	b	2	113	1	4	4^{hd}	$3^{1\frac{1}{2}}$	1^{3}	$1^{2\frac{3}{4}}$	Asmussen S M5	a-7.20
20Dec82 ^{3}Aqu^{2}	Mighty Hunter		2	118	9	12	11^{4}	6^{2}	3^{hd}	$2^{1\frac{1}{2}}$	Cordero A Jr	1.80
11Dec82 ^{2}Aqu^{6}	Pont D'Argent		2	118	5	3	$2^{1\frac{1}{2}}$	1^{hd}	$2^{1\frac{1}{2}}$	$3^{1\frac{3}{4}}$	Venezia M	6.20
17Oct82 ^{4}Aqu^{2}	Speed Letter		2	118	12	2	3^{1}	$2^{\frac{1}{2}}$	4^{2}	4^{nk}	Velez R I	2.10
20Dec82 ^{3}Aqu^{12}	Time Together	b	2	118	6	8	$8^{\frac{1}{2}}$	$8^{\frac{1}{2}}$	5^{2}	$5^{3\frac{3}{4}}$	Skinner K	84.30
20Dec82 ^{3}Aqu^{8}	Political Flight		2	113	3	7	9^{3}	10^{3}	8^{5}	6^{nk}	Davis R G5	101.90
23Dec82 ^{5}Aqu^{7}	Aldalco	b	2	118	7	5	1^{hd}	$4^{1\frac{1}{2}}$	$6^{\frac{1}{2}}$	$7^{\frac{1}{2}}$	Hernandez R	b-13.40
23Dec82 ^{5}Aqu^{5}	Cold Blade		2	111	4	9	$7^{\frac{1}{2}}$	5^{1}	$7^{1\frac{1}{2}}$	$8^{4\frac{3}{4}}$	Clayton M D7	15.20
22Dec82 ^{6}Aqu^{10}	Astuteness	b	2	118	2	10	14	11^{4}	9^{3}	$9^{2\frac{1}{2}}$	Santagata N	a-7.20
6Dec82 ^{4}Aqu^{4}	Plum Numb	b	2	118	11	1	6^{2}	7^{hd}	10^{hd}	10^{hd}	Migliore R	18.50
	Equivocate		2	118	10	14	$13^{\frac{1}{2}}$	14	$11^{\frac{1}{2}}$	$11^{\frac{3}{4}}$	Beitia E	61.50
20Dec82 ^{3}Aqu^{14}	Point of Exchange		2	111	14	13	$12^{2\frac{1}{2}}$	$13^{\frac{1}{2}}$	12^{3}	$12^{2\frac{3}{4}}$	Thibeau R J7	61.50
20Dec82 ^{3}Aqu^{10}	Kirbys' Punch		2	118	13	11	$10^{\frac{1}{2}}$	12^{2}	13^{3}	13^{4}	Vergara O	80.30
	Middle Patent	b	2	118	8	6	5^{hd}	$9^{\frac{1}{2}}$	14	14	Lovato F Jr	b-13.40

a-Coupled: Quadratic's Pride and Astuteness; b-Aldalco and Middle Patent.

OFF AT 2:00 Start good, Won ridden out. Time, :23⅗, :48⅖, 1:14 Track fast.

$2 Mutuel Prices:

1-(A)-QUADRATIC'S PRIDE (a-entry)	16.40	6.40	3.80
7-(J)-MIGHTY HUNTER		3.60	2.60
5-(E)-PONT D'ARGENT			3.20

$2 QUINELLA 1-7 PAID $16.40.

Ch. c, by Quadratic—Snared, by Insubordination. Trainer Hertler John O. Bred by K T Leatherbury Assoc Inc (NY).

$164.00. Instead of placing that other $10 on the nose, you had wasted it on an exotic bet and, in effect, lowered your odds from 7–1 to just 4–1.

On the other hand, had Quadratic's Pride run second to the horse you feared the most, you would have been protected, cashing the quinella ticket worth $82.00. Note that a $30 place bet on Quadratic's Pride would have returned more—$96.00—but without offering the opportunity for significantly larger winnings. Of course, Quadratic's Pride could have finished second to a horse other than Mighty Hunter, in which case the place bet would have been wisest.

Unless keying an exotic wager to a specific horse, the handicapper is best advised to leave some room for error. Criss-crossing his first two selections in each of the daily-double races (four tickets) allows the player to be wrong about one horse in each race, yet still cash a winning ticket. Likewise, boxing his first three selections in an exacta (six tickets) or quinella (three tickets) permits the handicapper to have been wrong about one of the horses, and still collect.

The triple (trifecta) can be approached in much the same way. The bettor can box his first four selections in the race, and collect if three of them run to expectations. However, a four-horse box requires the purchase of twenty-four tickets. While the potential payoff may be great, so is the risk—three horses must run well, or all is lost. One surprise horse placing in the money can ruin the whole bet.

Others approach the triple by attempting to reduce it to an exacta. If one horse appears a standout, they may box three others in the second and third positions (six tickets). If two horses look certain in the first two positions, they may be played both ways with (say) three horses in the third slot (again six tickets). As long as one has some opinion limiting the number of possible contenders, the triple can be played with a minimum number of tickets.

Many fields consist of two, three, or four horses coming from each of (perhaps) three different races. Should the handicapper determine that one of these races was clearly the strongest of the three, he may wish to box the horses coming out of that race in some form of exotic wager. Or he may wish to capitalize on his belief in the strength of his selection's most recent performance by hooking that animal up in an exacta bet with one or two other horses coming from the same race. However, because horses from the same race tend to become associated or connected in many players' minds, the odds of those combinations tend to suffer. This is a good technique for the exotics, from a handicapping standpoint, but an easy one for unsophisticated players to spot.

On biased racetracks, it is best to play exotics totally with the bias.

Play speed horses (or closers) in both ends of the double, and play two speed horses (or two closers) in the exacta. Under normal circumstances, though, it is wise to include at least one speed type in all exacta and quinella bets.

A horse's value in the exotic pools can be seen through its earnings box. One with a high percentage of wins and seconds is hard to throw out, while the horse with few such placings is not a likely candidate to win or place. Should you really like a horse, the exacta offers far more value than does the quinella. The same is true for horses with bridesmaid tendencies, which are best used as the bottom half of an exacta, and lose all value when played in a quinella.

Many players wheel their selection in doubles, exactas, or quinellas. Others routinely include the favorite as part of their exotic wagers. Their action causes both favorites and hopeless longshots to be underlaid in these pools. Smart players take advantage, excluding these horses whenever possible. They consider horses in the middle odds range to be the profitable ones in their exotic wagering.

☐ MONEY MANAGEMENT TECHNIQUES ☐

Traditionally, the term "money management" has referred to the optimal use of one's betting capital over a long series of wagers. How can the player make his money work best for him? How can he best use his capital to avoid the serious repercussions of the ups and downs that all gamblers face? How much should be bet, in relation to the size of the bankroll? Should the size of the bet be changed as the bankroll fluctuates? These are the questions that money management addresses.

The size of one's betting bankroll, and the selection of a unit bet as a percentage thereof, are both critically important. The bankroll guarantees the bettor a certain longevity, insurance that a succession of losing bets will not completely empty the till. Oversized bets can ruin any profitable method. On the other hand, overly conservative bets can fail to take full advantage of the player's handicapping expertise and bankroll. What is the ideal middle ground?

The most conservative betting methodology is the flat bet. The player decides to risk the same amount on each selection—say 5 percent of the original bankroll. If nothing else, a flat betting analysis will prove (or disprove) the profitability of the handicapping technique(s) employed.

At the opposite extreme are the "negative progression" techniques that require the player to increase his bet after each loss. Such methods can be financially and psychologically ruinous. If, for example, one were to "double up" (double his bet) after each loss, an original bet of $2 would grow to $2048 after ten consecutive losses. For a $2 bettor, this is quite a sizable bet. On the other hand, had the first bet been $100, the eleventh would be $102,400, enough to drastically alter the odds at most tracks, and likely leave the player behind overall even if the horse wins.

Experienced players realize that it is far better to increase the size of their bet when winning, and decrease it when losing. Betting a fixed percentage of one's current bankroll on each selection accomplishes both. In a paper entitled "Optimal Betting," Huey Mahl writes that the percentage which will produce the best results can be determined mathematically, according to a formula known as the Kelly Criterion:

$$Optimal\ percentage = W\% - L\%/average\ win\ odds$$

where W% is one's expected percentage of winning selections, and L% the expected percentage of losing picks. So if a handicapper's records show him capable of picking 30 percent winners at average win odds of 2.75 to 1, that player should bet

$$.30 - .70/2.75 = .05,$$

or 5 percent of his bankroll on each selection. The Kelly Criterion suggests that the player wager more as his advantage over the game increases. To demonstrate this and the three techniques that follow, and to help the reader be sure he understands the arithmetic involved, the details of a sequence of ten bets using each technique is shown in tabular form. In each sequence, we assume the second ($8.00), fifth ($12.00), and eighth ($6.00) plays were winners. With each technique, we assume a starting bankroll of $1000 and a base bet of $50—5 percent of the starting bankroll.

FIXED PERCENTAGE WAGERING

	Bankroll	Bet
1.	1000	50
2. Won at $8.00	950	47
3.	1091	55
4.	1036	52
5. Won at $12.00	984	49
6.	1230	61
7.	1169	58
8. Won at $6.00	1111	56
9.	1223	61
10.	1162	58
	1104	

In an original paper appearing in his *The Literature of Thoroughbred Handicapping 1965–1982*, James Quinn warns of the erosion on profits during long losing streaks when using fixed percentage betting. Quinn offers instead what he terms "Fixed Percentage—Minimum" wagering, where the player bets a fixed percentage of his bankroll after each winning bet, but only the base percentage of the original bankroll after each loss. His technique therefore is a combination of flat betting and fixed percentage betting. It is designed to take advantage of the streaks so common in the seasonal play of successful handicappers.

FIXED PERCENTAGE—MINIMUM WAGERING

	Bankroll	Bet
1.	1000	50
2. Won at $8.00	950	50
3.	1100	55
4.	1045	50
5. Won at $12.00	995	50
6.	1245	62
7.	1183	50
8. Won at $6.00	1133	50
9.	1283	64
10.	1219	50
	1169	

James Selvidge offers another variation of flat betting. He recommends that one's bet should equal the base bet (a fixed percentage of the original bankroll) plus the square root of the profits. Should there be no profits at any given time, the bet would simply revert to the base bet. Selvidge contends that his technique will generate the most profit, at the minimal risk.

BASE BET PLUS SQUARE ROOT WAGERING

	Bankroll	Profit	Bet
1.	1000	0	50
2. Won at $8.00	950	0	50
3.	1100	100	50 + 10 = 60
4.	1040	40	50 + 6 = 56
5. Won at $12.00	984	0	50
6.	1234	234	50 + 15 = 65
7.	1169	169	50 + 13 = 63
8. Won at $6.00	1106	106	50 + 10 = 60
9.	1226	226	50 + 15 = 65
10.	1161	161	50 + 13 = 63
	1098		

In his *Encyclopedia of Thoroughbred Handicapping*, Tom Ainslie, long an advocate of fixed percentage wagering, suggests another approach, which he calls "unit wagering in ratio to the odds." In deference to the reality that most successful player's seasonal profits come from winning selections at decent odds (say from 3–1 through 10–1), Ainslie recommends betting:

one unit at odds of 3–1 or lower
two units at odds of 7–2 or 4–1
three units at odds of 9–2 or 5–1
four units at odds of 6–1
five units at odds of 7–1 or higher

Ainslie also suggests that a betting unit represent only 1 percent of the player's current bankroll.

UNIT BETS AT THE ODDS WAGERING

	Bankroll	Bet
1. Lost at 2–1	1000	50
2. Won at $8.00	950	50
3. Lost at 4–1	1100	100
4. Lost at 5–2	1000	50
5. Won at $12.00	950	150
6. Lost at 7–1	1700	250
7. Lost at 1–1	1450	50
8. Won at $6.00	1400	50
9. Lost at 12–1	1500	250
10. Lost at 3–2	1250	50
	1200	

Which of these approaches produces the best results? And what percentage of one's capital should be risked on each bet? 1%? 2%? 5%? 10%?

To answer these questions, we turned to computer simulation. As our sample, we have taken the selections in seven hundred races produced by a multiple regression technique developed by the author. Our sample included 30.4 percent winning selections at an average payoff of $7.50 (average win odds of 2.75–1). The sample included runs of up to ten consecutive losing selections. These represent realistic and attainable results for experienced handicappers. They simulate a full season's play, with the player making two or three selections a day.

Our simulation included one thousand "re-creations" of the full season, each time with the seven hundred selections occurring in a different order. This averaged out any effect the placement of winners, especially those at long odds, might have had on the final results, and provided a fair test of all techniques studied.

Each system has been tested using each of 1%, 2%, 3%, 4%, 5%, and 10% as the base percentage of capital to be invested on each selection. We started each simulation with a bankroll of $1000. Here are the results, in tabular form:

FLAT BETS

Percent	Average Bankroll	Largest Bankroll	# Tapouts
1%	$1984	$1984	0
2%	$2968	$2968	10
3%	$3735	$3952	55
4%	$4442	$4936	100
5%	$4748	$5920	198
10%	$5583	$10840	485

FIXED PERCENTAGE

Percent	Average Bankroll	Largest Bankroll	# Tapouts
1%	$2278	$2278	0
2%	$3855	$3855	0
3%	$4991	$4991	0
4%	$5054	$5054	0
5%	$4075	$4075	0
10%	$70	$70	0

BASE BET PLUS SQUARE ROOT

Percent	Average Bankroll	Largest Bankroll	# Tapouts
1%	$3435	$4868	0
2%	$5122	$6419	13
3%	$6208	$8032	80
4%	$7087	$9390	137
5%	$7128	$10689	255
10%	$7438	$17226	538

FIXED PERCENTAGE—MINIMUM

Percent	Average Bankroll	Largest Bankroll	# Tapouts
1%	$2074	$2799	0
2%	$3297	$8580	7
3%	$4595	$17366	49
4%	$5544	$26699	105
5%	$6758	$122190	211
10%	$4954	$335039	675

AINSLIE'S UNIT BETS

Percent	Average Bankroll	Largest Bankroll	# Tapouts
1%	$3987	$3987	0
2%	$1303	$1303	0
3%	$75	$75	0
4%	$1	$1	0
5%	$0	$0	1000
10%	$0	$0	1000

The individual reader must decide for himself which approach best suits his own betting philosophy. He must weigh the average bankroll produced against the largest attained, and both against the frequency of ruin. We offer a few comments of our own. First, note what a 14 percent profit on paper really means. In most cases, we see the original $1000 bankroll growing to an average somewhere between $2000 and $7000—a profit margin, in the final analysis, between 100 percent and 600 percent.

Second, unless a long succession of losing bets leads to bankruptcy, both flat and fixed percentage wagering at any given level will always produce the same final bankroll, with that generated by fixed percentage wagering always the higher of the two. The order in which the selections occur does not matter.

Third, conservative players will note that there is very little, if any, risk of tapping out while betting any of these methods at the 1 percent level. The same can be said for fixed percentage wagering at any level between 1 percent and 10 percent, making it the safest approach.

Fourth, average profits are highest when using the Base Bet Plus Square Root method advocated by James Selvidge, except at the 1 percent level. At that level, Tom Ainslie's technique proved best. However, the Ainslie method was useless at 2 percent, and disastrous at anything higher. Also, the Selvidge method allowed the greatest risk of ruin when using between 2 and 5 percent of one's betting capital.

Fifth, James Quinn's FP-M method offered the greatest chance for large profits—when the winners come in streaks—although on the average it was well below the fixed percentage and base-bet methods.

Finally, the fixed percentage method achieved its greatest success when wagering 4 percent of capital, and not the 5 percent predicted by Huey Mahl's formula. Possibly, that formula failed to account for the increasing risk of ruin as the size of the bet increases.

There is one conceptual difficulty with this entire study, however. A player simply likes some of his selections better than others, yet each of these techniques treats them as equals. Some selections might rate "four stars," others just "one star." None of the techniques permits intuitive adjustments to weigh one more than the other. I myself advocate (and use) an approach similar to the Ainslie technique described above. One betting unit could be used for "play" bets, and five units for prime bets that start at reasonable odds. Two, three, and four units could be reserved for exotic wagers, or serious bets that do not qualify as prime bets. In other words, the largest bets should be reserved for those horses about whom you feel the strongest, and whose odds warrant the large investment.

Chapter 15

SUMMARY

My formative years as a handicapper were spent studying the many excellent books by Tom Ainslie. Most authors of current handicapping books learned from the same source. Tom Ainslie almost single-handedly took Thoroughbred handicapping from the Dark Ages and elevated it to the status it now enjoys—a semi-respectable art and/or science.

But Tom Ainslie did his job too well. Too many graduates of the Tom Ainslie School of Handicapping are studying the *Daily Racing Form* at the nation's tracks. Too many people can read the *Form*, and understand the implications of what they read. The information found in the *Form* is still of critical importance to handicappers, but it is no longer enough. Traditional logic nowadays all too often leads to the pari-mutuel favorite.

Most people can now understand what they read in black and white in the *Form*. But if there is something that is not visible, possibly hidden between the lines, that is where the advantage lies for those who are aware.

To remain competitive, the contemporary handicapper must do graduate work. He must be part researcher, part detective, and part investigative reporter. He must be willing and able to develop his own sources of information to supplement what he reads in the *Form*.

During the late 1970s and into the 1980s, speed handicapping was thought to be the answer. With accurate daily variants and homemade speed figures, the speed handicapper was able to take a giant step beyond the primitive speed ratings found in the *Form*. Unfortunately, speed handicapping has become too popular. Vast hordes of speed handicappers are killing the prices on the "numbers" horses. Perhaps the central conclusion of Handicapping Expo '83 was that in spite of its obvious merits, speed handicapping was no longer enough. Speed figures could no longer stand alone. They had to be placed in context. It was no longer sufficient to know how fast a horse ran. Equally important was knowing "how it ran fast." Trip handicapping is supposed to fill that void. Handicappers possessing trip notes, calculating pace figures, and aware of track biases will be the ones to prosper in the 1980s.

Many times over, the casual handicapper will wonder why the crowd is betting a particular horse. Five years ago, the answer was almost certainly "speed figures." Today, it may just as easily be "trips."

Another interesting development of the last couple of years is worth mentioning, and emphasizing. Should you hear the comment "The speed boys probably had that one" after a race, it may not mean what it once did. There is another school of handicapping around these days. Its major thrust is to locate the "main speed" in a race, the horse likely to dominate and control the early pace. They don't find a play in every race, but when they do, they are dealing with one of the most profitable and reliable aspects of handicapping. They have become so successful that they are being called the "speed boys," and the speed handicappers have been redubbed the "figure boys," or simply "the figs."

☐ MARKING THE PAST PERFORMANCES ☐

During the handicapping process, one scans the past performances of the horses, and especially the contenders, many times over—at home, then in the grandstand before the races, in the paddock between races, and while standing in line minutes before betting. It helps no end to mark the *Form*, making certain that key pieces of information stand out on subsequent readings.

We suggest the following procedure be followed on one's first reading of the past performances:

(1) Write the names of today's jockeys (or some abbreviations thereof) into the past performances, between the jockey column and the weight column. The records of horses giving a call to one of the meet's leading riders deserve close scrutiny.

(2) Read the race conditions carefully, especially if an allowance contest. Write the race classification in large letters—such as NW2 or

weak CLF—above the past performances. If certain horses might be disadvantaged because of age or sex conditions (such as three-year-old claimers competing against older horses, or fillies competing against males), circle the appropriate item in their past performances.

(3) Circle the name of any trainer among the leaders on the circuit, currently on a hot streak, or employing an angle he or she is known to use successfully.

(4) Cross out the earnings box of any horse that seldom wins—a win percentage considerably less than 10 percent—and disregard the horse unless some compelling reason demands its consideration. Circle the earnings box of any horse that wins a high percentage of its starts—at least 40 percent—and give the horse extra credit for its gameness and consistency.

(5) Draw a line across the past performances, immediately below the first race in the horse's most recent campaign. That line points out the horse's most recent layoff of more than thirty days, and helps highlight freshened horses likely to show improvement. If a horse is returning from a layoff, circle the date of its most recent start.

(6) If a horse is shipping in from another track, circle the name of the track at which it has been competing recently. The "ad-hoc" shippers discussed in Chapter 7 will stand out clearly.

(7) If a horse appears unsuited by the distance, circle its entire distance column. If today's race represents a change in distance from the horse's previous race, circle that distance.

(8) If a horse appears outclassed, circle its entire class column. If claimed recently, circle that and subsequent races. If dropping today, draw a downward-pointing arrow through the class column of its most recent races.

(9) Circle the running line from a horse's most recent race if it hints of improvement—possibly the horse bid, but hung, showed surprising speed, or any of the several other angles discussed in Chapter 3.

(10) Possibly the most important: glance through the early speed column of each horse, identifying those likely to contest the issue in the early stages. For these horses, write pace figures from their three most recent representative early speed efforts into their past performances. Or calculate speed points, as defined in *Winning At The Races.*

And now, for a few examples of annotated past performances:

ZEB'S HEL CAT, a relatively fresh ad-hoc shipper to Aqueduct with a high percentage of wins for his career-to-date, all positive signs.

Zeb's Hel Cat — Ch. g. 3, by Over Arranged—Hell Cat Lou, by Nasamo — $60,000 — Br.—Patterson T C (Md) — Tr.—Sedlacek Roy — 119
Own.—Hurst B J
Lifetime 7 3 1 2 $23,985 — 1983 2 1 0 1 $8,625 — 1982 5 2 1 1 $15,360

19Mar83- 8Pim	sly	6f	:22⅖ :45⅕ 1:10⅘	H Jacobs	2 5 45½ 411 410 38	Miller D A Jr	b 116	5.90	84-16 Emperial Age 116hd Unreal Zeal 1168 Zeb's Hel Cat 116½ Evenly 5
7Mar83- 7Bow	fst	6f	:22⅖ :45⅗ 1:11⅕	Alw 9000	6 4 12 16 12 1¾	Delgado A5	b 112	*1.80	84-27 Zeb's Hel Cat 112¾ Cutter Sark 1172 Vincennes Road1132 Driving 6
22Dec82- 8Lrl	fst	6f	:22⅗ :46⅗ 1:12⅖	Alw 9000	7 4 11½ 12½ 1hd 11½	Delgado A5	b 117	3.00	81-23 Zeb'sHelCat1171½IllustriousBoat1153½CenturyDouble114¾ Driving 8
4Dec82- 5Lrl	sly	6f	:22⅖ :45⅘ 1:11⅖	Alw 9000	3 5 1½ 21½ 24 27	Delgado A5	117	8.90	79-19 Noble Home 1197 Zeb's HelCat1172½Talkright119¾ Best of others 8
16Nov82- 8Lrl	fst	6f	:22⅗ :46⅘ 1:12⅖	Alw 9000	4 3 2hd 21 59½ 813	Delgado A5	110	3.50	68-25 DixielandBand1151AssaultLnding122¾MrchingForMrgy1153 Tired 9
24Oct82- 4Aqu	fst	6f	:22⅖ :46⅘ 1:12	Md 50000	7 3 11½ 11½ 14 14	Delgado A5	b 113	13.50	81-25 Zeb'sHelCat1134EighteenKrt114noBudgetCutter1132¼ Ridden out 13
30Jun82- 4Lrl	sly	5½f	:23⅗ :48 1:07⅕	Md 25000	4 6 58¾ 57¾ 49½ 37	Delgado A5	113	*2.10	80-22 Out Of Wedlock 118hd Crimson 1187 Zeb's Hel Cat 113½ Rallied 9

LATEST WORKOUTS Mar 5 Lrl 4f fst :49⅗ b Feb 25 Lrl 4f gd :50⅘ b Feb 18 Lrl 4f my :49⅗ h ●Feb 9 Lrl 4f fst :47 h

THREE RING CIRCLE, a disinterested type with one win lifetime that was returning from a layoff on March 24 at seven furlongs on the dirt, neither the distance nor surface being her forte. An obvious "throwout."

Three Ring Circle — Dk. b. or br. f. 4, by Circle—First Cue, by First Balcony — Br.—Spenwood Farm (Ky) — Tr.—Cincotta Vincent J — 117
Own.—Frisina R J
Lifetime 24 1 3 4 $37,919 — 1983 1 0 0 0 — 1982 23 1 3 4 $37,919 — Turf 14 1 2 4 $34,679

9Jan83- 5Aqu	fst	1 1/16 [•]	:48⅗ 1:13⅗ 1:46⅖	ⒻAlw 22000	5 5 88½ 813 829 830	Migliore R	b 117	31.20	51-17 BringMeFlowersII1124BckstgeWhisper117½LdyNoble1123 Outrun 9
30Dec82- 7Aqu	fst	1 1/16 [•]	:49 1:14 1:47⅕	3+ⒻAlw 22000	1 5 67½ 57 713 814	Migliore R	b 115	17.80	63-24 Beside the Point 112½ Ranch Mink 110nk Simhala 115¾ Tired 8
25Nov82- 7Aqu	sf	1⅛ Ⓣ	:48⅕ 1:13⅖ 1:54⅕	3+ⒻAlw 20000	5 2 39 37½ 53¾ 67½	Cordero A Jr	b 115	3.80	65-28 PoliticsNTricks1202¾LovingHomeII1101½SlaveNoMore115nk Tired 9
8Nov82- 6Med	fst	170	:45⅗ 1:11⅕ 1:42⅕	ⒻLakewood	3 6 720 715 812 814	Perret C	b 115	15.50	76-18 BrightChoice115nkNightHirss1141½DistinctivMoon1144 No Factor 8
13Oct82- 6Aqu	fm	1⅜ Ⓣ	:50 1:41⅖ 2:17⅘	ⒻAthenia H	6 5 54 31 21 44¾	Hernandez C	b 106	28.80	77-13 Mintage 114½ Doodle 1192¼ Street Dance 1122 Tired 8
13Oct82-Run in two divisions 6th & 8th races									
2Oct82- 1Bel	fm	1¼ [T]	:48⅘ 1:38 2:02⅗	3+ⒻAlw 21000	5 3 34 42½ 54½ 58¾	Migliore R	b 114	11.60	72-15 Great Nation 119nk Dorinade 1102¼MissFrampton1146¼ Weakened 6
18Sep82- 6Bel	fm	1 1/16 [T]	:48 1:12 1:43⅗	3+ⒻAlw 20000	2 3 42 42½ 31 33¾	Migliore R	b 115	13.80	79-08 FairRoslind117hdLdyMndrin1133¾ThreeRingCircle1151½ Weakened 6
1Sep82- 1Bel	fm	1⅜ [T]	:52⅗ 1:44⅖ 2:20⅖	3+ⒻMd Sp Wt	3 1 11 1hd 1½ 1½	Migliore R	b 118	2.40	55-27 Three RingCircle118½RowdyAngel118½SevenYearItch111¾ Driving 5
22Aug82- 5Sar	fm	1 1/16 Ⓣ	:46⅘ 1:10⅘ 1:42⅖	ⒻClm 55000	5 6 610 67¼ 42½ 33¼	Migliore R	b 112	9.10	82-11 Proteja 112no Mystery Witness 1123¼ThreeRingCircle112¾ Rallied 7
9Aug82- 1Sar	gd	1 1/16 [T]	:47⅗ 1:12⅘ 1:45⅖	ⒻClm 45000	1 6 512 54¾ 32 21¾	Migliore R	b 112	4.90	81-21 MysteryWitness1161¾ThreeRingCircl1123¼LdyAmzon1163¾ Rallied 10

LATEST WORKOUTS Mar 14 Bel tr.t 5f fst 1:03⅗ b Mar 6 Bel tr.t 5f fst 1:02⅘ h Feb 25 Bel tr.t 4f fst :51 b Jan 29 Bel tr.t 5f fst 1:05 b

DUCK CALL, a sprinter entered in a turf route at a claiming level above his proven capabilities. An obvious prep race, with no risk of being claimed.

Duck Call — Dk. b. or br. g. 4, by Rock Talk—Delta Duck, by Delta Judge — $45,000 — Br.—Walker Mrs J Jr (Pa) — Tr.—Picou James E — 113
Own.—Pambi Stable
Lifetime 29 8 6 3 $94,030 — 1983 4 0 1 1 $6,370 — 1982 17 7 5 2 $79,320

25Apr83- 2Aqu	my	6f	:22⅘ :46 1:11	Clm 30000	5 4 54½ 64¾ 53½ 32¾	McCarron G	113	10.90	83-20 Really Smart 1172¾ Bright Search 115hd Duck Call 113nk Rallied 9
2Apr83- 6Aqu	fst	6f	:22⅗ :45⅘ 1:11⅕	Alw 20000	5 2 2hd 21½ 21½ 43	McCarron G	117	6.00	82-23 Pams McAllister117nkHelloFederal1121½SkiJump1101¼ Weakened 8
4Feb83- 6Aqu	fst	6f [•]	:22⅘ :46⅕ 1:13⅗	Clm 25000	13 2 31 42 54 67½	Graell A	113	4.40	68-20 TermPaper1122¾CatchMatthew113¾T.V.Repairman117¾ Weakened 14
22Jan83- 2Aqu	fst	6f [•]	:23 :45⅘ 1:10⅗	Clm 25000	11 1 2hd 21½ 2hd 21¾	Graell A	117	4.60	89-07 Tolerable1171¾DuckCall117nkT.V.Repirmn1172¼ Led between calls 13
29Dec82- 8Med	fst	6f	:22⅗ :45⅗ 1:11⅕	Clm 25000	6 1 1½ 11 12½ 11½	Graell A	115	*2.30	87-18 Duck Call 1151½ Professor Vis 113¾ Pass TheLeader115no Driving 7
2Nov82- 7Med	fst	6f	:22⅖ :46 1:11	Clm 25000	3 4 52¼ 3½ 3nk 1nk	Graell A	115	*2.60	88-18 Duck Call 115nk Pass The Honey 115no Cold Trailin' 1106 Driving 8
11Oct82- 4Bel	fst	6f	:22⅗ :46⅕ 1:12	3+Clm 45000	4 4 56½ 48½ 59½ 812	Graell A	110	13.10	70-28 Speedy Reality 1095¾ Term Paper 117no Private Sun 1141¼ Tired 8
4Oct82- 3Bel	fst	6f	:23 :46⅖ 1:10⅗	Clm 35000	3 2 22 42 35½ 37¼	Graell A	117	*1.50	82-19 Flippydoo 1171¼ Big Win 1176 Duck Call 117½ Weakened 8
4Sep82- 9Bel	fst	6f	:22⅗ :45⅘ 1:11	Clm 35000	6 3 33½ 42½ 41 32	Graell A	117	*2.40	85-13 [D]Flippydoo 117no Hello Federal 1172 Duck Call 117hd Impeded 9
4Sep82-Placed second through disqualification									
27Aug82- 9Sar	fst	6f	:22⅗ :46⅕ 1:10⅘	Clm c-20000	7 1 3½ 11½ 14 16½	Graell A	119	*1.00	86-14 Duck Call 1196½ Blue's Choice 106½HeresAnthony113½ Ridden out 12

LATEST WORKOUTS Apr 14 Bel tr.t ~~5f fst 1:03~~ h Mar 23 Bel tr.t 5f fst 1:00⅖ hg

RAISE A BUCK, a recent claim that has soured after a promising start for his new trainer. The four consecutive drops in price, including the last two when prepping at sprint distances after a five-week freshening, are a very negative sign.

Raise A Buck
Own.—Twin Coasts Stable

B. g. 7, by Raise A Bid—Skyblue Pink, by My Babu
$20,000 Br.—Diamond C Farm Inc (Fla)
Tr.—DeBonis Robert

117

	Lifetime	1983	10	0	3	1	$17,150
	93 13 23 19	1982	17	2	7	1	$61,060
	$268,750	Turf	4	0	0	1	$3,960

18May83- 3Bel fst 6¼f	.23	.46¾ 1.17	Clm 25000	13 10 117¾128¾109¾ 96¼ Velasquez J	b 117	5.30	85-15 Cold Trailin' 117¹ DealingDiplomat115ⁿᵏHerefordMan117½ Outrun 14
5May83- 9Aqu fst 7f	.22½	.44¾ 1.22¾	Clm 30000	7 2 39 49 33½ 35½ Murphy D J⁷	b 106	11.80	83-21 Fanny's Fox 117⁵ Alec George 117⅓ Raise A Buck 106½½ Mild bid 10
29Mar83- 1Aqu gd 1⅛	.48	1.12¾ 1.57¾	Clm 40000	3 4 57¾ 56½ 47⅓ 57½ Smith A Jr	b 117	2.90	68-28 BrshrDoublocn117¾Strhtch117⁴½LttrFromLcy113² Lacked a rally 8
23Mar83- 6Aqu fst 1⅛	.49	1.14½ 1.53	Clm 50000	2 3 34⅓ 33 1ʰᵈ 2⅓ Smith A Jr	b 117	4.70	69-28 Clarinet King 110⅔ Raise A Buck117⁶FiddleFaddle114ⁿᵒ Game try 6
13Mar83- 5Aqu fst 1⅛	.49	1.14½ 1.50⅞	Clm 50000	4 2 2ʰᵈ 2ʰᵈ 33⅓ 48 Cordero A Jr	b 117	4.60	86-08 Class Hero 115ʰᵈ Clarinet King 110⁵⅔ To Erin 117²¼ Gave way 7
24Feb83- 3Aqu fst 170	⚫ .47¾ 1.13½ 1.44¼	Clm c-40000	2 4 33⅓ 31⅓ 21 2¹¼ Cordero A Jr	b 117	*2.10	80-24 Solid Credit 115¹¼ Raise A Buck 117³ Startog s Ace 115ⁿᵒ Rallied 9
17Feb83- 5Aqu fst 1⅛	⚫ .47¾ 1.12¾ 1.46	Clm 45000	3 4 54 41⅓ 2½ 2⅓ Diaz J R	b 113	8.20	82-17 Beguine 112⅓ Raise A Buck 113ⁿᵏ Minced Words 113½ Gamely 6
2Feb83- 10GP sly 1⅛	.47	1.12 1.44¾	Clm 35000	5 7 7¹⁰ 78⅔ 9¹¹ 7¹⁰ Fell J	b 117	5.50	68-20 Darby Gillic 117² Strictly Straight 115⅓ABigFortune113ⁿᵒ Outrun 10
22Jan83- 10GP fst 1⅛	.47⅖	1.11⅗ 1.43⅖	Clm 40000	9 5 31⅓ 53 58 69⅔ Fell J	b 114	4.30	72-16 Dragon Slayer 113³ Count Rebeau 117⅓ Mr. Monsenor114²⅓ Tired 11
7Jan83- 10Crc fst 1¼	.48½	1.13⅖ 1.46	Alw 18000	6 4 43⅓ 54 55⅓ 46 Rivera M A	b 114	10.00	83-10 Bolivar 109½ In All Honesty 114¹½ Command Attention114⁴ Tired 8

LATEST WORKOUTS   Apr 23 Bel tr.t 3f fst :39¾ b   •   Apr 13 Bel tr.t 3f fst :37¾ b

The thrust of one's handicapping then boils down to answering the following three questions:

(1) Does one horse outclass its field? Whether one makes this determination using speed figures, earnings, comparative handicapping, or eligibility conditions is one factor. Whether the horse is fit and ready to prove its class is another.

(2) Does one horse figure to dominate the pace? Should these two questions point out different horses, the "class" horse may not have the advantage one thinks. And should the "class" horse have a modicum of early speed, the "pace" horse might not have things so easy on the lead.

(3) Does one horse, more than the others, figure to be aided by existing track conditions? Or the probable pace? Is there a track bias, and which horses does it favor?

Should no clear-cut decision emerge from these questions, the handicapper may employ one of the following angles in an attempt to find a decent play at attractive odds:

(1) A freshened horse that may have raced only moderately well the first time back, possibly flashing high early speed or showing some sign of impending good form then (or since).

(2) A horse possibly on the rebound from a case of muscle soreness or bleeding.

(3) A horse that may have suffered a poor trip last time, the extent of which did not make the *Form* comments.

(4) A horse with grass bloodlines making its first attempt on that surface, or one bred for the slop set to race over a wet course.

(5) A horse with an established preference for specific track conditions, such as slop or soft grass.

(6) A horse with a proven trainer-angle in its favor, or one handled by a trainer currently "on a roll."

(7) A lightly raced horse with some potential that is donning blinkers for the first time.

(8) A shipper handled by an out-of-town trainer with a proven record at the local track.

(9) A horse taking a hidden class drop, or one dropping just when it appears to be coming into form.

(10) A horse with apparent poor form switching to a leading rider.

(11) A horse that was bet surprisingly heavily last time, or today, either in the straight win pool or in the exotics.

It is difficult to beat the horses grinding out a profit race after race using traditional methods. A few hot streaks, possibly coinciding with a track bias or the beginning of the grass racing season, help immensely. Being aware of a few "spot play" techniques the average bettor does not fully comprehend is the icing on the cake, adding several winners that mean so much over a season's play.

☐ THE NOTEBOOK ☐

Speed and pace figures are best kept in a notebook, along with track bias notes, and some indication of key races. Below is a sample page from the author's own notebook (for Aqueduct):

Race	Classification	Speed Figures		Par
1.	M20,000	99–96		98
2.	$30,000 √	104–106		105
3.	SCAP 10,000 √ √	MARATHON	1^2-SCAP	xx
4. *	NW1 √ √ √	105–98		99
5.	$25,000	107–106-104		106
6.	NW2	103–101	6^8-NW3	104
7.	CLF √	107–106		106
8.	STK √	110–113-112		112
9.	$10,000	98–100	4^5-13	100

Variants: 17–17
Speed: 4/5 (2.6)   2/3 (2.3)
Bias: positive rail
Shippers: SA 21/22   GP 19/19
            BOW 27/29   KEY 24/26

The classification (on the left) and par figure (on the right) are listed for each race, together with the actual speed and pace figures for the race.

An asterisk placed to the left of the race classification denotes a key race as defined in Chapter 10.

Checks placed next to the race classification signify horses that came out of the race to win, or at worst lose in a photo finish, in their next start. The performance of the race winner in its next start is recorded to the right of the race figures. The third race winner, for example, came back to win (again) in starter handicap company, this time by two lengths. The sixth race winner, however, ran a dismal sixth when moved up into NW3 company.

Beneath the figures for the day's races are the sprint and route variants for Aqueduct that day, as well as daily variants for other tracks of interest. In our case, variants from Santa Anita, Gulfstream Park, Bowie, and Keystone were calculated, and listed under the heading "Shippers."

The note "positive rail" means that horses racing along the rail that day did unusually well.

Under the heading "Speed," two numbers are shown describing how well early speed horses performed on the day in question. Four of the five sprints on the card were won by horses first, second, or third at the first call, as were two of the day's three routes (the third race marathon was ignored in these statistics). On a typical day, five of the nine races will be won by horses among the early leaders. Our day was slightly better than average in this respect. Also, the day's five sprint winners had an average first call of 2.6, while the three route winners averaged 2.3. The overall average for this statistic is approximately 3.5, so our day was also above average in this respect, favoring early speed.

Supplementing this information would be a "Horses to Watch" file, listing horses that recently participated in a key race, suffered a noticeably poor trip, or were penalized by a track bias. And, of course, a file on the local trainers, noting especially those with predictable (and profitable) *modus operandi*.

The comprehensive handicapper then would transcribe whatever significant information he uncovered directly into the past performances.

□ ART OR SCIENCE? □

Computers. Can they really handicap the races successfully? Is there really a science to Thoroughbred handicapping?

Computers certainly can be a valuable aid to the handicapper. They can store vast amounts of data, and retrieve or analyze all or part of it very quickly. As a source of information, the computer has no peer.

Imagine having all the facts and figures mentioned above, as current as yesterday's races, at one's fingertips. Type in the name of a horse, and the computer displays its recent record. For each of its latest ten races, the computer would display the date, track, distance, classification, trainer and jockey, odds, running line, pace and speed figures, trip information, and paddock appraisal. Participation in key races would somehow be flagged. Almost everything the modern handicapper needed to know would appear on the screen in an instant.

Sound impossible? Probably so, if any one individual had to input all the information required each day to keep the data bank up to date. But if there was a centralized data bank, available to subscribers via telephone-hookup to their home or office computer . . .

Computers are an invaluable research aid. They allow statistical analysis of handicapping factors, theories, or systems, based on thousands of races, in a matter of minutes. They make possible the application of statistical techniques such as multiple regression and factor analysis to produce comprehensive formulae for playing different types of races, and odds lines to help the player identify advantageous betting situations. Such formulae do exist, and are being used profitably as this is being written. Those published in *Winning at the Races* have received good reviews over the years. I receive mail regularly from people who are using them profitably.

The computer's major shortcoming is "limited vision." It can only process what it has been programmed to process. This it does relentlessly, race after race, without error, never forgetting to consider some piece of information it is programmed to consider. A computer, however, can't read between the lines. Its formulae cannot include every last piece of information, any one of which may be relevant to the race at hand. One or two, even five or six, formulae can't account for every type of race situation—grass, marathon distances, two-year-olds, and so on. Nor can they account for the nuances of individual tracks, unless based solely on data from that track.

Although there are numerous successful practitioners of scientific handicapping today, they are all missing out on one thing—the intellectual challenge of handicapping, the thrill of putting all of the pieces together correctly, and reaching the right conclusion. The computer, or formulae produced by a computer, does all their work, and makes their decisions, but so many aspects of the handicapping process require judgments based on years of experience that it is difficult to imagine a machine matching wits with a seasoned handicapper.

Above all else, Thoroughbred handicapping is an art—it demands creativity. As several have said before me, there is no one secret to beating the races. Racing is too complex for that. Rather, the successful player must be familiar with the techniques of all schools of handicapping. He must arm himself with as many weapons as possible—speed figures, trip notes, pace analyses, trainer techniques, bloodlines, angles, and so on. And then, he must decide which provides the key to solving the puzzle of the race at hand.

Thoroughbred handicapping is one of the most exciting and enjoyable intellectual pastimes man has yet devised. I can only hope that you will find it as stimulating as I do.

Appendix

EASTERN VS. WESTERN FORMS

For several years now, the *Daily Racing Form* has published past performance profiles in two different formats, one for players on the East Coast, and the smaller, more condensed version for the rest of the country.

The purpose of this Appendix is to point out the ways in which the Western editions differ from the Eastern format used throughout this book. This is done by presenting both Eastern and Western versions of the same past performances.

Above the running lines, note two differences. First, the horse's lifetime record appears immediately under the name of its trainer, rather than directly to the left of the rest of the earnings box. Second, the positioning of the weight assigned and claiming price for which the horse is

Campus Capers — Ch. g. 6, by Fast Hilarious—Pampas Flower, by Prince John — $40,000 — Br.—Drake Farm (Fla) — Tr.—Sedlacek Sue — 1125

Own.—Tresvant Stable

Lifetime							
29 7 7 4	1983	12	2	3	1	$61,890
$118,130	1982	13	3	3	3	$40,940
	Turf	13	5	2	4	$77,940

17Jun83- 8Bel	fm	1 1/16 (T):46⅖ 1:11 1:42⅗	3↑Alw 37000	7 4 46½ 5^5 54¾ 43¼	Murphy D J^5	b	114	11.00	80-12	Lamerok 119^3 Red Brigade 119^{nk} Half Iced 117^{hd}	Rallied	8
6Jun83- 2Bel	gd	1⅜ [T]:48⅖ 1:39⅕ 2:18	3↑Hcp 16000s	7 2 2^6 32½ 2^{hd} 1^1	Velasquez J	b	122	*1.20	67-31	Campus Capers 122^1 Could It Be 1141¼ Ardent Bid 120^3	Driving	11
25May83- 8Bel	gd	1 1/16 [T]:48 1:12⅖ 1:44⅗	3↑Handicap	1 4 43½ 62¾ 33½ 3^3	Velasquez J	b	113	*1.60	75-32	Ten Below 117½ Santo's Joe 1152½ CampusCapers113¾	No excuse	8
19May83- 8Bel	fm	1 1/16 [T]:48 1:11⅗ 1:43	3↑Alw 37000	3 3 2^1 2^{hd} 1^{hd} 2^{hd}	Murphy D J^7	b	110	6.60	86-24	Open Call 117^{hd} Campus Capers 110¾ And More1172¾	Drifted out	8
7May83- 6Aqu	fm	1 (T):47 1:12⅖ 1:38⅖	3↑Alw 37000	5 3 32½ 3^3 34½ 11½	Murphy D J^7	b	112	9.20	86-19	CampusCapers1121½Revoction119¾CnnonRoyl121½	Clear under dr.	10
22Apr83- 5Aqu	fst	1⅛ :47⅘ 1:12⅕ 1:50	Clm 70000	5 5 4^5 62½ 57½ 59¾	Thibeau R J^7	b	106	4.20	75-16	Account Receivable 1133¼ Irish Waters112½FourBases117^{no}	Tired	8
11Apr83- 8Aqu	my	1 :46⅘ 1:10⅗ 1:35⅕	3↑Alw 37000	3 3 21½ 36½ 46½ 59½	Thibeau R J^7	b	112	11.50	80-23	Mortgage Man 1162¾ A Magic Spray 119^2 And More 116^{nk}	Tired	6
1Apr83- 3Aqu	fst	1 :47⅖ 1:13⅕ 1:39⅕	Clm c-50000	5 4 4^7 3^5 31½ 2no	MacBeth D	b	117	4.10	70-30	Class Hero 119no Campus Capers 117^{nk} Subordinate 117^3	Tired	7
11Mar83- 8Aqu	sly	1 70 [•]:46⅗ 1:11⅕ 1:40⅗	Alw 37000	4 4 4^9 59½ 58½ 57¼	McCarron G	b	115	8.60	92-11	Skin Dancer 115^{hd} Ten Bore 115^2 Rain Prince 110½	Tired	7
18Feb83- 8Aqu	fst	1 1/16 [•]:48 1:13⅕ 1:45⅗	Alw 37000	6 4 52¼ 3^2 3^5 46¾	McCarron G	b	115	6.90	78-27	Deedee's Deal 115¾ Rain Prince 110^4 Daring Bet115^2	Faded in dr.	7

LATEST WORKOUTS Aug 9 Aqu 4f fst :49⅗ b

Campus Capers — Ch. g. 6, by Fast Hilarious—Pampas Flower, by Prince John

Own.—Tresvant Stable — 1125 — Br.—Drake Farm (Fla) — Tr.—Sedlacek Sue — $40,000

Lifetime 29 7 7 4 $118,130

1983	12	2	3	1	$61,890
1982	13	3	3	3	$40,940
Turf	13	5	2	4	$77,940

17Jun83-8Bel	1 1/16 (T):$46^2$1:11 1:42^3fm	11	114^5	46½ 5^5 54¾ 43¼	Murphy D J^7	Aw37000	80-12	Lamerok, Red Brigade, Half Iced	8
6Jun83-2Bel	1⅜ [T]:$48^2$1:$39^1$2:18 gd	*6-5	122	2^6 32½ 2^{hd} 1^1	Velasquez J^7	H16000	67-31	CmpusCpers,CouldItBe,ArdentBid	11
25May83-8Bel	1 1/16 [T]:48 1:$12^2$1:44^3gd	*8-5	113	43½ 62¾ 33½ 3^3	Velasquez J^1	Hcp0	75-32	TenBelow,Santo'sJoe,CampusCpers	8
19May83-8Bel	1 1/16 [T]:48 1:$11^3$1:43 fm	6½	110^7	2^1 2^{hd} 1^{hd} 2^{hd}	Murphy D J^3	Aw37000	86-24	Open Call, CampusCapers,AndMore	8
19May83—Drifted out									
7May83-6Aqu	1 (T):47 1:$12^2$1:38^2fm	9¼	112^7	32½ 3^3 34½ 11½	Murphy D J^5	Aw37000	86-19	CmpusCpers,Rvoction,CnnonRoyl	10
22Apr83-5Aqu	1⅛ :47^4 1:12^1 1:50 ft	4¼	106^7	4^5 62½ 57½ 59¾	Thibeau R J^5	70000	75-16	AccountReceivbl,IrishWtrs,FourBss	8
11Apr83-8Aqu	1 :46^4 1:10^3 1:35^1m	12	112^7	21½ 36½ 46½ 59½	Thibeau R J^3	Aw37000	80-23	MortgageMan,AMgicSpry,AndMore	6
1Apr83-3Aqu	1 :47^2 1:13^1 1:39^1ft	4	117	4^7 3^5 31½ 2no	MacBeth D^5	c50000	70-30	ClassHero,CmpusCpers,Subordinte	7

Aug 9 Aqu 4f ft :49^3 b

Copyright © 1984, by DAILY RACING FORM, INC. Reprinted with permission of copyright owner.

entered are reversed, with the weight appearing on the left and the claiming price to the right in the Western past performances.

Also note that the phrase "Latest Workouts" does not head the workout line beneath the running lines in the Western editions.

There are numerous differences in the format of the running lines themselves. We shall discuss these working left-to-right across the Eastern version. Differences noted, remember, are for the Western editions.

(1) The track condition field appears after the official running times, rather than before the distance. Track-condition abbreviations consist of only two letters rather than three—Ft represents a FAST track, and Sy denotes a SLOPPY track.

(2) Races run at "about" distances are indicated by the symbol *a* rather than the * used in the Eastern editions. (See Explosive Bid's races on January 13 and February 20.)

(3) The race classification field appears after the jockey field, on the right-hand side of the past performances, rather than on the left, following the running times.

Explosive Bid — Own.—Hawksworth Farm — **116**

Ch. h. 5, by Explodent—Golden Way, by Diplomat Way
Br.—Greiner-OclSTudInc-Wilkrson (Fl)
Tr.—Delp Grover G
Lifetime 38 9 11 5 $267,337

1983	6	2	3	0	$63,170
1982	16	4	4	3	$132,113
Turf	11	3	3	2	$101,123

8Aug83-5Sar	7f	:21^4	:43^4	1:22 ft	4	115	1^{1½}	1^{1½}	1^{1½}	2^{hd}	Guerra W A^6	Aw35000	92-12	StiffSentence,ExplosiveBid,Copeln	7
11Jun83-10LaD	6f	:22^3	:45^1	1:10^{3}ft	2	117	1^{2½}	1^{hd}	1^{hd}	1^{hd}	Franklin R J	Aw14500	90-14	ExplosiveBid,SwordDevil,SilentMan	6
30May83-10LaD	1$\frac{1}{16}$Ⓣ	:46^3	1:10^3	1:40^{4}fm	2½	114	1^{1½}	1^{1½}	2^1	2^5	FranklinRJ^7	Barksdale	96-04	PolicInspctor,ExplosvBd,CgyCougr	7
30Apr83-9LaD	1⅛	:47^2	1:11^1	1:50^{1}ft	2¾	113	1½	1^{hd}	3^{1½}	4^{5½}	Franklin R J^1	Arklatex	93-19	‡Rivlero,PoliceInspector,StgeRviwr	7
20Feb83-10FG	a1⅛Ⓣ			1:50^{3}fm	5½	118	2^{1½}	2^1	1^2	2^{¾}	FrnlnRJ^{12}	F G Classic	80-11	Listcpde,ExplosiveBid,CgeyCougr	13
13Jan83-9FG	a1$\frac{1}{16}$Ⓣ			1:42^{2}fm	*2	116	1^{1½}	1^2	1^5	1^{1½}	Franklin R J	Aw12500	103 —	ExplosivBid,Lstcpd,OccsonlyMondy	8
11Dec82-9FG	6f	:22^4	:46^1	1:11^{2}sy	*4-5	116	1½	1^{hd}	1^2	2^{nk}	Franklin R J	Aw14000	88-22	Jayme G., Explosive Bid, Princely	9
25Nov82-9FG	6f	:21^3	:44^4	1:10 ft	*6-5	119	1^{hd}	1^{hd}	2^{hd}	3^3	Franklin R J^2	HcpO	92-14	CherokeCircl,UpLimit,ExplosivBid	11

●Aug 5 Sar 4f ft :45^4 h

Six differences in race classification notation are worth noting:

(a) The symbol Clm does not precede the claiming price (see past performances of Marvelous Montauk).

(b) The symbol used for allowance races is Aw rather than Alw (see past performances of Explosive Bid).

(c) Maiden Special Weight events are denoted Mdn, rather than MdSpWt (see past performances of Try Gemini).

(d) Maiden claiming races are denoted M40000 rather than Md40000 (see past performances of Try Gemini).

(e) Overnight handicaps are denoted HcpO rather than Handicap (see past performances of Campus Capers on May 25).

(f) Starter handicaps are denoted simply H16000 rather than the more complicated Hcp16000s (see past performances of Campus Capers on June 6).

(4) No symbol, such as the familiar 3↑, is used to indicate that a race was open to both three-year-olds and older horses.

(5) There is no indication of a horse's position immediately after the break.

(6) The post position is separated from the rest of the running line, appearing instead as a superscript attached to the jockey's name. Apprentice allowances, which appear in this position in the Eastern edition, can be found instead affixed as superscripts to the weight carried.

Marvelous Montauk — Own.—Gee M Stable — **107^5**

Dk. b. or br. f. 3, by Thomasville—Miss Startop, by Sid's Gambol
Br.—Star L D (NY)
Tr.—Sallusto Justin
Lifetime 24 3 2 4 $32,265

1983	14	1	1	2	$13,445
1982	10	2	1	2	$18,820

26Jun83- 1Bel	fst	1$\frac{1}{16}$	:46⅗	1:12⅗	1:48	ⒻClm 20000	5	3	3^{3½}	3^{5½}	7^{11}	8^{24}	Santagata N	b	112	12.20	38-24	History Belle 116^{1¾} Gold Plated 109^2 Energetica 111½	Tired	8
23Jun83- 9Bel	fst	7f	:23⅖	:46⅘	1:25⅕	3↑ⒻⓈAlw 25500	6	1	6^{3½}	7^{7½}	8^{18}	6^{18}	Thibeau R J^5	b	104	13.40	58-22	Chaldea 109^{11} Three Dog Night 109½ Tiki Singh 111^{nk}	No factor	10
10Jun83- 5Bel	fst	6f	:23	:46⅗	1:12⅖	3↑ⒻⓈAlw 25500	1	3	7^{5½}	7^{3½}	2^4	3^4	Thibeau R J^5	b	104	14.70	76-11	AprilTarget104^{3½}Jazzerciser109½MrvelousMontuk104^{nk}	Weakened	7
5Jun83- 3Bel	fst	7f	:22⅘	:46⅕	1:25⅗	ⒻClm 14000	6	9	8^{7¾}	4^6	2^3	1^{hd}	Thibeau R J^5	b	107	39.00	74-17	MarvelousMontauk107^{hd}LilMissScrlet113^{1¾}MissB.P.116^{2¾}	Driving	11
1Jun83- 9Mth	fst	6f	:23⅕	:47⅕	1:13⅘	ⒻClm 14000	10	2	9^{6½}	8^{7¾}	8^{5½}	5^{2¾}	Gonzalez M A	b	111	21.20	68-24	Lady Linleigh 110^1 MusicMaker108^{nk}MyDearNurse115^1	No factor	11
26May83- 1Bel	fst	6f	:22⅘	:45⅘	1:12	ⒻClm 14000	3	3	6^7	7^{12}	8^{15}	11^{17}	McCarron G	b	112	12.30	65-21	Lil Miss Scarlet 109^7 Donna J. 111¾ Evening Run 116^{1¾}	Fell back	13
14May83- 2Mth	fst	6f	:22⅖	:46	1:13⅗	ⒻClm 12500	7	2	7^{8¾}	5^{4¾}	2^{1½}	2^2	McCarron G	b	115	3.20	70-20	Ya Bad Girl 113^2 MarvelousMontauk115½MollyMcGrew113^2	Hung	8
9May83- 5Aqu	fst	6½f	:23	:47⅗	1:19⅖	ⒻClm 16000	3	4	1^1	2½	6^6	10^{15}	McCarron G	b	116	5.30	63-25	Years Of Tale 111^5 Evening Run 116^{1¾} Vishnacka 112no	Stopped	10
23Apr83- 3Aqu	fst	1	:46⅕	1:11⅗	1:38⅘	ⒻClm 20000	5	1	1^{2½}	1^5	2^{hd}	5^{9¾}	Thibeau R J^7	b	105	7.70	62-24	Poster Princess 116^{2¼} Evening Run 107^4 Soucy 109^1	Used up	7
10Apr83- 3Aqu	sly	6½f	:23⅗	:47⅗	1:19⅖	ⒻClm 20000	5	6	4^{3¼}	5^{5½}	6^{7½}	6^{14}	McCarron G	b	112	6.50	64-23	RadcliffeGirl107^{6½}TenderReed116^{hd}LilMissScarlet111^{2¾}	Fin. early	7

LATEST WORKOUTS Jly 29 Sar tr.t 4f fst :52 b Jly 7 Bel tr.t 4f fst :49⅘ b

Marvelous Montauk — Dk. b. or br. f. 3, by Thomasville—Miss Startop, by Sid's Gambol
Own.—Gee M Stable — 1075 — Br.—Star L D (NY) — 1983 14 1 1 2 $13,445
Tr.—Sallusto Justin — 1982 10 2 1 2 $18,820
Lifetime 24 3 2 4 $32,265

26Jun83-1Bel 1 1/16 :463 1:123 1:48 ft 12 112 33 1/2 35 1/2 711 824 Santagata N5 Ⓕ 20000 38-24 HistoryBelle,GoldPlated,Energetica 8
23Jun83-9Bel 7f :232 :464 1:251ft 13 1045 63 1/2 77 1/4 818 618 ThibuRJ6 ⒻⓈAw25500 58-22 Chaldea,ThreeDogNight,TikiSingh 10
10Jun83-5Bel 6f :23 :463 1:122ft 15 1045 75 1/2 73 1/2 24 34 ThibuRJ1 ⒻⓈAw25500 76-11 AprilTrget,Jzzrcisr,MrvlousMontuk 7
5Jun83-3Bel 7f :224 :461 1:253ft 39 1075 87 3/4 46 23 1hd Thibeau R J6 Ⓕ 14000 74-17 MrvlosMontk,LIMssScrlt,MssB.P. 11
1Jun83-9Mth 6f :231 :471 1:134ft 21 111 96 1/2 87 3/4 85 1/4 52 3/4 GonzalezMA10 Ⓕ 14000 68-24 LdyLinleigh,MusicMker,MyDrNurs 11
26May83-1Bel 6f :224 :454 1:12 ft 12 112 67 712 815 1117 McCarron G3 Ⓕ 14000 65-21 LilMissScarlet,DonnJ.,EveningRun 13
14May83-2Mth 6f :222 :46 1:133ft 3 1/4 115 78 3/4 54 3/4 21 1/2 22 McCarron G7 Ⓕ 12500 70-20 YBdGrl,MrvlosMontk,MollyMcGrw 8
9May83-5Aqu 6 1/2f :23 :473 1:192ft 5 1/2 116 11 2 1/2 66 1015 McCarron G3 Ⓕ 16000 63-25 YearsOfTale,EveningRun,Vishnack 10
Jly 29 Sar tr.t 4f ft :52 b Jly 7 Bel tr.t 4f ft :494 b

(7) The weight and odds can be found on the left-hand side of the past performances, to the left of the running lines, rather than after the jockey's name on the right. The odds appear first, and in many cases are rounded to the nearest dollar.

Try Gemini — Dk. b. or br. c. 2, by Tri Jet—Dark Toast, by Duel — Lifetime 4 0 0 1 $1,260 — 1983 4 M 0 1 $1,260
Own.—Garren M M — Br.—Beresford Farm (Fla) — 118
Tr.—Puentes Gilbert

4Aug83- 4Sar fst 5 1/2f :22 2/5 :46 2/5 1:05 3/5 Md Sp Wt 11 2 12 1/2 1hd 44 1/2 1116 Ayarza I b 118 16.60 73-16 Don Rickles 1182 1/4 Hail BoldKing1182 3/4 MorningBob118 1/2 Angled in 12
13Jly83- 4Bel fst 5 1/2f :22 4/5 :47 1/5 1:07 Md 40000 4 5 2hd 11 1/2 31 1/2 610 Cruguet J b 118 5.50 70-24 Act Away 1131 1/2 Derby's Turn 1183 1/4 CutTheMusic1184 3/4 Gave way 9
1Jly83- 4Bel fst 5 1/2f :22 3/5 :47 1:06 3/5 Md 35000 4 4 13 12 2 1/2 36 3/4 Douglas R R7 b 111 3.00 75-16 Epilogue 1183 1/2 Act Away 1133 1/4 Try Gemini 111 1/2 Weakened 8
4Jun83- 4Bel gd 5f :22 1/5 :45 2/5 :57 2/5 Md Sp Wt 2 2 2hd 32 36 1/2 717 Davis R G b 118 8.90 85-08 DCountry Manor 1181 1/4 Go Go Regal1188NationalCity1184 1/2 Tired 8
LATEST WORKOUTS Aug 10 Sar tr.t 4f fst :49 3/5 b ●Jly 29 Sar tr.t 3f fst :35 h Jly 8 Bel 5f fst 1:01 2/5 h ●Jun 22 Bel tr.t 3f fst :35 1/5 h

Try Gemini — Dk. b. or br. c. 2, by Tri Jet—Dark Toast, by Duel
Own.—Garren M M — 118 — Br.—Beresford Farm (Fla) — 1983 4 M 0 1 $1,260
Tr.—Puentes Gilbert
Lifetime 4 0 0 1 $1,260

4Aug83-4Sar 5 1/2f :222 :462 1:053ft 17 118 12 1/2 1hd 44 1/2 1116 Ayarza I11 Mdn 73-16 DonRickls,HlBoldKng,MornngBob 12
4Aug83—Causedinterfernce
13Jly83-4Bel 5 1/2f :224 :471 1:07 ft 5 1/2 118 2hd 11 1/2 31 1/2 610 Cruguet J4 M40000 70-24 ActAway,Derby'sTurn,CutTheMusic 9
1Jly83-4Bel 5 1/2f :223 :47 1:063ft 3 1117 13 12 2 1/2 36 3/4 Douglas R R4 M35000 75-16 Epilogue, Act Away, Try Gemini 8
4Jun83-4Bel 5f :221 :452 :572gd 9 118 2hd 32 36 1/2 717 Davis R G2 Mdn 85-08 ‡CountryMnor,GoGoRgl,NtionlCity 8
Aug 10 Sar tr.t 4f ft :493 b ●Jly 29 Sar tr.t 3f ft :35 h Jly 8 Bel 5f ft 1:012 h ●Jun 22 Bel tr.t 3f ft :351 h

(8) There is no indication of whether or not a horse wore blinkers in any of the races appearing in its past performances.

(9) There is no indication of the margins between the first four finishers in each race, only the identity of the first three to finish. The weight each of the first three carried is also omitted from the Western editions.

(10) A trouble comment is not a standard part of the running line. Should a horse have had a noteworthy trip, a special comment will appear below that running line (see past performances of Try Gemini).

(11) Should a horse finish in a dead heat, the symbol ‡ will appear after its finish position (it appears after the weight in the Eastern edition), and a special comment will appear below the running line. No symbol appears next to the horse's name in the company field, however.

Tyrolean Miss Gr. f. 3, by Nodouble—Geneva II, by Gulf-Weed
Br.—Brant M (Pa)
Own.—Old Glory Stable Tr.—Martin Frank
112 Lifetime 14 1 3 0 $25,960 | 1983 9 1 2 0 $19,740 | 1982 5 M 1 0 $6,220 | Turf 1 0 0 0

6Aug83- 8Sar	fst	1¼	:48 1/5	1:36 2/5	2:02 2/5	ⒻAlabama	1	1	1½	57½	513	--	Cordero A Jr	121	4.60e		Spit Curl 1218½ Lady Norcliffe 121¾ Sabin 1216¾	Eased 5
9Jly83- 8Bel	fst	1½	:48 4/5	2:04 3/5	2:30 1/5	ⒻC C A Oaks	1	1	1½	713	1127	1237	Davis R G	121	14.30e	32-23	High Schemes 1217½ Spit Curl 1211¾ Lady Norcliffe121¾	Gaveway 16
25Jun83- 5Bel	fm	1 1/16 Ⓣ	:45 1/5	1:09 4/5	1:41 2/5	3↑ⒻAlw 21000	7	8	85¾	65½	87	88	Cruguet J	109	14.90	81-12	Jubilous 113hd Future Fun 111¾ Jolly Fast 1122	Outrun 11
11Jun83- 9Bel	fst	7f	:22 3/5	:45 3/5	1:23 3/5	3↑ⒻAlw 20000	6	7	87	78	711	713	Miranda J	111	6.90	71-14	Pride's Crossing 1127 Dollar Darling 109½ Descent 104¾	Outrun 12
28May83- 6Bel	fst	1 1/16	:46	1:10 2/5	1:43 2/5	3↑ⒻAlw 21000	2	1	16	14	11½	42½	Beitia E	109	6.30	82-18	Nimble Nova 114hd Gustavia 113nk Pentecost 1082¼	Weakened 7
4Apr83- 7Aqu	fst	1	:46 2/5	1:11 3/5	1:37 3/5	ⒻAlw 21000	4	1	1hd	1hd	2½	21¼	Miranda J	116	*2.10	77-21	Poppa's Big Lil 1161¼ Tyrolean Miss 116nk LadyD.1165	Held place 7
19Mar83- 4Aqu	my	7f	:22 4/5	:45 4/5	1:23 3/5	ⒻMd Sp Wt	5	2	11	11	13	12¼	Miranda J	121	*1.90	83-21	Tyrolean Miss 1212¼ Stark Drama 1217¼ Cajun Best 1213½	Driving 8
4Mar83- 4Aqu	fst	6f ⊡	:23	:46 3/5	1:11 4/5	ⒻMd Sp Wt	5	7	52¼	55	46½	23¼	Miranda J	121♦	12.70	82-19	Groom'sPride1213¼DHPrecipitate116DHTyrolenMiss1211¾	Rallied 14
4Mar83-Dead heat																		
14Jan83- 4Aqu	fst	6f ⊡	:23	:47	1:13 1/5	ⒻMd Sp Wt	4	7	41¼	106¼	1313	1314	Kaenel J L	121	*3.20	64-19	Poppa'sBigLil1212¼FlopTop1211¾Killthepinoplyer121hd	Brief foot 14
28Dec82- 6Aqu	fst	6f ⊡	:23 1/5	:47	1:13	ⒻMd Sp Wt	9	2	1hd	11½	11	2¾	Kaenel J L	117	15.50	78-22	Kl'sCornishGirl117¾TyrolenMiss117½WhtmiWood1172¾	Weakened 14

LATEST WORKOUTS Jly 5 Bel 4f fst :48 h Jun 21 Bel 4f my :51 b

Tyrolean Miss Gr. f. 3, by Nodouble—Geneva II, by Gulf-Weed
Br.—Brant M (Pa) 1983 9 1 2 0 $19,740
Own.—Old Glory Stable 112 Tr.—Martin Frank 1982 5 M 1 0 $6,220
Lifetime 14 1 3 0 $25,960 Turf 1 0 0 0

6Aug83-8Sar	1¼:481 1:362 2:022ft	4½e 121	1½	57½	513	—	CordroAJr1	ⒻAlabama	— —	Spit Curl, Lady Norcliffe, Sabin	5
6Aug83—Eased											
9Jly83-8Bel	1½:484 2:043 2:301ft	14e 121	1½	713	1127	1237	DvisRG1	ⒻC C A Oaks	32-23	HighSchems,SpitCurl,LdyNorcliff	16
25Jun83-5Bel	1 1/16Ⓣ:4511:0941:412fm	15 109	85¾	65½	87	88	Cruguet J7	ⒻAw21000	81-12	Jubilous, Future Fun, Jolly Fast	11
11Jun83-9Bel	7f :223 :453 1:233ft	7 111	87	78	711	713	Miranda J6	ⒻAw20000	71-14	Pride'sCrossing,DollrDrling,Dscnt	12
28May83-6Bel	1 1/16:46 1:102 1:432ft	6½ 109	16	14	11½	42½	Beitia E2	ⒻAw21000	82-18	Nimble Nova, Gustavia, Pentecost	7
4Apr83-7Aqu	1 :462 1:113 1:373ft	*2 116	1hd	1hd	2½	21¼	Miranda J4	ⒻAw21000	77-21	Poppa'sBigLil,TyroleanMiss,LadyD.	7
19Mar83-4Aqu	7f :224 :454 1:233m	*9-5 121	11	11	13	12¼	Miranda J5	ⒻMdn	83-21	TyroleanMiss,StarkDrama,CjunBest	8
4Mar83-4Aqu	6f ⊡:23 :4631:114ft	13 121	52¼	55	46½	23¼♦	Miranda J5	ⒻMdn	82-19	Groom'sPride,Prcipitt,TyrolnMiss	14
♦ 4Mar83—Dead heat											

Jly 5 Bel 4f ft :48 h Jun 21 Bel 4f m :51 b

Copyright © 1984, by DAILY RACING FORM, INC. Reprinted with permission of copyright owner.

(12) When a horse is disqualified, the symbol † appears after its finish position, and the symbol ‡ before its name in the company column.

Jazzerciser B. f. 3, by Tarleton Oak—Danseuse, by Jig Time
Br.—Stratford Farms Associates (NY)
Own.—Tamarind Tr.—Nash Joseph S
112 Lifetime 7 1 3 0 $30,460 | 1983 3 0 2 0 $11,220 | 1982 4 1 1 0 $19,240

15Jly83- 7Bel	fst	6f	:22 2/5	:46 2/5	1:11 2/5	3↑ⒻⓈAlw 25500	4	10	911	911	48	26¼	Davis R G	111	3.90	79-17	Sun Sounds 1136¼ Jazzerciser 1113 Regal Lady113nk	Wide, rallied 10
10Jun83- 5Bel	fst	6f	:23	:46 3/5	1:12 2/5	3↑ⒻⓈAlw 25500	3	7	64½	42½	45	23½	Davis R G	109	2.90	76-11	AprilTarget1043½Jazzerciser109½MarvelousMontuk104nk	Dwelt st. 7
14Feb83- 9Aqu	fst	6f ⊡	:23 2/5	:47 2/5	1:12 3/5	ⒻⓈAlw 25500	9	9	911	911	912	811	Cordero A Jr	116	2.10	70-13	SubversivChick111½AprilTrgt111¾Monrch'sMgic1163½	Dwelt start 9
15Dec82- 7Aqu	fst	6f ⊡	:23 2/5	:47	1:13	ⒻⓈAlw 26500	7	—	—	—	—	—	Cordero A Jr	121	*1.30	— —	RestlessGerry1211¾Enrgtic1161¾MrvlousMontuk1166½	Dwelt start 7
2Dec82- 4Aqu	my	6f ⊡	:23 3/5	:47 1/5	1:12	ⒻⓈMd Sp Wt	12	1	43½	22½	2hd	11¾	Alvarado R Jr5	112	*.80	84-13	Jazzerciser 1121¾ Gentle Game 1173¾DHRegalDowager117	Driving 14
31Oct82- 4Aqu	fst	6f	:23	:46 4/5	1:11 4/5	ⒻⓈMd Sp Wt	4	2	11½	14	11½	2nk	Alvarado R Jr5	112	1.60	82-18	Drakes Law 117nk Jazzerciser 1125¾ Bare Bikini 1076¼	Failed 8
16Oct82- 4Aqu	fst	6f	:23 1/5	:48	1:13 4/5	ⒻⓈMd Sp Wt	11	9	2hd	1½	14	12	Fielding R D7	110	21.60Ⓓ	72-26	ⒹJazzerciser 1102 Abraxis 1172¼ Bare Bikini 1071½	Came over 12
16Oct82-Disqualified and placed twelfth																		

LATEST WORKOUTS Aug 8 Sar 5f fst 1:01 4/5 h Jly 23 Bel 7f fst 1:31 3/5 b Jly 9 Bel 6f fst 1:15 4/5 b Jly 2 Bel 6f fst 1:14 3/5 hg

Jazzerciser B. f. 3, by Tarleton Oak—Danseuse, by Jig Time
Br.—Stratford Farms Associates (NY) 1983 3 0 2 0 $11,220
Own.—Tamarind 112 Tr.—Nash Joseph S 1982 4 1 1 0 $19,240
Lifetime 7 1 3 0 $30,460

15Jly83-7Bel	6f :222 :462 1:112ft	4 111	911	911	48	26¼	DavisRG4	ⒻⓈAw25500	79-17	Sun Sounds,Jazzerciser,RegalLady	10
10Jun83-5Bel	6f :23 :463 1:122ft	3 109	64½	42½	45	23½	DavisRG3	ⒻⓈAw25500	76-11	AprilTrget,Jzzrcisr,MrvlousMontuk	7
10Jun83—Dwelt st.											
14Feb83-9Aqu	6f ⊡:232 :4721:123ft	2 116	911	911	912	811	CrdrAJr9	ⒻⓈAw25500	70-13	SbvrsvChck,AprlTrgt,Monrch'sMgc	9
15Dec82-7Aqu	6f ⊡:232 :47 1:13 ft	*6-5 121	—	—	—	—	CrdrAJr7	ⒻⓈAw26500	— —	RstlssGrry,Enrgtic,MrvlousMontuk	7
15Dec82—Dwelt											
2Dec82-4Aqu	6f ⊡:233 :4711:12 m	*4-5 1125	43½	22½	2hd	11¾	AlvaradoRJr12	ⒻⓈMdn	84-13	Jzzerciser,GentleGme,ReglDowger	14
31Oct82-4Aqu	6f :23 :464 1:114ft	8-5 1125	11½	14	11½	2nk	AlvaradoRJr4	ⒻⓈMdn	82-18	Drakes Law, Jazzerciser,BareBikini	8
16Oct82-4Aqu	6f :231 :48 1:134ft	22 1107	2hd	1½	14	12 †	FieldingRD11	ⒻⓈMdn	72-26	‡Jazzerciser, Abraxis, Bare Bikini	12
†16Oct82—Disqualified and placed twelfth											

Aug 8 Sar 5f ft 1:014 h Jly 23 Bel 7f ft 1:313 b Jly 9 Bel 6f ft 1:154 b Jly 2 Bel 6f ft 1:143 hg

Copyright © 1984, by DAILY RACING FORM, INC. Reprinted with permission of copyright owner.

BIBLIOGRAPHY

The following books are all worthy of the serious player's attention:

Ainslie, Tom. *The Compleat Horseplayer*, New York: Simon & Schuster, 1966.

———. *Ainslie on Jockeys*. New York: Simon & Schuster, 1975.

———. *Ainslie's Complete Guide to Thoroughbred Racing*. New York: Simon & Schuster. 1968 and 1979.

———*The Handicapper's Handbook*. New York: Trident Press, 1969.

———*Theory and Practice of Handicapping*. New York: Trident Press, 1970.

———*Ainslie's Encyclopedia of Thoroughbred Handicapping*. New York: William Morrow, 1978.

Ainslie, Tom, and Ledbetter, Bonnie. *The Body Language of Horses*. New York: William Morrow, 1980.

Badone, Chuck. *Secrets of a Successful Race Handicapper*. Scottsdale, Ariz.: Pay Day Press, 1977.

Beyer, Andrew. *Picking Winners*. Boston: Houghton Mifflin, 1975.

———. *My $50,000 Year at the Races*. New York: Harcourt Brace Jovanovich, 1978.

———. *The Winning Horseplayer*. Boston: Houghton Mifflin, 1983.

Davidowitz, Steven. *Betting Thoroughbreds*. New York: Dutton, 1977.

Davis, Frederick. *Thoroughbred Racing: Percentages and Probabilities*. New York: Millwood Publications, 1974.

Fabricand, Burton. *Horse Sense*. New York: McKay, 1965.

Gaines, Milt. *The Tote Board Is Alive and Well*. Las Vegas: GBC Press, 1981.

Goodwon, Katcha. *A Thinking Man's Guide to Handicapping*. Newport Beach, Calif.: Westcliff Publications, 1978, 1983.

Jones, Gordon. *Gordon Jones To Win!* Huntington Beach, Calif.: Karman Communications, 1976.

Kuck, Henry. *Situation Handicapping.* New York: Woodside Associates, 1981.

Murray, William. *Horse Fever.* New York: Dodd, Mead, 1976.

Quinn, James. *Handicapper's Condition Book.* Las Vegas: GBC Press, 1981.

———. *The Literature of Thoroughbred Handicapping 1965–1982.* Las Vegas: GBC Press, 1983.

Quirin, William. *Par Times.* New York: Woodside Associates, 1978, 1981.

———. *Winning at the Races.* New York: William Morrow, 1979.

———. *Master Grass Sires List.* New York: Woodside Associates, 1982.

Scott, William. *Investing at the Racetrack.* New York: Simon & Schuster, 1981.

Selvidge, James. *Hold Your Horses.* Seattle: Jacada Publications, 1974, 1976.

Surface, William. *The Track—A Day in the Life of Belmont Park.* New York: Macmillan, 1976.

Taulbot, Ray. *Thoroughbred Horse Racing—Playing for Profit.* New York: Amerpub, 1959, 1973.

Zolotow, Maurice. *Confessions of a Racetrack Fiend.* New York: St. Martins Press, 1983.